CLOSE RELATIONS

An Introduction to the Sociology of Families

SIXTH EDITION

SUSAN A. MCDANIEL

UNIVERSITY OF LETHBRIDGE

LORNE TEPPERMAN

UNIVERSITY OF TORONTO

SANDRA COLAVECCHIA

MCMASTER UNIVERSITY

 Pearson

Toronto

Editorial Director: Anne Williams
Acquisitions Editor: Keriann McGoogan
Marketing Manager: Euan White
Content Manager: Madhu Ranadive
Project Manager: Ainsley Somerville
Content Developer: Rachel Stuckey
Production Services: iEnergizer Aptara®, Ltd.
Permissions Project Managers: Tanvi Bhatia and
  Anjali Singh

Photo Permissions Research: iEnergizer Aptara®, Ltd.
Text Permissions Research: iEnergizer Aptara®, Ltd.
Interior Designer: iEnergizer Aptara®, Ltd.
Cover Designer: iEnergizer Aptara®, Ltd.
Cover Image: Click Images/Shutterstock
**Vice-President, Cross Media and Publishing
  Services:** Gary Bennett

Pearson Canada Inc., 26 Prince Andrew Place, North York, Ontario M3C 2T8.

978-0-13-465229-0

Library and Archives Canada Cataloguing in Publication

McDaniel, Susan A., 1946-, author
    Close relations : an introduction to the sociology of families / Susan McDaniel,
    Lorne Tepperman, Sandra Colavecchia. – Sixth edition.
Previous editions authored by Susan A. McDaniel and Lorne Tepperman.
Includes bibliographical references and index.
ISBN 978-0-13-465229-0 (softcover)

    1. Families—Canada—Textbooks. 2. Textbooks.
I. Tepperman, Lorne, 1943-, author II. Colavecchia, Sandra, author III. Title.

HQ560.M82 2017   306.850971   C2017-906556-4

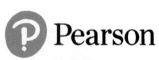

3 2019

Brief Contents

Chapter 1   Families and Family-Like Relationships
Definitions, Theories, and Research   1

Chapter 2   Historical Perspectives on Canadian Families
Demographic, Social, and Economic Origins and Trends   30

Chapter 3   How Families Begin
Dating and Mating   69

Chapter 4   Types of Intimate Couples
Marriage, Cohabitation, Same-Sex Relationships, and Other
Forms   108

Chapter 5   Happy and Healthy Relationships   145

Chapter 6   Parenting
Childbearing, Socialization, and Parenting Challenges   181

Chapter 7   Work and Family Life   219

Chapter 8   Stress and Violence
Realities of Family Life   254

Chapter 9   Divorce and Ending Relationships
Trends, Myths, Children, and Ex-Spouses   292

Chapter 10   Family Transitions and Diversity   338

Chapter 11   A Glimpse into the Future
Where Do Families Go from Here?   375

Contents

Preface *xiii*

Acknowledgments *xvii*

1 Families and Family-Like Relationships

Definitions, Theories, and Research   **1**

Introduction   **2**

The Importance of Family   **3**

What Is Family?   **3**

Defining the Family   **3**

Murdock: Three Relationships   **4**

    Census Family   5

    Household versus Family   5

    Process-Based Definitions   6

Common Elements of Family Life   **8**

    Dependency and Intimacy   8

    Sexuality   8

    Protection   9

    Power   9

    Violence   9

Kinship, Clan, and Community   **10**

New Ways to Understand Family Diversity   **11**

Theoretical Approaches to Understanding Families   **13**

    Theories of Family over Time   13

Basic Theoretical Approaches to the Family   **21**

    Structural Functionalism   21

    Symbolic Interactionism   23

    Marxist Theory of Family   23

    Feminist Theory   24

    Postmodern Theory   24

Variation despite Convergence   **25**

Life Course Theory   **26**

Concluding Remarks   **26**

Chapter Summary   27

Key Terms   28

Critical Thinking Questions   28

Weblinks   29

2 Historical Perspectives on Canadian Families

Demographic, Social, and Economic Origins and Trends   **30**

A Historical, Cross-Cultural Perspective   32

    Indigenous Peoples and Settlers: Contact and Conflict   32

    English and French Settlers   33

    The Transition to Industrialism   34

    The History of Immigration in Relation to the Family   36

    The History of Immigration Policies   38

    Wars   41

Variation in the Family Life Course   42

    The Impact of Modernization on Family Changes in
      Canada and Worldwide   44

    Changes in Sexual Attitudes and Courtship   46

    Changes in Attitudes toward Marriage   48

Declining Fertility and the Value of Parenthood   50

    The First and Second Demographic Transitions   54

    Contraception, Childbearing Choice, and Abortion   56

    Family and Household Size   58

Social Support and Regulation: The Role of the State in Families   59

    Child Support and Welfare Reforms in Canada   59

    Changing Nature of Elder Support by the State and the Family   62

    Families That Include Persons with Disabilities   64

    The Regulation of Divorce   64

Concluding Remarks   65

Chapter Summary   66

Key Terms   66

Critical Thinking Questions   67

Weblinks   67

3 How Families Begin

Dating and Mating   **69**

Love: A Recent Invention?   72

Theories of Mate Selection   72

    Complementary Needs Theory   73

    Exchange Theory   73

    An Evolutionary Perspective   73

    Social Role Theory   74

The Role of Gender Equality   74

Arranged Marriages and Love Matches   75

Internet Dating and Mating   77

Social Aspects of Finding a Mate   79

Dating and Disabilities   80

    Sexuality and Social Stigma   81

    Online Dating for People with Disabilities   83

The Sexual Double Standard: Fact or Fiction?   84
Dating in an Aging Society   88
Dating in a Multicultural Society   88
Same-Sex Dating   92
Dating for Overweight and Other Stigmatized People   93
Homogamy   94
    Educational and Other Status Homogamy   95
    Age Homogamy   96
    Ethnic Homogamy (or Endogamy)   96
    Religious Homogamy   98
    Endogamy for Indigenous People   98
The Ideals of Mate Selection   99
    Why People Do Not Optimize   100
Dating Violence   102
    Dating Violence for Obese and Other Stigmatized People   103
    Dating Violence for People with Disabilities   104

Chapter Summary   105
Key Terms   106
Critical Thinking Questions   106
Weblinks   107

4   **Types of Intimate Couples**

Marriage, Cohabitation, Same-Sex Relationships,
    and Other Forms   **108**
Introduction   109
Social Change in Close Relations   110
    Diversity and Fluidity   110
    Discontinuity   110
    Emerging Trends for Young Adults   111
    Emerging Trends for Older Adults   112
A Profile of Families in Canada Today   112
    Marriage   113
    Cohabitation   114
    Living Apart Together (LAT)   116
    Intersections of Sexual Relationships and Living Arrangements   117
    Single-Person Households   118
    Shifting Societal Views of the Unattached   119
    The Decision to Cohabit, Marry, or Remarry   121
    Divorce and Relationship Dissolution   121
    Remarriage and Blended Families   124
    LGBTQ Couples and Families   125
    Childbearing and Parenting   128
Diversity in Sexual Relationships   130
    Polygamy   131

Polyamory   132
Non-monogamy   133
Money Management   134
Relationship Status   134
Gender and Economic Inequality   135
Money and Economic Exploitation   136
Money and Relationship Dissolution   138
Technological Change   139
Concluding Remarks   142

Chapter Summary   142
Key Terms   143
Critical Thinking Questions   144
Weblinks   144

5   **Happy and Healthy Relationships   145**
Sociological Findings on Marital Quality   147
Close Relations, Good Health   149
Disability, Partnership, and Marriage   150
Good Marriage and Good Health   152
Types of Union and Relationship Quality   154
Homosexual versus Heterosexual Relationships   156
The Role of Homogamy   156
Marital Satisfaction among Immigrant Couples   157
The Life Cycle of a Marriage   157
Marriage Beginnings   158
The Introduction of Children into a Marriage   158
Infertility   161
The Midlife Marriage   162
What Makes a Marriage Satisfying?   164
Love   164
Sexual Satisfaction   165
Intimacy: Sexual and Emotional   166
Coping and Conflict Management   168
Domestic Violence   170
Gender Roles in Marriage   171
Work, Money, and Marital Quality   173
Verbal Communication   174
Nonverbal Communication   175
Communication and Gender   176
The Effects of Disabilities on Spousal Relationships   177

Chapter Summary   179
Key Terms   179
Critical Thinking Questions   180
Weblinks   180

6 Parenting

Childbearing, Socialization, and Parenting Challenges   **181**

Entering Parenthood   183

Entering Parenthood in the Past   183

Entering Parenthood Today: Family Planning   184

Entering Parenthood Young   184

Raising Children Alone   185

Adoption   186

Assisted Fertility   187

The Transition to Parenthood: Its Effect on Happiness   188

Coping with the Change in Marital Relationships   191

The Tasks of Parenthood   192

Socialization   192

Gender Socialization   193

Parenting Processes   194

Obesity and Parenting (for Mothers)   194

The Most Important Things Parents Give Children   196

Love and Attachment   196

Emotional Stability and Family Cohesion   198

Protection, Control, and Supervision   198

Fair and Moderate Discipline   200

Parenting Sick Children   203

Variations on a Theme   204

Disability and Parenting   204

Single Parenting   205

Parenting in Poverty   206

Gay and Lesbian Families   208

Indigenous Families   209

Cultural Variation   211

Parenting in the Internet Age   214

Chapter Summary   215

Key Terms   216

Critical Thinking Questions   217

Weblinks   217

7 Work and Family Life   219

Introduction   220

Change in Work and Family   221

Unpaid Labour, Domestic Labour, and Caregiving   222

Elder Care and Other Types of Caregiving   223

Unpaid Labour Is Multifaceted   224

Sick Days   225

The Multiple Meanings of Unpaid Labour   226

Stress and Conflict   227

      Physical and Mental Health   228

      The Skills Involved in Unpaid Labour   229

Key Findings Related to the Division of Household Labour   230

      Gender Inequalities in Unpaid Labour   230

      Factors Associated with the Division of Unpaid Labour   231

      Perceptions of Fairness   232

      Reactions to Gender Inequalities in Unpaid Labour   233

      Same-Sex Families   233

The Intersections between Paid and Unpaid Labour   234

      Gender Disparities in Earnings and Caregiving   235

      Primary versus Secondary Labour Markets   236

      Non-standard Employment and Precarious Work   236

      Occupational Sex Segregation   237

      The Needs of Children   238

      Parents of Children with Disabilities   239

      Barriers in the Labour Market   240

Work–Life Balance   241

Social Policy   242

      Neoliberalism   242

      The Limitations of Canadian Family Policy   244

      Typologies of Family Policy   245

      Parental Leave Benefits   246

      Child Care   247

Concluding Remarks   250

Chapter Summary   250

Key Terms   251

Critical Thinking Questions   252

Weblinks   252

8   Stress and Violence

Realities of Family Life   **254**

Stress   256

      Types of Stressors   257

      Caregiver Burden and Burnout   260

Family Violence   268

      Defining and Measuring Family Violence   268

      Causes of Violence   275

      Causes and Effects of Stress and Violence in Immigrant Families   282

      Effects of Violence   284

      Supporting Survivors   284

      Witnessing Violence   287

Concluding Remarks   288

Chapter Summary   288

Key Terms   289

Critical Thinking Questions   290
Weblinks   290

9 Divorce and Ending Relationships
Trends, Myths, Children, and Ex-Spouses   **292**
Divorce Rates   293
Divorce and Society   297
Separation and Divorce in the Immigrant Population   299
A Historical, Crossnational Overview of Divorce   300
Social Changes   300
Legal Changes   302
Causes of Divorce   305
Micro-sociological Causes   306
Meso-sociological Causes   307
Macro-sociological Causes   314
Effects of Divorce   316
Effects on Both Spouses   317
Effects on Women   321
Effects on Children   323
Relations with Parents   327
Effects on Older Adults   331
Concluding Remarks   332

Chapter Summary   334
Key Terms   335
Critical Thinking Questions   336
Weblinks   336

10 Family Transitions and Diversity   338
Introduction   339
What Is a Family Transition?   341
Social Change in Expected Transitions   343
Family Transitions in the Past   344
Family Transitions Past and Present: Immigrants and Transnational Families   345
Transitions during Childhood   347
Transitions to New Family Structures   347
Transitions in Care Arrangements   349
Delayed Home-Leaving   349
Smaller Households and Single-Person Households   351
Cohabitation, Marriage, and Relationship Dissolution   352
Remarriage and Blended Families   354
Money and Relationships   356
Indigenous Families   356
Lone-Parent Families   360
Families and Disabilities   365

New Contexts for Childbearing and Parenting   366
Transitions in Midlife and for Seniors   369
New Kinds of Close Relations   371
Concluding Remarks   372

Chapter Summary   372
Key Terms   373
Critical Thinking Questions   373
Weblinks   374

11 A Glimpse into the Future

Where Do Families Go from Here?   375
Family Life in the Twenty-First Century   377
Families in the Connected Society   380
  Technology and Family Relations   384
  Comparing Communication Technologies   385
  Communication Technology and the Forming of Relationships   388
  Technology for Family Caregiving   392
New Reproductive Technologies   394
The Growth of Individualization   396
A New Culture of Intimate Life   398
Likely Changes in the Future   401
  Dual-Income Families   403
  Refilled Nests   404
  Nominal and Virtual Families   404
  Increased Diversity   406
  Policy Challenges   406
Concluding Remarks   411

Chapter Summary   411
Key Terms   412
Critical Thinking Questions   413
Weblinks   413

References   415
Index   466

Preface

As can be imagined, discussing Canadian family lives and variations is challenging. That said, this sixth edition of our text has remained the same in its essential focus. Readers have agreed with our approach, which is to stress family processes over structure, diversity over uniformity, and reality over myth. This is a Canadian book, rooted in sociological research from around the world and reflecting concerns of the twenty-first century. It continues to cover the most important topics in the family literature and, as before, ends with a look at the future of families. As in previous editions, we are grateful to anonymous reviewers who have suggested ways to enhance this sixth edition of *Close Relations: An Introduction to the Sociology of Families*. We have followed their helpful suggestions. We also brought aboard a third author for this new edition, Sandra Colavecchia.

APPROACH

As recently as 40 years ago, books on the family were often simple "how-to" guides to family life. Sometimes called "matching, hatching, and dispatching" books, they often had chapters with titles such as "Dating and Courtship" and "Family and You." This approach seemed reasonable decades ago, since the ways in which people lived in families tended to be a little less diverse than it is now, and the diversity that did exist was not much portrayed nor celebrated in family texts. The supposed uniformity of families of four or five decades ago, on closer inspection, did not really exist. There are still books like this today, however, which tend to "sell" the so-called traditional North American way of family life. But, of course, shifting patterns and demands of work in postmodern societies create new kinds of family relations and forms, as we explore in this new edition.

Far more interesting than the regularities in close relations are the variations in family processes, forms, and structures. Twenty-first-century Canadian families are remarkably diverse. It was largely in response to this reality that we wrote the first edition of this text, and then revised it substantially with updated data and new insights about families in subsequent editions, and again in this edition. This text sets itself the task of being different from other family books in use today. Its focus is on applications and theory: what works for families, for us as individuals, and for society. Several themes continue to characterize our text.

■ Families are immensely varied and characterized more by processes than by the forms they take.

- Family is becoming more, not less, important to us as individuals and to society as a whole. Recent research and theory have clearly shown that family health affects individual health and longevity and the population health of entire countries. Yet we are at a point in history when more Canadians are questioning how they might be defined by their intimate relationships and family ties and what these relationships will look like.

- Old expectations about family may no longer work. New solutions to family problems, based on what is known from family research, are offered here.

- There is a constantly changing interplay among families, school, and work. Family is both part of the problem and part of the solution, as shown in this text in a variety of ways.

- Historical changes and cross-national comparisons help us to better understand and interpret families today.

Throughout this text, we look at families as plural and diverse. We focus on families in terms of what they do rather than the shape they take.

CANADIAN CONTENT

Speaking of diversity, this is a Canadian book intended primarily for Canadian students and classrooms. Although some findings based on American, European, or Asian research apply to Canadian situations, others do not. Our laws and policies are different, as are our histories, traditions, values, norms, and customs relating to family and marriage. At the same time, it is difficult to write a text based entirely on Canadian research. It must be noted, however, that both the volume of research on families in Canada and the scope of the topics covered have expanded enormously in recent years. To be useful, a Canadian text should rely on Canadian research and then incorporate findings from abroad. Thus, we attempt here a careful triangulation, using research from Canada, the United States, and the world. On the one hand, we try to offer international comparisons wherever they are important. On the other hand, we do not draw attention to the nationality of a finding if we think that doing so adds nothing to understanding the research on families.

WHAT'S NEW?

Throughout the book, we've added coverage of the role of disability in families and issues facing Indigenous families. We continue to discuss cultural variations among families (including cultural influences on mate selection, attitudes toward marriage and family, relations between parents and children, and so on). Chapters 4, 7, and 10 have been significantly revised to reflect current trends in intimate relationships, gender and labour, and family transitions. We've also retained and updated our discussion of media and its impact on the family, as well as the effects of population aging on families and our discussion of feminist theory. And of course, we've updated discussion, statistics, and references throughout the text and added new graphics, figures, and tables where appropriate.

FEATURES

Each chapter begins with a chapter outline and learning objectives. Throughout the chapters, figures and tables cover key current data on the topics, erroneous beliefs, international findings, major Canadian findings, and key statistics. Each chapter includes a number of boxes that contain interesting facts and observations drawn from other studies. Study tools at the end of each chapter include a chapter summary, key terms with definitions, critical thinking questions, and an annotated list of relevant internet sites.

Chapter 1 begins with an exploration of the variety of interesting shapes and processes of families and family-like relationships. We explore competing definitions of family and how families are seen through theoretical lenses. We also consider different research approaches to family work and what they enable us to see.

Chapter 2 opens the door to what we now know about families in the past. It offers an exciting glimpse of family diversity from a historical perspective, including more on Indigenous families. This discussion provides context for today's debates.

Chapter 3 explores how families begin by taking a look at dating and mating. A renewed emphasis on ethnic and other cultural differences is offered here; attention is also paid to same-sex dating.

In Chapter 4, we examine close relations today and the changes that have taken place in intimate partnerships, living arrangements, families, childbearing, and sexuality.

There follows, in Chapter 5, a discussion of ways of being close, in which we consider points of satisfaction and dissatisfaction, particularly in relation to communication, trust, and sex.

People sometimes think of real family life as beginning with the entry into parenthood—a time fraught with many new changes and challenges. That is the subject of Chapter 6. In this chapter, we also propose several approaches to parenting that are supported by research and offer some solutions to parenting problems.

In Chapter 7, we discuss the intersections between paid and unpaid labour and address the challenges faced by Canadians attempting to juggle paid work with the caregiving of children and ill, injured, disabled, aging, and dying family members.

An understanding of violence and stress in families, the topic of Chapter 8, is crucial if we are to solve or even ameliorate these problems. We describe some of the contexts in which stresses occur for families, including poverty, racism, alcoholism, and the particular challenges faced by Indigenous families. We also give attention to policies that attempt to reduce the negative situations with which families must cope.

In Chapter 9, the trends, myths, causes, and consequences of relationship dissolution and divorce are considered. Evidence that contradicts some of what is commonly said about the fragility of close relationships is presented.

Chapter 10 explores the varied family changes that occur when individuals transition from their families of origin to their own relationships, living arrangements, and families. Transitions have become more numerous, both during childhood and adulthood, due to the increasing instability of intimate partnerships and social change in how people view personal fulfillment, sexuality, and intimate and family relationships.

Chapter 11 takes a glimpse at families of the future, emphasizing how families create their own futures, influenced by both the opportunities and the constraints of society.

SUPPLEMENTS

These instructor supplements are available for download from a password-protected section of Pearson Canada's online catalogue (www.pearsoncanada.ca/highered). Navigate to your book's catalogue page to view a list of the supplements that are available. Speak to your local Pearson sales representative for details and access.

Test Item File. This test bank in Word format contains more than 700 multiple-choice questions, 70 short-answer questions, and 30 long-answer questions that correspond to the text. Designed to test students' comprehension of the material, this supplement contains the relevant page numbers for each question along with the correct answer for each multiple-choice question.

PowerPoint Slides. This practical set of PowerPoint slides outlines key concepts discussed in each chapter and includes selected tables and figures from the text. The slides have been specifically developed for clear and easy summary of themes, ideas, and definitions.

Learning Solutions Managers. Pearson's Learning Solutions Managers work with faculty and campus course designers to ensure that Pearson technology products, assessment tools, and online course materials are tailored to meet your specific needs. This highly qualified team is dedicated to helping schools take full advantage of a wide range of educational resources, by assisting in the integration of a variety of instructional materials and media formats. Your local Pearson Canada sales representative can provide you with more details on this service program.

Acknowledgments

The decision to prepare a sixth edition of this text, though welcome, came when all three authors were deeply involved in other projects. So, time spent working on this new edition was not as relaxed as we might have imagined or hoped for. Instead, this edition demanded intense work, for we resolved to continue improving the text even though our time was limited.

To achieve this goal, we relied on a team of research assistants to help us, and we were lucky to get excellent support from them. Our first thanks go to doctoral student Sophia Jaworksi and freelancer Nicole Meredith, who helped us update and upgrade the sixth edition by collecting and drafting new materials for inclusion. Thanks also go to Maja Jovanovic, who provided additional research assistance. We also thank undergraduate Teodora (Teddy) Avramov, who provided new materials and excellent help with the editing. These fine assistants gave us a huge leg up in the revision, and we thank them for helping so enthusiastically. Thanks also go to Jeffrey Bingley, master's student, at the Prentice Institute for Global Population and Economy, University of Lethbridge, who helped greatly with this edition. We thank him with enthusiasm.

We also want to thank the people at Pearson for their wonderful support from beginning to end—starting first with acquisitions editor Keriann McGoogan, who was helpful and supportive throughout. Rachel Stuckey, who oversaw the revision, made insightful comments and repeatedly shepherded us back toward efficient completion. Thank you, Rachel, for your help and patience. Thanks also to Susan Broadhurst and Seilesh Singh, who skillfully copyedited and proofread the text. Your help is much appreciated.

Finally, we are grateful to those colleagues who acted as anonymous reviewers for this edition, including:

Katie Aubrecht	Saint Francis Xavier University & Mount Saint Vincent University
Wei Wei Da	University of Western Ontario
Kathleen Moss	Carleton University
Kristin Ross	Camosun College

We hope our readers, new and old, will enjoy this edition of the text. Please let us know what you think about it.

Susan A. McDaniel,
University of Lethbridge

Lorne Tepperman,
University of Toronto

Sandra Colavecchia,
McMaster University

Chapter 1
Families and Family-Like Relationships
Definitions, Theories, and Research

Monkey Business Images/Shutterstock

CHAPTER OUTLINE

- Introduction
- The Importance of Family
- What Is Family?
- Defining the Family
- Murdock: Three Relationships
  - Census Family
  - Household versus Family
  - Process-Based Definitions
- Common Elements of Family Life
  - Dependency and Intimacy

- Sexuality
- Protection
- Power
- Violence
- Kinship, Clan, and Community
- New Ways to Understand Family Diversity
- Theoretical Approaches to Understanding Families
  - Theories of Family over Time

- Basic Theoretical Approaches to the Family
  - Structural Functionalism
  - Symbolic Interactionism
  - Marxist Theory of Family
- Feminist Theory
- Postmodern Theory
- Variation despite Convergence
- Life Course Theory
- Concluding Remarks

LEARNING OBJECTIVES

1 Learn different ways to define family.

2 Identify the three key relationships in a nuclear family.

3 Understand the connection between household and census family.

4 Learn the advantages of a process-based definition of family.

5 Define the common processes-based elements of family life.

6 Recognize the importance of intimacy and dependency.

7 Recognize how sexuality is regulated and protected in families.

8 Compare different theoretical approaches to family life.

9 Examine the contributions to theory after functionalism.

10 Consider the life course approach to family life.

INTRODUCTION

Among our deepest and most enduring human needs is to have someone close who understands and loves us and in whom we can confide and trust. In an uncertain and insecure world, we seek solace and hope in close relations, whatever form they might take.

Families belong to a group of relationships we characterize as "close," including intense friendships, love affairs, and long-term social or work relationships. These relationships are characterized by a strong attachment or bonding between the individuals. Not all family members feel strongly attached or bonded to each other. However, what people commonly imagine when they think of the word *family*—what the word *family* evokes in our culture—is attachment, sentiment, and emotional intensity. For most of us, families provide our most important relationships, our first connection to the social world, and a connection that remains important throughout our lives.

This text explores the changing dimensions of family relations and the ways in which they affect and are affected by school, work, society, and, perhaps most importantly, social changes. We examine the diversity of close relations and consider how families may be becoming more rather than less important in our lives.

THE IMPORTANCE OF FAMILY

Some people point to the upsurge in lone-parent households, increases in the number of children born outside legal marriage (Statistics Canada, 2012c), and high but declining divorce rates (Kelly, 2010) as evidence that the family is in trouble. At the same time, public opinion polls consistently find that family life is important to Canadians (Angus Reid, 1999; Vanier Institute of the Family, 2004)—perhaps increasingly important. Since the legalization of same-sex marriages in Canada in 2005, there have not been many polls asking Canadians about their views of families. Nonetheless, it is clear that despite negative trends in marriages, the majority of young Canadians still consider having a spouse and children an important aspect of their lives (Bibby, 2009).

People continue to value families because they provide emotional support and economic security in sharing resources. Perhaps most importantly, families give us grounding in an increasingly uncertain and chaotic world. The familiarity of family can be reassuring and, throughout our lives, gives us the confidence to explore new things.

WHAT IS FAMILY?

Many people think of families as groups of people related through marriage, blood, or adoption. Yet is that description contemporary enough? Is it inclusive enough?

To some people, the answer seems obvious. They propose that the word *families* should be used only to describe "traditional families." Fifty-eight percent of Canadians feel that a traditional family—with one husband, one wife, and children—is the ideal (Bibby, 2004). Yet families have varied in form throughout history, still vary from one society to another, and are different in societies like Canada and the United States. There is, in this sense, no traditional family.

In this text we examine the ways in which families are now viewed and lived. We see that family changes are closely tied to events in society and to what is seen as a social problem or concern.

DEFINING THE FAMILY

People tend to think that when they talk about family, everyone is talking about the same thing. "How's the family?" someone might ask, referring perhaps to one's spouse and possibly children. "I'm taking time now to have a family," says a woman to her co-worker. "My family came from the Ukraine," says another. A person with

Other things may change us, but we start and end with family.

—Anthony Brandt

Families are like fudge—mostly sweet with a few nuts.

—Author Unknown

To us, family means putting your arms around each other and being there.

—Barbara Bush

We cannot destroy kindred: our chains stretch a little occasionally, but they never break.

—Marquise de Sévigné

The family. We were a strange little band of characters trudging through life sharing diseases and toothpaste, coveting one another's desserts, hiding shampoo, borrowing money, locking each other out of our rooms, inflicting pain and kissing to heal it in the same instant, loving, laughing, defending, and trying to figure out the common thread that bound us all together.

—Erma Bombeck

Family life is a bit like a runny peach pie—not perfect but who's complaining?

—Robert Brault

What greater thing is there for two human souls than to feel that they are joined—to strengthen each other—to be at one with each other in silent unspeakable memories?

—George Eliot

A family is a unit composed not only of children but of men, women, an occasional animal, and the common cold.

—Ogden Nash

Source: www.quotegarden.com/family.html

human immunodeficiency virus (HIV) says, "My family are those around me now who support me." Immigration policy refers to "family reunification," where the concept of family has shrunk to include only close blood relatives and spouses and now includes fewer relatives. What do these images of family have in common? How differently do we see family?

Answers to questions about family are far from only academic. How family and other close relations are defined matters to us personally—to our values, our dreams, our hopes as individuals, and our identities.

Definitions are important also for our rights under the law and our claims to pensions, schools, child support, and many other social resources (Turner and West, 2014).

Debates rage about whether cohabiting spouses should have the same rights as married spouses, about parental rights for gays and lesbians, and about the financial responsibilities and the rights (to custody, access, and so on) of divorced people. Let's look now at some definitions of family.

MURDOCK: THREE RELATIONSHIPS

For many years, sociologists used as a benchmark George Murdock's (1949: 1) definition of family as a social group characterized by a common residence, economic cooperation and reproduction [including] adults of both sexes, at least two of whom maintain a socially approved sexual relationship, and one or more children, own or adopted, of the sexually cohabiting adults.

By this definition, three basic relationships—co-residence, economic cooperation, and reproduction—must all be present to qualify a social group as a family. Murdock's definition excludes many groups that most of us consider families: childless married couples, for example, and single parents and their children. Same-sex unions are excluded, as are married couples who are separated. Celibate couples, according to Murdock, cannot be a family even if they have children, live together, and share other kinds of intimacy. (This means questioning a couple about their sex life to find out whether they and their children make up a family.) Two sisters who live together cannot be a family, according to Murdock. Thus, Murdock's definition does not seem to allow for the variability that exists among families living in Canada today.

Census Family

Because the approach to defining family discussed previously is so limiting, Statistics Canada (2011a), the official census and survey agency for Canada, takes a much more inclusive approach. Statistics Canada defines family, for the Census, as comprising a married or a common-law couple (a couple can be opposite sex or same sex) with or without children, or a lone parent living with at least one child in the same dwelling. Married or common-law couple families with children refer to a family with at least one child age 24 or younger who is present in the home. This definition also includes children from either a current or a previous union, but excludes children who might have a permanent residence other than that of their parents at the time of the Census.

This definition is better, since it includes a wider variety of people. However, it still misses many groups that consider themselves families and are considered families by others outside of their household. This being so, many researchers have changed their focus to households for practical purposes.

Household versus Family

Market researchers and census-takers often try to sidestep difficulties of definition by focusing on "households" as though they were "families." Doing so allows us to talk about changes in households and imply changes in close relations without necessarily addressing changes in families or family life. Yet this approach also presents problems. As pointed out by Eichler (1997), many families live in separate households but maintain ongoing family relationships. The prime example is divorced families in which custody is joint or shared (Smart and Neale, 1999); the divorced parents and their child(ren) form at least one family and maybe more. For other trends in Canadian families, see "Six Trends for Canadian Families" on page 8.

A "household" may contain only one person or many unrelated members—roommates, boarders, or residents in a group home. Or it may contain a **nuclear family**, an **extended family**, or multiple families (e.g., co-ops, group homes, or families sharing living space to save money). Sharing living accommodations among generations is, as we shall see, a growing trend in Canada. Occasionally, these arrangements involve multiple families—parents, for example, with their parents or with their adult children's families. Conversely, a family may spread across many households, even households located in different countries. However, usually it is thought, whether true or not, that families and households coincide, resulting in "family households."

In the United States, family households are officially defined by the Bureau of the Census as married couples with or without children younger than 18 years or one-parent families with children younger than 18. As we shall discover, this definition may be problematic in that it excludes growing numbers of cohabiting couples. Family households also comprise other households of related individuals (e.g., two sisters sharing a household or a parent living with a child older than 17 years). Non-family households contain unrelated individuals or people who live alone. Canadian definitions from Statistics Canada and other official data-gathering organizations are similar but tend to be broader and more inclusive.

Process-Based Definitions

The Vanier Institute of the Family (2013a) uses a function- or process-based definition of family in Canada. This definition looks at the functions families perform, such as providing emotional, financial, and material support to its members, care of each other, transmission of cultural values, and personal development. In using this type of definition, the Vanier Institute is defining families in terms of their main shared processes, rather than in terms of structural features that they may not—and increasingly do not—share. The United Nations (2016) uses a similar approach to defining families.

In Canada, serious consideration has been given to the question of what family is and what families are. The question has been taken up by family researchers, the Vanier Institute of the Family, and the Canadian Committee for the International Year of the Family, on which one of the authors of this book (McDaniel) served. The conclusion is that ultimately families are defined not by the shape they take but by what they do (Vanier Institute of the Family, 2013a). As Moore Lappé (1985: 8) puts it:

> Families are not marriages or homes or rules. Families are people who develop intimacy because they . . . share experiences that come . . . to make up their

uniqueness—the mundane, even silly, traditions that emerge in a group of people who know each other. . . . It is this intimacy that provides the ground for our lives.

Over the past few decades, a broad process-based definition of family has become accepted by most Canadians (see Angus Reid, 1999; Vanier Institute of the Family, 2000, 2004, 2013a, 2016). Much of current Canadian family law and policy reflects the move toward inclusion of families that are diverse but similar in their processes, if not their structures (Kronby, 2010).

As one example, in 2003, Alberta passed the Adult Interdependent Relationships Act. The law defines relationship as "a range of personal relationships that fall outside of the traditional institution of marriage" (Alberta Justice, 2002). By doing so, it amends several statutes as they relate to people in non-conjugal relationships and recognizes financial and property benefits and responsibilities attached to these relationships.

Governments as well as various other organizations are trying to keep up with societal changes in the family. However, some groups oppose inclusive definitions, saying that changing the definition of family changes the nature of family itself. The diversity of families is controversial and continues to be a political issue, with groups squaring off in various levels of government. In 2016 alone, the family definition debate was part of a very divisive U.S. election. This and concerns in other countries led the United Nations Human Rights Commission to state that it is "not possible to give the concept (of family) a standard definition" (United Nations, 2016), and European policy vacillated on whether to validate or criminalize child marriage among arriving refugees, with human rights law being used both to support and to oppose such measures (BBC News, 2016; Charter, 2016; Parusel, 2016). Gay and lesbian families have also become a touchstone in the United States in many contemporary debates about what is and is not a family and what rights and entitlements those who are deemed family ought to have.

Remember that Statistics Canada, in its definition of census family mentioned earlier, includes same-sex families. Same-sex couples have had the option of legal marriage across Canada since 2005 and in several provinces prior to that. Similarly, immigration and growing ethnic diversity have challenged the ways in which we define family forms and maintain and connect in close relations. From the perspective of immigrants, the changing ways in which Canadians define and view family can also be challenging, and change tends to create stress between generations. How changes and adjustment are negotiated when differing cultural groups enter neighbouring space is the subject of acculturation theory. Overlapping interests in the definition of family matter greatly when policies and legislation are being planned, and these definitions may differ by cultural group.

How family is defined and thought about is a weather vane for social ideas and ideologies. The kind of research done in the study of families reflects the concerns of the day. We shall explore this idea in more detail later in this chapter.

- The number of common-law couple families increased 18.9 percent between 2001 and 2006, more than five times the increase for married-couple families. And from 2006 to 2011, the number of common-law couples rose again by 13.9 percent, more than four times the 3.1 percent increase for married couples (Statistics Canada, 2012a).
- In 2011, there were more census families that consisted of couples without children (44.5 percent) than those with children (39.2 percent; Statistics Canada, 2012a).
- Lone-parent families headed by men increased by 16.6 percent since 2001.

- In 2011, children age 4 years and younger were more likely to have a mother in her forties than they were in 2001.
- The proportion of children age 14 years and under who lived with common-law parents increased from 12.8 percent in 2001 to 16.3 percent in 2011.
- More young adults ages 20 to 29 years in 2011 were living in the parental home compared to 2001.

Source: Statistics Canada. 2012. *Family Portrait: Continuity and Change in Canadian Families and Households in 2006.* Ottawa: Statistics Canada. Catalogue no. 97-553-XIE.

COMMON ELEMENTS OF FAMILY LIFE

The social groups we think of as families typically share many features, and that commonality can help us begin to understand the nature of families. Because families are extraordinarily diverse in the twenty-first century, it is difficult to generalize about them. However, it is possible to focus our attention on some common processes.

Dependency and Intimacy

All close relations have in common attachment and some dependency or interdependency. This is not unique to families; most close friendships and social or work relationships also include a degree of emotional dependency, based on familiarity and expectations of reciprocity. However, family relations are special in that they tend to include long-term commitments, both to each other and to the shared family.

Sexuality

Adult partners within families typically have, or are expected to have, a long-term, exclusive sexual relationship, whereas among circles of friends or co-workers, sexual relations are expected to be either absent or of short duration. In families, sexual relations are allowed and expected between spouses but banned between other family members (e.g., parents, children, and extended family members). Norms of sexual propriety are much stronger in families than they are in friendship or work circles.

Taboos against sexual exploitation of children exist to prevent sexual relations with a family member other than a spouse. Nevertheless, sexual abuse of children and elders does occur within families, as we know.

Protection

Effective families keep their members under guard against all kinds of internal and external dangers. There is a clear cultural expectation that families will try to protect their members. Parents and relatives are supposed to keep children safe from accidents and household dangers, and away from drugs, alcohol, predators, and other forms of harm. As well, spouses are supposed to protect one another, and adult children are supposed to protect and help their parents. All this is an ideal. In reality, family members often fail to protect each other enough, and worse, some people neglect, exploit, or abuse family members. Others overprotect, hovering over children so the child has little independence. However, those who break the cultural rules face criticism and disapproval.

Power

Households and families are small social groups whose members spend time together and depend on each other to fill both economic and social needs. There are large differences in power, strength, age, and social resources among members. Ideally, the more powerful family members protect the less powerful ones. However, it is this imbalance in power that makes **patriarchy**—control of the family by a dominant male (typically, the father)—a central fact in the history of family life in most known societies. Simply put, men have dominated because they possessed and controlled more of the resources. And, in much of family law and policy, this domination over family by men was seen as a right, occasionally even a duty.

Families have been seen historically in practice and occasionally in law as men's places of domination and control. The often-heard phrase, "A man's home is his castle," reflects this. As we will see in this text, feminist scholarship and theory have taken us a long way in understanding the multiple ways in which patriarchy has shaped, and continues to shape, families.

Violence

Likewise, families—though idealized as peaceful and loving—are also marked by violence, perhaps to a higher degree than any other groups based on close relations. Violence has always existed in families, but in recent decades reports of violence within families have grown and received much more public and policy attention. The increase is likely the result of more reporting rather than an increase in violent acts. In fact, domestic violence against women has decreased since 2004 (Statistics Canada,

2016a). While a decrease is evident in the overall Canadian population, the rates of family violence among Indigenous people remains high. Usually the assailant is a spouse or boyfriend. As well, researchers estimate that one girl in four and one boy in ten is sexually abused before the age of 16, often by friends or relatives. Perhaps violence is more common in families than in other close relations precisely because, for many, the family is a place of intense emotions. Its patriarchal structure also is a contributing factor. Also, proximity makes it easy to inflict violence behind closed doors, and some family members are young or otherwise vulnerable and cannot easily escape.

KINSHIP, CLAN, AND COMMUNITY

So far, we have focused on families as they exist normatively in our own dominant culture. However, families vary from one society to another, just as they vary within our own society. In many societies, families exist within larger social networks—in kinship groups and clans—and we cannot understand how nuclear families function unless we also understand their place in these larger networks and in the community at large. The members of the household, whatever form that may take—for example, husband and wife, parent and child, brother and sister—are integrated into a larger web of kin—uncles, aunts, cousins, grandparents, grandchildren—and their lives cannot be understood without reference to this larger web.

A **kinship group** is a group of people who share a relationship through blood or marriage and have positions in a hierarchy of rights over the property. The definition of a kin relationship varies among societies; kin relationships may also influence where the members live, whom they can marry, and even their life opportunities.

Some societies count relationships through the male line, so that any individual's relationships are determined by his or her father's relationships; we call such kinship systems **patrilineal**. Others count relationships through the female line; these are **matrilineal** systems. Still others count relationships through both lines; they are **bilateral kinship systems**.

The Canadian approach is mildly patrilineal, but of course this is not the case for all recent immigrants. In a patrilineal system, a woman has historically taken her husband's family name, not the reverse, and this name is the one that passes to the children. However, this is not the case everywhere in the West. In Quebec, for example, the law prevents women from taking their husband's name on marriage. And some couples invent new names by hyphenating their names or choosing a new last name that everyone takes. There are also examples of men taking their wives' last name on marriage.

Our family system overall tends to follow the Western pattern, in which property is also typically inherited along the male line. Where families settle down is traditionally determined by the husband's job, not the wife's, although this is changing as more women in families become the main earner. However, our society also has certain matrifocal characteristics. Because women have been defined as the primary **kin-keepers**—the people who maintain family contacts—children tend to have stronger ties with their mother's kin than with their father's kin (Rosenthal, 1985; Thomson and Li, 1992: 15). Children also tend to preserve closer contacts with their mothers when the parents grow old (Connidis, 2001). When parents of grown children live separately, fathers are less often visited, called, and relied on than are mothers.

NEW WAYS TO UNDERSTAND FAMILY DIVERSITY

In this text, we will propose repeatedly that some of the older ways of understanding family life do not serve us well in a diverse, fluid, and increasingly global society such as Canada. As a result, we have adopted some new approaches to studying family life.

The life course approach is one way of studying family change. The pioneering study by Glen Elder of children in the Depression (Elder, 1992) opened the door to this approach to studying families. This life course perspective follows families and individuals over time, studying a variety of social and interpersonal dynamics of close relations (linked lives) and how these change throughout lifetimes (Bengston, Biblarz, and Roberts, 2002; Hofferth and Goldscheider, 2016; McDaniel and Bernard, 2011; Thomson, Winkler-Dworak, and Kennedy, 2013). Over time, families change—change is the nature of families—to meet new needs, such as the arrival, care, or departure of children; aging; and other life course changes. These changes have effects on the entire family system: on relations between spouses, parents and children, and siblings; and on the family's relations with the "outside world," such as parents' changing relations with their employers and their careers (Kruger and Levy, 2001; Martinengo, Jacob, and Hill, 2010; McDaniel and Bernard, 2011; McDaniel et al., 2013). More on this later in the chapter.

One newer approach recognizes that, within any given family, different members have different interests and experiences. Because different family members often have different interests, it is often inappropriate to speak of "the family" as though it has a single interest and acts in a unified way. Gazso and McDaniel (2010b, 2014) have used a similar approach by interviewing multiple members of families who by choice are living in low-income circumstances. Much family research in the past was done from a male perspective (Eichler, 2001; Giddens, 1992; Luxton, 1997). Instead, what do family life and changes in close relations among adults look like from the viewpoint of children, for example? Markedly different, as we are now discovering (Mason, Skolnick, and Sugarman, 2003; McDaniel, Gazso, and Duncan, 2016). Children live in many and varied kinds of families while still dependent, and changes in family are happening both earlier and later in their lives than occurred for children in times past. Looking at the changes in close relations among adults from the viewpoint of children gives us a new and important vantage point on families. For example, adults tend to worry that divorce is negative for children, and it can be at times, but some children see advantages in having more than two parents.

Another way to study family diversity is by exploring different groups in society in order to better understand how they function as families. This text, for instance, examines the way immigrant, rural, Indigenous, and gay and lesbian families work and the way historical and societal changes have shaped and influenced their family lives. Consider Indigenous families. Because of changes imposed on them by the Canadian government though the Indian Act, many Indigenous children were separated from their families involuntarily and shipped off to residential schools or to live with other Canadian families in an effort to integrate them into what was then seen as mainstream society. It was a long-standing policy—lasting more than a century—of forced assimilation (see King, 2012). In doing so, generations were disrupted, and many parents were unable to pass on important Indigenous traditions to their children or be the loving and caring parents they would have liked to have been. This, as was found by the Truth and Reconciliation Commission in 2015 and will be seen in the following chapters, has had lasting negative effects for Indigenous families.

By studying differences in families, we learn that families may look different today, but it is essentially the process of family life that is important to the health of the family and its members. For one, gay and lesbian families may not be structured like the "typical" heterosexual family, but more and more research shows that they provide security, love, and other fundamental family supports to their children and partners (Sullivan, 2012).

Another approach is to collect data in new ways so that family diversity can be studied over time. This is consistent with the life course perspective on families. Instead of studying families at one point in time, the interest with longitudinal data is to follow families over a longer span of time. Examples are Statistics Canada's National Longitudinal Survey of Children and Youth (NLSCY; Willms, 2002) and the Survey of Labour and Income Dynamics (SLID; Statistics Canada, 1996a), which build a picture of the changes in people's work and family lives over time. The NLSCY followed individual children as they grew, interviewing them and their families every two years. Data were collected[1] on family changes, schooling, health, and a range of variables that affect children's lives.

Findings from this survey have taught us that the effect on children of living with a lone parent is more than the result of the low incomes often faced by these families. In a study using the NLSCY data, researchers McIntyre, Williams, Lavorato, and Patten (2013) were able to isolate effects of child hunger as a contributor to depression and suicidal ideation in late adolescence. Maternal depression also clearly emerged through NLSCY data as a factor in the mental well-being of those who later become adolescents. Through longitudinal data we see that strengthening neighbourhood social cohesion seems to reduce mental health risks for children (Kingsbury et al., 2015). From the life course perspective and longitudinal data, we see that families

---

[1] The NLSCY has now been discontinued.

have different "life histories," and as these histories develop and change, they shape the prospects of their members, especially the youngest members. Understanding these dynamics gives society better tools to choose policies that will improve the prospects for society's newest members and their families.

A wealth of new insights is emerging about children's lives and how families and society can best benefit in the long run. The good news for both lone parents and for society from this longitudinal research is that good parenting can, largely, overcome these harmful effects. Much more is learned by following the same people (children or adults) over time and seeing whether they can, eventually, escape the disadvantages of a low-income childhood, and if so, how.

All families change, and the times change families. Whitehead (1996: 1) points out that families change with the times: "One day, the Ozzie and Harriet couple is eating a family meal at the dining room table; the next day, they are working out a joint custody agreement in a law office." Studying families in a context of change reminds us to stay away from simple definitions of family, or theories about family life and change that assume that all families are the same and stay the same, regardless of their socio-historical context.

THEORETICAL APPROACHES TO UNDERSTANDING FAMILIES

A theory puts things together in a way that helps us understand the social world. Theories may be only speculation about how things might work, although some are based more on evidence than others. Each theoretical approach is different, and each one may have a different insight to contribute to our understanding. In the following section, we discuss how the thinking about families and research on families have changed over time. These changes in thinking are closely tied to the events and climate in a society. Then, we highlight some basic theoretical approaches to understanding families. However, these are not all of the theoretical approaches. Each one of the approaches presented allows you to begin to see aspects of families that you might not have seen without the use of the theoretical lens. Theories offer a kaleidoscope of possibilities.

Theories of Family over Time

Thinking about families over time is challenging for sociologists for three linked reasons. First, there is new information, not only about families now but also about families in the past and how they lived. This new information challenges our understandings and shakes our beliefs about families and family change. Second, new ways to view families, socially and politically, are connected to new theories about families. If you think theories are only academic, think again! Feminist and gay and lesbian theories of family (often called "queer theories" in the literature) have been hotly contested by some interest groups and politicians. And the debate goes beyond family theory. New sociological and cultural studies theories and their proponents were blamed in part for the lack of simple political agreement on the causes of the terrorist attacks of September 11, 2001. Americans, and at times Canadians, too, were asked not only to denounce terrorists and terrorism but also to avoid postmodern social theorizing—theorizing that implied that societies are complex, with many factors leading to the taking up of terrorism. More recently, former Prime Minister Stephen Harper said publicly that discussing the "root causes" of terrorism was inappropriate, that we should simply condemn terrorism. He made clear that looking at root causes was sociology and that we should not "commit sociology." Theories are much alive and part of public debate. Third, changing family lives and changing ways to see families have risks and concerns that make us constantly question and revise our theories. Keep these challenges in mind as we outline how families have been viewed over time.

"The family" as we currently imagine it is a surprisingly recent social idea. Before the eighteenth century in Europe, for example, the term *family* was not necessarily used to refer to groups that today we see as nuclear families—parents with their children (Flandrin, 1979; Trumbach, 2013). More important then was the larger social grouping or the community. The focus was on how people lived, how they produced food and other necessities, and how they shared them. Therefore, much of the study of communities, and indirectly of families, has focused on sustaining life.

Anthropological, intensive studies of small communities have found that in foraging societies—which gathered food such as roots and berries—childbearing was more often postponed to later in life than in early agricultural societies (Fox and Luxton, 2001). There were few assets to inherit in societies that foraged, so it was proposed that, in theory, there were fewer restrictions on how children were viewed in relation to their parents. Families *per se* may not have been seen to "own children." Rather, children may have been seen as belonging to the community.

A well-known theory developed by Friedrich Engels ([1884] 1972), the theoretical collaborator of Karl Marx, in the late nineteenth century paints a picture of people living in a group without giving much importance to whose spouse was whose or which children belonged to which parents. The children were "parented" by the entire community, Engels asserts. All children were welcomed, and even though their biological parents may have been known, it didn't change how people lived. There was some evidence that communities like this did, in fact, exist. Some still live much like this, especially in poor urban neighbourhoods (see Edin and Kissane, 2010; Stacey, 1990), with entire communities raising children and little focus on nuclear family structures.

Once agricultural development began to yield a food surplus, people no longer consumed their food immediately but could save and store it. This led to the idea, according to Engels, of private property and new ideas about the organization of family life. Then, Engels says, it mattered much more who a child's parents were, as inheritance was to follow bloodlines. How these bloodlines were decided is unclear, according to Engels's theory. Men began to control the food surplus, it was theorized. Women were expected to be sexually faithful to their husbands, to ensure that the children they had were their husband's. Monogamy was born, this theory proposes, not because it was more moral than any other system of family or because living in families was a natural way to live. Monogamy was related to the economics of life at the time.

In part, many contemporary controversies about family life are efforts to wrest the family away from the effects of economic factors and commercial culture. For example, some conservative groups propose the family is more natural and fundamental than any economic change. Families, they propose, should resist pressures to change. In fact, research centred in Indigenous and ethnic minority paradigms finds that preserving familism is protective across childhood and adolescence (Stein et al., 2014). We are encouraged to be reflective about imposing Western values that tend to equate change with progress.

Another theory of family change parallels Engels's theory but follows a different thread at a different historical moment. The theory of Le Play proposes that families in feudal times were large and extended, with blood relatives and members of the community of the castle largely undifferentiated from each other. Large, extended families were not always happy. Some, for example, had many children not because they wanted them or could afford them. As a result, some large families lived in poverty with a mother worn down by childbearing. However, with the development of towns, trades, and markets, this kind of community "family" became awkward. It was not easily mobile. So, the smaller "stem family" emerged, a family that ran the farm or small shop while the rest of the family members moved on. It was this development that led, in large part, to a massive out-migration from Europe to North America in the nineteenth and early twentieth centuries, as more people without access to family enterprises sought opportunities in the "new world" of North America.

Prior to the 1850s, sociology was only in its infancy, as was thinking about family. Family theory consisted largely of Judeo-Christian religious belief. The biblical "begats" of the Old Testament characterized a patriarchal theory that saw an elder male as head of a community, clan, extended family, or even realm. In many ways, monarchies are remnants of this system. It is only rarely, in the absence of a male heir, that women become the heads of state and spiritual leaders of the realm. It was as recently as 2013 that the law was changed in the United Kingdom to eliminate male preference in the line of succession, a custom already in place in most other European monarchies. The system of male headship was more than familial and private; it was a system of governing before public systems of law and democracy were invented. In fact, the parliamentary system of government in Canada still parallels democracy with a ruling monarch who is Head of State. The extended-kin headship system was presumed to be natural and unchanging in both theory and practice. It was also, theoretically at least, presumed as a model for the emerging urban working class to follow.

In the middle of the nineteenth century, debates in society started to challenge old religion-based theories about family. This does not mean that religious beliefs or theories about family disappeared. In fact, they have continued to this day, some say even more actively as the twenty-first century began (Bibby, 2011).

The emerging debate in the 1850s occurred as societies were changing rapidly with industrialization and the beginning of capitalism. Social unrest was apparent, as were social movements that challenged prevailing beliefs. One belief actively challenged at that time was the role of women in family and society. New kinds of societies were springing up, based not on patriarchal authority, but on communal living arrangements in which women and men were more equal and children could be raised collectively (Luxton, 2001: 34). This experimental approach continued with the kibbutz or collective farming settlement in Israel; many there are still communal. Elsewhere, people lobbied for women's rights in both marriage and society. Married women at that time were not entitled to own property or to vote, or to have many other citizenship rights that women today take for granted.

Paralleling these changing social attitudes were changing sociological theories. Émile Durkheim, known as one of the founders of sociology, saw family as a social creation, not as something given by nature or religion. His theories about family had two aspects, and the two did not fit together well. First, he argued in favour of "the law of contraction," or that families were, in the middle of the nineteenth century, being reduced in size at the same time as family ties were being intensified. Second, he then theorized that relations between husbands and wives were organized by society as monogamous and "near perfect" (Sydie, 1987: 19–20). Durkheim saw the marriage relationship as permanent, unequal, highly regulated by society, and, crucially, the means of moral organization of all of society. Family was theorized as both less and more important than in earlier times. It was less important in that family sizes were reduced, but more important in that families' ties were strengthened. Key to Durkheim's contribution was his understanding of family as a social creation, not as something given by nature or religion.

As industrialization continued in the nineteenth century, family and work became more separate. Work, which had been an integral part of family life, was moved out of the family and into the marketplace. As work became separated from family, specialization of men in work and women in family began to emerge, creating the notion of separate spheres in which women were seen as being naturally suited to home life and raising children (private sphere) and men to the outside world (public sphere). Social theorists like Durkheim saw the bond between husband and wife as strengthened by this increasing specialization (Sydie, 1987: 22). The search began for biological differences between men and women to parallel the growing social differences in family and society. In hindsight, some of these searches were amusing. A Dr. Lebon is quoted by Durkheim as reporting, "The volume of the crania of men and women, even when we compare subjects of equal age, of equal height and equal weight, show differences in favour of man..." (quoted in Sydie, 1987: 22). We now know that this difference does not exist (McGlone, 1980), and many historians and sociologists are now recognizing that even during this period of separate spheres and biological determinism, women still held a great amount of independence and autonomy in running their own households, employing and managing servants, and being involved in charity work. Regardless, that social theories about family were linked to presumed biological differences between men and women was significant to later theories. It is also important to observe that sociological theories of the day were in response to the push in society for social change.

Most of the sociological theorists of the nineteenth century were white, middle-class men. Many, it has been proposed since, were keen to defend or promote the new capitalism and the new way to view marriage and family (Mandell, 2011). Some insisted the birth rate would fall if marriage were changed and if women were more equal to men. The argument is further made that the gender-differentiated responsibilities in marriage are natural and based on both biology and God's will. Other theorists—for example, Herbert Spencer—see this kind of family as a social construction that supports (and should support) capitalism. The patriarchal family was seen as the peak of social evolution (Luxton, 2001; Sydie, 1987). Had these social

The 1950s are occasionally seen as the "golden age" of the nuclear family, when suburbs were settled and the standard North American family (SNAF) was born.

Black and White Retro and Nostalgia/Mark Sykes/Alamy Stock Photo theorists been women, or working class or Indigenous or ethnic minorities, they might have viewed family differently. Writings from some social movements of that time seem less content with the patriarchal family (Dua, 1999; Eichler, 2001; Luxton, 2001; Sydie, 1987).

As society changed, so did the preoccupations of family researchers. For instance, in the 1920s when the Roaring Twenties overtook the Victorian era, sociologists turned their attention to dating and courtship. Women, previously so guarded in their appearance, dress, and behaviour, were dancing the Charleston in public, no longer wearing corsets, and showing not only ankles but also knees as they kicked up their heels! Speakeasy clubs, where men and women could drink, socialize, dance, and listen to music and entertainers, became popular. Society worried, caught up as always in concerns about social and family change. So, sociologists studied these changes by looking at relations among young people and changed dating practices.

The 1950s saw what many still consider the "golden age" of the nuclear family. The suburbs were created and nuclear families thrived, or at least seemed to. Moms did the child rearing and Dads commuted to work. Television programs such as *Father Knows Best, Leave It to Beaver,* and *The Adventures of Ozzie and Harriet* promoted a cultural ideal of family life. The standard North American family (SNAF) was born. As in previous eras, this kind of family had the support of family theory. The 1950s can be better seen as a response to a time of political insecurity and uncertainty after World War II that was, in general, an unusual decade in the twentieth century. This will be further discussed in Chapter 2.

In terms of family theory, the basic concept was that the family was an essential social institution, well adapted to fit into society. Furthermore, the nuclear family differentiated by gender was seen as a universal, something good for everyone. Earlier work by Malinowski among the Australian Aborigines lent credibility to the North American nuclear family form (Luxton, 2001). His views and assumptions about biological differences between men and women found their way into later theories of structural functionalists such as Talcott Parsons, a giant of twentieth-century sociology. Key to Malinowski's theory was that the nuclear family specialized by gender was essential for societies to function smoothly.

The advent of the structural functional theory (see page 21) led to research on men as breadwinners and less so on women as housewives. Research viewed families with a resolutely happy face. Until the late 1960s, there was nothing in the sociology of the family on family violence or on women's dissatisfaction with their families or their family roles. This is surprising, given what we know now of the "mad housewife" of the 1950s, the high teen pregnancy rate, and the unhappiness of many men with the breadwinner role of that time. But, so it was.

Structural functional theories of family were not used only to study families; the same theories shaped workplace policies. If women, for example, were theorized to specialize in family and men in work, then women were presumed not to be good workers. Married women were often fired from paid employment upon marriage, since it was thought that they were now to be housewives and dependent economically on their husbands. Women, who were, according to family theory at the time, emotional and centred on caring, were not thought to be appropriate candidates for jobs that required judgment or supervision. They were also excluded from jobs that involved risk, such as pilots, miners, soldiers, and much blue-collar work. That women had done a lot of this kind of work during World War II while the men who usually worked in these jobs were at war didn't seem to matter. Women were viewed as family specialists, unsuited by nature to working for pay, and certainly not suited to working for pay in high-paying jobs! Some of this thinking lingers in the twenty-first century.

Research using this theoretical approach was intensely focused on family dynamics and interactions and on how families around the world were becoming more similar and more like the U.S. ideal. Not surprisingly, other theories developed that let us look at these aspects of family more clearly. One of these was *symbolic interactionism*. While not fully disputing structural-functionalist theory, symbolic interactionists looked at how people interpret social organization and expectations. They focused on how we change our behaviours depending on how others behave and treat us. This is an "in the face" look at family interactions. Mothers' interactions with children was a favourite subject of research.

The concept of "roles" became a central part of the vocabulary of sociology of family. Society assigned the roles, but all of the roles were not the same in all aspects of our lives. So, a woman could play the mother role with her children and then the wife role with her husband. Increasingly, both were "scripted" by self-styled marriage and parenting experts who based the expertise they marketed on social theories of family. The role of the mother, for example, was scripted as caring, selfless, unassertive, and always there for the child. It became an ideal, something to be carefully worked toward by women, no matter what their individual inclinations might be. In its demands, the mother role also overshadowed everything else.

Beginning in the 1970s and continuing in the 1980s, there was what Cheal (1991) and others have called a "big bang" in sociological theories on families. So big was this "bang," proposed Cheal (2002), Giddens (1992), Fox and Luxton (2001), among others, that there was no turning back to previous ways of viewing families. All subsequent theories, states Cheal (2002), can be traced to this "big bang"—the feminist theories of families.

There is no single feminist sociological theory of family or of any other aspect of society: There are many. What is so different about feminist sociological theories of family is the opening of fresh new ways to regard families. Feminist theories, like family theories before them, grew out of the times. After the 1960s, there was increased political unrest in women's lives. The political push for daycare; for reproductive rights; for equal access to jobs, promotions, and benefits; for rights in marriage; for the right *not* to marry; for gays and lesbians; for older women; for the disabled; for children; and for the poor and disenfranchised led to the posing of "why" questions.

Why are all of these groups disadvantaged relative to straight, white, middle-class men with jobs? The answers called for new ways to see, new lenses through which to view the social and political landscape.

Feminist theories have several dimensions in common. For example, they all note discrimination and unequal advantage: Even in families, we find gendered social inequalities. They agree that no particular family form is God's will or written into our biology. There is a feeling that things we create, we can uncreate and recreate. Family, proposes much of feminist theory, is an ideology as much as a way to live. We owe concern and respect to the larger community, as well as to the members of our household. So, the nuclear family should not—cannot—be the extent of our social responsibility and affection.

A key insight of feminist theories of family is that the family is not private, but an important public social institution. Feminist theories reveal how families are power based. There are hierarchies of who has the money, who gets listened to, and who is more likely to be abused. The list is a long one, and we will explore many of these issues in this text.

Perhaps most fundamentally, feminist sociology opened new ways of thinking about sociological research on families. As a result, researchers now look through the feminist lens at the multiple ways to live in families, for example. Gay and lesbian families were studied for the first time as families, whereas previously they had been studied only through the sociology of deviance. Families were seen not as given but as being in constant change. People began to explore the ideology of the nuclear family and the denial of other ways to live. It is easy to see why so many see this theorizing as a "big bang."

For Canadian sociologists especially, immigration theories have become popular and an important part of understanding a large segment of our society. As of 2016, Canada welcomed 280 000 to 320 000 new immigrants per year (Immigration, Refugees and Citizenship Canada, 2016). They come seeking a new home and a new life (McDonald et al., 2010). Much of the research on immigrant families is concerned with acculturation, which is sometimes defined as the "process by which ethnic and racial groups learn and begin to participate in the cultural traditions, values, beliefs, assumptions, and practices of the dominant or host culture" (Lee and Edmonston, 2013). Most importantly, acculturation is a gradual process that often occurs more quickly for immigrant children than parents, since immigrant youth must adopt the language and culture of their new country quickly in order to succeed in school and social relations among peers. Also, children have an easier time learning languages and cultural habits than do older people.

Meanwhile, immigrant parents, facing considerable pressure to integrate successfully into the new country, often turn to their own cultural communities in search of knowledge about ways to start life anew and for financial and emotional support. Also, many immigrants live in extended family households and rely on kinship ties to face life challenges (Bastida, 2001).

As a result, over time an **acculturation gap** often emerges within immigrant families, meaning that there is distance between immigrant children and their parents in their language ability and cultural values; parents tend to rely more heavily on their former cultural views. According to Hwang (2006), this situation increases the risk for family dysfunction and potential health problems (see also Boyce and Fuligni, 2007).

Immigrant families are increasingly becoming part of the Canadian population, so their challenges and experiences are of essential importance to our society. The effects of acculturation and related topics on immigrant families will be further discussed throughout the text.

Lastly, in the latter part of the twentieth century and now in the twenty-first century, *postmodern* and *post-structural* theories of families have emerged (Cheal, 2002; Klein and White, 1996). With globalization, the spread of international capitalism, and the development of new, more controlling technologies, new theories of the family were needed. A central dimension of postmodernism and post-structuralism is the notion of flux or constant change. Family members today may live in multiple families and households that change in response to the changing circumstances around them. But we also change our families and households and our ways of being women and men in big ways—for example, through globalization, immigration, economic depression, and surges in unemployment. Topics researched from the point of view of these theories include sexuality, body images, cultural images, and representations, including theories and ideologies of families.

BASIC THEORETICAL APPROACHES TO THE FAMILY

Structural Functionalism

As shown in Table 1.1, there are various theoretical approaches to studying family life, and they proceed from somewhat different assumptions about the organization of social life more generally. Structural functionalism proposes that everything in society has a structure and purpose. It is up to us to see and understand those purposes. Structural functionalism is a theoretical approach developed in the first half of the twentieth century and applied to families by a variety of North American sociologists.

This approach directs us to view families in the light of how they benefit society, and how each member of a family fits in with the purposes that families serve. Why have nuclear families? From this standpoint, nuclear families are seen as useful because they are small, versatile, and mobile; when social change occurs, families can change easily. What purpose does a gender division of labour at home serve where women nurture children and men work for pay? Well, again the answer is simple and compelling. Women specialize in family and emotional relationships, while men specialize in work and relationships based on order and merit. Combining the two roles in a family makes the family stronger, structural functionalists propose, since women

Table 1.1 Sociological Theories on the Family

Structural Functionalism

- Elements in society have a structure and function (or purpose).
- Study of the family examines how family members fit together, given the purpose families have within a society.
- Gender division in the family is universal and probably inevitable.

Symbolic Interactionism

- Society is a product of face-to-face interactions between people.
- Understanding of the family requires studying the symbols and meanings shared among members.
- People depend on the labels of their roles to guide them.

Marxist

- The family exists in relation to economic systems.
- The family is a way to ensure that inheritance is passed down to the proper people; namely, rightful children.

Feminist

- Men and women negotiate with the resources and power they have.
- Women suffer more because they have fewer resources when they enter the family.
- Women take responsibility at home because society needs their unpaid labour, while men focus their efforts on paid work.

Postmodern

- Family is a social creation and changes are expected.
- Examination of family requires teasing apart the various components.
- Family members are aware of, and reflect on, family changes.
- Convergence theory (a branch of structural functionalism) presents a rosy picture of family modernization, as though families and individuals are choosing to change and are all changing effectively.
- Changes in society are part of a universal progress that will result in a single worldwide culture of modernity.
- Economic development requires specific kinds of families and family roles.

Life Course

- Human development is lifelong.
- People construct their own life courses.
- History shapes lives.
- Timing of events matters.
- Lives are linked, especially in families.

and men complement each other. Competition between women and men, it is thought by this reasoning, is not beneficial to families or to work.

The theoretical approach of structural functionalism has dominated family research for decades. Although much criticized in recent times, structural functionalism is and has remained the dominant theoretical approach to understanding families in North America. Its semblance of common sense captivates even those who criticize it. Everything about families has a structure and a function. Family relations are orderly and neat. This approach inspires us to find out how and why families act the ways they do.

The trouble with this approach is that it may be too captivating. It doesn't allow for conflict and social change. When women work in the paid labour market like men, what, then, for families? Do they fall apart because there are no longer complementary roles in family and society? Some might respond, "Yes, this could be a problem." Others might say, "Wait a minute. Societies change. Women and men change. Where is that change allowed for in structural functionalism?"

This theoretical approach dominated family research through much of the twentieth century and is still important today because it tries to answer one important question: Why is gendering so common throughout the world?

Symbolic Interactionism

Symbolic interactionism (Rock, 2016) depends not on structure or function but on sharing. The key to understanding families, this theory proposes, is that family members share symbols and meanings. So, for example, the word *dad* is not something that you alone understand, but is a symbol shared by others. The shared meaning makes family experience more universal, and more understood by others whose experience may be a little different than yours.

People are not passive recipients of social meanings, but work to make those meanings their own. They then interact with others on the basis of their own meanings. For example, the meaning of *dad* is changing. In this way, meanings become new realities in families.

Marxist Theory of Family

Many readers know Karl Marx as a political theorist or activist. In fact, Marx was a great thinker, a sociological theorist who conceptualized family in relation to economic systems. His thinking led him to see the nuclear family as specialized so that women would have to be faithful to their husbands to benefit economically. Originally, Marx and his collaborator, Friedrich Engels, imagined women and men living together freely in groups. They would have sex and children but not worry much about whose children they were. Then, with agricultural surpluses, the notion of private property developed. Men had to know who their own children were so that only those children could inherit their rightful surplus of food (dried root crops, dried animal meat, and so on). The only way men could know who their own children were was to demand sexual faithfulness from women. Thus, it is theorized, women traded free and open sexual relations for economic benefit for themselves and their children. The notion of women's sexual faithfulness to men in monogamous marriage was born in this way. Notably, it was not individual preference or religion or anything other than economics that created this system.

Feminist Theory

Feminist sociological approaches view family as a place of discussion and negotiation. Men and women come to family with different resources and power. Therefore, they negotiate from different places.

Women, feminist theorists propose, do not enter family with resources comparable to men's. They therefore suffer inequality in close relations and, if the relationship breaks down, are more likely to be in poverty. In fact, lone mothers with children have the highest family poverty rate in Canada, something we discuss in subsequent chapters. The following chapters will describe in more detail the major issues that mothers confront in negotiating the relationships among employment, domestic work, child and elder care, and family life. Important to these discussions will be the idea that women's decision-making processes in each of these domains are not isolated to an individual family but, instead, are embedded in a social context and a political ideology.

Feminist theories propose that women are taught to see family work as based on love and social expectation. It may be based as much or more on the need of society and of men for cheap labour to keep society going. So, women take on the major responsibilities for child and elder care as well as for housework, thus freeing men to focus more fully on paid work. Similarly, women's preoccupation with child rearing and unpaid housework compromises their capacity to work for pay outside the home.

With respect to housework, as an example, feminist theories reveal how women's lower pay at work is linked to the domestic division of labour—why they do more work at home and men do less. Recognition of the unpaid work done largely by women in families has led to inclusion of unpaid work on the Census of Canada and to policies that increasingly recognize the importance of unpaid work. The question about unpaid work, however, was removed from the Census subsequently and asked instead in a survey in which more fulsome responses were possible (Statistics Canada, 2015, 2016b).

Postmodern Theory

Postmodernists see that numerous ways of understanding and viewing family coexist. The new social, economic, and political dimensions of a globalized world reveal new identities (active disabled, transgender, immigrant, and so on) and new ways to live in families. This is not a crisis in any way, but something natural and vital to understanding life and society in the twenty-first century.

Key to the postmodern theoretical approach to family is that nothing can be taken for granted. Instead, all must be subject to being taken apart, or deconstructed, in order to be explained. Families and men's and women's relations to families are seen as social creations, subject to constant change and re-examination. Family members become part of the process. They re-create themselves and their ways to relate as they examine and re-examine what they are doing and why. Their senses of self form in response to this constant process of reflecting, responding, and re-examining.

When applied to the study of families, postmodern theories look at the meanings of mothering, both individual and social. They look at body images and at sexuality in relation to family. Nothing is taken as given by postmodern theory.

VARIATION DESPITE CONVERGENCE

As we have seen throughout the chapter, changing economies and societies, as well as changing approaches to seeing family, play a major role in changing the form and content of family life, both in countries just becoming industrialized and in the Western world, where economic change continues. Many social scientists see these changes as part of an inevitable and universal progress toward a single worldwide culture of modernity, in which families have a distinct and different form compared to traditional families. This approach has several pitfalls. First, it assumes that all modern families are similar to one another and different from all traditional families. Second, and equally important, it assumes that all modern families "choose" their new forms, and that these forms are necessarily better.

Convergence theory presents a rosy picture of family modernization, as though families and individuals are choosing to change and are all changing effectively. In fact, modernization forces families to change. William Goode (1982: 57–58), a structural functionalist, proposes that families change when societies industrialize precisely because industrialism "fails to give support to the family." He gives several reasons for this conclusion:

1. The industrial system fires, lays off, and demands geographical mobility by reference to the individual, ignoring the family strains these actions may cause.

2. The economy increasingly uses women in the labour force, and thus puts a still larger work burden on them, but few corporations have developed programs for helping women with child care or making it easier for men to share in these tasks.

3. The industrial system has little place for the elderly, and the neolocal, independent household, with its accompanying values in favour of separate lives for each couple, leaves older parents and kin in an ambiguous position.

4. The family is relatively fragile because of separation and divorce, but the larger system offers little help in these crises for adults and their children.

Industrialization produces not only great opportunities but also great perils for families and family life. Some societies, and some families, respond better than others. Some industrial states provide much more support for the family than others. By its laws and policies, a state influences the costs associated with marriage, divorce, childbearing, child rearing, and elder care. In this way, the state influences the patterns of family life in that society. That is, in part, why industrial societies do not have identical family forms.

Major forces of change like industrialization, urbanization, and education certainly affect family life; yet the relationships are not simple, nor are the outcomes predictable. In two of the most industrialized countries, Japan and Sweden, we find different family forms. In Japan, traditional family and gender norms persist. In Sweden, by contrast, there are high rates of cohabitation and of women working in the paid workforce (although mostly in traditional female sectors). Throughout this text, we propose that many family forms are not only possible but also desirable and that they work well—in Canada and throughout the world.

No simple conclusions can be drawn about what a family is, what causes families to change, or whether family life is getting better or worse. Those who want simple answers may find this ambiguity disappointing. Those who want to understand the modern family will find that the many open questions make for an exciting and intellectually challenging area of sociology.

LIFE COURSE THEORY

The life course perspective is commonly used to understand families and family change. This was not always the case, however. Life histories and connections between individuals and history used to be neglected in studies of family.

The life course perspective consists of five principles. First, human development is seen as occurring throughout life. In families, this matters because adults as well as children are part of family change. Second, people construct their own lives through choices and actions. In families, choices matter greatly to outcomes and happiness. Third, people's life courses are shaped by the times in which they live. Good economic times shape our families, as do wars, depressions and recessions, and tough times. Fourth, the same events affect individuals and families differently depending on when they occur in the life course. For example, having a baby at age 18 is different in terms of the rest of a woman's life than having a baby at age 28 or 38. Fifth, and importantly for the understanding of family lives, is that lives are linked. Nowhere is this truer than in families. Transitions in one person's life in a family can affect all members of the family, as well as the family itself. These five principles of the life course perspective, taken together, lead to a focus in family studies on social contexts as well as life change and choice (Elder, Johnson, and Crosnoe, 2004; McDaniel and Bernard, 2011). It is a powerful theoretical lens.

CONCLUDING REMARKS

It seems that, everywhere, family relationships are in flux. Around the world, industrialization and urbanization are transforming extended kinship networks and drastically changing the nature of family obligations. In North America, people value family life, but they are spending a smaller fraction of their lives in anything resembling whatever might be viewed as a traditional family. North American families today show signs of stress and conflict as well as greater freedom and happiness. How are these observable realities connected to one another?

Current family trends are the result of long-term worldwide changes in social life. New laws and new contraceptive technology have given rise to new sexual permissiveness. Fertility has continued to fall for more than a century. Divorce rates, once at historically high levels, have now stabilized and declined, while legal marriage rates have continued to drop. These long-term trends have been boosted by rapid increases in the labour force participation of mothers of young children. As an outcome of the struggle for gender equality that began two centuries ago, there are fewer social and legal constraints on types and duration of relationships. In turn, less rigid social and legal definitions of gender and family obligations open topics for research, accommodating greater variation (Turner and West, 2014). Families are less reliant on social, cultural, and legal institutions that used to define, protect, and promote only families that fit certain structural types. Through the work of defining and portraying their relationship boundaries and obligations internally and externally, families are maintained increasingly by mutual agreement and less by social norms (Galvin, Braithwaite, and Bylund, 2015).

As we will see, the process of societal development has set in motion irreversible social forces that have transformed, and continue to transform, the content of close relations in everyday life. These include the development of a consumer culture; a market economy; welfare states; and a mobile, urban, globalized population. As well, new technologies prolong life, prevent unwanted births, and can create life outside the womb as well as, of course, greatly enhancing communicative potential. With fluid boundaries, diversity, globalization, and industrialization have come cultural stresses felt in society's institutions and in familial relations. Institutions and families respond to the stress of change by innovating to make the most of the possibilities set in motion by multiple processes.

CHAPTER SUMMARY

In this chapter, we discussed what families are and how they are viewed. We explored how defining families is a challenge because both families and how they are seen are constantly changing. Families, for most of us, are our most important social relationships, defining who we are and providing emotional attachment.

This chapter examined the complexity of what families are, why they are interesting to study sociologically, and how they have changed and are still changing. Family is as important to people as ever, but it has changed. Even the Census of Canada has broadened its definition of family to include common-law unions, including same-sex unions, and adult children living with parents.

We have seen that sociologists are moving away from defining families by the shape they take. This is a recurring theme throughout the text, as we will see when we explore the ways in which Indigenous people, gays and lesbians, and immigrant families, to name a few, function and care for their family members. In doing so, it will be clear that families are more often now defined by what they do for us and for society. The common elements of family living—dependency and intimacy, sexuality, protection, and power—are explored.

The key to understanding families is how families are theorized. This chapter followed a brief journey through the major changes in theorizing families from the early days of Western social thought to media imagery.

We have set the stage for an in-depth examination of family change and family diversity in subsequent chapters.

Key Terms

acculturation gap The gap between immigrant children and their parents with regard to language ability and cultural values. Parents tend to rely more heavily on their former cultural views, while immigrant children adapt more easily to the values of the new country.

bilateral kinship system Kinship through both the male and the female lines.

extended family A family system in which three or more generations of family members live together and have social rights and obligations.

kin-keeper The family member who maintains and nurtures family contacts.

kinship group A set of people who share a relationship through blood or marriage and have positions in a hierarchy of rights over property.

matrilineal kinship system Kinship through the female line.

nuclear family A family group that consists only of spouses, or spouses and their children.

patriarchy A system in which family decision making is dominated by males, most typically by fathers.

patrilineal kinship system Kinship through the male line.

Critical Thinking Questions

1. Why is studying the family so complicated in society today?
2. What are the benefits of a function-based definition of the family and a structural-based definition? What are the drawbacks of each?
3. In this chapter we discussed what the Census of Canada defines as a family. What would you add or remove from this definition and why?

4. Why have feminist theories become so prominent in recent decades? Do feminist theories improve our understanding of family life?

5. Predict some future changes that will likely occur for Canadian families in the next five years.

6. We discussed some theoretical approaches to family in this chapter. Which theoretical approach do you think is the most useful for studying the family today? Which do you think is the least useful?

7. Why are gay and lesbian families of particular interest for sociologists studying family?

8. People often refer to the increase in divorce, delaying marriage, and common-law unions as proof that the value of family is decreasing in our society. Do you think these trends prove that the family is becoming less important, or even unimportant? Do you think the changes improve the quality of life or improve opportunities for members of families?

Weblinks

The Vanier Institute of the Family
www.vifamily.ca
This Ottawa-based independent organization has a wealth of information, new studies, and data on families in Canada. The site has many links to other sources of information on families.

Institute of Marriage and Family Canada
www.imfcanada.org
After February 9, 2016, this site amalgamated into Cardus.ca/family. The new site leans more toward faith-based perspectives on family.

Childcare Resource and Research Unit
www.childcarecanada.org
This site focuses on providing up-to-date resources that deal specifically with child care issues and family policy in Canada and internationally.

First Nations Child & Family Caring Society of Canada
www.fncfcs.com
This site offers academic information regarding the issues facing First Nations families today. It provides links to community projects that focus specifically on First Nations youth and children's rights volunteer opportunities and *First Peoples Child & Family Review*, an interdisciplinary research journal overseen by First Peoples.

Government of Canada—Immigration and Citizenship
www.cic.gc.ca
This site provides new Canadian immigrants with a location-specific list of resources to assist in settling into Canada and information such as how to set up a business.

Government of Canada—Youth
www.youth.gc.ca
This site focuses on a variety of youth issues facing Canadian teenagers. One of the best features of the site is that it targets unemployed, immigrant, and disabled youth issues and provides easy-to-understand tips on how to find jobs and earn an education.

Chapter 2
Historical Perspectives on Canadian Families
Demographic, Social, and Economic Origins and Trends

Lebrecht Music and Arts Photo Library/Alamy Stock Photo

CHAPTER OUTLINE

- A Historical, Cross-Cultural Perspective
  - Indigenous Peoples and Settlers: Contact and Conflict
  - English and French Settlers
  - The Transition to Industrialism
  - The History of Immigration in Relation to the Family
- The History of Immigration Policies
- Wars
- Variation in the Family Life Course
  - The Impact of Modernization on Family Changes in Canada and Worldwide

- Changes in Sexual Attitudes and Courtship
- Changes in Attitudes toward Marriage
- Declining Fertility and the Value of Parenthood
  - The First and Second Demographic Transitions
  - Contraception, Childbearing Choice, and Abortion
  - Family and Household Size
- Social Support and Regulation: The Role of the State in Families
  - Child Support and Welfare Reforms in Canada
  - Changing Nature of Elder Support by the State and the Family
  - Families That Include Persons with Disabilities
  - The Regulation of Divorce
- Concluding Remarks

LEARNING OBJECTIVES

1 Identify and discuss key historical factors that influence Indigenous families in Canada.

2 Understand the impact of the "mechanization" of housework on families.

3 Distinguish the role of immigration in Canada's past, present, and future families.

4 Analyze how past patterns of courtship, marriage, and divorce have affected present family patterns.

5 Identify the key aspects of an aging population and assess how an aging society may change Canadian families.

6 Explain how the definition of family has changed over time.

7 Describe how resources affect individual and family transitions.

8 Define and evaluate the role of social policy for families, both at individual and societal levels.

In this chapter, we look at families through a sociological lens. We emphasize the big changes in society, such as contact and ongoing relations between Indigenous peoples and settlers, industrialization, large-scale immigration waves, and wars. We consider how families in the past connect to some of today's patterns and how contemporary socio-economic changes have altered families and our views of them. We also focus on the multicultural families that have been part of Canada since its beginnings. Historical dimensions of families are explored more specifically in the chapters that follow.

A HISTORICAL, CROSS-CULTURAL PERSPECTIVE

Indigenous Peoples and Settlers: Contact and Conflict

Indigenous families in what was to become Canada have always been diverse. First contacts between Indigenous peoples and foreigners were with male explorers, followed by fur traders and missionaries, and lastly by women and families who settled in Canada. Such contacts changed Indigenous family practices, as they did the family practices of some of the settlers. Early settlers in Canada developed strong relationships of mutual aid with their Indigenous neighbours. Blood First Nations women helped homesteading women on the prairies with childbirth and with building houses that would help them stay warm and survive the harsh winters. The settlement of New France (now Quebec) and Upper Canada (now Ontario) brought together the families of the Indigenous groups and the colonists. In the early days, children born to unmarried settler women were often adopted by Indigenous families.

The relationships in those days between settlers and Indigenous peoples cannot be characterized as simply good or bad. Some explorers and fur traders married or cohabited with Indigenous women (Van Kirk, 1980). Some of these relationships were committed and long-lasting, while others were short-term and exploitative, with men from afar taking advantage of differences in culture and status between themselves and the local women (Brown, 1980). This is a common story of colonialism, occurring throughout the world and leaving a legacy of combined racism and sexism toward Indigenous women.

Not sanctioned by church or society, the unions were also disapproved of by fur trading companies, notably Hudson's Bay Company, which banned these men from taking their "country wives" and families back home with them upon retirement (Van Kirk, 1980). Some of the men simply abandoned their Canadian families. Others, however, remained in Canada with their families, adapting to Indigenous societies. One couple, William Hemmings Cook and his wife, Agatha, made a fresh start by marrying after living together according to the "custom of the country" for years (Van Kirk, 1992: 79). Still others provided for their country wives in their wills or organized to find them new husbands to ensure that they would be provided for.

Unlike the Europeans, relatives of the Indigenous women often did support the relationships. The Huron, for example, saw ties between French men and Huron women as a way to develop kinship alliances. Many thousands of Canadians today can trace their ancestry to the British and French fur traders and Indigenous women of the seventeenth to nineteenth centuries.

However, the children of unions between European men and Indigenous women suffered a significant strain. Some, especially boys, left their familiar lives at a young age, sometimes going abroad to their father's relatives to be educated. Daughters more often stayed with their mothers and the mother's culture (Brown, 1992). Efforts were made at various times, notably in the 1820s, to organize and to "civilize" what were seen as mixed-race families and communities. This resulted in officials making new laws and in missionaries working to sanction relationships. One outcome was a sense of *in loco parentis*, whereby family life was controlled by others who regulated and governed the Indigenous children as needing discipline and order.

Other family issues that arose with early contact between Indigenous peoples and Europeans have to do with kinship ties. For hundreds of years, Indigenous cultural beliefs and practices around family and family issues had been developing and changing, and were widely divergent throughout Canada. Indigenous peoples viewed kinship, the basis for assigning rights and duties, more flexibly than did European settlers. Kinship regulated relations with others without courts and states per se. Decisions about justice and about compensation were often filtered through kinship rules, with different outcomes than might have resulted from following European rules. Some of the conflicts that resulted are continuing to this day.

Another large difference between the early Europeans and Indigenous peoples was in gender roles. Although societies always seem to organize rights and responsibilities by gender, they differ significantly in the way gender is employed. Bradbury notes that "[i]n most Aboriginal societies women appear to have been able to exercise greater power than their European counterparts . . ." (2001: 72). This system led some European observers to shocked reactions.

Finally, Indigenous peoples and early Europeans had divergent views on the relationship of family to its community, and of both to property. To the colonial settlers, property, whether it was land, money, or goods, was private and to be traded in a market economy. Assets belonged to individuals and nuclear families. This was not the case with Indigenous groups, whose extended kinship groups often determined who would be eligible for the benefits of a hunt, for example. These different viewpoints created a clash of values, posing some difficulty in the fur trade. The concept of furs for sale was a new one to many Indigenous peoples. Ritual exchanges among Indigenous family groups, such as the potlatches of the peoples of the west coast, were seen as dangerous by the colonials, both to their economic values and to their sense of righteousness. In fact, potlatches were outlawed by authorities, and in some villages all the goods to be exchanged were symbolically burned (Dickason, 2002).

English and French Settlers

Interestingly, the conflicts between colonists and Indigenous peoples over family and kinship relations parallel the conflicts between British and French settlers. English Common Law, from which many of the modern understandings of marriage, family, inheritance, and property rights came, tended to concentrate power, authority, and property in male heads of households. For women, marriage meant the "suspension of independent existence" (Bradbury, 2001: 74).

For a long time (until the early part of the twentieth century), married women could not own property, sign a contract, or sue. Like children, they had no rights under law. In contrast, in New France, which became Quebec, rules governing marriage and family were guided by the Custom of Paris (Bradbury, 2001: 75). This set of legal codes was much more egalitarian than English Common Law. Property was seen as shared between husbands and wives, even if controlled by husbands. And children, regardless of gender, could share inheritances.

After the Battle of the Plains of Abraham in 1760, known in Quebec as the Conquest, the English tried to impose their version of family law and practice on the French. This attempt failed immediately and has never succeeded for political reasons. As early as 1774, it was agreed that Quebec would have its own legal code regarding family matters, though all criminal law would follow the English practice. Even today in Quebec, we see different approaches to family than in the rest of Canada. One major family difference is that the Québécois/Québécoise (Quebec men and women) are significantly more likely to live in common-law unions than other Canadians. Another difference is that a Québécoise does not take her husband's name on marriage. Both of these points will be discussed in the chapters that follow.

Also after the Conquest, there was a significant gender imbalance in New France, with a much higher proportion of men than women. The low birth rate in the new colony threatened the success of territorial expansion. In response, about 770 young women were imported to New France from the streets of Paris between 1663 and 1673 (Landry, 1992). These women were called *les filles du roi* (daughters of the King). Many were orphans, some were illiterate, all were poor, and, despite their name, none was even remotely related to royalty. The *filles du roi* were expected to find marriage partners quickly, and most did. Out of the whole group, only 15 percent of the marriages were annulled, the equivalent of divorce in Catholic New France at the time (Huck, 2001: 14). Of those, most remarried, and seven even married for a third time. Many Quebeckers today can trace their ancestry to the unions of original French settlers and the *filles du roi*.

The Transition to Industrialism

Before Canada industrialized and urbanized, families were the primary unit of production. Most families were rural, and work and family were found in the same space. Therefore, the two were inseparable. Each person, old or young, had a role to play as defined by society.

In this way, agricultural work depended on the formation of extended families. Farm work—based on land and animals—could not be moved, so people mostly stayed in one place. Exceptions were non-inheriting children, who often migrated or emigrated in search of their own land. People who stayed formed strong bonds among neighbours and generations. This led to the formation of a **gemeinschaft** type of community typical of pre-industrial rural life: that is, one in which everyone knows everyone else and people share common values. Since limited social safety nets existed, families largely had to create their own. Aging grandparents helped busy parents to care for the many children and often provided housing and money when needed (McDaniel and Lewis, 1998).

When many of the Europeans migrated to Canada and established an agricultural way of life, the conventional division of labour was altered. Even though most early settlers to Canada preferred a strict division of labour at home (as in their native countries), they often could not manage this divide. As a result, land was sometimes owned and worked by unmarried women, for example, a practice unheard of in the "old country." This change was motivated less by an interest in gender equality than by a desire to increase agricultural output. At the same time, men's and women's work was still largely separate in pre-industrial times. The husband was usually responsible for representing the family in public. However, men also had domestic responsibilities such as farm work, child discipline, and some provisioning. The wife, on the other hand, was mainly responsible for the private domain. Besides doing housework and taking responsibility for child care, women at this time also took care of farm animals, manufactured needed household items, and provided social services to those in their community (Cross and Szostak, 1995). When, often, men had to leave their farms and shops to work at other jobs, women would often supplement household income with home-based businesses.

This provided a small source of income for women that contributed to the family and to their pride. It also gave some women considerable power and autonomy both in their families' enterprises and in the wider society. However, with industrialization many women could not continue such work. For instance, zoning bylaws might prohibit non-family establishments in some neighbourhoods, and in this way they would prevent separated, divorced, and widowed women from taking in boarders to make ends meet (Bradbury, 1984).

With the advent of industrialization, the agricultural family and way of life drastically changed. First, industrialization drove many individuals and families out of the countryside and into the new towns and cities. Some families became migratory, moving where work was available. Since this was almost impossible to do with an extended family, the smaller, compact nuclear family became the more common family form. It was also more specialized. Everyone had a role to fill, although the roles were different from those in an extended family.

A new image of childhood emerged, as many nuclear families couldn't survive with only one or two people working for wages. Children worked in factories or on the street selling papers, shining shoes, or looking after younger children so that mother could work. Children often sought to keep some or all of their wages, moving out of their home and staying poor to gain their independence. Clearly, children in an industrializing society were more independent. Thus, a significant change occurred in relations between older and younger generations, and a new image of childhood emerged. Increasingly, children became a liability. So, parents started to have fewer children.

As well, the Industrial Revolution, which began in Canada only in the mid-1850s, moved the productive activity of men outside the household. Increasingly, people began to work *with* strangers and *for* strangers. Family life was their own private business, and work life was, if they wished, outside the family's purview. A clear line between work and family life, in the way that we perceive them today, only appeared with the coming of industrialization.

Then, in the beginning of the twentieth century, industrialization of household technology brought new and unexpected dimensions to family life, especially changing what families expected of women. Vacuum cleaners, for example, brought the possibility of cleaning a house more readily than by sweeping or taking heavy area rugs out to the yard to be beaten with brooms or paddles. Yet expectations about cleanliness also rose, so there was no reduction in the housework to be done. Similarly, refrigerators replaced wells, cold storage areas, and iceboxes. Fridges saved the worry and the trouble of food storage in homes but created the necessity to shop longer and with greater care because meals were expected to be more complex and elegant than they had been before.

Thus, the growing availability of new "labour-saving devices" raised standards of living and increased the time women spent shopping. Homes quickly shifted from small-scale production units into showplaces of consumer goods. In the new domestic division of labour, women were no longer producers of goods to sell on the market, but rather specialists in the consumption of goods aimed at making houses "homey." This shift sharpened the domestic division of labour by gender. It was the precursor to the modern "domestic goddess" movement, spearheaded by Martha Stewart.

Campaigns to promote new household technologies stressed the "love" part of housework out of fear that women might abandon their domestic work with the "mechanization" of housework (Fox, 1993: 151). Home economists worked to raise the esteem of homemakers by promoting the idea that the new home technologies required skilled operators. Health came to be associated with extreme standards of cleanliness. Homemakers were therefore expected to master household technology and promote family health—complex but unrewarded increases in responsibility. The scientization of housework was complete, and women were cast into the role of preserving the home as their central life work, with limited access through their homemaking skills to the markets they had enjoyed before industrialization. They had been transformed into domestic engineers, responsible for all things related to family and the household.

The History of Immigration in Relation to the Family

People often think of family change and family transitions as recent occurrences. In reality, family changes are nothing new. Immigration has been a significant part of Canada since before Confederation. Early immigrants, mainly from the colonizing countries of Britain and France, arrived in search of opportunities for work, land ownership, and a new life. These goals were pursued, in part, as the means to start or support a family. Despite the notable change in other aspects of recent immigration—such as changed countries of origin—many immigrants continue to see economic advancement as a means to ensuring family welfare.

In the eighteenth century, the American Revolution brought to Canada the United Empire Loyalists, including significant numbers of African Americans. The latter settled largely in Nova Scotia and southern Ontario. Many black families did not fit the expected family model. For instance, black women often worked outside the home to earn enough money to get by. "[F]or African-Nova Scotian men in the early 1800s, many families practised gender interdependence and reversals of traditional gender roles in the division of labour" (Calliste, 2001: 402). This reflects, in part, a need that resulted from discrimination. But it may also be reflective of the West African cultural tradition in which women are both more economically and more sexually independent of men and families.

Later, in the early twentieth century, African American families settled as homesteaders in central Alberta. In *The Keystone Legacy: Reflections of a Black Pioneer* (1997), author Gwen Hooks, daughter of original homesteaders in that area, describes how settlers banded together in families and communities to make a new and happy life on the prairies. Hooks also states that homesteaders of all ethnic origins banded together to build community facilities such as schools. Later immigrants to Canada's West have included people from all regions of the world, seeking a better life and bringing along rich family traditions and strong values and beliefs. With time, some of these family practices have changed or even disappeared, whereas others influenced the practices of people with whom they came in contact.

Immigration from Europe has also had a long history in Canada, beginning with colonialism and expansion. Canada continued to receive European immigrants from strife-torn, and sometimes poverty-stricken, countries throughout the first half of the twentieth century. Immigrants and refugees from Europe are still coming, as strife and economic difficulties recur, and have now been joined by people from Africa, Asia, and Latin America fleeing an old life or seeking new opportunities.

Today, South Asian families form a large portion of new immigrants in Canada. As such, they experience unique difficulties in their immigration experiences. South Asian women, in particular, face significant problems in adjusting after immigration because of the rigid gender roles in their home countries (Samuel, 2010). A study by Ahmad and colleagues (2004) found that South Asian women face stress-inducing factors that include loss of social support, economic uncertainties, downward social mobility, and health problems associated with climatic and food changes. Equally important, these women feel they cannot turn to professional health workers for help with these concerns for fear of disgracing their families. This inability to seek help is aggravated by the fact that immigrant women already face a lack of resources with the loss of family and friends from the homeland.

The isolating experience of South Asian women migrants highlights the need for health care professionals to provide and understand the specific challenges and needs of recent immigrants in order to offer necessary support and care for this vulnerable population. Inevitably, life in the new country forces families—both parents and children—to live in new ways. These family changes are demanded by the process of immigration and the contact with new ways of living in close relations.

The History of Immigration Policies

As Canadians, we like to imagine that our country helps people in need, and occasionally these imaginings prove justified. However, Canada's past immigration policies undermine this idealistic point of view. For example, during the early periods of Chinese immigration to Canada, racially discriminatory laws such as the head tax were imposed in the period of 1885 to 1923 (Man, 2001). As well, the Chinese Exclusionary Act strictly prohibited Chinese workers (including those who built the railroads and worked in the early mines) from bringing in their wives and children. In this way, their harsh, impoverished lives were made even harder by Canadian immigration laws.

This example reminds us that Canadian immigration laws were not, and are still not, primarily philanthropic or immigrant focused: They were intended to supply needed labour power and little more (Green and Green, 2004). The labourers were admitted into Canada historically specifically to build the Canadian Pacific Railway (Comeau and Allahar, 2001). Then, in the 1920s, in the 1950s, and again in the 2000s, immigration was used to meet demands for labour in resource sectors. In the 1960s and 1970s, increasing skill level among occupational workers was the goal. In the 1980s, immigrant labour was sought to compensate for the large population of aging baby boomers in the native-born population. And in the 2000s, the belief is that immigrants are filling skills shortages in Canada. The large inflows of immigrants at these times were permitted mainly to fill shortages of specific kinds of labour.

At other times, immigration inflows were significantly cut back, and entry restrictions ensured that groups that were not needed were turned away (McLean, 2004). This method of controlling immigration reflects a concern with Canada's absorptive capacity—that is, "only accepting the number of immigrants that the Canadian economy [can] easily absorb" (Green and Green, 2004: 135). Yet through the 1980s, 1990s, and 2000s, this short-term focus on labour demand shifted to a long-term one that considered immigration as essential to longer-term economic growth and prosperity. This policy allows for immigration inflow even during economically difficult times, which has inevitably helped immigrant families start new lives in Canada. However, in the second decade of the twenty-first century, short-term economic objectives have returned to centre stage in immigration policy, with various programs such as the Temporary Foreign Worker Program and the explicit stating of labour needs by employers who can then request suitable immigrants.

Along with changes in policy, the source countries of Canada's immigrants have changed. In 2011, 19.1 percent of Canadians (1 in 5) were visible minorities (what Statistics Canada used to refer to as non-white; Statistics Canada, 2013g). This compares to 12.4 percent in 1971. Among the G8 countries (the most advanced countries in the world), Canada had the highest proportion of foreign-born population in the early 2010s (20.6 percent), well above the shares in Germany (13.0 percent) and the United States (12.9 percent; Statistics Canada, 2013g).

Asia, including the Middle East, remains the most significant source of immigrants to Canada, accounting for 56.9 percent of all immigrants arriving between 2006 and 2011 (Statistics Canada, 2013g). In the 2011 National Household Survey (NHS), more than three-quarters of the immigrants who reported coming to Canada before 1971 were from Europe. The share of European-born immigrants from subsequent periods of immigration has declined steadily. The 2011 NHS showed a slight increase in the share of immigration from Africa, the Caribbean, and Central and South America during the past five years. The Philippines was the leading country of birth among people who immigrated to Canada between 2006 and 2011.

With the development of feminist theory in the 1970s to 1990s, strong efforts have been made to understand the unique experiences of immigrant women. This has signalled a shift away from the initially male-focused experience of migration that deemed women largely invisible and their experiences the same as those of men. Previously, when women's motives for immigration were taken into account, they were seen as based on family responsibilities, rather than on independent choice or labour opportunities in the receiving country. Today, scholars are more likely to examine female migration as a complex and gender-specific experience based on a complex set of factors, including the gendered restrictions that often exist in a women's home culture that either encourage or inhibit immigration and family change (Boyd and Grieco, 2003; Nesteruk and Gramescu, 2012; Samuel, 2010).

The immigration policy of a home country can affect migrants in various ways. First, migration policies sometimes assume a "dependent" status for women and an "independent" status for men (Boyd and Grieco, 2003: 4; Tastsoglou and Dobrowolsky, 2006). Women, therefore, are more likely to be classified in relation to their family and husbands, rather than independently (Samuel, 2010). Second, the differences between dependent and independent status can automatically place women within a family role and men in a market role. This can reinforce patriarchal relations between spouses and also shut women out of important economic roles and a chance for bargaining power within the home. More important, this power imbalance accounts for much of the social vulnerability of migrant women (Samuel, 2010). Thus, although immigration policy may be seen as "gender neutral," the entry status of men and women can have important implications for the experience of new immigrants, especially of women.

The mid-1850s created a paradigm shift from agriculture to industrialism. Families were driven into urban settings, where men left the house to work in factories.

Brand X Pictures/Stockbyte/Getty Images

The differences in the rate of uptake of Canadian culture create some tension on the intergenerational relationships between family members of newly arriving Canadians. Immigrants nonetheless enjoy freedom of choice within the family in how they approach adjusting to culture change. We noted earlier that Indigenous families adapted to contact with European cultures in various ways, including intermarriage. There was also commercial interdependence. However, shortly after Confederation, Indigenous and mixed-marriage families had that freedom to choose how to adapt taken from them. It seems unthinkable that the government of the day could strip away the right to control identity from one group of people, while laying wide open the vast expanse of lands they had offered to share instead for the exclusive settlement by those seeking freedom from similar persecutions in their own former homelands. Yet it was so (Truth and Reconciliation Commission of Canada, 2015).

After the signing of the treaties that did not give Canada control over Indigenous families, offer them citizenship, or in any way bring them under the Dominion of Canada, the federal government began an unlawful program of forced assimilation in which Indigenous children were removed from their families and other traditional influences and placed in isolated residential schools (Truth and Reconciliation Commission of Canada, 2015). These Indian Residential Schools were operated by churches and inadequately funded by government at a fraction of that which was provided for education of non-Indigenous children. Many of the children died of malnutrition and disease from overcrowding in inadequate facilities. In addition, a shocking number of Indigenous children experienced physical and sexual abuse within residential schools. Such traumas were exacerbated by being far from parental and community emotional support, and without recourse to justice or to adequate care and protection. This is now well documented by the Truth and Reconciliation Commission of Canada (TRC, 2015).

Prevailing policy-makers hoped that forced conversion through the churches operating the schools would lead Indigenous children to participate in the modern industrial economy and leave behind their claim to the reservation land, which could then be redistributed. In residential schools, corporal punishment was used to penalize children for speaking their Indigenous languages and to shame Indigenous practices, values, and spirituality.

The residential schools left a legacy of traumas. Many of the approximately 150 000 children who experienced residential school returned as outsiders to their families and communities and with deep emotional scars. They had been taught to feel ashamed of their traditional culture and at the same time felt resentful of the culture and values of their oppressors.

Steps toward healing were advanced in 2007 when the federal government, in reaction to losing the largest class action lawsuit in history for its complicit role in abuses in residential schools, established the TRC and issued a formal apology for the Indian Residential School system (Government of Canada, 2008). The TRC documented the experiences of survivors as well as some statements by instructors and has collected documents associated with residential schools in an effort to bring closure to this chapter of Canadian history (Truth and Reconciliation Commission of Canada, 2015). These resources are available at the National Centre for Truth and Reconciliation (www.nctr.ca).

Wars

The two world wars of the twentieth century had profound impacts on families. They also had an influence on women's social roles and responsibilities. World War II brought an influx of women into the labour force, as men were sent away to fight. Women were employed in jobs that they had previously been excluded from due to their gender, such as work involving manual labour (Coontz, 2005: 221). More important, the government supported and encouraged both single and married women to join the labour force, and many women even earned men's wages.

However, upon the return of the men, women had to give up their jobs and resume a domestic way of life.

However, families did not effortlessly pick up where they left off before the outbreak of war. For one, marriage experts worried that women had become too independent during wartime and would subsequently demand more autonomy and authority within the household (Ravanera, Rajulton, and Burch, 1998: 223). This would threaten the male breadwinner model of the nuclear family.

Moreover, the experience of families during the 1950s was not as simple or happy as has been believed and portrayed in some media. Although some women willingly embraced domesticity and were pleased to revert back to more traditional gender roles within the household, others resented their exclusion from the labour force and missed the independence they enjoyed during the war years (LaRossa, 2004: 50).

For men, the changing role of the father came to emphasize children's socialization more than in the past. Popular sitcoms such as *Leave It to Beaver* and *Father Knows Best* also reflected the role of the father within the household and as a participant in raising children. However, the "father" that was popularly promoted during the 1950s was a traditional, patriarchal version of the role demanding clear gender lines. In fact, the popular image of a nuclear family during this time—particularly rigid and stereotypical—reflected the need many people felt for stability and clarity during an insecure, fearful Cold War period.

World War II had profound effects on Canadian families who had come from Axis power countries (i.e., Germany, Italy, and Japan), Canada's opponents during combat. For instance, between 1941 and 1949, approximately 27 000 Japanese Canadians were forced to leave their homes, deprived of possessions and civil rights, such as the right to vote. Some were even deported to Japan, even if they were Canadian citizens (Kobayashi, 1992). The Canadian government committed these acts under the pretense that Japanese Canadians posed a threat to national security during World War II, despite claims to the contrary by the military and the Royal Canadian Mounted Police (Sunahara, 1981). The geographic dispersal of these people was meant to distribute them across the country in such a way that they could be easily assimilated into Canadian culture, undermining the likelihood that they would retain traces of their own traditions and culture (Sugiman, 1983). These actions had a deep impact on the attitudes of Japanese Canadians growing up in those times, and the effects of World War II policies continue to be felt by the older generations today.

The effect of these actions is shown in a study by Sugiman and Nishio (1983), which examined the attitudes of aging (51 to 67 years old) Japanese Canadians in Toronto toward old age and dependency of the aged. In traditional Japanese culture, care of the elderly by their children or grandchildren is viewed positively, as it is considered a repayment of the older individual's life work. Yet, though it is the norm in traditional Japanese culture, Japanese Canadian aging persons prefer not to rely on younger generations for care. In their study, Sugiman and Nishio find the values of aging Japanese Canadians somewhat ambiguous. They report detecting traces of the Japanese upbringing in the participants, but also attitudes that coincide with Anglo Canadian views. Much like their Anglo Canadian counterparts, the Japanese Canadian respondents dislike the prospect of growing dependent on their children and demonstrate a preference for living alone in old age (Sugiman and Nishio, 1983).

Wars and the experiences associated with them directly affect entire generations and their families, but also affect future generations indirectly, by influencing beliefs and attitudes. Currently, there are many Canadians in the Canadian Forces serving overseas in various roles, including combat roles. Large numbers of Canadian families are affected by this military service, even though Canada does not see itself as a military power. Deborah Harrison (2002), along with colleagues (see Harrison et al., 2011) has extensively studied the effects of military deployments in the Canadian Forces on families and children.

VARIATION IN THE FAMILY LIFE COURSE

In the past century, families have changed significantly, as we can see by examining changes in the timing and sequencing of major life course events. People born between the two world wars married younger, and most married over a narrow spread of ages. For these cohorts, the transition to adulthood was compressed into a relatively short period of completing formal education, entering the labour force, leaving home, setting up a nuclear household, and having a first child.

In contrast, later cohorts have experienced a lengthening of this time sequence. In addition, the events themselves are less clearly defined and their sequencing is more diverse. This timing of transitions involves trade-offs. Waiting longer to have children allows greater investment in oneself before investing in reproduction. However, delay may mean having no children at all. Later transitions enable more transfers from parents to children, allowing recipients to benefit more from resources, but this may reduce the potential for the parents to invest in their own retirement. Thus, these children enter work life later but better equipped.

As well, couples in the past spent a much longer period of time having and raising children than they do now. When we look at a woman's age at last birth across cohorts, we see a fundamental change in family lives. Women having children in the 1950s had their last birth at the same age as women a hundred years before had their first birth. Even more striking is the huge difference in the timing of last births: at age 40 in the mid-nineteenth century compared with at age 26 a hundred years later. Over a 100-year period, families reduced the time they spent having and raising children by more than 10 years! Recall that this happened at a time when life expectancy was increasing substantially. The result is that the portion of life spent as a parent with dependent children has been sharply reduced. By contrast, the portion of life spent married with no children at home, or at least no juvenile children, has sharply increased from zero to almost a quarter of a century. (We shall see in Chapter 10 that in the 2000s there is a significant difference between when children become adults and when they leave home.) See Figure 2.1 for more detailed information about recent changes in the number of families with and without children.

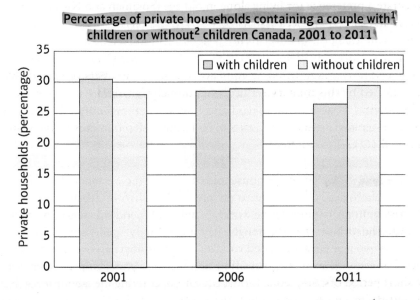

Figure 2.1 Percentage of private households containing a couple with[1] children or without[2] children, Canada, 2001 to 2011.

[1]With at least one child aged 24 years and under.

[2]Without at least one child aged 24 years and under; includes families with all children aged 25 and over (Statistics Canada, 2011b).

Source: Statistics Canada. *Census of population 2011.* Catalogue no. 98-315-XWE. Retrieved January 2013 from www12.statcan.gc.ca/census-recensement/2011/dp-pd/vc-rv/index.cfm?LANG=ENG&VIEW=C&TOPIC_ID=3&GEOCODE=01&CFORMAT=jpg#f3_1. Reproduced and distributed on an "as is" basis with the permission of Statistics Canada.

Given these trends, it may not be surprising that having second or even third families was more characteristic of families in the past than we sometimes admit today. In some ways, widows in the past were similar to single mothers today, both in the economic vulnerability they and their children faced and in the social challenges they experienced (Gordon and McLanahan, 1991). Widows often fell into poverty and had to rely on charity or the generosity of the state or family members to survive. In Chapter 9, we will see the differences in children's lives between the loss of a parent to death and the loss of a parent to divorce.

In the past, people expected a certain sequencing of family-related events. They expected, for example, young people to complete their education before marrying, to marry before having children, to get old before becoming a grandparent, and so on. So predictable were the patterns that sociologists spoke confidently about a normal life cycle of family events. Today, the timing and sequencing of events are too varied to be easily categorized. A woman can be a grandmother and a mid-career professional at the same time, or a new mother at midlife while starting a career. Patterns of family life have evidently become more complex—even "individualized."

The Impact of Modernization on Family Changes in Canada and Worldwide

Many changes in close relations accompany modernization. Struggles to define and redefine families continue throughout the industrialized world (Baker, 1995). Indeed, industrialization, as we have seen, has had a huge impact on family living. In addition to industrialization, urbanization has also had a great effect on family life (see Finlay, Velsor, and Hilker, 1982). That is mainly because households—or who lives with whom—are determined by property ownership arrangements, which vary between urban and rural areas. Typically, households are larger (i.e., extended) and family life is more psychologically important to people in rural than in urban areas—or so we usually think. In many parts of the world, people still spend substantial parts of their lives in extended households, though they increasingly spend significant parts of their lives in nuclear families.

Along with industrialization and modernization, women's roles and responsibilities are changing. Most significantly, women increasingly seek higher education and careers (Divale and Seda, 2001). By means of their higher education and job participation, women are now more able to control their childbearing and to support themselves economically, and they may also delay marriage. Marriages are showing more egalitarianism than in the past, meaning that family power is shared between spouses. Not that all are equal, but more men are seeking wives who are educated and nearer their own age. This trend is occurring throughout the world. In Brazil, for example, there are more women than men seeking job opportunities in cities rather than living the traditional rural life. This is in part because of patriarchal norms still in place that prevent women from inheriting land. Because they have fewer job prospects at home, many women move to urbanized centres (Brumer, 2008).

As in the Brazil example, these and other societal changes can be observed in other parts of the world, wherever modernization has affected social and cultural life. In many modern Arab societies, modernization is associated with smaller family sizes, a higher literacy rate, and a better economy (Ajrouch et al., 2013; El-Ghannam, 2001). Moreover, Schvaneveldt, Kerpelman, and Schvaneveldt (2005) have noted that in United Arab Emirates (in the Persian Gulf), a modern industrial economy, university education, and global media access mean that young women have different attitudes toward choice in mate selection, fertility practices, and egalitarianism in child care than do their mothers. Better-educated young people today, exposed to higher standards of living and individualism, can come into conflict with parents or other institutions of power as they seek to change their lives. A well-known example is the youngest Nobel Peace Prize winner, Malala Yousafzai. These changes may be especially challenging in countries where the state and religion are not separate, such as Iran or Israel. Yet outcomes are not preordained; there is no certainty, for example, that the family in a modernizing Muslim region will be identical to the modern Christian, Hindu, or Jewish family.

Some of the impacts of modernization on other cultures can be predicted since, along with industrialization and individualism, modernization alters traditional customs and norms in foreseeable ways. For instance, in Asian countries where filial piety is a traditional value, massive and sudden modernization in recent years (Quach and Anderson, 2008) has also resulted in negative experiences for families with older relatives (Chappell, 2013; Ding, 2004). The family remains the main support for aging relatives, but providing for them is becoming increasingly difficult, especially because children are pursuing higher education and are influenced by individualistic notions of the West. Families in many parts of the world are experiencing similar challenges (McDaniel and Zimmer, 2013; Zimmer and McDaniel, 2013).

As another example, consider the effects of modernization in India. Here, modernization has arguably had a very significant impact on society, or at least on parts of the society. And, of course, families are hugely affected by this social and political shift. Before modernization, even over its expansive history and countless societal changes, the family as a unit in India remained fairly stable. With industrialization and urbanization, however, as well as the growing influence of Western markets and ideologies, the traditional customs of marriage, family, and kinship have changed significantly. Some of the changes are viewed as positive, yet this is so only for a small percentage of the population. Many more people have been marginalized as a result of modernization and have experienced suffering (Kashyap, 2004). Women, in particular, have been affected in both good and bad ways. As more jobs open, women have many more opportunities. Yet these very opportunities can clash with older cultural values, leading to increased violence against women who are seen as stepping away from traditional values and patriarchy (Chibber et al., 2012; Kimuna et al., 2012).

Another factor that changes family life is political will and ideology. China, for example, has mobilized families and citizens in support of social and economic development. State planning of family life has gone hand in hand with dramatic economic and political change (Wang, 2016). Both hardship and progress as a result of this are apparent (Xie, Jiang, and Greenman, 2008). Conditions of life in China for many, particularly in rural areas, remain difficult, yet for some, quality of life has been hugely enhanced. And there are indications that family life is improving, especially for women. State efforts to regulate marriage, fertility, and the rights of women are starting to pay off with smaller families and increased gender equality, though at the expense of personal liberty (Attané, 2012). And of course, smaller families are more amenable to urban living, as has been true of every modernizing society.

Moreover, even in the smaller, more isolated rural areas of the world, where traditional family forms persist most strongly, parent–child relations are changing with modernization (Caldwell, Reddy, and Caldwell, 1984; Trommsdorf, Kim, and Nauck, 2005). Children, on average, are gaining more autonomy and power in interactions with parents. These changes show the pervasive influence of Western cultural notions, specifically notions about childhood and adolescence, but also, more generally, notions about the life cycle. They also show the growing importance of education and media even in rural areas, and the socialization of new generations in preparation for an urban, industrial lifestyle.

Changes in Sexual Attitudes and Courtship

As sociologists have known since the founding works by Durkheim, there is an important connection between population size, population diversity, specialized roles, and changing attitudes. So, let us begin this section by noting, as shown in Figure 2.2, that Canada's population has grown continuously and dramatically over the past 100 years. For that and other reasons, family forms and practices have changed, diversified, and specialized as well.

Before the nineteenth century, sex was strongly associated with the wedding night, and virginity was hugely valued. Then, newlyweds had no privacy. They were accompanied into the matrimonial bedroom by relatives and friends and, of course, rude jokes. In some cultures, the bloodied sheets of a virgin "deflowered" would be tossed from the window to the cheers of crowds of relatives and friends below. However, in the nineteenth century, the Victorians "de-sexed" the honeymoon. Isobel March, a newly married young woman in 1871 in Niagara Falls, cited by Dubinsky (1999: 27), "did all she could to avoid the horror of being an 'evident bride.'"

In the Victorian era, the banishing of sex from public view reached its peak. Legs on tables were covered for fear that, in their naked state, they would make people

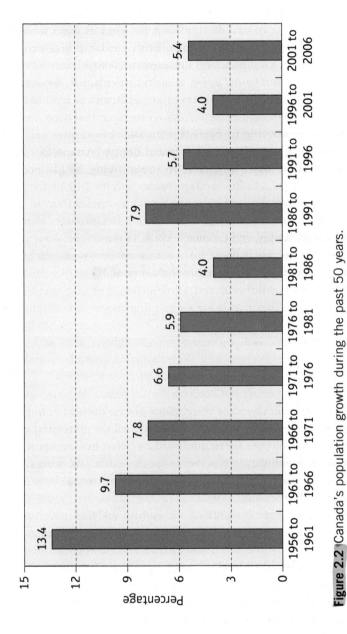

Figure 2.2 Canada's population growth during the past 50 years.

Source: Statistics Canada. *Censuses of population 1956 to 2011.* Retrieved January 2013 from www12.statcan.gc.ca/census-recensement/2011/dp-pd/vc-rv/index.cfm?LANG=ENG&VIEW=C&TOPIC_ID=1&GEOCODE=01&CFORMAT=jpg#f1_1. Reproduced and distributed on an "as is" basis with the permission of Statistics Canada.

think of sex! Pregnancy was disguised, hidden, or denied. Nonetheless, during this period a world of men's pubs and clubs flourished, as did a thriving prostitution trade and lurid romance novels. Sex did not cease to exist.

By the late nineteenth century, sex began to be seen as a central part of marriage and sexual attraction as a crucial part of courtship. Sex is considered to have "come out" in the 1920s (Dubinsky, 1999)—heterosexuality in a married relationship, that is. Soon, sex experts and romance filmmakers invented the sexual honeymoon. Sexuality and sexual attraction began to occupy a more central place in modern ideas of personality and identity, and sexual happiness came to the fore as a primary purpose of marriage (Dubinsky, 1999).

At the beginning of the twenty-first century, marriage is seldom considered rationally by sentimental youth, who are often engaged not in planning lives together, but in planning romantic—and increasingly costly—white weddings. Interestingly, in weddings today, all but the most ultra-modern brides still look like fairy princesses, and grooms remain one step short of riding in on white horses (but, of course, in some ethnic groups, that is exactly what grooms still do). Brides are still "given away" by their fathers (or both parents) to their husbands. And the important ritual of uniting the couple sexually—sending them on the expected honeymoon—as well as socially is shared by families brought together for the wedding.

Changes in Attitudes toward Marriage

Traditionally, marriage was viewed largely in terms of rights, duties, and obligations to each other's families. Throughout the West, a major attitude shift has placed greater emphasis on the personal or emotional side of close relations.

Why, then, do so many people still keep up the old forms? Why do so many still get married, many of them in churches or religious places, dressed in hugely expensive white bridal gowns and formal black tuxedos, or in all the glitter and gold of the Hindu wedding? We shall discuss these questions in detail in Chapter 4. In short, formal weddings and the legal ceremony have more to do with marking a life transition or gaining social approval than with emotional commitment. Many people still find the idea of legal marriage compelling, despite what they know about the realities of marriage and divorce (Vanier Institute of the Family, 2004). Enormous numbers of North Americans are neither rejecting the family or other long-lasting, close relationships nor accepting family in a traditional form. Most are hoping to revitalize and reinterpret family (Scanzoni, 2000; Vanier Institute of the Family, 2004), making families suited to themselves and their needs.

Although many people still get married, one significant change in family life in the Western world has been an increase in cohabitation—people living together without being legally married. Cohabitation, or the "common-law union" as it is also called, used to be more prevalent among working-class people. It also used to be seen as a lesser form of relationship than marriage—the practice was sometimes referred

Changes in the Marriage Rate in the Twenty-First Century

■ In 1986, with amendment to the divorce law, the percentage of those married over age 15 decreased to 61.4 percent. Married couples made up 80.2 percent of all Census families. Lone-parent families accounted for 12.7 percent, and cohabiting couple families for only 7.2 percent, rates that both increased substantially in 2006 (Statistics Canada, 2006a).

■ By 2011, married couples remained the predominant family union at 67 percent, while those cohabitating rose 13.9 percent since 2006, an increase more than four times that of married couples. These couples, in the 2011 Census, accounted for 16.7 percent of all families (Statistics Canada, 2011a).

■ The number of same-sex married couples nearly tripled between 2006 and 2011, reflecting the first five-year period for which same-sex marriage was legal across the country. Of all same-sex couples, 32.5 percent were married and those in cohabitating relationships accounted for 67.5 percent (Statistics Canada, 2011a).

■ For the first time, in 2006, the number of unmarried people (meaning those never married, divorced, separated, or widowed) over age 15 surpassed the number of married people, at 51.5 percent (see Figure 2.3; Statistics Canada, 2006a).

■ In 2011, those who were single, as defined above, were difficult to assess, as the Census did not isolate that portion of the population as a discernible group. The number of respondents who declared being single, and not living common law, was 39.8 percent; however, there is no way to determine if they had ever been married or not (Statistics Canada, 2011a).

■ Canada's declining marriage rate is similar to that in other Western countries, including the United Kingdom, Australia, and the United States. In the United States in 2001, the number of married-couple families was 70 percent, down from 83 percent in 1981, and common-law families increased from 6 percent to 14 percent in the same period (Statistics Canada, 2006a).

---

to as "living in sin" or "shacking up." Now, however, cohabitation has lost some of its stigma and is much more accepted. In Quebec, cohabitation has become the norm for younger couples, while legal marriage is decidedly less preferred (Vanier Institute of the Family, 2004). These trends are discussed further in Chapter 4.

It may be coincidental that the growth in cohabitation has coincided with later marriage (since the 1960s and 1970s), higher divorce rates, and lower rates of childbearing. More and more often, people think of spousal relations as being about love and sexual attraction, not about childbearing and creating family alliances. People have come to expect more satisfaction of their emotional and psychological needs in their close relationships. Women, particularly, are less economically dependent on their partners than they used to be. These shifting norms, opportunities, and expectations have all contributed to a decline in the stability of married and cohabiting life. But both continue and for the majority seem to work and work happily.

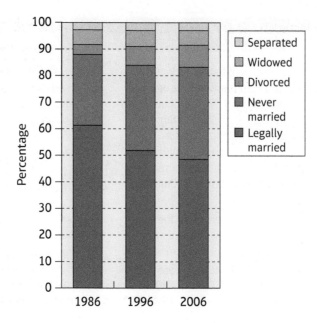

Figure 2.3 For the first time, the legally married population age 15 and over fell below 50 percent in 2006.

Source: Statistics Canada. *Censuses of population 1986 to 2006.* Retrieved from www12.statcan.ca/census-recensement/2006/as-sa/97-553/figures/c7-eng.cfm. Reproduced and distributed on an "as is" basis with the permission of Statistics Canada.

DECLINING FERTILITY AND THE VALUE OF PARENTHOOD

There can be no denying the dramatic changes that have occurred in family life—especially, in the size, structure, and composition of Canadian families—even in the last 20 to 30 years (on this, see the data in Table 2.1 below). However, it is important to note that these recent changes are rooted in dramatic changes that began more than a century ago and took place, at differing rates, in all modern industrial societies.

One of the most marked changes in family life has been a change in family size over the past century or so. Since the 1870s, fertility in the West has declined steadily. Birth rates in Canada hit a record low in 2000, after 10 straight years of decline. A total of 327 882 babies were born in 2000, down 2.8 percent from 1999 and the lowest number since 1946 (Statistics Canada, 2002e). Today, most European and North American countries are at, or just below, population replacement levels. While Canada is still showing some population growth, it is steadily decreasing, and growth is due more to immigration than to births. This means that unless there is a radical shift in fertility or immigration in the future, Western populations will get smaller and older during the next century. This process is already well underway in Sweden,

Table 2.1 Selected Trend Data, 2011, 2006, 2001, and 1996 Censuses

	Census Year			
	2011	**2006**	**2001**	**1996**
% of couples (married & common-law) with children (of any age)	n/a	54.3	56.7	59.3
% of couples (married & common-law) with at least one child under 24 years of age	39.2	49.2	51.7	54.7
% of one-person households	27.6	26.8	25.7	24.2
% of households containing a couple with children	26.5	28.5	30.5	32.9
% of households containing a couple without children	29.5	29.0	28.0	26.8
Average household size	2.5	2.5	2.6	2.6

Source: Data from Statistics Canada. *Census trends for Canada, provinces and territories, census population 2011.* Catalogue no. 92-596-XWE and catalogue no. 98-312-X-2011001. Retrieved April 15, 2009, and January 2013 from www12.statcan.ca/english/census06/data/trends/Index.cfm and http://www12.statcan.gc.ca/census-recensement/2011/as-sa/98-312-x/98-312-x2011001-eng.cfm.

France, and Japan. Whether this is a problem—for families and for societies—depends on who is deciding and how the situation is defined. It is a topic to which we will return.

A significant blip on this downward fertility curve was the post-war "baby boom." The baby boom, however, was only a temporary reversal of the long-term trend and was largely confined to North America. The "boom" was also misnamed. Higher birth rates were the result not of increasing family size alone but also of compressing two decades of births into a decade and a half (roughly 1947 to 1962). In other words, while fertility did increase somewhat, the boom was more the result of postponed fertility due to World War II. Several different age groups then had their desired number of children within a short time frame, leading to a dramatic increase in birth rate for those years. Largely, the long-term downward trend in fertility over the course of the twentieth century never really ceased (see Figure 2.4). Married-couple families with children age 24 and under is no longer the largest family structure.

Family size and birth rates in Canada have always been political issues, as we mentioned earlier. The term used to describe Quebec's historically high birth rates (before they fell sharply from the late 1950s on) was "the **revenge of the cradle**," reflecting the belief that Quebec's long-standing sense of political injustice might be countered by having more Quebec (French-speaking) citizens (see Henripin and Peron, 1971). Early birth-control promoters, such as A.R. Kaufman of Kitchener, Ontario, were concerned about the French in Canada "outbreeding" the English (see McLaren and McLaren, 1986: 124).

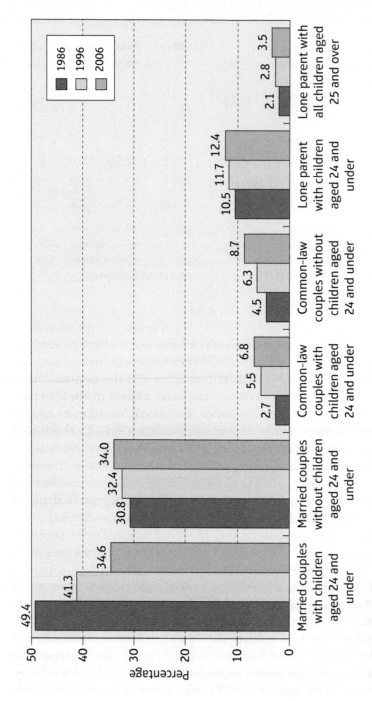

Figure 2.4 Married-couple families with children age 24 and under is the largest family structure, but declining.[1]

[1]Historical comparisons for Census families, particularly lone-parent families, must be interpreted with caution due to conceptual changes in 2001.

Source: Data from Statistics Canada. *Censuses of population 1986, 1996, 2006, and 2011.* Catalogue no. 98-312-X2011001. Retrieved May 2013 from http://www12.statcan.ca/census-recensement/2006/as-sa/97-553/figures/c1-eng.cfm and http://www12.statcan. gc.ca/census-recensement/2011/as-sa/98-312-x/2011001/fig/fig1-eng.cfm.

■ At the start of the Great Depression in 1931, women were having fewer than three children. During the baby boom of 1946 to 1965, however, alongside a higher percentage of married people, the number of children born increased to three children per woman on average. Most of these children were born to young mothers in their early twenties (Statistics Canada, 2006a).

■ With the legalization of contraception in 1969, the number of children born decreased and has continued its decline over the past half-century. In fact, 1971 marked the last year during which the birth rate was at replacement level (Statistics Canada, 2006a).

■ There are now more couples without children than with children. For the first time, in 2006, there were slightly more couples without children than with children (less than 1 percent). In 2011, this trend became more firmly entrenched, with the gap between the two groups widening.

■ Women today are having children at increasingly older ages. Number of births by women in their thirties rose from 23 percent in 1982 to 44.8 percent in 2002 (Statistics Canada, 2004b). Whereas in 2001, 7.8 percent of children age 4 and younger had a mother age 40 to 49, in 2006 this percentage increased to 9.4 percent (Statistics Canada, 2006a).

The Quebec government awarded prizes in the 1930s and 1940s to women who bore many children. Their photos would appear in newspapers. Both the church and the government encouraged families to have more children. This policy was formalized with baby bonuses, which increased with each extra child born. The shift from large to small families in Quebec has occurred rapidly indeed, leaving many Quebec families with older and younger generations of vastly different sizes. Quebec's birth rate remains a political issue in the 2000s. Family researchers who study birth rates—known as **demographers**—are household names to Quebeckers; not so in the rest of Canada.

Indigenous peoples in Canada also had high birth rates in the past. In the 1970s and into the 1980s, births to Indigenous peoples started to decline. Recently, however, First Nations birth rates have since increased and are now the fastest growing in Canada (Vanier Institute of the Family, 2004). The current fertility rate among Indigenous peoples is around 1.5 times the overall rate among Canadians (Statistics Canada, 2005d), with 10.5 percent of the Indigenous population being in the youngest age group (0 to 4 years old) compared to only 5.3 percent of the Canadian population at large (Statistics Canada, 2005c).

Although Canadians are having fewer children than before, expectations of marrying and having children remain strong. When asked by family researchers, most young people say that they expect to get married and have children (Vanier Institute of the Family, 2004). Interestingly, few expect ever to be divorced, despite the high divorce rate in modern society. Moreover, in the late nineteenth century

Recent Statistical Trends in the Indigenous Population

We should note that Indigenous peoples are variously located in different Canadian provinces and territories (see Figure 2.5): In some, they are a tiny minority, while in others they are a large minority or even a majority. Moreover, Indigenous bands vary quite markedly in size and prosperity. So, it is difficult to generalize about Indigenous peoples in Canada, but we will venture a few generalizations nonetheless.

■ The number of Indigenous peoples in Canada—including the First Nations, Métis, and Inuit—is now almost 1.5 million. Indigenous peoples make up 4.3 percent of Canada's total population, compared to 2.8 percent in 1996. The population has been increasing significantly and grew by 20.1 percent between 2006 and 2011, compared with 5.2 percent for the non-Indigenous population (Statistics Canada, 2013a).

■ Eight in ten Indigenous people lived in Ontario and the western provinces (Manitoba, Saskatchewan, Alberta, and British Columbia) in 2011. Indigenous people made up the largest shares of the population of Nunavut and the Northwest Territories (Statistics Canada, 2013a).

■ By 2017, the number of Indigenous young adults ages 20 to 29 years ready to enter the labour market is projected to increase by more than 40 percent, compared to the 9 percent of the same age group from the general population (Statistics Canada, 2005b).

■ The percentage of Indigenous peoples in Canada is similar to that of New Zealand, Australia, and the United States. Canada's Indigenous population is second to New Zealand's, where the Maori population accounts for about 15 percent of the total population (Statistics Canada, 2006a).

and the early part of the twentieth century, many more people than now never married at all, a fact contrary to the common assumption that everyone in the past got married. For example, Gee (1986: 266) finds from historical records that in 1911, 12 percent of Canadians had never married. This compares with only 5.8 percent in 1981. Today, fewer than 2 percent of Canadians are likely to remain single their whole lives (neither marrying nor cohabiting). Not marrying in the past generally meant not entering parenthood. So, in fact, parenthood in the past was not part of as many people's lives as it is now. In the past, a lower percentage of the population got married, but those who did had many more children, on average, than couples do today.

The First and Second Demographic Transitions

The **demographic transition** from high mortality and fertility to low mortality and fertility transformed the social meaning of children, child rearing, and women's place in the family. The transition to low fertility in the West, which began around 1870, is called the *first demographic transition*. It brought births into line with a sharply reduced death rate. Since 1965, we have seen a new force for lower fertility in the West.

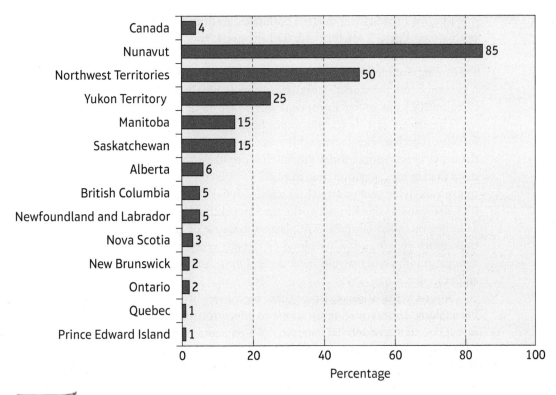

Figure 2.5 Percentage of Indigenous peoples in the population, Canada, provinces and territories, 2011

Source: Statistics Canada. *National Household Survey 2011*. Retrieved May 2013 from http://www12. statcan.gc.ca/nhs-enm/2011/as-sa/99-011-x/2011001/tbl/tbl02-eng.cfm. Reproduced and distributed on an "as is" basis with the permission of Statistics Canada.

Demographers have called this new phase the *second demographic transition* (Van de Kaa, 1987). This contemporary transition brought birth rates into line with new lifestyle goals and family practices. Wherever we find the second demographic transition well advanced, we find a profusion of new ("non-traditional") family styles, women working in the paid labour force in large numbers, and people seeking autonomy and fulfillment in their personal lives.

The second demographic transition is especially advanced in Northern and Western Europe. Renewed concerns have been expressed in these regions about depopulation and a shortage of young people in the future. In Europe, the fertility rates needed to replace the population—about 2.1 lifetime births per woman—are found only in Ireland, Malta, Poland, Albania, Turkey, and some new countries in Eastern Europe. None of these countries is a highly industrialized, Protestant country. All of them have made a virtue of large family size or limited access to birth control. It must be remembered that Canada did this as well until recently.

In most Protestant industrial countries, fertility rates hover around 1.5 children per woman. Japan's fertility rate had dropped, too, from an annual level of 2.1 in 1973 to 1.29 in 2004 (BBC News, 2005, June 1), the lowest ever recorded there. A continuing decline in fertility will leave Europe's population with a growth of only 6 percent while the world's population overall nearly doubles. As a result of low fertility, by 2025 one in five Europeans will be age 65 or older.

The effects of this transition are both profound and subtle. A long decline in fertility, together with increased life expectancy, has led to an aging population. On the other hand, people today are much more likely to have many generations alive at once than at any previous time in history, with some families having as many as five or even six living generations (McDaniel, 1996a). Remarried, step-, and blended families also expand our kin networks into stepchildren and stepgrandchildren, as well as larger extended families. And, largely because of urbanization and industrialization, more people today live alone or outside conventional families than their parents or grandparents would have done. Domestic lives are becoming more varied and complex.

Several explanations exist for these recent fertility declines. For one, women have been taking advantage of more access to education and employment. Another factor is that couples have delayed marrying. When people delay marriage, they are likely to have fewer children. At the same time, the costs of raising children, both economic and social/personal, rose dramatically during the twentieth century. Children are especially expensive if they need daycare by someone other than the mother (whose child care in the past was presumed to be costless) or if caring for them means forgoing a parent's income and career aspirations for several years. Moreover, parents usually spend increasing amounts of money on children's lessons, camps, and education. As well, children today remain in a state of economic dependency for longer than in the past, sometimes for surprisingly long times, as we shall see in later chapters. Finally, children often contribute less to the family economy than they used to in pre-industrial times and in the early part of the twentieth century. We will discuss these issues further in Chapter 6.

Contraception, Childbearing Choice, and Abortion

In the past, women found a major source of identity in having children and being mothers. This was the case in such different situations as urban Quebec in the seventeenth century and the early frontier societies in the Canadian West. Silverman (1984: 59) explains that giving birth and raising children was the answer often given to the question "What are women for?"—an answer given by women as well as by men (also see Mitchinson, 2002). Until recently, both women and men agreed that childbearing and child rearing gave women's lives meaning. Entering parenthood was also vital to populate Canada, especially in settling the West and, as we have seen, in the earliest settlements in Quebec.

However, there have always been attempts, some of them successful, to regulate pregnancy and births. Although it was officially illegal in Canada until 1969, some couples tried to use birth control to choose how many children they would have and when they would have them. Among the most common birth control methods in the past were abstinence and prolonged breastfeeding. Other popular birth control methods used in the past included barrier methods, timing or rhythm approaches, withdrawal, abortion, and, as one wise adviser to young married women suggested in her 1908 marriage manual, "twin beds" (McLaren and McLaren, 1986: 19–20).

Abortion was also common in previous centuries, with methods of "bringing down the menses" routinely advertised in daily newspapers and early magazines (McLaren and McLaren, 1986: 33–35). It is only in recent decades that abortion has come to be seen as an important public and moral issue. Interestingly, several of the well-known nineteenth-century **abortifacients** (herbs or potions that brought on a miscarriage) are still in use today for inducing labour.

During the 1960s, however, safe, reliable, and easily available contraception methods were invented. This technological shift significantly changed the concept of birth control and so contributed to the decline in fertility rate. Therefore, the first demographic transition was accomplished through a combination of strategies, including late marriage, abstinence from sex, awkward methods of birth control, and dangerous, illegal abortion. The second demographic transition has occurred in the midst of a liberalizing sexual revolution and new, accessible means of contraception. The pill and other relatively readily available forms of contraception—including IUDs (intrauterine devices), spermicidal gels and foams, and higher-quality condoms—allow women and couples to choose if and when to become pregnant.

Contraceptive devices, for example, were generally scarce in Eastern Europe under communism. As a result, the average woman in the former Soviet Union and Romania in the mid-1960s would have had seven abortions during her lifetime. Van de Kaa (1987) notes the dramatic rise in third and higher-order births after the repeal of legal abortion legislation in Romania, while the Ceausescu regime maintained an iron-fisted stance against birth control in a deliberate effort to increase the birth rate. What this shows is that, before the ruling of abortion, this method had been playing a large role in controlling fertility where other means of birth control were unavailable. Consequently, many people abandoned their babies to the care of the state. The net result was a huge number of Romanian babies and children crammed into orphanages under appalling conditions.

Up to the 1890s, abortion was tolerated in many jurisdictions, including Canada. Women who wanted to end their pregnancies could do so with the assistance of surgeons, herbalists, or midwives. Abortion was in fact legal in most North American states until the 1890s. Then it became illegal for 70 years, as a result of pressure exerted by social purity movements. Legalizing abortion once again made the process safer and more medically controlled. The (legal) abortion rate rose briefly after the mid-1960s, with a more liberal interpretation of the laws, but the rate soon tapered off (McLaren and McLaren, 1997). The most important factor promoting a decline in the incidence of abortion is the use of contraception, which enables avoidance of unwanted pregnancies. As contraceptive knowledge and use have spread, abortion has become a less often relied-upon means of limiting fertility. Yet there is a renewed focus on women's reproduction and reproductive rights and access, particularly apparent in the United States, where many states have sharply limited women's access to abortion and simultaneously reduced their access to contraception. These changes have also influenced people's ideas about love, sex, and intimacy in ways that would have been hard to imagine.

Family and Household Size

As fertility has declined, so has the number of people in the average Canadian household. It has shrunk by 50 percent, from around six people in 1961 to now two or even one today. In addition, complex family households, containing people not part of a traditional nuclear family, had almost vanished by 2001, but now it seems that those multigenerational households are on the rise, perhaps as a result of tough economic times (McDaniel, Gazso, and Um, 2013).

A major change in family life is a rise in the proportion of single-person households (Statistics Canada, 2012a)—this more than tripled from 1931 to 2011, to 13.5 percent of the population age 15 and over, while the proportion of people overall living in families declined since 1981 (Vanier Institute of the Family, 1994: 29). In 2011, there were more than three times as many one-person households as those with five or more people (see Figure 2.6; Statistics Canada, 2012a). Curiously, while households have been growing smaller, houses have been growing bigger. Victorian-era single family houses, where as many as 15 people lived at the peak of immigration, today are often occupied by couples with fewer than three children or no children at all (Iacovetta, 1992).

> ### ⟫⟫ Decrease in Family Size
>
> - The size of families in Canada is continually decreasing. Whereas in 1961, 32.3 percent of all families were made up of five or more persons, half a century later the percentage is only 8.4 percent (Statistics Canada, 2012a).
>
> - Along with the size of families, the size of households has been declining over the past half-century. The average size of the Cana- dian family decreased from 3.9 people in 1961 to 2.5 in 2011 (Statistics Canada, 2012a).
>
> - One-person households are more common. The percentage rose from 9.3 percent in 1961 to 25.7 percent in 2001. In 2011, it was at 27.6 percent, three times that of those households consisting of five or more people (Statistics Canada, 2012a).

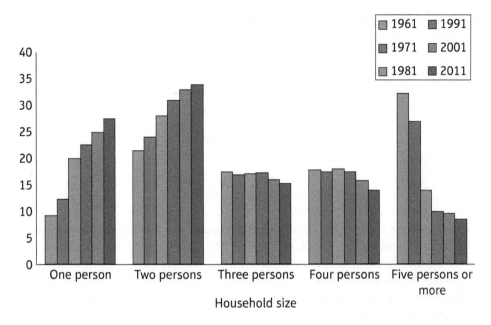

Figure 2.6 Distribution, in percent, of private households by household size, 1961 to 2011

Source: Statistics Canada. *Censuses of population 1961 to 2011*. Catalogue no. 98-312-X-2011003. Retrieved January 2013 from http://www12.statcan.gc.ca/census-recensement/2011/as-sa/98-312-x/2011003/fig/desc/desc3_1-4-eng.cfm. Reproduced and distributed on an "as is" basis with the permission of Statistics Canada.

SOCIAL SUPPORT AND REGULATION: THE ROLE OF THE STATE IN FAMILIES

As families have changed and evolved with respect to meeting people's needs for support, state support also changed and has now shrunk significantly. For example, state support in Canada for lone mothers changed from being largely supportive of widows with dependent children, enabling them to be "stay-at-home" mothers, to encouraging today's lone mothers (who are more often never married, divorced, or separated) to work for pay while their children are young (Baker, 2005b; Gazso and McDaniel, 2010a, 2010b). In the second decade of the twenty-first century, there is little doubt that Canada has become less supportive of families overall (Vanier Institute of the Family, 2006), despite words to the contrary. Major cycles of change in state support for families have occurred through recent times, with sharp reductions occurring at the present.

Child Support and Welfare Reforms in Canada

At the beginning of the twentieth century and especially during the Great Depression, child poverty and support for low-income mothers remained a low priority on the political agenda. Instead, legislation of the 1930s tended to reverse earlier progress toward a universally protected childhood (Strong-Boag, 2000). Change began after World War II under the Mackenzie King government, which recognized the state's role in supporting its young citizens and introduced **family allowances**. These monthly payments, based on the number of children at home, went to all women with children—but only to women, never to men. For many women who worked solely at home, this was their only independent income. In a way, family allowances were given to women as a way to compensate and recognize their important role in child rearing.

During the 1980s, the publication of Lenore Weitzman's book *The Divorce Revolution* sparked widespread concern that rising divorce rates together with inadequate child support were responsible for poverty among single mothers and their children. One of the most notable findings was that "a woman's standard of living decreases by 73% after divorce, while a man's increases by 42% on average" (Millar and Gauthier, 2002: 140). This led to a re-evaluation of child support guidelines in Canada and the United States. In 1989, the Canadian government announced its mandate to erase child poverty by the year 2000 (Crossley and Curtis, 2006). That said, there was almost no change in the proportion of children under age 18 living in a low-income family from 1989 to 2004, despite government interventions and a strong economy since 1990–1992 (Fleury, 2008).

What followed was a number of tax and benefit policy changes. In 1990, parental benefits were added to the unemployment insurance (UI) benefits. The federal program of family allowances was discontinued in 1992 and was replaced by the Child Tax Benefit program, which aimed to provide relief for low- and middle-income families in Canada (although Quebec adopted its own guidelines; Millar and Gauthier, 2002). Finally, the National Child Benefit program was established in 1998 to support low-income families that move from welfare into the labour market (National Child Benefit, 2009). Despite these state interventions, child poverty increased from about 1 in 7 in 1989 to 1 in 5 in 1999 (Strong-Boag, 2000).

Critics argue that these reforms do little to relieve child and women's poverty (Gazso and McDaniel, 2009; Williamson and Salkie, 2005). Rather, they fuel the privatization of social benefits, increase economic stratification, and are not responsive enough to changing family circumstances (Millar and Gauthier, 2002). Today, only Quebec continues with some form of family allowances in Canada (LeBourdais and Marcil-Gratton, 1996; Milligan, 2005; Milligan and Stabile, 2011). The Quebec program of baby bonuses is intended both to increase the number of births and to provide support for women raising children. The amounts paid, however, in no way compensate for the costs involved in raising a child.

It is important to note that child poverty is not equally distributed in society. Poverty rates are consistently higher among young, single-parent, immigrant, and Indigenous families (Prentice, 2007; Statistics Canada, 2012c). For example, in 1997 only 13.7 percent of *all* children lived with a single mother, compared to 41 percent of *income-poor children* and 49.8 percent of children in *deep poverty* who lived in this family type (Kerr and Beaujot, 2003: 327). The rates among Indigenous populations are as high as 52 percent, and roughly 43 percent of visible minority children experience child poverty (Strong-Boag, 2000: 125).

The rise in lone-parent households, neoliberal economic reforms, and the retrenchment in the welfare state may contribute to the persistence of child poverty (Kerr and Beaujot, 2003). Interesting patterns are found when low income is examined among groups at risk of social exclusion: seniors, children, lone parents, Indigenous peoples, immigrants, unattached non-elderly people, and people with activity limitations. In the past few decades, measures have improved somewhat for seniors and lone parents; however, low income was still high relative to the other groups (Statistics Canada, 2012c). As children are included in nearly all groups, their situation is the most desperate. Debates on how to define and measure child poverty make it difficult to evaluate the efficacy and success of government policies.

"Welfare-to-work" initiatives of the 1990s added a new dimension to the plight of low-income families and their children. Prior to the 1990s, single mothers across Canada "could provide full-time care to their children and receive social assistance until their youngest child was at least school age" (Williamson and Salkie, 2005: 56). However, in the mid-1990s, Canadian policy-makers sought to reduce the proportion of welfare recipients by mandating them to find work or take part in employment-related

The Imbalance of Indigenous Poverty

Ongoing socio-economic struggles among the Indigenous population in Canada continue to go unrecognized by the general population, and solutions are limited and unsatisfactory. The negative impacts of extreme poverty, which is experienced by disproportionately high numbers of Indigenous children, encompass far more than hunger. These impacts are extensive and pervasive. Statistics Canada (2006) finds that more than half of First Nations children live in low-income families. Compare this with 21 percent of non-Indigenous children. Most Canadians are not aware of the extreme poverty these children, especially those living in remote areas, are subjected to. Growing up in a system that clearly does not understand how to deal with their needs, these children are more likely to experience a number of impacts: family violence, family structure breakdown, lower educational attainment, high suicide rates, widespread alcohol and solvent abuse, undiagnosed mental health issues, and low chance of improving socio-economic situation. "Aboriginal children are one of the most marginalized and oppressed populations within Canada. Their rights . . . are regularly being violated and they are extremely overrepresented in the child welfare system. Allowing communities to take on [self-governing child welfare] responsibility . . . is a step in the right direction" (Jones, 2010: 21, 27).

Melanie Jones. 2010. Systemic/social issues: Aboriginal child welfare. *Relational Child & Youth Care Practice* 23(4) 17–30. http://encore.uleth.ca:50080/ebsco-web/ehost/pdfviewer/pdfviewer?sid=b97fd556-b536-460a-beef-cc17aa7bac1e%40sessionmgr114&vid=2&hid=123

programs (e.g., job training). Contrary to original goals, these welfare reforms did not improve children's well-being (Gazso and McDaniel, 2010a, 2010b).

Instead, impoverished children are now more likely than before to have parents who are trying to balance work with employment, and they are more likely to live in families that secure income from the labour market rather than social assistance. Therefore, elimination of child poverty will likely entail the integration of several carefully planned and evaluated social policies—not only child support benefits and welfare-to-work initiatives, but also those associated with social assistance incomes, higher minimum wages, affordable housing, and more accessible and universal child care (Lloyd, 2008).

Changing Nature of Elder Support by the State and the Family

Traditionally, support of older individuals was provided by what is sometimes referred to as the "three-legged stool" of responsibility—namely, government, employers, and families (Salisbury, 1997). However, efforts to reduce government spending, the precarious nature of employment markets, and changes in family life have altered the support received by the elderly (Kemp and Denton, 2003).

The Canadian welfare state, which developed during and immediately after World War II, underwent a progressive expansion, culminating in a full-blown Canadian social security system in the 1970s (Li, 1996). Given its supply of economic, medical, and social assistance, the system was especially important for older people, who were now supported by the government. Two other main sources of support were available in later life—the market and the family (Esping-Andersen, 1999). The financial services market provided plans such as life insurance and private pension policies, while the family, often mainly through the efforts of women, provided care for infirm older adults.

The post-industrial society, however, brought with it changes to the traditional sources of support for the aging portion of society. Because of changes in the labour market and demographic transformations, the state, the market, and the family started limiting their provision of welfare compared to their contribution in the past (Esping-Andersen, 1999). Beginning in the 1980s, a concern with the overextension of the welfare state and with the public expenditure implications of an aging population took over in the political realm. This led to decreased spending, terminated social programs, and streamlining of services (Baines, Evans, and Neysmith, 1998; Brotman, 1998). Such changes caused a greater responsibility for late-life provisions to fall on the shoulders of the family and the market.

However, the high levels of unemployment that have characterized the past few decades have forced many into early retirement or chronic unemployment, often with insufficient financial resources (Curtis and McMullin, 2016; Kohli, Rein, Guillemard, and Van Gunsteren, 1991). The trend toward early retirement in Canada has recently turned around, however, with people working longer (Statistics Canada, 2012c) due to necessity or preference. Furthermore, the new face of the labour market, which included interrupted employment patterns, contract work, and part-time employment, also began limiting the support of employers through private pension plans and insurance programs (McDaniel, 1997).

The socio-demographic changes during this time, mentioned earlier in the chapter, reduced the availability of relatives able to provide support for older family members. Such changes included a rise in single-parent families, substantially increasing female participation in the labour force, as well as the geographical dispersion of family members. Thus, overall, the post-industrial society and the changes it brought with it have translated to a shift in responsibility for the care of the elderly from the state, market, and family to the elderly trying to take care of themselves.

These circumstances become evident when examining the attitudes and beliefs of today's middle- and old-age population. Kemp and Denton (2003) investigated the way in which midlife and late-life Canadians discuss and allocate responsibility for the provision of social, financial, and medical supports in later life. The answer was clear: Care for the elderly is the responsibility of the elderly. Recall the example of the Japanese Canadian and Canadian seniors discussed previously. Their reports were similar to those of the participants in this study. Most respondents in this study assumed personal responsibility for later life, citing individual planning and preparation as necessary tasks to secure against the perceived risks associated with becoming or being old. Furthermore, most participants rejected the notion that family members should provide housing, financial support, or personal care and were generally seen as a source of emotional support (Kemp and Denton, 2003).

Even though studies have shown that the senior population is not responsible for escalating health care costs or depletion of the Canadian pension fund (see Barer, Evans, and Hertzman, 1995), the shift to greater individual responsibility for societal and personal social security remains significant today. It has been argued that this can lead to increased social and financial risks in old age (e.g., Esping-Andersen, 1999).

Because of aging population, the payments for Old Age Security and Guaranteed Income Supplement for low-income seniors are expected to quadruple (or double, accounting for inflation) between 2009 and 2036. There is pressure to improve these programs soon. One idea is to implement a penalty for those receiving benefits early and create a bonus for those who delay payments until 70 years of age. Bigger challenges include individual preparedness for retirement and the cost of federal public service pensions. The challenges of seniors and health care that need to be addressed will depend on things external to the aging population per se: Economic growth, innovations in health care delivery that improve cost-effectiveness, individual health status, and trade-offs among coverage, taxation, and debt financing are some of the issues facing the future of Canadian health care in general (Coyte and McKeever, 2016; Echenberg, Gauthier, and Léonard, 2011).

Families That Include Persons with Disabilities

About 14 percent of Canadians age 15 years and older reported having a disability in 2012. The Statistics Canada survey on disabilities collected information on types of disability, age, employment, and income. Most disabilities were related to mobility, dexterity, flexibility, or pain, and these disabilities become more common with age. Disability was seen to affect employment: 49 percent of those with disabilities reported being employed, compared with 79 percent of Canadians not identifying as having a disability being employed. In addition, persons with disabilities have a median personal income that is half that of other Canadians. Social acceptance of persons with disabilities remains a problem in Canada. Of the 2.3 percent of Canadian adults who have a learning disability, half (49.8 percent) said they have experienced bullying at school (Statistics Canada, 2012g).

The quality of life of families and persons living with disability in Canada has seen gradual improvement over time, much of it the result of activism of family members of those with disabilities. In the early days of the disabilities rights movement, mothers of children with disabilities led grassroots efforts to de-institutionalize those with disabilities. They made the case that segregating and institutionalizing those with disabilities is discrimination and an abuse of human rights (Panitch, 2008; Prince, 2009). An important milestone was reached in 1985 when the Canadian Charter of Rights and Freedoms forbade discrimination on the basis of disability. Recently, in 2013 and 2016, class action lawsuits alleging mistreatment of developmentally disabled persons in 14 Ontario government institutions between 1945 and 1999 were successful (Ballingall, 2016). More will be understood in future years as the relatively new scholarship of disability uncovers more details on how some persons with disabilities were marginalized, segregated, and institutionalized in Canada's past (Reaume, 2012).

The Regulation of Divorce

Marriage dissolution is of great interest to the state. In fact, at the turn of the twentieth century, divorce in Canada could be granted only by an Act of Parliament. Marriage was considered a crucial part of the social fabric, not to be tampered with by the parties involved.

However, marriage failure and divorce did not, as some might think, begin recently. There have always been men who deserted their families (some women deserted, too) and couples who agreed mutually to separate (Gordon and McLanahan, 1991). Some Canadians went to the United States to seek divorce when it was not attainable in Canada (Bradbury, 1996: 72–73). In some provinces, such as Quebec, where divorce was almost impossible to obtain until well into the mid-twentieth century (and was frowned upon strongly), some women slipped into Ontario and declared themselves widows.

In 1968, greater access to divorce was made possible under the Divorce Act. This led to a fivefold increase in divorce between the late 1960s and the mid-1980s. Immediately following the revised 1985 Act, divorces again rose sharply, but much of this increase appears to have been accounted for by people who put off divorcing in 1984 and 1985, in anticipation of the revised legislation, and then initiated proceedings once the new law was enacted. By the late 1980s, the rate was declining.

These changes did not come to all parts of the Western world at the same time. For example, divorce remained illegal in Ireland until 1995. A referendum on the topic in that year defeated existing laws by a narrow margin. The pressure to liberalize Irish divorce laws contributed to a wide-ranging discussion of **secularization** (a move away from religion as an organizing principle of society) and the nature of social and familial change. People have also begun to reconsider the connection between moral and constitutional matters, or the church and state. Ireland is not yet a secular society (Wills, 2001). However, it is more pluralistic and tolerant than it was a decade ago. Individual Catholics, in Ireland as elsewhere, no longer completely embrace all the doctrines of the Church (though it may well be that, in practice, they never did so entirely).

CONCLUDING REMARKS

A long and complex process has marked efforts to reform government policies concerned with family life. One reason that government policies often do not meet the needs of Canadians is that most are based on the outdated assumption that all families are alike. Canadian sociologist Margrit Eichler (1997), among many others, argues that there are increasingly complex ways to live in families and for family life to connect with work life. Thus, her starting point is to recognize the fact that families and work–family relationships vary widely. So must models of the family and state responses to family life.

Furthermore, the Canadian family is not a static entity; rather, it is a product of a unique history of ethnic relations, transition to industrialism, wars, and demographic changes. The historical analysis outlined in this chapter shows how broad cultural, social, and economic changes can redefine traditional notions of courtship, marriage, family, parenthood, and gender relations. Informed by the successes and oversights of the past, we may begin to develop more effective policies and interventions to suit the changing nature of families in modern society. No doubt, the changing social and political landscape of the twenty-first century will have its own influence on the future of the family. The following chapters will discuss in detail the trends in our modern understanding of family norms, structures, and processes.

What the reader should take away from this chapter is the sense that family forms and structures have always varied. They have varied throughout history, and they vary today, cross-nationally and cross-culturally. They vary because different circumstances call on families to perform different social tasks, often with different kinds and amounts of support. As a result, families have always had to adapt—to be almost infinitely flexible and resourceful. Keep this in mind when, in the chapters that follow, we examine the ways in which different "kinds" of families—legally married and cohabiting, one-parent and two-parent, single-earner and dual-earner, same-sex and opposite-sex, and so on—try to grapple with their changing circumstances.

CHAPTER SUMMARY

Historically, families have been important bases for identity and for resource allocation. In many cultures, broader family structures, such as kinship groups and clans, have played a large role in determining relationships and social positions.

We have seen in this chapter that families are always and have always been changing in response to societal shifts, changing attitudes and expectations of women and men, and altering roles and views of and toward children. We have seen that contact with new cultures, either through colonization or through immigration, brings about inevitable change that has both micro and macro implications.

Immigration has been part of Canada since its beginning, and changing immigration policies reflected Canada's positions toward new people coming to live in this country, positions that, as we saw, were not always admirable. We have also seen how politics, economic circumstances, state regulations and reforms, wars, and consumerism shape families and family change, and the long-term impacts of these changes. We explore the effects and significance of such changes in more detail in later chapters.

Key Terms

abortifacients Herbs or potions that bring on a miscarriage.

cohort A group of people who experience some major demographic event, typically birth, migration, or marriage, within the same year or period.

demographic transition The transition to low fertility in the West, which began around 1870, is called the first demographic transition. This brought births into line with a sharply reduced death rate. A second demographic transition, more contemporary, has brought birth rates to a low level and, it is theorized, into line with new lifestyle goals and family practices.

demographers Those who study population changes such as births, deaths, and migrations.

family allowances Monthly payments started in Canada after World War II as a way to give women compensation as well as recognition for child rearing. They were based on the number of children at home and went to all women with children, but not to men.

gemeinschaft A type of community typical of pre-industrial rural life; that is, one in which everyone knows everyone else and people share common values.

"mechanization" of housework The introduction of new home technologies. Home economists worked to elevate the esteem of homemakers by promoting the idea that the new home technologies required skilled operators.

revenge of the cradle An expression reflecting the belief that Quebec's long-standing sense of political injustice might be countered by having more (French-speaking) citizens.

secularization A move away from religion as an organizing principle of society.

Critical Thinking Questions

1. Families adapt when societies change as they come into contact with other cultures through colonization or immigration. The Indigenous peoples of Canada and their families have been greatly affected by colonization. What is the significance of the original contact and conflict between English and French colonizers and the Indigenous peoples on today's Indigenous families? How do social policies affect Indigenous families?

2. As we have seen, immigration has been part of Canada since its founding and is still an important aspect of our country. However, some of Canada's past policies do not cast our country in a favourable light. In recent years, these policies have improved, shifting to a long-term perspective that considers future growth and prosperity. Is it likely that future circumstances can alter this perspective? Do you think Canada may revert to its previous position? How important is immigration to Canada's present and future families? Can you identify some of the issues recent immigrant families may experience?

3. Courtship, marriage, childbirth, and divorce have all experienced changes in the past decades. From definition to legality, our close relations are quite different than those of our grandparents. Increases in cohabitation and childless unions, as well as legalization of same-sex marriage, are a few of the changes we have experienced. In the past, the primary reason for lone motherhood was widowhood; at present, it is divorce. Why? Why is this important when considering social support in families? What other examples of changing relationships can you think of?

4. To make good policy decisions, governments need to have good data and an understanding of society as it changes and ages. What changes has our society experienced, and what can we expect to experience in the future?

5. The typical life course of an individual is less predictable than in the past. What are the implications for families? What must be considered when developing definitions, generalizations, and predictions about families?

Weblinks

Library and Archives Canada
www.collectionscanada.gc.ca/index-e.html
Library and Archives Canada has an incredible amount of resources, primary and secondary, about the history of Canada and its people. It features publications, photographs and other

images, audio, and internet resources. It provides links to other Canadian government websites. Also visit www.archivescanada.ca for the Archives Canada portal, "your gateway to Canada's past."

Our Roots
www.ourroots.ca

This site features a search system for information about local communities and the histories of specific Canadian families. It also provides a search engine for Canadian books that is frequently updated with new and rare material. For students, several interactive educational resources are available. The collection has both French and English information and documents.

Multicultural Canada
www.lib.sfu.ca/about/initiatives/collaborations/multicultural-canada

This site contains a wealth of information about the history of immigration to Canada and how it has affected people from diverse backgrounds. It includes newspapers, photographs, book references, legal documents, audio files, pamphlets, and other materials, most of which are in languages other than English.

Multicultural History Society of Ontario (MHSO)
www.mhso.ca

MHSO is a "not-for-profit educational institution and heritage centre" founded by Professor Robert F. Harney in 1976. Ontario has had a rich history of multiculturalism, and this site provides information about cultural issues and links to publications and exhibit information at the Oral History Museum in Toronto.

Quebec History
http://faculty.marianopolis.edu/c.belanger/QuebecHistory/index.htm

This site is intended for a post-secondary school course in Montreal. It covers the history of Quebec people and culture from the mid-eighteenth century (after the fall of New France) to the present. It includes supplementary sections on important issues, biographies, statistics, documents, and images. It is updated on a regular basis.

The Global Gathering Place
www.mhso.ca/ggp

Related to the MHSO, the Global Gathering Place is an interactive site with an aim to educate Canadians about the diversity of Canadian people through documents, images, videos, and audio material. It has information about immigration, ethnicity, community and family life, labour, and Canadian citizenship.

First Peoples' Cultural Council
www.fphlcc.ca

The First Peoples' Cultural Council is an organization based in British Columbia that works to promote First Nations culture and language and to improve the well-being of First Nations peoples. It works in conjunction with the First Peoples' Cultural Foundation as well as First Voices, organizations that "raise awareness and funding for Aboriginal language revitalization." Both also have interactive and informative sites. Visit www.fpcf.ca and www.firstvoices.com for more information.

Chapter 3
How Families Begin
Dating and Mating

Terry Vine/Blend Images/Alamy Stock Photo

CHAPTER OUTLINE

- Love: A Recent Invention?
- Theories of Mate Selection
    - Complementary Needs Theory
    - Exchange Theory
    - An Evolutionary Perspective
    - Social Role Theory
- The Role of Gender Equality
- Arranged Marriages and Love Matches
- Internet Dating and Mating
- Social Aspects of Finding a Mate
- Dating and Disabilities

- Sexuality and Social Stigma
- Online Dating for People with Disabilities
- The Sexual Double Standard: Fact or Fiction?
- Dating in an Aging Society
- Dating in a Multicultural Society
- Same-Sex Dating
- Dating for Overweight and Other Stigmatized People
- Homogamy
  - Educational and Other Status Homogamy
  - Age Homogamy
- Ethnic Homogamy (or Endogamy)
- Religious Homogamy
- Endogamy for Indigenous People
- The Ideals of Mate Selection
  - Why People Do Not Optimize
- Dating Violence
  - Dating Violence for Obese and Other Stigmatized People
  - Dating Violence for People with Disabilities
- Chapter Summary

LEARNING OBJECTIVES

1 Distinguish between the various theories of mate selection.

2 Identify the social influences affecting how people meet potential mates.

3 Describe how dating and mating are different for older adults.

4 Develop a multicultural viewpoint of dating and mating practices.

5 Differentiate between the mate preferences of men and women.

6 Argue against seeking an optimal mate, and argue for satisficing.

"How will I find the right person to marry?" That question—which many young people think about today—is profoundly modern. No one would have asked this question through most of human history, for reasons we will explore. And that's why the idea that marriages commonly grow out of long, complicated rituals of dating and mating would have seemed absurd to most people before the Industrial Revolution. (A nice description of sixteenth-century [preindustrial] marriage, life, and death in England and Western Europe is provided by historical demographer Peter Laslett [1965] in *The World We Have Lost*.)

Population numbers tell us the reason. For most of human history, people lived in small agricultural communities, small villages, or towns; or in small neighbourhoods within preindustrial cities. They would have typically known about 300 to 400 people in total, and their mobility—their ability to visit other communities—would have been limited to an 8- to 16-kilometre radius: the distance a person can walk easily in a day. They would likely have met and married someone from among the 300 to 400 people they knew. And since most of them would have chosen someone of the opposite sex, someone not a blood relation, and someone roughly their own age—give or take 10 years—the pool of potential mates would have numbered at most about 40 to 50 people.

Of course, since death rates were high in preindustrial populations, new candidates—widows and widowers—regularly became available. So, people's marriage pools weren't stagnant, but they were small. To deal with this limitation, people settled for the best available candidate at a given moment. If a preferred candidate was unavailable or unwilling, they would marry someone less satisfactory or (sometimes) go unmarried.

However, in later centuries, as people became more mobile and moved into larger, more diverse cities, the range of mating choices increased. Increasingly, people fled farms, small towns, and villages and headed for big cities. Only in the context of large, fluid marriage pools—large sets of eligible marriage candidates—did people begin to think about "seeking" a perfect or even compatible mate. Likewise, only in this context of variety and choice does the notion of romantic love make much sense. So, dating and mating, for most of humanity, began only about a century or two ago.

What happens where people live in small, isolated communities that have some (though limited) access to the outside world? Who do people marry then? A classic study of marriage by Yonina Talmon (1964) looked at mating patterns among Israeli youth who lived on kibbutzim—small agricultural collectives with strong socialist ideologies. She found a wide variety of endogamous and exogamous practices in the 125 couples from whom she collected data. By "endogamous," we mean mates chosen from within one's own community; by "exogamous," we mean mates chosen from outside one's own community.

To summarize, Talmon found that roughly a third of the couplings were endogamous (i.e., intra-kibbutz) while two-thirds were exogamous. There seemed to be an unspoken expectation that you not marry someone from within the kibbutz, if possible. In fact, she found "deep-lying tendencies during the process of maturation" that made "newcomers, outsiders and strangers more desirable" as potential mates (Talmon, 1964: 501). So, perhaps romance and love thrive on strangeness, as well as choice. But only within the context of choice can romantic love (as we understand it today) flourish.

Question to consider: Reflect on marriage as you know it (or imagine it) today, and consider how it differs from marriage in the past. What has changed and what has stayed the same, in your view?

LOVE: A RECENT INVENTION?

The idea of love, as we know it today, emerged from courtly love, the likely origin of **romantic love** that appeared in Europe in the Middle Ages. Courtly love was the dating and mating behaviour of aristocrats, nobility, and gentry—people who did not have to work long days to support themselves and therefore had time available to meet new people, flirt, attend parties, and have leisurely sexual encounters. In the Middle Ages, only very few people had the time, let alone money, to indulge these tastes, until the twentieth century. The rise of dating as we know it today only emerged with the rise of a large middle class with leisure time and money to spend, especially a large middle class of youth for whom leisure was prolonged by the extension of education.

Through most of history, marriages were arranged in ways that were mutually profitable for families that owned land or other property. Historically, marriage sealed an exchange of property between families, and this property exchange between families mattered more than whether the couple loved each other romantically.

Feudalism ended and the market economy began to grow around the fifteenth century. Then, according to Morton (1992), Western European households, which had previously included many unrelated people, began to shrink. As well, people began to question the traditional basis of marriage—the melding of households for economic or political reasons. Choice—not accidents of birth—came increasingly to be the basis on which families began.

The emergence of the idea of romantic love changed social roles, especially for women. Increasingly, in relationships, women became less valued for their position as partners in work and more valued as passive decorations (Abu-Laban and McDaniel, 2004). As such, in prosperous families, women's adornment and appearance mattered more than their contributions to the family's material well-being. With this gendering of roles, the social differences between men and women were exaggerated. Men gained more and more social and economic power in the family—a process that reached its peak with industrialization in the nineteenth and twentieth centuries. A division of labour developed between marriage partners, including different sexual norms for men and women and gendered inheritance patterns.

THEORIES OF MATE SELECTION

Increasingly, mating came to include an elaborate set of courtship rituals by means of which the powerful male aimed to capture the appealing and fertile female. Using the term *mate selection* to describe this process may seem odd, given all the constraints on our choices, both logistical and social.

Whether we examine heterosexual or same-sex couples, a central feature of couple relationships in Canada today is a commitment to the ideals of romantic love. In our society, the ideals of marriage are framed through the ideological rhetoric of romance. Most people marry because they feel they are in love with someone. Often, they feel they have discovered the best—even the perfect—mate. That said, mate selection cannot be described simply as the result of two people falling in love. It is a more complex process, and various theories have been developed to explain it.

Complementary Needs Theory

An early theorist, Robert Winch (1962) proposed that, in mating, a person is typically drawn to someone whose needs are opposite and complementary to his or her own. People commonly referred to this as the "opposites attract" phenomenon. For example, a person who wants to provide care—to be a "white knight"—would be attracted to someone who is imagined to need care. According to this theory, people choose mates different from themselves in hopes of filling in the "missing pieces" in their own lives or personalities.

Exchange Theory

Exchange theory, for its part, describes the mechanism that makes the mating of opposites work. The exchange perspective sees marriage as give-and-take, where each partner gives something and gets something. The stability of a close relationship is thought to depend on how well a balance is maintained in exchanges between partners—that is, how well what is given matches what is received. Or, stated in terms of Winch's theory, how well what is given satisfies the needs and weaknesses of the mate.

The exchanges imagined in exchange theory fall into two categories. **Expressive exchanges** are exchanges of emotion between partners. They include hugs and kisses, sexual pleasure, friendship, a shoulder to lean on, empathy, and understanding. Expressive exchanges affirm the affection and love that each partner has for the other, and presumably each spouse gets the amount and kind of affection that is needed. By contrast, **instrumental exchanges** involve tangible or material support (Muncer et al., 2000). These include contributions of money and time, with couples sharing household duties and tending to practical matters such as housework, paying the bills, and looking after the children.

An Evolutionary Perspective

Developed from Charles Darwin's nineteenth-century theory on the evolution of species, the perspective of evolutionary psychologists and sociologists sees human mating as guided by principles that maximize survival advantages. Presumably, people are programmed to mate in ways that ensure the production and survival of offspring, since this gives their genes the best chance of surviving over generations.

However, genetic survival strategies differ for men and women, because their reproductive potential differs. Men, who can easily father many children over their lives, are genetically programmed to seek women who appear to be fertile, as shown by their youth and sexual attractiveness. However, women must be more selective. Giving birth to each child represents a major investment of time and energy for a woman, so women are genetically programmed to seek men who can supply social and economic advantages to their children. Said another way, women will inevitably seek mates who can be good and reliable providers. As such, women, in the evolutionary perspective, will prefer men with a higher-than-average social and economic status (Doosje, Rojahn, and Fischer, 1999).

Data showing a tendency of men to prefer younger and fertile women, and women to prefer successful and possibly older men, support this evolutionary theory. Evolutionary theory also receives support from the fact of a gendered division of labour in the workplace. This gendering of roles in both the private and the public sphere can be said to ensure that young and vulnerable children will receive the best possible care from (what many believe to be) the most caring parent—the mother.

Social Role Theory

According to social role theory, men and women are socialized to prefer partners whose attitudes are congruent with these gendered social distinctions (Doosje et al., 1999). The more traditional the gender ideology in a community or society, the greater likelihood that sex-typing will guide mate preferences in the selection process (Eastwick et al., 2006), such that older men select younger wives and women seek stable and prosperous (or, at least, potentially prosperous) husbands.

However, modern marriages, increasingly based on dual-earner parents, struggle with these traditional, gendered social roles. Increasingly, present-day men may look for an ambitious and career-oriented woman when they are choosing a mate. Because of the influence of traditional social roles, they may also expect the same woman to fit into a stereotypical housewife role. This contradiction often creates role conflict at home. It produces conflict between ideal and real family lives and between men and women. In turn, this conflict often leads to high rates of frustration, divorce, and even violence.

THE ROLE OF GENDER EQUALITY

The growth of gender equality in our society has had a profound influence on mate selection. In less traditional, more gender-equal societies such as Canada, people tend to look for different qualities when choosing a mate (Moore, Cassidy, Smith, and Perrett, 2006).

In particular, well-educated women with access to good jobs put less importance on earning potential in their mate (Koyama, McGain, and Hill, 2004). They are more likely than in the past to look for partners who are near in age and education to themselves (Moore et al., 2006). And, given their own economic and social independence, women today are even likely to engage in short-term sexual relationships without fearing this will harm their marriage chances (Stanik and Ellsworth, 2010). In these and other respects, women take on more male-typical mate preferences and, accordingly, place a larger emphasis on physical attractiveness during mate selection (Moore and Cassidy, 2007).

In societies with a high level of gender equality, men and women tend to look for similar qualities in a mate—for example, they focus similarly on personality and value compatibility. In one cross-national study, Zentner and Mitura (2012) assessed mate preferences in 10 countries. They found that societies with the most gender equality, such as Finland, Sweden, and Norway, had higher-than-average gender similarity in mate selection practices. In other words, in these egalitarian countries men and women put a similar emphasis on the importance of qualities like physical appearance and financial prospects during mate selection, as well as on social and educational similarity.

Countries with slightly lower levels of gender equality, like Canada, put slightly less importance on gender parity in mate selection. Finally, countries that scored the lowest in gender equality (e.g., Iran) had the lowest levels of gender parity and, conversely, showed the greatest difference in how men and women chose mates.

As suggested earlier, the range of ways to meet one's life partner has widened in recent years. Today, many couples meet in places of shared activities—in schools and universities, workplaces, religious places, neighbourhoods, sporting groups, or events. Others meet through common friends or relatives. Increasingly, cyberspace is a popular way for people to search for and meet new partners. However, in some societies, relatives still bring singles together in arranged or semi-arranged marriages.

ARRANGED MARRIAGES AND LOVE MATCHES

A society that practises *arranged marriage* puts parents and other kin at the centre of the matchmaking process. Today, even in Canada, arranged marriage remains popular among certain ethnic communities, including South Asians and Orthodox Jews (see Howell, Albanese, and Obosu-Mensah, 2001; Weinfeld, 2001).

However, for most people in societies like Canada, the nuclear family is more important than the extended family, and most unmarried people's lives revolve around school or work. In these countries, people are likelier to choose their own partners, whether in Japan, China, Europe, India—or Canada. School and work are important to mating in these societies, because they offer young people a place to meet and become acquainted, often across ethnic, racial, and class lines. Here, in situations of social discovery, themes of romantic love and dating are most important for mating (Ghimire, Axinn, Yabiku, and Thornton, 2006).

By contrast, arranged marriages are most common in preindustrial or less economically developed societies where people are organized around extended family,

- Children of South Asian and Chinese immigrants to Canada put a greater value on chastity in a mate than their European Canadian peers, though they are still more sexually liberal than their parents. This shows that young adults from some Eastern cultures are caught between local and traditional norms about dating and marriage choices (Lou, Lalonde, and Wong, 2015).

- Traveller communities, or Gypsies, as they are known in Britain, commonly practise "grabbing," a dating ritual at weddings where women are physically grabbed by men and forced to kiss them (McDonald, 2011). In other cultures, women are kidnapped and raped, then married afterward to legitimize the relationship.

- Most people in Western cultures value physical attractiveness and passionate feelings in their partners. However, people in Eastern cultures put a higher value on family wishes in selecting a mate (Bejanyan, Marshall, and Ferenczi, 2015; Zhang and Kline, 2009).

- Even in Nepal, urbanization and new media technologies have led to the emergence of a new dating culture (Regmi, van Teijlingerm, Simkhada, and Acharya, 2011). In the past, the transition to adulthood was marked by early marriage and childbearing. Today, young people wait longer to get married, stay in school longer, go on dates, and even engage in premarital sexual behaviours.

relationships. The stated reasons for arranged marriage vary from one culture to another. Some groups want to ensure that a certain religion or ethnic culture is carried on from one generation to the next. Others want to ensure that land is passed from one generation to the next within the extended family line. Others still think the choice of marriage partners is far too important to be left to the whims and passions of youth. In all of these cases, spouses are chosen by the family because the union is economically valuable or because of friendship or kinship ties between the parents.

In Chinese-influenced cultures, Confucian ideology stresses the importance of family survival. However, recent trends show steep declines in arranged marriages in those cultures. For example, in China, friends and colleagues have taken over the matchmaker role formerly played by parents. Family remains the main pillar of the community, but the nuclear family has become more important and the extended family less so. And, as has happened in other parts of the modern world, educated young people are putting a higher value on a partner's education and a lower value on his or his family than in the past (Xu et al., 2007).

Sometimes, in societies with arranged marriage, people marry mates they have never even met. Today, however, few marriages are "arranged" in the traditional sense. Even in arranged marriages, young people are getting more say in the process today. Note, finally, that arranged marriage today is very different from "forced marriage," which still happens to a small minority of women in Canada (Husaini and Bhardwaj, 2010).

INTERNET DATING AND MATING

The search for a compatible mate has increasingly drawn on a wider and wider mating pool, through internet dating. In an early study of the topic, Brym and Lenton (2001) proposed the following reasons for the growth of internet dating:

- As career and time pressures increase, people look for more efficient ways of meeting potential intimate partners.
- Growing sensitivity about workplace sexual harassment has led to a decline in workplace romance.
- Because of job market demands, single people are becoming more mobile, making it harder to meet dating partners.

According to a 2015 survey by the Pew Research Center, the use of online dating sites has increased rapidly. In 2013, 10 percent of young people ages 18 to 24 reported using online dating, but by 2015 that number had nearly tripled to 27 percent. In every other age group, there were slightly less dramatic, but still considerable increases over the same two-year period. As a consequence, there has also been a rapid increase in the proportion of people who have met their partners online, as we see in research by Rosenfeld and Thomas (2010). This increase has been particularly dramatic for same-sex couples, and most of this change has taken place since 2000.

According to a study by Ward and Terence (2004), many people prefer online dating to traditional dating because it allows them to develop a relationship in a safe and comfortable setting. In particular, it allows people to establish communication and awareness before meeting face to face. The internet also provides a larger pool of people to choose from than a person would normally meet in everyday life.

The internet enlarges the pool of potential mates within socially preferred categories by reducing the factor of distance. As Sprecher (2009) puts it, people are more likely to find their perfect mate online than offline. Later in this chapter, we talk about the impossibility of finding the "ideal" mate. That said, online dating improves the odds by introducing people to a massive database of potential mates. By giving each user a profile of potential partners, it allows daters to search and match based on these ideal traits. Internet dating also increases the potential for cross-cultural (i.e., inter-ethnic, interracial, and inter-religious) romance (Yum and Hara, 2005).

When people go online to find a mate, they are usually looking for qualities that could, in principle, be found through traditional dating practices. Similarity remains the major predictor of early attraction for internet daters, as it does for face-to-face daters (Baxter and West, 2003). Online contacts usually judge one another according to criteria that have always been important to them, such as physical attractiveness, income and occupation, hobbies, smoking status, and desire for children (Sprecher, 2009). These are the same traits that are important to traditional daters. However, certain factors are unique to online dating—notably, a different emphasis on response time, writing style, and honesty (Baker, 2007).

Men prefer ads in which women claim to have intrinsic values—honesty, integrity, and the like—but they also pay more attention to looks and physical features (weight, height, ethnicity, even eye and hair colour) than women do. Even before the rise of online dating, research showed that men preferred women whom they described as "attractive," "slender," "petite," or "sexy" (Coltrane, 1998: 47; Smith, Waldorf, and Trembath, 1990). Though old, this finding is supported by a literature review of 14 000 text messages 10 years later that shows women use more words related to psychological and social processes, whereas men refer more to object properties and impersonal topics in their advertisements (Newman, Groom, Handelman, and Pennebaker, 2008).

So, in its use of language, the online method of mate seeking may play to gender stereotypes even more than conventional mating practices do. Recent online dating "apps" such as Tinder confirm the continuing influence of traditional mating practices. Men are more likely than women to report using an app for casual sex. However, both men and women report having a stronger "love motivation" to use Tinder than a "casual sex" motivation (Sumter, Vandenbosch, and Ligtenberg, 2017).

>>> Dating and Mating Myths

The myth: Older couples are likelier than other couples to express negative views about their mates, since they have lived together for a longer time and are well past the early infatuation stage of a romantic relationship.

- **The reality:** Older couples are likelier to view their partners positively and develop something like an automatic response to handle negative traits in their partner. Said another way, older adults tend to stress the positive aspects of their partner and their relationship (Fingerman and Charles, 2010; Perunovic and Holmes, 2008; Story et al., 2007).

The myth: Meeting people online is more dangerous than meeting people in the "real world."

- **The reality:** Despite potential dangers associated with meeting people online, online dating is reportedly no riskier than dating people in the "real world" and taking safety precautions

is just as important in both situations (Mock, 2011). For example, some counsel always meeting in a public area on the first few dates, and letting a friend know about your plans for the date.

The myth: People with disabilities are not interested in activities of a romantic or sexual nature.

- **The reality:** This is evidently not true. For example, a Dutch study found that most young adults with cerebral palsy were thoroughly interested in sex and fantasized about love-making (Wiegerink, Roebroeck, Van, Stam, and Cohen-Kettenis, 2010). They had fewer romantic relationships or sexual experiences than other young adults of the same age. However, they valued these things and sought them by participating in peer groups. We will say more about this topic shortly.

This is not to say that people insist on the qualities they initially look for, and often, regardless of their mating strategy, they settle for something else. When researchers follow up with participants to find whether these were the characteristics of the people they actually dated, they found that participants often met and went on dates with people who differed from their stated ideals (Eastwick and Finkel, 2008). As we will see shortly, reality works this way: We state ideals of perfection but act in ways that satisfy us, however imperfectly.

Online dating has also become a popular method for gays, lesbians, and bisexuals to connect with one another. Because of their smaller total numbers, these groups often use the internet as a meeting space. A 2008 study found that gays, lesbians, and bisexuals are even likelier than heterosexuals to meet in person, have sex with, and have a long-term relationship with someone they meet online (Lever, Grov, Royce, and Gillespie, 2008).

SOCIAL ASPECTS OF FINDING A MATE

Whether participants admit it or not, rating and ranking are part of the search for a mate. The processes of meeting, mating, and marrying involve a giant sorting process whereby our "market values" are matched with the market values of others. Sometimes, this can be a cold calculation, as when a man seeks a wife who will "look good on his arm." We call such women "trophy wives," for their purely decorative value in the relationship. Interestingly, we do not have a name for the men who seek them.

Good looks make a difference—for men and women, heterosexuals and gays—in getting attention in the mate market. Immense amounts of time, effort, and money go into the construction of attractiveness. Many women pluck, wax, and shave unwanted hair, and carefully groom the wanted hair. Through workouts and other unnatural processes, they shape and flatten unwanted bulges and enhance wanted ones. Men increasingly focus on their appearance, and the recently coined term *metrosexual* is used to describe a straight young man (typically city dwelling and wealthy) who takes great interest in his image.

People often use personal decoration as a means of communicating their status on the mate market. The engagement ring is one common example. A woman wears the ring as a symbol with many meanings: It signals that she is desirable on the mate market, that her intended mate makes sufficient money (or comes from sufficient family money) to afford the ring, and that she can be decorated well. This suggests that she will be "kept well" during their married life and announces to all who see her ring that she has made a "good catch."

This idea is supported by research on the amount men spend on engagement rings. A study found that men marrying younger women spent more. The same was true for men who earned more money and whose fiancées earned more money (Cronk and Dunham, 2007). This finding is consistent with the theory that the engagement ring is a symbol of mate quality. Yet, despite ideas that the marriage industry promotes, the longevity of marriage is not directly related to the amount spent on an engagement ring. Other, more directly important factors are the suitability (or compatibility) of partners and wedding-related debt stress (Francis-Tan and Mialon, 2015).

In the mate market, flirting matters. Flirting is still an important part of the meeting and mating scenario. Men tend to report that women display more sexual interest in cross-sex interactions than women admit to displaying. This has been explained by findings that behaviour that men view to be sexually motivated is attributed different motivations by women (Henningsen, Braz, and Davies, 2008). So, it seems that flirting has a lot to do with views that are not always agreed upon by everyone involved. This may partly be due to the persistence of men's greater acceptance of casual sex over the past two decades, despite the degree of this belief being dependent on ethnic group membership (Sprecher, Treger, and Sakaluk, 2013).

Where people meet potential mates is also an important factor in mate selection. Lampard (2007) studied trends in where couples report having met. He notes that a decreasing number of couples report first meeting in settings such as restaurants, bars, and clubs, whereas an increasing number of couples report first meeting at places of work and education.

DATING AND DISABILITIES

Typically, people mate with others who are socially similar to themselves: They spend their time in social settings, such as schools, workplaces, and neighbourhoods, that allow them to meet people who are similar to themselves. These individuals share interests, goals, and backgrounds, so interaction is easy, they come to like and attract one another, and they enjoy each other's company. However, factors such as isolation, stigma, and lack of social capital can play an important role in limiting these opportunities—especially for people with physical or mental disabilities.

Research repeatedly confirms that people with disabilities often feel isolated, lonely, and marginalized (Crawford and Ostrove, 2003; Di Giulio, 2003; Slayter, 2009). People with significant injuries tend to spend less time with non-injured people in social settings such as schools, workplaces, and recreational venues (Davies, 2000). For example, the majority of Crawford and Ostrove's (2003) participants reported that they lived or worked almost entirely with other people with disabilities. People with disabilities are likely to spend more time in private places such as the home or in public places where other injured people are present, such as hospitals and doctors' offices. As a result, they meet fewer people altogether and a higher-than-average number of people with disabilities.

This kind of segregation means that people with disabilities are less likely to come into repeated or long-term contact with able-bodied people, as often precedes the establishment of an intimate relationship (Crawford and Ostrove, 2003). Instead, they tend to share more experiences, interests, goals, and identities with other people with disabilities. Their interactions with able-bodied people will be more difficult as a result, whereas interactions with other people with disabilities will be easier and more familiar. As such, people with disabilities are more likely to meet and get along well with other people with disabilities.

Since people with disabilities tend to be more socially isolated, they have fewer chances to interact with and learn from their peers (Di Giulio, 2003). For this reason, disabled teens tend to have less accurate knowledge about sexuality in comparison with the general population (Isler, Tas, Beytut, and Conk, 2009). Reduced interaction with peers restricts their opportunities (1) to learn about sexual behaviour, (2) to participate in social activities wherein one might meet a potential sexual partner, and (3) to experiment sexually (Isler et al., 2009).

Sexuality and Social Stigma

Most young people develop questions and concerns—especially about dating and intimacy issues—around the development of relationships (Gordon, Tschopp, and Feldman, 2004). However, adolescents with disabilities may experience heightened concerns because, due to their social isolation, they may have limited opportunities to develop dating skills or to even think of themselves as potential dating partners. The characteristics of their disability might prevent them from dating, but the messages they receive from others (such as parents, teachers, and peers) may also make the notion of dating and sexual activity seem unfeasible.

Like everyone else, people with disabilities develop their sense of self and self-esteem largely through interactions with others (Howland and Rintala, 2001). However, the response to their disability by family, friends, and society in general deeply influences patterns of dating behaviour for physically disabled women. Davies (2000) notes that people with disabilities often become ashamed of their "abnormal" bodies. Not only do they lack the self-esteem to pursue sexual partners, but they may also come to feel as though they are incapable of engaging in sexual relationships altogether. Caregivers, parents, siblings, friends, and other family members often overlook or even discourage the sexual desires of people with disabilities (Giulio, 2003). As a result, people with disabilities often come to believe that they are "asexual," incapable of establishing intimate relationships (Hassouneh-Phillips and McNeff, 2005).

In some respects, newly acquired disabilities are even more problematic than congenital disabilities. In addition to making it more difficult to find new sexual partners, acquired disability often alters intimate relationships that were established pre-injury. While physical limitations restrict sexual activity among many people with disabilities, other injury-related factors also reduce a sense of intimacy between partners (Di Giulio, 2003). Financial struggles, changes in the division of housekeeping responsibilities, and new caregiving duties change the ways in which couples lived their lives together pre-injury. Sexual activity often decreases dramatically following the onset of disability due to changes in either partner's perception of sexual attractiveness or assumptions that the disabled individual is incapable of taking part in mutually satisfying sexual activities.

Another factor that limits people with disabilities in their search for dates and mates is that of social stigma. Many people are unable to imagine social or sexual relationships with people with disabilities, as they are often thought to be significantly unlike other people. As well, many people express discomfort with people with disabilities engaging in certain sexual acts that they would consider acceptable for able-bodied people. Many believe that people with disabilities are incapable of having "responsible" sexual relationships, which explains some of this disapproval.

Stigmatization varies according to the type and degree of disability (Miller, Chen, Glover-Graf, and Kranz, 2009). People with physical disabilities are reportedly the least stigmatized, followed by people with cognitive disabilities (e.g., blind or deaf people). People with intellectual disabilities (e.g., with memory or judgment problems) are the next most stigmatized, and people with psychiatric disabilities (e.g., with severe depression or anxiety issues) are subjected to the most intense stigmatization. People with more severe disabilities, especially those requiring assistance with daily care activities, are less likely to have partners or spouses than less severely disabled or able-bodied people.

To illustrate these ideas, consider the following study of college students: In a study of social distance from people with disabilities, 305 students ranging in age from 19 to 58 years completed a questionnaire designed to test their willingness to form a variety of relationships with people with disabilities. Participants said that they were willing to become friends and acquaintances with people with disabilities, but they were less willing to date and least willing to marry them. As the severity of disability increased, people's willingness to establish a relationship decreased, with willingness ratings highest for people with mild disabilities and lowest for those with significant disabilities. Furthermore, participants said that they were willing to become friends or acquaintances even with people with severe disabilities, but they were almost entirely unwilling to date or marry a person with disabilities, regardless of the severity of the condition (Miller et al., 2009).

People in this study were most willing to form relationships with people struggling with sensory and health disabilities, followed by those with physical and cognitive disabilities, and least willing to do so with those with psychiatric disabilities. Miller and colleagues (2009) conclude that the stereotypes, stigmas, and negative attitudes held by able-bodied people severely hinder people with disabilities from establishing intimate relationships.

As a result of such stigma and prejudice, dating and mating are less common among people who are physically or mentally disabled, compared to people of the same age who are not disabled. In this sense, people who are disabled and people who are able-bodied have quite different experiences: They are subject to a double standard in the mating market. However, an even more common "double standard" applies to men and women.

Online Dating for People with Disabilities

One might imagine that online dating would significantly improve the mating possibilities of people with disabilities. However, a recent study shows that online dating is a complex terrain for all people, and particularly for people with disabilities. Researcher Natasha Saltes (2013) conducted interviews with 108 self-identified disabled participants ranging in age from 18 to 75 years. She was interested in the ways in which people with disabilities "reconstruct" their identities online. Did the interviewees conceal their disabilities from potential dates, as prominent disability scholarship suggested they would?

For example, Dobransky and Hargittai (2006: 316) have argued that "the most striking part of online communication for people with disabilities is the ability it affords the user to hide aspects of him or herself." Barney (2004:152) agrees, contending that "the disclocation, disembodiment and opacity of network communications can enable a high degree of anonymity and fluidity in the social construction of our selves." Likewise, Yurchisin, Watchravesringkan, and Brown McCabe (2005: 737) suggest that the internet provides a space where people with disabilities can try out different identities, or different "possible selves."

However, in interviews with 108 disabled participants, Saltes (2013) found that the majority of participants did *not* want to try on a different "possible self" to disguise their disabilities. As one participant reports, "I feel very comfortable [with my disability] because this is part of who I am" (Saltes, 2013: 101). Another participant made sure to include two photographs of himself in his wheelchair (Saltes, 2013: 103). A third respondent acknowledged her disability but did it on her own terms; as Saltes (2013: 103) notes, she

> avoided medical terms and the word "disability" or "impairment" and provided a description of her attributes in her own words: "I usually mention that I'm 'oddly brained' or make a vague reference to my shyness or lack of eye contact. I also talk about how to talk to me."

A fourth respondent stated explicitly that she was a "post-polio quadriplegic" who used a ventilator. Summing up, one participant declared, "My disability is obvious to anyone that meets me so I see no point in not disclosing" (Saltes, 2013: 105).

On the other hand, a few respondents felt uncomfortable disclosing their disability. As one of them stated, "I do not disclose my disability, as I figured it would turn off most potential mates" (Saltes, 2013: 103). Another said, "I have trouble . . . being motivated to pursue relationships. I often feel that I don't have as much to offer as normal people" (Saltes, 2013: 104). Others do not want to disclose their disability but feel that they ought to: As one participant put it, "If I don't disclose my disability, how would they know what's wrong with me?" (Saltes, 2013: 104).

Overall, then, although a minority of participants resisted disclosing their disability online and embraced the internet's cloak of anonymity, a majority of participants in

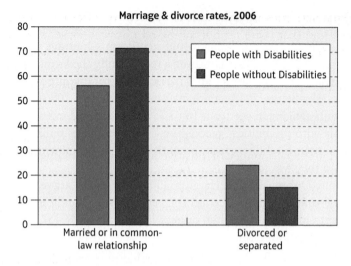

Figure 3.1 Marriage and divorce rates among younger working age adults (25–54) with and without disabilities, 2006

Source: Data from Human Resources and Skills Development Canada (2011). *Disability in Canada: A 2006 Profile*, pg. 32.

this study did disclose their disabilities online, some sooner and others later. This shows that, as Saltes (2013: 107) puts it, "people with disabilities are forced to confront their impairment" even in the disembodied online sphere.

As we see in Figure 3.1, this has consequences for the probability of meeting and marrying a partner. People with disabilities are much less likely than people without disabilities to be in a marital or common-law relationship and much more likely to be separated or divorced.

THE SEXUAL DOUBLE STANDARD: FACT OR FICTION?

In many societies, a **sexual double standard** rewards men for sexual activity but criticizes women for the same activity. However, the research findings on this topic have been, and continue to be, confusing. For example, qualitative studies continue to find evidence of the double standard, but more recent experimental vignette designs often fail to do so.

Part of the problem may be what psychologists call a "confirmation bias," such that people tend to notice information that confirms the double standard and fail to notice information that refutes it. Aubrey (2004) conducted a content analysis to examine how the media present the sexual double standard. Specifically, the researchers looked at scripts from prime-time television dramas that featured characters between the ages of 12 and 22 years. They found that female characters who initiated sexual activities in these stories tended to suffer emotional and social consequences, and that these far outnumbered physical consequences. Generally, negative consequences were more common in scenes where females initiated sexual activities than in scenes where male characters did so. Thus, the media conformed to traditional cultural beliefs about dangers of violating the sexual double standard.

Two experimental studies by Marks and Fraley (2006) tested this so-called confirmation bias. In both studies, subjects read vignettes about a target man or woman that contained an equal number of positive and negative comments regarding the target's sexuality. Participants recalled more information consistent with the double standard than inconsistent with it (Marks and Fraley, 2006). Thus, for example, they were more likely to remember positive characteristics of men who were depicted as having many sex partners than they were to remember positive characteristics of women who depicted in the same way.

This kind of evaluation and labelling also takes place outside the laboratory. In another study, Kreager and Staff (2009) directly measured the social status of sexually permissive youth, using data collected from the National Longitudinal Study of Adolescent Health. They found that boys with a large number of sexual partners were highly accepted by their male peers, but girls with a large number of sexual partners were not as highly accepted by their female peers. This was particularly true of youth from lower-income backgrounds, suggesting more traditional gendered thinking on sexual matters in this income group.

However, within couples, the consequences of violating the double standard are not as severe. In a study of 698 heterosexual couples (Greene and Faulkner, 2005), women reported more equal sexual negotiation than their male partners. People with less traditional attitudes toward gender roles and sexuality discussed more sexual issues and disclosed more sexual information to their partners than people with more traditional attitudes. In the end, the couples with more sexual communication and sexual assertiveness also reported more relationship satisfaction.

To determine whether a sexual double standard exists in practice, Marks and Fraley (2005) asked both undergraduate (n = 144) and internet (n = 8080) participants to evaluate (imaginary) experimental targets (i.e., potential mates) who were described as either male or female and as having a high or low number of sexual partners. They found that subjects were more likely to criticize targets with high numbers of sexual partners, but this effect held for both male and female targets. These results suggest that people do evaluate others as a function of sexual activity—being more likely to criticize people with a lot of sexual partners—but they do not necessarily hold men and women to different sexual standards.

Partly supporting this finding, Milhausen and Herold (2002) studied young people ranging in age from 18 to 28 years, from three university classes and two community-based dating bars. Most of the respondents—especially the women—reported thinking that, in our culture, the double standard still exists. On a personal level, however, most respondents said that they did not hold men and women to different standards of evaluation themselves. Men were slightly more likely than women to endorse a traditional double standard. Women, for their part, were more likely than men to endorse a reverse double standard, which evaluated men's sexual promiscuity more harshly than women's.

In the end, Jackson and Cram (2003), however, disagree. They note that despite significant changes in attitudes over the past two decades, much research suggests that young women's negotiations of sexual relations remain dominated by the sexual double standard. Where this sexual double standard prevails, men who actively seek sexuality are positively regarded, but women who do so are criticized.

In short, our sexual attitudes have changed in the past two or three generations, but remnants of the double standard persist. We can see this persistence in the language used to describe sexually experienced males and females. Terms used to describe women who have had many sexual partners—for example, *slut, promiscuous, loose,* and *easy*—have negative connotations. Compare these to the terms used for men with many sexual partners—for example, *stud, stallion,* and *playboy*—and we can see that more positive connotations are associated with male sexual promiscuity. The sexual double standard is weaker today, as more young people are sexually active before marriage. Research by Rotermann (2012) shows that, in Canada, at least one-quarter of both boys and girls have had sex by the age of 17.

A traditional sexual double standard was the premise for dating rituals (or "scripts") that existed in North America from about the 1920s through the 1950s and most of the 1960s (despite popular images of that decade as the era of "free love"). **Sexual scripts** saw boys as initiators, calling girls for dates and often paying for the date. Some of these expectations persist today; however, patterns of meeting and dating have also changed over time. With greater equality between men and women, women are less likely to wait for men to ask them out, although some women still wait for men to initiate dating. Often, also, the man still picks up the woman and pays for the first date (Serewicz and Gale, 2008). This persistent expectation is part of a traditional dating script.

The question remains whether "wooing"—or romantic seduction—is more equal today than it was in the past. However, a gender imbalance remains. Studies of first-date initiation still find that men are more likely than women to view a woman who asks a man out as showing sexual interest, or even being sexually forward (Serewicz and Gale, 2008). Despite recent variability in women initiating first dates, overall a dominant dating script of men asking first persists (Eaton and Rose, 2011). Women who initiate dates are reportedly seen as being more sociable and more liberal but as less physically attractive than the person being asked. Despite a growing tendency toward more equality in dating initiatives, women who initiate dates are still viewed differently from men, who are expected to do the asking.

The initiation of sex is also strongly gendered. The media and other cultural factors play an important role in the age of first sexual activity. Some express alarm about the increasingly sexually overt nature of all types of media, specifically the manner in which women are represented. However, parents serve to mediate the connection between media influences and youthful behaviour. Fingerson (2000), for example, discovered that teens do what they think their parents would do, not what they say. In addition, having a good relationship and open communication with their mothers is associated with a lower likelihood of teens having sex, and having fewer partners if they do choose to have it. In contrast, Regnerus (2006) finds that among adolescents in intact, two-parent biological families, closeness of daughters to fathers rather than to mothers postpones coital debut and reduces risky sexual behaviour.

On balance, research findings support the notion that parental monitoring, adolescents' perception of their parents' disapproval, and adolescent sexual attitudes (mediated by parent–child communication) are important predictors of later age of sexual initiation (Regnerus, 2006). Overall, teens report that their parents are the biggest influence on their decisions about sex.

The threat of acquired immune deficiency syndrome (AIDS) and other sexually transmitted infections (STIs) also has a large influence on sexual practices. In the latter part of the twentieth century, STIs were widely known and reported to be a serious threat. Certain social groups continue to engage in risky sexual behaviour despite the high prevalence of human immunodeficiency virus (HIV)/AIDS and STIs in their populations (Singer et al., 2006). Interviews with a sample of these young adults uncover an underlying cultural logic being followed in their dating and mating lives. In particular, participants said that their assessment of risk for STIs, and therefore their viewed need to use condoms, was based on beliefs about "who is safe" rather than "which behaviors are risky" (Singer et al., 2006: 1018).

The greater ease associated with sexuality in current dating does not, however, seem to have produced a strong trend toward open relationships, one form of which is sometimes called "polyamory." Research on polyamory and other "open" or non-exclusive sexual relationships recognizes several common tensions. One is the asymmetry between partners, where one partner is more committed to exclusivity than another partner and less comfortable with relationship "openness." Another is the disagreement among people who practise polyamory themselves, as to what (if any) the ethical requirements of this practice are. As Klesse (2006: 565) points out in a study of bisexual polyamorous people,

> love, intimacy and friendship are salient themes in polyamory discourses. An exploration of the question of how respondents define polyamory with regard to different "styles of non-monogamy" reveals that the boundaries of polyamory are contested within the movement that has formed around this concept. The prevalent definition of polyamory as "responsible non-monogamy" usually goes hand in hand with a rejection of more sex- or pleasure-centred forms of non-monogamy, such as "casual sex", "swinging", or "promiscuity".

DATING IN AN AGING SOCIETY

Most sociological research focuses on the dating lives of adolescents and young adults, but a growing number of older adults are also dating these days, and the number of seniors in Canadian society is growing as well. Clearly, however, adults and seniors are at a different point in their lives than adolescents, so different rules and priorities shape their dating activities.

Increasingly, seniors (65+ years of age) are a large segment of society and, therefore, a large part of the dating market. However, seniors face particularly pressing problems in relation to dating. As people age, they find it much harder to develop new relationships. Obstacles include shrunken social networks, retirement from paid work, geographic relocation, and the death of friends and loved ones (Alterovitz, Sheyna, and Mendelsohn, 2011).

For women, the problems are even more pressing, as the pool of eligible dates shrinks considerably more than for men, since women live longer. This leaves a shortage of men at every age over 40. For people over 65 years of age, the sex ratio is roughly one man for every three women (Thies and Travers, 2006). In addition, seniors are usually less willing to date outside their culture, race, or religion, thus eliminating even more potential partners. On the other side, seniors are reportedly more willing to travel substantial distances to meet a date (McIntosh, Dawson, and Locker, 2011).

We all know the qualities younger people look for in their mates (physical attractiveness, for example), and research shows that seniors look for many of the same things. Even age preferences of seniors reflect youthful patterns: Men prefer younger women, and women prefer older men (although they prefer younger men after the age of 75) (Alterovitz, Sheyna, and Mendelsohn, 2011). The reason women prefer younger men after age 75 is because they do not want to end up as caregivers.

A big difference between young daters and senior daters is the reversal of traditional dating roles, however. Among younger people, typically men want casual relationships and women want serious ones. By contrast, among older people, men tend to approach dating with intentions of marriage, since they have grown accustomed to the stability and comfort that comes with it (McWilliams and Barrett, 2014). By contrast, older women want to avoid these responsibilities and seek more casual relationships, or companionship without demanding care roles.

DATING IN A MULTICULTURAL SOCIETY

In Canada, especially, immigrants make up a large part of modern society, and the children of immigrants, whether born in Canada or in their home country, are one of the fastest-growing populations. According to King and Harris (2007), because this demographic shift is so recent, researchers today know little about the social development of these youth during the critical life stage when dating and mating occur. Moreover, most of the sociological research on ethnic romantic interactions focuses on sexual behaviour (e.g., Raffaelli and Ontai, 2001).

Many factors are associated with the dating practices of immigrants in their new country. Dating people of a different culture requires language competence, for example. Other factors that bear on the possibility of successful dating include an understanding of a person's cultural background, family beliefs and values, and the expectations of peers in their school or community. Here, a conflict may occur between the dating norms that prevail in Canadian society and the norms of the culture within which the potential date has grown up (Howell et al., 2001: 135). And these differences are real enough: For example, research shows that first-generation (immigrant) adolescents are less likely to enter romantic relationships with dates than adolescents in native-born families (King and Harris, 2007).

Immigrant youth date less often than their peers, for many reasons. Many new immigrant families have less money or many dependent relatives and are isolated from English-speaking society for linguistic reasons (King and Harris, 2007). Other factors increase the likelihood that an immigrant teenager will have more household responsibilities than his or her peers and therefore less time for dating. However, those immigrant adolescents who do decide to engage in romantic relationships do so as readily as any host-country youth, most likely because they are more integrated in the culture of their new country.

Many immigrants to Canada come from cultures in which youth have little say in choosing their dating partners and long-term mates: cultures where, for example, arranged marriages are common. Even if their families are not as traditional as others in the same culture, they are likely to be more rigid in their beliefs than are families of North American adolescents. Likewise, many immigrants and their children retain traditional attitudes toward women and dating (Mchitarjan and Reisenzein, 2014, 2015). Many young women, such as those in the study by Espiritu (2001) of Filipino immigrants, believe that abstaining from casual intercourse is declarative of their moral superiority over the dominant culture of the West. However, the same study shows that this outlook may be enforced by a patriarchal society aiming to restrain girls from seeking autonomy.

Sometimes, children follow the cultural rules and practices taught to them by their parents. In one study, groups of Chinese and European Canadians were asked to respond to a scenario in which a young adult was having a conflict with his parents over interracial dating. In reviewing this scenario, Chinese Canadian respondents gave much more support to the parents than did European Canadians, who gave more support to the choice of the young adult (Uskul, Lalonde, and Cheng, 2007). In other cases, parents who try to control or supervise their children may increase the likelihood that they will go against their family's wishes and engage in unwanted romantic relations (King and Harris, 2007). Also, if immigrants (or children of immigrants) have close friends who date, they are much more likely to do so, too.

Continually growing immigration and ethnic diversity in Canada predicts that we will see even greater shifts in dating and mating practices in the future (Zhenchao and Lichter, 2007). One effect of growing up in a multicultural society, and of an ever-growing change in dating and mating, is the rise of interracial dating. Increased acceptance of interracial dating may also contribute to this trend. Generally, people tend to seek mates within their own race.

However, interracial marriage in Canada is becoming more common with each decade and with each generation an ethnic group spends in the country. It is especially common among people with higher education. Some groups (e.g., Japanese Canadians) are more likely than others to marry outside their own race, and to a degree, this pattern reflects the relative availability of potential mates of the same race. So, it seems that younger, more educated, more popular people are engaging in interracial dating (Fleras and Elliott, 2003). However, a poll of people of Chinese and South Asian origins in British Columbia found that around 37 percent of Chinese males, 19 percent of Chinese females, and 35 percent of South Asians experienced dating discrimination, suggesting that discrimination may still be preventing interracial dating (Insights West, 2014).

In many cultures, parents are concerned about the ethnic, religious, or racial background of their children's partner and try to influence their choice. This parental tactic is sometimes successful. In general, groups that are especially concerned about their ethnic community's survival place a premium on dating others from within the same ethnic group. For example, this is the case among Jews in Canada (Weinfeld, 2001). Similar findings can be found in other ethnic groups.

Acceptance of interracial dating in Canada varies regionally. Nearly three-quarters of respondents in the Atlantic provinces (72 percent) and in British Columbia (73 percent) said that they would be comfortable being in a romantic relationship with someone from a different ethnic background, compared with only 65 percent in Ontario and 63 percent in Quebec. Likewise, in the Atlantic provinces, 86 percent said that they would be comfortable if someone from a different ethnic background married their best friend, whereas in the Prairie provinces that figure dropped to 71 percent (CBC News, 2014).

However, we should note that interracial mating has been going on since even before Confederation. On this, historian Sylvia van Kirk (2002: 1) notes

> over the course of the colonial period, from the early seventeenth to the late nineteenth centuries, the practice of Aboriginal/non-Aboriginal marriage shifts from "marrying-in" to "marrying-out." Especially in the fur trade context, a major impetus for such unions came from Aboriginal groups themselves. The idea was to create a socioeconomic bond that would draw the Euro-Canadian male into

Native kinship networks. However, by the end of the colonial period, intermarriage had been transformed by settler society into "marrying-out." Aboriginal women lost their Indian status if they married non-status males. Aboriginal groups were deprived of any say in the matter and their kinship structures were ignored.

Only gradually did prejudices and preventive measures develop to discourage marriage between Indigenous and non-Indigenous people in Canada. But so common was the practice, for a time, that it produced an entire population of Canadians known as Métis.

As we see in Figure 3.2, an increasing number of Canadians are in racially or ethnically mixed unions, especially in Canada's largest cities, where they are most likely to meet people from different social backgrounds. In the United States, a similar process has been going on (Rosenfeld, 2008), and data going back more than half a century show that the process started in the 1950s. From then onward, we see a marked decline in the percentages of Hispanic and Asian men and women who married members of their own racialized group. A similar decline among blacks began only in the 1970s and progressed much more slowly.

As we see in Figure 3.3, in Canada, families play an indirect though important role in this process of out-marriage (**exogamy**). Looking at Muslim young adults, researchers find that highly cohesive (or allocentric) families are more able than other families to enforce a strong religious identification among their members and, in this way, discourage dating outside their religious group.

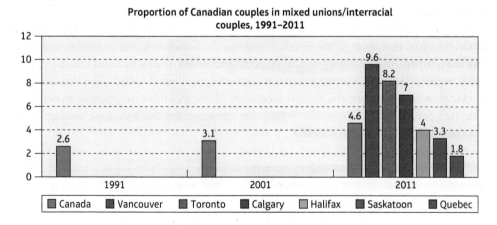

Proportion of Canadian couples in mixed unions/interracial couples, 1991–2011

Legend: Canada, Vancouver, Toronto, Calgary, Halifax, Saskatoon, Quebec

1991: 2.6
2001: 3.1
2011: 4.6, 9.6, 8.2, 7, 4, 3.3, 1.8

Figure 3.2 We can see that there appears to be regional differences in the proportion of interracial couples in Canada, with some cities such as Vancouver and Toronto having almost double the national average.

Source: Data from Statistics Canada. *Census 1991, 2001 & National Household Survey 2011.*

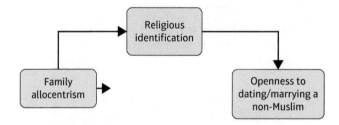

Figure 3.3 The indirect effect of family connectedness on personal openness to dating or marrying a non-Muslim.

Source: Based on Cila, Jorida, & Richard N. Lalonde. 2014. Personal openness toward interfaith dating and marriage among muslim young adults: The role of religiosity, cultural identity, and family connectedness. *Group Processes and Intergroup Relations 17*: 357–370. Web.

SAME-SEX DATING

Much like interracial dating, same-sex dating is becoming more mainstream and accepted. One instance was even covered by the media extensively, leading to the production of a TV movie about the case: *Prom Queen: The Marc Hall Story.* Marc Hall, a student at Monsignor John Pereyma Catholic Secondary School in Oshawa, Ontario, was prohibited from bringing his 21-year-old boyfriend to the prom. Officials from the Durham Catholic District School Board admitted that Hall had a right to be gay but proposed that allowing the date would send a message that the Church supported his "homosexual lifestyle." On May 10, 2002, Ontario Superior Court Justice Robert McKinnon ruled that a gay student had the right to take his boyfriend to the prom. Hall went to the dance (CBC News, 2005).

Where gays and lesbians meet and mate has changed over time. In 1990, gay bars were the most common first meeting place, regardless of whether people were looking for a short- or long-term relationship (Berger, 1990). Today, gay and lesbian youth have many other avenues open to them, including well-established subcultural institutions (bars and nightclubs, theatres, comedy clubs, gay travel tours, and so on) and internet dating. However, so far, little research has been done comparing same-sex and opposite-sex dating practices.

One interesting finding shows an important difference between heterosexual and same-sex couples. Previous research has shown that in heterosexual couples, conflict and even divorce result when the husband and wife earn similar amounts of money. Some have taken this to prove that complementarity (i.e., a husband–wife division of labour) is the way to ensure marital stability, whereas others have taken it to prove that husbands resent having to compete with their wives for income superiority, in violation of traditional (unspoken) gender expectations. On the other hand, Weisshaar (2014) finds that, in same-sex couples, equal earnings are associated with relationship stability, cohabitation, and marriage and that unequal earnings have an opposite association (see Figure 3.4).

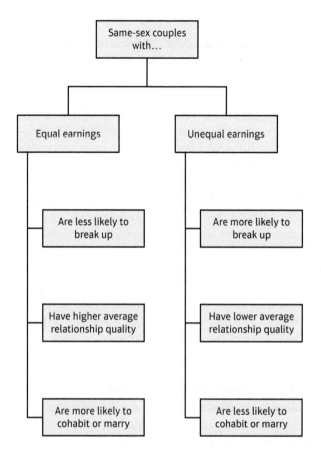

Figure 3.4 Factors affecting same-sex mating decisions and outcomes

Source: Based on Weisshaar, Katherine. 2014. Earnings equality and relationship stability for same-sex and heterosexual couples. *Social Forces* 93(1): 99.

DATING FOR OVERWEIGHT AND OTHER STIGMATIZED PEOPLE

In our society, above-average weight is often criticized and obesity is stigmatized. So, what is dating like for overweight and obese women? Given the importance that men attach to physical appearance in their dating preferences, excess weight should be even more problematic for single women than it is for single men.

To find out the answer, Jeannine A. Gailey (2012) interviewed 36 self-identifying fat North American women and found that 34 of them (94 percent of the sample) felt shame about their bodies. They also reported that their relationships suffered as a result of their excess weight. However, Gailey found that when they began to embrace their size rather than reject it, the women reported having better body images and sex lives.

In extensive interviews with Gailey, these women recalled many negative dating experiences. Many reported being the "target" (Gailey, 2012: 119) of men who specifically fetishized fat women. As "Karen" explained, "for most of those men, fat was a fetish. It wasn't, like, an acceptable thing. It was a fetish thing. Like, 'obviously, lady, I would never date you, but I will screw you because I have this weird fetish thing'" (Gailey, 2012: 119). Another interviewee, Beth, noted that "in our society, it's a shameful thing to be attracted to a fat woman—there's got to be something the matter with you" (Gailey, 2012: 120). And Abigail said, "I always thought when I was younger, that men don't want to sleep with fat girls. But it's the opposite. It's just that they don't tell anybody about it" (Gailey, 2012: 120).

However, Gailey notes a dramatic turnaround in body self-acceptance when the women begin to gain a sense of communal awareness among overweight people. For Marissa, participation in the fat acceptance movement led to "an epiphany moment where I said, 'my God, I've spent my entire life worrying about whether I'm fat or not. I think I'm going to stop'" (Gailey, 2012: 121). Another participant notes that the movement has helped women end bad relationships with men who mistreated them. Yet another participant revealed that the movement "really helped the whole process [of sex] be very positive" (Gailey, 2012: 122). For Jessica, the fat acceptance movement made wedding planning an enjoyable experience, as she was able to "completely ignore all of the standard messages of losing weight before the wedding" (Gailey, 2012: 122).

Overall, when fat-identified women were imprisoned by societal norms that stigmatized their size, they were unhappy in all aspects of their dating life. But when they rejected these conventional standards of beauty and embraced the size acceptance movement, their self-esteem and relationships improved accordingly.

HOMOGAMY

The theory of **homogamy** proposes that people tend to fall in love with people who are socially like themselves, as defined by class, educational level, religion, and race or ethnicity. This tendency of like marrying like—also referred to as assortative mating—is found for a wide variety of characteristics: age, geographic location, various physical traits and overall physical attractiveness, and mental traits, including attitudes, opinions, and personality (Furnham and McClelland, 2015).

People are homogamous for many good reasons. First, **propinquity (closeness) theory** states that people are more likely to find a mate among those with whom they associate. Given the social circles within which we move, we are more likely to meet others who are (at least socially) like ourselves than to meet people unlike ourselves. Second, we like people who think the way we do and act the way we expect them to; indeed, we feel comfortable in their presence. Third, instrumental and expressive exchanges are easier to balance when like is marrying like. That's because people are bringing similar, and therefore more equal, qualities and resources to the marriage.

Educational and Other Status Homogamy

Some characteristics of prospective mates are more important than others in determining mate selection. For example, in our society, education—an achieved status—is a more important criterion in the selection of marriage partners than racial, religious, or social class origins, which are ascribed (i.e., inherited at birth). Educational homogamy has become the most relevant aspect of homogamy in Canada and the United States. Since 1960, educational homogamy has continued to increase.

Someone with a low level of education is especially unlikely to "marry up" educationally—that is, marry someone with more education. University graduates are much more likely to marry each other, rather than others with less education (Schwartz and Mare, 2005). There may be several explanations for this, including the increased importance of educational attainment for upward mobility and the increased numbers of young people who prolong their education through secondary school, college or university, and even postgraduate programs. These young people who spend a longer period of time within these institutions are more likely to meet and date people in the same settings who often have similar interests.

Increasingly, people marry spouses of the same or similar educational attainment, most likely because of extended education and postgraduate programs.

Gina Smith/Shutterstock

Age Homogamy

In the days when marriage meant financial security rather than romance, women tended to look for a financially secure man who could provide for them. So, younger women tended to consider older, more established, and more mature men the most suitable marriage partners. This gendered age difference—the so-called marriage gradient—in mating persists even today, although it is far weaker than it once was.

Whatever reasons there may be for marrying someone of older, younger, or similar age, in Canadian society today, people do not tend to have as strong age preferences as they once did. For a variety of reasons, age today plays less of a determining role in marital relationships than it did in the past. This marks a major difference worth noting in marriage patterns: the decline of the marriage gradient. First proposed by sociologist Jessie Bernard (1973), the **marriage gradient** meant that people sorted themselves into couples not only by age but also by differential status. Men, on average, married women with a little less education or a lower occupational status than their own, following this pattern. Women, on average, married (typically older) men with a little more education or a little higher occupational status than their own.

Today, the marriage gradient is much less marked, but it persists in some societies and more traditional ethnic groups, and there, it often gives rise to difficulties. Men left out of marriage by the marriage gradient are those at the bottom of the socio-economic ladder (e.g., men with less education) who can find no one of lower status to marry. Women left out of marriage by the marriage gradient are those at the top of the ladder who can find no one of higher status to marry.

This has become extremely consequential in societies or communities where women have started to attain higher levels of education than men and have been reluctant to marry "down" to men who are less educated. As a result, in East Asia (for example) many well-educated women go unmarried and many less-educated men have to find mates outside their own country (e.g., through mail-order brides from poorer Asian countries.)

Despite a continued (small) marriage gradient in Canada, research shows great and increasing age and educational homogamy. This age and educational similarity hints at a decline in women's reliance on men as "breadwinners."

Ethnic Homogamy (or Endogamy)

At the turn of the twentieth century, endogamy was strong among all North American ethnic groups. Ethnic homogamy—also known as **endogamy**—was strongest for new immigrants from Southern and Eastern Europe, with weaker endogamy in the second generation. Today, ethnic intermarriage (or out-marriage) is more common for all groups, as we have already noted. Second-generation European Canadians and Americans marry increasingly out of their ethnic group, and the

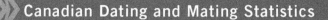

Canadian Dating and Mating Statistics

- Slightly more than half of Canadian couples (58 percent) are three years apart or less in age, and just over 40 percent are four or more years apart (Boyd and Li, 2003). Recently, there has been a trend of a narrowing age gap among seniors: 49 percent had an age difference of three years or less in 2001, compared with 40 percent in 1981 (Milan, Wong, and Vézina, 2014).

- Interracial marriage in Canada is on the rise. In 2011, there were 360 045 mixed-race couples in Canada, comprising 4.6 percent of all married and common-law couples. By comparison, couples in mixed unions accounted for 2.6 percent of all couples in 1991, 3.1 percent in 2001, and 3.9 percent in 2006. In most of these interracial couples (85 percent), one partner is white and the other is from a visible minority group. The remaining 15 percent are couples in which both partners are from different visible minority groups (e.g., black and Asian).

- Common-law relationships have increased over the past few decades, but marriages still account for the majority of Canadian unions (CBC News, 2005). Between 2006 and 2011, the number of common-law couples rose 13.9 percent, to 16.7 percent of all families (Statistics Canada, 2011a).

- The 2011 Census counted 64 575 same-sex couple families, up 42.4 percent from 2006 (Statistics Canada, 2011a).

- In Canada, Japanese people are most likely to enter mixed-race unions (79 percent). Next are Latin Americans (48 percent) and blacks (40 percent). South Asian and Chinese people are least likely to form a union with a partner outside their own ethnic or racial group (Statistics Canada, 2011a).

ethnic boundaries that separate potential mates have weakened over time (Kalmijn and Van Tubergen, 2010).

That's likely because people from different ethnic backgrounds are, during adolescence and early adulthood, attending educational institutions together. There, they meet and mate with others of similar age and educational status, typically regardless of ethnicity. As a result, between 1970 and 2000, the number of interracial marriages rose tenfold, with many saying that this signifies increasing status equality between Caucasians and minorities (Fu, 2008).

Between groups of equal status, people in interracial marriages tend to be from the higher strata of their group (Fu, 2008). This pattern of individual status matches results in the perpetuation of income and poverty inequality among ethnic groups. "Low-status minority families that carry on their racial and ethnic heritages through endogamy tend to have lower status within their group, while those with higher status tend to marry out and no longer carry the sole racial and ethnic heritage to the next generation. If this pattern persists, underprivileged minorities may suffer from low family resources across generations" (Fu, 2008: 152). In this way, intermarriage poses a social dilemma. On the one hand, it can foster greater acceptance between ethnic and racial groups, while at the same time preserving ethnically and racially defined social classes.

Religious Homogamy

Just as more people are marrying across racial lines, so too they are marrying across religious lines. Among Jews, a group that is especially concerned about its group survival, a high degree of homogamy is maintained, at least in part by increased acceptance of religious conversion, before or after marriage (Weinfeld, 2001: 154–160).

Intermarriage between Protestants and Catholics grew dramatically after the 1920s and continued growing slightly in the last few decades (Sherkat, 2004). Education has largely replaced religion as a key factor in spouse selection, so that people who marry across religious lines share a similar educational attainment (Kalmijn, 1991). However, conservative (i.e., highly observant) people are much less likely to marry across religious lines than people who are less conservative. For example, conservative Protestants have a much stronger preference for religious homogamy than mainline Protestants (Logan, Hoff, and Newton, 2008).

Although in the past people thought that crossing religious lines would hurt a marriage, the research on religious homogamy and its effect on marital satisfaction is mixed. In general, the link between religious homogamy and marital satisfaction seems to have weakened over the past 50 years. There has been an overall decline in perceptions of religious authority among younger generations, causing less importance to be placed on religion and its traditions (Myers, 2006).

Endogamy for Indigenous People

Endogamy remains an important aspect of dating life for many Indigenous peoples in Canada. Yet, as studies have shown, ethnic intermarriage is generally on the rise in Canada. For example, a 2014 Statistics Canada report found that there were more than 360 000 mixed-race couples in Canada as of 2011, which comprises 4.6 percent of all Canadian couples (Maclean's, 2014). Perhaps more important, endogamy among Indigenous peoples in Canada occurs because many Indigenous youth grow up and live in small communities where they mainly meet and date other Indigenous youth.

Some Indigenous people in Canada resist intermarriage, as they feel that they have an obligation to carry on their bloodline. As Anishnawbe artist Sarain Fox puts it, "It's absolutely vital for us to actively be thinking of keeping our bloodlines strong, within all aspects of our life" (Charleyboy, 2014).

In this respect, Indigenous endogamy is mixed up with the history of discrimination against Indigenous peoples throughout Canadian history and with complications of Indigenous status in Canada. New Fire host Lisa Charleyboy (2014) explains her dating preference this way:

> I want to partner with a Native man, and one who has Indian status. I also would love if he is connected to his culture and has over 25 per cent blood quantum. My father's Tsilhqot'in from Tsi Del Del reserve in the interior of British Columbia, and my mother was a Christian missionary born in California who came to the reserve on

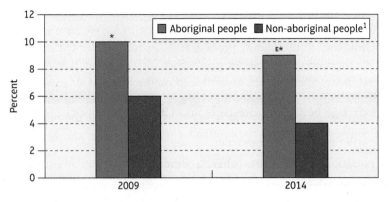

Figure 3.5 Aboriginal and non-Aboriginal victims of self-reported spousal violence, 2009 and 2014

Note: Includes legally married, common-law, same-sex, separated and divorced spouses who reported having experienced violence within the five-year period preceding the survey. Data for the territories will be published at a later date.

Source: Data from Statistics Canada. *General Social Survey 2009 & 2014.*

a mission . . . She fell head over heels with my father, they got married and she moved to the rez. But back in those days, there weren't a lot of interracial marriages. My mom never really fit in, despite her best efforts. And my father really struggled to find a balance between being a good Christian man and being a Tsilhqot'in Chief rooted in culture. When I was four my father committed suicide and my mother was blamed.

My two brothers and I left the rez fast and furious and I was raised in the suburbs . . . separate from my culture and my Tsilhqot'in family. I have felt that loss my entire life. . . . Eventually I found my way back home. I don't want that feeling of loss for my future child. I want them to feel grounded and connected to culture and community. Which is why I choose to "date Native."

A problem associated with Indigenous couples, however, is the high risk of domestic violence. Using a variety of measures, we find higher rates of reported spousal violence among Indigenous people than among non-Indigenous people. And although Figure 3.5 shows a drop in self-reported spousal violence between 2009 and 2014, the drop is smaller for Indigenous victims than it is for non-Indigenous victims.

THE IDEALS OF MATE SELECTION

As stated at the beginning of this chapter, we live today in an age of romantic choice. This opportunity to choose, combined with mass media depictions of passionate love, leads many to think that marriage has passionate love as its goal. Thus, some believe that mating and marriage are about the capture and possession of "erotic property" (Collins, 1992). This view is consistent with what we have said so far about the role of romance in the mating process and can account for the complicated and unreal beliefs that people hold about mating.

However, many relationships are smashed on the rocks of unreasonable expectation. Experts who provide premarital counselling note a variety of unrealistic beliefs commonly held by people when choosing mates. They include the beliefs that:

- People will find the perfect partner
- Only one good partner exists for each person
- Love is enough to smooth over the rough patches in a relationship
- When all else fails, the mates will try harder and succeed
- Opposites complement each other (i.e., heterogamy is better than homogamy)

People tend to hold such beliefs because, for many, mate selection is the capture of erotic property, and people's ability to reason about mate selection is often clouded by passion.

Why People Do Not Optimize

Despite the romantic ideals that many hold about marriage, and the problem posed by a sexual double standard, people do not seek an ideal or **optimal mate**. They do not try to optimize; rather, they satisfice. They seek a "good enough" mate within the constraints life has handed them (March and Simon, 1958). The difference between optimizing and satisficing is the difference between searching a haystack for the sharpest needle and merely searching for a needle that is sharp enough to sew with. For most purposes, whatever satisfies us is ideal.

Suppose that, as an idealistic teenager, you had listed 10 qualities you felt you absolutely must have in a mate. If we assume that 1 in 5 people has each of these qualities, and the qualities you are looking for in a mate are uncorrelated, only 1 person in 5 to the 10th power—1 in 9.8 million—will meet all of your requirements. That may be less than one adult person of the right sex, ages 20 to 60, in all of Canada. Equally, there is only one chance in 9.8 million that your "perfect mate" will consider you the perfect mate. So, in this scenario, the chances of meeting and marrying the perfect mate are 1 in 9.8 million squared (or nearly zero).

Even more modest goals cannot be optimized. Suppose that, instead of needing your perfect mate to be among the top fifth in attractiveness, you need him or her to be only in the top half. You similarly lower your standards for your other requirements. This makes your mating problem more manageable: Now, you only need to look for that one "perfect" person in a thousand (i.e., 2 to the 10th power).

With this in mind, you may try to solve the problem by reducing the number of qualities you look for in a mate. Suppose your potential mate has to excel in only one respect and satisfy you in four others. Now you and your perfect mate are each looking for someone who is in the top fifth in one quality and in the top half in just four other qualities. The likelihood of finding a person with the qualities you seek is 1 in 1250. The likelihood that you will satisfy his or her needs is also 1 in 1250. Even so, the chance of meeting and mating is still well below 1 in 1 million (i.e., 1 in 1250 squared).

>>> Dating and Mating Trends

- The term *hooking up*, commonly used by young adults, is deliberately left ambiguous, telling us little about what sort of intimate activity it describes (Bogle, 2008; Strokoff, Owen, and Fincham, 2015). This ambiguity allows young adults to adhere to the traditional sex roles of our society. Girls can use the term to downplay their sexual experience, whereas boys can use it to pretend greater sexual expertise.

- Similarly, the expression "friends with benefits" allows flexibility in a relationship and minimal commitment while maintaining physical encounters. One study found that 54 percent of male respondents and 43 percent of female university student respondents had participated in a friends-with-benefits relationship in the past 12 months (Owen and Fincham, 2010).

- In seeking mates, men tend to put the highest priority on facial attractiveness in long-term relationships and the highest priority on bodily attractiveness in short-term relationships (Confer, Perilloux, and Buss, 2010, Wagstaff, Sulikowski, and Burke, 2015). Women, on the other hand, tend to show no preference for facial or bodily attractiveness in their choices.

- College and university students reportedly use cigarettes as part of their mating strategy (Jones and Figueredo, 2007). Specifically, students who are actively looking for a mate are likelier to smoke—or at least try to smoke—cigarettes in social settings. However,

women perceive men who do so as more short-term oriented, and men also see it as more of a short-term strategy (Vincke, 2016).

- Both men and women use conspicuous consumption as a mating strategy, as it gives them an opportunity to show off their wealth, status, and taste (Sundie, 2003). Indeed, people seeking a short-term sexual partner—men particularly—are most likely to engage in conspicuous consumption, compared with people seeking a long-term marriage partner.

- Compared to men, women are more likely to want to be asked for consent before sexual involvement and endorse more explicit forms of communication of consent (Humphreys and Herold, 2007, Muehlenhard, Humphreys, Jozkowski, and Peterson, 2016).

- Men and women typically have different mating goals when they use online dating websites. Research shows that women mainly use online dating in search of a long-term partner, whereas men more often use it to build casual relationships (Alam, Yeow, and Loo, 2011; Gatter, Hodkinson, and Kolle, 2016). Online dating is a unique and evolving terrain for finding a partner and can often involve a degree of deception about one's appearance or personal characteristics (Toma and Hancock, 2012).

- As adolescents grow older, they are more likely to engage in sexual intercourse but also more likely to use a condom when they do so (Saewyc, Taylor, Homma, and Ogilvie, 2008).

However you revise the list and extend your range and number of contacts, the chance of finding the perfect mate this way is nearly zero. Most people cannot and do not find a mate in this way. Rather, people fall in love with those who are close at hand. As in so many areas of life, we come to value what we know best and have available: people like ourselves. We become satisfied with the possible, not the ideal; and then we come to love the person who satisfies us.

DATING VIOLENCE

Unfortunately, every discussion of dating and mating must include a discussion of dating violence. This is ironic because, as we said at the beginning of this chapter, dating in our society is charged with romantic illusion and emotional intensity.

A Canadian study reports that 33 percent of high school students had at least one experience of aggression with a current or past partner (Connolly et al., 2010). Estimates from the survey show that nearly 1.5 million women in the United States are raped or physically assaulted annually. Another survey of adolescents in Atlantic Canada found that around 60 percent of both boys and girls had experienced a form of psychological violence, with more boy (41 percent) than girl (29 percent) victims of physical aggression, and around 40 percent of each had experienced sexual coercion (Sears and Byers, 2010). This shows the importance of recognizing that women also commit acts of physical violence, a fact often ignored in popular conceptions of abuse.

The survey also examined violence among gay and lesbian dating partners, finding that lesbian couples were significantly less likely to experience violence, whereas the opposite was true for gay men. Men in homosexual couples experienced more partner violence than men in opposite-sex partnerships. This would support the findings that men are the main perpetrators of dating violence. However, more research is needed on same-sex relationships.

People who are dating, and not yet married or in a committed relationship, are especially vulnerable to partner violence—especially when relationships are in the process breaking up. In dating relationships, girls are much more likely than boys to report physical violence and psychological abuse by their partner (Swahn, Simon, Arias, and Bossarte, 2008).

About 14 percent of all female victims of violent crime in Canada are assaulted by a current dating partner, while another 8 percent are assaulted by a former dating partner. As we see in Figure 3.6, women are always more likely than men to be victims of violence by an intimate partner, and the risks of assault by a spouse are highest.

Where violent abuses are concerned, women are more than twice as likely as men to admit their occurrence. Where less violent abuses are concerned, men and women admit them equally often. The 2004 General Social Survey (Statistics Canada, 2005c), the most comprehensive survey on family violence in Canada, found a clear inconsistency in the reports by women and men. These disturbing findings reveal that violent abuse on dates is not only physical but also sexual. Date rape is a growing concern

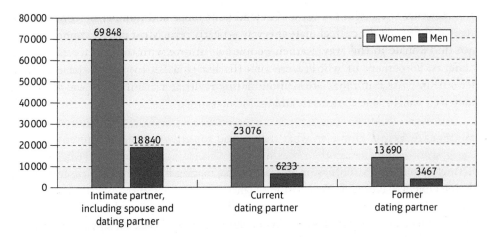

Figure 3.6 Number of victims of dating violence by gender, Canada, 2014

Source: Data from Boyce, Jillian. *Victimization of Aboriginal People in Canada, 2014.* Juristat: Canadian Centre for Justice Statistics (2016).

among sociologists. But in this area of research, getting good data is difficult, because young men and women disagree about what happens on dates. Bear in mind, too, that most instances of forced sexual activity occur between people who know each other, so there may be sentiments of liking as well as fear attached to these experiences.

The result is, too often, that women blame themselves for the experience. Since they know the assailant, they often react passively to the sexual assault and thus blame themselves for not reacting more forcefully. A few even continue the dating relationship. Some girls tolerate sexually coercive behaviour because non-physical coercive tactics are seen as socially acceptable. For example, many girls find it hard to deal with being verbally pressured into unwanted sex because verbal pressure is not identified as overt abuse. However, the results are real. Verbal sexual coercion is associated with relationship dissatisfaction and troubles with sexual functioning that each leads to further negative consequences (Katz and Myhr, 2008).

Social position often plays a factor in dating violence. Foshee and colleagues (2008) found that adolescents from minority families or single-parent families, or whose parents have lower educational attainment, report significantly more experiences of physical dating violence. Typically, this also connotes an acceptance of dating abuse and gender stereotyping in less educated, minority populations (Foshee et al., 2008).

Dating Violence for Obese and Other Stigmatized People

As we noted earlier, overweight and obese people are often stigmatized, and sometimes this can lead to low self-esteem and mistreatment. In a troubling study, researchers Farhat and colleagues (2015) found a correlation between weight and dating violence. Specifically, they found that white girls who consider themselves overweight (regardless of whether they actually were) and Hispanic girls who are overweight run a much higher risk of domestic violence victimization than their non-overweight peers. The researchers used a nationally representative sample of students, 56 percent of whom were girls (Farhat et al., 2015). From these respondents, they collected information about dating violence victimization, weight status, perceived weight, and various demographic measures.

Among boys, they found no correlation between actual weight and domestic violence victimization. However, what they found for girls was quite different. One in 4 girls who overestimated their weight—that is, viewed themselves as obese—were victims of violent victimization, in comparison with only 1 in 10 girls who did not overestimate their weight. Yet most girls who were actually in the obese weight range had lower odds of victimization than non-obese girls who *thought* they were obese. Only for Hispanic girls was actual overweight status, as opposed to perceived overweight status, associated with victimization.

From these findings, the researchers concluded that (inaccurate) weight overestimation is associated with low self-esteem and depression, which are in turn associated with violent victimization.

Dating Violence for People with Disabilities

Risk of dating violence is also higher for people with physical or mental disabilities. For example, Weiss and colleagues (2011: 564) found that "youth with a borderline-to-mild intellectual disability reported significantly more victimization and perpetration of relationship violence" than their non-disabled peers. Similarly, researchers Monika Mitra and colleagues (2013: 1090–1091), using data from the Massachusetts Youth Health Survey (MYHS), found that "respondents who had a disability were more likely than those without disabilities to have reported ever having experienced dating violence." What's more, *both* boys and girls with disabilities were more likely than boys and girls without disabilities to report dating violence victimization.

Finally, researchers Hahn and colleagues (2014), using data from the U.S. National Epidemiological Survey, found that people reporting physical impairments were more likely than people not reporting physical impairments to be victims of violent victimization. Overall, there remains a problematic link between dating violence and social vulnerability (including stigmatization and exclusion) of all kinds.

Just as all women generally have higher risks than men of violent victimization on dates, girls with disabilities have higher risks than boys of violent victimization. However, what is most striking is the information that girls with disabilities have three times as high a risk of violent victimization on dates as do girls without disabilities. The effects of such dating violence for youth with disabilities are very serious (see Figure 3.7); they may include feelings of sadness and hopelessness, suicide ideation (i.e., thoughts of death and suicide), and drug use (Mitra, Mouradin, and McKenna, 2013).

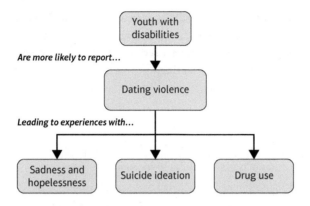

Figure 3.7 Effects of dating violence

Among high school students who had ever been on a date, girls and boys with disabilities were more likely than girls and boys without disabilities to report dating violence.

Source: Based on Mitra, Monika, Vera E. Mouradian, & Maria McKenna. 2013. Dating violence and associated health risks among high school students with disabilities. *Journal of Maternal Child Health* 17: 1088–1094.

CHAPTER SUMMARY

The way we choose a mate has changed from when romantic love emerged during the Middle Ages. As we look at our dating and mating rituals in the courtly love tradition, we see the origins of the sexual scripts of men and women. These dating rituals contributed to a sexual double standard in which boys were the initiators and girls were the receivers of romantic attention. Love is the ideal basis of a marriage in the Western tradition, though in other traditions a material exchange is more important.

In the modern "mate market," we compare our marketability on the basis of physical features, earning potential, and personality; we search for "the one" on campus, in workplaces, among friends, on the internet, or on holiday. In mating, we follow certain predictable patterns that govern whom we are most likely to date and mate with. Like marrying like, or homogamy, is one way the exchange process of dating becomes apparent. Similarity seems to play a large role in whom we choose to mate with. Educational homogamy has increasingly become an important factor in dating. Couple happiness is deeply connected to the social similarity of the partners.

Dating and mating sometime end in violence. In this chapter, we have noted repeatedly that certain socially vulnerable groups—among them, Indigenous people, overweight people, people with disabilities, and women of all kinds—are at particular risk of dating violence. Sociologists face many problems in getting reliable data about violence, because victims are unlikely to report it. But we can have no doubt about the widespread prevalence of this "dating" problem.

Key Terms

endogamy Marriage to a member of one's own tribe or social group.

exogamy Marriage outside of one's own tribe or social group.

expressive exchange An exchange of emotional and sexual benefits.

homogamy The selection of a mate with similar social attributes, such as class, education level, religion, race, or ethnicity.

instrumental exchange An exchange of practical and useful benefits, such as unpaid work or financial support.

marriage gradient A systematic difference between mates, such that men are typically older and of higher social or economic status than their female partners.

optimal mate One's theoretical ideal mate.

propinquity (closeness) theory A theory of mate selection that people are more likely to find a mate among those who are geographically nearby.

romantic love An idea of love that is influenced by idealistic concepts of mating, such as chivalry and a search for one's soul mate.

sexual double standard The application of different rules, or standards of sexual behaviour, to men and women.

sexual scripts Attitudes and activities that a culture links to each gender or that are typically expected of members of a particular gender in regard to dating.

Critical Thinking Questions

1. Name the two or three most important ways in which dating and mating have changed in the past hundred years. How do you account for these changes?

2. Why do some people participate in mate selection online instead of through more traditional methods? Is it possible to form a serious relationship using the internet?

3. In what ways do parents influence the sexual behaviour of their teenage children?

4. What are some of the obstacles facing older adults who wish to find new intimate relationships, and does internet technology overcome these?

5. What are the different types of homogamy? Specifically, discuss the importance of educational homogamy and the effect it may have on social inequality and social segregation.

6. What unrealistic beliefs do people possess about choosing mates? Why do these beliefs persist, despite evidence to the contrary?

Weblinks

Pew Research Center: Online Dating

www.pewInternet.org/topics/Dating.aspx

This website presents numerous articles that provide information about online dating and relationships.

New Directions

www.newdirections.mb.ca

This non-profit agency funded by the United Way provides information on families and parenting.

Second Wives Club

www.secondwivesclub.com

This site provides an array of articles, information, and discussion for remarried women and stepmothers, as well as links to other family- and woman-oriented advice and information sites.

Match.com

www.match.com

This dating site caters to all types of singles in many areas, including lesbian and gay people.

Matchmaker.com

www.matchmaker.com

This fun, less traditional dating service allows you to participate in a trial match without spending money or giving away personal information. The site categorizes its participants by gender, sexual orientation, expected level of commitment, and ethnic and religious backgrounds. Ironically, it does not sort its participants by occupation or interests/hobbies.

Do Something

www.dosomething.org

This site encourages teens to become empowered agents of change in their own communities and includes a large section on dating violence aimed at adolescents. The Teen Dating Bill of Rights and Pledge encourages respect and responsibility in relationships.

About: Relationships

http://about.com/people

This site provides a vast array of information, including data on dating and relationships, marriage, divorce, homosexual life, and senior life.

Chapter 4
Types of Intimate Couples
Marriage, Cohabitation, Same-Sex Relationships, and Other Forms

Inti St Clair/Blend Images/Getty Images

CHAPTER OUTLINE

- Introduction
- Social Change in Close Relations
  - Diversity and Fluidity
  - Discontinuity
  - Emerging Trends for Young Adults
  - Emerging Trends for Older Adults
- A Profile of Families in Canada Today
  - Marriage

- Cohabitation
- Living Apart Together (LAT)
- Intersections of Sexual Relationships and Living Arrangements
- Single-Person Households
- Shifting Societal Views of the Unattached
- The Decision to Cohabit, Marry, or Remarry

- Divorce and Relationship Dissolution
- Remarriage and Blended Families
- LGBTQ Couples and Families
- Childbearing and Parenting
- Diversity in Sexual Relationships
  - Polygamy
  - Polyamory
  - Non-monogamy
- Money Management
  - Relationship Status
  - Gender and Economic Inequality
  - Money and Economic Exploitation
  - Money and Relationship Dissolution
- Technological Change
- Concluding Remarks

LEARNING OBJECTIVES

1 Identify the changes that have taken place in intimate relationships, marriage, living arrangements, sexuality, and childbearing.

2 Recognize emerging trends in close relations for young and older adults.

3 Learn how sexuality and sexual relationships have changed.

4 Explain the causes of the changes we have seen in intimate relationships, living arrangements, sexuality, and parenting.

5 Consider how technologies like the internet and social media transform intimate relationships.

6 Consider how family law affects relationship formation and dissolution.

7 Understand money management in relation to relationship status, income, and gender.

INTRODUCTION

At no other time in history have there been as much variety, choice, and fluidity in different aspects of private life and close relations, including relationship status, living arrangements, family structure, childbearing, parenting, sexual orientation, sexuality, and emotional intimacy. What is particularly remarkable about this seismic societal shift is that it has happened in a relatively short period. This chapter takes a look at close relations today and the changes that have taken place in intimate partnerships, families, childbearing, and sexuality. It is becoming normative for people to experience more numerous intimate relationships, living arrangements, and family reconfiguration. The private and family lives of Canadians today contrast with those of earlier generations who had fewer choices around intimate relationships and family life. This chapter discusses the social, economic, political, legal, and technological changes that have facilitated changes in private life in Canada.

SOCIAL CHANGE IN CLOSE RELATIONS
Diversity and Fluidity

Throughout most of the twentieth century, heterosexual marriage was the benchmark by which people were judged (Adams, 1997; Coontz, 1992). Social pressure to pursue conventional family life continued even into the closing decades of the twentieth century, when the decline of the traditional nuclear family was cause for concern among politicians, journalists, and some sociologists (Popenoe, 1993). There is greater diversity in the twenty-first century in the decisions Canadians make about their intimate relationships and the close relations they build. Non-marital childbearing, cohabitation, living apart together (LAT) relationships, divorce, living alone, non-monogamy, voluntary childlessness, new reproductive technologies, and LGBTQ (lesbian, gay, bisexual, transgender, queer, and questioning) families are examples of trends in family life that represent new choices for Canadians. In the twenty-first century, there is greater fluidity in the lives of Canadians as they change their life circumstances, living arrangements, family structure, intimate partnerships, and sexual relationships. Fluidity also exists in sexual relationships and sexual orientation—for example, individuals who have experienced opposite-sex and same-sex relationships and individuals who have experienced monogamous and non-monogamous relationships. Change in close relations occurs as relationships end and new relations are established.

The terrain around emotional intimacy has shifted as individuals no longer rely on traditional marriage or romantic partnerships to establish emotionally intimate relationships. Non-monogamous individuals and polyamorists develop emotional intimacy with multiple partners. Canadians, including unattached Canadians, have emotionally close relations with relatives, friends, and others and do not define emotional intimacy solely in terms of sexual and romantic relationships. Intersections between relationship status and living arrangements are more diverse, as being in a romantic relationship does not always mean co-residence or monogamy. Changing societal attitudes, increased secularism, social movements for LGBTQ rights (Fetner, 2008), and new technologies are just some of the causes of the changes we see in private life.

Discontinuity

It is becoming normative for people to experience more numerous intimate relationships, living arrangements, and family reconfiguration. This is true for all age groups: children, young adults, adults at midlife, and seniors. A greater number of Canadian children experience changing family structures due to parental relationship dissolution (Ambert, 2012; Juby, Marcil-Gratton, and Le Bourdais, 2004; Wu and Schimmele, 2009). Younger generations experience a prolonged transition to adulthood, as increased credentialism and the requirements of postsecondary education often result in the postponement of marriage and childbearing. Earlier generations faced a more continuous life course trajectory of completing their education, seeking employment, getting married, and having children. Younger generations are more likely to experience a discontinuous life course trajectory wherein the sequencing of phases is less straightforward than it was for earlier generations. For instance, young adults may return to postsecondary education to further their careers or to build new careers once they already have a family they need to support. They may do so because of unemployment, underemployment, blocked job opportunities, low incomes, health issues, economic restructuring, corporate downsizing, or job dissatisfaction.

Emerging Trends for Young Adults

Today's young adults are more likely to delay marriage, remain single, have fewer children, cohabit, and experience relationship dissolution or divorce as compared to those in earlier generations. They are more likely to have children within the context of a cohabiting relationship, to have children with different partners, and to be a stepparent as compared to earlier generations. They are more likely to pursue LGBTQ relationships (Statistics Canada, 2011a) and polyamorous relationships (Boyd, 2017). A growing number of Canadian children are born to unmarried parents, particularly in Quebec (Laplante, 2014). One in three births in Canada are to unmarried women, most of whom are cohabiting (Marcil-Gratton and Le Bourdais, 1999, 2004). In Quebec, this rate is approximately 60 percent (Marcil-Gratton and Le Bourdais, 1999, 2004). Young adults are more likely to cohabit than get married in their first relationship and to experience numerous relationships throughout their lives.

Young adults experience transitions that look different than those of their parents' and grandparents' generation. Unlike their parents' generation, young adults in their early twenties are more likely to live with their parents rather than a partner (Milan, 2016; Statistics Canada, 2012a). Young adults are more likely to be in a LAT relationship. Not only are young adults living with their parents longer, but some are returning to live with their parents after living on their own. This is true in Canada and other industrialized countries. They may do so for financial reasons, such as an inability to afford a household on their own, unemployment, or the need to return to school (Mitchell, 2006; Stone, Berrington, and Falkingham, 2014). They may return for emotional support after relationship dissolution or for assistance with childcare (Stone et al., 2014). More men in their twenties live with their parents than do women of the same age (Milan, 2016). Culture is also important; some ethnocultural groups place a strong emphasis on adult children, particularly daughters, continuing to live in the parental home until marriage.

Emerging Trends for Older Adults

Family transitions continue throughout adulthood after divorce or widowhood as individuals pursue later-life relationships. One change from earlier generations is the increase in divorce among older people. Phrases like "grey divorce" and "silver separations" describe older couples who divorce after long marriages (LaRochelle-Côté, Myles, and Picot, 2012). Rates of remarriage for divorced or widowed individuals decline with age, yet many senior Canadians repartner. A significant recent change is that rates of remarriage or cohabitation following divorce are declining (Ambert, 2009). Divorced Canadians are taking longer to remarry or cohabit with a new partner, and an increasing number of divorced Canadians, particularly those with children, are not repartnering (Ambert, 2009; Vanier Institute of the Family, 2010). More women are living alone following marital dissolution (Vanier Institute of the Family, 2010).

Increasing divorce rates and life expectancy mean that the proportion of Canadians over age 65 who are divorced has risen. Some older couples who are alone after widowhood or divorce may choose to repartner but keep separate households in order to maintain continuity in their living and financial arrangements and to avoid conflict with their children about loyalties and inheritance (Borell and Karlsson, 2002). Studies of seniors in France (Caradec, 1997) and Sweden (Borell and Karlsson, 2002) found diversity in living arrangements and relationship status, as some were married, others cohabited, and others maintained two homes and alternated time between households. Similar trends are apparent among older Canadians (Statistics Canada, 2012b). LAT is increasingly common in Canada not only for those with jobs in different cities, but also for those who prefer to maintain separate homes (Statistics Canada, 2013a).

A PROFILE OF FAMILIES IN CANADA TODAY

The majority of families in Canada are married-couple families, although the proportion of married-couple families is declining. In 2001, married couples represented 71 percent of all census families, and this number had dropped to 67 percent by 2011 (Statistics Canada, 2012b). Married-couple families have declined because there has been an increase in cohabitation, lone-parent families, and people living alone. In 2001, common-law couples represented 14 percent of census families, and this number had increased to 17 percent by 2011 (Statistics Canada, 2012b). Lone-parent families had always been more common in Canada than common-law couple families, but this changed in 2011 when the number of common-law couples was higher than the number of single-parent families. Common-law couples are increasing at a faster rate than married couples. Lone-parent families are also increasing (Statistics Canada, 2012b). Approximately 16 percent of families are single-parent families, and about 80 percent of these are headed by women (Statistics Canada, 2012b). While there are more female lone parents than male lone parents, the growth in male lone-parent families in the twenty-first century has been faster than the growth in female lone-parent families (Statistics Canada, 2012b).

Stepfamilies, in which at least one child preceded the relationship, were counted for the first time in the 2011 Census. Statistics Canada refers to families in which children are raised by their biological or adoptive parents as intact families, although some view the word *intact* as problematic. Of all families with children, 13 percent were stepfamilies and 87 percent were intact families (Statistics Canada, 2012b). Stepfamilies are less likely to be married than intact families. A higher proportion of same-sex couples with children are stepfamilies (Statistics Canada, 2012b), reflecting the reality that some Canadian children have been raised by both opposite-sex and same-sex step-parents. There are provincial differences, as stepfamilies are more common in Quebec; several areas in Quebec have significantly higher levels of stepfamilies than the rest of Canada (Statistics Canada, 2012b).

Marriage

Most Canadians marry; 2001 data show that 80 percent of the Canadian population age 25 and over had married at least once (Clark and Crompton, 2006). The rate of marriage is declining as Canadians cohabit or remain unattached (Vanier Institute of the Family, 2010). Most divorced Canadians repartner by getting married a second time or by cohabiting. Cohabitation is more common than remarriage, and divorced men are more likely to repartner than divorced women. An increasing number of divorced Canadians remain unattached, and this is particularly true for single parents and for women (Vanier Institute of the Family, 2010). Married-couple families, although declining as a proportion of all households, remain the most common family form in Canada (Statistics Canada, 2012b). The major changes we have seen in marriage include Canadians delaying marriage, as evidenced by a higher age at marriage for males and females; Canadians foregoing marriage to remain single and live alone; people opting to cohabit rather than marry formally; an increase in LAT couples; and an increase in same-sex marriages. Marriages between individuals of different ethnicities and races are becoming more common. According to the 2006 Census, approximately 4 percent of couples were interracial unions (Statistics Canada, 2011b). The increase in interracial relationships is due to the overall increase in the visible minority population in Canada and to increased opportunities for people of different races to meet and interact.

The decline in the number of married Canadians reflects the higher age at marriage, increases in divorce and cohabitation, and an increase in the number of young adults who live in the parental home. The number of Canadians in their twenties and thirties who have never been married has increased dramatically in the past several decades. In 1981, only 26 percent of Canadians in their mid- to late twenties had never married, but this number increased to 73 percent by 2011 (Milan, 2013). In the

1980s, common-law unions were more popular for Canadians in their twenties and uncommon among Canadians in older age groups. Now they are common among older age groups, including Canadians in their fifties and sixties. The proportion of Canadians in a married or common-law union increases with age; for instance, half of Canadian women ages 25 to 29 are in a union, and 75 percent of women ages 45 to 49 are either married or in a common-law union (Milan, 2013).

Marriage continues to be more common than cohabiting relationships, although cohabitation is more popular among younger groups. Women with a university education are more likely to marry than cohabit (Milan, 2013). There has been an overall decline in the number of married people in Canada. In 1981, 61 percent of the population was married and 39 percent was unmarried (Milan, 2013). By 2011, a greater number of people were unmarried: 54 percent were unmarried and 46 percent were married (Milan, 2013). Marriage rates have varied historically due to economic factors, and they have declined over the last 40 years in Canada. Historically, the age at marriage is higher for men by two years (Milan, Keown, and Covadonga, 2011). The age at marriage has increased; in 2008, women married at almost 30 years of age on average and men married at 31 years of age (Milan, Keown, and Covadonga, 2011). This contrasts with earlier decades, when men and women got married in their mid-twenties. The pursuit of educational and career goals leads to the postponement of marriage for both men and women.

Earlier generations of women were dependent on marriage for economic support (Luxton, 1980). While many women still rely on a male partner for economic support (Sassler and Miller, 2011), more women have the economic means to forego marriage. Intimate relationships, and marriage in particular, have always reflected economic relations. In a study of lesbian mothers, Dunne (2000) argues that the ability to pursue a lesbian relationship—which implies the absence of a male partner's economic support—is an economic accomplishment. That gender, sexuality, and economics are interconnected processes is revealed when relationship formation and dissolution are considered. The relative economic insecurity of women channels women into intimate relationships (Sassler and Miller, 2011) and motherhood (Fox, 2009; Gerson, 1985), and relationship dissolution leads to economic hardship (Richards, 2010; Sev'er, 1992) and repartnership (Richards, 2010).

Cohabitation

A growing number of couples, particularly younger Canadians, are cohabiting, and an increasing number of children are being born to cohabiting couples. Cohabiting relationships tend to be less stable than marital relationships, partly because cohabiters tend to hold less traditional ideas about family life and are less likely to believe in marital permanence (Wilson, 2009). Studies comparing relationship stability for common-law versus married couples after the birth of a child find that common-law parents have higher rates of relationship dissolution than married parents

(Manning, Smock, and Majumdar, 2004; Osborne, Manning, and Smock, 2007; Tach and Edin, 2013). However, a more recent Canadian analysis by Ménard (2011) found that children and stepchildren increased the stability of common-law relationships, whereas among married couples relationship stability was enhanced only when children were conceived after the marriage. Various explanations have been advanced to explain the higher rate of relationship dissolution among cohabiting couples. Individuals who have experienced parental divorce are more likely to experience relationship dissolution and are more likely to choose cohabitation over marriage (Bumpass, Raley, and Sweet, 1995; Hamplová, 2003; Liefbroer and Dourleijn, 2006). However, parental divorce is also a risk factor for divorce (Amato and Hohmann-Marriott, 2007). Age is an important variable; young people are more likely to cohabit and more likely to experience relationship dissolution as compared to older people (Raley and Bumpass, 2003). There is greater relationship stability among religious individuals, and individuals who cohabit are less religious and more accepting of cohabitation and divorce (Clark and Crompton, 2006).

While cohabiting relationships are more unstable than marital relationships, relationship stability is affected by race, education, substance abuse, and previous relationship history. Osborne, Manning, and Smock (2007) found that, in the United States, children of common-law couples are five times more likely to experience the dissolution of their parents' relationship as compared to children of married couples. The difference in stability between cohabiting and married parents was greater for white children than it was for black or Mexican American children. Parental education, paternal substance abuse, and prior marriage and children predicted relationship dissolution among white children of cohabiting parents, but these variables did not predict relationship dissolution among non-white children.

Relationship dissolution can adversely affect the well-being of children. In a study of the impact of parental relationship dissolution on young children, Osborne and McLanahan (2007) found that children born to unmarried parents experienced more parental relationship dissolution and partnership changes than children born to married couples. These partnership changes resulted in increased behavioural problems in children, but the association between partnership changes and behavioural issues was mediated by the level of stress experienced by mothers and the quality of parenting by mothers. The authors suggest that the well-being of children can be enhanced with policies that address maternal stress and relationship instability.

There is some evidence to suggest that cohabiting couples are more gender egalitarian than married couples, particularly in their willingness to resist the idea of the male breadwinner. However, when it comes to the division of unpaid labour, cohabiting couples resemble married couples in that women do a disproportionate amount of unpaid labour. Entries into either cohabiting or marital relationships typically involve women doing more unpaid labour and men doing less unpaid labour (Gupta, 1999; Smock, 2000). Common-law unions are becoming more stable over time and are shaped by socio-demographic factors, regional variation, and time period (Liefbroer and

Dourleijn, 2006). For Canadian children born between 1989 and 2004, Pelletier (2016) found the risk of relationship dissolution converging for common-law and married parents. With the exception of Quebec, residents of other provinces and territories experienced lower rates of divorce but higher rates of common-law relationship dissolution. The risk of divorce was higher when children were conceived before marriage and when stepchildren were present (Pelletier, 2016). Among cohabiting couples, the presence of children and stepchildren was associated with relationship stability.

The fact that most cohabiters have never been married and half of cohabiters marry their partners supports the notion that cohabitation is often a trial phase before marriage (Wilson, 2009). For others, particularly divorced Canadians, cohabitation is an alternative to marriage. In Canada, rates of cohabitation are exceptionally high in Quebec (Laplante, 2014). The high rates of cohabitation in Quebec reflect a rejection of Catholicism (Laplante, 2006, 2014) and increasing secularism. They also reflect stronger family policy such as affordable childcare, flexible eligibility criteria to allow more parents to qualify for parental leave benefits, higher benefit levels, and special leaves for fathers (Tremblay, 2014). Le Bourdais and Lapierre-Adamcyk (2004) argue that there are regional differences in cohabitation, namely that cohabitation represents an alternative to marriage in Quebec, whereas in the rest of Canada cohabitation is often a phase before marriage and childbearing.

There has been an increase in the number of common-law unions among older Canadians, and part of this is because of an increase in all living arrangements due to the large size of the baby boom cohort (Milan et al., 2011). Stigma around cohabitation has declined, and older Canadians are more willing to accept cohabitation. Individuals who started living together when they were in their twenties or thirties may continue to live common-law, and many divorced Canadians are selecting cohabitation over remarriage.

Living Apart Together (LAT)

Couples who are in a relationship but do not live together are referred to as **living apart together (LAT) couples**. LAT relationships are often viewed as a temporary phase prior to cohabitation or marriage. An alternative interpretation is that LAT relationships represent a new family form that allows individuals to experience both the advantages of being part of a couple and preserve their independence and pre-relationship lives, including financial autonomy, pre-existing responsibilities, and investment in family and friends (Duncan and Phillips, 2010). Individuals in LAT relationships may prioritize family and friends over romantic relationships, and maintaining separate households facilitates this independence. Seven percent of Canadians over the age of 20 were in a LAT couple (Turcotte, 2013). It is more common among people in their twenties, and 80 percent of these young adults state that they want to live with their partner one day (Turcotte, 2013). One in three Canadians ages 20 to 24 are in a LAT couple, and many of these young adults live with their parents.

Only 5 percent of Canadians in their thirties are in a LAT relationship. For young adults most LAT relationships are temporary before cohabitation or marriage, whereas for older Canadians this type of relationship lasts longer. For young Canadians the decision to live in separate households is often made because the individuals are pursuing postsecondary education and cannot afford to live together.

An increasing number of older Canadians are pursuing LAT relationships. Of all adults age 60 and older in Canada, the percentage in LAT arrangements grew from 1.8 percent in 2001 to 2.3 percent in 2011 (Turcotte, 2013). Older Canadians may be in a LAT relationship because they cannot find jobs in the same area or simply because they prefer to maintain separate households. The desire to keep finances separate reflects a wish to protect financial assets for children and grandchildren. LAT relationships result from issues related to immigration or health. According to the General Social Survey, 28 percent of LAT couples were apart because their partner had not immigrated to Canada (Turcotte, 2013), 8 percent were apart because their partner was in a nursing home, and 8 percent were apart because their partner was in a medical care facility.

Much of the care that aging Canadians who are facing health issues require is performed informally in the home by a spouse. The rise in older LAT couples raises questions about whether LAT partners will provide the same level of care that spouses normally provide. This question was investigated by De Jong (2015) among a sample of older LAT couples in the Netherlands. Half of the LAT couples anticipated providing medical care to each other if needed in the future, whereas the other half did not think they would rely on each other for care if medical problems arose. More specifically, individuals were willing to provide care to their partner if needed but were not interested in receiving care from their partner should they become ill and need assistance. This represents a departure from the common pattern of spouses providing care to each other when faced with health issues. However, all of the LAT couples in De Jong's (2015) study who had already experienced illness or injury of a partner had provided care to their partner in need. The willingness to provide care reflects the commitment of LAT couples even though they maintain separate homes.

Intersections of Sexual Relationships and Living Arrangements

Living alone can be a temporary and transitional stage to a new relationship or a permanent arrangement, either by choice or because of the end of a relationship or the death of a partner. Among those who live alone are individuals who would prefer to live with a partner but are not in a relationship, individuals who are in a relationship but prefer to live alone or for whom circumstances are preventing them from living with a partner, and individuals who want to live alone regardless of their current or future relationship status. Relationships used to be premised on co-residence, but this is no longer true, as more couples live apart (LAT), either in monogamous or non-monogamous relationships. Some people opt to live alone but have sex either within or outside of a relationship.

Diversity in sexual relationships means that there are more possibilities for individuals in terms of deciding whether and how their sexual relationships might intersect with their relationship status or living arrangements. Among couples who live apart, some involve individuals who have children from previous relationships and prefer not to disrupt their children's lives by merging households. This decision may be based on direct knowledge of their children's wishes and perhaps instances of conflict between different sets of children, which serves as an obstacle to a blended family arrangement. There are individuals who have attempted to cohabit, found that it did not work out, and decided to go back to living separately while maintaining the relationship across two different households. There is greater opportunity for experimentation, as contemporary relationships are more fluid and diverse compared to relationships in the past. Individuals who live alone, even those for whom it is a permanent arrangement, are often embedded in families or relationships. Families and households are not synonymous. Families can exist across households, and as transnational families illustrate, families can overcome vast geographic distance.

Single-Person Households

Lone-person households now outnumber families. Among single-person households, some individuals were once married or cohabiting. The reasons for this trend include greater societal acceptance of living alone, increasing divorce and relationship dissolution, increased financial independence for women, and longer life expectancy. The growing number of people who live alone reflects the fact that many people do not repartner after relationship dissolution or death of a partner (Skew, Evans, and Gray, 2009). Living independently necessitates economic resources, and many Canadians cannot financially sustain a household on their own. Living with a partner reduces the likelihood of poverty due to pooled incomes and shared housing expenses. The financial security of partnership is greater for women who have been in longer marriages or in longer second marriages (van Eeden-Moorefield, Pasley, Dolan, and Engel, 2007).

Canadians may cohabit with a romantic partner or spouse, family member, or roommate because they do not have the financial means to live independently. Individuals who live alone are at greater risk of low income and poverty. Senior women's greater likelihood of living alone has consequences for their economic well-being, as many live on low incomes. Senior women who were not in paid employment earlier in their lives due to childbearing and caregiving face lower retirement income through private company pensions and the Canada Pension Plan. Economic disadvantage is also experienced by single mothers who do not repartner; they are more likely to have low incomes compared to mothers who repartner. The ability to live alone and maintain a high standard of living is a privilege experienced by Canadians with greater economic resources. As more women attain financial independence, the possibilities of living independently expand for women. This represents a significant departure from earlier generations of women who needed marriage for economic survival.

Shifting Societal Views of the Unattached

Just as economic resources facilitate the opportunity of living alone, so too do changes in societal values and ideas about people who remain unattached. At one time there was considerable stigma associated with remaining single, and that stigma coerced men and women into marriage. Mary Louise Adams (1997) has written about the pressure to conform to heterosexual marriage and family life during the height of the Cold War in the 1950s, when there was enormous fear of Russia and fear that Canadians could be influenced by communist thinking or become communists themselves. According to Adams (1997), government officials believed that Canadians who did not conform to traditional marital and family roles were more likely to be communist sympathizers. Government officials were more likely to investigate Canadians who did not fit this model of the good citizen. Gays and lesbians, single people, and even childless couples were viewed with suspicion as possible communists. Gays and lesbians and other non-conformists working in the civil service could and did lose their jobs if they were thought to be communists and threats to national security (Adams, 1997).

The discourse surrounding remaining single, particularly for women, has shifted in a short period of time. In popular culture, singlehood is addressed; sometimes it is critiqued, but it is also celebrated. Celebrities have spoken out on the benefits of remaining unattached and have argued that women should not be defined by their marital or motherhood status (see the box below).

⟫⟫ Female Singlehood

Female singlehood has been highlighted and supported in popular television programs and films such as *Sex and the City* and in bestselling books such as the *New York Times* bestseller *Spinster: Making a Life of One's Own* by Kate Bolick. As mainstream media and celebrities highlight the rewards of remaining single, more unattached people feel supported in their choice. Female celebrities have spoken out on women's roles in society, critiquing the idea that women need to be married or have children to be fulfilled and feel valued. For example, on July 12, 2016, American actress Jennifer Aniston wrote an op-ed in the *Huffington Post* in response to ongoing false tabloid stories about whether she might be pregnant. Her essay argued that women should not be judged on their marital status, childbearing, or appearance and that women can define happiness on their own terms. Similarly, American comedian and actress Chelsea Handler celebrated female singlehood in an editorial she wrote for *Time Magazine* on May 11, 2016. In the editorial, Handler disclosed that she had chosen to remain single and encouraged readers to congratulate rather than question or criticize single women. In true comedic fashion, Handler likened engagement and wedding rings to a "male paperweight" weighing women down.

Apart from celebrities, there are more role models of singlehood today than in the past, which reduces stigma and results in greater numbers of individuals deciding to remain single. The decision to remain single, either temporarily or permanently, may be a strategy used by individuals to meet their own occupational or personal goals. Individuals who do not want to compromise in terms of how they spend time or money, or perhaps do not want to assume the emotional weight of dealing with a partner's personal problems, may opt to remain unattached or pursue casual dating or sexual relationships instead. Some individuals prefer to avoid the financial entanglements that come with cohabitation and marriage. Individuals who have gone through a divorce and experienced financial losses that take years to recover from may decide to live alone in order to avoid the potential of experiencing such financial losses again. Individuals who have lost half of the equity in their home, lost half of the value of their pension, and may pay ongoing child and spousal support may feel that they cannot take the financial risks associated with remarriage. Millennials face the highest student debt in history. Young adults who are saddled with their own debt, or who have painstakingly worked to pay off their debt, may not want to get involved with someone who brings debt to a relationship.

Beyond economic issues, remaining unattached affords autonomy in decision making, particularly when it comes to professional pursuits. In the context of scarce employment opportunities, the need to be geographically mobile in order to get a job, and the ability to travel extensively for some positions, relationships may be seen as an obstacle to professional success. More women today reject the idea that they are defined by their relationship status; they do not feel the need to have a boyfriend or husband as compared to earlier generations. Expectations of a partner are higher today than they were in earlier generations, and people are less willing to settle when it comes to mate selection. People who have lived independently for a period of time may feel less inclined to share their living space if they have grown accustomed to their own space, routines, and habits. New reproductive technologies reduce pressure about when and if children are a possibility, allowing individuals the opportunity to postpone or forego marriage or cohabitation.

As the number of people who live alone or remain unattached increases, societal views shift and there is greater social acceptance of this choice. This creates new possibilities for people to choose to remain unattached, an option that would have been met with stigma and disapproval among earlier generations for whom this was not a realistic option. A small but growing number of single people, and women in particular, are celebrating their singlehood through self-marriage, which is also referred to as **sologamy** (Lytton, 2017). These celebrations reaffirm self-acceptance, autonomy, and self-love yet do not preclude an individual from dating or pursuing relationships in the future. Critics have described sologamy as "a sad trend" and a reflection of women putting their careers ahead of their personal lives (Prestigiamo, 2017), a disturbing perversion of marriage (Justice, 2016), and a reflection of narcissm (Dunetz, 2017).

The Decision to Cohabit, Marry, or Remarry

Decisions about whether to merge households among couples who were previously divorced or bring children into a new relationship are influenced by factors such as whether various family members might get along, existing custody arrangements, and financial considerations. These decisions are also shaped by family law, which can sometimes deter cohabitation or marriage. For example, custody agreements that prohibit a distant residential move may preclude relationship formation among partners who live far apart. Among couples in which one partner has far greater financial resources, maintaining separate households can be a strategy to protect assets in the event of relationship dissolution and to ensure that assets will go to one's own children and grandchildren. This is particularly salient for older Canadians in their fifties, sixties, and seventies who risk losing a lifetime of assets, including a pension, to a failed later-life relationship. Even if the new relationship survives, older Canadians risk losing their assets to their new spouse if they predecease that spouse. This is problematic for older Canadians who prefer that their assets are inherited by their children and grandchildren. If a divorced individual has previously had to equally divide assets such as a matrimonial home with an ex and pay ongoing child or spousal support, they might decide that they do not want to risk additional financial losses in the event of a second divorce. Parents who are paying child support to a former spouse may be required to pay child support to stepchildren in the event of a second divorce. Family law determines the financial consequences of relationship dissolution, and these potential consequences may deter subsequent relationships.

Divorce and Relationship Dissolution

An increasing number of Canadians have experienced relationship dissolution due to the higher rate of divorce, increase in cohabitation, and greater instability of cohabiting relationships as compared to marital relationships. Historically, the Canadian divorce rate was low until legislation was liberalized in 1925, 1968, and 1986 (Sev'er, 1992). Prior to the 1968 Divorce Act, few Canadians could divorce due to social stigma and prohibitive legislation. The 1968 Divorce Act provided "no fault" divorce, and subsequently divorces increased dramatically. In 1986, the Divorce Act was further modified to permit divorce after a one-year separation, and divorces again rose after this new legislation. The divorce rate has been stable in the past two decades. For divorces occurring in 2006, the average age at divorce was 42 years for women and 44 years for men. Thirty-eight percent of Canadian couples divorce by their thirtieth anniversary, and 30 percent of Canadian children experience a parental separation or divorce before the age of 16 (Ambert, 2012; Juby et al., 2004; Sev'er, 1992; Wu and Schimmele, 2009). The fact that a sizable number of children will experience a parental separation or divorce before reaching the age of 16 means that family change is normative for many young Canadians (Juby et al., 2004).

The likelihood of getting a divorce is higher for individuals who get married younger—for instance, in their late teens or early twenties—and for people who have a low level of educational attainment (Clark and Crompton, 2006). Couples who live together before marriage have higher rates of divorce than couples who do not (Xu, Hudspeth, and Bartkowski, 2006), and this might reflect the fact that individuals who choose to cohabit have more liberal views toward the institution of marriage and divorce (Clark and Crompton, 2006; Le Bourdais, Neill, and Turcotte, 2000). In the same way that premarital cohabitation increases the risk of divorce, post-divorce cohabitation also increases the risk of a second divorce (Xu et al., 2006). The idea that relationships that follow too quickly after a divorce (sometimes referred to as rebound relationships because of the speed with which they take place) are likely to fail is not supported by research that analyzed the timing of subsequent relationships and second divorces (Wolfinger, 2007).

Marriages of longer duration have a lower likelihood of divorce than marriages of shorter duration, and the presence of children is associated with a lower rate of divorce among first marriages (Clark and Crompton, 2006). Couples who attend religious services have a lower rate of divorce than couples who do not attend religious services (Clark and Crompton, 2006; Jensen, Shafer, Guo, and Larson, 2017). The economic benefit of remarriage is greater for women than it is for men (Ozawa and Yoon, 2002). Infidelity can lead to divorce, and women are more likely to initiate divorce if their husband has been unfaithful (Amato and Previti, 2003). Infidelity has also been linked to the relative incomes of husbands and wives; when men are the breadwinners they are more likely to cheat, whereas when women are the breadwinners they are less likely to cheat (Munsch, 2015). Breadwinning wives' fidelity may be a strategy that women engage in to deal with concern about violating gender norms and straining marital relations (Munsch, 2015). Economically dependent spouses are more likely to cheat, and this is true for both men and women, leading Munsch (2015) to argue that economically dependent spouses cheat to regain equity in the relationship. However, the relationship between economic dependency and infidelity is stronger for men, perhaps reflecting the fact that economic dependency may undermine masculinity and self-identity. Cheating is a strategy that economically dependent men may use to distance themselves from the reality of having a breadwinning wife (Munsch, 2015).

Marital dissolution is linked to opportunities for infidelity and opportunities for married people to find a new partner. South and Lloyd (1995) found that the risk of divorce is higher for married couples living in areas that have higher numbers of unmarried women in the workplace. Women in the workplace increase interactions between married men and unmarried or married women where infidelity can occur and new partners can be chosen (South and Lloyd, 1995). Women's increased labour force participation and postsecondary education raise the marriage age, which increases the supply of unmarried women in the workplace. Thus, a greater number of unmarried women in the workplace increase the probability of married men seeking a divorce because they have found an alternative to their wife (South and Lloyd, 1995).

In a study of married couples who divorced, Amato and Hohmann-Marriott (2007) found that some were high-conflict marriages and others were low-conflict marriages. Divorces happened in both high-conflict and low-conflict marriages; both groups shared similar risk factors, such as young age at marriage, having divorced parents, believing in divorce, the presence of stepchildren, cohabiting with other partners prior to the marriage, and holding more liberal views (Amato and Hohmann-Marriott, 2007). Amato and Hohmann-Marriott (2007) suggest that individuals in high-conflict marriages resort to divorce because of poor relationship quality, whereas individuals in low-conflict marriages divorce because of a weak commitment to marriage and the existence of alternative partners. In fact, the majority of individuals in the low-conflict group who divorced had engaged in infidelity and had new partners before their divorce. Divorce is associated with both positive and negative health outcomes. These outcomes may be associated with the quality of the marital relationship; Amato and Hohmann-Marriott (2007) found higher happiness levels among individuals who had been in high-conflict marriages, whereas individuals who had been in low-conflict marriages experienced declines in happiness after divorce.

Divorce is linked to inequality in housework, unmet expectations (Riessman, 1990), and how couples spend time together (Kalil and Rege, 2015). In a study of American couples who had divorced, Riessman (1990) found that couples divorced because their spouse did not meet their expectations for a marriage based on companionship and shared interests. Men had expectations of emotional exclusivity with their wives and were unhappy when their wives spent too much time with others, including friends and family. Wives, on the other hand, did not have the same expectation of emotional exclusivity. Australian researchers found that time spent together having family meals was a significant predictor of divorce (Kalil and Rege, 2015). Eating dinner together improved how women evaluated their marriages and improved their mental health. All of these factors—time spent eating meals together, perceptions of satisfaction with the marriage, and better mental health—reduced relationship dissolution.

Are the predictors of relationship dissolution the same for married and cohabiting couples? Some predictors, such as young age at onset of relationship, short duration of relationship, and parental divorce, are similar for married and cohabiting couples. Tach and Edin (2013) found that marriages were more likely than cohabiting relationships to end due to relationship and financial problems. Tach and Edin (2013) suggest that the greater resiliency of cohabiting relationships to withstand financial and relationship problems reflects the very high standards that individuals have for marriage. Individuals who cohabit believe in a "marriage bar," which is a threshold at which a divorce would be warranted (if they were married). Cohabiters are willing to stay in a cohabiting relationship despite financial and relationship problems, but they understand that they would not tolerate these problems if they were married. Cohabiters tolerate problematic circumstances because their expectations of a cohabiting relationship are more flexible; what they will tolerate in a cohabiting relationship is not something they would tolerate in a marriage (Tach and Edin, 2013).

Relationships are complicated, and couples may break up and get back together again; some may stay in the relationship after a reconciliation, whereas others may break up a second time after experiencing a reconciliation. Couples can experience multiple breakups and reconciliations that can be of any duration. The term *on–off* has been used colloquially to describe couples who experience a series of breakups and reconciliations. Moreover, some people have had sex with a former partner, which may or may not lead to a reconciliation. Binstock and Thornton (2003) found that for a majority of individuals, either cohabiting or married, a breakup due to conflict was a strong predictor of permanent relationship dissolution. Marriages were characterized by greater stability than cohabiting relationships, including experiences of breakups and reconciliations (Binstock and Thornton, 2003). Cohabiting couples who later married experienced greater stability in their relationships, including higher rates of reconciliation after marriage. In a study of sexually active teens, Halpern-Meekin, Manning, Giordano, and Longmore (2013) found high rates of relationship instability, breakups, reconciliations, and individuals having sex with an ex. Half of the teens had experienced breakup and reconciliation, and more than 25 percent had had sex with a former boyfriend or girlfriend after a breakup.

Remarriage and Blended Families

High divorce rates have made remarriage more common. While second marriages have a higher rate of divorce than first marriages (Jensen et al., 2017), the risk of divorce declines as age at remarriage rises (Clark and Crompton, 2006). The higher rate of divorce in second marriages reflects selection effects, such as level of religiosity, which increase the likelihood of divorce, rather than a direct causal link between marriage order and divorce (Jensen et al., 2017). As the age of marriage has increased, so too has the average age of divorced men and women. Remarriage typically happens in the mid to late forties for individuals who have previously divorced, whereas it happens later, in the late fifties, for Canadians who have been widowed (Milan et al., 2011). Women are less likely to remarry following the death of a spouse as compared to men (Schimmele and Wu, 2016; Watkins and Waldron, 2017). Only 5 percent of widows remarry as compared to 24 percent of widowers (Schimmele and Wu, 2016). Canadian and European women are less likely to repartner following the dissolution of a cohabiting relationship or marriage, particularly if they have children (Poortman and Hewitt, 2015). Following divorce, men are more likely to repartner and remarry than women and do so more quickly (Schimmele and Wu, 2016). There has been an increase in the number of divorced Canadians who do not cohabit or remarry following divorce, and this is more common among single parents and women. An increasing number of previously divorced Canadians opt for cohabitation rather than marriage.

The likelihood of remarriage is lower for single mothers, even those with adult children living in the home. Women's caregiving of young children reduces the time available for dating, whereas adult children in the home provide companionship that may change women's feelings about dating or repartnership. Women find the social support they need living with adult children and may not want to risk a new partner who has the potential to disrupt daily routines, use up resources of time and money, add domestic labour to a single mother's already heavy workload, or damage existing family relationships and harmony. The introduction of a husband or cohabiting partner can risk women's emotional or financial stability and have consequences for their children. A family unit of mother and child(ren) that has functioned smoothly and happily without a husband or male partner is an accomplishment that many women are proud of and have no interest in jeopardizing.

Blended families occur when individuals with children from previous relationships merge households. Blended families are more unstable than families that do not involve stepchildren (Cherlin, 2009; White and Booth, 1985). Blended families face challenges such as differences in parenting styles and difficulties between children and step-parents and step-siblings (Cherlin, 2009; White and Booth, 1985). Blended families report having greater financial problems as compared to nonblended families (Vezina, 2012). In a Statistics Canada study asking people whether they had not been able to pay one or more bills such as rent, mortgage, or utilities, blended families reported greater difficulty in meeting all household bills and financial obligations (Vezina, 2012). Financial difficulty may stem from larger family size or may reflect the long-term economic disadvantage of previous relationship dissolution. Relationship dissolution, whether the relationship is cohabiting or marital, is costly, as individuals are confronted with various costs such as moving, legal costs associated with union dissolution and the selling and buying of a new home, child support, and spousal support. It may be that these costs create financial setbacks that are difficult to recover from or that take a long time to recover from.

The decisions people make about relationship formation, cohabitation, marriage, or remarriage are shaped by family law. Even though prenuptial and cohabitation agreements are possibilities for individuals who come into a relationship with a higher net worth and want to preserve this for themselves, and possibly for their children and grandchildren, these agreements can be challenged. The costs associated with going to court may make some people provide a financial settlement despite having a prenuptial or cohabitation agreement or may make some people decide not to cohabit. Decisions such as whether to live with a partner are affected by the rules of family law. For instance, a new marriage makes any pre-existing will invalid, and some Canadians have seen the estates of their parents and grandparents inherited by new spouses, even new spouses of marriages of short duration.

LGBTQ Couples and Families

Same-sex married couples were first counted in the census in 2006 after same-sex marriage was legalized in 2005. Same-sex cohabitation and marriage, with and without children, have increased in Canada. The number of same-sex married couples tripled between the 2006 Census and the 2011 Census, and the number of same-sex common-law couples increased 15 percent (Statistics Canada, 2015a). The raising of children by LGBTQ parents predates same-sex marriage legislation, but it has been only recently that same-sex parents are able to foster and adopt children through the Children's Aid Society. Despite this change in legislation, LGBTQ adoptive parents face barriers to adoption (Ross et al., 2008).

Same-sex couples represent about 0.8 percent of all couples in Canada, which is comparable to the rate in other countries (Milan, 2013). According to the 2011 Census, 68 percent of same-sex couples are common-law couples and 33 percent are married (Statistics Canada, 2011a). There are more male same-sex couples than female same-sex couples; 55 percent are male couples and 46 percent are female couples (Statistics Canada, 2011a). Same-sex couples tend to be younger than opposite-sex couples. Ten percent of same-sex couples are raising children (Statistics Canada, 2011a).

LGBTQ parents are often more educated and established and tend to plan their children and pregnancies; these characteristics in and of themselves are associated with better outcomes for children, regardless of the sexual orientation of parents (Biblarz and Stacey, 2010). Research on lesbian families suggests that some involve the added participation of men who were chosen as sperm donors; these men play an active role in the lives of their children, who receive support from three parental figures (Dunne, 1997, 1998). LGBTQ couples are characterized by greater sharing of unpaid labour, caregiving, and paid employment as compared to heterosexual couples (Bauer, 2016; Civettini, 2016; Dunne, 1998; Gotta et al., 2011; Nelson, 1996). Dunne (1998) found that the lesbian couples she studied rejected materialism and high standards of housework to achieve better work–life balance. The women were devoted to caregiving while maintaining financial independence by working part-time. The preservation of financial independence among these lesbian couples challenges the conventional pattern of couples prioritizing the career of a higher-earning spouse at the expense of a lower-earning spouse.

LGBTQ families may provide children with greater opportunities to challenge traditional gender role expectations (Averett, 2016; Biblarz and Stacey, 2010; Epstein, 1999), but these processes are also shaped by class, race, and other variables. In a study of LGBTQ parents, Averett (2016) found that while parents wanted to challenge traditional processes of gender socialization—for instance, in toy and clothing selec-tion—their social location shaped the extent to which they explicitly challenged tradi-tional ideas about gender. Race, social class, and family and community support shaped parents' willingness to challenge traditional gender socialization processes (Averett, 2016). White, higher-income parents with family and community support were most willing to challenge gender socialization practices, while visible minority, lower socio-economic status parents without family or community support were less able to challenge these socialization practices. Averett's (2016) research highlights the importance of social location and intersecting inequalities in understanding family processes and parenting practices. In a study of LGBTQ youth raised by lesbian or bisexual mothers, Kuvalanka and Goldberg (2009) found that LGBTQ parents positively affect children's sexual and gender identity development, but that societal pressure and scrutiny adversely affected LGBTQ youth. Some of the LGBTQ youth felt pressure to be gender conforming and heterosexual because of their mother's sexual orientation.

Research on LGBTQ families suggests that many have created new families and extended family based on close friends and, to a lesser extent, supportive members of the family of origin. Yet LGBTQ families remain constrained by the past and by traditional notions of family and blood relations as reflected in research which suggests that biological grandparents of lesbian parents are more involved in the lives of their grandchildren as compared to nonbiological grandparents (Nelson, 2000). Opponents of LGBTQ families have argued that children are adversely affected by being raised by same-sex parents and have argued that the sexual orientation of parents should be considered in child custody cases. Research comparing children raised by same-sex parents and opposite-sex parents finds no differences that would warrant discrimination against a parent based on sexual orientation (Biblarz and Stacey, 2010). Children raised by same-sex parents are similar to those raised by opposite-sex parents in terms of various outcomes, such as mental health, academic achievement, behavioural issues, and quality of parent–child relationships (Biblarz and Stacey, 2010). In a study of parents of LGBTQ children, parents reported closer parent–child and family relationships along with other positive aspects of raising an LGBTQ child (Gonzalez, Rostosky, Odom, and Riggle, 2013). The fact that children raised by LGBTQ parents have done so well despite the social stigma and discrimination they face is a testament to the quality of parenting by LGBTQ parents. Much of the explanation for why children of LGBTQ parents do well relates to the fact that same-sex parents tend to differ from heterosexual parents in ways other than sexual orientation that make them good parents. Among opposite-sex parents, there are higher proportions of unplanned pregnancies, young parents, and parents with low socio-economic status, and these factors are associated with poorer outcomes for children.

Wider societal homophobia affects LGBTQ parents who face stigma and discrimination. In a study of LGBTQ parents of disabled children, Gibson (2016) found that parents experienced challenges in trying to access services and support for their children. To receive support, such as a tax credit, children require a diagnosis, and this means that parents must fill out many forms and deal with professionals to get a diagnosis. LGBTQ parents reported having to navigate a problematic system that includes homophobic professionals and outdated forms that assume opposite-sex parents. LGBTQ parents understand that assessments are read by future school and health professionals who may be biased due to the inclusion of unnecessary information such as the sexual orientation of parents or that a child was donor conceived.

A history of some LGBTQ individuals being pathologized makes them concerned about getting a diagnosis for their child because they worry that a label may harm their child (Gibson, 2016).

Childbearing and Parenting

Childbearing and parenting are no longer inextricably linked to intimate relationships and marriage. There has been a long-term trend of declining fertility and smaller families in Canada. Most families today are one-child or two-children families. The trend of declining fertility is linked to delayed marriage and childbearing, which shortens women's reproductive years; women's paid employment; the high costs of raising a child; higher rates of relationship dissolution; and greater access to contraception and abortion. Approximately 100 104 abortions were performed in clinics and hospitals in 2015 (Abortion Rights Coalition of Canada, 2017). A significant trend in parenting is the increased involvement by fathers in childcare. This includes an increase in the number of fathers taking parental leave (Marshall, 2008), especially in Quebec (Statistics Canada, 2015b); an increase in single fathers; and the increasing prevalence of stay-at-home fathers (Doucet, 2006).

Reproductive technologies, such as in vitro fertilization (IVF), offer new possibilities for creating life and in the process transform how we define and understand parenthood. Increasingly, parenthood is detached from biology as individuals and couples who cannot reproduce biologically use adoption, surrogates, and sperm, egg, and embryo donors (Baker, 2009). While still relatively rare, **embryo adoption** allows different sets of parents to raise genetic siblings. The adopted embryos are extra embryos from couples who have used IVF but have completed their families and do not wish to have any more children. These embryos are implanted in another woman or in multiple women, creating genetic siblings. Some of these parents may decide to foster a relationship between siblings raised in different homes (Teotonio, 2017). Collard and Kashmeri (2011) conducted interviews with men and women who had participated in embryo adoption in California either as adoptive parents or as donor (placing) parents and found variation in how relationships between genetic siblings were understood and managed. Parents wanted to wait until their children were older to disclose embryo adoption and the nature of the genetic sibling relationship. Not all of the placing or adoptive parents explicitly referred to genetic siblings as siblings; siblings were also presented as friends or cousins. Collard and Kashmeri (2011) described how some of the placing and adoptive parents did not pursue contact between the genetic siblings and favoured delaying the sibling relationship until the children were older.

Marriage and fertility are becoming increasingly uncoupled; more people have children outside of marriage, either as single parents or in a cohabiting relationship, and an increasing number of married couples are voluntarily childless. Childless marriages offer a challenge to the traditional idea that having children is the goal of marriage and that children provide marital satisfaction and fulfillment. Although childlessness has increased internationally since World War II, rates of childlessness were also high for people born between 1880 and 1910 (Rowland, 2007). Thus, high rates of childlessness are not new. Voluntarily childless couples face stigma and are sometimes viewed as selfish, as illustrated in a 2012 *National Post* article titled "Trend of Couples Not Having Children Just Plain Selfish" (O'Connor, 2012). Park (2002) found that voluntarily childless men and women face social stigma and engage in a variety of strategies when interacting with others to deflect that stigma, including denying that their childlessness is voluntary. Survey data from 25 European countries asking participants for their views on voluntarily childless couples found a double standard in that men were judged more harshly for being voluntarily childless as compared to women (Rijken and Merz, 2014). It may be that women who choose not to have children are judged less harshly because the costs of childbearing and caregiving are generally greater for women whose paid employment and career success may be adversely affected by motherhood. Voluntary childlessness is more common among women with higher levels of education; no relationship between education and childlessness exists among men (Waren and Pals, 2013). Moreover, voluntarily childless women have higher income and socio-economic status, more work experience, and lower levels of religiosity as compared to other women (Abma and Martinez, 2006). In an analysis of increasing childlessness in the United States, Hayford (2013) found that the increase in unmarried women was the largest factor explaining increasing childlessness, followed by an increase in women pursuing post-secondary education.

The proportion of families with children has decreased over time. The number of households consisting of couples without children exceeded the number of households with children for the first time in the 2006 Census. This trend continued and intensified with the 2011 Census (Statistics Canada, 2012b). These census data include empty nesters, individuals who have children who live with a previous partner, and adults who may have children in the future. More families are pursuing unconventional parenting arrangements, sometimes outside the traditional boundaries of an intimate romantic relationship. **Co-parenting** arrangements facilitate parenting by two individuals who are not in a relationship. Co-parenting arrangements can be informal or formal and can be established before the birth of a child or after; for instance, in 2017 two best friends fought a legal battle to be officially recognized as co-parents to one of the woman's disabled son (Ireton, 2017). It is the first time in Canadian history that two friends have been legally recognized as parents. Co-parenting may also occur in multifamily households—for instance, where two nuclear families, related or not, share a home. Multifamily households may or may not be biologically related and may include multigenerational families. Multigenerational families are increasing in Canada; between 2001 and 2011, there was a 40 percent increase in multigenerational families in Canada (Battams, 2017). Co-parenting by related and unrelated adults also occurs in a myriad of unconventional families.

For example, one of the unconventional families studied by Fox and Fumia (2001) included a grandmother, her two adult daughters, and a grandchild. More children are being raised by multiple parents: blended families with one or more step-parents, same-sex families (e.g., children raised by lesbian mothers who co-parent with the children's biological father), and children raised by multiple adults in polyamorous, or multipartner, relationships.

Adoptions are increasingly common and can take different forms, such as closed or open (where the identity of birth parents is known to children), and some adoptive parents may agree to allow birth parents to participate in the life of their biological child (Goldberg, Kinkler, Richardson, and Downing, 2011). Single parents and couples of any sexual orientation can adopt (Goldberg, Smith, and Perry-Jenkins, 2012; Goldberg et al., 2011; Raleigh, 2012). Research by Hamilton, Cheng, and Powell (2007) finds high levels of parental investment in adopted children, challenging previous sociological explanations that predicted parental investments would be strongest in parent–child relationships based on biological connection. Adoptions can be domestic or transnational. Transnational adoption has been critiqued on the basis that it reinforces inequalities between the Global South and Global North. In interviews with 30 Canadian women who had adopted one or more children from China, Lockerbie (2014) found that infertility led women to adopt and that these women invoked pregnancy metaphors in describing their adoption processes. Lockerbie (2014) argues that the value of biological parent–child relations is maintained due to the emphasis placed on infertility, adoption after all options for having biological children were unsuccessful, and the use of pregnancy metaphors.

DIVERSITY IN SEXUAL RELATIONSHIPS

There is unprecedented diversity in sexual relationships as individuals have more partners throughout their lives and more Canadians experience sexual activity outside of a relationship context. The lives of most Canadians, in young adulthood through their senior years, are characterized by serial monogamy. Serial monogamy refers to having one monogamous relationship at a time; however, a person might have a number of different partners over a lifetime because of relationship breakup, divorce, or death of a partner. Yet non-monogamy is a reality for both unattached and partnered individuals of all sexual orientations. Many individuals, some of whom are previously divorced, opt for dating rather than maintaining a monogamous relationship with one person.

Sexual relations occur outside of a relationship context. This is true not only for childless singles; single parents may opt for sexual relations outside of a relationship in order to maintain a separation between their family roles and their sex lives. The time pressures of single parenting may preclude romantic relationships, while some individuals prefer to have sex outside of a relationship context. These sexual relationships take varying forms, including "one-night stands" or "hookups" for casual sex (Bogle, 2008; Paul, McManus, and Hayes, 2000) and "friends with benefits" (Epstein, Calzo, Smiler, and Ward, 2009), where two people who already know each other participate in a temporary or ongoing sexual relationship without the requirement of a relationship or monogamy. Casual sex or sex outside of a relationship context is also common among adolescents. Among sexually active teens, sexual experiences occur in romantic or dating relationships and also outside of a relationship or dating context (Manning, Longmore, and Giordano, 2005). A majority of teens are having sex, and a majority of sexually active teens have had a sexual experience in a non-romantic relationship (Manning, Giordano, and Longmore, 2006; Manning et al., 2005). In a study of casual sex among young adult Americans, Lyons, Manning, Giordano, and Longmore (2013) found an inverse relationship between educational attainment and casual sex; more highly educated respondents had fewer casual sex partners. Yet the relationship between educational attainment and number of casual sex partners was mediated by attitudes toward sex and casual sex.

While the term *casual sex* may be fairly recent, its practice is not a new social phenomena (Reay, 2014). Despite the paucity of information about nonmarital sex in earlier historical periods, we know that both men and women engaged in premarital sexual activity before the sexual revolution of the 1960s (Reay, 2014). The famous Kinsey reports, the first scientific study of sexual activity conducted in the 1940s, uncovered considerable premarital sexual activity among men and women (Kinsey, Pomeroy, and Martin, 1948; Kinsey, Pomeroy, Martin, and Gebhard, 1953). The term *casual sex* was not used, but other terms such as *petting* were used and referred to all kinds of sexual activity excluding sexual intercourse. Petting with multiple people was prevalent among both men and women; thus, many women who were technically virgins when they married had considerable sexual experience prior to marriage (Kinsey et al., 1953).

Polygamy

Polygamy involves being married to more than one person at a time (Canada, Department of Justice, 2006; Eichler, 2012) and is prohibited by Canadian law (Omand, 2017). **Polygyny** is the marriage of one husband to multiple wives (Sociology Dictionary, 2017). **Polyandry** is marriage between one woman and more than one husband. The term **group marriage** has been used to describe a marriage involving multiple husbands and wives. Polygamy gained media attention in Canada when members of the Mormon community of Bountiful in British Columbia were prosecuted for polygamy (Heath, 2016); specifically, they were practising polygyny involving one man and multiple wives. One of the men charged was Winston Blackmore, head of Bountiful (Crawley, 2017). He was accused of marrying 24 women, one of whom was only 15 at the time she married (Crawley, 2017). Mormons refer to polygyny as plural marriage. The polygamists argued that plural marriage reflected their Mormon fundamentalism and that prosecution violated their right to religious freedom. The courts ruled against polygamy and argued that it adversely affected children and women. Protection for women and children was motivated by the young age of some of the wives and concern that legalization of polygamy would put teens at risk of exploitation and abuse (Eichler, 2012). The court ruling stated that the law should not be used to criminalize the teen wives in polygamous marriages or individuals involved in polyamorous relationships (Eichler, 2012). The Mormons of Bountiful are not the only Canadians who practise polygyny; the practice is also found among a small number of Muslim Canadians (Javed, 2008).

Polyamory

Polyamory involves intimate relationships between multiple partners where the relationships are agreed upon and transparent and where both men and women have access to additional partners outside of a committed relationship. Relationships are typically organized such that individuals negotiate specific rules such as safe-sex practices and schedules (Scheff, 2014). Polyamorous relationships vary in terms of the number of individuals involved and the duration of these relationships (Boyd, 2017). Unlike polygamists, polyamorists are not always married, and unlike in polygamy, where wives are expected to be monogamous to their husband, both female and male polyamorists are non-monogamous (Scheff, 2014). Polyamory is further differentiated from polygamy in the degree of gender equality that exists, as both men and women are able to pursue sexual intimacy with other partners. In contrast to polygamy, which is often based on religion and includes marriage, polyamory is not based on religion and does not always include a marital relationship (Boyd, 2017). Polyamorous relationships are most common in Australia, Canada, the United States, and Western Europe (Scheff, 2014).

Polyamorists engage in a variety of relationships that involve both sexual and emotional intimacy; however, it is not always the case that an individual in a polyamorous relationship will have sexual intimacy with his or her partner's partner. The term *polyaffectivity* was coined by Elisabeth Scheff (2014) to describe emotionally intimate but sexually platonic relationships within a polyamorous grouping. For instance, an individual might be emotionally intimate but sexually platonic with his or her partner's partner. There is tremendous variety and polyaffectivity does not exist in all polyamorous relationships. Polyamorous relationships vary in terms of the number of partners, duration of relationships, and experiences of sexual and emotional intimacy between partners (Boyd, 2017; Scheff, 2014). Some individuals who engage in polyamory are raising children (Boyd, 2017; Scheff, 2014), and the degree to which polyamorous adults co-parent children varies. What distinguishes polyamorous relationships from other kinds of non-monogamous relationships is that they are consensual, transparent, and negotiated.

Some couples who become polyamorous return to monogamy. They may do so for a variety of reasons, including unsuccessful relationships or dissatisfaction with polyamory (Boyd, 2017; Scheff, 2014). Polyamory challenges long-standing and deeply entrenched ideas about the sanctity of marriage premised on monogamy. It also challenges ideas about sexual jealousy and partner satisfaction. Polyamorists sometimes refer to **compersion**—the happiness they experience when their partner finds love and happiness with someone else (Scheff, 2014). Compersion contrasts with sexual jealousy, which is associated with infidelity in monogamous relationships.

Non-monogamy

Polyamory can be distinguished from non-monogamous sexual relationships—either infidelity in monogamous relationships or consensual non-monogamous relationships (see the box below). Non-monogamous sexual activity is sometimes referred to as "swinging" or "partner swapping," whereby single people and partners in relationships engage in sexual activities with others. The emphasis in swinging is

>>> Polyamory

Statistics on the prevalence of polyamory—consensual, transparent, multipartner relationships—are unavailable, and individuals in polyamorous relationships may hide their relationships due to social stigma and fear of repercussions such as harassment or loss of friends, family, or job. A study of 547 individuals who were currently or had previously been in a polyamorous relationship found that polyamorists are generally younger, are more highly educated, and have higher incomes as compared to the general Canadian population (Boyd, 2017). Twice as many of the respondents identified as female, and approximately equal numbers of respondents indicated that they were heterosexual or bisexual (Boyd, 2017). Sixty-five percent of survey respondents said that their relationship involved three people, 18 percent said their relationship involved four people, and 14 percent said that their relationship involved six or more people (Boyd, 2017). Living arrangements also varied, with 20 percent of respondents reporting that the members of the relationship lived together, 44 percent reporting that they lived in two households, and 22 percent reporting that they lived in three households (Boyd, 2017). Twenty-three percent of respondents had a child living in the home full-time, and 9 percent had a child living in the home part-time.

Polyamory is likely to affect social policy and family law in the future. Family law related to issues of relationship dissolution such as the division of property and assets, spousal support, and child support has the potential to be challenged to accommodate polyamorous relationships (Boyd, 2017). For example, upon relationship dissolution, child support or spousal support from more than one relationship partner may be sought. Pensions, government plans (such as the Canada Pension Plan survivor benefit and Old Age Security spousal allowance), medical benefits, and tax deductions for dependent partners are currently oriented to two-person relationships, and they have the potential to be challenged by polyamorous relationships (Boyd, 2017).

on sexual activity rather than on building emotionally supportive and emotionally intimate relationships. Swinging focuses on sexual variety and is often less accepting of emotional intimacy (Scheff, 2014). Some couples who swing explicitly forbid emotional intimacy with additional sexual partners (Scheff, 2014). Early research on swinging suggested that it reflected men's greater power and decision making in marriage (Henshel, 1973) and that men were more likely to initiate conversations and decisions about swinging. More recent research challenges the idea that married women are coerced into swinging by their husbands (Bergstrand and Williams, 2000) and suggests that husbands and wives report equal levels of satisfaction with swinging (Fernandes, 2009).

MONEY MANAGEMENT

Relationship Status

Money management practices such as joint versus separate bank accounts vary across different types of families and relationships (Burgoyne and Morison, 1997; Fishman, 1983; Lown and Dolan, 1995; Singh and Lindsay, 1996; Treas, 1993). Relationship length and status shape how couples organize their banking, spending, and saving. The pooling of incomes into joint accounts is more typical in relationships of longer duration and among married couples than among cohabiting couples (Singh and Lindsay, 1996; Vogler, 2005). Perceptions of relationship permanence shape whether individuals view incomes as jointly or separately owned. Separate bank accounts are more common among new relationships (Colavecchia, 2005), common-law relationships (Heimdal and Houseknecht, 2003; Singh and Lindsay, 1996; Treas and Widmer, 2000; Vogler, 2005), and relationships where one or both spouses have previously been divorced (Burgoyne and Morison, 1997; Fishman, 1983; Lown and Dolan, 1995; Pasley, Sandras, and Edmondson, 1994). The way that separate accounts are used varies by gender; women are more likely to use separate bank accounts for collective expenditures, such as to save for family vacations, whereas men are more likely to use separate bank accounts for personal expenditures (Burgoyne, 1990; Pahl, 1999; Tichenor, 1999; Treas, 1993). This is consistent with the finding that women are more family focused in their spending (Blumberg, 1991; Nyman, 1999; Pahl, 1999; Phipps and Burton, 1998; Stamp, 1985; Wilson, 1987).

The opening of a joint bank account, or a shift toward viewing individual income as collective money, may accompany the transition to a cohabiting or marital relationship (Lyssens-Danneboom and Mortelmans, 2014; Singh and Lindsay, 1996). In a study of LAT couples in Belgium, Lyssens-Danneboom and Mortelmans (2014) found that couples who anticipated cohabitation were more likely to engage in financial support of each other as compared to couples who anticipated that they would continue to maintain separate households. As some of the relationships headed in the direction of cohabitation, money was viewed in collective terms. An important gender difference was noted; LAT women with children were unwilling to give money or belongings to a partner, even one who they anticipated living with. These women viewed their income as money for themselves and their children.

Gender and Economic Inequality

Many women experience economic inequality in intimate relationships, which can include lower levels of personal spending as compared to that of husbands or partners, financial deprivation, lack of access to a male partner's income, and lack of decision-making power over financial matters (Ayers and Lambertz, 1986; Colavecchia, 2005; Fleming, 1997; Pahl, 1999; Vogler and Pahl, 1994; Wilson, 1987; Woolley and Marshall, 1994). One of the ways that a woman can experience economic inequality is through adoption of the allowance system, whereby a woman does not have access to her male partner's income but instead receives a monthly or weekly allowance. The allowance system, while less common today, is associated with economic inequality for women. Vogler, Brockmann, and Wiggins (2006) found that cohabiting couples who shared a biological child were the most likely to use the allowance system and that women experienced financial deprivation with this particular allocative system.

The system of partial pooling whereby couples keep incomes in separate bank accounts but contribute equally to shared household expenses has increased alongside increases in cohabitation and female labour force participation. However, given that women earn less than men on average, partial pooling systems reinforce women's economic inequality since contributions to shared expenses are not proportional to income, resulting in lower levels of personal spending and saving for women (Vogler et al., 2006). Drawing on British data from 1994 and 2002, Vogler Brockmann, and Wiggins (2006) investigated whether relationship status and money management were related and found that partial pooling had increased, particularly among childless cohabiting couples who had significant differences in income. Childless couples with similar incomes were more likely to use joint accounts and not keep incomes separate. Partial pooling puts a lower-earning spouse at a disadvantage, and because women typically earn less than men, partial pooling systematically disadvantages women.

Vogler, Lyonette, and Wiggins (2008) argue that even though electronic banking has changed how people manage their money, gender-based inequalities in control over finances and financial decision making persist, even among cohabiting couples who articulate values of sharing and equality in their relationships. Money can cause conflict in a relationship, and Vogler, Lyonette, and Wiggins (2008) found that unilateral decisions about spending lead to dissatisfaction with the relationship and with life in general. They suggest that intimate relationships are increasingly coming to resemble business relationships in so far as couples adhere to a 50/50 strategy of sharing collective expenditures even when significant income differentials exist. When large income differentials are not considered, lower-earning individuals can experience a lack of financial equality in their ability to spend and save.

Research on women's experiences of financial deprivation in marriage parallels research on family food consumption, which indicates that in order to save money, some women serve their husbands more food and better-quality food than they serve themselves and their children (DeVault, 1991). Early sociologists like Rowntree (1910) wrote about the "**secondary poverty**" that women experienced as a result of men not sharing their pay equitably with their families. Young (1952) argued that when husbands gave inadequate spending allowances to their wives, this left wives with no choice but to seek paid employment. Male entitlement to personal spending money is also found in more contemporary descriptions of family life (Cantillon and Nolan, 2001; Pahl, 1999; Stamp, 1985; Vogler and Pahl, 1994; Woolley and Marshall, 1994). Women's restraint in personal spending often follows the transition to parenthood (Colavecchia, 2009; Nyman, 1999).

Financial practices such as the type of bank accounts used vary according to the relative incomes of each partner (Phipps and Burton, 1998). Women in paid employment may have greater involvement in financial management (Cheal, 1993; Fleming, 1997) and have greater access to their husbands' wages, but women who outearn their husbands do not always use their higher earnings to claim greater power in the marital relationship (Hertz, 1986; Tichenor, 1999). The fact that women's higher earnings do not translate into higher levels of personal spending or greater control over financial decision making, as is the case for men, reflects gender norms in society. West and Zimmerman's (1987) conceptualization of "doing gender" is useful for understanding how women with higher earnings achieve a more conventional marriage by deferring to husbands over money matters and not using their economic power to claim greater decision-making power in the marriage. Pooling incomes into joint accounts can obscure a woman's higher earnings (McRae, 1987) and has been cited as a means for women to minimize their own power in the marital relationship and to protect a husband's self-respect (Hertz, 1986; McRae, 1987; Pahl, 1999). Another strategy used by wives to avoid having too much power is to relinquish control over family finances (Hertz, 1986; McRae, 1987). Hertz described some women as being "squeamish" (Hertz, 1986: 104) about money and not wanting to understand finances even when husbands wanted them to be more actively involved. This is consistent with Wilson's (1987) finding that women who earned high incomes and managed their finances prior to marriage are unwilling to get involved in financial matters after they marry.

Money and Economic Exploitation

In the past, marriage provided economic opportunism that was experienced by entire families, as individuals would marry within their own social class to solidify each family's social standing. Homogamy refers to marriage between two people who share similar backgrounds in terms of socio-economic status, but it also extends to include socio-demographic variables such as race, ethnicity, culture, and religion. Historically, parents had an interest in ensuring that their children married within the same social class. Economic opportunism within relationships and marriages still exists but is more likely to be experienced by individuals who "marry up" rather than by entire families. "Marrying up" occurs when an individual of lower socio-economic status marries an individual of higher socio-economic status and, in doing so, improves his or her socio-economic status.

That marriage and money are inextricably linked means that some relationships have the potential to be economically exploitive and that sometimes an individual pursues marriage solely for economic gain. The concepts of **"predatory marriage"** (see the box below) and **"sexually transmitted debt"** (see the box on the next page) are recent cultural constructions; however, they reflect the interconnections between money and marriage that have existed since the emergence of private property (Engels, 1884/2010). *Predatory marriage* is a term associated with marriages where an individual pursues marriage solely for financial gain. Often this involves a younger person marrying an older individual with the objective of assuming control over the spouse's financial affairs and gaining access to the spouse's assets, pension, or property. The term *sexually transmitted debt* typically refers to debt that accrues between two people who are in an intimate relationship.

▶▶▶ Predatory Marriage

What do predatory marriages look like? Predatory marriages involve an individual who is preying on the advanced age and needs of an individual solely for his or her own financial reasons. Sometimes the offending spouse attempts to isolate the new spouse from family members, including adult children, so that financial transactions remain hidden. The topic has gained media attention in Canada as more cases have surfaced, and the courts grapple with the question of whether older individuals have the mental capacity to enter into new marriages and forego control over their financial affairs to a new spouse. Dagmara Wozniak is a Canadian lawyer who has written about predatory marriage. Wozniak (2014) gives us an idea of what this type of exploitive marriage looks like:

> The term "predatory marriage" has been coined to refer to a marriage entered into for a singular purpose of exploitation, personal gain or profit. Frequently, it involves an interested party (i.e. friend,

neighbour etc.) assuming the role of a caregiver and persuading a vulnerable person to marry. Often, the victim is elderly, dependent and suffering from some degree of cognitive impairment. After marriage, the "predatory spouse" takes advantage of the vulnerable victim spouse, and assumes control and management of the victim spouse's financial affairs.

Predatory marriages are not limited to older Canadians and are not a recent phenomenon, although the heightened media attention paid to them is more recent. These kinds of cases highlight the conflicts and opposing interests of new spouses and existing family members, namely adult children. They raise questions about financial obligations to new or subsequent spouses versus pre-existing adult children and grandchildren. They also raise questions about the extent to which financial obligations are inherent in intimate relationships, marital or nonmarital, and the financial considerations that factor into Canadians' decisions about relationship formation.

Sexually Transmitted Debt

The term *sexually transmitted debt* is frequently used to describe the situation of women who lack knowledge about financial matters and sign financial documents, such as business loans, with husbands or common-law partners that make the women responsible for the debt. In these kinds of scenarios, financial transparency is typically absent and women are removed from the financial and business affairs of their husbands or boyfriends. Elements of control and abuse sometimes operate to give men leverage and keep women in the dark about the extent of the financial risk they are exposing themselves to.

Men can be victims of sexually transmitted debt, and financial exploitation is not exclusive to intimate partner relationships. Financial risk and debt can be experienced by any family member, such as when a parent co-signs for a business loan, car loan, mortgage, or credit card for an adult child and ends up carrying the debt because the adult child cannot make the payments. Debt that stems from intimate relationships or family relationships is different than debt between business partners who are not family. Emotional coercion may be used so that the person who is assuming potential debt feels enormous pressure to do so. Family or relationship dynamics such as abuse, guilt, feelings of obligation, family history, or, in the case of an intimate relationship, a promise of a future together or the threat of a breakup may be at work. A parent may feel obligated to co-sign a business loan or mortgage out of worry about the welfare of his or her child or grandchildren. Individuals can use emotional coercion on a family member or intimate partner in pursuit of their financial interests.

Money and Relationship Dissolution

Canadians often assume that the law treats cohabiting and married couples in the same way when relationships end and financial matters need to be sorted out. This assumption is incorrect, and there are also provincial differences in how cohabiting versus legally married couples are treated. Married and common-law couples are treated differently when it comes to determining the division of matrimonial property. An equal division of equity in the matrimonial home is only provided for legally married couples; there is no equal division of equity in a shared home for common-law couples in all provinces, with the exception of British Columbia. In 2013, British Columbia introduced legal reform to address issues such as property division among cohabiting couples who break up. It allowed individuals who had cohabitated some rights to the division of assets in their home. This was done in response to concerns that family members, particularly women and children, were left economically vulnerable following relationship breakdown. Spousal support and child support provisions extend to common-law couples in Canada. Legal scholars have described how the courts in Canada, including the Supreme Court of Canada, have expanded obligations for spousal support and child support, including the support of stepchildren. Some writers, such as legal scholar Mary Jane Mossman (2003), attribute these changes to **neoliberalism** and a retreat by the state in providing support to families. The result is that individuals are likely to face continued economic obligations following relationship dissolution.

Until recently, property laws for most Canadians did not apply to Indigenous people living on reserves. Prior to 2013, homes on reserves were owned by husbands, and women had no automatic property rights following relationship dissolution. In 2013, new property laws were established to give Indigenous women in marital or common-law relationships equal property rights (Indigenous and Northern Affairs Canada, 2015).

TECHNOLOGICAL CHANGE

Technologies such as the internet, smartphones, and social media have affected intimate relationships (Bergdall et al., 2012) and families. Most of us are aware that social media have revolutionized dating. A growing number of people use online dating to find new partners, and there are dating sites for particular groups such as seniors, single parents, professionals, and individuals who identify with specific religions. There are sites for individuals pursuing relationships, marriage, casual sex, and sexual practices that have historically been stigmatized, such as sites for swingers (Serina, Hall, Ciambrone, and Phua, 2013). New technologies and social media are implicated in relationship dissolution (see the box on the next page). Social media have been blamed for harming marriage and intimate relationships by providing greater and more convenient opportunities for individuals to find new partners or be unfaithful. One of the most well-known examples of this is the website Ashley Madison, which was developed explicitly to help married people cheat on their spouses. Individuals are increasingly consuming software technologies to hide or uncover infidelity (Gregg, 2013). In a study of perceptions of cyber-cheating, Whitty (2005) found that online affairs and emotional infidelity were viewed as being just as serious as offline affairs and sexual infidelity. Women were more likely to view emotional infidelity as problematic and a cause for divorce (Whitty, 2005), although both men and women viewed cyber-affairs as equally damaging as offline affairs. Social media are used to find partners, identify one's relationship status to the world, and highlight changes in relationship status, such as relationship dissolution. Individuals can use online forums such as Facebook to navigate their contact with a former partner after a breakup. For example, LeFabvre, Blackburn, and Nicholas (2015) explored how individuals used features in Facebook, such as unfriending and limiting profile access, to modify their contact with an ex after a breakup.

Social media provide new ways for people to pursue varied sexual relationships and encounters; for instance, couples can find others interested in threesomes or people interested in polyamory (consensual, non-monogamous, multipartner relationships). The internet provides opportunities for individuals to pursue sexual interests, such as casual sex, or to pursue particular sexual practices and interests, such as BDSM (bondage, discipline, dominance, submission, sadomasochism). People can

Smartphones and social media affect how individuals in intimate relationships communicate; for instance, the term *sexting* refers to the exchange of sexually explicit messages or images, typically using cellphones (Choi, Van Ouytsel, and Temple, 2016; Lee and Crofts, 2015). Sexting by adolescents raises concerns around youth not understanding laws related to child abuse and child pornography (Lee and Crofts, 2015). Moreover, there are concerns that youth may experience adverse consequences such as emotional harm or risk to their social reputation as a result of sexting (Lee and Crofts, 2015). Scholars have explored gender differences in sexting, specifically whether females experience coercion when it comes to sending or receiving such messages. Choi, Van Ouytsel, and Temple (2016) explored females' experiences with offline and online sexual coercion and suggest that sexting may be an extension of offline sexual coercion. Lee and Crofts (2015) argue that while some adolescent females experience coercion, this is not the case for the majority of females who participate in sexting.

Social media have transformed relationship dissolution (Bergdall et al., 2012). For example, the term **ghosting** has gained traction as a breakup method. Ghosting occurs when a person who wants to end contact with someone he or she has been involved with ignores all forms of communication and does not respond to texts, phone calls, and other messages. It is done without explanation or warning. A growing number of people report having experienced it or doing it to another person (Hayes, 2017). The unpredictability of ghosting often leaves people feeling confused, rejected, hurt, and uncertain not only about future relationships but also about their own ability to read social cues. It has been suggested that ghosting reflects a new era in which relationships are disposable. Social media and online dating facilitate ghosting because people who meet online often do not have shared social circles; if they ghost the person they have been involved with, they probably do not need to worry about mutual friends finding out (Hayes, 2017). Ghosting is seen by some as highly problematic because it can cause emotional harm to the person who is ignored (Vilhauer, 2015).

The term **zombieing** is used to describe a related phenomenon: a dating partner who resurfaces long after he or she ghosted a former partner. The term **benching** or **cushioning** refers to individuals who lead others on without any intention of a relationship (Hayes, 2017). The individual might send texts or messages, even flirtatious messages, yet does not make any moves in the direction of a relationship. Just as the person on the receiving end of this gives up hope, he or she receives another message that makes him or her hopeful again (Bennett, 2016). Benching or cushioning is a strategy used so that people have backups in the event that things do not work out with their primary interests. **Breadcrumbing** occurs when a person puts in minimal effort, such as irregular flirtatious texts, with the hope of luring a sexual partner. The contact can be very sporadic, such as a few texts every few weeks or months (Bennett, 2016).

use dating websites for non-dating purposes, such as looking for new friends to go out with or friends who can help them explore specific issues—for instance, an individual who wants to explore a different gender or sexual identity and does not have anyone he or she can share this with. Thus, dating sites can be used for non-dating purposes. Dating sites offer anonymity and privacy—for example, to couples who are looking for discreet sexual encounters or to LGBTQ individuals who want privacy.

Individuals can use multiple social media platforms such as dating sites, Facebook, Instagram, Snapchat, and Twitter in their dating relationships.

Romance apps are popular and profitable in countries like Japan, which has a high rate of nonmarried people in their twenties and thirties, many of whom have not had any sexual relationships (Marsh, 2016). Romance apps are marketed to single women and allow for user-driven storylines. They provide users with text messages and emails from their fantasy boyfriends or lovers. Users pay for extras such as additional chapters that provide simulated sex or online features such as makeup so that their characters can look more appealing to their love interests. Users are presented with numerous love interests and choice in their romance fantasies. Romance apps are said to provide comfort to young women experiencing loneliness or disappointment from real-life relationships, leading some to worry that real-life men cannot compete with perfect, fictional romance characters (Usher, 2016). Focus groups and other forms of market research are used by software companies to better understand the desires of female consumers and how these vary cross-culturally (Marsh, 2016).

One advantage of romance apps is that they allow users to pursue romances they understand would be too emotionally dangerous to pursue in real life and to not have to deal with the drama, heartache, and rejection that accompanies real-life dating relationships. Women may use romance apps in place of real-life relationships, to supplement real-life relationships, during lonelier periods when they are in between real-life relationships or dealing with a breakup, and perhaps even to figure out what kind of man they want and then apply this online experience to real-life dating. Romance apps are hugely popular in countries like Japan, China, and South Korea, and they are becoming increasingly popular in the United States. It may be just a matter of time before they become popular in Canada.

The internet has transformed childbearing, parenting, and new reproductive technologies. There are websites to help people find donor eggs, sperm, embryos, and surrogates. Andreassen (2017) explored how families with children conceived using donor sperm connect via Facebook and, in the process, form alternative kin based on their shared experience. These online communities are virtual alternative families that experience intimacy online yet can also pose challenges or threats to existing family relations (Andreassen, 2017). There are also websites for people interested in co-parenting that provide information about co-parenting agreements and profiles of people interested in co-parenting. The term co-parenting is commonly used to describe how divorced couples share parenting of their children after divorce. Co-parenting also refers to two individuals who are not in a relationship with each other agreeing to raise a child together. Co-parenting agreements are often made in advance of the birth of a child to determine access schedules, decision making, and financial obligations. Social media also allow transnational and extended families to stay in contact and can be used to forge new familial or kin relationships. For example, there are websites to help match young families with older people who are willing to act as surrogate grandparents.

CONCLUDING REMARKS

Until very recently, Canadians faced societal pressure to conform to conventional family life organized around heterosexuality, marriage, monogamy, and parenthood. The early twenty-first century represents a much different social landscape of greater choice in intimate relationships, family structure, childbearing, and sexuality. Divorce, cohabitation, remaining unattached, non-monogamous relationships, LGBTQ relationships, and an uncoupling of marriage and fertility are just some of the trends in close relations that have become commonplace in Canadian society. Because relationships and families are often economic units, the significance of financial matters such as access to income, financial decision making, and economic equality cannot be overlooked. New technologies have transformed dating and parenthood and have altered how couples meet, interact, communicate, and even break up. Changing family law affects relationship formation and dissolution and provides economic security for children and adults. It isn't just young people who are experiencing change in living arrangements, sexuality, and family reconfiguration; older Canadians are also experiencing profound change in their close relations (Humble, 2013). The pace of change has been rapid and intense; relationships and families in the coming decades are sure to change even more with technological advancement and broader economic, political, and social changes.

CHAPTER SUMMARY

This chapter examined the changes that have taken place in intimate relationships, marriage, families, childbearing, living arrangements, and sexuality. Canadians experience greater choice and fluidity in their private lives than ever before, and this is reflected in the diversity we see in close relations and family life. The range of options available to young and older adults is much wider than it was for earlier generations, and the stigma surrounding non-traditional family arrangements has eroded over time. Technology has transformed relationship formation and dissolution, as have changes in family law. It is normative for Canadians to experience family reconfiguration and numerous intimate relationships over their lifetime, and there is greater latitude for individuals to make decisions about how they want to live and the close relations they build. This chapter also examined how issues related to money—banking, spending, decision making, and inequality—affect relationships and families. There are myriad intersections between intimate relationships, living arrangements, parenting, and sexuality, which provide Canadians with opportunities to structure private life in unique ways that reflect the needs and desires of individuals and family members.

Key Terms

benching/cushioning Occurs when individuals lead others on without any intention of a relationship by sending intermittent texts. Individuals who are being benched are backups in case the person doing the benching is unsuccessful with others.

breadcrumbing Occurs when a person puts in minimal effort such as irregular flirtatious texts with the hope of luring a sexual partner. The contact can be very sporadic, such as a few texts every few weeks or months.

compersion Among polyamorists, happiness that is experienced when a partner finds love and happiness with someone else.

co-parenting Individuals who are not in a relationship who decide to raise a child together. Often, co-parenting agreements are signed to set out clear expectations around access, decision making, and financial support.

embryo adoption Embryos created through in vitro fertilization that are implanted in another woman or in multiple women, creating genetic siblings.

ghosting Describes how a person who wants to end contact with someone he or she has been involved with ignores all forms of communication and does not respond to texts, phone calls, and other messages. It is done without explanation and warning.

group marriage A marriage involving multiple husbands and wives.

living apart together (LAT) Couples who are in a stable relationship but do not live together.

neoliberalism A retreat by the state away from providing support to families.

polyamory Multipartner relationships that are agreed upon, negotiated, and transparent and that involve sexual and emotional intimacy.

polyandry Marriage between one woman and more than one husband.

polygamy Being married to more than one person at a time.

polygyny Marriage between one man and more than one wife.

predatory marriage An individual who pursues marriage for financial gain. Often, this involves someone who marries an older person and tries to take control of the new spouse's financial affairs.

secondary poverty The poverty that women experience as a result of men not sharing their pay equitably with their families.

sexually transmitted debt Debt that accrues between two people who are in an intimate relationship.

sologamy Self-marriage or marriage by a person to oneself. These celebrations reaffirm self-acceptance, autonomy, and self-love and do not preclude future relationships.

zombieing A dating partner who resurfaces long after he or she ghosted a former partner.

Critical Thinking Questions

1. How have intimate relationships and living arrangements changed compared to those in earlier generations?

2. In what ways do we see greater diversity, choice, and fluidity in close relations, sexuality, and family life today?

3. What are the emerging trends for young adults as they establish new relationships and living arrangements?

4. In what ways have technology and social media improved or harmed intimate relationships and family life?

5. What accounts for the increasing number of Canadians who are opting to live alone?

6. What are the issues to consider when thinking about money in relationships?

Weblinks

Ministry of the Attorney General: What You Should Know about Family Law in Ontario
www.attorneygeneral.jus.gov.on.ca/english/family/familyla.html
Outlines rights and responsibilities and covers issues such as cohabitation agreements, spousal support, and child support.

CoParents.com
www.coparents.com/laws/canada.php
Information on co-parenting, surrogacy, and sperm, egg, and embryo donation.

Re:searching for LGBTQ Health
http://lgbtqhealth.ca/resources/lgbtqfamiliesandparenting.php
Research on LGBTQ families, including parenting and adoption.

Government of Ontario: Getting Married.
www.ontario.ca/page/getting-married
The rules and procedures for getting married or remarried in Ontario.

Statistics Canada: Divorce
www.statcan.gc.ca/eng/help/bb/info/divorce
Information and statistics on divorce, child support, and second marriages.

Statistics Canada: Debt and Family Type in Canada
www.statcan.gc.ca/pub/11-008-x/2011001/article/11430-eng.htm
Information and statistics on financial insecurity and debt among Canadians. Data for younger families, older Canadians, single-parent households, and changes over time are provided.

Government of Canada: Innovation, Science and Economic Development Canada
www.ic.gc.ca/eic/site/oca-bc.nsf/eng/ca02108.html
Information and data on issues like financial security, assets, pensions, registered retirement savings plans (RRSPs), and investment products among Canadians.

Chapter 5
Happy and Healthy Relationships

Maridav/Shutterstock

CHAPTER OUTLINE

- Sociological Findings on Marital Quality
  - Close Relations, Good Health
  - Disability, Partnership, and Marriage
  - Good Marriage and Good Health
- Types of Union and Relationship Quality
  - Homosexual versus Heterosexual Relationships
- The Role of Homogamy
- Marital Satisfaction among Immigrant Couples
- The Life Cycle of a Marriage
  - Marriage Beginnings
  - The Introduction of Children into a Marriage
  - Infertility
  - The Midlife Marriage
- What Makes a Marriage Satisfying?
  - Love

- Sexual Satisfaction
- Intimacy: Sexual and Emotional
- Coping and Conflict Management
- Domestic Violence
- Gender Roles in Marriage
- Work, Money, and Marital Quality

- Verbal Communication
- Nonverbal Communication
- Communication and Gender
- The Effects of Disabilities on Spousal Relationships
- Chapter Summary

LEARNING OBJECTIVES

1 Distinguish between the types of intimate unions that people engage in.

2 Describe how relationship quality varies from one relationship to another.

3 Identify the stages of the life cycle of marriage and their characteristics

4 Describe what a relationship needs to satisfy the people involved.

5 Show how gender roles affect the experience of a close relationship.

6 List the rules for successful communication.

The world can be a cold, lonely place for people on their own, without a close intimate relationship. That may be why, over the course of their lives, most people enter one or more intimate relationships. Yet, despite the benefits, no relationship is perfect and no long-term relationship is easy to preserve. Close relations can be frustrating, boring, irritating, exhausting, and disappointing. People in close relations can sometimes feel just as alone as single people. Yet most people enter and remain in these relationships and, if the relationships end, people seek new ones.

This chapter is about why people enter and stay in close intimate relations—what benefits they receive by doing so—and how some manage to "succeed" in these relations more than others do. We also study the reasons people in committed long-term relationships are, on average, happier and healthier than unattached people—despite the many difficulties associated with setting up and preserving intimate relations. We will not claim that close, intimate relations are the only factor in happiness and a good, healthy life. Obviously, many other factors—including health, job security, and social integration—also affect people's well-being. However, in this chapter we focus on the important role of relationship satisfaction, since no other single factor is more important.

SOCIOLOGICAL FINDINGS ON MARITAL QUALITY

Among Canadians, marital status is a consistently strong predictor of life satisfaction (otherwise known as happiness, emotional well-being, or contentment). Compared to married Canadians, and controlling for a wide variety of other characteristics (e.g., age, sex, health status), unmarried Canadians are less satisfied. This is true of common-law (or cohabiting) couples; widowed people are *much* less satisfied, never-married people are even less satisfied, and separated or divorced people are the least satisfied of all adults. According to data published by Bonikowska, Helliwell, Hou, and Schellenberg (2013), all of these differences in life satisfaction are strong and statistically significant, meaning that they are unlikely to have arisen by chance.

However, some social scientists have disputed the claimed link between marriage and well-being, pointing to a prejudice against singlehood in our society. So, for example, De Paulo and Morris (2006) state:

> People who are single are targets of singlism: negative stereotypes and discrimination. Compared to married or coupled people, who are often described in very positive terms, singles are assumed to be immature, maladjusted, and self-centered. Although the perceived differences between people who have and have not married are large, the actual differences are not. Moreover, there is currently scant recognition that singlism exists, and when singlism is acknowledged, it is often accepted as legitimate.

This supposed prejudice is supported, the authors say, by flawed social science findings that conclude that marriage is the cause (rather than a consequence) of health and happiness. In this chapter, we argue otherwise, looking at various studies, both longitudinal and cross-sectional, that show marriage does indeed increase people's happiness and well-being.

In fact, sociologists have been studying this link between marriage and well-being for more than a century, using various data sources from various countries. They have done so in at least three different ways: (1) by examining the suicide rates of married and unmarried people; (2) by asking married and unmarried people to report their feelings of happiness or satisfaction with life; and (3) by looking at people's mental or physical health, according to their marital status. Interestingly, these different methods have yielded similar results. Let's consider each of these sources of data in order.

One of sociology's earliest empirical studies—Émile Durkheim's classic work *Suicide*—looked at patterns of suicide rates in late nineteenth-century France. In doing so, Durkheim found that socially integrated—that is, socially attached and regulated—people are less likely to kill themselves than socially isolated and unregulated people. The more attached and regulated they are—as spouses or parents, for example—the less likely people are to commit suicide. Married people, as the most integrated and regulated of all people, were least likely to commit suicide.

Here's the explanation: People who are isolated and unregulated often suffer from rootlessness and aimlessness, which Durkheim called **anomie**, a condition that increases the risk of suicide. Marital relations reduce this risk by providing attachment and care. Marital relations also provide order. They set healthy limits on people's hopes and ambitions. Strong emotional ties connect people to those they live with. Duties to protect and support these people regulate their lives.

On the other hand, unattached people—especially people with no partner, children, or other close family (e.g., dependent parents, brothers, or sisters) to care for—can go where they want, when they want, with whom they want. At first, this sounds pretty good. However, with less integration and regulation, these same people are more likely to commit suicide than married people. Thus, having fewer limits imposed on them carries risks as well as benefits for people.

Today's statistics continue to support Durkheim's theory. Suicide rates are higher among unmarried people than among married people, just as they were a century ago. However, researchers rarely rely on suicide statistics to measure people's well-being. Suicide may be a sign of unhappiness, but few people who are unhappy commit suicide. Besides, divorce and singlehood are not the only causes of suicide. Therefore, sociologists have developed other ways to measure health, happiness, and life satisfaction. As the reasoning runs, good marriages should provide more health and happiness benefits than bad marriages or no marriages at all. This reasoning can be subjected to empirical analysis.

Cross-sectional data from the U.S. National Health Survey (2011), as published by the National Center for Health Statistics, show that married people are much more likely to be healthy than their non-married (i.e., single, separated, divorced, or widowed) peers. However, these data—being cross-sectional—obscure causality, leaving us to wonder whether marriage leads to happiness or happiness leads to marriage.

A study by two Canadian social scientists (Grover and Helliwell, 2014) may help answer this question. Their study used various cross-sectional and longitudinal data sources from various countries. Using the British Household Panel Survey, the researchers controlled for premarital well-being and found that married people are still more satisfied than unmarried people, which suggests a causal effect (Grover and Helliwell, 2014). So, with high-quality panel (i.e., longitudinal) data, the authors showed that marriage leads to increased satisfaction and well-being.

Second, they noted that people's life satisfaction tends to fall as people move toward middle age, something we will discuss later in this chapter. However, using data from the United Kingdom's Annual Population Survey, the researchers found that married people experience less of a "mid-life dip" in satisfaction (Grover and Halliwell, 2014). Thus, marriage provides protection against the inevitable drop in life satisfaction that accompanies aging (and, for many, parenthood).

Third, the researchers examined the role of friendship in life satisfaction. They found that the positive effects of marriage are twice as large for those couples who consider each other their best friend. In other words, marriage is good for people because it gives them the social support and social cohesion people get from close friends. People in a good marriage have an on-site close friend, according to these data.

Fourth and finally, the researchers asked whether these are universal facts about marriage or are limited to a few societies. They examined data from the Gallup World Poll and found that in different cultural contexts, the well-being effects of marriage vary, but marriage does seem to ease the "mid-life dip" in all regions, except Sub-Saharan Africa. In short, marriage is good for people's happiness and well-being (almost) everywhere.

Close Relations, Good Health

Because marriage contributes to people's well-being, we should expect to see people's well-being increase as the closeness (or quality) of their closest relationship increases. Said another way, we should expect to find that people who are wholly isolated are worst off, people who are in weak and unstable relationships are better off, and people who are in good, stable marriages are best off, in terms of well-being. So, we expect to find that, other things being equal, married people are happier and healthier than people in less stable relationships.

To simplify, imagine that there are four kinds of close relationship statuses: single, dating, cohabiting, and married. By "dating" we mean being involved in an intimate relationship with someone who lives in another household, and by "cohabitating" we mean being involved in an intimate relationship with someone who lives in the same household. How do these statuses compare in health terms? A study looking at data representing 500 million people found that single (or never-married) people have a 24 percent higher chance of early death than married people (Roelfs, Shor, Kalish, and Yogev, 2011). The same study finds that the "hazard ratio," or risk of early death, for women who are *not* married has increased over time more rapidly than for men, causing the hazard ratio for men and women to be roughly equal in recent years.

So, for both men and women, marriages—despite the effort they take and the conflict they often breed—are healthy and life-enhancing for people. Committed marriages can do people a lot of mental and physical good, although bad ones can do them a great deal of harm. Best of all, most of the time people can choose the people they want to join in close relations and can improve their relationship if it starts to produce unhealthy results. As the data in Figure 5.1 show, married people are much more likely than other adults to have excellent health and are much less likely to have only fair or poor health.

High divorce rates in North America may cause people to have more skeptical ideas surrounding marriage. What's more, recent Pew Institute survey results for the United States note a considerable rise in the ages at which people marry. This all means that present-day adult North Americans spend a smaller fraction of their adult lives married than their parents or grandparents would have done. That said, most people still marry, and marriage continues to have strong benefits for those people. The benefits of marriage for some groups have even increased over the past several decades. The link between marriage and health is mediated by the quality of the

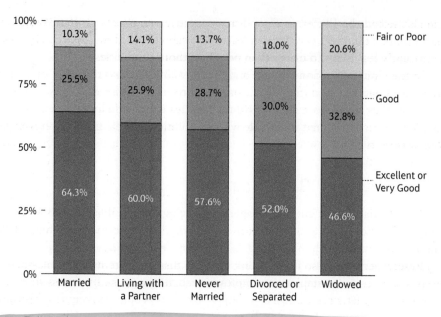

Figure 5.1 Age-adjusted current health conditions by marital status
Source: National Center for Health Statistics, National Health Interview Survey, 2011.

relationship, however—that is, by how a couple gets along. The higher the quality of the relationship, the stronger is its positive effect on health.

The likeliest explanation for the link between marriage and health is that a good marriage provides emotional and economic support. Emotional stability strengthens the immune system, making partners more able to avoid or recover from illness. It also increases the will to live and promotes prudence and self-care. As for economic support, married people who live together can pool their funds to avoid economic hardship: They share what lawyers call "interdependent revenue." This increases their access to health care and also permits them to focus on healthy lifestyles. These two factors are likely the best explanation for the good health of people in good marriages.

Disability, Partnership, and Marriage

People with a disability are especially likely to benefit economically and emotionally from marriage. However, many studies show that having a disability decreases one's chances of getting married and, thereby, of benefiting from a happy marriage. For example, Tumin (2014), analyzing data from the U.S National Health Interview Surveys (1997 to 2013), found that adults with childhood-onset disabilities were less likely to marry than their non-disabled peers. Similarly, MacInnes (2011) found a negative correlation between disability and marriage. In her analysis of data from the National Longitudinal Study of Adolescent Health, she found that people with a disability have a smaller chance of marrying than people who do not have a disability,

She also noted that different disabilities had different effects on the likelihood of marriage. For example, people with learning disabilities and multiple disabilities are significantly less likely to marry than people without disabilities.

In the United Kingdom, Clarke and McKay (2014) studied the effect of disability on people's dating and marital lives, using data from the British Household Panel Survey. First, they found that people with disabilities stay single longer than their non-disabled peers: 35 percent of people with disabilities in their thirties were single, in comparison to 18 percent of people without disabilities. What's more, 18 percent of people with disabilities in their forties were single, in comparison to 12 percent of people without disabilities. When they were married, people with disabilities were more likely to get divorced than people without disabilities. As a result, in this sample 37 percent of people with disabilities between the ages of 30 and 59 were married, compared to 57 percent of people without disabilities—a 20 percent difference (Clarke and McKay, 2014: 550).

Researchers have also found a link between disabled parents and joblessness, for reasons such as "discrimination, employer recognition of skills, access to training, combining care services and employment, benefit concerns and access to appropriate

Couples therapy may help resolve issues when the well-being of a relationship is threatened.

Kzenon/Shutterstock

childcare" (Clarke and McKay, 2014). Even when people with disabilities do have jobs, they are more likely to hold insecure, low-paid, and part-time work than their non-disabled peers. This link between disability, joblessness, and precarious and low-paying work can, as the researchers note, lead to marital strife, and even to divorce. As a result, people with disabilities in this study are twice as likely to be divorced than people without disabilities: 20 percent of people with disabilities compared to 10 percent of people without disabilities.

Good Marriage and Good Health

In short, marriage contributes to people's emotional and economic stability. Of course, not every marriage is an equally "happy" or "good" marriage. Some marriages are beset by endless conflict and even violence. Common sense tells us that bad marriages are less likely to enhance a person's happiness than good marriages. In fact, some people might even be better off unmarried than married to the wrong person. For this reason, data from the longitudinal Marital Instability Over the Life Course Study show that declines in "marital quality" result in declines in marital happiness and physical health, other things being equal (Miller, Hollist, Olsen, and Law, 2013).

Of course, people in happy marriages sometimes get sick and people in bad marriages are often perfectly healthy. But marital quality, personal stress, and well-being are all correlated. That's why signs of poor health such as depression, lack of sleep, and poor eating—not to mention signs of physical violence—may reveal that the marriage is in trouble.

Marital stressors are related to both mental and physiological problems (Kiecolt-Glaser and Newton, 2001). The cause-and-effect relationship goes both ways: For example, psychiatric symptoms can lead to marital difficulties, and marital difficulties can lead to psychiatric symptoms. In fact, people in unhappy marriages often show signs of psychological difficulty. The symptoms include a weaker will to live, less life satisfaction, and reported poorer health, compared with people in happy marriages. People with higher marital quality, on the other hand, have lower rates of illness and mortality and better self-reported health—even lower cardiovascular reactivity during interpersonal conflict (Robles, Slatcher, Trombello, and McGinn, 2014).

A good marriage is especially important to people who are vulnerable, whether because they are elderly, sick, disabled, or pregnant. For example, pregnant women benefit from being in a good marriage with a kind and understanding partner. Emotional closeness with and global support from one's partner protect against perinatal depression and anxiety (Pilkington et al., 2015). Intimacy gives both partners health protection within a stable and caring family environment. Emotional intimacy may also mediate the association between spouses' appraisal of their partners' communication and their own relationship satisfaction (Yoo, Bartle-Haring, Day, and Gangamma, 2014).

However, intimacy is a complicated matter, as we see in Figure 5.2. It includes intention (or commitment), the expression of emotional feelings, involvement

- Similarities in cognitive style may increase the chance of a successful marriage, where cognitive style refers to the strength of a person's desire for structure when confronted with change (Skinner and Iaboni, 2009).

- The complementarity of interpersonal coping styles, such as "dismissive, adaptive, and anxious/expressive," also predicts relationship quality (Chow, Buhrmester, and Tan, 2014).

- Humour is important in helping a marriage to work, but the worst humour style for a relationship is antisocial or aggressive instrumental humour; it predicts greater apathy during conflict resolution (Campbell and Moroz, 2014).

- Sharing of all kinds—including ideas, thoughts, worries, and dreams—with one's partner leads to more marital satisfaction and intimacy (Duffey, Wooten, and Lumadue, 2004).

- Partners who share on a regular basis are usually more able to resolve conflicts effectively (Knee, Lonsbary, Canevello, and Patrick, 2005).

- More frequent positive problem solving can improve relationship satisfaction regardless of conflict resolution style (Sierau and Herzberg, 2012).

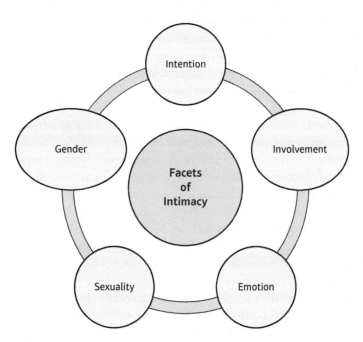

Figure 5.2 Faces of intimacy

Source: Data from Greeff, Abraham P., & Hildegarde L. Malherbe. 2001. Intimacy and marital satisfaction in spouses. *Journal of Sex & Marital Therapy 27*: 247–257. Web.

with the other partner, and satisfying sexual engagement. What makes this even more complicated is that men and women tend to bring different expectations about intimacy to the relationship and express their needs and feelings differently as well.

The same positive effects of marriage that are found among married heterosexual couples are also found among gay and lesbian married couples (Wienke and Hill, 2009). Whether heterosexual or homosexual, couples benefit from couplehood. Research shows that this is true whether we ask people about their life satisfaction, whether they consider their life worthwhile, whether they were happy yesterday, and whether they were anxious yesterday (Dush and Amato, 2005). No matter how we phrase the question of well-being, when compared to married people, non-married people score much worse. They show less life satisfaction, less happiness, and more anxiety.

TYPES OF UNION AND RELATIONSHIP QUALITY

As we have seen, reported well-being varies from one relationship to another—for example, from marriage to cohabitation to dating. Likely, people in different kinds of relations bring different standards to bear when evaluating their relationship and their lives within them. As well, people who choose marriage are more inclined to long-term relationships than people who choose cohabiting relationships. Perhaps as a result of this, cohabiting unions typically last a shorter time and yield less satisfaction than legal marriages. Studies comparing marital quality between three types of marriage—long-term cohabiting, married, and remarried—reveal that cohabiting couples have the least happiness (Skinner, Bahr, Crane, and Call Vaughn, 2002).

We must bear in mind that cohabiters are more likely than married people to be young, since for many people cohabitation is equivalent to "trial marriage." As well, people who cohabit may differ in various social and psychological ways from people who marry legally. So, comparing cohabitation and marriage is, in one sense, like comparing apples and oranges. That said, people tend to behave differently in cohabiting relationships and legal marriages. For example, as we see in Figure 5.3, cohabiting people are more likely to be regular (i.e., daily) drinkers of alcohol. This suggests that they are under greater strain. Cohabiters typically report less relationship commitment than married people, as well as greater conflict frequency (Stafford, Kline, and Rankin, 2004).

However, cohabitation provides enormous benefits of the kind that marriage also provides. First, cohabitation provides people with companionship without the formalities of marriage and the accompanying legal responsibilities. Second, even though they are living together, cohabiting people can still maintain financial autonomy if they wish, to protect their offspring's inheritance. Third, since cohabitation

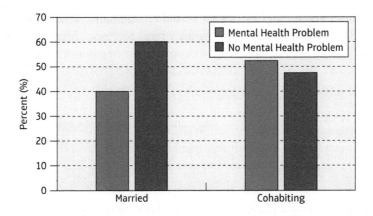

Figure 5.3 Mental health problems of parents (including alcohol use) by relationship status

Source: Based on DeKlyen, Michelle et al. 2006. The mental health of married, cohabiting, and non–coresident parents with infants. *American Journal of Public Health 96*(10): 1836–1841. PMC. Web. January 16, 2017.

avoids the commitment demands of marriage, there is no risk of a costly divorce. So, in some senses, cohabitation provides many of the benefits of marriage without all of the risks.

For all of these reasons, cohabitation is similar to legal marriage and is becoming more similar all the time. Studies find a declining difference between cohabiting relationships and marriages in terms of emotional satisfaction, relationship quality, and associated well-being. In a recent longitudinal study comparing legal marriage, cohabitation, and singlehood, Mernitz and Kamp Dush (2016)

> examined the change in emotional health across the entrance into first and second unions, including cohabiting unions, direct marriage (marriage without premarital cohabitation), and marriage preceded by cohabitation. Using the National Longitudinal Survey of Youth, 1997, a nationally representative panel study of youth born between 1980 and 1984 in the United States, pooled fixed-effects regression models indicated that entrance into first cohabiting unions and direct marriages, and all second unions, were significantly associated with reduced emotional distress.

Since "reduced emotional distress" can be interpreted to mean "more happiness" and "more well-being," the data show that cohabitation, like marriage, confers benefits in the form of health and happiness. However, the authors note an interesting difference between men and women in these data. By entering into their first union, men gained the emotional health benefit (i.e., reduced distress) only if they married without cohabiting. In contrast, women who entered into their first union gained equal measures of benefit from both direct marriage and cohabitation.

Homosexual versus Heterosexual Relationships

Some people imagine that homosexual marriages are markedly different from their heterosexual counterparts. However, sociological evidence implies that the same kinds of marriage dynamics are found in all couples, regardless of their sexual orientation. For example, gays and lesbians, like heterosexuals, tend to find partners who match them in age, race, education, and income (Jepson and Jepson, 2002). However, owing to the continued stigma of homosexuality in some circles, "coming out" affects the relationships of homosexuals in a unique way.

Specifically, homosexual relationships work best when both partners "come out" and neither is trying to hide his or her sexual orientation from friends and family members. It is essential for the quality of the marriage that the partners reveal their sexual orientation to their families. Gay men who openly reveal their sexual orientation to friends and family are more likely to sustain a long-term marriage than men who do not (Eaton, 2000). Similarly, lesbians who come out to friends and family report more satisfaction in their marriage than those who do not (Jordan and Deluty, 2000).

If one partner is openly gay to friends and family but the other is still hiding his or her sexuality, conflict can result and marital quality can decrease (Mohr and Fassinger, 2006). In this circumstance, one partner may feel that he or she is not getting the needed social support or may feel insulted by the other partner's refusal to openly acknowledge the marriage. As for heterosexual marriages, so for homosexual marriages, declaring the importance of the relationship to friends and family marks a turning point in the relationship. It signals a commitment and invites public support. Both commitment and support strengthen a couple's closeness and increase satisfaction with the marriage.

The Role of Homogamy

In Chapter 3, we noted the importance of homogamy in mate selection: People tend to seek, find, and marry people like themselves in important respects (e.g., age and education). Not surprisingly, researchers find a strong connection between spousal similarity and later marital satisfaction. Gaunt (2006), for example, reports that for both men and women, similar personality traits and values are strongly and consistently associated with happiness and marital satisfaction. Gaunt finds that similarity in self-direction, conformity, and achievement values are most important for wives' satisfaction and well-being. In most domains, according to Gaunt's findings and consistent with other research, marital satisfaction shows a strong and consistent association with couple similarity.

The reasons are simple: Homogamy increases marital satisfaction by reducing the number of issues on which the couple may disagree. Just as important as actual similarity is perceived similarity: Partners who *think* they are alike are more satisfied with their marriage than partners who think they are different (Blackmon, 2000; Decuyper, De Bolle, and De Fruyt, 2012; Yaffee, 2003).

Marital Satisfaction among Immigrant Couples

Many Canadian families are made up of people who were born elsewhere and immigrated to Canada. This fact is important because the experience of immigration is stressful, and stressful experiences strain close relations. Hyman, Guruge, and Mason (2008) identify many of the negative effects of immigration on marital satisfaction. One source of strain is conflict that results from a change in gender roles and responsibilities after migration. Often, migration changes the balance of employment and income between spouses, or calls for changes in the domestic division of labour. Often, these changes happen just as the couple has lost much of its social support network—its family and friends back home—by moving to Canada. However, in some strongly cohesive families, immigration can occasionally strengthen the bonds of marriage by increasing interdependence and intimacy (Hyman et al., 2008).

So, what does a marriage need in order to survive immigration? Most essential are communication and trust, as in all marriages. As well, the immigrant couple needs flexibility: an ability to adjust to changing gender roles and responsibilities in the new society. It may also need new ways of coping with stress and managing conflict (Cheung, 2008; Huang and Akhtar, 2005; Hyman et al., 2008). External factors are also important; these include striking a good balance between old and new cultures and being able to build new support networks (Cheung, 2008).

THE LIFE CYCLE OF A MARRIAGE

Many happy couples expect that their marriage will become even happier as they enter and pass through each successive stage of life. However, here people's expectations may be unrealistic. Most marriages have predictable difficulties connected to new obligations they take on over the passage of time.

Most marriages follow a familiar pattern of marital happiness, depicted in Figure 5.4. They start out at a high level of satisfaction—even joy and contentment. These feelings of satisfaction decline more or less steadily over the next 25 years, with the birth and socialization of children. With the departure of children, feelings of marital satisfaction begin to rise again and reach a plateau in old age, typically the retirement years. One of the earliest studies to reveal this pattern was a classic Canadian study by University of Calgary sociologists Eugen Lupri and James Frideres (1981). Lupri and Frideres related this pattern directly to the effects of parenthood and showed that the decline in satisfaction and subsequent rebound were dramatically steeper for couples who had borne children than for couples who had not. Many researchers have replicated that finding in the decades that followed.

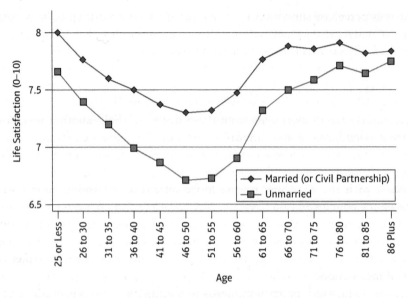

Figure 5.4 Overall happiness of married versus non-married persons

Source: This figure is adapted from Figure 1 of S. Grover & J.F. Helliwell. 2014. *New Evidence on Marriage and the set Point for Happiness.* NBER Working Paper 20794. With permission of the authors and the NBER. © 2014 by Shawn Grover and John F. Helliwell. http://faculty.arts.ubc.ca/ jhelliwell/papers/w20794.pdf

Marriage Beginnings

In the beginning, sex is especially important for marital satisfaction. The quality and frequency of sexual intercourse becomes an important indicator of couple satisfaction and relationship quality. People come to marriage with preconceived notions about sexual behaviour, and these notions will influence the way sexual activity plays out in the relationship. For example, a sexual double standard, as discussed in Chapter 3, may influence the sexual activities of a couple, especially in the beginning stages of a marriage. Nevertheless, both men and women tend to find that sexual satisfaction is important for marital satisfaction, whatever notions they bring to the relationship.

The Introduction of Children into a Marriage

In general, the transition to parenthood is associated with less frequent sex and, therefore, steeper declines in marital satisfaction, compared to couples who remain childless (Lawrence et al., 2008). To some degree, the effect of children on the relationship depends on whether their arrival was desired and planned. Not surprisingly, couples who plan for the pregnancy experience less decline in marital satisfaction than couples whose pregnancy is unplanned and unexpected (and possibly unwanted).

As mentioned, in all couples, marital satisfaction declines gradually with the passage of time. This occurs whether the couple bears children or not, and it occurs for both husbands and wives. However, the decline is less for couples who do not bear children. Lawrence and colleagues (2008: 41) note that "parenthood hastens marital decline—even among relatively satisfied couples who select themselves into this transition—but planning status and prepregnancy marital satisfaction generally protect marriages from these declines." Said another way, couples who are getting along poorly before parenthood or have not planned (or even desired) parenthood will show the largest declines in marital satisfaction after the birth of a child.

Today, with the economy posing more difficulty for young people starting careers, young couples are still having children, but they are having their first children (on average) at later ages than in past generations. This marks the continuation of a long process by which women are entering parenthood at later ages, to allow them to complete a longer education and, often, to gain a foothold in the job market before taking on motherhood.

On the other hand, parenthood leads to a lot of new responsibilities and challenges, including many new chances to "fail" (see Figure 5.5). No wonder that people who feel they are failing as parents feel badly about their lives. And lest you

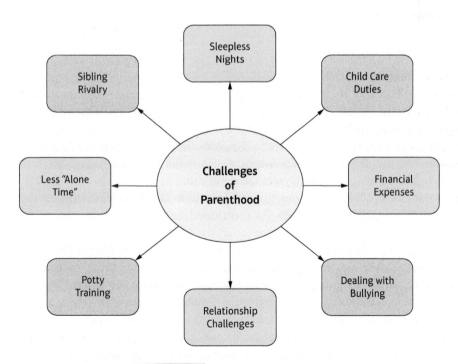

Figure 5.5 Challenges of parenthood

imagine these feelings are limited to male–female relations, the same trend is found in lesbian couples. Shortly after the birth of a child, lesbian couples report less love and more conflict in their marriage (Peplau and Fingerhut, 2007). Therefore, despite the (typically) more egalitarian division of labour in lesbian homes, children are nonetheless stressful.

Researchers have offered at least four explanations for this near-universal decline in marital satisfaction following childbirth (Twenge, Campbell, and Foster, 2003):

1. *Role conflict model*: The arrival of children often leads to changes in social roles, bringing them closer to the traditional ones—wives providing child care and husbands being the breadwinner.

2. *Restriction of freedom model*: Children drastically reduce the time wives have for their husbands or themselves. The presence of a preschool-aged child reduces significantly the activities wives do alone or parents do as a couple or with non-family members. This radical shift from spousal (adult-centred) activities to parenting (child-centred) activities creates an emotional distance the partners find hard to bridge.

3. *Sexual dissatisfaction model*: With the presence of children, sleepless nights increase. Privacy, and often romance, disappears. It is more difficult to have sexual relations.

4. *Financial cost model*: Children are expensive, and the costs involved in raising them often constrain family resources.

After the birth of a baby, mothers, usually the main providers of child care, have to change their time use much more than fathers do. According to the role conflict model, mothers may have to give up previous jobs in exchange for household and caregiving duties. Their happiness decreases if they resent the fact that they had to give up their careers. Fathers, on the other hand, may have to spend more time at work to meet increased financial needs. Some studies have also pointed to changes in the domestic division of labour as a source of new conflict in the marriage. As well, access to and ability to afford daycare are significant.

Bonnie Fox (2001) points out that the transition to parenthood often increases gender inequality in the marriage. As mentioned, many women put their jobs on hold to stay home with the newborn (even if it is just during maternity leave). Child care is difficult and time-consuming work, so typically mothers have to devote more time to their infant and less time to their husband. Fox's study found that husbands often resent this change in marital attention (and sexual opportunity). To appease their husbands and keep the family together, many wives end up catering to their husband's needs at the expense of their own needs for rest and leisure.

In short, how a woman experiences mothering is largely a product of negotiation with her partner. Intensive mothering requires considerable support, which depends on gaining the consent and active cooperation of the partner; in turn, this need for cooperation can cause all sorts of subtle new inequalities in the relationship (Fox, 2001: 11–12). As well, partners with young children are often too busy to spend even limited "quality time" with each other. Sexual activity falls off dramatically and may never return to its original level. With preschoolers present in a household, sexual inactivity is likely and prolonged. New sources of conflict emerge for the couple (Wadsby and Sydsjoe, 2001). Both husbands and wives often become anxious about new troubles associated with financial matters, family relations, work, and social isolation.

Having children can even affect the mental and physical health of a couple. Children younger than age 18 take time and work, create feelings of overload, and lower marital quality—all of which can cause depression in the caregiving parents (Najman et al., 2014). Single parenthood—meaning an absence of partnership—is especially associated with increased rates of all common mental disorders (Helbig, Lampert, Klose, and Jacobi, 2006).

A good marriage can decrease the risk of postnatal depression in first-time parents. Many couples also come to rely on their parents—especially their mothers—for practical help and emotional support (Matthey, Barnett, Ungerer, and Waters, 2000). As mentioned, a husband's participation in pregnancy and parenthood is essential in helping to keep the marriage healthy. Wives in strong, supportive marriages are more likely to view the baby in a loving, warm, and joyful way, for example. They are also less likely to feel abandoned by their husbands during pregnancy (Sitrin, 2001).

Infertility

Having young children commonly increases stress and marital problems, even when the children are wanted. But ironically, couples who want children but cannot have them because of involuntary (or unwanted) infertility also suffer increased stress and anxiety. In recent decades, this problem of unwanted infertility has become a more common issue. On average, Canadian women are waiting longer to have children as they complete their education and work toward establishing careers. But when wives wait too long, they can encounter difficulties getting pregnant due to age-related infertility. Often, infertile women experience high levels of stress and depression because of this inability.

Couples, and especially women, are caught in a bind. Biologically, women and men are in their prime childbearing stages in young adulthood, but culturally, they are now expected to wait longer in order to ensure that they are socially and economically "ready." As a result, infertility that results from waiting "too long" is an increasingly important cause of marital strain. This strain is increased by the financial costs of expensive infertility treatments. The industry catering to infertile couples is booming as couples spend hundreds of millions of dollars on fertility treatments that, often, do not work (BioPortfolio, 2006).

Facing infertility can cause intense feelings of powerlessness; however, as with all other marital stressors, coping abilities are key. As with other strains, couples cope with the stress brought about by infertility in many ways, some more effective than others. Active coping means asking for advice, trying to solve the problem, and discussing feelings about infertility. Meaning-based coping involves trying to grow as a person in other ways and redirecting life goals. Both approaches have their merits and shortcomings (Peterson, Pirritano, Christensen, and Schmidt, 2008).

In recent years, with the widespread growth of obesity in our society, researchers have studied the causal link between obesity and infertility. According to Orkun Tan and Bruce R. Carr (2012: 517), "obesity-related infertility is one of the most common problems of reproductive-age obese women who desire childbearing." For this problem, they recommend various bariatric surgeries, which are surgeries that limit a woman's caloric intake. These surgeries either reduce the size of an individual's stomach or reduce the length of the person's intestinal tract. The researchers report that bariatric surgeries not only are successful in helping patients to lose weight, but also help to normalize menstrual cycles and improve pregnancy rates.

Obesity reportedly causes an increase in testosterone levels in women and a decrease in sex-binding hormones. This hormonal imbalance, in turn, can disrupt a woman's menstrual cycle and induce irregular bleeding. Following this lead, researchers found a 60 percent improvement in menstrual regularity in adolescents after bariatric surgeries and a 33 percent improvement in adults (Tan and Carr, 2012). They also found that 71.7 percent of women who were not able to ovulate before their operation were able to have regular periods afterward (Tan and Carr, 2012).

The Midlife Marriage

As children enter school and the demands for round-the-clock caregiving diminish, marriages face new kinds of problems. For example, many couples have to take on new caregiving responsibilities for their aging parents. As well, married couples in their forties and fifties report problems with financial matters, sexual issues, and ways of dealing with adolescent children. Compared to newlyweds, these couples are less likely to report problems with values, commitment, spiritual matters, and violence (Henry and Miller, 2004).

As children approach late adolescence and start to leave home, marital satisfaction usually starts to increase. Once the children leave home, creating what is often called an "empty nest," many marriages improve nearly to newlywed levels of satisfaction. Parental and work responsibilities also decline around that time, partly explaining this return of marital satisfaction (Bouchard, 2014).

Many husbands and wives now "rediscover" each other because they have more leisure time to get reacquainted. Compared with younger married couples, older couples report much less anxiety about the relationship, less desire for change in their marriage, and a more accurate understanding of the needs of their partners. In part, this is due to constructive communication by wives, which has been shown to improve and regulate the emotional content of successful long-term marriages for older couples (Bloch, Haase, and Levenson, 2014). Of course, the experience of positive changes is not universal. Sometimes the departure and absence of children have an opposite effect, resulting in feelings of loneliness. Emotional loneliness is especially common among women in second marriages (de Jong Gierveld, Broese van Groenou, Hoogendoorn, and Smit, 2009).

Even later, married couples enjoy more relationship satisfaction during their retirement years than do unmarried (i.e., cohabiting or dating) couples (Price and Joo, 2005). Because social networks tend to shrink over the life course, marriages increasingly become a source of well-being in post-retirement years (Kupperbusch, Levenson, and Ebling, 2003). The amount of psychological well-being people gain from their marital relationship depends largely on how they assess their personal resources after retirement as compared to before retirement (Wang, 2007)—whether, for example, they feel socially isolated by their retirement from work or liberated from meaningless work-related interactions.

Among Canadians ages 50 to 74, relationship satisfaction is highest when both members of the couple are retired, compared to when they are both in the labour force. When they are both retired, they are best able to coordinate their interests, activities, and time use patterns. The least amount of work-induced stress impinges on the family relationship at this time. Note also that relationship satisfaction is highest among these people when no children are living with the couple and lowest when two or more children are living with them (Chalmers and Milan, 2005).

Within marriages, couples tend to have more time to share activities after their retirement, leading to greater social cohesion in the relationship (Fitzpatrick and Vinick, 2003). Also, after retirement, most husbands generally involve themselves more in household tasks (Kulik, 2001). That said, many aspects of the marriage do not change after retirement, and marital quality remains more or less the same (Fitzpatrick and Vinick, 2003). For example, power relations tend to remain similar before and after retirement, although spouses have more independence in how they use their time (Kulik, 2001). And some aspects of a marital relationship may even decline. For example, many wives report feeling that their retired husband now impinges on (or disrupts) their comfortable personal and social world (Bushfield, Fitzpatrick, and Vinick, 2008).

Nonetheless, the need for companionship in later life is strong for both men and women. For instance, in a qualitative study of middle-class seniors over the age of 65, Schlesinger and Schlesinger (2009) found that the main reason senior men enter a new union after the death of a spouse is to alleviate loneliness. Women, on the other hand, enter a new marriage for various reasons that include companionship, sexuality, friendship, shared intellectual interests, and support for children and grandchildren. Regardless of the reasons, these new unions bring well-being in various ways to both senior men and senior women.

WHAT MAKES A MARRIAGE SATISFYING?

At every stage of the life cycle, the same elements are crucial for marital satisfaction. Chief among these are love, sexual satisfaction, intimacy, and conflict management. We discuss each of these in turn.

Love

People vary culturally in the qualities they look for when selecting mates (Rothbaum, Pott, Azuma, Miyake, and Weisz, 2000). As we noted in Chapter 3, North Americans consider love an essential part of the mating choice; to marry without love seems almost immoral. Traits people look for when forming a relationship typically include personal attraction, trust, and romantic love.

What, then, of marriages that are not based on romantic love? In many societies, arranged marriages are the norm. Arranged marriages in China, the Indian subcontinent, and the Middle East are often built on parents' views about important qualities in future partners. In arranging the marriage, parents usually choose carefully—and homogamously—for their children. As a result, arranged marriages tend to be stable and sometimes happy. But are they happier than love marriages?

Westerners tend to assume that they cannot be. Cultures that support arranged marriages say that arranged marriages become, over time, even more satisfying than love marriages. Allegedly, arranged marriages "heat up" with time, while love marriages "cool down." Research on this idea is mixed. A study of Indian couples in the United States found no significant differences between arranged marriages and love marriages in terms of marital satisfaction, commitment, companionate love, and passionate love (Regan, Lakhanpal, and Anguiano, 2012). In China, where the arranged marriage has a long history, a survey by Xiaohe and Whyte (1990) found that love marriages are more satisfying than arranged marriages at every stage or duration. However, another study of people from 12 different countries and 6 different religions found that love grew significantly over time in arranged marriages (Epstein, Pandit, and Thakar, 2013).

In Canada, most people marry for love. They see love as the basis of their union, without which the marriage would not satisfy either partner. According to our ideology about marriage, people are not supposed to think about other things when assessing a partner for romantic compatibility. However, people do not ignore practical considerations, such as the earning power or social status of a potential mate. People who must live hand to mouth especially cannot afford to think as much about love; often, they have to be more practical. Therefore, the more financially secure people feel, the more willing they are to indulge romantic impulses: They can afford to indulge their emotions.

Ironically, people who assign the most importance to love as a basis for happiness also have the highest divorce rates (Campbell and Wright, 2010). They are likely to look for and find flaws in their love marriage. As well, a marriage based on romantic ideals may not be able to weather the often-harsh realities of the situations couples must face together.

In marital relations, feelings of love and companionship usually continue throughout life, yet some types of love are more common than others at particular stages of a marriage (Sumter, Valkenburg, and Peter, 2013). Late adults (age 50+ years) may have lower levels of sexual passion and intimacy but similar levels of commitment compared to young (age 18 to 30 years) and middle adults (age 30 to 50 years). This type of companionable love is more common later in a romantic marriage, compared with sexual love, which flourishes earlier in the relationship.

Sexual Satisfaction

Sex may be most important in the early years of marriage; however, it is still important in middle age and beyond. In middle-aged couples, sexual satisfaction continues to make an important contribution to couples' positive evaluations of their marriage. In turn, marital satisfaction also has an effect on the frequency and satisfaction of sex.

With increased life expectancy, couples now live together longer and remain sexually active longer than in the past. The association between sexual activity and marital satisfaction may be weaker for seniors than for younger couples, but sexual frequency and happiness are still correlated for older adults (Karraker, DeLamater, and Schwartz, 2011). It is not a lack of desire that typically causes a decline in the frequency of sexual interaction in older adults. For many older women, the decline is due to a lack of opportunity: As they age, women are more likely (than men) to be widowed and often have a hard time finding a sexual partner. For older men, the decline in sexual activity is typically due to a decline in libido and physical health.

An authoritative international study of men and women between the ages of 40 and 80 found that sexual well-being remains strongly related to overall happiness. The study, by Laumann, Mahay, and Youm (2007), found that most middle-aged and older respondents with partners remain sexually active. A more interesting finding is that people in countries with a culture of gender equality are most likely to report being sexually satisfied. Of the 29 countries surveyed, Canada ranked third in these respects, behind only Spain and Austria. The lowest rankings on equality and satisfaction were for Japan and Taiwan. However, a literature review by another researcher found that other factors also play a part in sexual satisfaction. They include sociodemographic and psychological characteristics, physical and psychological health status, and variables associated with intimate relationships. Factors related to social support and family relationships also play an important role (del Mar Sánchez-Fuentesa, Santos-Iglesiasb, and Sierraa, 2014).

Finally, a global study of 29 countries found that sexual difficulties are common among senior adults across the world, with important gender differences. Among women, age is an important correlate of lubrication difficulties among women; among men, age is also an important correlate of other sexual problems, including a diminished interest in sex, the inability to reach orgasm, and erectile difficulties (Laumann et al., 2004).

Men and women experience sexual pleasure differently. They want, need, and expect different things. This gendered difference has consequences in every aspect of a marriage, including sex. For example, wives typically report less sexual satisfaction than do husbands (Laumann et al., 2004). As well, the predictors of sexual satisfaction are different for husbands and wives (Shoenfeld et al., 2016). For women, sex occurs within a gendered or gender-unequal society. Many women have to find sexual pleasure within a marriage that also provokes feelings of powerlessness, anxieties about contraception, and exhaustion from child care and outside employment.

Intimacy: Sexual and Emotional

We should not confuse sexual satisfaction with intimacy, because the two are different. "Intimacy" comes from the Latin word meaning "inward" or "inmost." To become intimate with someone else means allowing them access to our private world, and trusting them with the things that are important to us, whether that be valued material possessions or property of a more emotional nature. Building this intimacy with a partner is the key to a mature, surviving marriage.

Intimacy is not mainly about sex. Many sexually active couples are not truly intimate with each other, and many who are intimate have no sexual relations. Consider the odd status of friendship—especially same-sex friendship—in our culture; friendships are sometimes far more intimate (in the original sense of the word) than marriages.

The Importance of Intimacy

- Size matters: As the size of a family household increases, intimacy between the partners typically decreases and pleasure, including sexual pleasure, declines (de Munck and Korotayev, 2007).

- Equality matters: In societies where men and women are of equal status (or of almost equal status), male–female romantic relationships are more likely to be intimate and satisfying (de Munck and Korotayev, 2007).

- Trust matters: In romantic relationships, most people seek and desire a partner with qualities that inspire confidence and (thereby) facilitate intimacy (Johnson and Anderson, 2013).

- Patriarchy matters: Traditional gender ideologies generally result in lower levels of couple intimacy by inhibiting self-disclosure, which hinders the development of intimacy (Marshall, 2008).

A loving, committed couple can have problems establishing and maintaining emotional intimacy for many reasons. For example, one or both partners may have never learned how to express their feelings and respond to a partner's expression of feelings. Couples can also have problems with sexual intimacy when they have different levels of desire. Gender can moderate associations between individual sexual desire discrepancy (SDD) and reported couple communication. Specifically, negative associations between individual SDD and communication in one study were especially strong when husbands reported high discrepancies between desired and actual sexual frequency (Willoughby, Farero, and Busby, 2014). This can be a problem since North American culture places a high premium on sex, both as a source of pleasure and as an indicator of trust and intimacy.

Besides, as we have seen, sexual satisfaction contributes significantly to marital satisfaction (McNulty, Wenner, and Fisher, 2016). Couples in which sexual satisfaction is low and one or both partners show little sexual desire may have problems getting along together.

Problems with intimacy sometimes lead to marital infidelity. Typically, men consider cheating by their partner to mean sexual interaction with another man. Women may consider cheating by their partner to mean emotional intimacy with another woman, whether sexual relations occur or not. In good marriages, we find intimacy of both kinds, sexual and emotional. Satisfied partners are more sexually intimate with each other, as measured by how often they display affection physically, touch each other, kiss each other, cuddle, and have sex. These loving behaviours are mutual. Shows of affection by one partner in a good marriage usually prompt shows of affection by the other partner. Intimacy grows naturally in a sympathetic marriage.

A new obstacle to intimate fidelity is posed by internet chat rooms and other online forums, such as MySpace and Facebook (Hoffner, 2008). These have made it easier than ever to enjoy the stability of marriage and the thrills of the dating scene at the same time (Mileham, 2007). Often, emotional infidelity comes in the form of anonymous online interactions of a sexual nature. Anonymity makes the internet a seemingly "safe place" for infidelity for married people. Sometimes people turn to these online forums to satisfy emotional needs that their current partner is not fulfilling, and sometimes, despite initial intentions, such communications transform into close and intimate relationships (Hoffner, 2008).

Online relationships can be just as rewarding and intimate as face-to-face relationships. As a result, even though a person may participate with pure intentions, unexpected intimacies may evolve nonetheless (Hoffner, 2008). Married people tend to rationalize this behaviour as innocent and harmless. Even people who report happy marriages have joined chat rooms for these purposes (Heiman et al., 2011). As we see in Figure 5.6, women are much more likely to be upset by emotional infidelity than men, and men tend to place a higher priority on sexual infidelity.

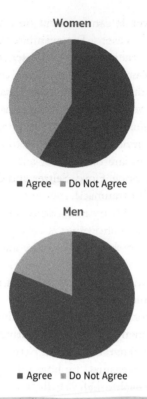

Women

■ Agree ■ Do Not Agree

Men

■ Agree ■ Do Not Agree

Figure 5.6 Responses to online infidelity "My partner's sexual involvement would upset me more than my partner's emotional bonding with someone else."
Source: Based on Groothof, Hinke A.K., Pieternel Dijkstra, & Dick P.H. Barelds. 2009. Sex differences in jealousy: The case of Internet infidelity. *Journal of Social and Personal Relationships* 26(8): 1119–1129. Web.

Coping and Conflict Management

How well a couple manages the conflicts that arise in their marriage also shapes their marital satisfaction, and these conflicts and stresses come in many forms. Some couples avoid discussing important aspects of their marriage, such as their financial situation and their children, and they are more likely just to make small talk, but this avoidance of conflict does not lead to marital satisfaction (Nielsen, 2002). When talking about important or conflictual issues, couples with low marital satisfaction do so more negatively than couples with high marital satisfaction, reminding us that it is important not only what is said, but how it is said (Nielsen, 2002).

Health-induced strains also reduce marital satisfaction. Taking care of a severely ill partner puts an enormous chronic strain on a marriage. This leads to dissatisfaction, especially for the caregiving partner. However, research finds gender differences: One study reports that marital conflict may be more likely for wives whose husbands are in poor health, but not the other way around (Iveniuk et al., 2014). However, another study conducted over 20 years found no differences among gender, but instead that marital happiness is associated with health in early life and that marital problems are associated with health in midlife (Miller et al., 2013).

Traumatic events in the course of a marriage lead to distress, which has effects on marriage. For example, the death of a child reduces marital satisfaction by straining emotional and sexual intimacy for years afterward. Often, marriages fall apart after a child's death. Partners have a hard time thinking and talking about their suddenly changed lives, with their child missing. The grieving parents often need help reorganizing the ways they think and talk about themselves and their family and may have a lower health-related quality of life in the long term (Song, Floyd, Seltzer, and Greenberg, 2010)

When strains are chronic or traumatic, they are distressing and increase the likelihood of marital conflict. Married people cannot avoid conflicts, whatever their cause, and trying to avoid disagreements altogether is unwise. Marital well-being is affected less by the presence or absence of hardship than by marital skills and beliefs, or coping abilities. With the passage of time, many couples figure out how to defuse and laugh at their disagreements. In older couples, conflict resolution is usually less hostile and more loving than in middle-aged couples.

Styles of conflict resolution vary by gender, and this difference causes more conflict. Yet, as both men and women age, levels of negative characteristics (e.g., hostility) lessen, and average levels of positive characteristics (e.g., warmth, affiliation) increase, as a result of fine-tuning of emotional regulation and mood stability in later years (Henry, Berg, Smith, and Florsheim, 2007; Story et al., 2007).

Which is better—making a fuss or refusing to say anything at all? Research suggests that becoming quiet and withdrawn does the most to keep the peace and preserve marital happiness, providing this is not just a means of avoiding the discussion of problems. Many new parents cope (effectively) with the increased stress that accompanies childbirth by adopting this strategy of quiescence. However, this short-term coping strategy is only effective temporarily while the couple decides how to address their problem in a more useful way. In the long run, people in more equal power relationships need to use fewer avoidance strategies (Worley and Samp, 2016).

An important process affecting marital well-being is forgiveness. Husbands and wives who can forgive each other for past transgressions are much happier than couples who cannot do so. Studies have found that strategies of nonforgiveness—for example, retaliation and avoidance—not only fail to resolve conflicts, but also make conflicts worse. Unresolved conflicts then spill over into future conflicts and create a negative cycle of continuing—and even worsening—conflict (Fincham and Beach, 2006).

We should remember that, as tempting as this may seem, walking away from issues and troubles is not a good practice in the end. Neither is hostile argument a good practice. It neither makes the disagreement disappear nor improves the marriage. Each partner responds to the other's comments with one-upmanship, and the argument escalates, sometimes even resulting in violence. Violence, as we will learn in Chapter 8, is never a satisfactory way to deal with marital conflict. Fortunately, older adults find forgiveness, cooperation, and coping more useful than control when dealing with interpersonal problems (Smith et al., 2009).

In short, successful and happy couples practise a mixture of emotional expression and emotional restraint under conditions of stress. They try to discuss their disagreements in a calm, friendly way. Most important, they understand that each has his or her own way of dealing with the stress and show each other patience and sympathy.

Domestic Violence

We discuss domestic violence at length in a later chapter, but it should be noted here in passing that domestic violence is a widespread and significant problem for many Canadian couples. In many couples, domestic violence is the opposite of peaceful conflict resolution, and domestic violence against Indigenous women is one of the most talked-about problems facing women in Canada today. The violence that Indigenous women in Canada face is unprecedented; Amnesty International dubbed it a "national human rights crisis" (Amnesty International, 2014). Indigenous women are significantly more likely than non-Indigenous women to be the victims of domestic violence, sexual violence, and murder. A 2011 Statistics Canada report notes that, in 2009, 15 percent of Indigenous women had experienced domestic violence, in comparison to only 6 percent of non-Indigenous women (Statistics Canada, 2011g).

In fact, studies have shown that both Indigenous men and women are more likely to be victims of domestic violence than non-Indigenous men and women. Yet we too often ignore the extent of domestic violence against Indigenous men. In a study of intimate partner violence among Indigenous men in Canada, Douglas A. Brownridge (2010) analyzed Statistics Canada data from 1994 to 1999 and found that 6 percent of Indigenous men reported domestic violence victimization, in comparison to 1.7 percent of non-Indigenous men. Indigenous men were much more likely to experience each type of 10 individual forms of violence. For example, compared to non-Indigenous men, Indigenous men were twice as likely to be physically threatened and to have something thrown at them; three times as likely to be kicked, hit with a fist, or bitten; and four times as likely to be slapped. They were a staggering 10 times more likely to be choked, to be threatened with or have had a knife used against them, and to be beaten (Brownridge, 2010: 229–230).

In Canada, as in the United States and elsewhere, Indigenous people are overrepresented as victims of violence, even including intimate partner violence (Brzozowski, Taylor-Butts, and Johnson, 2006). In fact, the number of victims of violence among Indigenous people significantly exceeds the number of victims among non-Indigenous people.

In 2009, Statistics Canada reported that more than one-third (37 percent) of the Indigenous population age 15 years or older living in Canadian provinces has been victimized, in comparison to about one-quarter of non-Indigenous Canadians. The most common forms of victimization among Indigenous people include theft of personal property, robbery, and physical and sexual assault (Perrault and Brennan, 2010). Indigenous people are also significantly more likely to be victims of homicide. Between 1997 and 2000, the homicide rate for Indigenous people was seven times higher than the rate for non-Indigenous people (Perreault, 2011). No other minorities, immigrants or native-born, are at the same risk for victimization.

What makes Indigenous victimization more likely? Male unemployment is linked to an increase in violent victimization for Indigenous men, as is heavy drinking. Both Indigenous and non-Indigenous men have a higher chance of victimization if they were previously married, but previously married Indigenous men were still more likely to experience domestic violence than previously married non-Indigenous men.

So-called "location theory" helps explain these high rates of Indigenous victimization. Over the past century, Indigenous people have continued to live in worse social and economic conditions than non-Indigenous people, on average. Persistent social and economic inequalities have continued to involve Indigenous people in criminal incidents, either as victims or as perpetrators. Factors such as poor living conditions situated in crowded areas, unemployment, lack of education, and low income have continued to expose them to crime (La Prairie, 2002; Reading and Wien, 2009). These factors have also increased the risk for domestic violence, which occurs at a high rate in Indigenous households.

Indigenous people have also continued to maintain high-risk lifestyles that include drugs, alcohol, and "hanging out on the streets" (Brady, Dawe, and Richmond, 1998; Perkins et al., 1994). This is especially true of Indigenous youth. Students of the victimization literature know that high-risk lifestyles lead to high-risk situations, which increase the likelihood of victimization.

Gender Roles in Marriage

We noted earlier that gender equality tends to improve people's sex lives. However, we can make an even stronger point that gender equality tends to improve people's marriages—at least, among people who have been raised to expect equal treatment. People are more satisfied with a marriage that meets their expectations of what a marriage should be and how a partner should treat them. Increasingly, this means that, in our society, people, especially women, are much more satisfied when their partner treats them as an equal in the marriage.

Do women in families have less power than men? That question is surprisingly difficult to answer, even if we just limit ourselves to an examination of domestic labour. As we will see in Chapter 7, women still do most of the housework in Canadian families, even if they also work for pay outside the home. Not surprisingly, when the household division of labour is unequal (favouring husbands), wives—especially employed wives—are likely to become unhappy and depressed (Kalmijn and Monden, 2011). However, the issue is not merely who does more minutes of housework per day than whom; the issue is whether and to what degree this difference is viewed as unfair or inequitable.

The most dissatisfied wives today are younger mothers who do most of the household work—often, far more than their husbands do—as well as work for pay outside the home. The more involved women are in the labour market, the more women and men are likely to report one person doing a larger proportion of the housework as unfair (Jansen, Weber, Kraaykamp, and Verbakel, 2016). It is not just the objective reality of wives doing more housework, but the wife feeling she is under-rewarded and undervalued that is the problem (DeMaris, 2007).

Despite being labour intensive, housework is not regarded as "real work" by most people in our society. Household labour is therefore not recognized and rewarded in the way that workplace labour is; in fact, it is generally unpaid when done by a family member. Increasingly, this gender inequality leads to marital conflict.

The distribution of domestic work between men and women has scarcely changed in recent decades. Between 1998 and 2010, husbands increased their time spent on domestic work by a mere 15 minutes per day, while for women the amount of time spent on domestic labour did not change at all. Specifically, the average length of time men spent doing household work increased from 2 hours and 51 minutes per day in 1998 to 3 hours and 4 minutes in 2010. For women, the average duration remained unchanged at 4 hours and 15 minutes per day (Marshall, 2011). Likewise, in 2010, women were more likely than men (91 versus 81 percent) to have done household work on the diary day (see Figure 5.7).

Couples today argue more about household work than about paid work or anything else, as we will see in Chapter 7, which discusses the work-family conflict so common in Canadian homes. Child care is an area of particular conflict when household work is discussed. For example, a larger discrepancy between ideal and actual division of labour in male same-sex couples can lead to lower relationship quality, less expression of affection, and less relationship agreement (Tornello, Kruczkowski, and Patterson, 2015).

Bulanda (2011) reports an inverse relationship between marital satisfaction and power inequality. That is, happy couples more often share the power. Equality brings couples closer together, so partners are better able to support each other (Knudson-Martin, 2013). Equal partners are more satisfied with their marriage and better adjusted (Glenwright and Fowler, 2013); they also report using fewer power strategies to get their way. Support from partners of work careers promotes higher marital satisfaction (Bakker, Demerouti, and Burke, 2009) and reduces work–family conflict (Gareis, Barnett, Ertel, and Berkman, 2009).

Despite increases in the fairness of domestic labour, the division of household labour in heterosexual marriages remains less equal than the division of labour in same-sex marriages. In same-sex marriages, household tasks are divided more equally, though in different ways: Lesbian partners tend to share the same tasks, whereas gay men tend to specialize in different tasks (Peplau and Fingerhut, 2007).

Summing up to this point, marriages in our society are still better for men than for women (Jackson, Miller, Oka, and Henry, 2014). Married people are, on average,

Figure 5.7 Average minutes per day men and women spent in household activities, 2010

Source: American Time Use Survey. 2010. Charts by topics: Household activities. Bureau of Labor Statisitics. www.bls.gov/tus/charts/household.htm.

Note: Data include all noninstitutional persons age 15 over. Data include all days of the week and are annual averages for 2012. Travel related to these activities is not included in these estimates.

healthier than unmarried people. Significantly, this is truer for men than it is for women. Interestingly, women are more likely than men to think that both men and women can have satisfying lives without marriage, while at the same time they are also more likely to think that only women can have satisfying lives without marriage (Kaufman and Goldscheider, 2007). Indeed, men and women often have different experiences of marriage. Conflicts in marital relations can take a greater toll on women, especially when coupled with conflicts at work. This may be because women are more likely than men to blame themselves for marital conflict.

Work, Money, and Marital Quality

With more women entering the workforce and the subsequent rise of dual-earner families, the influence of work and money on marital quality deserves a more detailed discussion. As Dakin and Wampler (2008: 300) point out, "because money is woven into many parts of the family and marital fabric, it is essential to better understand this family financial phenomenon." They contend that disagreements over finances are among the top reasons for divorce.

Financial stress can lead to spousal hostility and a decrease in spousal warmth (Dakin and Wampler, 2008). It can also increase the likelihood of depression in both partners. The process is circular and reciprocal: Depression can lead partners to withdraw their social support and undermine each other. These behaviours, in turn, reduce marital satisfaction and intensify the depression. Depression can also increase levels of stress and hostility and increase interpersonal stress (Rehman, Gollan, and Mortimer, 2008). For families living in poverty, financial problems constitute one of the most significant stressors, as these families find it difficult to meet their basic economic needs.

Religiosity can buffer the negative effects of economic stress on married couples, if the spouses share similar beliefs, pray together, or attend religious services together (Lichter and Carmalt, 2009). These results show that social institutions, shared beliefs, and engagement in common activities may have the capacity to enhance and strengthen marital bonds independent of financial circumstances. A study conducted by Ipsos Reid for Calgary-based accounting firm MNP Ltd. found that 20 percent of Canadians polled who were married or living common-law said that their relationship problems were due to their current debt situations. And 27 percent said that financial stress has left a negative impact on their relationships (Nguyen, 2013).

The stresses of work can also reduce marital satisfaction. Unemployment because of job loss is known to increase marital conflict, because of either the loss of ordinary ways of family living or an unwanted role reversal (especially for males). Retirement from work can either increase or decrease marital satisfaction. Leaving a high-stress job normally increases satisfaction. However, poor health and other changes that often cause or accompany retirement reduce satisfaction (Forman-Hoffman et al., 2008; Wickrama, O'Neal, and Lorenz, 2013). Retirement, like unemployment, may also reverse gender roles or reduce social support. In general, people need to prepare for retirement and, often, adjust their marriage to handle their new situation.

Verbal Communication

As already noted, communication is important for marital satisfaction. Both the quantity and the quality of communication are important in a marriage. The quality of spousal communication includes (1) how open partners are, (2) how well they listen, (3) how attentive and responsive they are, and (4) to what extent they confide in each other. These are all important to establishing a good, satisfying marriage.

Quantity means how often partners talk with each other. Successful couples talk a lot, even if they have tight schedules and little time to spend together, and even if the topics of conversation are trivial. Satisfied couples engage in much more communication than dissatisfied couples, who engage in little communication on most of the topics commonly discussed by satisfied couples (Hawkins, Blanchard, Baldwin, and Fawcett, 2008). A feeling of social support from family and friends for same-sex couples is directly related to well-being, and social support from one's partner is protective against the negative impacts of stress (Graham and Barnow, 2013).

Satisfied couples chit-chat; they make small talk, banter, and joke around. Dissatisfied couples talk less or mainly talk about weighty matters when they talk at all. Couples do not all have to communicate at the same rate to be successful; however, the couples' sensed quality of communication contributes significantly to marital satisfaction. A word, phrase, or even type of body language can have intensely different meanings for different people. Partly to avoid these problems, and partly to separate themselves from others, many couples develop their own private **idioms**. These idioms take various forms: special pet names for each other; inside jokes; and words or phrases for intimate activities, special activities, or places. Couples in the earliest stages of marriage report using the most idioms, and those in later stages use the fewest, for various reasons. One is the arrival of children. When teaching children to speak, you want to teach them words that will help them in the outside world. Family idioms will not do that.

At the beginning, however, the use of idioms improves communication because the couple has defined their meanings together. As a result, satisfied couples use more idioms than couples who report lower levels of marital satisfaction. For interracial couples who may have grown up in different cultures, the use of idioms can reduce conflict and increase openness by creating a language with which both parties are now familiar (Shi, 2000).

A common style of communication that increases marital conflict is the "demand/withdrawal pattern." In this pattern, one party—the demander—tries to establish communication by nagging, bullying, or criticizing the other partner. Partners with more power in the marriage are more likely to be the demander. The withdrawer, on the other hand, tries to avoid such discussions through silence, defensiveness, or withdrawal (Schrodt, Witt, and Shimkowski, 2014).

Like any behaviour that reduces marital satisfaction, the demand/withdrawal pattern of communication has health outcomes. Among married couples ages 23 to 71 years old, withdrawers—nagged spouses—had higher blood pressure and heart rate reactivity than the other groups. Husbands of withdrawer wives had even higher blood pressure than the husbands of demander wives. Demander (i.e., nagging) husbands with withdrawer wives experienced the highest blood pressure of all groups (Denton, Burleson, Hobbs, Von Stein, and Rodriguez, 2001).

This implies that neither nagging nor being nagged is a recipe for good communication. Partner communication patterns must be effective and similar enough to uphold marital quality and couple happiness. If partners discuss this problem, and what both parties want, their commitment to their marriage will increase.

Nonverbal Communication

Another important part of successful communication is the encoding and decoding of nonverbal information. Nonverbal communication includes all forms of communication that do not use verbal speech. These include posture, the direction of the gaze, and hand position, for example. Dissatisfied couples are especially prone to misunderstanding each other's nonverbal cues. This lack of understanding can cause problems, especially when a person's nonverbal cues contradict his or her verbal cues.

For example, if one partner is apologizing sincerely, and the other partner misreads the nonverbal signals as insincerity, a simple miscue can turn into a full-blown argument. Long-term couples may also ignore each other's verbal cues and rely mostly on nonverbal ones, causing more misunderstanding. Older long-married couples display lower frequencies of responsive listening than do younger couples, which can increase conflict in a situation where a partner uses verbal cues. Nonverbal accuracy increases over time in marriages, but it increases more for people who are satisfied with their marriages.

Communication and Gender

Communication is a gendered marital challenge, in that women sense more communication problems than men do and are more likely to see men as the source of these problems. Men and women speak differently, and this difference can become a problem. Consider an important form of marital communication called debriefing—conversation about what happened during the day. Men view their debriefing talk as having an informative report role; that is, to bring their partner up to speed on current events. In women's view, the talk may be about current events at home or at work, but the real purpose is downloading grievances, receiving and providing support, and renewing contact with the mate.

Studies show that women, more than men, are sensitive to the interpersonal meanings that lie "between the lines" in the messages they exchange with their mates. Societal expectations often make women responsible for regulating intimacy, or how close they allow others to come. For that reason, women pay more attention than men do to the underlying meanings about intimacy that messages imply. Men, on the other hand, are more sensitive than women are to "between the lines meanings" about status. For men, societal expectations are that they must negotiate hierarchy, or who's the captain and who's the crew (On this, see the classic study by Tannen [1993] and much additional research since then.)

Women tend to be the marriage specialists, and men tend to be task specialists. Women are typically the experts in "rapport talk," which refers to the types of communication that build, maintain, and strengthen marriages. Rapport talk reflects skills of talking, nurturing, emotional expression, empathy, and support. Men are typically the experts in task accomplishment and in addressing questions about facts. They are experts in "report talk," which refers to the types of communication that analyze issues and solve problems. Report talk reflects skills of being competitive, stifling sentimentality, analyzing, and focusing aggressively on task completion. These differences can create specific, and commonly experienced, misunderstandings (Torppa, 2002).

Myth: Love marriages are bound to be happier than arranged marriages.

■ **Reality:** The evidence is mixed on this. Some studies have shown no difference in marital satisfaction between love (or choice) marriages and arranged marriages (Myers, Madathil, and Tingle, 2005). In one study, Asian Indians who lived in North America were more satisfied in their arranged marriages than North American counterparts were in their love marriages (Madathil and Benshoff, 2008).

Myth: Intimate relationships in which the woman is older than the man do not work out well.

■ **Reality:** Relationships in which the woman is older have the highest level of romantic satisfaction, equality, and commitment (Lehmiller and Agnew, 2008). Perhaps, given the stigma associated with women-older relationships, couples only enter into such relationships if they plan to be committed and feel confident that the benefit will outweigh the cost (Lehmiller and Agnew, 2008).

Myth: Financial troubles will not hinder marital satisfaction, if the people involved love each other enough.

■ **Reality:** Poor people have more and worse marital conflicts because they are more stressed about problems caused by lack of sufficient income. The shortage of money leads to hostile emotions and thoughts of divorce, for example (Grable, Britt, and Cantrell, 2007).

THE EFFECTS OF DISABILITIES ON SPOUSAL RELATIONSHIPS

Many Canadians live with disabilities for their whole lives. They include blind people, deaf people, people with mobility issues or physical impairments, and people with intellectual or developmental delays. Often, the rest of the population pays little attention to them, or stigmatizes them. Often, they dismiss the idea that people with disabilities fall in love, get married, have kids, and worry about their marriage, just the same as everyone else.

As well, many Canadians' family lives are altered dramatically by an injury or disabling condition that arises after marriage. All severe injuries, illnesses, and disabilities strain spousal relationships. Obviously, the effects on a spousal relationship are greatest and harshest where the injury or illness is most severe. As an example, consider the effects of traumatic (or acquired) brain injury (TBI) on spousal relationships. Such brain injuries (or concussions) are an all-too-common result of automobile accidents, interpersonal violence, or contact sports (such as football or hockey), although they are less common than routine bone fractures or bruising.

Brain injuries can have an impact on the survivor's family that is dramatic, consequential, long term, and life altering. The physical, cognitive, emotional, and behavioural changes experienced by the brain-injured person can lead to a loss of employment or educational opportunities, family financial drain, reduced satisfaction in family interactions and intimacy, loss of social supports, change in family roles, and poorer family functioning. Alongside these changes in social relations come increased stress, anxiety, and depression for the spouses and family members who provide care for the survivor of a TBI.

TBI, like many other physical and mental disabilities, has the following effects, each of which places significant strain on intimate relations: increased financial hardship, psychosocial restrictions on the day-to-day physical functioning of the survivor, a heavy burden in caring for an injured spouse, and a limitation of social life and a peer-based, supportive relationship. Just as they need to adjust their housekeeping roles, couples dealing with injury or disability often need to adjust their sexual roles. However, this can be challenging given the relative inflexibility of gender roles in our culture (and many others). Many people find it hard to accept women doing what are traditionally seen as "men's" tasks, and vice versa. Perhaps because of these gendered stereotypes, men are less willing to fill the caregiving role and to take on domestic responsibilities in comparison to women (Glantz et al., 2009). As such, women are more likely to accept, and adapt to the (gendered) burdens of caregiving for an injured or ill partner, while men are more likely to terminate a relationship that would require such duties.

Couples experiencing the pressures associated with caregiver burden are especially vulnerable to relationship dissolution. Moreover, the frustration and stress that accumulate in caregivers over time can result in their negative—or even abusive—treatment of the injured individual. Irritability and exhaustion can lead caregiving spouses to vent their frustrations violently, using their partners as targets. Getch (2012) finds that support systems, counselling, and therapy are essential in helping spouses (and survivors of TBI) to manage their emotions in healthy ways in order to prevent such negative responses to anxiety.

In many societies, disabled or handicapped people are severely stigmatized. For example, a report by UNICEF (2004) notes that, in Afghanistan, people with disabilities face "verbal and physical abuse, lack of access to education and livelihood opportunities, lack of social opportunities (marriage, family life, etc.), lack of appropriate healthcare and treatment, abandonment (for intellectually people with disabilities), and discrimination." In the West, attitudes are less stigmatizing. For example, Chen, Brodwin, Cardoso, and Chan (2002) compared the attitudes of American, Taiwanese, and Singaporean college students toward people with disabilities, using the Attitudes Toward Disabled Persons Scale and the Attitudes Toward Dating and Marriage Scale. The study revealed that American women showed the most favourable attitudes toward people with disabilities.

That said, people with physical disabilities are likely to suffer considerable exclusion and stigmatization around sexual matters. Taleporos and McCabe (2003; also, McCabe and Taleporos, 2003) found that people with a physical disability, especially a severe disability, are more likely than other people to be single, and this is especially true of disabled men. A large part of the problem is sexual frustration or lack of sexual well-being. But even married people with physical difficulties report lower-than-average levels of sexual satisfaction. In large part, this is due to low levels of sexual esteem, body esteem, and sexual satisfaction, which in turn predict low self-esteem and high risk for depression among people with physical disability, compared to able-bodied people (Taleporos and McCabe, 2001).

CHAPTER SUMMARY

This chapter showed that relationships are complicated. Some factors make marriages highly successful, while other factors can cause the whole relationship to collapse. To navigate through close relationships successfully, couples should anticipate the inevitability of conflicts and learn how to manage them successfully.

Life means dealing with the unexpected. Negotiation is key to working out problems in marriages. Interestingly, the fairer the distribution of power seems to the partners, the more satisfied they will be.

As we have seen, married people—and others in enduring close relations—tend to live longer, happier lives. Satisfaction in a marriage means different things to men and women. Men value emotional independence in their wives, while wives feel happiest when their husbands are "there for them," or emotionally available.

The life cycle of a family is full of difficulties; for example, planning to have a child and then setting out to produce one increases marital happiness. Yet marital happiness usually decreases once the child arrives or if that goal is unable to be met, as in the case of infertility.

Intimacy is an important part of a good marriage. Sexual intimacy is a reliable sign of happiness throughout a marriage, although after children appear, sexual activity typically decreases, often for extended periods of time.

One cause of increased marital satisfaction is homogamy—similarity in attitudes, interests, and behaviours. Not only do people tend to date people like themselves, they usually end up happier after marrying people like themselves. If partners disagree on a woman's role, the marriage is often less happy.

Communication is the key to a successful marriage, but, like many skills, it is easier to applaud than to acquire. Good communication may seem irrelevant to couples who choose to divorce and start afresh. Others face their problems squarely, with the help of counsellors who may help them communicate and solve their troubles.

Key Terms

anomie According to Durkheim, a lack of control, or a lack of norms.

idioms Various verbal forms, including pet names and inside jokes, that couples use to separate their relationship and define themselves as a couple.

Critical Thinking Questions

1. How do Western and Eastern cultures differ in terms of what a marriage has to fulfill in order for it to be considered satisfying?

2. Why does cohabitation tend to lower life satisfaction even more in collectivistic societies than in individualistic societies?

3. What is the greatest source of marital conflict for immigrant couples?

4. At what stage of raising children is marital satisfaction the lowest, and when does it start to increase again?

5. What is the difference between immature and mature love, and when does each tend to develop in the marriage?

Weblinks

The American Communication Association (ACA)
www.americancomm.org
The ACA was created to promote academic and professional research, criticism, teaching, practical use, and exchange of principles and theories of human communication. This resourceful educational site offers up-to-date information on communication.

Professor's House: Marriage Advice
www.professorshouse.com/category/relationships/marriage-advice/
This link provides information on marriages and includes various articles that cover a wide range of phenomena related to marriage.

Ask the Internet Therapist
www.asktheInternettherapist.com
This resource provides a new and original form of marriage counselling. For people with time constraints or those who are unwilling to physically visit a therapist, a new option is online counselling. For a fee, the site offers on-the-spot counselling from an array of medical professionals. The professionals also offer phone and video counselling.

Chapter 6

Parenting

Childbearing, Socialization, and Parenting Challenges

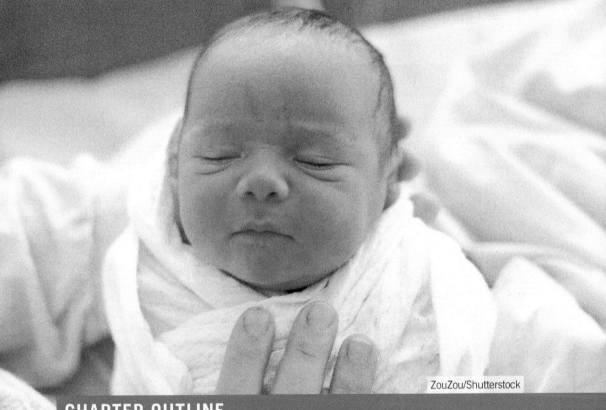

ZouZou/Shutterstock

CHAPTER OUTLINE

- Entering Parenthood
  - Entering Parenthood in the Past
  - Entering Parenthood Today: Family Planning
  - Entering Parenthood Young
- Raising Children Alone
- Adoption
- Assisted Fertility

- The Transition to Parenthood: Its Effect on Happiness
  - Coping with the Change in Marital Relationships
- The Tasks of Parenthood
  - Socialization
  - Gender Socialization
  - Parenting Processes

- Obesity and Parenting (for Mothers)
- The Most Important Things Parents Give Children
  - Love and Attachment
  - Emotional Stability and Family Cohesion
  - Protection, Control, and Supervision
  - Fair and Moderate Discipline
  - Parenting Sick Children
- Variations on a Theme
  - Disability and Parenting
  - Single Parenting
  - Parenting in Poverty
  - Gay and Lesbian Families
  - Indigenous Families
  - Cultural Variation
- Parenting in the Internet Age
- Chapter Summary

LEARNING OBJECTIVES

1 Sequence a brief and general history of fertility rates and their causes in Canada.

2 Prioritize the factors that influence marital satisfaction after entering parenthood.

3 Identify the features of authoritarian, authoritative, unengaged, and permissive parenting.

4 Explain how family dysfunction differs in families with runaways and sick children.

5 Relate historical events to the obstacles facing Indigenous families today.

6 Explain how immigration policies influence the functioning of immigrant families.

Looking at the big picture, it's easy to see why parenthood is an important topic for families and for society. If, tomorrow, the world decided to outlaw parenthood, in just over 100 years the human race would be extinct. We need children—and parents—to perpetuate the human race. If, tomorrow, Canada—like China in the second half of the twentieth century—decided to limit parents to one child, we would soon see a drastically aging society and aging parents without children to care for them. Finally, if, tomorrow, Canada (or its provinces) decided to undermine parenthood by reducing family benefits and daycare spaces, we would soon see a dramatic uptick in stressed parents, domestic violence, divorce, and poorly cared-for children.

So, parenthood makes a difference. Yet, today, parenthood is considered less important than it was a generation or a century ago. In the days of your great-grandparents and before, it was assumed that people would marry and—as soon as it was affordable—start producing children. Marriages without children were considered to be scarcely marriages at all. Today, we think differently about these matters. We do not assume that everyone will want to have children or start having children soon after marriage. Similarly, we no longer assume that a family without children is no family at all.

We shall see many reasons for the dramatic changes in family life and, especially, dramatic changes in women's social roles in the past century. Today, with the availability of good contraception, couples are better able to decide whether and when to have children, and the reasons they should or should not do so. And with good educational and occupational opportunities open to them, many women find parenting less attractive than it once was. Although most women want to have at least one child, few women want four, five, or six children, as in the past.

ENTERING PARENTHOOD

Entering Parenthood in the Past

Childbearing today is much less common than it was in the past, the result of a slow and (almost) consistent decline that took more than a century. Historical records show a marked, gradual drop in the Canadian **birth rate** from the mid-nineteenth to the mid-twentieth century in average numbers of children per family. Women born in Canada between 1817 and 1831, for example, bore about 6.6 children, whereas women born between 1947 and 1961 bore only 1.7 children—less than one-third as many. And for the past 50 years, the number of births has continued to fall or remain constant—not rise—especially among native-born, highly educated women.

Part of this drop in the fertility rate is due to the improvement of birth control technology, but even more important has been significantly changed views about the value of children. As Canadian society industrialized, fewer parents needed children to work on the farms. Children cost more to raise in towns and cities than they did on farms, and they brought their parents fewer economic benefits. As a result, children in cities changed from an economic benefit to an economic liability.

So, childbearing trended downward from about 1871 to 1946, with only a brief interruption—the so-called "baby boom," between 1947 and 1967. After the baby boom, this downward trend continued. In 2008, the average number of births per woman was 1.68, a slight increase from more recent years (Statistics Canada, 2011) but below the so-called "level of replacement"—meaning that the Canadian population would shrink without immigration. Despite a brief blip due to the high number of women at childbearing age, overall the fertility rate is still declining (Vanier Institute of the Family, 2010a). In recent decades, women have started their childbearing at older average ages. Today, the age of women with the highest fertility rate in Canada has shifted from the 25 to 29 age group to the 30 to 34 age group. Thus, not only are women having fewer children today, but they are also having their first (and sometimes only) child later in life.

Entering Parenthood Today: Family Planning

Improved birth control was not the only reason for fertility decline, but we should not underestimate its importance. In Canada, contraception is widely understood and widely practised (Roterman, Dunn, and Black, 2015). The widespread availability of effective contraception has allowed women to limit the total number of children they bear. It has also allowed them to space these children as they wish. Even more important, contraception has allowed a separation of sexual intercourse from pregnancy, making sexual activity a form of recreation and self-expression, not merely a means of reproduction.

In North America, three-quarters of women of reproductive age use contraception. By contrast, only 40 percent use modern contraception in the world's lower-income countries, and just 33 percent do so in Africa (United Nations, 2015). Despite its widespread popularity, contraceptive use varies within Canada, with lower rates in rural areas compared to cities, in part because accessing health care and contraceptive advice is more difficult in rural areas. As Sutherns and Bourgeault (2008) discovered, finding out about birth options is harder in rural Canada than in the country's urban areas. Access to secondary care is also insufficient in many rural areas, with the result that one finds more troubled pregnancies and sickly infants in these areas.

Entering Parenthood Young

Today, we are still concerned about children who have children. In many cases, this means that young women are interrupting their education and taking on parental responsibilities before they are fully mature themselves. Yet the fertility rate of Canadian teenagers has dropped steadily since 1975. As a result, the proportion of Canadian live births accounted for by teenagers dropped from 6 percent in 1991 to 3.4 percent in 2012 (Statistics Canada, 2012a).

Teen fertility rates vary enormously across Organisation for Economic Co-operation and Development (OECD) countries. In 2009, Switzerland had the lowest rate and the United States had the highest, at 39.1 births per 1000 teenage girls (World Bank, 2011). By contrast, Canada's teen birth rate in 2009 was 13 births per 1000 teenage girls (World Bank, 2011). How do we account for these large international variations? A study that interviewed pregnant or parenting adolescents found that four factors predict risky sexual behaviour that could lead to teenage pregnancy: presence of a family member with a drinking problem, physical assault by a family member, (early) age of first drunkenness, and (early) age of first wanted sexual experience (Kellogg, Hoffman, and Taylor, 1999). Another study found that less-educated, high-sensation-seeking adolescents who come from less-cohesive families are more likely than other children to engage in sexually risky behaviour (Baumgartner, Sumter, Peter, and Valkenburg, 2012).

Comparative research (Jones et al., 1993; Wright, 2011) suggests that another source of sexual risk-taking is cultural—namely, excessive sexualization of the mass media combined with a relative absence of sexual education in the schools and access to contraception in the community. However, these same mass media, especially social media and text messaging, can also be used to provide sexual health education interventions (Jones, Eathington, Baldwin, and Sipsma, 2014).

Adolescent parenting poses important risks for both child and parent. Children born to teen mothers are more likely to have behavioural disorders, especially during preschool years, and to have poor listening vocabulary on entering school (Dahinten and Willms, 2002). As these children enter adolescence, they tend to have significantly lower math scores and commit more property offences than children born to older mothers (Dahinten, Shapka, and Willms, 2007).

A compilation of studies (e.g., Ashcraft and Lang, 2006; Levine and Painter, 2003) showed that coming from a low-income background may increase the risk of both teenage motherhood and low income after childbearing (cited in Luong, 2008). However, women from disadvantaged backgrounds are more likely to have low incomes even if they do not have children before the age of 20, because people from disadvantaged backgrounds get less education, on average. If they manage to get more education, they overcome this income hurdle, even if they had a first child as a teenager (Gaudie et al., 2010; Luong, 2008).

We know far less about the fathers of babies born to teen mothers. Using birth records, Millar and Wadhera (1997) found that more than three-quarters of births to teen mothers involved men who were older by an average of 4.1 years. Many of these fathers fail to stay around to raise and support the child. Likely, employment opportunities influence fathers to stay or leave: They are more likely to stay if they can find a job. For those young men who do stay, teenage fatherhood may decrease their years of schooling and future earning potential (Fletcher and Wolfe, 2012).

Teen pregnancy can be unexpected and unwanted, adding further complexity to the parenting situation. People who enter parenthood often unexpectedly find parenting more stressful and more difficult than other parents. This is especially true of teen mothers, who are still forming their own identities. The result is greater stress associated with parenting. However, interventions can improve parent responsiveness to the child, infant responsiveness to the mother, and parent–child interaction (Barlow et al., 2011).

RAISING CHILDREN ALONE

According to the 2011 Census, lone parents and their children make up 21.5 percent of families in Canada. This followed a steady long-term increase from 11 percent in 1981 (Vanier Institute of the Family, 2010b) and 6.4 percent in 1961 (Statistics Canada, 2011). Women head most (81 percent) of these lone-parent families, but the percentage headed by men is increasing (Vanier Institute of the Family, 2010). Some (37.2 percent) of these lone-parent families result from teen pregnancies or unwed (often unplanned) pregnancies, although most (56.2 percent) result from the dissolution of a relationship (Statistics Canada, 2011).

- For the first time in 2011, more census families comprised couples without children (44.5 percent) than those with children (39.2 percent).

- With increases in maternal education and age of childbearing, a higher proportion of children age 4 and younger live with mothers in their forties.

- The upward trend for lone parents grew 8 percent between 2006 and 2011, with more never-married lone parents and fewer widowed ones.

- Average household size continues to decline, with a large increase in the number of one-person households.

- An increasing proportion of children age 14 and younger live with common-law parents, and today common-law couple families (16.7 percent of census population) surpass the number of lone-parent families (16.3 percent).

- More young adults ages 20 to 29 are living in the parental home today because of extended education or because they are "boomerang children."

- Between 2006 and 2011, the number of common-law couples rose 13.9 percent.

- Same-sex couple families increased 42.4 percent between 2006 and 2011, reflecting the legalization of same-sex marriage.

- Stepfamilies, recorded in the census for the first time in 2011, comprise 12.6 percent of all families, meaning that 10 percent of all children age 14 and under live in a stepfamily.

Source: Statistics Canada. 2012. *Portrait of families and living arrangements in Canada: Families, households and marital status.* 2011 Census of Population. Catalogue no. 98-312-X2011001. Ottawa: Author.

Single mothers are of concern because they face a higher-than-average risk of physical and mental health problems. Their children also face an increased risk of social, academic, emotional, and behavioural difficulties. We will talk about this issue again later in the chapter.

ADOPTION

For various reasons, some people choose to adopt children. With increases in cross-cultural and cross-national adoption, and in cross-racial adoption within Canada, interest in the policies surrounding adoption has increased.

Not long ago in North America, officials handled adoption in secrecy and kept their records secret from the child, the adoptive parents, and the biological parents. Many children were never even told that they had been adopted. However, most family researchers today agree that it is better to tell children that they have been adopted when they are old enough to understand what it means. By openly talking to the child about his or her adoption, parents can make it a positive fact of the child's life.

Some people think that open (i.e., non-secret) adoptions reassure the birth parents about their child's genetic health and help adopted children to form a secure identity. Others, however, think that contacts with birth parents interrupt and destabilize the adopted family and confuse the child's sense of identity. More research is needed before

Especially in Canada and the United States, adoptive parents may belong to a different ethnic or racial group from their adoptive child. This results in a blend of identities for the child.

Kathy Dewar/E+/Getty Images

we can say much with certainty about the conditions under which adopted children benefit from linking with their natural parents (Miall and March, 2005a).

We see more tolerance today for cross-ethnic and cross-racial adoption than in the past. Especially in Canada and the United States, adoptive parents may belong to a different ethnic or racial group from their adoptive child. This results in a blend of identities for the child. An increased awareness of the value of the child's ethnic or racial identity encourages adoptive parents to go beyond their own community in search of their child's original community. Such parents generate a blend of identities for their children, often involving representatives of the child's original community. That said, Indigenous and African Canadian communities have increasingly criticized the adoption of their babies by parents of another ethnic or racial origin. That matter is far from resolved.

ASSISTED FERTILITY

Most Canadian women expect to bear one or more children, but the norms about family size are much weaker in Canada than one finds in pronatalist societies with higher rates of childbearing. In pronatalist societies, people expect all women to bear many children and stigmatize women who fail to produce them. In these high-fertility cultures, most women fully internalize and support the pronatalist discourse (Remennick, 2000).

Women who are infertile are stigmatized and, to cope with stigma, develop strategies that include secrecy and selective disclosure about their "hidden disability."

Even in our society, infertility is often associated with lower levels of marital satisfaction. Infertile women older than age 30 have an even more negative vision of the future than infertile women younger than age 30 (DeBoer, 2002). Many Canadian women regret their inability to become pregnant and seek medical help—often in the form of long-term and burdensome infertility treatments at high personal and financial costs.

Assisted human reproductive (AHR) technologies can help couples who face infertility or sterility. According to information from the Canadian Fertility and Andrology Society (CFAS), rates of assisted reproduction in Canada are high and rising rapidly. However, the success rate of many of these procedures is not high at all. In 2010, for example, the live birth rate for in vitro fertilization (IVF) per cycle for women under age 35 was only 38 percent—which translates to a 62 percent failure rate per attempt. This failure rate sharply increases as a mother's age increases (Orfali, 2011).

On the other hand, for some women, the new technology succeeds too well and they bear far more children than they had bargained for. Typically, births of three, four, or more children may result from such assisted fertility.

The success rates have steadily increased in recent years, and the number of multiple births has decreased, too, though at a less consistent rate (Gunby, Bissonnette, Librach, and Cowan, 2010). However, a successful outcome is not the only factor affecting women's reaction to their experiences with assisted fertility. Some women resent the experience of male domination in fertility clinics (Birenbaum-Carmeli, 1998) or find the clinic experience humbling. Others appreciate the importance of medical skills, respect, coordination, accessibility, information, comfort, support, partner involvement, and a good relationship with fertility clinic staff (Dancet et al., 2011).

The biggest problem with IVF is the associated cost of each treatment. This cost is always high, since it involves careful treatment by highly trained professionals; however, the cost varies dramatically from one country to another. As we see in Figure 6.1, the cost of a single IVF treatment can vary from more than $12 500 in the United States to less than $4000 in Japan, with Canada at the higher end (at $8500).

THE TRANSITION TO PARENTHOOD: ITS EFFECT ON HAPPINESS

When it comes to having children, one of the most commonly shared myths is that having children increases a person's level of happiness. As we saw in the last chapter, however, the evidence is mixed on this subject. Here, we expand on the relationship between parenting and marital satisfaction, since it is so central to so many families. What's more, the stresses associated with a transition to parenthood not only affect parents, but affect children as well.

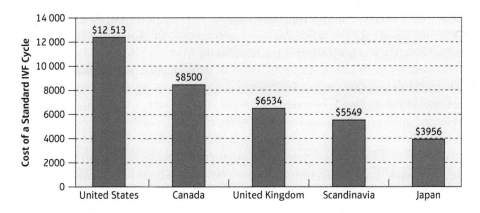

Figure 6.1 Average cost of a standard fresh IVF cycle ($US 2006)

Source: Data from Chambers, Georgina M., Elizabeth A. Sullivan, Osamu Ishihara, Michael G. Chapman, & G. David Adamson. 2009. The economic impact of assisted reproductive technology: A review of selected developed countries. *Fertility and Sterility* 91(6): 2281–2294.

Parenthood has different kinds of effects on men and women, and it varies as well according to the type and quality of the relationship between the spouses. As Moller and colleagues (2006) report, "Attachment styles significantly predicted dissatisfaction in couple relationships for the second but not for the first time parents . . . [I]nsecure attachment was significantly linked with dissatisfaction in couple relationships after transition to parenthood."

According to Myrskylä and Margolis (2014), happiness tends to increase in the years around the birth of a first child. This increase, however, is only temporary and soon decreases to before-child levels. And even if one child briefly adds to a family's happiness, two children, let alone three, are not even more happy-making. A couple's first two children may add to the happiness of the parents, but having more children (i.e., having a third child or more) does not have the same effect. Research shows that there are diminishing rates of return (in the form of diminishing increases in happiness) with additional children beyond the first two.

There are also gendered differences in parents' levels of happiness after having children. Having children comes with a lot of stress, because of the enormous time commitment. Parenthood is typically harder on women than on men, since women usually act as the primary caregiver, often leaving paid work, especially when the child is young (Myrskylä and Margolis, 2014). Therefore, young mothers may often find the parenting experience less enjoyable than do young fathers.

Bonke and Jensen (2012), for example, found that having children reduces the time women spend in the labour market, but does not have the same effect on men. To care for their children, women take time away from both paid work and leisure; by contrast, men take time to spend with their children mainly from their leisure time. As a result, women often experience an increase in work–family stress. In addition, women may feel more socially isolated than men after childbirth if they end up staying at home to care for the child. For these reasons, women tend to have larger drops in life satisfaction after having children than do men (Myrskylä and Margolis, 2014).

Increasingly, in Western industrial nations, parenting has put pressure on mothers, in particular, to take responsibility for more and more aspects of their children's behaviour and outcomes. The tendency toward what Annette Lareau (2005) has called "concerted cultivation" places the most stress on middle-class mothers, which may also explain why they experience lower levels of life satisfaction after having children than do fathers. In Canada, for example, mothers are encouraged to spend a lot of one-on-one quality time with children (especially during the early years) to "stimulate brain development and future brain potential" (Wall, 2010). The idea is that, through nurture, parents can shape their child's future intellect and personality.

Many women in Canada and other Western countries feel this cultural pressure to be an intensive parent. The result is that many mothers find themselves spending a significant amount of time planning and managing a schedule for their children that is filled with cultural and physical activities that will broaden their children's experiences and enhance their abilities.

Mothers who fail to spend a lot of time with their children may come to feel guilty. Our current notion of "good motherhood" seems to demand this intensive involvement, and mothers who fail to provide it may think they are not fulfilling their role as mother. One mother explains, "The pressure is there, just by the way other parents talk . . . if you don't do it, all these activities with your kid, you feel guilty about it. You have some parents whose kids are in karate and soccer and (they ask) 'have you signed up your kid for soccer or swimming yet? Ballet?'" (Wall, 2010: 259).

To meet the time demands of intensive parenting, many mothers cut back on paid work, take part-time work, or take a leave from paid work entirely. Some mothers even cut back on sleep and personal relaxation so that they can give undivided attention to their children. Mothers often find that these changes keep them from meeting their own needs. However, intensive parenting demands that mothers put their personal needs and wants "on the back burner" (Wall, 2010: 260).

If mothers put their own needs first, they may experience guilt and failure; so, a mother must choose between feeling like a failure and feeling the exhaustion that comes with intensive parenting. As a result, child rearing can take a huge toll on mothers' mental, emotional, and physical health, causing high levels of stress, anxiety, guilt, and exhaustion.

New mothers are quick to note this loss of personal freedom. One mother explains, "When I first had [a child], I must admit I wanted to go out sometimes with my friends, like I used to just get up and go but I couldn't. I couldn't even go to the mall because it was too cold or raining. It has changed my life, but it doesn't bug me anymore. I brought it on myself. I can't blame anybody" (Bassey Etowa, 2012: 31). Similarly, another woman complains that "the minute your baby comes, your life stops, and it's surrounded by him. Everything that happens, happens with him. [Y]ou have to make the best of it". For these women, the loss of freedom that comes with motherhood is a source of unhappiness. For other women, having the responsibility of caring for a child is grounding and enjoyable, and increases their overall level of happiness. Some women think that having children allows them to fulfill their "gender role," so they see having children as the purpose of their lives.

Like women, men also experience changes in identity and happiness after becoming parents, for several reasons. For one thing, fewer wives are stay-at-home wives today. As more mothers have remained in the workforce after childbirth, parental roles have become more equal and more demanding for men. Like new mothers, new fathers often have fewer opportunities to take part in leisure physical activity. They both have less time to invest in moderate to vigorous physical activity (MVPA) and sports once they have children (Pot and Keizer, 2016). Some men do not mind this, but fathers who see MVPA as an important part of their daily life and identity may experience an unhappy change.

The level of happiness new parents experience varies not only according to gender, but also according to the parents' age and education level. Older and better-educated parents tend to experience an increase in well-being after having children, while younger and less-educated parents feel either no increase in happiness or even a decrease in happiness (Myrskylä and Margolis, 2014). Parents with less education and lower incomes tend to experience higher-than-average levels of post-birth depression. Research suggests that younger mothers are less ready to have children and therefore feel more stressed once they have them. By postponing childbirth, mothers are often able to attain more social capital, a higher status at work, and more financial flexibility and options for child care. These resources make the transition to parenthood much easier for these older, more educated women.

We all know that children today make fewer economic contributions to families than in the past. Cognitive dissonance theory suggests that children's declining *economic* value may be one of the reasons that parents exaggerate the *emotional* value of child-bearing (Eibach and Mock, 2011). When parents realize that the economic incentives for raising children are negligible, they convince themselves that parenthood will yield large emotional rewards instead. For similar reasons of dissonance, the more time parents spend with their children, the more time they will say they want to invest in their children in the future, and the more likely they are to tell prospective parents that having children has huge emotional rewards. In this way, the idealization of parenthood is self-perpetuating, even under gruelling conditions.

Coping with the Change in Marital Relationships

Despite a momentary rise in people's happiness after the birth of a child, parenting typically has a negative long-term effect on marital relationships, as we mentioned in the last chapter. To repeat, parents typically report lower marital satisfaction than childless couples (Twenge, Campbell, and Foster, 2003). As well, researchers find additional decreases in marital satisfaction as the number of children increases. Children may be cheaper by the dozen (as a famous old book once claimed)—due to economies of scale in raising them—but not better for the marital relationship.

Couples with infants face various new concerns: disappointed expectations, problems with returning to work, reductions in sexual intimacy, new intrusions by (and reliance on) in-laws, a reduction of sleep and leisure time, and problems communicating all these concerns to one's partner. Preserving closeness is critical to keeping marital satisfaction alive during the new transition to parenthood. Couples have trouble doing this, especially if they start out with low levels of attachment or have childhood memories of their parents lacking attachment (Curran, Hazen, Jacobvitz, and Feldman, 2005). Typically, these problems do not diminish as the children get older. Often, parent–child conflicts introduce or intensify parent–parent conflict, reducing marital satisfaction even more (Hiotakis, 2005).

Some couples learn to lower their expectations so that they can take more satisfaction from their new lifestyle. For example, couples who place a lower importance on sexuality intimacy and a higher importance on building a future together can preserve a higher level of marital satisfaction. Preserving a secure sense of attachment also makes it easier for a couple to endure the strains and disruptions associated with new parenthood (Simpson, Rholes, Campbell, Tran, and Wilson, 2002), as does strong support from family and friends (Schulz, Cowan, and Cowan, 2006).

THE TASKS OF PARENTHOOD

Socialization

Children do not arrive "ready to go" but must be carefully taught—i.e., socialized—to take part properly in families and in society. Sociologists define **socialization** as the social learning a person goes through to become a capable, functioning member of society. The **primary socialization** of children is usually the responsibility of the child's family. It has a deep impact on future life by helping to set the child's future values, goals, and, to a certain extent, personality. It is in the family that a child first learns how to gain rewards by doing set tasks and following rules.

Typically, parents base their socialization practices on particular cultural or traditional values. Parents also choose skills and behaviours to teach their children that they think will help them become healthy and successful members of society. Finally, parents provide their children with love as well as learning; children in well-functioning families soon learn that they are valued human beings. Thus, socialization is the beginning of social acceptance in the family and the community—and in this way, the beginning of self-esteem. The well-functioning family encourages each step in the child's physical, emotional, and moral development. In every aspect of this development, good communication plays an important part. Like the spousal relationship, the parental relationship relies on good communication.

Myth: Peers invariably reinforce gender-normative behaviour in their friendship groups.

■ **Reality:** Gender socialization by peers can yield varying results. Boys whose friends are mostly male are likely to respond to harassment in ways that society considers "masculine." Boys whose friends are mostly female, however, are more likely to respond to harassment in ways that society might even consider feminine. Thus, children conform to the norms of their peer group. They are socialized by their peers, not by abstract notions of "maleness" or "femaleness" (Lee and Troop-Gordon, 2011).

Myth: Socialization is always a process of downward transmission, from parent to child.

■ **Reality:** Socialization is often a bidirectional process, especially in immigrant families. Many parents of immigrant families socialize their children through discussions about their country of origin. Children, at the same time, socialize their immigrant parents by explaining the politics of the host country (Wong and Tseng, 2008). Thus, socialization is reciprocal, not one-way, especially if children are politically active (Terriquez and Kwon, 2015).

Myth: The effects of gendered socialization are always harmful for girls, since gender roles are grounded in gender inequality.

■ **Reality:** Even by kindergarten, girls are likely to have positive attitudes toward school, whereas boys are likely to have negative attitudes (Orr, 2011). These attitude differences lead to differences in grades: Positive attitudes lead to better grades for girls, while negative attitudes lead to lower grades for boys. As a result, the gender roles of girls—more cooperative and submissive, for example—predispose them to respond better to the school environment, while the male gender role can cause difficulty for boys.

Those are some of the general facts about socialization. The box above lists some popular myths about parenthood, peer influences, and child socialization.

Gender Socialization

Sex is inborn, but gender is not; instead, people learn gender-based ways of behaving through **gender socialization**. In various ways, they learn the cultural meanings of femininity and masculinity and the performances that their culture and society expect of typical females and males. The major agents of socialization—family, peer groups, schools, and the mass media—all serve to reinforce cultural and conventional definitions of femininity and masculinity.

Gender socialization starts at birth and continues throughout life. Young children learn gender identities by watching others at nursery school or daycare, role-playing games, and experimenting with hair, clothing styles, and body decoration (for example). At home, parents routinely assign cleaning, child care, and meal preparation tasks to daughters and fixer-upper tasks (or heavier work) to sons. Not surprisingly, children often learn traditional, gender-based attitudes toward housework well before the end of high school. Men, older people, and less-educated people are especially likely to hold and teach these traditional, gendered attitudes.

Learned gender differences extend well beyond our housework attitudes to our intimate relations—for example, to our communication practices. For example, we teach women to behave in a demure, innocent, and disinterested fashion when discussing sex with men. (Women are more forthcoming in discussions with other women.) Learned patterns of communication create and preserve distinctions between women and men and reinforce social expectations between the sexes.

Parenting Processes

Of course, parents may differ in how they want their children to turn out. Some parents put a high value on obedience, for example, while other parents value independence highly. Some parents want their children to be cooperative and adaptable; others want their children to be competitive and ambitious. Some of these different perspectives on children are echoed in the box given on page 197.

However, most members of a given society agree on what constitutes "good parenting." In Canada, for example, most parents aim to produce children who are healthy, law abiding, and successful at school. When a child is failing, delinquent, or disturbed, this signals poor parenting. Of course, many factors besides parenting can increase the risks of childhood failure, delinquency, ill health, and depression. That said, parents still play a large part in creating the "right" conditions for a child's best emotional and cognitive development. These "right" parenting conditions include love and attachment, emotional stability, protection and control, and fair and moderate discipline.

OBESITY AND PARENTING (FOR MOTHERS)

Inevitably, any discussion of parenting raises questions about the "right" and "wrong" ways to raise children. Often, these parenting rules are (inappropriately) geared specifically toward mothers. An example of this can be seen in childhood obesity discourse, which dictates that mothers are responsible for their child's weight.

Excessive weight is a big issue today for several reasons. First, public health and medical researchers have increasingly called attention to the role of excessive weight (and improper eating) in the development of heart disease, diabetes, and other avoidable ailments. Increasingly, governments have urged us to improve our eating practices and to exercise to counteract some of the negative effects of unhealthy eating and too much sedentary activity. Second, our culture has increasingly lavished praise on people—especially women—with slender, fit bodies. Adults and even children who fail to fit this profile are often ridiculed, excluded, and stigmatized by the media and in social interaction. So, people in our society are strongly motivated to think about—even worry about—their own and their children's weight.

Both academic scholarship and popular media have unduly blamed mothers for their children's weight issues. Consider, for example, research by Mainland, Shaw, and Prier (2015) and Freidman (2015) that examined the underlying messages of print media (and, in Friedman's case, scholarly sources). They concluded, as Friedman, citing Herndon, puts it, that "'parents (and largely mothers) [are] responsible for any difficulties experienced by the young people in their care,' which suggests that the real concern is about maintaining normative bodies and mothering practices and *not* making children's health a central concern" (Friedman, 2015).

To reach this conclusion, Mainland, Shaw, and Prier (2015) analyzed four issues of *Parents* and *Today's Parent*, American and Canadian parenting magazines, respectively. They found an overwhelming tendency to hold mothers, and not fathers, accountable for their children's health, including weight. For example, one advertisement shows a mother solely defending her child against non-nutritious food: "dressed in a warrior outfit, the mother stands in front of her child, protecting him from a cartoon made out of doughnuts, candy bars, and other junk food" (Mainland et al., 2015). Advertisements that hold fathers accountable for their children's eating habits are noticeably absent. This suggests that, in North American culture, fathers do not have the same parenting responsibilities as their spouses.

What's more, one article even assumes that fathers will not readily participate in a healthy living environment at home. It makes mothers responsible for ensuring that their spouses participate at home. As the article puts it, "sometimes the biggest roadblock to getting your partner involved in your parenting could be you" (Mainland et al., 2015).

Friedman, mentioned earlier, stresses that, "while the scholarly and news articles under review suggest overarching parental failing, the explicit focus is often on the mothers" (Friedman, 2015: 20). First, Friedman notes that maternal blame has historical precedent. Dating back to the 1930s, renowned physician Dr. Hilde Bruch placed the blame for overweight children on "permissive parenting" and "smothering mothers". Friedman also cites studies that correlate childhood obesity with maternal employment (Friedman, 2015: 21). To repeat, parents—and, in particular, mothers—are held responsible for the weight of their children.

Some blame the loss of good, wholesome cooking by modern mothers. For example, in an editorial for *Childhood Obesity*, Dr. Keith-Thomas Ayoob, Associate Professor of the Albert Einstein College of Medicine, indirectly blames mothers for childhood obesity. He writes that having more families with a single working parent or two working parents increases the number of meals eaten away from home, thus increasing the prevalence of obesity. Ayoob explicitly declares that today's culture is "not optimal" and is "not our mother's culture anymore" (Ayoob, 2011). Some research finds support for this connection between bad cooking and increasing obesity: Researchers Summin Lee and colleagues (2012), using survey data, found that girls whose mothers worked only part time or stayed at home had a lower risk of excess weight gain than did girls whose mothers worked full time.

Other researchers more explicitly correlate mothers with childhood obesity, and date this relationship all the way back to the womb. This idea is commonly referred to as "fetal programming theory." As Parker (2014) puts it, "the theory . . . effectively positions the fat pregnant body as the origin, not only of the 'obesity epidemic,' but of a wide range of population health problems, and thus also the focus of efforts to combat them". As another researcher succinctly declares, "we must look at the womb to understand what is producing today's obesity" (Leibowitz, quoted in McNaughton, 2011: 1).

To blame mothers for obesity and "fat shame" poses several problems. First, as Friedman (2015) notes, focusing on parents takes the focus away from structural factors (e.g., media advertisements of fast food) that may negatively affect a child's weight. Second, as both Friedman (2015) and Parker (2014) note, by focusing on households that do not provide their children with nutritious food, the obesity literature puts undue emphasis on lower-income and marginalized households. Third, Parker (2014: 180) warns that blaming women for "obesity" can open up "new and disturbing opportunities for the surveillance, regulation, and disciplining of 'threatening' (fat) female bodies."

This debate about the parental influence on eating and obesity can serve as an example of a more general point: Namely, that whenever children turn out imperfectly, there is a tendency to blame the parents for raising them wrongly. We will say much more about this issue of parental influence later in this chapter. Note, for the time being, that although parenting fashions vary over time and from one culture to another, certain perceptions of parents and children have remained fairly constant, as we see in the box on the next page. Parents and scholars have talked about the interesting (and sometimes odd) characteristics of children for millennia. Read the quotes on the next page, from different times and places, and ask yourself whether they are arriving at more or less the same general conclusions.

THE MOST IMPORTANT THINGS PARENTS GIVE CHILDREN

Love and Attachment

The most important things parents can give their children include love, stability, protection, and supervision. Of all of these, the single most important gift is love. No doubt, many parents make an imperfect job of raising their children; yet most parents probably love their children. Often, however, parents do not know how to express this love, or how to raise their children properly—and many parents fall into these categories.

Of all the errors parents can make, loving their children insufficiently is probably among the worst. Children who feel unloved by their parents suffer emotional damage that may be long-lasting. That is because the emotional bond that parents form with their children is, usually, a model for all of the other important social and emotional relationships these children will form in their lifetime. And in the end, the

Of all the animals, the boy is the most unmanageable.

—Plato

If children grew up according to early indications, we should have nothing but geniuses.

—Goethe

Healthy children will not fear life if their elders have integrity enough not to fear death.

—Erik Erikson

What's done to children, they will do to society.

—Karl Menninger

Children are remarkable for their intelligence and ardour, for their curiosity, their intolerance of shams, the clarity and ruthlessness of their vision.

—Aldous Huxley

Children have never been very good at listening to their elders, but they have never failed to imitate them.

—James Baldwin

Children have no use for psychology. They detest sociology. They still believe in God, the family, angels, devils, witches, goblins, logic, clarity, punctuation, and other such obsolete stuff.

—Isaac Bashevis Singer

Source: http://www.famousquotesandauthors.com/topics/children_and_childhood_quotes.html

Children's talent to endure stems from their ignorance of alternatives.

—Maya Angelou

Source: http://www.oxfordreference.com.myaccess.library.utoronto.ca/views/SEARCH_RESULTS.html?y=14andq=childrenandcategory=t93andx=19andssid=308183164andscope=bookandtime=0.733832986209592.

Happiness is an imaginary condition, formerly often attributed by the living to the dead, now usually attributed by adults to children, and by children to adults.

—Thomas Szasz

Source: www.oxfordreference.com.myaccess.library.utoronto.ca/views/ENTRY.html?entry=t115.e3145andsrn=25andssid=236191040#FIRSTHIT.

ability to form mature and meaningful social bonds comes down to being able to experience attachment.

John Bowlby (1969), a British psychoanalyst, was the first to state a formal theory of attachment. While trying to understand the distress that some infants suffered after a separation from their parents, Bowlby noted that these infants would make great efforts to prevent separation from their parents or to re-establish closeness after a separation. Research showed that, far from being unusual, such behaviours were common to various mammals. In fact, they may be necessary adaptive responses to separation from a primary attachment figure—someone who regularly provides the support, protection, and care on which a helpless infant depends: That is, they may have significance for the evolution of human beings and other animal species.

According to Bowlby, infants often want to know whether the attachment figure is nearby, on hand, and attentive. If the answer is yes, the child feels loved, secure, and confident, and is likely to explore the environment, play with others, and be sociable. Otherwise, the child suffers anxiety and is likely to search for and call to the missing parent. These behaviours continue until the child is near the attachment figure again or until the child "wears down." In the latter case, the child is likely to experience despair and depression.

Warm parental support and encouragement are important in creating this sense of attachment. Remember that people of all ages form judgments about themselves by responding to how others treat them. This insight goes back to research by the seminal sociologist Charles Cooley, who in 1902 wrote about "the looking-glass self." Children with kind, encouraging parents usually get higher grades at school, have more social competence, and get into less trouble with teachers. They have learned that people in authority—first their parents, then their teachers—are there to help them, not hold them back. Even in adolescence, often a time of big changes and doubts, children whose parents are encouraging do better. Adolescents with unsupportive parents are more likely than other adolescents to start smoking cigarettes and engage in other risky behaviours. Parenting style, therefore, has a significant influence on child behavioural outcomes (Hoeve et al., 2009). We will say more about parenting style shortly.

Emotional Stability and Family Cohesion

Emotional stability is another key contributor to the healthy development of children. Without stable, consistent support from a parent, the child runs a higher risk of school problems, delinquency, low self-esteem, or diminished well-being.

Factors that reduce the stability and cohesion of a family can include parental addiction, depression, illness, and spousal conflict. For example, spousal conflict can cause parents to spend too little time with their children because they are depressed, stressed out, and distracted by their own problems. As well, marital conflict disrupts normal practices of discipline in the household. This can create uncertainty and decrease child–parent attachment.

On the other hand, many family practices help to strengthen family stability and cohesion. For example, family rituals are important—things like regular family meals and conversations, family outings, and vacations. **Family cohesion** is a sense of attachment among members of a family, preserved and represented by shared activities, self-identification as a family member, and signs of familiarity and liking. As a simple example, consider family meals. The importance of family meals is more symbolic than practical. Family meals are signs of family cohesion that contribute to the healthy emotional development of children. At the same time, researchers (see, e.g., Evans and Rodgers, 2008; Franko et al., 2008) have noted that family meal routines make an important contribution to family cohesion and children's health.

Protection, Control, and Supervision

No less important than loving stability is parental **control and supervision**—how firmly, consistently, and fairly parents enforce rules for the child.

Good rules guide and protect the child. They show the parents' concern and attachment. Children are less likely to become delinquents if their parents keep an eye on what they are doing, offer them support, and give them a chance to discuss whatever is bothering them. This is true of children in two-parent families, mother-only families, and mother–stepfather families. In forming and socializing healthy children, the quality of family relationships counts more than the number of parents.

According to research over many decades, the **authoritative parenting** style (high acceptance, high control) does best, turning out children who achieve the highest levels of academic performance and mental well-being. By comparison, other forms of parenting produce less desirable outcomes. For example, **authoritarian parenting** (low acceptance, high control) keeps children from independence and learning to express themselves. Children whose parents are authoritarian—controlling but not caring enough—are more likely than children of authoritative parents to become delinquents and to use drugs.

As we see in Figure 6.2, authoritative parenting style is quite different from authoritarian parenting style, and the two styles have different consequences. Children who receive authoritarian parenting are much more likely to develop low self-esteem and engage in delinquent behaviour, for example.

However, lax parental control is no better. **Unengaged parenting** (low acceptance, low control) can also be harmful. **Permissive parenting** (high acceptance, low control) may produce poor results, too. Permissive parenting produces poor grades, and low-achieving students are more likely to come from families with permissive parenting styles (Chan and Koo, 2011; Vergun, Dornbusch, and Steinberg, 1996).

Authoritarian parenting is probably more harmful in some cultures than others. Specifically, it is more harmful in cultures that encourage child independence and self-expression, and less harmful where children grow up expecting to be treated in a cool, more controlling manner. So, for example, Dwairy and Menshar's (2006) study of parenting in Egypt found that, in rural communities, the authoritarian parenting style is common among Arabs, especially for the parenting of male adolescents. Parents—especially fathers—are likely to use an authoritative style with girls and an authoritarian style with boys (Dwairy and Menshar, 2006). However, parenting styles are adjusted to environment—whether rural or urban—and reflect variations in the need for control and obedience among sons and daughters in these contexts. As a result, parents use an authoritarian parenting style with girls in urban communities, but not with boys.

In short, one parenting style may not work well under all circumstances. However, in North America, researchers find that children whose parents are authoritarian, unengaged, or permissive are more likely to show problems of adjustment, poor academic achievement, or substance abuse than children whose parents are authoritative. In North America, the authoritative parenting style offers the best mixture of acceptance and control—not too much or too little of either. This seems to be as true of immigrant minorities in Canada as it is of native-born Canadians (on this see Garg,

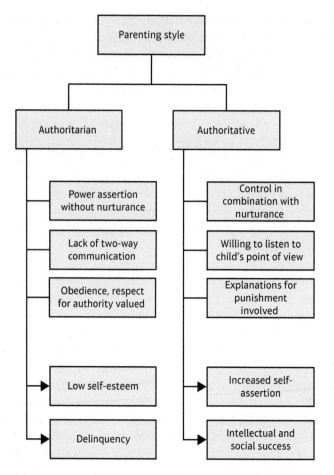

Figure 6.2 Parenting styles and their effects on children

Source: Based on Coplan, Robert J., Paul D. Hastings, Daniel G. Lagacé-Séguin, & Caryn E. Moulton. 2002. Authoritative and authoritarian mothers' parenting goals, attributions, and emotions across different childrearing contexts. *Parenting: Science and Practice 2*(1).

Levin, Urajnik, and Kauppi, 2005, although Liu and Guo, 2010 offer an alternative view). We will say more about this later in the chapter.

Fair and Moderate Discipline

Related to control is the issue of discipline. Overzealous or unfair discipline may wipe out the benefits of control, as may lax discipline. The trick is to provide the right amount of discipline and provide it in the right way—that is, the trick is using the right technique.

Induction teaches children correct behaviour by stressing examples and principles. They learn not only that some behaviour is bad, but also *why* it is bad. When children who were raised inductively break the rules, they know they are contributing to another's distress and feel guilty. Feelings of guilt, unlike feelings of fear or anxiety, exercise an **internal moral control** over their behaviour. Inductive discipline—teaching good behaviour by setting a good example, then rewarding imitation—is better for the child than **power assertion** because it is internalized. Once rules are internalized, the child motivates himself or herself to behave properly. Thus, inductive discipline fosters more consistent compliance (Hoffman, 1979).

However, teaching through inductive techniques can be time-consuming since this method obliges parents to explain and model good behaviour. Not surprisingly, many parents—whether because they are short of time or impatient—continue to use some degree of physical punishment—a form of power assertion—as a disciplinary tool. Physical punishment and power assertion appeal to parents who were raised this way themselves or who do not have the time, patience, and inclination to teach rules inductively. In general, parents tend to raise children the way they were raised, often with the same unfortunate consequences—yelling, spanking, and fighting, among others (Barnett, Quackenbush, and Sinisi, 1996). However, sometimes this intergenerational pattern can be disrupted if there is a co-parent on the scene who demonstrates a warm and supportive parenting style instead (Conger, Schofield, and Neppl, 2012).

Spanking and other forms of corporal punishment continue to be prevalent in Canada, as revealed in a review of the literature by the Global Initiative to End All Corporal Punishment of Children (www.endcorporalpunishment.org). Corporal punishment remains one of a host of risk factors related to child maltreatment (Stith et al., 2009). It is also the form of socialization that is most distant from induction, since it teaches not by example and precept but by threat and violence.

When parents threaten physical punishment as a form of discipline, they typically want compliance with some simple demand. For example, the parent may want the child to sit still, be quiet, come with the parent, or stop touching things. Children typically respond by ignoring the parent. About half of the adults making these threats also hit the children. What we learn from this scenario is that when parents use physical punishment routinely, it is routinely ineffective! Unfortunately, some parents may continue to use physical punishment, believing that it is instrumental in achieving parental goals such as teaching life lessons, respect, and safety. They may also continue to use corporal punishment if they see it as normal and expected in their ethnic group, religious group, or family of origin (Taylor, Hamvas, and Paris, 2011).

As we see in Figure 6.3, corporal punishment is likely to produce immediate compliance and even the learning of moral values. However, it also has side effects that include aggression, delinquency, poor mental health, a poor relationship with the parent, and a high probability of using corporal punishment in adulthood, against one's own children.

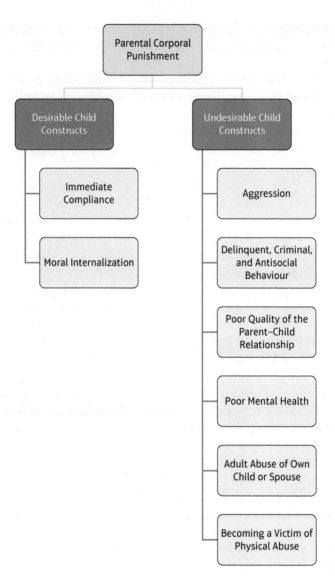

Figure 6.3 Effects of corporal punishment on child development

Source: Based on Gershoff, Elizabeth Thompson. 2002. Corporal punishment by parents and associated child behaviours and experiences: A meta-analytic and theoretical review. *Psychological Bulletin* *128*(4): 539–579.

At its worst, harsh childhood discipline produces delinquency and low self-esteem (Peiser and Heaven, 1996), and relational aggression in children (Kawabata et al., 2011; Taylor, Manganello, Lee, and Rice, 2010). A broad range of studies has also found harmful outcomes in adulthood, including depression, alcoholism, aggressive behaviour, suicide, and a tendency to physically abuse one's family. Some children

- Researchers have estimated 150 000 homeless youth across Canada, a number that is likely increasing.

- Researchers also estimate that 60 to 70 percent of homeless youth leave family environments where they have experienced interpersonal violence, including physical, sexual, or emotional abuse.

- Gay, lesbian, bisexual, and transgender youth are over-represented among the homeless youth population, along with those who have been involved with the child welfare system (41 to 43 percent in a sample of studies).

- Fifty-eight percent of the children in the runaway category in 2014 were females and 42 percent were males.

- Roughly 12 to 36 percent of youth age 18 or 21 exiting the foster care system become homeless, which in 2010 translated to approximately 28 000 youth (Dworsky et al., 2012). Runaways make up the greatest number of missing persons reports, at 76 percent.

- Thirty-nine percent of participants in one study of homeless youth in Canada had been physically assaulted in the last 12 months, and males reported higher rates of physical assault than did females (51 percent versus 27 percent). Thirty-nine percent had experienced physical abuse and 23 percent had experienced sexual abuse in their lifetime, with significantly more females experiencing sexual abuse than males (31 percent versus 15 percent).

Sources: Karabanow, Jeff & Allyson Marsolais (Eds.). 2013. *Youth Homelessness in Canada: Implications for Policy and Practice.* Toronto: Canadian Homelessness Research Network Press. http://www.homelesshub.ca/sites/default/files/Youth- Homelessnessweb.pdf; Dworsky, Amy, Keri-Nicole Dillman, Robin M. Dion, Brandon Coffee-Borden, & Miriam Rosenau. 2012. *Housing for Youth Aging out of Foster Care: A Review of the Literature and Program Typology.* Washington, DC: Office of Policy Development and Research, U.S. Department of Housing and Urban Development.

respond to persistent abuse by running away from home and even living on the street. Thus, we learn a lot about the failures of socialization caused by bad parenting by studying street youth (see the box above).

Parenting Sick Children

Parenting sick children is especially difficult and stressful for parents, so family researchers have given much attention to the stress caused by a severely ill child. Not surprisingly, the illness is stressful for the sick child: Many children who become chronically ill by age 15 also suffer from serious psychological and behavioural problems as a result. Often, other family members suffer health problems as well, or at least emotional and psychic depletion—most of all, the main caregiver. The more severe the decline of the caretaker parent and the longer the illness goes on, the more strain the entire family experiences and the more difficulty it has coping.

Caregiving for the sick child, among other things, deprives other family members of the care and attention that they crave, too. High levels of parenting stress result, as well as poor psychological adjustment in caregivers and children (Cousino and Hazen, 2013). Fathers may come to feel estranged from their wives, while healthy siblings may feel estranged from their parents. Often, siblings have a hard time giving voice to their feelings and wishes under these conditions. Serious behavioural problems at home and school may result, and often parents may be unaware of the reasons.

The problems faced by families with disabled or chronically ill children deserve our attention because they illustrate two important principles: First, all families have to cope with crises of shorter or longer durations in connection with their child rearing. Second, families develop different strategies for dealing with these crises. For example, different families deal with childhood illness and caregiving in different ways. Caregiving and crisis management are influenced by various cultural, ethnic, or socioeconomic factors, but all such issues interfere with normal family life and the pursuit of life satisfaction (Stenberg, Ruland, and Miaskowski, 2010).

VARIATIONS ON A THEME

As noted, all families face obstacles from time to time, but some families face more obstacles than others—whether for reasons of time restraint, shortage of money, or social exclusion. However, as long as they follow the basic principles of good parenting mentioned above, they can function well, despite these obstacles.

Disability and Parenting

As already suggested, parenting is a physically demanding and emotionally draining task for everyone, but especially so for disabled parents. To illustrate this, Zelkowitz and colleagues (2013) studied patients with inflammatory arthritis and found that parents with the condition reported unusual parenting stress and depression. Out of 257 patients enrolled in the McGill Early Arthritis Registry (McEAR), 80 of them had children, and 29 of them had children who were 18 years of age or younger and living with them at home. The researchers found that disabled parents with young children at home experienced a great deal of parenting stress. In turn, this led children to internalize and externalize behavioural problems.

Let's unpack this finding a bit, because it is important. Children, as we have said, need and want love, protection, and supervision. When they don't get enough of these things, even if the parent is blameless, they feel cheated, angry, and resentful. They may not be aware of these feelings and, if confronted, might even deny having these feelings. Some of their confusion or anger is internalized (i.e., directed inward), such that the child feels as though he or she somehow deserves to be treated this way. Some is externalized (i.e., directed outward) in the form of misbehaviour and attention-getting. In both ways, family life becomes more conflictual; often, the disabled parent becomes more stressed, feeling guilty about the inability to give his or her children what they need.

Single Parenting

Similar problems arise in families led by a single parent. Because one parent must do the work of two parents—providing love, protection, and supervision, as well as income and domestic amenities (meals and the like)—the custodial parent is often stressed, does an inadequate job, and feels guilty about doing so. Again, the children may feel deprived, angry, or resentful about this.

On the other hand, some single-parent families—especially those that result from a divorce or separation—are superior to conflictual two-parent families. Here, single-parent families provide children with a significant decrease in conflict, anxiety, and depression. This in turn leads to better, more consistent parenting and a closer bond between the children and the custodial parent. "Despite their problems, these families can be viewed as representing a stage of one's life or a preference to marriage,

---

⟩⟩⟩ Myths and Facts about Single Parenting

Myth: Since single mothers have significantly improved their financial condition in the past 30 years, they will continue to become more involved in the economy and other aspects of public life.

■ **Reality:** Between 2007 and 2010, the poverty rate of lone-parent families fell from 21.4 percent to 18.7 percent: a good sign. However, the lack of readily available community support and affordable child care limits how many women can pursue education, enter the labour market, and increase their working hours. Participation in the public sector may stall until these problems facing single-parent families are addressed. Lone-parent families are one of the groups most likely to experience longer spells of poverty (Citizens for Public Justice, 2012). As of 2012, the median after-tax income for lone-parent families headed by a woman was $39 100 (Statistics Canada, 2014).

Myth: Financial resources are more important than effective parenting in preventing the problems that children in single-parent households tend to face.

■ **Reality:** Positive parenting practices play a larger role than financial resources in reducing emotional disorders in children from single-parent households (Abada and Gillespie, 2007). Only hostile and ineffective parenting—not income—affected the risk of destructive and physically aggressive behaviour in children from single-parent households. These results are mirrored by McConnell, Breitkreuz, and Savage (2011), who found that the relationship between socio-economic status and child difficulties was mediated by financial hardship and parenting stress.

Myth: The main reason adolescents in single-parent families are more likely than other teenagers to engage in drug use is that they have poor relationships with their parents.

■ **Reality:** Adolescents in single-parent families are more likely to use substances than those in intact families (Crawford and Novak, 2008). These results have been replicated in a study of Latino adolescents with single parents (Wagner et al., 2010). Nevertheless, higher parental education and income are associated with higher rates of binge drinking, marijuana, and cocaine use in early adulthood (Humensky, 2010).

rather than as a failure or a disaster . . . [and] a viable alternative to other ways of carving out a life for oneself and one's children" (Lynn, 2003).

For reasons already mentioned, lone parents often have a harder time than couples preserving a high quality of life for themselves and their children. In large part, the problems result from a single parent having to do the earning and parenting work of two people—a nearly impossible job. As we see in Figure 6.4, a significantly higher proportion of female-led lone-parent households occupy the lower family income groups. What makes this gender imbalance more troublesome is that females head 81 percent of lone-parent families (Statistics Canada, 2015). Female-headed lone-parent families, where most children with lone parents live, are significantly more likely to experience financial hardship than male-headed lone-parent families.

Statistics Canada data from 2015, for example, show that lone-parent families have an average family income of $43 630, compared to an average income of $88 610 for two-parent families (http://www.statcan.gc.ca/tables-tableaux/sum-som/l01/cst01/famil106b-eng.htm; http://www.statcan.gc.ca/tables-tableaux/sum-som/l01/cst01/famil106a-eng.htm). As we see in Figure 6.4, less than one lone-parent family in five earns this amount or more per year.

Low income for many single mothers is a direct outcome of divorce (Duffy and Mandell, 2001). Such low incomes have important consequences for family members. For example, low income is likely to hinder the school performance of children in single-parent families. However, data from the National Longitudinal Survey of Children and Youth (Lipman, Offord, Dooley, and Boyle, 2002) show that income disparities account for only a part of the variation in school readiness between children in single-parent families and those in two-parent families.

Even controlling for (low) income, children in single-parent families are much more likely than children in two-parent families to present emotional, behavioural, and academic problems. Gender also plays a part, with boys in single-parent families being especially prone to behaviour problems. This may reflect the shortage of parental supervision (as well as income) in lone-parent families. It may also reflect mental health problems that often accompany loneliness, stress, and a shortage of income.

Parenting in Poverty

Often, parents who are unable to supply the basic needs for their family experience despair, depression, and social isolation and think they are inadequate caregivers. They describe their financial situation "as a struggle, a fight, a daily preoccupation that consumed parental time, strength and patience" (Russell, Harris, and Gockel, 2008: 93).

Other things being equal, children who grow up in low-income families are at higher risk of behavioural and cognitive problems from preschool onward (Noel, Peterson, and Jesso, 2008). Poverty often deprives parents of access to educational resources and activities and gives them less opportunity to pursue educational activities

	2010	2011	2012	2013	2014
	Lone-Parent Families[1]				
	Number of Families				
Total, all income groups	1 401 870	1 403 940	1 410 890	1 408 400	1 404 010
Under $5000	61 810	61 420	62 710	60 640	53 710
$5000 and over	1 340 060	1 342 520	1 348 180	1 347 760	1 350 300
Under $10 000	-	-	-	-	-
$10 000 and over	1 288 350	1 291 040	1 300 310	1 300 610	1 302 870
$15 000 and over	1 210 150	1 212 840	1 230 400	1 233 300	1 240 990
$20 000 and over	1 091 990	1 096 810	1 120 660	1 128 530	1 141 570
$25 000 and over	969 060	976 960	1 004 210	1 015 680	1 034 680
$30 000 and over	849 700	862 050	891 160	904 550	926 130
$35 000 and over	741 610	757 740	787 530	802 160	824 650
$40 000 and over	644 050	662 810	693 620	710 910	733 210
$45 000 and over	553 590	573 210	604 750	623 940	647 030
$50 000 and over	475 010	494 620	523 840	543 890	565 960
$60 000 and over	353 730	373 230	396 810	415 940	435 650
$70 000 and over	-	-	-	-	-
$75 000 and over	229 300	247 330	266 650	283 280	300 250
$80 000 and over	-	-	-	-	-
$90 000 and over	-	-	-	-	-
$100 000 and over	108 010	120 400	133 370	144 740	156 680
$150 000 and over	-	-	-	-	-
$200 000 and over	-	-	-	-	-
$250 000 and over	-	-	-	-	-
			$		
Median total income	37 050	37 900	39 350	40 380	41 780

-: not available for any reference period.

Note: Family income is the sum of the incomes of all members of the family.

1. A lone-parent family is a family with only one parent, male or female, and with at least one child.

Source: Statistics Canada, CANSIM, table 111–0012.

Last modified: 2016-07-14.

Find information related to this table (CANSIM table(s); Definitions, data sources and methods; The Daily, publications; and related Summary tables).

Figure 6.4 Family income, lone-parent families, 2010 to 2014

Source: Data from Statistics Canada website—Summary Tables: CANSIM table 111-0012. Family income by family type (lone-parent families). http://www.statcan.gc.ca/tables-tableaux/sum-som/l01/cst01/famil106b-eng.htm

with their children (Ermisch, 2008). Sometimes, this disadvantage can be overcome by especially skillful parenting. For example, research shows that the effect of economic disadvantage on preschool child cognitive performance is mediated by parenting quality (Lugo-Gil and Tamis-LeMonda, 2008).

In this way, the disadvantages of poverty pass from one generation to the next (Scaramella, Neppl, Ontai, and Conger, 2008). It's easy to trace the chain reaction. For example, economic disadvantage predicts a higher risk of mental health problems and maternal stress. In turn, this reduces the quality of parenting and decreases the child's life chances, thus perpetuating poverty (McLanahan, 2009).

Social support from others—family, friends, and social services—may reduce the harmful effects of poverty by providing financial, child care, or housing support (McLanahan, 2009). For example, by reducing parental stress, such support improves the home environment for the child and therefore his or her school achievement. However, a literature review by Attree (2005) found that low-income single mothers have smaller support networks than mothers in two-parent families. As well, the most socially isolated women—women with the smallest support networks—are least likely to seek professional help in parenting. They are likely to feel that the services do not cater to their specific needs and fear being labelled as "inadequate" parents.

The duration of poverty, and not only its extent, is a problem, however. Long-term poverty has especially harmful outcomes for children (Jones et al., 2002). Persistent poverty increases parental stress and family conflict. These, in turn, increase the likelihood of parental depression and hostile and ineffective parenting patterns—yelling, smacking, and providing no quality time or even time to help a child with homework. Poor parenting behaviours, in turn, produce undesirable child outcomes: reduced mental health (e.g., more depression), worse physical health (e.g., more physical injuries), and poorer school performance (e.g., more school absences).

The effects of poverty are worst in neighbourhoods characterized by high levels of violence, social disorder, and fear, where children experience greater risks of anxiety and depression (Caughy, Nettles, and O'Campo, 2008). Low-income families often find themselves in these economically impoverished communities with a negative social climate. Positive **parental involvement** can mitigate the harmful neighbourhood effects on behaviour problems, to some degree. However, the responsibility for doing so puts an enormous burden on the shoulders of parents who are already stressed by poverty, unemployment, or underemployment.

Gay and Lesbian Families

In past decades, people were inclined to imagine that gay and lesbian families were different from opposite-sex families in important ways, with harmful consequences for children who lived in these families. Even today, we see vestiges of stereotypical views about these families among people with little or no first-hand familiarity. Such vestigial views include the beliefs that homosexual parents create a dangerous environment for the child, provide a less secure home, and offer less emotional stability. Yet, as research has shown for more than a decade, gay and lesbian parents raise healthy, successful children just as often as heterosexual families do (Wainwright, Russell, and Patterson, 2004).

According to the research literature, children raised by homosexual parents have the same behavioural and educational outcomes as children of heterosexual unions and feel just as loved and accepted by their parents (Mattingly and Bozick, 2001). Likewise, the self-esteem levels, the levels of functioning at home and in school, and the romantic lives of these adolescents are the same, regardless of family type (Wainwright et al., 2004). Finally, there is no more chance of children growing up gay or lesbian in a same-sex family than in a heterosexual family (Fitzgerald, 1999; Mooney-Somers and Golombok, 2000). However, children who grow up in same-sex households feel less pressure to conform to gender stereotypes and are less likely to experience their gender as superior, and these may be positive effects of being raised in a lesbian household (Bos and Sandfort, 2010).

Indigenous Families

Indigenous families in Canada are as varied as other Canadian families, and they face many of the same problems. However, on average, they also face more severe problems than other Canadian families, and this translates into higher-than-average rates of domestic violence (as we will see in Chapter 8). It also translates into higher-than-average rates of child abuse.

As we see in Figure 6.5, child abuse is apparently more common in Indigenous families than it is in non-Indigenous families. An expert report on the topic finds that

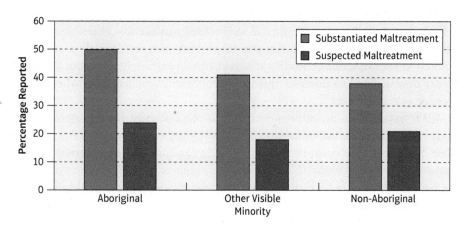

Figure 6.5 Suspected and substantiated maltreatment of Aboriginal and non-Aboriginal children, 1998

Source: Based on Blackstock, Cindy, Nico Trocme, & Marlyn Bennett. 2004. Child maltreatment investigations among Aboriginal and non-Aboriginal families in Canada. *Violence Against Women 10*(8): 1–16.

"Compared to non-Aboriginal and Other Visible Minority children, maltreatment was more often substantiated for Aboriginal children (38% for non-Aboriginals, 41% for Other Visible Minorities, and 50% for Aboriginal children) or remained suspected (24% for Aboriginal children vs. 21% for non-Aboriginals and 18% for Other Visible Minorities" (Blackstock, Trocme, and Bennett, 2004).

Understanding the problem of child abuse and the problematic parenting of Indigenous families means taking into account the long-term effects of conquest, colonization, and discrimination. As Frideres (2007) has noted, the familial organization of Indigenous families has been profoundly altered on two separate occasions since Confederation.

First, from the late nineteenth century onward, many Indigenous children were forcibly removed from their families and moved to residential boarding schools under a government policy of assimilation. During the process, Indigenous children were no longer allowed to speak their own language or practise their spiritual values (Frideres, 2007). The teachers, often members of religious groups or orders, served as "parents" to the children, who did not see their natural parents for up to 10 months a year. In fact, for reasons of distance, some children never saw their parents during the years they attended residential schools.

These residential school "parents" were strict disciplinarians—perhaps best characterized as authoritarian parents who used techniques of power assertion to teach the children good behaviour. Harsh punishment was meted out to children who failed to obey their schoolmasters quickly enough (Bradbury, 2001). The historical concept of "good parenting" that informed these policies was shaped by particular cultural ideals associated with Western colonizers. By contrast, today we see a push to prioritize Indigenous parenting practices that do not perpetuate problematic stereotypes about child rearing.

The government policy of forced assimilation destroyed nearly three generations of Indigenous families through forced separations and the forcible removal of children from their parents' care. Equally important, the residential schooling also imposed European ideals of marriage, sexuality, and patriarchy (Bradbury, 2001: 71). We are now inclined to think of this as a form of cultural genocide, whether it was intended as such or not.

This "experiment" in cultural domination was a disaster for Indigenous families and communities, who lost cultural traditions and social ties (Bradbury, 2001; Dickason, 2002). Survivors have continued to make claims against the federal government for compensation for the abuse they suffered as a result of Canada's policy of assimilation (see the Assembly of First Nations' website at www.afn.ca for details). Understanding historical trauma helps us take into account how the consequences of numerous and sustained attacks against a group may accumulate over generations and interact with proximal stressors to undermine collective well-being and stable family life (Bombay, Matheson, and Anisman, 2014).

Second, during the 1960s and 1970s, another series of social service initiatives by provincial governments led to the removal of Indigenous children from their

Lineage Ties in the Indigenous Culture

Lineage ties hold great importance in all Indigenous groups. As well, some Indigenous peoples have a clan system that connects all members of a clan and involves each clan in certain responsibilities within the community. Clan systems vary among the Indigenous peoples that have them. For example, the Oneida clans include the following and their traditional roles:

- Turtle Clan: Keepers of knowledge and all to do with the environment

- Bear Clan: Keepers of the medicine
- Wolf Clan: The pathfinders; those who guide others to live their life in the way that the Creator intended

Clan systems indicate not only traditional roles in the community, but also who can marry whom.

Source: Based on Filion, Barbara, et al., *Indigenous Beliefs, Values, and Aspirations* (Toronto: Pearson Canada, 2011).

homes to live with non-Indigenous families (Frideres, 2007). This, too, has reportedly had a harmful effect on Indigenous families and parenting practices. Cheah and Chirkov (2008: 407) note that the separation of Indigenous children from their families has undermined traditional Indigenous child-rearing patterns and hindered the spread of cultural knowledge from one generation to the next. In turn, some claim that this has led to an increase in drug and alcohol dependency and high rates of suicide among the Indigenous population (Cheah and Chirkov, 2008; Elias et al., 2012).

Current Indigenous scholarship about the well-being of Indigenous people in Canada, however, warns against the perspective that positions an entire population as "traumatized," as it may, in fact, perpetuate victimhood (Maxwell, 2014). It may also reinforce negative stereotypes of Indigenous people as pathological, childlike, and in need of the guardianship (or wardship) of the state. So, although it is important to recognize the historical trauma that Indigenous people in Canada have experienced, we must also avoid promoting a view of Indigenous "deviancy" (DeLeeuw, Greenwood, and Cameron, 2010). This poses a dilemma for those who, following the *R v. Gladue* decision, want to focus on the harm done by historical mistreatment in explaining crimes committed by present-day Indigenous people.

Cultural Variation

Like poverty and cultural genocide, immigration can pose many difficulties for parenting attitudes and practices. In some instances, the problems are a result of economic difficulties that immigrant parents face on their arrival in North America. In other cases, the problem is cultural, owing to different ideas about parenting in Canada and the country of origin. This is especially marked when cultural differences arise between the parents and their more acculturated child.

This and related issues of immigrant family life were highlighted a century ago in one of the first major studies of immigration in North America, William I. Thomas and Florian Znaniecki's multivolume *The Polish Peasant in Europe and America* (1918–1920). This study examined the social and family lives of Polish immigrants—specifically why they often struggled and failed to overcome the challenges of assimilating into a new culture.

The authors noted that many peasants came to America with expectations of success. Yet they often had trouble altering their social customs—a necessity if they were to assimilate into North American culture and achieve economic success. Social marginality resulted; the results of this marginality included poverty, delinquency, mental illness, marital conflict, and social isolation. Immigration demands prodigious change and adaptability from the immigrant, yet society provided none of the means to help bring this about. The stresses and difficulties—especially the conflicts between spouses and between parents and children—that Thomas and Znaniecki described are still common among new immigrants to Canada today.

For their part, the children of immigrants were (and still are) often challenged by the need to balance two cultures. If parents show understanding, the children's problem is solved more easily; but often, the parents are themselves struggling with a problem of cultural balance. Fathers can be especially important in this regard, as their patriarchal status in the family is often placed at risk by immigration (Abad and Sheldon, 2008).

As mentioned earlier, parenting styles often differ between Western and other cultures. For example, Hispanic and Asian families often use authoritarian practices more readily than do North Americans of European descent (Pong, Hao, and Gardner, 2005; Varela et al., 2004). As well, Chinese adolescents may report that their parents, though warm, are too controlling.

In keeping with our earlier discussion of parenting styles, we would characterize these Chinese parents as falling somewhere between authoritative and authoritarian. Another study finds that cultural variation in parenting is also mediated by stress and social support. There is a difference even between Mainland Chinese mothers and Chinese Canadians in terms of their levels of authoritarian and authoritative parenting of children ages 2 to 6 (Su and Hynie, 2011). Authoritarian so-called "tiger parenting" may not actually be the most typical type of parenting, however, with supportive parenting also appearing frequently. That said, "tiger parenting" may not lead to optimal adjustment among Chinese American adolescents (Kim et al., 2013).

Canadian research by Ho, Bluestein, and Jenkins (2008) illustrates the complexity of this problem. Their study used parent and teacher data for nearly 15 000 children from the National Longitudinal Survey of Children and Youth to examine the relationship between children's aggression and emotional problems, and parenting styles. It found that the statistical association between parental harshness and child aggression differed between ethnic groups and across informants. According to teacher reports of the children, parental harshness was positively related to child aggression in European

Canadian families but negatively related in South Asian Canadian families. According to parental reports of the children, parental harshness was positively related to children's aggression, although relationships varied in strength across ethnic groups.

Why do we see these variations in parental severity? Immigrants to Canada face various problems when they move here: problems that affect their family relations. In general, cultural values related to parenting tend to persist after immigration, due to efforts many parents make to retain their authority and promote traditional values. So, for example, South Asian mothers in North America often adapt their parenting styles to achieve their parenting goals of building a collective cultural identity for their children (Maiter and George, 2003). The mothers sometimes instill even stricter moral and religious practices in their children—to create a sense of belonging to their cultural group and to build character—than they would have if they had remained in their home country.

Acculturation of some kinds (e.g., economic) may erode some of the cultural values of Chinese immigrants but have little effect on their parenting beliefs and goals (Costigan and Su, 2008). A study by Su and Hynie (2011) showed the persistence of traditional parenting beliefs and goals despite external pressures for change. In fact, external pressures increased the tendency of Chinese Canadian mothers to practise authoritarian parenting. It was only with less external pressure and more acculturation

Parenting Proverbs across Time and Space

Just as the famous quotations about children in the box on page 197 gave us the sense that people have been viewing children similarly for a long time, the "parenting proverbs" below lead to somewhat similar conclusions about the universal nature of parenthood. Can you identify the universal conclusions contained in these words of wisdom?

Every beetle is a gazelle in the eyes of its mother.

—Moorish proverb

God could not be everywhere and therefore he made mothers.

—Jewish proverb

A father is a banker provided by nature.

—French proverb

Source: http://www.famousquotesandauthors.com/topics/children_and_childhood_quotes.html.

Children are a poor man's riches.

—Danish proverb

More precious than our children are the children of our children.

—Egyptian proverb

Source: http://creativeproverbs.com.

Do not confine your children to your own learning, for they were born in another time.

—Chinese proverb

It is the duty of children to wait on elders, and not the elders on children.

—Kenyan proverb

Source: http://creativeproverbs.com.

Respect for one's parents is the highest duty of civil life.

—Chinese proverb

Source: Aboriginal and non-Aboriginal families in Canada.

that they were more likely to practise more flexible, authoritative parenting (Su and Hynie, 2011). Yet, despite their behavioural changes, cultural parental beliefs and goals did not change.

PARENTING IN THE INTERNET AGE

Although parenting and parenting issues are ancient, new communication technologies provide both new opportunities and new dangers for parent–child relationships. As we all know, information communication technologies (ICTs) give people the ability to communicate easily and quickly, wherever they are. ICTs include smartphones, social media, and various other forms of internet communication.

Take smartphones. As Ling, Julsrud, and Yttri (2005) point out, smartphones are a mode of communication that is increasingly under the control of adolescents, since most adolescents today own a smartphone or have access to one, uncontrolled by their parents. This new element has many effects on parental authority and communication in the parent–child relationship. Williams and Williams (2005) found that smartphone use by teens leads to an increased pattern of authoritative parenting, compared to authoritarian parenting. That is because smartphone use promotes parent–child negotiation, a defining element of authoritative parenting. Smartphones provide a new means for these negotiations to take place. For example, they allow parents to check up on where their children are, and this makes parents more likely to give their children more freedom. In this sense, smartphones are negotiation tools for the parent–child relationship.

However, often parents and adolescent children have trouble reaching agreement about the use of this freedom and the use of these devices. According to Ling, Julsrud, and Yttri (2005), most parents accept the consequences of children having control over their means of communication, but only in exchange for an increased scope of monitoring opportunities. For their part, teens accept the need to be constantly accessible to their parents in exchange for the freedom that smartphones allow. Of course, smartphones don't always guarantee that parents will know and supervise their child's whereabouts. A study by Weisskirch (2009) found that parental knowledge depends on the teens' willingness to initiate frequent phone calls. By contrast, a high frequency of parent-initiated phone calls is likely to result in the teens being secretive toward their parents.

Besides helping parents to monitor their children, smartphones also help parents and children to maintain emotional connections. Blair and Fletcher (2011) found, for both mothers and children, that smartphones signify (or symbolize) emotional ties with other family members and adolescent autonomy. A study by Wei and Lo (2006) examining how college students use smartphones found that affection was the most usual motivation for (and predictor of) smartphone calls from students to their parents.

At the same time, Ling, Julsrud, and Yttri (2005) found that, for teens, smartphones tend to strengthen ties with peers at the expense of ties with parents. The fact that teens can communicate with their friends at any time means that they can be distracted at any time from family functions such as holidays and dinners. This increase in distraction can undermine the sense of family solidarity that normally results from these family rituals. So, it would be fairest to say that the increasing availability of smartphones creates a constant tug of war between families and peer groups for the attention of the adolescent phone-owner.

A similar pattern is found with the use of the internet—especially social media—for communication purposes, even among elementary school students. Lee and Chae (2007) note that time spent online communicating is associated with a (small) decline in family communication. That is, online communication with friends reduces the amount of communication with family members. However, use of the internet for reasons other than communicating with friends—for example, to do homework assignments—does not affect family communication to the same degree.

ICTs take on a different role when families are separated geographically. A study by Hughes and Funston (2006) found that teens whose parents had separated valued smartphones even more than teens from residentially intact families, as they used their phone for purposes of private communication. In particular, ICTs allowed them to talk easily to the nonresidential parent without the residential parent knowing. Similarly, teens whose nonresidential parent lived far away valued internet communication with parents, for the obvious reason that no other communication was as easy.

Other studies have replicated this finding about the value of internet communication in long-distance parent–child relationships. For example, Baldassar (2007) found that internet communication, including social media and web video conferencing, allowed transnational families to provide each other with emotional support and advice (Bacigalupe and Lambe, 2011). The authors note that, for us to fully appreciate the benefits of internet communication for families, we need to rethink our views on "proper" family communication, which (for many) is currently limited to face-to-face communication (Bacigalupe and Lambe, 2011).

CHAPTER SUMMARY

In this chapter, we examined parenthood from the perspective of societies, families, parents, and children. Today, most people have fewer children, reproduce at a later age, and compress their parenting into a smaller time frame than in the past, allowing more time for careers and family. We can plan our families in this way because reliable contraceptive devices allow us to do so.

Reliable contraception, for example, has helped to reduce the risk of teen pregnancy. As a result, the teen pregnancy rate is low in Canada, compared with the United States and many lower-income societies. Teen pregnancy is to be avoided, as it can lead to many difficulties later. For example, many teenage mothers never make up their lost opportunities. They may also be unable to provide good parenting, so it is good that this social risk has been reduced.

Once you have a child, you must be a parent, and as a parent, you are responsible for primary socialization during your child's first years. One of the jobs of the parent is to ready the child for entry into formal schooling and society, and some parents do this badly. The research leaves us with little doubt about the difference between good parenting and bad. For example, runaways are children who have judged their parents' parenting styles as so inadequate that they prefer life on the streets to life in the home of the parents.

Although class and cultural variations in styles of parenting remain, they are narrowing in many ways. The same principles of good parenting apply whatever the cultural group or class. Good parenting has social desirable results, while bad parenting has the opposite, at least in terms of North American cultural values. Our goal as sociologists is to publicize our findings about good and less-good parenting and to promote social policies and programs that make it easier for less-advantaged families—for example, lone-parent families, low-income families, immigrant families, and Indigenous families—to surmount the parenting difficulties they often face.

Key Terms

authoritarian parenting Parenting characterized by low acceptance and high control, which can hinder the development of expressiveness and independence in children.

authoritative parenting Parenting characterized by high acceptance and high control, which produces the best results in children.

birth rate Number of births per 100 000 people in a given year.

control and supervision The extent to which parents oversee and censure their children's behaviour.

family cohesion A sense of attachment and relatedness among members of a family, both maintained and signified by shared activities, self-identification as a family member, and signs of familiarity and liking.

gender socialization The social learning process a person goes through to acquire gender roles and gender-based habits. This is done through family, peer groups, schools, and the mass media.

induction A form of discipline focused on using reason to encourage children to behave in certain ways in order to benefit themselves or others. For example, a child will be told to put away her toys so that others will not trip over them.

internal moral control An emotional feeling, such as guilt, that pushes people to obey the rules.

parental involvement Spending time with children, talking about them, and thinking about them.

permissive parenting A type of parenting with high acceptance and low control.

power assertion Threatening a child with punishment, usually in physical form, for noncompliance.

primary socialization Learning that takes place during childhood.

socialization The social learning process a person goes through to become a capable, functioning member of society; to prepare for life in society.

unengaged parenting A type of parenting with low acceptance and low control.

Critical Thinking Questions

1. Why and how might the ways a society defines family affect people's attitudes toward child-bearing, contraception, adoption, and abortion?

2. Do the issues that arise with adoption and assisted fertility serve as evidence that the traditional idea of family is still influential in some ways? Explain.

3. How and why do parents socialize their children? How and why do children socialize their parents?

4. Research two distinctly different cultures. How might different styles of parenting yield the same results (i.e., adjustment, academic achievement, and not abusing substances) in these two cultures?

5. Can different kinds of families—for example, two-parent versus one-parent families, cohabiting versus married-parent families, heterosexual versus homosexual families, native-born versus immigrant families—parent their children equally well? Explain your answer.

6. Research one key issue facing Indigenous people in Canada. How can you connect residential schools and non-Indigenous foster families to this problem?

Weblinks

Planned Parenthood
www.plannedparenthood.com
For more than 90 years, Planned Parenthood has promoted a common-sense approach to women's health and well-being, based on respect for each individual's right to make informed, independent decisions about sex, health, and family planning.

Daily Strength
http://dailystrength.org/support-groups/Childrens-Health-Parenting
This site offers parents free, anonymous online parenting advice from "people just like you," on topics that include children's mental and physical health and developmental and learning disorders. Discussion groups are designed for various family types, including gay, military, single-dad, and adoptive families.

Health Canada: Just for You—Parents
www.canada.ca/en/health-canada/services/healthy-living/just-for-you/parents.html
Health Canada is the federal department responsible for helping Canadians to maintain and improve their health, while respecting individual choices and circumstances. This webpage includes information on child development and effective parenting, healthy lifestyles, work–life balance, prenatal health, mental health, and more.

The Young Mommies Homesite
www.youngmommies.com
This website run by young mothers offers support and information to mothers and pregnant women in their teens and twenties. Teen pregnancy statistics, an article database, a resource directory for Canada and the United States, message boards, and chat rooms are just some of the resources offered.

Journal of Family Issues

http://jfi.sagepub.com

Journal of Family Issues (JFI), published monthly, provides up-to-date research, theory, and analyses on marriage and family life, including professional issues, research, and interdisciplinary perspectives on family studies, family violence, gender studies, social work, and sociology.

Family Relations

http://onlinelibrary.wiley.com/journal/10.1111/(ISSN)1741-3729

An applied journal of family studies, *Family Relations* is mandatory reading for all professionals who work with families, including family practitioners, educators, marriage and family therapists, researchers, and social policy specialists. The journal's content emphasizes family research with implications for intervention, education and public policy, and publishing.

Journal of Marriage and Family

http://onlinelibrary.wiley.com/journal/10.1111/(ISSN)1741-3737

For more than 70 years, the *Journal of Marriage and Family (JMF)* has been a leading research journal in the family field, featuring original research and theory, research interpretation and reviews, and critical discussion concerning all aspects of marriage, other forms of close relationships, and families.

Chapter 7
Work and Family Life

Jupiterimages/Pixland/Getty Images

CHAPTER OUTLINE

- Introduction
- Change in Work and Family
- Unpaid Labour, Domestic Labour, and Caregiving
  - Elder Care and Other Types of Caregiving
  - Unpaid Labour Is Multifaceted
- Sick Days
- The Multiple Meanings of Unpaid Labour
- Stress and Conflict
- Physical and Mental Health
- The Skills Involved in Unpaid Labour

- Key Findings Related to the Division of Household Labour
  - Gender Inequalities in Unpaid Labour
  - Factors Associated with the Division of Unpaid Labour
  - Perceptions of Fairness
  - Reactions to Gender Inequalities in Unpaid Labour
  - Same-Sex Families
- The Intersections between Paid and Unpaid Labour
  - Gender Disparities in Earnings and Caregiving
  - Primary versus Secondary Labour Markets
- Non-standard Employment and Precarious Work
- Occupational Sex Segregation
- The Needs of Children
- Parents of Children with Disabilities
- Barriers in the Labour Market
- Work–Life Balance
- Social Policy
  - Neoliberalism
  - The Limitations of Canadian Family Policy
  - Typologies of Family Policy
  - Parental Leave Benefits
  - Child Care
- Concluding Remarks

LEARNING OBJECTIVES

1 Describe the activities involved in unpaid labour, domestic labour, and caregiving.

2 Identify the various meanings and challenges associated with unpaid labour.

3 Understand the challenges facing Canadians who provide child care or elder care.

4 Describe men's and women's participation in unpaid labour and the inequalities that exist with respect to gender.

5 Consider how paid and unpaid labour are mutually reinforcing; how women's experiences in the labour market shape their domestic labour, and how women's family responsibilities affect their paid employment.

6 Outline features of the labour market that present challenges for caregivers.

7 Analyze family policy in Canada and the limitations of Canadian social policy.

INTRODUCTION

This chapter explores intersections between paid and unpaid labour, which is referred to as domestic labour. The terms *unpaid labour*, *domestic labour*, and *caregiving* intersect and overlap. Unpaid labour refers to any unpaid work to care for family members and maintain a household. Unpaid labour can thus include tasks such as cleaning, but it can also include child care and elder care. It may be done in a different household, such as when elder care is done in a parent's home, hospital, nursing home, or long-term care facility. In the past, sociologists used the term *domestic labour* to refer to all of the work involved in maintaining a home, including caring for family members. Caregiving involves the care of children or ill, disabled, injured, elderly, or dying family members. This care work can include tasks like helping an elderly parent with banking, personal care, and housework.

The chapter begins by taking a close look at what unpaid labour entails, how it is viewed in society, and the challenges faced by Canadians juggling unpaid and paid labour. The contemporary social context is one in which Canadians seek solutions to address the incompatibilities between caregiving and paid work. The chapter will highlight how unpaid labour is gendered and how women continue to perform a disproportionate amount of unpaid labour despite their participation in paid work (Duxbury and Higgins, 2012a). Paid and unpaid labour are mutually reinforcing, as women's responsibility for their families affects their decisions about paid employment and ideas about women's family roles serve as obstacles to career progression (Eichler, 1983; Fox, 2009; Sinha, 2013). Elder care and caregiving for ill, injured, disabled, and dying family members are also addressed throughout this chapter. Family policy is outlined in a comparative context, which highlights the limitations of family policy in Canada.

CHANGE IN WORK AND FAMILY

In the last several decades, there has been a steady increase in female labour force participation and dual-earner families. In 1976, 53 percent of two-parent families in Canada were male-breadwinner, female-homemaker families, and one-third of families were dual-earner couples (Uppal, 2015). By 2014, almost 70 percent of two-parent families in Canada were dual-earner families and, among these, 75 percent were couples where both parents worked full time (Uppal, 2015). In comparing late baby boomers (born between 1957 and 1966) to generation Xers (born between 1969 and 1978) to millennials (born between 1981 and 1990), men's and women's participation in paid work and domestic labour became more similar over time (Marshall, 2011). Even though there has been a narrowing of the differences in paid and unpaid labour over time, men continue to spend more time in paid labour and less time in unpaid labour (Marshall, 2011). Our population is aging, and from 2011 to 2016 our country saw the largest increase in the number of seniors since Confederation (Statistics Canada, 2017a). According to the 2016 Census, there are more seniors in Canada than children (Statistics Canada, 2017a). As our population gets older, caregiving needs will intensify, yet government-funded home care is inadequate and the historical trend of smaller families means that there are fewer adult children available to share elder care.

UNPAID LABOUR, DOMESTIC LABOUR, AND CAREGIVING

Domestic labour entails caring for family members and maintaining a household to facilitate the care of family members. The term **social reproduction** has been used by sociologists to describe the varied facets of caring work that entail the intergenerational care of family members (Fox and Luxton, 2014). If domestic labour cannot be done by a family member—for instance, because of disability or because of time spent in paid work—sometimes it becomes necessary to hire someone to do this labour. Domestic labour includes finding and organizing care by a paid employee. Sociologists more commonly refer to domestic labour as unpaid labour because under industrial capitalism this labour is unpaid unless an individual decides to outsource this labour to individuals such as personal support workers, nurses, house cleaners, landscapers, babysitters, and nannies. When unpaid labour is outsourced, it is commonly outsourced to women who come from more marginalized backgrounds, including newcomers, migrant labour, women of colour, and poor women. The wages paid to these women are considerably lower than the average wage earned by Canadian women because this labour is defined as women's work and because the pay grade is oriented in relation to women's salaries. Often decisions about paying for child care are made by comparing the cost of child care to the salary of the mother. When salaries of working mothers do not cover work-related expenses, including child care, mothers may opt to leave the labour force (Zhang, 2009).

Apart from child care, caregiving extends to adults. Caregiving for one or more ill, injured, aging, disabled, or dying family members or friends is prevalent. In a study of more than 25 000 Canadians employed full time, Duxbury and Higgins (2012a) found that a majority provided care to elderly relatives, half provided elder care to more than one person, and one-third were providing both child care and elder care. Almost half of Canadians will at some point in their lives care for an ill, injured, aging, disabled, or dying family member or friend (Sinha, 2013). Twenty-eight percent of respondents to the 2012 General Social Survey had cared for an ill, disabled, or older family member or friend in the previous year, 27 percent reported caring for two people, and 15 percent reported caring for three or more family members or friends (Sinha, 2013). Twenty-eight percent of caregivers cared for a terminally ill family member or friend at some point in their lives (Sinha, 2013). Caregiving has financial costs, and it affects the health and well-being of caregivers, particularly when the care work is more time intensive (Sinha, 2013).

While caregiving can be emotionally rewarding, not all aspects of caregiving or other types of domestic labour are rewarding. Domestic labour can be physically and emotionally taxing, unpleasant, monotonous, and repetitive. Domestic labour extends beyond the more obvious kinds of tasks like caregiving. It is gendered, as it is performed disproportionately by women (Milan, Keown, and Covadonga, 2011), even when they are employed full time. Domestic labour includes child care, meal preparation, the work involved in cleaning and maintaining a home and surrounding yard or property, and taking care of the needs of individual family members, such as ensuring that they are clothed and fed, and that their physical and emotional needs are met. It entails the care of children and ill, injured, disabled, or older members of a family. Domestic labour is most time-consuming when children are young and declines as children get older (Milan et al., 2011). Women spend more hours on child care than men; even among dual-earner couples where both parents are working full time, women spend twice as many hours on child care per week than men do (Milan et al., 2011: 20). With an aging population, time spent on elder care has increased, and women spend more time on elder care than men do (Cranswick and Dosman, 2008; Duxbury and Higgins, 2012a; Milan et al., 2011: 21; Sinha, 2013).

Elder Care and Other Types of Caregiving

Canadians caring for older, ill, injured, disabled, or dying family members face two major challenges: caregivers are often in full-time employment (Pyper, 2006; Sinha, 2013) with inflexible employment schedules (Duxbury and Higgins, 2012b), and there have been significant cuts to government-sponsored home care as a result of neoliberal economic policy. Canadians care for family members themselves because the cost of paying a professional is prohibitive and there are long wait lists for spots in long-term care facilities. Many elderly Canadians prefer professional care because they do not want to impose on family, but private care is unaffordable for most Canadians (McDaniel, 1992). In some respects, elder care is harder emotionally as compared to caring for children because it involves declining physical and perhaps cognitive abilities and unpredictable medical crises (Church, 2016). As older care recipients experience declining mobility, the physical demands of elder care increase. Caring for older, ill, disabled, or dying family members has time and financial costs and has consequences for the health and well-being of caregivers (Turcotte, 2013), particularly women, who do more of this work (Duxbury and Higgins, 2012a). It can affect women's employment, and some women have to reduce their hours of paid work in order to perform elder care (Pyper, 2006). In a study of middle-aged women in Alberta, 60 percent considered quitting their jobs because of family responsibilities (McDaniel, 1992). The term **sandwich generation** is used to describe individuals who are caring for children and aging parents simultaneously. With longer life expectancy, more Canadians are living into their eighties and nineties. Canadians who work past the age of 65 are less available to care for elderly parents who may be frail and in need of considerable personal care and assistance. Fifty-seven percent of seniors in their nineties live in households rather than in nursing homes, and 29 percent live alone (Statistics Canada, 2012). Seniors in their eighties and nineties who live on their own require care from family, friends, or paid help.

Unpaid Labour Is Multifaceted

Unpaid labour encompasses mental, physical, emotional, and spiritual aspects. Consider the task of grocery shopping. Grocery shopping entails the physical labour of lifting and carrying groceries, unloading groceries, and putting away purchased items. If you've ever done a large amount of grocery shopping and filled an entire grocery cart, you have firsthand experience with the physical requirements of grocery shopping. Grocery shopping requires mental labour, such as identifying items that need to be replenished, writing a list, meal planning, reading food labels, and calculating the cost of groceries in order to stay within one's food budget. Grocery shopping requires emotional labour, such as considering the likes and dislikes of various family members (DeVault, 1991) and considering health-related issues such as food allergies or intolerances and the nutritional needs of family members with specific health issues, such as chronic illnesses like diabetes or obesity. It includes being concerned about things like staying under budget, following the Canada Food Guide, or considering whether one is purchasing the healthiest foods for one's family members. More of us spend time thinking about our food purchases because of media exposure to trends such as eating clean, veganism, vegetarianism, eating locally grown food, organic foods, superfoods, non–genetically modified organism (non-GMO) foods, and non-processed foods. It seems as though we are inundated on an almost daily basis with new research about nutrition and health and feel pressure to be responsible food consumers. Grocery shopping might require that an individual conform to the food requirements of a religion or a spiritual practice, such as avoiding specific foods or ensuring that foods adhere to certain requirements, such as purchasing food that is halal or kosher.

Unpaid labour is not always easily noticeable (Eichler et al., 2010) and is challenging to measure (see the box on the next page). For instance, pet care takes time, energy, and money, but pet care is a less visible form of unpaid labour. Pet care includes predictable tasks such as providing water and food, walking a dog, and arranging care when one is unavailable, such as when one goes on vacation. Pet care can sometimes be unpredictable, such as when a pet becomes ill or injured and needs to be cared for. The unpredictable nature of pet care applies to most forms of unpaid labour, which is one of the reasons that unpaid labour is challenging for those who perform it. Not knowing when a family member might become ill or hospitalized, be in need of a doctor's or dentist's appointment, or be in need of emotional support makes unpaid labour challenging and fundamentally incompatible with the more structured orientation and demands of the labour force. Illnesses, injuries, medical treatment, and recovery are unpredictable processes that are incongruent with the realities of most workplaces.

The invisibility of unpaid labour (Eichler et al., 2010) means that sometimes the labour is acknowledged and appreciated only when someone stops performing that labour. Consider the experience of going to use a washroom only to discover,

Sociologists have used participant observation, interviews, surveys, and time-use diaries (which note how a participant spends time over a 24-hour period) to collect data on unpaid labour. Time-use diaries are superior to merely asking a participant how much total time is spent on housework in a day or week, yet they are limited because participants do not always have the interest or capacity to record their activities with the level of care and detail researchers prefer. Moreover, this method does not always capture multitasking, such as when a mother is working on her computer at home while keeping an eye on her children and interrupting her work to load and unload the dishwasher, washing machine, and dryer. Sociologists have used self-report surveys, which ask participants specific questions about who performs various tasks, such as vacuuming, cooking dinner, and caring for sick children. This method requires that participants be accurate, and unfortunately some men overestimate how much they do while women underestimate how much they do.

perhaps too late, that there isn't enough toilet paper within reach. That someone had routinely ensured that there was sufficient toilet paper is labour that probably goes unnoticed. Yet the moment the toilet paper is gone, one is put in a difficult spot, and one might realize that this was labour that someone else was doing all along without one noticing it. Another example involves the work of kin-keeping: ensuring that relatives, even distant relatives, stay connected through activities such as sending holiday cards, making phone calls, or planning events such as annual family picnics and gatherings. Kin-keepers are more likely to be female. It isn't until the kin-keeper no longer performs this labour, perhaps due to death or disability, that family members realize that the connection between relatives has been lost and understand the value of this invisible labour. Another less visible form of domestic labour is financial labour, such as the work involved in paying bills, creating and monitoring budgets, overseeing investments and debt repayment, and tracking savings and spending.

Sick Days

Most Canadian parents are working parents, yet employees are not always able to miss work to care for a family member. Because of the lack of formal workplace support, Canadians who need to stay home to care for a sick or injured family member often use their own vacation days or sick days to do so or take unpaid time off work. Workers who have more sympathetic employers or who are more secure in their employment might be in a better position to be honest and transparent about needing to miss work to care for a family member, yet workers who have precarious employment cannot be honest and transparent with their employer about absences from work. The lack of formal sick days for family care means that Canadians cannot be honest with their employers about needing to miss work to care for a family member.

This puts Canadians in the position of having to lie to their employers and say that they are too ill to work rather than admitting that they need to care for a family member. Two-parent homes benefit from being able to negotiate or trade off which parent will stay home to care for a child so that job security is not compromised, but single-parent homes do not have this advantage and single parents may compromise their employment by caring for a sick or injured child. Self-employed workers and workers who run small businesses or who are in temporary, seasonal, or contract employment may jeopardize their businesses or employment if they miss work. Non-salaried Canadian workers with low hourly wages or financial problems may find it difficult to pay their monthly bills if they lose even a day's worth of wages. Parents may go to work when they themselves are sick because they have used up their own sick days to care for their children.

Daycares and schools mandate that children with certain symptoms such as fever, vomiting, or diarrhea stay home, and parents who cannot miss work might need to pay a babysitter to care for their ill child in addition to paying their regular daycare costs since daycares do not reduce fees for absences. Parents who are stressed about losing their jobs may resort to desperate measures, such as not disclosing symptoms like diarrhea or giving a child fever-reducing medication like children's Tylenol or Advil before dropping them off at daycare, knowing that once the medication wears off the fever will return and the daycare will call them to pick up their child. Parents who are worried about getting fired may feel that they need to show up at work, even for a few hours, rather than miss an entire day's worth of work. Canadians struggling financially to pay for daycare are further stretched financially by having to pay for a babysitter when they cannot send a child to regular daycare. Bezanson (2014) has written about the findings of two longitudinal studies of Ontario families that explored how neoliberal economic policy, cuts to social assistance, and insecure employment affected working parents. These Ontario families struggle to make ends meet and to juggle paid work and caregiving. Many Canadian women, particularly those with two or more preschool-aged children, spend most of their incomes on daycare. When children are too ill to go to daycare and a babysitter must be paid to care for those sick children, some Canadian women might not earn any income for those days above what they have had to pay for unused daycare and a backup babysitter (Bezanson, 2014).

The Multiple Meanings of Unpaid Labour

Unpaid labour is simultaneously valued and devalued. It is valued subjectively in that most people would agree that we need unpaid labour to ensure that family members are cared for. Yet the fact that we do not pay family members to perform this labour, and pay very low wages when the work is outsourced to people such as house cleaners and nannies, suggests that the labour is economically devalued. The lack of universal affordable child care in Canada suggests that unpaid labour is not a political priority.

Multiple meanings are associated with unpaid labour. Some view it as an expression of love. For example, an individual who cooks an elaborate dinner for a family member or for a holiday such as Thanksgiving might do so as an expression of their love, caring, and commitment. Preparing and cooking for a holiday such as Thanksgiving or Christmas can be a way to create a sense of "family." The work involved in organizing and preparing a birthday celebration might be an expression of love, despite the fact that it takes time, energy, and labour. We can contrast the work of preparing a Thanksgiving meal to the work of shovelling snow, taking out the garbage and recycling, mopping floors, and scrubbing toilets. These tasks are essential and are commonly viewed as unpleasant chores or absolute drudgery rather than an expression of love.

Stress and Conflict

Although in some respects unpaid labour is invisible labour, it is also the case that some domestic labour, such as caring for young children, needs to be performed daily and cannot be postponed or set aside to be done at a later time. The never-ending nature of housework can be a source of stress because, unlike other tasks, it is rarely completely finished, and even if a person is able to complete all housework, a home will stay clean only for a short period of time, as daily life quickly creates more housework. The repetition and monotony of household tasks that are done daily or multiple times daily can affect the emotional well-being of those who perform it. Housework is a source of conflict between spouses and between other family members, such as between parents and older children (Anderssen, 2013). Conflict arises as individuals avoid doing unpleasant or unfulfilling housework and housework is not fairly shared. Gender differences in how the home is viewed and how tasks like meal preparation are experienced can produce tension and conflict. In Luxton's (1980) study of three generations of housewives, women felt preoccupied with housework and found it difficult to relax or pursue sexual intimacy with husbands because of their worries about children's needs and unfinished housework. The house was a site of work, which made leisure in the home more complicated than it was for husbands, who left their work in the mines and returned home for rest and leisure. In Riessman's (1990) study of people who divorced, she found gender differences in how leisure was defined; husbands preferred dinner at home, whereas wives viewed dinner at home as work and defined leisure as going out for dinner. The meanings attached to domestic labour can influence how family members get along, and a perceived lack of fairness in unpaid labour can lead to relationship conflict.

Newcomers, families with a disabled family member, and lone parents experience greater challenges juggling unpaid and paid labour. The settlement process is difficult as newcomers look for work and housing and navigate educational, health, and social services to meet the needs of family members. Immigrants in the past several decades have faced employment difficulties because foreign educational and work credentials are not always recognized by Canadian employers (Reitz, 2007; Statistics Canada, 2015b; Tyyska and Colavecchia, 2003). Unpaid labour may increase without the help of extended family members from the country of origin (Man, 2004). Canadian families that have a disabled family member face tremendous challenges in meeting the health needs of the disabled family member and also meeting other obligations, including care of other family members and employment. Cutbacks to government-funded home care mean that many Canadian families do not receive any government help for home care and must do this care work themselves or pay someone to do this work. Canadian parents of disabled children experience challenges, and mothers commonly reduce hours of paid work to care for a disabled child on their own. Lone parents do not have the benefit of a partner who can offer some reprieve from unpaid labour. Unpaid labour and caregiving are intensified in Indigenous families, which have more children on average than non-Indigenous families and many are headed by young single mothers who face economic insecurity (Statistics Canada, 2008a).

Physical and Mental Health.

There is an inverse relationship between caregiving and health; as caregiving intensity increases, psychological and physical health declines (Schulz and Sherwood, 2008; Turcotte, 2013). Unpaid labour affects women's emotional and physical well-being (Duxbury and Higgins, 2012b); well-being is lowest and depression is highest among wives whose husbands do little housework. Marriage benefits men's health, as married men report better health than non-married men (Harvard Men's Health Watch, 2010). The same is not true for women; single women report better health than married women. Marriage offers a protective health benefit for men, yet the burden of housework and child care has a detrimental impact on married women's health. Housework and child care reduce the time that women can spend on self-care, leisure, sleep, exercise, and medical appointments.

Guilt is a common theme in research on motherhood (McMahon, 1995; Walzer, 1998) and for individuals engaged in elder care, particularly those who spend more hours doing elder care while engaged in paid work (Pyper, 2006). Unpaid labour—and caregiving, in particular—can invoke stress, worry, and anxiety (Turcotte, 2013). Elder care is particularly emotionally challenging as caregivers cope with declining physical and mental abilities and respond to medical emergencies (Church, 2016).

Research on the organization of family finances finds that women who oversee family budgets experience stress and worry as a result of their responsibility for financial management (Burgoyne, 1990; Colavecchia, 2005, 2009; Nyman, 1999). Even tasks that we might think are optional or enjoyable might cause worry if deadlines are not met—for instance, ordering your child's school pizza before the deadline, ordering a Christmas or birthday gift so that it arrives on time, or registering your children for summer camps and extracurricular activities before the spaces fill up. Failure to meet these deadlines has real consequences for children, such as not getting pizza when other classmates do, not getting a gift on time, not being able to play a much-loved sport, or not being able to go to the summer camp that a best friend is attending. These examples reveal that failure to perform unpaid labour has consequences for family members. Sometimes these consequences are minor, but sometimes they are more serious, such as failure to address the medical needs of a family member before a medical problem becomes more severe or even life-threatening. Caregivers experience stress in trying to determine the seriousness of medical problems, such as evaluating whether a medical issue is improving or worsening, and have the responsibility of following up with doctors and other health professionals if they believe that their family member needs additional medical care. Medical conditions are unpredictable, which creates the added stress of trying to juggle medical appointments and perhaps long waits in waiting rooms or hospital emergency rooms with paid work and other responsibilities.

The Skills Involved in Unpaid Labour

The extent to which domestic labour constitutes skilled or unskilled work is debated. Some argue that domestic labour requires skill, expertise, hard work, intelligence, the ability to plan and organize, and attention to detail (Eichler et al., 2010). Even though domestic labour is unpaid, sometimes it can achieve goals related to cost-cutting measures for the family and reduced expenditures (Luxton, 1980). For example, in a study of the organization of family finances among a sample of married couples with children, it was found that a number of the women engaged in highly detailed budgeting to track family spending (Colavecchia, 2005, 2009). Some women used Excel spreadsheets to track every dollar made and spent. This kind of high-intensity budgeting requires time, focus, and attention to detail and ultimately can have the effect of helping families to stay on track financially (Colavecchia, 2005). Yet this financial labour led to feelings of worry, stress, and anxiety (Colavecchia, 2005, 2008). There were emotional costs to the time, energy, and focus these women devoted to organizing and overseeing their family budgets. Women engaged in other cost-cutting measures, such as making items instead of buying them, finding and using coupons, consignment clothing shopping where they could buy and sell clothing, getting price adjustments when items they had purchased went on sale afterward, and cooking from scratch to reduce food costs. Others refute the argument that unpaid labour is skilled labour and argue that almost anyone can do this work because it does not necessarily require a great degree of skill or expertise. Along these lines, the low pay given to house cleaners, nannies, and babysitters is offered as evidence for the low skill associated with domestic labour.

KEY FINDINGS RELATED TO THE DIVISION OF HOUSEHOLD LABOUR

Gender Inequalities in Unpaid Labour

Productive labour includes both paid work and unpaid work. Some researchers suggest that when we measure total hours of productive labour, men and women do equal amounts of productive labour; however, men tend to do more hours of paid work, whereas women do more hours of unpaid labour (Beaujot, 2000; Statistics Canada, 2011b). Children increase the time spent on unpaid labour (Marshall, 2006). However, there is a fair amount of evidence that women perform a disproportionate amount of unpaid labour, even when they work the same number of full-time hours as their husbands (Milan et al., 2011; Young, Schieman, and Milkie, 2014; see the box below). Gender inequalities are greater at midlife as women care for both children and aging parents. Gender segregation in tasks is common— for instance, men being responsible for yard work and women being responsible for grocery shopping, meal preparation, and child care. There is gender segregation in elder care, with women doing more personal care and emotional care and men doing more home maintenance and repair. Women are more likely to notice that an aging parent needs care.

⟫⟫ The Second Shift

Arlie Hochschild's *The Second Shift: Working Parents and the Revolution at Home* (1989) is perhaps one of the best-known pieces of sociological scholarship on unpaid labour. Hochschild (1989) conducted participant observation of heterosexual American couples with children where both the husband and the wife worked full time. She coined the term **second shift** to describe the greater share of housework and caregiving that women performed, likening it to a second shift of work when women returned from their first shift in paid work. Hochschild found that these couples believed in egalitarianism and constructed relationship myths in order to reconcile the gap between their egalitarian beliefs and the inequity in their division of household labour. One of these myths was a willingness to see domestic labour as shared because men performed outdoor tasks such as car maintenance and yard work while women performed indoor labour such as cleaning and child care. Even though the indoor labour that women performed took more time, these couples used the indoor–outdoor distinction as a way to rationalize their division of labour and make it seem more equitable than it was. The couples embraced what Hochschild (1989) called "an **economy of gratitude**" whereby wives felt lucky and grateful for having husbands who did any amount of domestic labour because they were aware that not all husbands did. Husbands embraced this economy of gratitude and made wives aware of the fact that they did labour that not all husbands do.

Factors Associated with the Division of Unpaid Labour

The division of unpaid labour varies depending on the presence and ages of children, the employment status of spouses, educational attainment, and age. Women in male-breadwinner families who are not employed do more unpaid labour than women in dual-earner families (Milan et al., 2011). Women in dual-earner families who work part time do more unpaid labour than women in dual-earner families who work full time (Milan et al., 2011). Men in dual-earner families do more unpaid labour than men in male-breadwinner families where women are not employed outside the home. Gender inequalities in the division of household labour are narrowing over time; men are doing more now than they have done in the past (Marshall, 2006; Milan et al., 2011; Statistics Canada, 2011b). This narrowing gap cannot be explained solely by increases in the time men spend on household labour; much of the narrowing gap is due to women reducing the time they spend on household labour. Women spend less time on household labour (Statistics Canada, 2006) because they modify their approach to housework, lower their standards for cleanliness, and rely on convenience items such as prepared foods and eating out (Marshall, 2006). In a crossnational study, Altintas and Sullivan (2016) found that there has been a trend over the last 50 years toward convergence in the time that men and women spend doing housework, yet there has been a slowing of this trend in countries where men's and women's participation in housework is more equal. Moreover, there has been more of a change for women than for men and greater crossnational variation in women's participation in housework than in men's participation. These crossnational findings suggest that change has occurred in men's participation in housework, yet there is evidence for what Arlie Hochschild (1997) called a "stalled revolution"; despite women's advancement in paid employment, men have not made the same kind of advancement in terms of their participation in unpaid labour.

Class differences exist, as middle-class women outsource housework by paying other women for house cleaning and child care (Statistics Canada, 2006). High-income families where wives earn more than husbands are more likely to outsource housework and child care than high-income families led by male breadwinners (Palameta, 2003). Outsourcing does not always translate into greater equality in the time men and women spend on unpaid labour, however. Craig and Baxter's (2016) study of more than 900 Australian couples revealed that outsourcing did not necessarily lead to greater equality in the amount of time husbands and wives spent on unpaid labour. This is because gardening and maintenance, typically undertaken by men, was outsourced as frequently as cleaning, typically undertaken by women. This resulted in time reductions for men but not for women. Younger couples are more likely to have greater sharing of household labour, and more highly educated women tend to spend less time on household labour than do women with less education (Marshall, 2006). The costs of household labour are higher for more highly educated women, and this serves as a deterrent; these women likely have greater economic resources to resist household labour. In their research on newcomers to Canada, Frank and Hou (2015) found that women who came from countries that embraced more traditional gender roles were less likely to be in paid labour. Change over time among newcomers was evident, particularly among immigrant women who married non-immigrant men or who married men from a different country than their source country.

Perceptions of Fairness

Even though women perform more unpaid labour, a majority of Canadians report that they feel that their division of labour is fair (Baxter, 2000; Lennon and Rosenfield, 1994; Schieman, Young, and Glavin, 2014; Young et al., 2014). How might we reconcile this contradiction? It may be that women have attempted and failed to get their husbands to do more and resign themselves to an unequal division of unpaid labour. Women may view child care as an extension of their identity as mothers, thus inequality in child care may be more acceptable to women. Women may ascribe to Hochschild's economy of gratitude and feel lucky to have their husbands do any household labour (Hochschild, 1997). Women may be reluctant to acknowledge the inequality because they don't want to accept that their husbands don't care enough about the relationship to do more. Women may feel economically coerced to stay in a marriage or decide to stay in a marriage for the sake of their children, believing that a two-parent family is better than a single-parent family. They may realize that lone parenthood will lead to a much lower standard of living and even more housework and child care. The gulf between perceptions of fairness and the reality of inequality parallels research on money in families, which suggests that despite believing that incomes should be shared equally, many women experience economic inequality in marriage (Burgoyne, 1990; Colavecchia, 2009; Fleming, 1997; Nyman, 1999; Pahl, 1983; Singh, 1997; Wilson, 1987). In a study of married couples, Wilson (1987) found that women supported the dominant ideology that couples should share incomes, but this belief was never actually tested because women restrained their personal spending. Wilson (1987) and others (Colavecchia, 2005; Nyman, 1999) suggest that women's lower levels of personal spending and conflict avoidance come about because women are aware of the level of financial insecurity they face after divorce (Beaujot, 2000).

Among couples who have an unfair division of household labour, it is difficult to change that pattern once it is established. Parenthood can exacerbate the unequal division of household labour, as children increase the amount of housework in a household (Marshall, 2006). The transition to parenthood can restructure how couples undertake housework and a new form of labour: caregiving. In a study of new parents, Fox (2009) found that new mothers took on additional housework following the birth of their baby in order to give husbands more time with the baby. The new mothers attempted to facilitate a stronger father–baby bond by ensuring that the baby was fed, changed, and in a good mood before spending time with dad. For some women, housework was a welcome break from baby care.

Reactions to Gender Inequalities in Unpaid Labour

Men's success in resisting an equitable division of household labour reflects hidden power in marriage (Komter, 1989). In her research on married couples, Komter (1989) described a kind of hidden power that is revealed by inconsistencies in husbands' and wives' perceptions. Komter found that even though women reported dissatisfaction with housework, couples suggested that women derived more pleasure from doing housework than their husbands. Komter interprets this as a form of hidden power because it allowed inequalities in housework to continue even though women had clearly expressed their dissatisfaction with the division of household labour. Women's reactions to inequalities in household labour include both protest and conflict avoidance. Conflict avoidance by women has been documented in studies of other areas of family life where inequalities exist. Studies of money in marriage find that many women engage in conflict avoidance when faced with economic inequality in marriage as a way to preserve marital harmony (Komter, 1989; Nyman, 1999; Wilson, 1987). Some women view fairness in housework as relevant to the viability of a marriage, and lack of sharing is interpreted as an expression of disrespect and lack of caring. Unequal sharing of domestic labour may help to explain why women are more likely to initiate divorce than men. Yet the detrimental economic repercussions of divorce prevent women from demanding a more equitable arrangement from their husbands.

Same-Sex Families

Research on same-sex couples finds greater sharing of unpaid labour as compared to opposite-sex couples (Bauer, 2016; Gotta et al., 2011; Nelson, 1996). Gotta and colleagues (2011) used archival data from 1975 and 2000 to investigate the division of housework among 6864 participants that included lesbians, gay men, and heterosexuals. The researchers found greater equality in the division of housework among lesbians and gay men as compared to heterosexual individuals. In a crossnational study of housework in seven countries, Bauer (2016) found greater equality in housework among gay and lesbian couples than among heterosexual partnerships. In a qualitative study of 10 South African, interracial, gay, cohabiting partners Adeagbo (2015) found that domestic labour was shared equally regardless of income, race, class, and status. The presence of children increases domestic labour; in a study of newly adoptive parents, Goldberg and colleagues (2012) found that lesbian and gay couples were more likely to share child care and housework than heterosexual couples. Same-sex couples are less constrained by traditional gender roles, which construct unpaid labour as women's labour. However, ideas about gender can shape the division of household labour among same-sex couples. In a study of same-sex cohabiting couples, Civettini (2016) found a tendency toward egalitarianism in the division of housework yet also found evidence that housework reflected non-normative gender displays. Specifically, women who had more masculine traits took on a smaller share of housework than women who had fewer masculine traits, and men who expressed more stereotypically feminine traits did more housework than men who expressed lower levels of these traits.

In a study comparing lesbian couples to the larger British population, Dunne (2000) found greater equality in unpaid labour among lesbian couples who also spent more time on caregiving than housework. In contrast, women in the larger British population spent more time on housework than child care. The ability of lesbian women to relax standards of cleanliness reflects shared interests but also bargaining power. The fact that the wider population of women spends more time on housework may reflect a lack of bargaining power, and it may also reflect how definitions of femininity are constructed in relation to domesticity. Dunne's participants reduced their full-time employment to part-time employment and believed that lower-earning spouses needed to maintain and protect their paid employment. This contrasts with heterosexual couples, who often fail to protect the careers or employment opportunities of lower-earning spouses, who are typically the mothers.

In contrast to Dunne's participants, voluntary part-time employment is not common among heterosexual couples. The growth in non-standard employment and involuntary part-time employment in Canada has the potential to transform the division of unpaid labour among heterosexual couples. The degree of economic parity experienced by Dunne's participants was important; other sociologists have argued that economic parity is central to creating egalitarian relationships (Blaisure and Allen, 1995; Fox and Fumia, 2001; Risman and Johnson-Sumerford, 1998). When both parents have a secure attachment to the labour market, this affords a level of financial protection in the event of divorce, death, or disability of a partner. Yet in most heterosexual relationships, women typically have labour force interruptions and make concessions to facilitate their caregiving responsibilities. This creates long-term economic risk for women in the event of divorce or of the death or disability of a husband. The economic vulnerability of women has a cumulative effect, as many senior women live on low incomes and have insufficient retirement income due to decisions made earlier in life.

THE INTERSECTIONS BETWEEN PAID AND UNPAID LABOUR

Paid and unpaid labour are mutually reinforcing; low earnings or blocked job opportunities may result in women taking on more unpaid labour than their male partners (Fox, 2009; Gerson, 1985); likewise, women's responsibilities for caregiving may limit her choices around paid employment (Leach, 1999) and career advancement (Sinha, 2013). Results of the 2012 General Social Survey reveal that 10 percent of employed caregivers turned down or did not pursue a new job or promotion because of their caregiving responsibilities; survey participants who spent more time on caregiving were more likely to delay or decide against career opportunities (Sinha, 2013). Four in 10 caregivers switched to a less demanding job because of caregiving (Sinha, 2013). In a study of the impact of economic restructuring and manufacturing job loss on rural Ontario families, Leach (1999) found that women faced greater challenges in finding new employment because of their caregiving responsibilities. Jobs that required long commutes were not feasible for women with young children, limiting their opportunities for new employment. Economic restructuring and job loss adversely affect women who become vulnerable and dependent on a male partner's financial support. Leach (1999) argues that one consequence is that abused women or women in problematic or unhealthy relationships do not have the economic resources to leave and may feel coerced into remaining in these relationships.

Women have made tremendous progress in terms of their representation in postsecondary education and the labour market. More women than men graduate from Canadian universities (Statistics Canada, 2011a), and women have entered historically male-dominated professions like medicine and law. Compared to earlier generations of women, women today are increasingly following unique paths through education, child rearing, and employment. In a study of working mothers, Jones, Marsden, and Tepperman (1990) argued that there has been increased individualization in women's lives as women are more likely to follow a discontinuous life trajectory—for instance, returning to school after they have started a family. In comparing Canadians today to earlier generations, there is greater diversity in the timing and sequencing of life events and pursuits such as caregiving, education, and employment, and this is more true of women than men because women's lives are more directly affected by childbearing (Jones, Marsden, and Tepperman, 1990).

Gender Disparities in Earnings and Caregiving

Despite the progress that women have made in postsecondary education and the labour market, gender disparities in earnings have been a historical constant. Women have always earned less than men, even when employed in a similar job or field. Gender disparities in earnings are narrower when comparing single women to single men; they widen when married women's incomes are compared to married men's incomes. This difference reflects the fact that marriage leads women to undertake more caregiving and housework. Women with children earn less, on average, than women without children (Zhang, 2009), and the gap widens for lone mothers, mothers with additional children, mothers with longer labour force interruptions, and mothers who are more highly educated (Beaupré and Cloutier, 2007). This earnings gap between mothers and childless women is sometimes referred to as the "child penalty," "family gap," or "motherhood earnings gap" (Beaupré and Cloutier, 2007).

Decisions about who will stay at home to care for a baby or young child are commonly based on financial considerations; lower-earning spouses tend to stay home while higher-earning spouses remain in paid employment (Fox, 2009). Given that many Canadian women earn lower incomes than their husbands, they are more likely to have labour force interruptions to care for children. More women than men take parental leave, although Quebec has seen a dramatic rise in the number of men taking parental leave after the province introduced a new policy to encourage fathers to do so (Statistics Canada, 2015a). Women provide more care to aging, ill, and disabled family members (Sinha, 2013). A major challenge is that most caregiverss are in full-time employment. The stress of attempting to care for an ill, aging, or disabled family member while employed leads women to reduce their hours of employment, retire early, or consider leaving the labour force (Pitrou, 2005).

Primary versus Secondary Labour Markets

Why have gender disparities in earnings persisted despite women's advancement in education, employment, feminism, and the implementation of policies like pay equity? **Pay equity** legislation provides that women and men receive the same pay if they are working in jobs that are of equal value. The Employment Standards Act states that women should receive equal pay for work that requires the same skill as work done by men (Ontario Ministry of Labour, 2015). Gender parity has not been achieved with this protective legislation, although progress has been made and explicit gender discrimination in hiring, promotion, and termination is prohibited. Part of the gender gap in earnings can be explained by how the labour market is structured and where women tend to be positioned in the labour market. The labour market is not one entity; it can be internally divided into a primary and secondary labour market. The **primary labour market** generally contains highly skilled and well-educated workers employed in large companies where job security, good wages, benefits, opportunities for advancement, and unionization are more common. The **secondary labour market** contains more unskilled workers employed in smaller companies where wages are low, employment is precarious, few opportunities for promotion exist, and workers do not often have medical benefits or the protection of unionization. Women are more likely to be in the secondary labour market.

Non-standard Employment and Precarious Work

We can understand the organization of the labour market by distinguishing between standard and non-standard work. Whereas **standard employment** typically means working full time year-round for the same company and enjoying benefits such as health benefits, **non-standard work** includes part-time employment that is often involuntary because full-time employment is not available. Non-standard employment includes working multiple jobs, temporary and seasonal work, contract employment, and self-employment. Non-standard employment tends to be precarious work where employees do not have a salary, job security, or any guarantees about the hours of work they can expect to receive. Fluctuations in weekly hours of work are problematic because they make it difficult for employees to pay their bills or plan their schedules. Employees may be given very little advance notice about their work schedule, which is stressful and affects workers' ability to plan their private lives. For working parents, unpredictable employment schedules make it difficult to arrange child care.

Distinctions between non-standard and standard work and between primary and secondary labour markets are important because we see certain social groups disproportionately represented in non-standard work and the secondary labour market. These include women (Young, 2010), immigrants (Reitz, 2007), ethnic and racial minorities, students, and young workers. Some women may opt for employment in the secondary labour market, such as service sector employment or non-standard employment, to facilitate their caregiving responsibilities. Canadian mothers sometimes choose part-time evening and weekend employment, so that they are at work when their husbands are home from work and available for child care. Couples may adjust their work schedules so that one parent is always home, either to reduce child care costs or because they prefer parental care.

Occupational Sex Segregation

The gender gap in earnings reflects horizontal and vertical occupational sex segregation. **Horizontal occupational sex segregation** refers to the fact that men and women tend to work in different jobs (Statistics Canada, 2017b) and that some fields are male dominated, such as trucking and skilled trades (Statistics Canada, 2011a), or female dominated, such as nursing and social work. Economists have described the concept of a **"wage penalty"** for anyone working in a traditionally female-dominated field, as these jobs are less valued and receive less financial compensation than jobs that have not been traditionally female dominated. **Vertical occupational sex segregation** is the gender disparity that exists within the same field; for instance, consider pharmacy or law. Females comprise at least 50 percent of the graduates of pharmacy and law programs, yet they earn less, on average, than their male counterparts, and much of this difference is due to the fact that females are less likely to own pharmacies or become partners in law firms and do not share in the profits of business ownership. The causes of these discrepancies in fields like pharmacy and law are multifaceted; the nature of employment in these fields may not align with the needs of mothers, or it may be that women are not offered opportunities for partnership or business ownership because of biases against them. Owners of smaller businesses may worry that hiring young females may hurt them financially because they anticipate that women will eventually take time off for parental leave or other time off to care for children.

The Needs of Children

Motherhood and women's responsibilities for caregiving and domestic labour may lead some women to scale back their careers (see the box below). Women with young children or with children with special needs may decide not to accept positions that

---

⟫⟫⟫ The Underrepresentation of Women in Corporate Leadership

In 2013, Sheryl Sandberg, CEO of Facebook, wrote *Lean In: Women, Work, and the Will to Lead*, which examined women's underrepresentation in corporate leadership. It became a best-seller and garnered tremendous media attention and criticism. Despite acknowledging workplace barriers like sexism and sexual harassment, Sandberg wrote that the underrepresentation of women in corporate leadership was caused by women's own decision making and actions. Sandberg believes that women hold themselves back from pursuing leadership positions because they believe that corporate success and motherhood are incompatible and unattainable.

Sandberg believes that the lack of women in leadership roles is due to women prematurely forgoing career advancement to pursue marriage and children. According to Sandberg, young women do not believe that they can adequately balance a highly prestigious, lucrative, or demanding career with motherhood and thus do not pursue career advancement. In a sense, women are complicit in their career underachievement and responsible for taking on a disproportionate amount of child care and housework. For Sandberg, the shortage of female executives in corporate America is the result of women holding themselves back and scaling back their career ambitions. She advises women to "lean in" to career success. Sandberg encourages women to overcome their insecurities and the imposter syndrome, the feeling that they are not competent enough for leadership positions. She offers advice such as the importance of mentoring and of selecting a spouse who is willing to share parenting, as she did with the father of her children, Dave Goldberg, CEO of Survey Monkey.

Critics charge that Sandberg's perspective is aligned with corporate America in offering an individual-level self-help approach rather than addressing the structural barriers that women face, such as an absence of family policy to support working mothers (Geier, 2013). The critics of *Lean In* believe that the way to shatter the glass ceiling is to develop collective solutions such as universal child care, parental leave, and changes to the workplace and working hours—the kinds of family-friendly policies that already exist in many European countries (Geier, 2013). In a *New York Times* book review, Ann-Marie Slaughter (2013) argued that rather than women needing to "lean in" to their careers, businesses need to "lean in" to support working mothers. Pulitzer Prize–winning journalist Susan Faludi (2013) took aim at *Lean In* for not addressing the realities of single mothers, who cannot share parenting with a partner and may not be able to "lean in" as Sandberg advises.

Recently, Sandberg addressed her failure to acknowledge the challenges faced by single mothers after the unexpected death of her husband in 2015. Goldberg's death left Sandberg as the single parent of two children. Sandberg's lack of attention to race, class, privilege, and intersectionality was raised by critics, including celebrated writer bell hooks (2013). Sandberg concedes that her white and class privilege shield her from the poverty and marginalization that many American mothers face in trying to raise their families while working. Despite the shortcomings of *Lean In*, Sandberg created a dialogue about the underrepresentation of women in leadership positions and the unequal division of unpaid labour that undermines women's career advancement.

---

require travel, overnight absences from home, long working hours, or long commutes. Most daycares and home daycares do not offer child care in the evenings, on weekends, or overnight. Working mothers and single mothers may not be able to accept work in the evening hours unless they have alternative child care, such as help from relatives or a nanny or babysitter who is willing to work in the evening. Low-income working mothers who do not receive child care subsidies may not see any financial benefit from working after paying for child care. Parents make decisions about child care and absences from children based on economic factors and on the individual needs and abilities of their children. Some children are more resilient and better able to withstand disruptions in their daily routines, such as having a parent or both parents regularly travel for work and be away from the home. Other children are less resilient and may need more consistency—for instance, needing to see a parent in the morning before they go to daycare or school or needing to see a parent at bedtime. The needs of children inform the decision making of women, who tend to be the primary caregivers of children.

Parents of Children with Disabilities

Parents of children with disabilities face challenges in finding suitable care for their children. Approximately, 3.7 percent of Canadian children under the age of 15 have one or more disabilities (Statistics Canada, 2008b). The severity of a child's disability has consequences for the entire family. More severe disabilities often necessitate greater care from parents—from mothers, in particular—which reduces hours in paid employment and household income (Statistics Canada, 2008b). The lower income of such families is due to the higher costs associated with the child's disability. These families are much more likely to live below Canada's low income cut-off; about 1 in 5 children with a disability involving an activity limitation live in a household that falls below the low income cut-off as compared to only 13 percent of children in households without a disabled child (Statistics Canada, 2008b). Finding suitable child care for disabled children is more challenging, and this is why parents are more likely to reduce their hours of employment to undertake caregiving on their own. Parents often seek the help of family members and paid professionals in the care of a child with a disability. For children with milder disabilities, family members such as grandparents help with care. For children with more serious disabilities, paid professionals tend to be sought (Statistics Canada, 2008b). Paid care is expensive; parents with a disabled child often report needing more affordable assistance. In the absence of this support, most parents, namely women, care for their disabled children themselves, reducing their availability for paid employment and household income. The challenges faced by families experiencing the disability of a family member extend beyond low income and affect other aspects of the health and well-being of family members (see the box given on the next page).

The parents of children with disabilities face difficulties that increase stress and reduce well-being. A child's disability is associated with a decline in marital satisfaction and stability, and this is even more pronounced among families with children who have a more severe disability (Statistics Canada, 2008b). Caring for any child is physically, emotionally, and mentally taxing; caring for a child with a disability presents even greater challenges. Caring for a child with a disability negatively affects parental physical and emotional health and lowers the self-reported life satisfaction of parents (Statistics Canada, 2008b). Parents of children with disabilities experience high levels of stress; the more severe the disability is, the greater the self-reported stress of parents (Statistics Canada, 2008b). The stress has several causes, including greater levels of exhaustion, inadequate sleep, and work and financial problems (Statistics Canada, 2008b). Parents have less personal time, time that is needed for self-care and other activities that benefit physical and emotional well-being, such medical appointments and leisure and social activities (Statistics Canada, 2008b). The work of caring for a child with a disability might be 24 hours a day, 7 days a week; even among parents who are able to find suitable child care, they are ultimately responsible for caregiving in the evenings, on weekends and holidays, and when children are too ill to go to daycare or school.

Barriers in the Labour Market

Glass ceiling, *glass escalator*, and *maternal wall* are some of the phrases used to describe the inequalities that women face in the labour market. The **glass ceiling** is the notion that there are very few women in senior management and executive positions and there seems to be an invisible ceiling above which women cannot rise. Women are less likely to be in positions of authority over co-workers or to supervise others. When women do serve in supervisory roles, they are more likely to supervise other women than men; in contrast, men are more likely to supervise both male and female co-workers (Jarman, Blackburn, and Racko, 2012). The **glass escalator** is the idea that men in female-dominated professions such as teaching and social work are disproportionately overrepresented in upper-level management or supervisory positions. They seem to ride an invisible escalator to the top of their organizations, bypassing female colleagues. The **maternal wall** refers to the obstacles to career advancement that women face once they become pregnant or have children. Motherhood is a wall or barrier to advancement because supervisors assume that women will have less time for their careers or will be less dependable or less devoted to their careers once they have a child (England, 2005). Sexual harassment is a barrier that women, and some men, experience. Sociologists who have studied sexual harassment describe quid pro quo sexual harassment and hostile or poisoned environment (Welsh, 1999). Quid pro quo sexual harassment occurs when sexual threats or bribery are used as a condition of employment decisions, such as in decisions about promotion or termination. A hostile or poisoned work environment is uncomfortable or threatening because of inappropriate conduct, comments, or touching.

WORK–LIFE BALANCE

Most Canadian employees have caregiving responsibilities, yet most work full time and have little flexibility in their hours of work. In a study of 25 000 Canadians working full time, Duxbury and Higgins (2012b) found that 65 percent of participants worked 9 to 5, 15 percent worked a compressed workweek, 14 percent had flextime schedules, fewer than 1 percent were able to work from home, and no one in the sample participated in job sharing. Moreover, 60 percent worked more than 45 hours per week, and more than half also took work home with them (Duxbury and Higgins, 2012b). In comparing their study findings to earlier studies, Duxbury and Higgins (2012b) concluded that workers have less flexibility in hours of work, hours of work have increased, absenteeism has increased, and mental health has declined. This profile of the Canadian labour market suggests that the inflexibility of paid employment presents challenges to workers who provide child care or elder care. Juggling paid employment and caregiving is difficult, and the demands of paid employment can affect how family members spend time together. Figure 7.1 illustrates how work hours can reduce the time available for activities such as caring for a sick child, extracurricular activities, and family dinners.

Individuals trying to juggle paid work and caregiving may experience stress related to a lack of time. The term **third shift** was coined by Hochschild (1997) to describe the mental and emotional energy involved in dealing with the challenges of severe time shortages experienced by contemporary working parents. According to Hochschild, working parents experience a time famine, which means that they must follow strict schedules in order to meet work and family obligations. This entails keeping children on strict schedules and being attentive to the clock, which is in contrast to children, who are not always willing to adhere to rigid schedules. In *The Time Bind*, Hochschild (1997) provocatively argues that sometimes working parents prefer being at work because their home life is perceived to be more stressful than the workplace. Women feel more time-stressed than men (Marshall, 2006; Zukewich, 2003). In a study of 1955 dual-earner Danish parent couples, mothers who were self-employed were better able to control their daily schedules, and this lowered the time pressure they experienced. In a study of more than 24 000 employees across 27 European countries, Lunau and colleagues (2014) found that poor work–life balance due to long working hours and inflexible work schedules was associated with more health problems.

Canadian survey data show that a majority of Canadian parents say that they are satisfied with the balance between their jobs and family life; however, mothers express lower levels of satisfaction than do fathers (Statistics Canada, 2016). The main source of dissatisfaction is lack of time; working parents would like more family time. Women who work part time are happier with their work–life balance and feel less time pressure than full-time working mothers (Marshall, 2006). Shift work reduces work–life satisfaction, heightens stress (Williams, 2008), and reduces health and well-being (Shields, 2002, 2006). Groups that have lower levels of work–life satisfaction

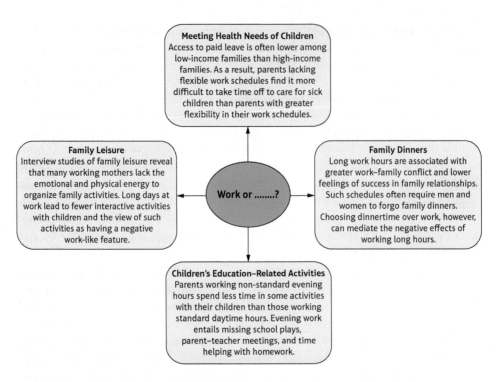

Figure 7.1 Choices faced by working parents

Sources: Based on Clemans Cope, L., et al. 2008. Access to and use of paid sick leave among low-income families with children. *Pediatrics 122*(2): 480–486; Jacob, Jenet I., S. Allen, J. E. Hill, N. L. Mead, M. Ferris. 2008. Work interference with dinnertime as a mediator and moderator between work hours and work and family outcomes. *Family and Consumer Sciences Research Journal 36*(4): 310–327; Wight, Vanessa R., Sara B. Raley, & Suzanne M. Bianchi. 2008. Time for children, one's spouse and oneself among parents who work nonstandard hours. *Social Forces 87*(1): 243–271; Shaw, Susan M. 2008. Family leisure and changing ideologies of parenthood. Sociology Compass 2: 1–16.

include lone parents, individuals caring for both children and aging parents, and employees who do not have flexibility in their employment schedules.

SOCIAL POLICY

Neoliberalism

The trend toward **neoliberalism** in the past several decades has led to less state support for families, who are viewed as being responsible for their own welfare. The burden of care and responsibility has shifted away from the state and toward individual family members, and this caregiving work is undertaken disproportionately by women. Home care is given in a patient's home and includes tasks such as personal care (e.g., bathing), meal preparation, and paying bills. Individuals eligible for home care include older Canadians, those with disabilities, and patients who are terminally ill. In 2012, 8 percent of Canadians received home care (Turcotte, 2014); however, an additional 500 000 Canadians needed home care but did not receive it. Others received inadequate levels of home care. Home care allows Canadians to stay in their homes and reduces the costs associated with hospitalization, palliative care, and other forms of institutionalized care. Despite the fact that Canada's population is aging and demands for home care are increasing, the ability of Canadians to access home care is declining. Reduced home care over the last few decades means that family members have increasingly had to care for ill or disabled family members on their own or pay privately for care. Many Canadians receive insufficient home care, and there is evidence that insufficient care adversely affects mental health (Turcotte, 2014).

In 2004, the Canadian government introduced the Compassionate Care Program, which gave financial benefits to family members who took time off work to care for a terminally ill family member. Initially, the program limited eligibility to specific family relationships, but it has since expanded the eligibility criteria to permit Canadians to care for anyone they consider to be a family member. Despite this improvement, the Compassionate Care Program requires recent labour force participation in order to receive benefits. Women who do not have recent labour force participation because they have been at home caring for children are ineligible to receive benefits to care for a gravely ill family member. Although the Compassionate Care Program is beneficial in recognizing that sometimes family members wish to care for a dying family member, it shifts the economic burden from state-supported hospitals, palliative care centres, and home care toward family members, who bear the economic brunt of end-of-life care.

The last several decades have seen the introduction of welfare reforms that require participation in employment training or volunteerism as a condition of eligibility for financial benefits. Canada, the United States, the United Kingdom, Australia, and the Netherlands are just a few of the nations that have introduced "workfare" policies aimed at getting welfare recipients, including lone parents, back into the labour force. In the mid-1990s, Canadian provinces began introducing various workfare policies for social assistance recipients, such as the Ontario Works program, which requires recipients to engage in various activities such as employment training, community placements, and employment placements in order to qualify for benefits. These workfare policies have been critiqued for offering benefit levels that are below Statistics Canada's low income cut-offs and inadequate child care subsidies for single parents (Gazso and McDaniel, 2010). Some of the more dire consequences of these workfare programs are increased food insecurity, use of food banks, and women returning to abusive ex-partners in order to escape poverty (Critically Thinking About Policy, 2008).

The Limitations of Canadian Family Policy

Given Canada's universal health care system and high standard of living, it is often assumed that the Canadian government offers generous supports for families and children. Yet when we consider the high rate of child poverty in Canada (Albanese, 2009), it becomes clear that our country's family policy does not adequately support vulnerable groups. Crossnational comparisons of family policy reveal that many European countries offer much more generous benefits to families, more inclusive eligibility criteria to receive government support, and greater supports to facilitate parents being in full-time employment. Benefit levels in Canada are lower than the levels in Sweden, Denmark, Germany, and Norway (Phipps, 2009) and historically have been taxable income, which reduces the amount of money families receive. In fact, benefit levels are even lower than in some poorer Eastern European countries such as Romania, Lithuania, and Slovenia (McGill Institute for Health and Social Policy, 2012). Some Canadians return to work before the end of parental leave because they cannot afford to meet all of their financial obligations with parental leave benefits (Beaupré and Cloutier, 2007).

Canadian policy uses stricter eligibility criteria, making it difficult for families to qualify for support (Colavecchia, 2016; Phipps, 2009; Tremblay 2014). Canadian parental leave, for example, requires recent labour force participation to qualify for support, and this means that women who have been at home caring for young children do not qualify. Women who have children close in age may have to decide between returning to work before the end of a parental leave in order to qualify for support for a subsequent child or staying home and forgoing benefits for the subsequent child. Flexible eligibility criteria in European countries make it easier for a larger number of families to qualify for support, even when women do not have recent labour force participation (Phipps, 2009). Many European countries offer longer paid and unpaid parental leaves. For instance, the Netherlands gives unpaid leave for parents with children under the age of 8, and Spain offers three-year unpaid leave (Organisation for Economic Co-operation and Development, 2011). Crossnational variation in rates of poverty among single parents reflects differences in family policy (Phipps, 2009). In countries like Sweden and Finland, lower rates of poverty, including child poverty, reflect more comprehensive family policies to support mothers' employment. The economic security of single-parent families is improved when parents are in paid employment and there is sufficient support, namely child care subsidies, to facilitate caregiving and employment. (Albanese, 2009; Phipps, 2009).

In 2017, Prime Minister Justin Trudeau extended Canada's parental leave program from 12 months to 18 months. Although there is no increase in benefit levels, the program gives parents choice in terms of whether they would prefer to receive higher benefits over the first 12 months of parental leave or lower benefits spread out over the entire 18 months. The new policy has been criticized for not increasing benefit levels, and analysts suggest that parents would be further ahead financially by receiving benefits for the first 12 months rather than receiving lower benefits over the entire 18 months. The new parental leave program is seen as addressing the problem of a scarcity of daycare spots for infants under the age of 18 months, but critics charge that the real solution would be to ensure daycare for infants rather than expect parents to stay out of the labour force longer (Cleland, 2017).

Canada's system offers fathers parental leave, but it is mostly mothers who take it. In other countries and in Quebec, fathers are offered a leave for fathers only. The fact that so few men take parental leave stems from societal attitudes about men's and women's roles and from the fact that women tend to earn less than men; gender disparities in the labour market channel the lower-earning spouse, typically the woman, into parental leave. For most couples, the decision about who should take parental leave is made on a purely economic basis rather than by taking into consideration the aptitudes, dispositions, and desires of the spouses. In addition to lengthening parental leave, Prime Minister Trudeau eliminated a taxable, modest universal child care allowance introduced by former Prime Minister Stephen Harper and replaced it with a tax-free Child Tax Benefit that gives higher benefit levels to lower-income Canadians. Supporters of this policy change argued that Harper's allowance was too minimal to help low-income families and that high-income Canadians did not need the money. Other supports for parents that exist in Canada include deductions for families caring for a child with a disability and income support for parents caring for a child who is critically ill or injured or who have a child who has been murdered or is missing.

Typologies of Family Policy

Sociologists who have conducted crossnational comparisons of family policy have developed different conceptual typologies to highlight the main differences between countries. One typology makes distinctions between "private family," "family-oriented," and "state-based" policies. Private family policy describes those countries, such as the United Kingdom and the United States, where the state offers very little because the family is viewed as being able to take care of itself (Korpi, Ferrarini, and Englund, 2013; Lesemann and Nicol, 1994). In other countries, such as France, the government is viewed as having a public interest in families and provides generous benefits. This has been described the family-oriented model. Quebec diverges from other Canadian provinces in the extent to which the government supports families and children and aligns more closely with the family-oriented model. In some countries, the state intervenes in very significant ways to promote women's employment and gender equality in the labour market. Sweden, Denmark, and Norway are examples of countries that fit with this state-based model of family policy. Policies in Canada fall between the family-oriented and state-based models, but the lack of a national child care strategy, low benefit levels for parental leave and other income supplements, and strict eligibility criteria to receive financial benefits position Canada well behind most European countries.

A second typology makes distinctions between "work–family balance," "work–family alternating," and "non-interventionist" policy (Tremblay, 2014). Countries like Sweden, Norway, Finland, and Iceland have policies to help parents remain in the labour force, even if they have young children. The kinds of policies that help to support parents include accessible and affordable child care, longer paid and unpaid parental leaves, and shorter work days. This model of promoting labour force participation while offering good supports has been described as the "work–family balance" model (Tremblay, 2014). Some countries, such as Germany, France, and the Netherlands, have developed policies to support women staying at home to raise young children but then also to support them as they re-enter the labour market. In this "work–family alternating" model, individuals are viewed as entering and leaving the labour market as their caregiving needs change. A final "non-interventionist" model characterizes countries like the United Kingdom and the United States that do not have policies such as parental leave or child care. Canada's parental leave distinguishes it from the "non-interventionist" model, but the absence of other policies such as affordable child care places us closer to the "work–family alternating" model. Policies in Quebec are markedly different than in the rest of Canada and align with the "work–family balance" model. Quebec offers more support to working parents and more generous benefits. For example, Quebec offers affordable child care, more flexible eligibility criteria to allow more parents to qualify for parental leave benefits, higher benefit levels, and special leaves for fathers (Tremblay, 2014).

Parental Leave Benefits

One of the main criticisms of how Canadian maternity and parental benefits are determined is that Canada requires recent labour force participation and links benefits to earnings in the previous year only. Our laws preclude women from receiving benefits for second and third children if they have not worked in the year before giving birth. This eligibility requirement forces women to decide between (1) returning to work sooner than they would like to so that they can qualify for benefits for a subsequent child, or (2) forgoing benefits altogether so that they can stay at home with their children. In many European countries, parental leave can be taken by parents even if they lack a recent history of employment, and this results in more families qualifying for benefits. Other family-friendly policies that exist in some Western European countries but not in Canada include the option of parents working shorter work days and taking paid sick days to care for sick children at home. These crossnational differences underscore how the larger social context informs private decisions, such as whether or how long a parent can stay at home with a baby or sick child.

In 2008, 80 percent of new mothers who had been employed before giving birth received Employment Insurance parental leave benefits; the other 20 percent did not qualify for benefits, either because they were self-employed or because they lacked sufficient insurable earnings to qualify for support (Marshall, 2010). After Quebec revamped its parental leave program in 2006, more women, including self-employed workers and women with fewer insurable earnings, qualified for benefits, which increased the national average (Marshall, 2010). Benefit levels are higher in Quebec than in the rest of Canada. Of the women who received Employment Insurance benefits, 1 in 5 received an additional employer "top-up" to these benefits (Marshall, 2010). More women in Quebec receive employer top-ups, as do women working in the public sector, women working in large companies, and women who earn higher wages. These factors suggest that Canada has a two-tier system, with higher benefits going to employees who are already the most advantaged in the labour market.

Child Care

Canada lacks a nationwide system of universally accessible, affordable, high-quality, regulated daycare (Langford, Albanese, and Prentice, 2017). Some analysts argue that universal child care offers short-term and long-term benefits to our economy; others say that the costs are prohibitive. Our government's willingness to fund daycare during World War II to entice women to work in munitions factories and take other jobs to help the war effort suggests that universal child care can be implemented if there is sufficient political will. During World War II, the Dominion-Provincial War Time Agreement established funding for child care for women working in wartime industries (Friendly, 1994). Funding was cut at the end of the war, despite opposition and protest (Wartime Day Nurseries Are Boon, 1944).

The significance of political will is most evident when we consider how Quebec has made child care a political priority. In Quebec, parents have access to regulated and affordable child care. Initially, daycare cost $5 per day, then it increased to $7 a day, and in 2017 it was modified again so that cost is based on household income. For families earning less than $51 000 annually, the cost is $7.75 per day (Finances Quebec, 2017). The cost increases gradually as income increases to a maximum cost of $21.20 per day which would apply to families earning more than $161 380 per year (Finances Quebec, 2017). Families that have two children pay only 50 percent of the daily cost for their second child, and families that have more than two children do not pay for third or subsequent children (Finances Quebec, 2017). Throughout the rest of Canada, child care is much more expensive, although daycare fees vary by region and by the age of the child. Child care costs are highest for youngest children because younger children require more care and lower staff-to-child ratios. Daycare fees for infant care in Toronto are the highest in the country and average just over $1600 per month; in most other Canadian cities, monthly daycare costs for one infant exceed $1000 per month (Macdonald and Friendly, 2014). In Quebec, the costs are about $152 per month. Parents of toddlers (18 months and older) in Quebec pay $152 per month, whereas parents in most other Canadian cities pay between $800 and $1000 per month (Macdonald and Friendly, 2014). Often there are long wait lists for licensed daycare centres, leaving working parents with no guarantee that they will have care set up before they return to work. Parents sometimes take more time out of the labour force because care is not yet available. Parents resort to informal care in unregulated settings by relatives, friends, neighbours, nannies, and home daycares because of lowered cost or because regulated, licensed care is unavailable.

A majority of Canadian children are taken care of in their first year of life by mothers on maternity leave. However, some women cannot take maternity leave or may need to shorten the length of their leave, either because they do not qualify for benefits or because they cannot afford to stay home to care for their baby (Beaupré and Cloutier, 2007). This includes self-employed women and women who do not have sufficient recent labour force participation to qualify for Employment Insurance benefits because they are caring for other children at home. Quebec offers more generous benefits; in Quebec, women can qualify for Employment Insurance benefits with fewer insurable hours as compared to women outside of Quebec, and Quebec offers a special paternity leave benefit for fathers (Tremblay, 2014). Most Canadian children experience transition at the age of 1 from care by their mother to another kind of care, as a majority of women return to the labour force following the end of their maternity leave. Family income predicts the type of child care used. Data for 2011 show that middle-income Canadians (household incomes between $40 000 and $100 000) typically use home daycares, which are less expensive than licensed daycare centres (Sinha, 2014a). Regulated care in a licensed daycare centre is most often used either by low-income families that receive government subsidies or by Canadians with household incomes above $100 000 (Sinha, 2014a). Canadian children experience a lack of continuity in care and possibly in quality of care, as informal care arrangements do not have the same level of oversight as regulated, licensed daycare facilities.

The lack of affordable child care leads some Canadian parents to try to adjust their work schedules so that one parent is home to care for children while the other is at work. The benefit is saved child care expenses, but parents must often forgo time with each other, sleep, and leisure time to accommodate both child care and work. This affects the quality of care and the level of parental supervision that children receive, as well as the physical and emotional well-being of parents, who may be chronically sleep deprived or have insufficient time for self-care, including exercise and medical appointments. A severe time crunch emerges, and this creates conditions of high stress that may adversely affect the parent–child relationship, the marital relationship, and the emotional and physical well-being of all family members. Many Canadians rely on free or inexpensive child care provided by relatives, neighbours, and friends.

Fathers Providing Care   Even though caregiving is performed disproportionately by women, more fathers are caring for their newborn children and more fathers are becoming "stay-at-home fathers." According to Statistics Canada, 20 percent of fathers received parental leave benefits in 2006, compared to only 3 percent in 2000

(Marshall, 2008). Sometimes fathers become caregivers because of unemployment, but sometimes they actively decide to become the primary caregiver. In 2014, 27 percent of Canadian families were single-earner families; 16 percent had a stay-at-home mother and 2 percent had a stay-at-home father. Stay-at-home fathers tend to be older and have less education than fathers who are in paid employment (Uppal, 2015). Andrea Doucet (2006) studied 118 Canadian fathers who were the primary caregivers of their children and found that men provide care that is similar to the kind of care provided by mothers. This group of fathers had fewer role models for fathering in this way. This is an example of how Canadians are forging new possibilities for themselves absent role modelling from earlier generations.

Earlier literature on fathering after divorce highlighted that most fathers became absent in the lives of their children or had little contact with their children (Arendell, 1992). One of the reasons that fathers became absent in the lives of their children after divorce is the lack of role models of other divorced dads who actively parent. As more fathers continue to participate in their children's lives post-divorce, there are more role models to help other men to do the same. Legislated child support affects fathers' decisions about time spent with children after divorce; some fathers opt to share access time with children to avoid or lower their child support obligations. Results of the 2011 General Social Survey reveal that most children live with their mother following divorce and that 18 percent of nonresident parents had not spent time with their children in the year prior to the survey (Sinha, 2014b). While custodial parents are overwhelmingly female, the number of single fathers in Canada is increasing.

The Live-in Caregiver Program   In the absence of a universal child care system, Canadians have relied on the Live-in Caregiver Program as a way of offering affordable child care to working parents. This program allows women from foreign countries such as the Philippines to work as nannies, with the objective of receiving permanent resident status after two years of such work. Faced with dire economic need in their countries of origin, women who come to Canada under this program have often left their own children to care for Canadian children. Workers can be exploited and abused by their employers but are unable to do anything about their situation because of their immigration and economic status (Arat-Koc, 2001). Various elements of this immigration policy are problematic and lead to the exploitation of domestic workers (Hsiung and Nichol, 2010). The requirement that foreign workers live with their employers increases workers' vulnerability to abuse and exploitation. There are few measures in place to ensure that domestic workers have job security and are paid a fair wage, including for overtime hours. Moreover, there are no protections to ensure that domestic workers are not overworked or mistreated and are given adequate shelter, food, and privacy. Domestic workers have little power to respond when employers do not meet their contractual obligations, such as adequate pay and shelter. The term **transnational mothering** describes women who have left behind young children to care for Canadian children (Arat-Koc, 2001). Despite the geographical separation, these women try to mother from a distance and stay connected to their children using technologies like Skype, Facebook, and other forms of social media. The experience of leaving behind a baby or young children can cause psychological trauma and mental health issues as these women endure grief and loss (Pratt, 2009). Domestic workers endure this trauma because of the economic pressures their families face. Reunification can be fraught with difficulty, as children may have been separated from their mothers for years.

CONCLUDING REMARKS

Domestic labour is essential for the well-being of families, yet much domestic labour is invisible (Eichler et al., 2010), devalued, and undertaken by women. The persistence of gender inequalities in unpaid labour raises important questions about power, feminism, and gender roles in contemporary society. In the absence of sufficient government support, families must navigate the daily dilemmas of juggling paid labour and caregiving by relying on individual rather than collective solutions. Even if we do not see ourselves as caregivers, most of us will care for a child or one or more aging, disabled, or dying family members at some point in our lives and will do so in a less-than-ideal context of insufficient government support. Those of us who have cared for children, adults, or both simultaneously can attest to the enormous stress, strains, and costs of doing so. This care work affects marital relations, family relationships, and the health and well-being of both patients and caregivers. An analysis of the intersections of paid and unpaid labour reveals the myriad challenges facing Canadian families in the twenty-first century.

CHAPTER SUMMARY

This chapter defined unpaid labour and explored the multifaceted nature of unpaid labour or domestic labour. It examined caregiving and the challenges faced by working Canadians who are juggling the competing demands of paid employment and caregiving. The chapter outlined gendered inequalities in unpaid labour and described the ways in which paid and unpaid labour are mutually reinforcing, as responsibilities for domestic labour affect the decisions women make about employment and career advancement. At the same time, the realities of the labour market, including occupational segregation and gender disparities in earnings, reinforce women's responsibilities for domestic labour and caregiving. Canadians face enormous challenges in balancing paid and unpaid labour, and these will intensify due to our aging population. The stresses for working parents and those with caregiving responsibilities can be intense due to the inflexibility of the labour market and the absence of family-friendly workplace policies such as paid or unpaid days off to care for a family member or sick child. Crossnational comparisons of family policy reveal the limitations of policies in Canada. As our population ages, it seems likely that greater media and political attention will be paid to the challenges faced by working parents and working caregivers who are trying to cope with caring for their loved ones.

Key Terms

economy of gratitude A term coined by Arlie Hochschild that refers to wives feeling grateful for having husbands who do any amount of housework. Wives compare their husbands to other husbands rather than to their own contributions to housework.

glass ceiling The notion that there are very few women in senior management and executive positions and there seems to be an invisible ceiling above which many women cannot rise.

glass escalator The idea that men in female-dominated professions such as teaching and social work are disproportionately overrepresented in upper-level management or supervisory positions. They seem to ride an invisible escalator to the top of their organizations, bypassing female colleagues.

horizontal occupational sex segregation The fact that women and men tend to work in different fields. For instance, more men work in manufacturing and skilled trades and more women work in education.

maternal wall The obstacles to career advancement that women face once they become pregnant or have children.

neoliberalism A set of economic and social policies whereby governments reduce spending on social services and health care. Neoliberal economic policy shifts the burden of responsibility for caregiving away from the state toward individual family members.

non-standard employment Non-standard work includes part-time employment that is often involuntary because full-time employment is not available. It also includes working multiple jobs, temporary and seasonal work, contract employment, and self-employment. It tends to be precarious work where employees do not have a salary, job security, or any guarantees about the hours of work they can expect to receive.

pay equity Legislation that provides that women and men receive the same pay if they are working in similar jobs that are of equal value.

primary labour market The primary labour market generally contains highly skilled and well-educated workers employed in large companies where job security, good wages, benefits, opportunities for advancement, and unionization are more common.

sandwich generation Individuals who care for children and aging parents at the same time.

second shift Describes the greater share of housework and caregiving that women perform in the home after completing their first shift in paid employment.

secondary labour market The secondary labour market contains more unskilled workers employed in smaller companies where wages are low, employment is precarious, few opportunities for promotion exist, and workers do not often have medical benefits or the protection of unionization.

social reproduction Describes the many facets of caring work that families undertake, including the intergenerational care of family members.

standard employment Typically means working full time year-round for the same company and enjoying benefits such as job security and medical benefits.

third shift Refers to the mental and emotional labour involved in dealing with the challenges of severe time shortages experienced by contemporary working parents.

transnational mothering Domestic workers from foreign countries who have left their children in their country of origin attempt to mother from a distance as they care for their employers' children in Canada. Economic pressures necessitate the geographical separation, and mothers use social media to stay connected to the children they had to leave behind.

vertical occupational sex segregation Refers to the lower pay and lower prestige women experience within the same occupational type, such as law.

wage penalty Wages tend to be lower in traditionally female-dominated fields, as these jobs are less valued and receive less financial compensation than jobs that have not been traditionally female dominated.

Critical Thinking Questions

1. What are the ways in which domestic labour is both valued and devalued in society?

2. Why is unpaid labour peformed disproportionately by women?

3. Domestic labour and caregiving can be stressful for Canadians. What are the factors that make domestic or unpaid labour stressful or challenging for Canadians?

4. Our population is aging at a time when most adults are in full-time employment. Given this context, what are the challenges faced by Canadians who provide care to a child or to an aging, disabled, ill, or dying adult?

5. Paid labour and unpaid labour are mutually reinforcing. How do women's experiences in the labour market reinforce their responsibilities for unpaid labour, and how do women's responsibilities for unpaid labour reinforce their position in the labour market?

6. How does family policy in Canada compare to that in other industrialized nations?

Weblinks

Canadian Centre for Policy Alternatives
www.policyalternatives.ca/
The Canadian Centre for Policy Alternatives is a research institute providing research on social, economic, social justice, and environmental issues facing Canadians.

Statistics Canada
www.statcan.gc.ca/eng/start
Canadian data on a wide variety of issues related to families, the labour market, caregiving, and unpaid labour.

Childcare Resource and Research Unit
http://childcarecanada.org/
Information and research on child care and resources for educators, parents, and policy-makers.

Government of Canada: Family Benefits
www.canada.ca/en/services/benefits/family.html
Lists all of the benefit programs in place for Canadian families, including parental leave, tax deductions for parents caring for a child with a disability, and income support for parents of children who are critically ill, injured, murdered, or missing.

Canadian Mental Health Association
http://toronto.cmha.ca/programs_services/family-support/#.WQnuP4jys2w
The Canadian Mental Health Association offers support for Canadians caring for someone with a mental health issue.

Canadian Hospice Palliative Care Association
www.chpca.net/
The Canadian Hospice Palliative Care Association provides education, research, fundraising, advocacy, and support on issues related to end-of-life care.

Chapter 8
Stress and Violence
Realities of Family Life

Gladskikh Tatiana/Shutterstock

CHAPTER OUTLINE

- Stress
  - Types of Stressors
  - Caregiver Burden and Burnout
- Family Violence
  - Defining and Measuring Family Violence
  - Causes of Violence
- Causes and Effects of Stress and Violence in Immigrant Families
- Effects of Violence
- Supporting Survivors
- Witnessing Violence
- Concluding Remarks

1 Use the ABCX family crisis theory to model family adaptations to stress.

2 Discuss how illness and health issues affect all members of a family.

3 Provide data about how common acts of family violence are in society.

4 Discuss how gender is related to intimate partner violence.

5 List the types of abusive relationships that occur within families.

6 Explain the traumatic effects of witnessing family violence.

Close relations are hard work, as we've noted repeatedly throughout this book. Solving conflicts and communication problems, raising children effectively, earning an income, and getting the household work done—these tasks are hard to do. They can be frustrating, draining, and upsetting. No wonder people get ill and depressed when faced with so many tasks, so often. Family life gives people a lot, but it also takes a lot.

For some, families and homes can even be danger zones. People's closest, most intimate relations are with their family members. In this vulnerable setting, people reveal their true selves, invest themselves, and, in so doing, leave themselves open to much stress, and even to violence.

In this chapter, we examine various forms of family stress and violence. We consider why family life often leads to stress, how this stress affects family relations, and why some families are better able to cope than others. We also examine the types of physical and emotional violence that occur all too often within families. Finally, we review some of the many attempts by researchers to explain why **domestic violence** is much more common than we would expect or hope.

By discussing stress and violence in the same chapter, we are *not* claiming that stress is the only or even the main cause of domestic violence. Stress does not always lead to violence, nor does violence always result from stress. Stress is often an effect of as well as a cause of family violence. However, these two topics are related in that both stress and violence reveal the striking gap between an idealized, sentimental fantasy about family life and the way that flesh-and-blood families actually work.

Few people, when they form a family, imagine how stressful family life is going to be at times. But for some families, a high degree of stress is recurrent or continuous. And few people, when they form a family, imagine there to be a risk of violence. Since most people consider family life a private matter, family violence is often hidden. We rarely know when it is going on in other people's lives, and we keep other people from knowing if it is going on in our own lives.

Neither violence nor stress fits into the romantic ideal of family life that most of us have learned to imagine. So, for some readers, this chapter will be a shocking wake-up call. For others, it may confirm what they already know from their own firsthand experience. But we cannot stress enough that violence is *not* a normal, everyday incident. Some types of stress are normal and common, but violence is never normal and should never be endured lightly.

STRESS

Family stress arises in response to a **stressor**: a demand that threatens the relations between family members (Hall et al., 2012). Only by using family resources can the stress be relieved, and in this chapter we describe those resources (Joseph, Goodfellow, and Simko, 2014).

To explain how stressors affect families, most researchers use updated versions of the **ABCX family crisis model** first elaborated by Reuben Hill in 1949. Hill used the model to explore how families adjusted to wartime separation and reunion. Since then, sociologists have adapted the model to examine differences in the ways families cope with other hard, stressful problems.

In the ABCX model, stressors (labelled A) interact with the family's coping resources (labelled B) and with the family's subjective interpretation of the stressor (labelled C). The result of these three interacting variables—labelled X—is the resulting family crisis (Joseph et al., 2014).

To understand the distinction between A and C, recognize that events can be both objectively and subjectively stressful. Through careful observation and data collection, a researcher can objectively evaluate a given stressor—the so-called A in the model. To do so, the researcher will measure things like how long the stress has endured and the frequency with which it has recurred. Typically, the longer a stressor lasts, the more severe its effects will be. And the more often it recurs, the more it will strain a family's resources, decreasing the family's ability to cope successfully.

Family members themselves also evaluate the stressor, and their evaluation may be different from that of the researcher. How family members view and define a stressful event shapes how they will react to it. And what they think about the stressor will influence its effect on the family. Families may exaggerate or downplay a stressor, compared with the researcher's evaluation. And like any self-fulfilling prophecy, the family members' belief in their ability to cope increases their ability to cope.

Sociologists have used versions of this model to study how stress changes the roles and relationships that make up a family. For example, they study how stress changes the ways that spouses connect with each other, parents connect with children, children connect with parents, and siblings connect with one another. They also study the ways stress affects communication among family members, marital satisfaction, and parenting abilities.

Often, extreme stress reduces a family's ability to work well in these respects. For that reason, sociologists are interested in how family members cope with and adjust to a long-term stressor. As mentioned, such coping depends on the strength or quality of a family's crisis-meeting resources. Typically, those that cope well already have important resources—especially cohesion and flexibility—before the stresses began. We find systemic differences between the families that pull together and the families that fall apart under different stressors.

Types of Stressors

Common causes of family stress fall into at least four categories:

1. *Major upheavals*, such as war and natural disasters that affect many people simultaneously
2. *Major life transitions*—acute disruptions that affect some family members but not others—such as the birth of a child, the death of a parent, divorce, and retirement
3. *Chronic stressors*, such as disability, severe physical or mental illness, drug and alcohol abuse, occupational problems, unemployment, or imprisonment of a family member
4. *Occasional stressors*, such as car accidents, burglaries, and seemingly pleasant but stressful stimuli like family vacation trips. We do not discuss these occasional stresses in this chapter, since they may be briefly severe but depart without permanent harm.

Major Upheavals   For North American families, the financial crisis of 2007–2009 was a stressor that caused widespread unemployment and poverty. In the United States, home foreclosures and personal bankruptcies affected many American families; in Canada, southern Ontario's automobile industry was devastated, as was the forestry and lumber industry in British Columbia (Dubé and Polèse, 2015). Families in both nations are still feeling the effects. Today, we see echoes of this economic disaster in the high unemployment rates of young people. Many young adults, unable to secure a job, have moved back in with their parents. Older parents have had their retirement plans sabotaged by these so-called "boomerang kids" or by their own reduced earning power in our post-recession economy. Middle-aged, working adults are the most stretched, as they struggle to find or keep their own jobs as well as to provide financial and instrumental support to their young children and aging parents (McDaniel, Gazso, and Um, 2013).

Major Life Transitions   Many life transitions are predictable and expected in average families: birth, death, marriage, divorce, retirement, the empty nest, and so on. They all have disruptive, stressful effects, even though they are common and foreseeable. In Canada and other societies with large immigrant populations, it makes sense

Generation Boomerang

It's so normal for millennials to move back home after flying the coop that people across the world have developed special names to describe this group of dependent young adults. North Americans have dubbed them "boomerang kids," while Italians call them "Bamboccioni," or big babies (CBC.ca, 2016). In the United Kingdom, they're known as "Yuckies": Young, Unwitting, Costly Kids (CBC.ca, 2016).

Just one of many reasons for millennials' failure to launch is education: A university degree is the new high school diploma. However, getting that education saddles young adults with significant debt, and it does not guarantee them a job in today's tough labour market. The unemployment rate in Canada among 15- to 24-year-olds is 14 percent—twice as high as it is among the general population (CBC.ca, 2016). With tens of thousands of dollars to pay off and no significant or stable income, free room and board at home is the only option for many millennials.

For others, it's the most comfortable option. Research shows that children of parents with greater economic resources fly the coop later and move back home earlier (Sandberg-Thoma, Snyder, and Jang, 2015). They are likely to have postsecondary degrees and may even have decent jobs, but these young adults are often wary of our unstable post-recession economy and nervous to commit to a lease or mortgage when they could easily lose their unstable positions. Not to mention, staying put in mom and dad's spacious house beats paying huge sums for a bachelor apartment.

Millennials struggle to enter and stay in the job market, but baby boomers are having a hard time leaving it. Sixty-two percent of Canadians in the baby boom generation report that supporting their adult children is keeping them from saving for retirement (Wright, 2017). It's a big enough problem that we've coined a special phrase for this phenomenon too: "deja-boom."

Sources: CBC.ca. 2016. Generation boomerang. Retrieved from http://www.cbc.ca/doczone/episodes/generation-boomerang; Sandberg-Thoma, S.E., A.R. Snyder, & B.J. Jang. 2015. Exiting and returning to the parental home for boomerang kids. *Journal of Marriage and Family 77*(3): 806–818; Wright, L. 2017. Retirement vs. "boomerang" kids. *TheStar.com.* Retrieved from https://www.thestar.com/business/2017/01/29/retirement-vs-boomerang-kids.html.

now to also include migration as a typical family transition—one that is common if not always foreseeable and that often disrupts family life in stressful ways.

Immigrant families typically face **acculturative stress** because of the strains of adapting to a new society. On arrival, many newcomer parents struggle to find work, as they are not fluent in English or French and their foreign educational credentials are often not recognized (Pitt, Sherman, and Macdonald, 2015). On top of this financial stress, immigrants feel the loss of friends and families they left behind and often report feeling lonely and isolated in their new home societies as they adjust to new cultural norms and expectations. Prolonged stress of this kind can harm a family. Therefore, time spent in a new homeland can cause anxiety and depression for both parents and children (Islam, Khanlou, and Tamim, 2014).

Immigration affects the members of a family in different ways. In a sense, children have the easiest time: At school, they will learn English, make new friends, and grow used to social and cultural norms more quickly than, say, their grandparents, who may spend more of their time alone at home. Yet children are more pressured to adopt the new culture (if not assimilate socially). Integration into a new culture may be stressful, as youth feel caught between the old and the new. In a study of Southeast Asian youth who had immigrated to British Columbia, Hilario and colleagues (2014) found that their respondents experienced reduced stress and emotional despair if they had good social support from their peers—and especially if they felt connected to and supported by their parents.

However, since youth typically assimilate quickly, tension and conflict can arise between immigrant parents and their children. For example, a study of Chinese immigrant families in British Columbia found such tension between parents, who preserved more traditional values, and their adolescent children, who assimilated in their efforts to fit in to their new communities (Costigan and Dokis, 2006). The parents in this study stressed the importance of getting good grades, staying close to the family, and remaining respectful toward and obedient of authority, but youth participants wanted the greater independence that North American teens typically enjoy. These discrepancies are often stressful, as parents struggle to understand their child's new behaviours and begin to question their own parenting abilities, and children worry that they are disappointing their parents by failing to meet their expectations (Ho, 2013).

Adolescent women may have especially strained relations with their immigrant parents. Immigrant parents may keep traditional views on dating and teach their daughters that their male peers are "distractions" who can tarnish the family's reputation, yet daughters may adopt an openness to dating and even to sex from their new culture (Qin, 2009).

Chronic Stressors   Chronic stressors confronting families include "economic stress," which can refer to unemployment, job insecurity, too little income, and the like. These problems increase stress, reduce resilience, and hinder every part of a family's well-being, including the physical and mental health of each member. Chronic stressors can develop because of the major upheavals discussed above. The financial crisis of 2007–2009, for example, officially ended years ago, but many North American families are still reeling in its aftermath.

Sociologists find that economic pressure on a family increases parental unhappiness and marital conflict (Minnotte, Minnotte, and Bonstrom, 2015). Many researchers use the notion of "spillover" to explain these results: External variables, such as work- and money-related stress, often spill over into one's marriage (Randall and Bodenmann, 2009). For example, long hours spent at the office can detract from time spent at home, causing feelings of loneliness and resentment among those who sense they are being "left behind" or ignored. Or, when work-related concerns become overwhelming, people with otherwise effective communication skills can find themselves unable to express themselves to their loved ones, leading members to feel alienated from one another. For these reasons, chronic economic stress can eventually cause marriages to dissolve and parent–child bonds to decline.

Single mothers are especially vulnerable to economic and social stress. One study of 674 employed Canadian mothers found that single mothers experience significantly higher levels of psychological distress than their married counterparts (Dziak, Janzen, and Muhajarine, 2010). The reasons for this are rooted in the disadvantage of being the sole breadwinner and caregiver, having to balance work and parenting strain. So, married and single mothers are similar in their ability to react to and cope with stress, but single parents are more consistently exposed to stressful life events. What's more, they do not have a partner to support them emotionally, financially, or in other ways through these difficulties.

Children and teenagers feel the effects of their single mothers' economic and personal stress. Those who live in persistent poverty are at a significantly higher risk for depression when they enter adulthood (Mossakowki, 2008). The more extended the period of poverty, the more likely it is their mental health will suffer. However, closer and more frequent contact between a single mother and her adolescent child is likely to reduce stress from other sources. During early adolescence, closer supervision by single mothers may increase their awareness of adolescent stress and, in turn, may buffer the negative effects of stress on adolescent adjustment (Hartos and Power, 2000).

Racism is another source of chronic stress, especially for racialized minorities. For example, Indigenous peoples have been the targets of exploitation and abuse since Canada's founding. Today, they remain disproportionately likely to endure the economic stress described above and are often blamed for their own hardships. Indigenous youth are over-represented as offenders in the criminal justice system and are three times as likely as non-Indigenous youth to be targets of violent crime (Scrim, 2016).

Indigenous peoples and other racialized minorities in Canada need social support to help them cope with these problems of racism, isolation, and poverty. For example, many Somali immigrant families rely on their religious and cultural traditions to keep them feeling united. Mensah and Williams (2013) found that Somali newcomers to Toronto often struggle to secure housing because of racial discrimination and financial disadvantage. To manage the resulting stress, participants reported that they would convert areas of the homes they eventually gained into prayer spaces and make an effort to enjoy cultural dishes at home with their families. Participation in these familiar, comforting activities fostered feelings of solidarity among family members that help them to cope with chronic, external stressors.

Caregiver Burden and Burnout

Caregiving is most often associated with supporting aging, infirm parents, but many different family members often need care. The responsibility for providing that care typically falls on particular family members, who then experience unique types of stress—and who rely on different coping methods—depending on the nature and duration of the caregiving.

Recipients of Care Caring for aging parents is often stressful, so an aging, longer-living adult population will experience more family stress for longer periods of time. In 2012, 13 million Canadians said that they had acted as caregivers at some point in their lives (Sinha, 2012b). Two in three of these people are caring for their elderly parents or parents-in-law (Vezina and Turcotte, 2010).

Parents' different needs influence the amount of stress felt by their caregivers. For example, minimal stress may arise if adult children need to begin checking in on their aging parents a few times a week. However, more intense, prolonged stress may arise among adult children who are acting as caregivers for parents with severe health issues, such as dementia. They often report heightened feelings of stress and even depression because of their parent's aimlessness, aggressive behaviours, forgetfulness, and restlessness (Chen, Uzdawinis, Scholmerich, and Juckel, 2014).

At the other end of the age range, infants and youth need much care and supervision as well. In turn, working-age parents have become members of the "sandwich generation," discussed in Chapter 7. More than a quarter of the Canadian women who provide care for their parents or spouses are also main caregivers for their own children (Sinha, 2012b).

Children with disabilities need unique types of caregiving. Depending on the nature of the disability and the child's needs, caring for a child with a disability may need attention and energy 24 hours a day, 7 days a week, for the child's entire life.

Finally, when any family member experiences severe illness and needs prolonged care, the provider of that care is likely to endure stress. The effect of such family strain varies with the nature, severity, and duration of the illness.

What's more, growing numbers of older parents and young children are in need of care today because of changes in Canada's social policies (Giesbrecht, Wolse, Crooks, and Stajduhar, 2015). Institutional care used to be common in the past, both for older adults and for people with disabilities. But today, these groups are more likely to continue living in their own homes or with their families (Williams et al., 2011). Some families prefer to provide care for their relatives personally, at home, but clawbacks for social services of all types have made it more difficult for overwhelmed families to access caregiving support (Canadian Centre for Policy Alternatives, 2004). The result is a growing number of older adults, severely ill people, and people with disabilities who must rely on increasingly exhausted, stressed family members for care (Lilly, Robinson, Holtzman, and Bottorff, 2012).

Providers of Care The "caregiving family" in our North American culture contains both people who provide assistance and people who have some duty to provide help but do not. Certain family members are more likely to provide care—and experience stress as a result of providing care.

In Canada, women are more likely than men to be caregivers (Guerriere et al., 2016). Women also devote greater amounts of time to caregiving: Women often spend 20 hours or more fulfilling their caregiving responsibilities each week, while men are more likely to spend 1 hour or less (Sinha, 2012b). In this sense, **caregiver burden** and burnout are gendered stressors: They are more likely to affect women than men, and as we see in Figure 8.1, the number of Canadian involved is quite high (Chappell, Dujela, and Smith, 2015).

Older adults are more often recipients—rather than providers—of care, and the caregiving role can pose unique challenges for them. Often, older women take responsibility for providing care for their aging husbands. The greater needs of the older recipient, coupled with the older woman's own increasing, age-related needs, make this caregiving arrangement especially burdensome (Williams, Giddings, Bellamy, and Gott, 2016). Yet older caregivers spend the greatest number of hours per week providing care (Sinha, 2012b).

Consequences of Caregiving   Sociologists have been researching the challenges and rewarding experiences of caregivers for years. This research has long shown that caregiver burden—a blanket term describing the emotional, physical, and financial toll of caregiving—is common. Burden is especially common among caregivers who devote more time to the recipient and when the recipient's needs are many and intense (Chappell et al., 2015).

Caregiver burden can cause anxiety, depression, exhaustion, poor physical health, emotional distress, and overall reduced quality of life (Guerriere et al., 2016).

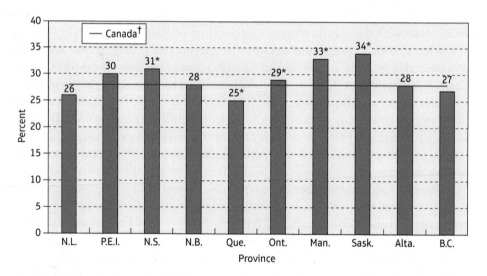

† reference category
* significantly different from reference category (p < 0.05)

Figure 8.1 Percentage of Canadians providing care, by province, 2012
Source: Sinha, M. (2012). *Portrait of Caregivers, 2012.* Statistics Canada. Reproduced and distributed on an "as is" basis with the permission of Statistics Canada.

Fifty-five percent of Canadian caregivers report symptoms associated with caregiver burden, including feeling anxious and worried (Sinha, 2012b). Continued efforts to provide care in the face of these negative effects can result in moments of "crisis." **Crisis episodes** in caregiving have been defined as significant events that are likely to lead to seeking help from professionals (Betts Adams, 2006) or changing caregiving conditions (Usita, Hall, and Davis, 2004).

In a study of 5496 Canadian caregivers, Sims-Gould, Martin-Matthews, and Gignac (2008) analyzed crisis episodes among employed caregivers. They found that these episodes occur in two forms. First, crises can be enduring (chronic) or they can be temporally bounded (acute). Second, crises can be predictable or unpredictable. For instance, the authors classify a knee surgery needed by the cared-for individual as temporally bounded and predictable, whereas they classify a depression diagnosis as enduring and unpredictable. Similarly, events taking place in the caregiver's life can lead to crises.

However, shifting one's caregiving responsibilities post-crisis does not always reduce stress. For example, many wives experience reduced anxiety when their aging or chronically ill spouse is hospitalized, but others suffer ambivalence. On the one hand, they feel relieved that they need no longer provide difficult home-based care and grateful that their husband is receiving excellent care. But on the other hand, they feel guilty that they are failing to provide that care themselves. As a result, in the first weeks after admission, wives often display poor physical health, low morale, and high levels of depression.

Parents of people with disabilities experience similar ambivalence. If parents decide that their child needs more full-time care than they can provide, they may place the child in a home that specializes in supporting people with disabilities. This transition relieves the burden of care, but it can create new stressors, including financial strain (as parents must now save for an unanticipated set of services) and a sense of loss (as parents are physically separated from a child they expected to have in their home). Alternatively, if a child's disability rules out income earning and independent living, parents may need to adjust their own careers, retirement plans, and lifestyles indefinitely. For these reasons, concern for the future of a child with a disability has been the greatest source of stress for parental caregivers (Hall et al., 2012).

Caregiving can also be financially costly. Most caregivers accrue hospital bills or pay out of pocket for prescription medications not covered by the Canadian health care system. Those who devote significant amounts of time to caregiving are also likely to suffer work-related consequences. Employed caregivers say that their caregiving responsibilities routinely interrupt their paid work: They arrive at the office late, leave early, or are forced to take time off to attend to the recipient of care (Sinha, 2012b). Many are forced to reduce their paid working hours, which often leads to their health care benefits being withdrawn and to a decline in their household income. Some caregivers even say that they have turned down promotions and new work opportunities because of their caregiving responsibilities, whereas others actively seek less demanding (and therefore lower paying) work to accommodate their caregiving duties.

Finally, the caregiving role can detract from the time and energy available for other family members. Half of Canadian caregivers say that their caregiving responsibilities force them to spend less time with their children, and half of married Canadian caregivers say that the responsibilities cut into the time they spend with their spouses (Sinha, 2012b).

Caregiving parents of a child with a disability sometimes worry that their other children will feel left out or abandoned as they devote so much time and attention to the child with a disability (Hall et al., 2012). Others suggest that their marital satisfaction declines, as they have more conflicts over the best way to care for their child and less time to spend together as a couple (Hartley, Papp, and Bolt, 2016). Overall, some parents report that having a child with a disability can restrict their freedom and make them feel like their child's needs occupy much of their lives (Miranda et al., 2015).

Caregiver burden is so common and so well documented that research has shifted gears and now focuses on exploring solutions: initiatives that may better support caregivers (Lilly et al., 2012). For example, Guerriere and colleagues (2016) propose that professional help from personal support workers could ease the burden experienced by many caregivers, while allowing recipients of care to continue living at home. As we see in Figure 8.2, the more hours that family members spend providing care, the more stress they suffer.

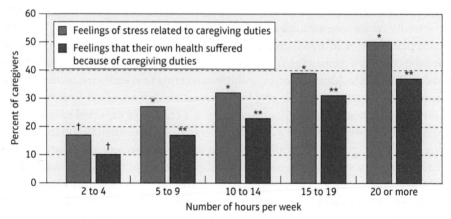

† reference category
* significantly different from reference category - feelings of stress for 2–4 hours of caregiving per week (p < 0.05)
** significantly different from reference category - feelings health suffered for 2–4 hours of caregiving per week (p < 0.05)
Note: Questions on the impact of caregiving responsibilities were only asked of those caregivers providing care for 2 or more hours per week.

Figure 8.2 Caregiver stress and health, by hours of care per week

Source: Sinha, M. (2012). *Portrait of caregivers, 2012.* Statistics Canada. Retrieved from: http://www.statcan.gc.ca/pub/89-652-x/89-652-x2013001-eng.htm#a2. Reproduced and distributed on an "as is" basis with the permission of Statistics Canada.

Coping with Caregiver Stress   Caregiving causes stress, but many families cope successfully; they find ways to return to normalcy, although the stressor may still be present. Two types of resources—material and emotional/psychological—determine which families can withstand crises and which cannot. Material resources refer to things like time and money (Giesbrecht et al., 2015). These make it easier for a caregiver to afford hospital stays and medications for the care recipient and to avoid burnout. However, such material resources are not equally available to all Canadians.

Emotional resources are internal abilities to withstand misfortune. They may include coping skills that have been learned and cultivated, as well as personality traits such as self-confidence, calmness, and bravery. Emotional resources also include feelings of trust and affection for other family members, an ability to communicate openly, and a willingness to risk change for the collective good. In this sense, family members can contribute to each other's emotional resources by listening well and offering encouragement.

The more time devoted to caregiving, the more material and emotional resources are needed. One in 10 caregivers who spend 20 hours a week or more on caregiving tasks say that they are not coping with the stress well (Sinha, 2012b). Greater efforts must be made to support the many caregivers who feel overwhelmed (Lilly et al., 2012).

However, for those who come to manage caregiving stressors successfully, the role can be rewarding. For one, when caregivers can effectively meet the needs of the care recipient, their family member may be able to remain at home longer, as opposed to being placed in a hospital or care facility (Guerriere et al., 2016). Providing care and support can also help bring family members together and forge closer bonds. Lastly, successfully coping with the stresses of caregiving can teach family members—including those who provide minimal caregiving help themselves but watch the caregiving duties of others—important skills like resilience, compassion, and responsibility.

Nowhere are these positive caregiving experiences more consistently documented than in the literature on parents of children with disabilities. Not all of the effects are negative, as one might expect. Many of these parents report great personal growth, heightened sense of purpose in life, stronger and more rewarding relations with others, and a deeper emotional connection with their child (Hall et al., 2012). Parents who have learned to cope with the stress related to raising a child with a disability also focus on the benefits to the child's other siblings, such as learning compassion and patience. When parental caregivers find such positive meanings in their child's disability, rather than viewing it only as a burden, they are better able to cope with related stress.

Social Support Networks   Like responses to all stressors, the ability to cope and enjoy these positive results depends on a family's resources (Miranda et al., 2015). The most important resource a caregiver can have is a large, strong social support network. These networks can be made up of family, friends, and community agencies, all of which help to buffer the strain of caregiving, working, and fulfilling one's other roles. Overall, caregivers with larger support networks report lower levels of stress and better overall health (Giesbrecht et al., 2015).

As mentioned above, caregiving duties often preclude caregivers from spending as much time with their friends and families as they may like. In turn, social support networks shrink precisely when caregivers need them most (Lai and Thomson, 2011).

Social support is more than information diffused through social channels. To be useful, social support must give caregivers the right information and encouragement at the right time. Social interaction and positioning in a network of relations give meaning and value to health information. The information is confirmed by acquaintances the listener trusts and respects.

Illness and aging are partly biological events and partly social performances, and family and friends play an important part in this culturally scripted drama. Through interaction in social networks, people recognize (or admit) health problems, contact health professionals, and comply with medical advice. A key player in this drama is the sick person's main caregiver, who often finds herself or himself needing support.

Sometimes, people can get this support from their doctor. However, doctors remain main advisers to resolve confusion over conflicting information, despite being sometimes averse to information from outside sources. Interpersonal trust depends on the degree to which patients see their doctors as competent, responsible, and caring. Continuities of care, meeting times that allow opportunities for response, patient instruction, and patient participation in decision making all encourage trust.

Other increasingly common sources of support include online groups that people connect with through social media platforms. These groups set up virtual communities for people suffering from a chronic illness or for their caregivers. These may only be virtual relationships, but they provide the same kinds of moral support as face-to-face interactions. In one study, Chou, Hunt, Beckjord, Moser, and Hesse (2009) found that online support group users are mainly people with minimal education, poor health, a personal cancer experience, or psychological stress. The participants came together around a shared health-related problem to exchange useful, practical information they had gathered through personal experience or to provide emotional support for one another. Caregivers often find such support groups especially helpful; they are remotely accessible and available 24 hours a day, 7 days a week, meaning that participation can be easily incorporated into caregivers' hectic schedules.

However, people get far more of the information and encouragement they need from their personal networks than from special-purpose support groups. Physically present social contacts can boost caregivers' material and emotional resources. For example, in addition to providing emotional comfort and solace, husbands can provide financial support, take on more household chores, and assume more child care responsibilities to help support their wives as they care for aging parents (Tsimicalis et al., 2012). People with large, cohesive social networks filled with genuinely caring people are also more likely to address their own needs by using health care services regularly (Richmond, 2009). Caregivers risk burnout if they neglect their own health as they try to improve that of others. Finally, these large networks typically promote higher levels of social participation, leading to higher levels of overall well-being and life satisfaction.

Family cohesion is especially crucial for parents of children with disabilities. Families that are cohesive before the child is born—or that come together in response to the child's birth—are better able to cope with related stressors (Hall et al., 2012). By contrast, mothers who feel that their partners are less encouraging, committed, and willing to help care for a child with a disability report feeling more stressed. Parents who report that their child's disability is stressful typically say that they and their children feel lonely, isolated, and excluded from groups beyond their immediate family; that they lack support; and that they are disappointed that their child is missing developmental milestones. These social costs of caring are elaborated on in the box below.

⫸ The Costs of Caring

Caregiving is nothing new. Most adults today have taken on—or intend to take on—the responsibility of supporting their aging parents. However, the huge need for care today could become too great for families to meet. As our population ages, more and more people require care. Yet the people who have traditionally cared for them are becoming less available: Smaller family sizes mean fewer adult children to look after their aging parents. Similarly, women's greater participation in the labour force means that they have less time and energy to devote to caregiving. The result is a "caregiver squeeze," where the demand for caregiving outstrips its supply (Taylor and Quesnel-Vallee, 2017).

Making matters worse is the reality that many adults who are expected to care for their aging parents have young children as well. This "sandwich generation"—largely composed of women—tries to split its time between caring for parents or in-laws, raising children, and, often, working a full-time paid job (Steiner and Fletcher, 2017).

Improved access to formal caregiving services may help to alleviate the pressures on this sandwich generation, but we lack the resources needed to make those services more widely available. Family members perform 10 times as many hours of caregiving as paid caregivers do (Fast, 2016). That makes their labour worth more than $66 billion. Our already overburdened health care system cannot absorb their efforts.

With so much time and energy going into informal caregiving, we cannot continue to view it as a personal obligation, or a labour of love (Fast, 2016). Rather than assuming that adult children will always be willing to devote their time, money, and energy toward caregiving, we need to develop structured ways of providing them with support and acknowledging the importance of their work.

Sources: Fast, Janet. 2016. We need to start caring for caregivers. *Toronto Star.* Retrieved from https://www.thestar.com/opinion/commentary/2016/01/21/we-need-to-start-caring-for caregivers.html; Steiner, A.M., & P.C. Fletcher. 2017. Sandwich generation caregiving: A complex and dynamic role. *Journal of Adult Development 24*(2): 133–143; Taylor, M.G., & A. Quesnel-Vallee. 2017. The structural burden of caregiving: Shared challenges in the United States and Canada. *The Gerontologist* 57(1): 19–25.

FAMILY VIOLENCE

Before delving into statistics, definitions, and sociological analyses of causes and effects, several themes surrounding family violence warrant mentioning. The first is that, to repeat, violence is not always a direct result of family stress. All families experience stress at one time or another, but not all families resort to violence. Second, people who are targeted by and live through violence should be considered survivors, not victims. A growing literature documents the ways in which abused and oppressed family members resist and fight back against abuse, even while they remain locked in cycles of violence they cannot escape and can scarcely avoid. Finally, victim-blaming accounts remain popular in our society, but survivors of violence are never to blame. One can never excuse violence or the idea that the targets of violence bring that violence on themselves.

Defining and Measuring Family Violence

How big of a problem is family violence in our society? Collecting exact statistics is hard, partly for methodological reasons. To begin with, we have the problem of defining violence. What counts as violence varies from one culture to another, and often from one family to another. Is female circumcision family violence? What about infant male circumcision?

Also lacking is a widely accepted definition of what exactly defines a family. Students of family violence come at the issue from a host of disciplines that include anthropology, sociology, psychology, social work, medicine, and criminology. Disciplines differ in what they count as family violence and use different ways of measuring its extent.

To resolve these definitional issues, family violence is now understood as an umbrella term that covers different kinds of violence among different sets of family members. We begin by outlining several types of violence before noting which family members are most likely to perpetrate and be targeted by violence.

Physical Violence   The oldest recognized form of violence is physical: the intentional use of physical force by one family member aimed at hurting or injuring another family member. Physical violence can involve hitting; kicking; biting; choking; burning; throwing things; the use of a knife, gun, or other weapon; and so on (Broll, 2014).

Sexual Violence   Researchers classify sexual violence separately from non-sexual physical violence and study it in its own right. Sexual abuse includes nonconsensual sexual interaction, including touching, photographing, self-exposure, harassing comments intended to embarrass or intimidate, and intercourse (Brozowski and Hall, 2010). Perpetrators may use physical violence, verbal threats, or emotional manipulation to force compliance.

Emotional or Psychological Violence   Emotional abuse entails efforts to degrade, belittle, undermine, intimidate, and weaken a target's sense of self. It can include financial exploitation, verbal insults, destruction of property, name-calling, shaming, neglect, efforts to isolate the target, and efforts to rob the target of his or her dignity (Kaukinen, Powers, and Meyer, 2016). Emotional abuse can also involve threatening someone with physical or sexual violence.

Abuse—physical, sexual, or emotional—may happen once, or it may occur in a repeated and intensifying pattern over months or years. Different types of abuse can be inflicted in combination and can also change over time. Family violence is far from a uniform experience; each targeted individual experiences it differently.

Measuring the frequency with which these different types of violence are inflicted is challenging because we often lack access to hospital records and case files gathered by social workers. What's more, violence typically takes place in private, as part of a continuing intimate relationship. Perpetrators (and sometimes survivors) often try hard to keep it hidden.

Despite these difficulties, sociologists have developed better techniques for estimating its prevalence. One reliable and valid scale for measuring family violence, the **Conflict Tactics Scale**, measures verbal aggression and physical violence on a continuum (Moreau, Boucher, Hebert, and Lemelin, 2015). It looks at two aspects. One is whether there have been three or more instances of violence in the previous year. The other is the severity of the act or acts. Factors included in the scale include the use of a weapon; injuries needing medical treatment; the involvement of a child, an animal, or a non-family member; drug or alcohol involvement; extreme dominance, violence, or surveillance; forced sex; extensive or repeated property damage; and police involvement (Straus, 1996). Yet as we see in Figure 8.3, victimized family members have many reasons for not wanting to report spousal violence to the police.

Types of Abusive Relationships   Certain family members are more vulnerable to violence and abuse than others. The first more vulnerable group is children. In 2010, 74 000 cases of physical violence against children and youth were reported to police (Sinha, 2015). Family members committed 25 percent of these violent acts. Children are also five times more likely than adults to be the targets of a sexual offence. Boys may be more likely to endure physical abuse, but girls are at a much higher risk of sexual abuse.

Abuse of older adults is another all-too-common form of family violence, typically perpetrated by caregivers, including spouses and adult children (Lai, 2011). Sometimes, older adults are physically and sexually abused because they are seen as easy targets: too frail to defend themselves. They are also at risk of financial abuse: theft, fraud, forgery, or extortion (Tyyskä, Dinshaw, Redmond, and Gomes, 2012). For example, caregivers may steal their money, pension cheques, or other possessions; sell their homes or other property without their permission; fail to use their assets for their benefit; or wrongfully use a power of attorney.

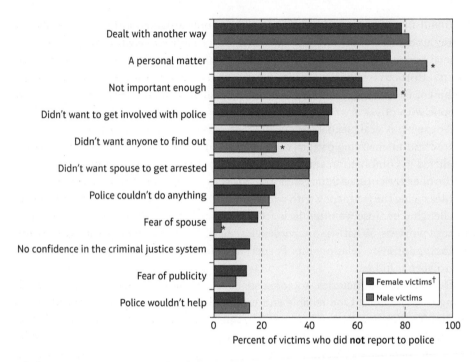

† reference category
* significantly different from reference category (p < 0.05)
Note: Includes legally married, common-law, same sex, seperated and divorced spouses who experienced spousal violence within the previous 5 years and who indicated that the violence did not come to the attention of police. Figures do not add to 100% due to multiple responses. Data from the Northwest Territories, Yukon and Nunavut were collected using a different methodology and are therefore excluded.

Figure 8.3 Reason for not reporting spousal violence to police, by sex of victim, Canada, 2009

Source: Sinha, M. (2015). *Responses to violence against women.* Statistics Canada. Retrieved from: http://www.statcan.gc.ca/pub/85-002-x/2013001/article/11766/11766-4-eng.htm#a3. Reproduced and distributed on an "as is" basis with the permission of Statistics Canada.

Finally, many dependent older adults who cannot meet their own needs are neglected. For example, they may be denied adequate nutrition; personal care; a safe, clean place to live; or access to health care services. Despite its many forms, abuse of older adults often remains hidden because of their typically smaller social networks and isolation (Taylor-Butts, 2014). Often, their main contacts are the family members perpetrating the abuse.

Since the 1999 General Social Survey on Victimization, there has been an increase from 280 reported family cases of abuse of older adults to 2400 cases in 2009. A Statistics Canada report, based on police statistics, revealed that about one-third of violent incidents against older adults were committed by family members. Older women were prone to abuse by both spouses and grown children, whereas older men suffered abuse by their grown children (Sinha, 2012a).

Also, since immigration trends have contributed significantly to Canada's eth-nocultural diversity among seniors, the issue of abuse of older adults has to be studied in different cultural environments (Lai, 2011). Added to the risks of abuse that older adults in the general population face are factors unique to the immigrant population: language barriers, social isolation, and socio-cultural factors (Tyyska et al., 2012). The same barriers can also prevent survivors from seeking help: They may be unaware of their legal rights in Canada, unfamiliar with formal services that can intervene, or unable to access those services because of language barriers (Yoshioka, Gilbert, El-Bassel, and Baig-Amin, 2003). Legal sponsorship—wherein Canadian citizens and permanent residents can assist their parents, grandparents, and other relatives to immigrate to Canada as well—can make older adults depen-dent on younger generations. Some may abuse that power imbalance, and older adults may be unable to report abuse at the hands of their sponsors for fear of los-ing their residency.

When it comes to abuse of older Indigenous people in Canada, the research is scarce. One report notes that, as in the general population, older Indigenous people are more vulnerable to abuse if they have medical conditions or are dependent for basic care (Beatty and Berdahl, 2011). We lack the data needed to determine whether abuse is more commonly perpetrated against Indigenous or non-Indigenous older adults, and whether abuse is more common on or off reserves. However, researchers note that low socio-economic status (SES) typically predicts abuse; given the low SES of many Indigenous peoples—especially those living on reserves—we may expect a higher risk of abuse among older adults in this population.

Another type of violent relationship is that between siblings. Many people excuse violence between children by claiming that they don't know better. The simi-lar reasoning that kids will be kids—and therefore bickering and squabbles will inevi-tably result—has contributed to the dearth of literature on this type of family violence. In general, the sibling relationship has been less studied than abuse perpe-trated between parents and children, and between spouses. We are far from knowing the full extent of sibling abuse, as well as its long-term effects.

By contrast, extensive research has been conducted on **intimate partner violence (IPV)**. Today, IPV is a more widely used term than the older language of wife batter-ing, spousal violence, marital abuse, and so on. As an umbrella term, IPV accounts for the many intimate relations that underpin families today, including same-sex, common-law, cohabiting, and other types of couples, as well as relations between former partners who have dissolved their relationship.

As mentioned, researchers have a hard time finding out how common IPV is because people make concerted efforts to hide such behaviour. Most of our data come from police reports. However, survivors may be reluctant to report violence to the police for fear that their abuser will retaliate with even greater violence. Thus, IPV (and other forms of family violence) may be even more common than our sta-tistics suggest.

Among heterosexual couples, women are most often the targets of IPV. In 2013, women accounted for 80 percent of the targets of acts of IPV that were reported to police in Canada (Beaupré, 2015). Sexual offences, forcible confinement, kidnapping, beating, choking, and threatening with a gun or knife are among the intimate partner offences most likely to be committed against women (Statistics Canada, 2016). As we see in Figure 8.4, young women—ages 20 to 35—are the most commonly reported victims of partner violence; as women age, their risk declines dramatically.

Women are also most likely to suffer the most extreme form of IPV: homicide. From 2003 to 2013, 960 homicides were committed against intimate partners. Of these, 747 were committed against a woman, making women the victims of more than three-quarters of IPV homicides.

We are not saying that men are never targets of IPV, or that women are incapable of perpetrating violence (Baker, Buick, Kim, Moniz, and Nava, 2013). Research confirms that IPV is as prevalent among LGBTQ (lesbian, gay, bisexual, transgender, queer) people as it is among heterosexual people (Gabbay and Lafontaine, 2017). Up to 43 percent of

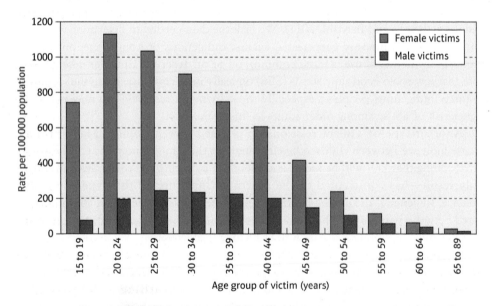

Note: Rates are calculated per 100 000 population. Polpulation figures are based on July 1st esimates from Statistics Canada, Demography Division. Intimate partner violence referes to violence committed by married, separated or divorced person, common-law partners (current and former), dating partners (current and former) and other intimate partners. Includes victims aged 15 to 89. Excludes incidents where the age or sex of the victim was unknown and where the relationship between the victim and the accused was unknown. Victims aged 90 years and older are excluded because of possible instances of miscoding of unknown age within this age category.

Figure 8.4 Survivors of police-reported IPV by sex and age

Source: Data from Sinha, Maire. 2012. *Family Violence in Canada: A Statistical Profile, 2010.* Ottawa: Canadian Centre for Justice Statistics.

self-identified lesbians and 26 percent of self-identified gay men report having been physically or sexually abused by an intimate partner in their lifetime (Cannon and Buttell, 2016).

Research on the sex of IPV perpetrators has yielded conflicting results: Some studies find that men and women are equally likely to perpetrate IPV, while others find a disproportionate number of female survivors and male perpetrators. These different findings are the result of different definitions of violence (Johnson, 2011). Physical and sexual abuse intended to achieve control and dominance over a target are committed by men against women (although there are exceptions). However, men and women are equally likely to commit "situational couple violence"; these violent acts are not part of a broader pattern of systemic abuse and domination, but rather the result of conflict that progresses to violence (Richards, Tomsich, Gover, and Jennings, 2016). The actual behaviour can be as severe as tactics used to show control. However, in this case, high emotions and tension drive one or both partners to violence. Situational couple violence is the type of violence that men and women are equally likely to commit. Thus, data collection methods that distinguish between these different types of IPV are more reliable and can help us understand the root causes behind violence perpetrated by men and women.

Research finds that both men and women may use a weapon in their violence, but the proportions are different (Beaupré, 2015). For example, Statistics Canada (2016) finds that women are two times as likely as men to be threatened with a gun or knife by their intimate partners, while men are three times as likely as women to be hit with something. On the one hand, women may feel that they need a weapon to balance differences in strength between themselves and their male partners. But on the other hand, greater use of weapons by males would be consistent with their tendency toward committing more serious acts of violence more often over prolonged periods of time (Serran and Firestone, 2004).

To repeat, men are much more likely than women to commit IPV homicide. Women who do kill their partners do so for different reasons than men. Men typically kill partners who have left them, who have tried or are planning to leave them, or who they think have been unfaithful. Their motives are more likely to include jealousy, rejection, and a sense of ownership over their partners, whom they view as their sexual "property" (Belknap et al., 2012). Statistics Canada reports that the risk of being killed by one's partner is six times higher for legally separated women than for legally married women (Sinha, 2015). Jealousy of the legally separated woman was reported to have played a role in 25 percent of the homicides of legally separated women. By contrast, women are most likely to kill their partner if they have been suffering continued abuse, are prevented from leaving, and must retaliate in self-defence. After coming to realize that the abuse will never end, some women eventually think the only way to escape the cycle of violence is to kill their partner (Johnson, 2011).

One study of police-reported IPV in Canada shows that younger people in their late twenties and early thirties are more likely to be targeted by IPV

Men and women are equally as likely to commit small acts of violence; the greatest predictor is previous experience of violence at the hands of a mate or spouse or a parent, or witnessing such violence.

Iakov Filimonov/123rf.com

(Sinha, 2015). However, research suggests that household income and education are not related to IPV, although these factors may have been decades ago (Statistics Canada, 2016).

Indigenous people in Canada are also at a heightened risk for IPV. Statistics Canada (2016) reports that people who self-identify as Indigenous were more than twice as likely to have experienced IPV in the past five years, compared to non-Indigenous people. Therefore, Indigenous communities face particular social and situational factors that increase the likelihood of IPV. For one thing, the Indigenous population is younger, on average, than the general Canadian population. Indigenous people also have higher rates of unemployment, are more likely to live in rural areas, have higher rates of alcohol abuse, and have higher fertility rates than non-Indigenous Canadians—all factors that increase the risk for IPV.

However, much of the elevated risk for IPV among Indigenous women has been linked to the colonization of Indigenous peoples, which has negatively affected the community and its members' health, as discussed later in this chapter.

Causes of Violence

Family violence raises many questions. Why would a person abuse someone they have chosen to share their life with, or the children they are supposed to love and nurture?

Researchers continue to debate the causes of family violence. Possible contributors include personal factors, such as a history of abuse, and broader cultural conceptions of families and "discipline." However, various strains of feminism have emerged as the most popular and widely accepted approaches for explaining family violence. Much of the following discussion therefore draws on feminist theories to help explain the underlying causes of violent relations.

Power and Control A recurrent theme in the literature is perpetrators' quest for power and control over their targets (Basile, Hall, and Walters, 2013). This cycle is often represented in the Power and Control Wheel, popularized by the Duluth Model, a domestic abuse intervention approach developed in Duluth, Minnesota. The wheel illustrates the different aspects of power and control that are used in family violence situations, including coercion and threats; intimidation; emotional abuse; isolation; minimizing, denying, and blaming; children; male privilege; and economic abuse (DAIP, 2017).

Feminist theory proposes that patriarchal attitudes are an important determinant of power-motivated IPV (Cheung and Choi, 2016). Patriarchy refers to the various popular beliefs, values, and social arrangements that privilege men and allow for the subordination of women. In patriarchal societies, IPV is one of many strategies men use to exert control over women (Peters, Shackelford, and Buss, 2002). This control over women, by means of violence, in turn reinforces the traditional patriarchal family structure (Felson and Messner, 2000).

Some view IPV as a defence of patriarchy by men who fear that women's increasing economic and social independence is eroding their dominance (Johnson, 2011). For example, gender traditionalism—or belief in traditional gender norms and roles—predicts male IPV toward women, especially when a man with traditional views on gender is coupled with a woman who has non-traditional views on gender (Cheung and Choi, 2016). Since employment is a symbolic resource in relationships—a source of status, power, and economic resources—some men may commit IPV against women partners who can find jobs while they remain unemployed or against women partners who earn more money than they do (Paterson, 2011). In these circumstances, violence is used as a means to reassert dominance, or to put the woman back in her "place" (Basile et al., 2013).

Men who abuse their partners would not often explain their motivations in patriarchal terms. Instead, they often use elaborate excuses to justify their violence (Whiting, Oka, and Fife, 2012). For example, they often dehumanize and objectify their victims, thus minimizing the violence in their own eyes. Some women survivors of IPV, trapped in the cycle of violence, similarly excuse their abusers' behaviour (Crawford, Brown, Walsh, and Pullar, 2010). They make sense of the brutality they endure by reasoning that they must have done something to bring it on them-selves. In this way, many perpetrators of IPV obtain the authority and control over their targets that they set out to achieve.

Certain types of internet abuse help show the search for power that often under-lies IPV. Social media sites allow perpetrators to contact, harass, threaten, incite fear, and otherwise abuse their targets from a distance, at any time (Lee and O'Sullivan, 2014). By making their targets feel like they cannot escape, perpetrators can gain dom-inance and control over the relationship (Fraser, Olsen, Lee, Southworth, and Tucker, 2010). Abuse via social media often occurs among couples who have separated: The perpetrator feels as though he is losing control over the relationship and attempts to reassert his dominance.

One common use of social media sites for abusive purposes is called cyberstalk-ing: The perpetrator gathers personal information about a former partner via social media, then uses it to bully, threaten, or intimidate her or him (Southworth, Dawson, Fraser, and Tucker, 2005). In some instances, cyberstalkers impersonate the victim and post damaging information about her or him on social media sites (Fraser et al., 2010). Some websites are devoted to abusing former partners and are places where people can post damaging information or photographs for a wide audience to see. Other perpetrators use social media to locate their exes, or partners trying to flee their abuse (Southworth et al., 2005). In these cases, cyberstalking is often a strong predictor of other forms of violence; once they have determined their target's loca-tion, perpetrators can commit physical, sexual, or emotional attacks.

A few myths about feminist theories of family violence are worth mentioning. First, some misinterpret feminist theories, claiming that they frame men as power-hungry abusers and women as their helpless victims. However, many feminist scholars have drawn attention to the inaccuracy of these reductive stereotypes. Most people who perpetrate IPV in a quest for power and control are men, but most violent men do not perpetrate this particular type of IPV (Johnson, 2011). The more detailed, methodologically rigorous studies described above suggest that situational violence—where heated conflicts intensify, finally resulting in violence—is the most common form of IPV and is perpetrated equally by men and women (Richards et al., 2016).

Situational violence is not used to gain power or control. However, some women perpetrate IPV to gain dominance. This female group is statistically smaller than the male group of power-seeking abusers, and they also use different methods to achieve the sought-after control (Bair-Merritt et al., 2010). Women tend toward minor to moderate types of physical abuse—such as throwing things—and emotional violence. By contrast, men are more likely to sexually abuse, seriously physically abuse, and eventually kill their partners.

To some degree, the difference between male and female perpetrators of power-seeking IPV may reflect the support they receive from society. Compared to male aggressors, female aggressors lack the support of a patriarchal power structure, and this prevents them from taking total control over their male partners (Swan and Snow, 2002). Men, on the other hand, receive at least some support in their quest for power because their community members see them as the rightful heads of their homes and families.

Feminist scholars also draw attention to two important things about women targeted by IPV. First, those who are targeted do not always passively stand by and allow the abuse to continue. Many develop strategies to resist, fight back, and finally escape (Paterson, 2011). And, in the instances that women do physically fight back, feminist scholars do not (necessarily) praise this violence as somehow excusable (Johnson, 2011). Self-defence and the rejection of oppression are offered as explanations of some women's IPV. However, just as a history of childhood abuse helps to explain—but does not excuse—IPV, violent retaliation against one's abuser helps to explain much woman-perpetrated IPV. That said, it does not justify violence, which is always an objectively poor result.

Second, some scholars have suggested that IPV among LGBTQ people challenges feminist theories of family violence. If patriarchal values and gendered power relations lead to IPV, then why do LGBTQ couples experience IPV at similar rates? In response, many have pointed to many "shades" of feminism, each exploring a different intersection of oppression, and these include those to do with sexuality and queerness (George and Stith, 2014). Recall that IPV (and family violence of any kind) is inflicted on different people, for different reasons, with different results. It would be excessively simple to reduce IPV to men's plain wish for power and dominance over women. Rather, a feminist perspective recognizes that perpetrators want to enforce compliance with their traditional conventions, values, and beliefs.

For example, beyond the more universal predictors of IPV that we outline below, we see also some unique causes of IPV among LGBTQ couples (Edwards, Sylaska, and Neal, 2015). One is homophobic control: a particular form of psychological abuse used to assert control and power over the target (Badenes-Ribera et al., 2015). Some examples of homophobic control include threatening to reveal the target's sexuality to their family, friends, or colleagues; reiterating homophobic views by saying that the target brought the abuse on himself or herself by choosing an "abnormal" sexuality; harassing the partner by questioning if he or she is a "real" gay; or forcing the partner to display affection in public. The common theme is that an intimate partner exploits popular homophobic views to induce feelings of shame, fear, and indignity. Homophobic control perpetrated by one lesbian against another is obviously not caused by a patriarchal man's quest for dominance, but it does involve the traditional views on sex, gender, and sexuality that feminists think are problematic.

Third and finally, critics of feminist theories contend that the feminist literature ignores other well-documented causes of abuse, insisting that patriarchy is the sole cause of IPV. However, one of the central and most widely celebrated tenets of feminism today is intersectionality: the ways in which many different factors intersect to cause unique experiences. So, many feminists have conducted research on the variables discussed below, studying how several factors combine in unique ways to produce IPV (George and Stith, 2014).

Previous Experience of Violence   Violence breeds more violence. The single best predictor of violence toward a partner is having experienced or witnessed violence as a child. One half of all the people who report having been abused by intimate partners say that they were also physically or sexually abused as children (Statistics Canada, 2016). Researchers sometimes refer to this as "victim-offender overlap" (Richards et al., 2016).

Abused people often abuse others who are even more vulnerable than themselves. Thus, husbands may abuse wives, and wives may abuse children or older parents. Abuse is rarely directed only toward one particular family member. People who abuse their spouses often abuse their children as well; the more often someone uses violence against a spouse, the more likely that person is to also use violence against a child. This relationship is especially strong for men. Thus, children in abusive households are likely to both witness and experience domestic violence firsthand. This perpetuates the **cycle of abuse**, as these children are more likely to grow up to abuse their own spouses and children. However, as the box on the next page points out, we should always question stereotypical notions about domestic violence.

Children learn many of their behaviours by watching their parents. When it comes to abuse, in some families they learn that violence is an appropriate way to resolve disputes and vent frustration (Richards et al., 2016).

Many children who suffer or witness abuse never become abusive adults, however. Boys are more likely to respond to violence with violence and grow up to become abusive toward their own families. Girls more often internalize their problems, resulting in depression and anxiety.

Interactional Styles   As noted above, research finds that men and women are equally likely to commit certain types of IPV. Some researchers propose that, in these cases, violence is an interactional problem: a result of dysfunctional relations. This type of violence can arise when couples lack healthy strategies for coping with their stress; their conflicts can intensify into physical or emotional abuse (Richards et al., 2016).

Emotionally abusive men and women typically share some personality traits, including jealousy, suspicion, immaturity, and insecurity (Vall, Seikkula, Laitila, and Holma, 2016). Thus, they may lash out at each other if they think that either partner has been unfaithful, for example. Many couples struggle to communicate their concerns and frustrations in healthy, effective ways and, when frustrated, turn instead to cruel language intended to hurt their partners (Johnson, 2011). Others express their anger and frustration by physically attacking their partners, such as by slapping or shoving them.

Because, for so long, domestic violence has been deemed a private, family issue to be dealt with behind closed doors, it remains poorly understood by the public. Consider just two of the harmful ways in which many people respond to news of abuse.

First, some mistakenly think that domestic violence happens only in certain "types" of families or in "bad" neighbourhoods (Yonas et al., 2011). Celeste Yawney's experiences demonstrate that domestic violence can happen to anyone (Saywell, 2017). Yawney's boyfriend had been repeatedly arrested for assaulting her and was eventually charged with her murder. The twist? Yawney worked in a women's shelter in Regina, where she counselled other women who had survived abuse.

Second, many people wonder why battered women do not leave their abusive partners. Lesley Ackrill, who has worked in a Toronto shelter for abused women and children for more than three decades, highlights that attempts to flee from, break up with, or divorce an abusive partner may spark even greater violence (Pelley, 2016). These efforts can make the abuser sense that his control over his victim is wavering and, in turn, make him attempt to reassert that control through more frequent or more violent attacks.

In many cases, we fail to acknowledge the violence being committed against a woman, and the fear in which she lives every single day, until she has been killed (Saywell, 2017). Part of the problem are the popular misconceptions of domestic violence that make it difficult for survivors to get the help and protection they need.

Sources: Pelley, L. 2016. Leaving relationship is "most dangerous time" for domestic violence victims, experts say. CBC News. Retrieved from http://www.cbc.ca/news/canada/toronto/domestic-violence-victims-1.3885381; Saywell, S. 2017. The war at home. CBC News. Retrieved from http://www.cbc.ca/firsthand/episodes/the-war-at-home; Yonas, M., A. Akers, J. Burke, J. Chang, A. Thomas, & P. O'Campo. 2011. Perceptions of prominent neighborhood individuals regarding neighborhood factors and intimate partner violence. *Journal of Urban Health* 88(2): 214–224.

Status Inconsistency   **Status inconsistency** describes the condition in which a person with high status on one dimension has low status on another. Some research shows that status inconsistency can drive people to perpetrate all types of abuse, including life-threatening violence. Status inconsistency can undermine self-esteem and cause feelings of inadequacy, jealousy, and possessiveness (Shackelford and Mouzos, 2005). For example, some men may perpetrate IPV if their wives land a job when they cannot; the wife's new, higher status causes her husband's self-esteem to drop, and he may seek to rectify that power imbalance through violence.

However, research on status inconsistency has yielded mixed results. Some studies find that wives' employment and higher earnings can make some men feel threatened, leading them to lash out to defend their power and authority in the relationship (Terrazas-Carrillo and McWhirter, 2015). Others, however, find that employment and higher earnings protect women against IPV, as they become less financially dependent on their husbands and therefore less willing to tolerate abuse (Crawford et al., 2010).

Women at all income levels experience violence, but some research suggests that rates of IPV are especially high among low-income and homeless women (Bassuk, Dawson, and Huntington, 2006; Morrow, Hankivsky, and Varcoe, 2004; Purvin, 2007). Less educated, younger women with weak social networks are even more likely to experience severe and recurring violence (Frias and Angel, 2007). These women may also be unable to flee abusive partners if they have no economic alternatives.

Alcoholism and Drug Abuse   Alcohol consumption is a significant, though modest, predictor of both IPV and child abuse (Devries et al., 2014). Many drugs (including alcohol) are disinhibitors: They cause people to relax their restraints against violence. Other drugs increase adrenaline levels and, in this way, may cause anger or frustration levels to spiral out of control. For these reasons, acts of violence committed when one or both partners have been drinking are often more severe—more brutal and likely to cause serious injury—compared with acts of violence committed when neither partner had been drinking (Graham, Bernards, Wilsnack, and Gmel, 2011).

Sometimes, one or both partners excuse violence because of drinking or another extenuating circumstance. In this sense, alcohol does not cause IPV; instead, it can provide perpetrators with a "shield," allowing them to identify not as an abuser, but instead as someone whose alcoholism can cause them to behave in ways they often would not (Javaid, 2015).

Lack of Coping Resources   A lack of healthy, effective coping resources also increases the likelihood of family violence. The World Health Organization (2012) reports that financial strain can lead to conflict and dissatisfaction in a relationship. Without the means to cope with these stressors, couples may turn to violence as a means of venting their frustration.

Social Isolation   Lack of social ties and support is a common predictor of abuse. Families that live in poverty are likely to lack formal and informal support networks, which can lead to all types of abuse but especially to neglect (Doherty and Berglund, 2012). For example, impoverished families are often isolated from their communities, lacking access to parks, child care services, preschool programs, recreational facilities, and other services that could ameliorate child neglect. Research finds that mothers who neglect their children report having fewer people in their social networks and less contact with them. They also report that their limited contacts are less sympathetic and that they receive less emotional and financial supports than mothers who do not neglect their children. Thus, both practical support from work or school associates and emotional support from nurturing people can reduce the risk for child abuse.

Cultural Attitudes   Attitudes that support violence as a whole, or violence against women and children in particular, also contribute to family violence. A society that overlooks violence may end up encouraging it. For example, in certain cultures, a husband may publicly beat or kill his wife if she has done something to dishonour their family (Shankar, Das, and Atwal, 2013). In North America, these so-called "honour killings" are not considered acceptable, let alone legal (Vandello and Cohen, 2003). However, as a nation with a large population of immigrants, these violent norms are sometimes imported into Canada and can contribute to the violence perpetrated in immigrant families discussed below (Aujla and Gill, 2014).

Some Indigenous communities also stress male authority while restricting women's activities. This can lead to violence against women as men seek to preserve their power and authority, as described above. However, these factors vary widely across Indigenous groups. For example, some Indigenous groups practise matrilineal descent, while others are patrilineal, and this diversity has far-reaching implications for the community context in which family violence occurs. An approach that integrates both feminist and community perspectives is best suited to address the problem of family violence among Indigenous people in North America.

Before the colonization of Indigenous peoples, many communities were egalitarian and, as far as we can tell from records and reports, levels of IPV were low as a result. Violence in the home reportedly started when colonizers created hierarchies between men and women, and husbands were taught to aim to control their wives' and daughters' sexuality. Violence by the state also helped create violence in the home. So, it should not be assumed that Indigenous people in North America are prone to violence, nor that their culture promotes violence; rather, colonizers introduced this habit or at least reinforced it.

For these reasons, some researchers have proposed that instances of IPV that seem culturally determined—including honour killings—may be better understood using the notions of power-seeking discussed above (Aujla and Gill, 2014). At stake in these violent meetings is the man's dominance and authority, which he tries to reassert through the attack. As we have seen, the search for power over women arises in any patriarchal society; no particular ethnic, cultural, or religious group has a monopoly on it (Shalabi, Mitchell, and Andersson, 2015).

Traditional Family Values   The feminist research cited above that draws attention to abusers' desire for power and control also notes an association between traditional values and family violence. Namely, IPV can be more common among couples who endorse traditional family values, such as male dominance, and a gender-based division of labour. Men who commit IPV are likely to support a patriarchal ideology, including approval or acceptance of marital violence—for example, thinking that it is acceptable for men to beat their wives (World Health Organization, 2012).

Some traditionalists also hold proprietary or "coercively controlling" attitudes: They think that their partners are their sexual and emotional property. This group of psychologically and physically abusive men may become jealous easily, fearing they may lose their partner, who they think "belongs" to them. In an effort to prevent this loss, an abusive partner may oversee his spouse or girlfriend, monitor and control her activities, limit her contact with family or friends, insist on knowing who she is with and where she is at all times, and prevent her from knowing about or having access to the family income. This type of controlling behaviour is abusive in itself, but it may also lead to other types of abuse, such as physical and sexual violence.

Finally, people who hold traditional values are more likely to think that violence is an acceptable means of conflict resolution, at least in particular circumstances. For example, IPV is sometimes seen as an appropriate response to a wife who has violated her prescribed roles, including "good mother" and "loyal wife." In these instances, survivors may be seen as "deserving" the abuse, and the abuser is not thought to have done anything wrong (Doherty and Berglund, 2012).

Some recent immigrants may import these traditional values and maintain them for years after their arrival in Canada.

Causes and Effects of Stress and Violence in Immigrant Families

For any family, immigration poses major life challenges and causes much related stress. This stress may never diminish, even after many years of living in the new country. A study by Mirdal (2006) showed that the financial situation of immigrant women and their families had significantly improved in the years after immigration. Nonetheless, these women still experienced a high level of stress regarding their immigrant status and the challenges of living in a country they felt they were still becoming accustomed to.

Many immigrants anticipate and try to reduce this stress by moving to areas that will be more familiar, both in language and in culture, to their old communities. The many cultural neighbourhoods of the Greater Toronto Area illustrate this strategy. There, immigrants find social support from other immigrants and are less distressed by acculturation. Immigrant parents, for instance, then feel less pressured to fit in quickly and can instead focus on providing support for their assimilating children (Thomas and Choi, 2006). In turn, these children can go on to integrate smoothly with peers in school and pursue higher education and employment in the new country. Research has shown that good family relations are fundamentally important in the acculturation of immigrant children (see Birman and Taylor-Ritzler, 2007 for information about acculturation of adolescents from the former Soviet Union).

On the other hand, studies have also found that less acculturated children experience less discrimination and psychological distress (Buddington, 2002). This may be because they retain their cultural identity by befriending peers of the same cultural background or find other ways of staying connected to their indigenous culture.

Not all stress intensifies into family violence, but some evidence shows that stress related to immigration can lead to abuse, especially among families from traditional, patriarchal societies (Abraham and Tastsoglou, 2016; Shankar et al., 2013). For example, stress is common among immigrant families that resist acculturation and feel uneasy in adapting to their new environments. Conservative immigrant families that feel culturally alienated or discriminated against often turn inward to preserve the family's ethnic identity, values, and culture (Meetoo and Mirza, 2007). Their conservative values become enlarged and, often, the male family members work harder to control the behaviour of their wives and daughters. Women in these families who do not behave according to the traditional value system may be violently punished—even killed—to uphold the family's "honour."

This response is more likely in certain families and settings than in others. A study by Kim-Goh and Baello (2008) found that immigrant men with low education are most likely to approve of violence, especially toward noncompliant wives. Therefore, the risk factors for abuse in immigrant families include patriarchal authority, strict gender roles, lack of education, women's financial dependence on partners, and women's insecure immigration status and dependence on a partner for sponsorship (Ammar, 2007; Anitha, 2011; Hadas, Markovitzky, and Sarid, 2008).

So, how are wives of such husbands to respond to this abuse, especially if they are economically and emotionally dependent? Bui and Morash (2007) claim that social networks within immigrant communities are most helpful for these women. The support of family and friends can help alleviate the distress associated with abuse for any survivor, since many women may be unable or unwilling to access formal supports. In some traditional, patriarchal cultures, family matters—even violence and abuse—are considered strictly private, to be dealt with at home (Holtmann, 2016). So, family and friends often discourage women from using legal services to deal with abuse, as that would mean sharing private concerns with public officials. It would also mean undermining the traditional gender roles and responsibilities typically endorsed by such traditional, patriarchal societies (Shankar et al., 2013).

Social isolation has been an important predictor of violence among immigrant women (Anitha, 2011). Having left their friends and family behind, newcomer women lack the large support networks that could help them cope with family violence, or prevent it from happening at all (Shankar et al., 2013). And, because many do not speak the local language, newcomer women may struggle to forge new friendships or feel unable to access formal support services even if they wanted to (Godoy-Ruiz, Toner, Mason, Vidal, and McKenzie, 2015).

Finally, immigrant and Canadian-born survivors alike receive less support if they live in societies that overlook or dismiss violence. In the past, many Canadians refused to accept family violence as a serious problem, let alone offer their support for laws and institutions designed to protect and assist survivors. Contributing to this apathy were the myths that women provoke violence and that family violence is a "private affair" that police should stay out of (Meyer, 2012). We have taken big steps forward by acknowledging that family violence does occur with alarming frequency in Canada. However, much more remains to be done. To understand the prevalence of family violence in our society, we must understand popular attitudes toward intimacy, gender, family roles, and violence. Even those who have never perpetrated violence may unwittingly support it through their ways of thinking.

Effects of Violence

We know far too little about the thoughts and feelings of people targeted by domestic violence. Many survivors struggle to verbalize their thoughts and feelings, which can be a symptom of post-traumatic stress disorder (PTSD). Sixteen percent of spousal violence survivors in Canada report three or more of the long-term symptoms associated with PTSD (Burczycka, 2014).

Not all violent events produce PTSD, but many survivors struggle with poor mental health effects. PTSD is a frequently cited consequence of abuse because it shows that negative results can persist for years (Ansara and Hindin, 2011). Sometimes, people assume that violence only produces immediate, short-term results. For example, physical violence may leave survivors with bruises, broken bones, lacerations, and similar injuries that will heal within weeks or months (Burczycka, 2014). But physical violence can also cause permanent damage, by damaging vision and hearing, causing traumatic brain injury, or leaving survivors with chronic conditions—for example, chronic pain. Sexual abuse can also have permanent physical effects, including sexually transmitted infections or irreparable damage to a woman's reproductive organs that could prevent her from having children in the future.

All types of violence—be it physical, emotional, or sexual—can affect survivors' mental health (Godoy-Ruiz et al., 2015). IPV survivors are more likely to experience depression, phobias, anxiety, and thoughts of suicide than those who have never experienced such violence (Ansara and Hindin, 2011). These people are also more likely to begin engaging in unhealthy activities, such as drug and alcohol abuse, cigarette smoking, self-harm, and unsafe sexual behaviour (Burczycka, 2014).

In less clinical terms, sustained violence of any kind breaks a survivor's spirit. Abused women typically have lower self-esteem and less faith in their own efficacy than non-abused women (Kim and Gray, 2008). In turn, survivors may struggle to achieve their goals, such as finishing school or setting up a career (although they may not directly blame these results on their abuse). Women survivors of IPV also commonly report struggling to connect with and feel comfortable with other men (Ansara and Hindin, 2011). For those who eventually escape their abusive partners, this can make it hard for them to forge new relations. This difficulty of starting a new life is made all the harder by a shortage of shelters in Canada, as discussed in the box on the next page.

Supporting Survivors

Contributing to the myth that survivors bring abuse on themselves is the reality that many struggle to leave their abusive partners. Survivors often stay in relationships with their abusers for years, and those who leave are likely to return (Meyer, 2012). So, why do some stay? Where do others find the strength and support they need to leave?

⟫⟫ Canada's Shelter Shortage

Every day, about 415 Canadian women and children show up at a shelter, hoping they've finally escaped their abusers (Grant, 2016). Seventy-three percent are turned away because the shelter is at capacity or under-resourced.

The need for shelter space is especially strong in the North. Nunavut, for example, has the highest rate of police-reported IPV in Canada (Zerehi, 2016), but only four shelters operate there (Government of Canada, 2016). Similarly, Indigenous women are at a disproportionately high risk of going missing or being murdered, but shelters are scarce in many remote areas and communities with large Indigenous populations.

Lise Martin, executive director of the Canadian Network of Women's Shelters and Transition Houses, says that most women see shelters as last resorts (Grant, 2016). They've tried many alternatives already, including staying at home and suffering through the abuse. That's why it's so important for shelters to have space for women: When they arrive at a shelter, women feel they're out of options.

Despite the urgent need for more shelters, funding has posed an ongoing challenge. In addition to an overall shortage, many of our existing shelters are quickly deteriorating, having been constructed in the 1970s and 1980s (CBC, 2016). In an effort to address these issues, the federal government dedicated close to $90 million to build and repair shelters for survivors across Canada. The funding will go a long way toward refurbishing or constructing more than 3000 shelters over 2 years, but not all existing shelters will get access to the money, given their provincial (rather than federal) funding.

Sources: CBC. 2016. Federal budget funding to help build, repair women's shelters. Retrieved from http:// www.cbc.ca/news/canada/sudbury/federal-budget-womens-shelters-1.3510308; Grant, T. 2016. Canadian shelters forced to turn away most women and children in need. *The Globe and Mail.* Retrieved from http:// www.theglobeandmail.com/news/national/canadian-shelters-forced-to-turn-away-majority-of-women-and-children-in-need/article29779517/; Zerehi, S.S. 2016. Territories have highest family violence rates in Canada: Report. CBC News. Retrieved from http://www.cbc.ca/news/canada/north/family-violence-rates-in-territories-1.3417850; Government of Canada, Department of Justice. 2016. Making the links in family violence cases: Collaboration among the family, child protection and criminal justice systems. Retrieved from http://www.justice.gc.ca/eng/rp-pr/cj-jp/fv-vf/mlfvc-elcvf/vol2/p12.html

First, abusers who seek to gain power and control over their targets are often successful: They make their victims feel powerless, helpless, unable to control their futures, and therefore unable to leave (Kim and Gray, 2008). Second, those who may not feel emotionally helpless may be financially helpless. Many women remain in abusive relationships because they lack the economic stability needed to support themselves (Lacey, Saunders, and Zhang, 2011). They may have limited resources, and they may not have anywhere else to go. Third, those with children may fear that they will be unable to care for them alone or that they may lose custody if the courts were to discover the abuse that had been occurring in their home. Fourth, many women fear increased abuse, for themselves or their children, if they leave; in these cases, blackmail and threats are not uncommon (Meyer, 2012). Fifth, some women feel that they deserve the abuse. Episodes of leaving or thinking about leaving are embedded in cycles of abuse (see Figure 8.5).

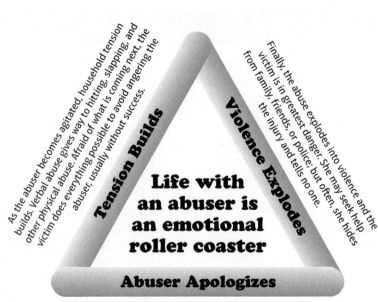

Text within figure:

Tension Builds — As the abuser becomes agitated, household tension builds. Verbal abuse gives way to hitting, slapping, and other physical abuse. Afraid of what is coming next, the victim does everything possible to avoid angering the abuser, usually without success.

Violence Explodes — Finally, the abuse explodes into violence and the victim is in greatest danger. She may seek help from family, friends, or police; but often, she hides the injury and tells no one.

Life with an abuser is an emotional roller coaster

Abuser Apologizes

The abuser apologizes for past misbehavior, offering gifts and kind words; he promises to change, and often the victim believes him. She wants to believe that change is coming and she can trust the abuser.

Figure 8.5 The cycle of violence

Source: Adapted from *Domestic Violence: Eastern Regional Committee Against Violence* ISO-8859-1. http://www.ercav.ca/mwm_files/home/sys/media/1247162361.gif

Sixth and finally, abusers are often able to manipulate their targets into staying. Commonly, after an abusive episode, the perpetrator apologizes, showers the victim with gifts and affection, and promises it will not happen again. Survivors may be convinced that they have suffered for the last time, that their abuser has changed, or that he did not mean to be violent. Also, people feel social pressure to stay committed to their relationship: the common view that marriage is for better or for worse and that one ought to stick it out because marriage and family are the bedrock of society.

Women with disabilities may also find it hard to leave a violent relationship. Hassouneh-Phillips and McNeff (2005) found that women with severe physical disabilities were more likely to feel that they were unattractive and sexually inadequate than did women with mild disabilities. Low self-esteem and a strong desire to be partnered, especially with men without disabilities, increased the likelihood that women with disabilities would enter and stay in abusive relationships over time.

By contrast, survivors who come to feel angry at their abusers—as opposed to attached to and dependent on them—are more likely to leave (Lacey et al., 2011). Mothers may also leave their abusive partners out of fear that they will start targeting their children or to protect their children from more abuse than they have already suffered.

Witnessing Violence

Fifty-two percent of Canadian parents who reported suffering spousal violence said that their children heard or saw the abuse (Sinha, 2015). Witnessing violence between parents can harm children's emotional and behavioural development. In particular, it can lead to delinquency, feelings of anxiety and depression, PTSD symptoms, and lowered self-worth (Burczycka, 2014; Royal Canadian Mounted Police, 2017).

Witnessing abuse can derail a child's future. Clements, Oxtoby, and Ogle (2008) note that children exposed to violence at a young age may develop difficulties trusting others, making it hard for them to interact at school and elsewhere. The negative physical and emotional effects also detract from a child's ability to perform well academically (Burczycka, 2014). They may struggle to pay attention in class, lash out at their peers, become isolated, or fail to attend school at all (Royal Canadian Mounted Police, 2017).

Children regularly exposed to violence at home are more likely to become aggressive and physically violent themselves. In a study of factors contributing to youth violence, Ferguson, San Miguel, and Hartley (2009) examined the effect of external influences such as family, the media, and peers. They decided that childhood delinquency and violence result mainly from family violence, more than from television, video games, or social media.

Children respond to violence in different ways depending on whether they were also abused, their sex and age, and the amount of time since their last exposure to violence. Exposure to physical abuse produces open hostility in children and a tendency to flare up in anger without a specific provocation. On the other hand, exposure to emotional abuse is more likely to produce shame, hostility, and anger—both expressed and unexpressed. Often, the results of domestic violence are gender specific. Females often internalize their emotions, reporting higher levels of shame and guilt. Males are more likely to lash out or abuse alcohol.

As mentioned, exposure to violence can set in motion a vicious cycle of abuse that predicts violence later in life. One in five Canadians who suffered IPV in the last five years say that they also witnessed abuse perpetrated by a parent, step-parent, or guardian when they were children (Statistics Canada, 2016). Thus, abused girls and daughters of abused mothers can become abused women, and male children of abusive fathers can become abusive fathers themselves. The connection between childhood abuse and adult abuse may lie in interpersonal functioning. Children who grow up in abusive families do not learn how to conduct their lives, or their marriages, in nonabusive ways, or how to prevent the escalation of violence or abuse. Given its severe and often longlasting consequences, research suggests that allowing a child to witness abuse is a form of abuse in and of itself (Royal Canadian Mounted Police, 2017).

CONCLUDING REMARKS

We can learn a great deal from research about the best ways to intervene to solve problems of family stress and violence. First, we learn that violence is a major factor causing women to leave their marriages and children to leave their parents' home. Second, programs that address abuse directly—such as civil restraining orders, treatment programs for batterers, and policies requiring compulsory arrest and no dropped charges—are not often effective in solving the problem of family violence (Vittes and Sorenson, 2008).

Third, we must actively address problems like stress and violence. If we want to reduce family stresses, we must create a family-friendly society with increased social support for working parents with small children. Fourth, research shows us that the health and social service professions are, sadly, far behind the times. Without well-planned assistance from these professionals, we have little hope of creating such a family-friendly society.

Fifth, research shows us that personal lives, and families, are increasingly diverse. Because of linguistic, cultural, and immigration issues, newly arrived immigrant and refugee women have needs that differ markedly from those of native-born women targeted by IPV. Along similar lines, LGBTQ people are less likely to use formal support services that were designed for heterosexual women fleeing their abusive husbands or boyfriends. We must therefore try to expand the resources available to survivors of family violence, so that all targets may have their diverse needs met.

In the end, however, we must recognize that there will be no major decline in family violence until societies reduce the stresses on family members and increase the personal value of all people—especially children, women, older adults, the poor, immigrants, sexual minorities, and people with disabilities. Societies must also reject the cultural justifications for domestic violence and deprive violent people of opportunities to hide or repeat their behaviour. Ending domestic violence must be a societal project, one that receives the same attention as other recognized social problems and is not hidden away in the privacy of the home.

CHAPTER SUMMARY

We have discussed two realities—stress and violence—that reveal the dark side of close relations.

Stress, as we have noted, is a normal part of family life. We may have trouble coping with it, but stress can never be eliminated. Common causes of family stress fall into at least four categories: major upheavals, major life transitions, chronic stresses, and occasional stresses. Any of these stressors has the potential to tear families apart if family members lack resources such as cohesion that can help them to cope effectively.

Violence is a potential result of family stress, but violence is never wholly the result of stress, nor is stress wholly the cause of violence. Domestic violence comes in many forms and affects people in every part of our society. Family violence can be physical, sexual, or emotional. It can be an isolated incident, but often family violence is part of a multigenerational cycle, with childhood abuse predicting more abuse later in life.

Men perpetrate many cases of IPV against women, but women also abuse their male partners, and LGBTQ couples abuse each other. Other types of violence include those committed between siblings, parents against infants, and grown children against their adult parents. Certain populations, including immigrants and Indigenous people, are especially vulnerable to various forms of violence. Often, family violence is spurred by a wish to prove one's power and to control behaviour that the perpetrator finds problematic.

Last, the effects of family violence are severe and widespread. They include depression, PTSD, social isolation, destroyed self-esteem, and permanent physical injury. Children exposed to abuse are more likely to become abusers themselves, perpetuating the cycle of violence.

Key Terms

ABCX family crisis model A model of stress in which *A*, which represents the stressor event, interacts with *B*, the family's crisis-meeting resources, and with *C*, the family's interpretation of the event, to produce *X*, the crisis.

acculturative stress Stress originating from the challenges involved in adapting to a new society.

caregiver burden Stress that caregivers experience while caring for an infirm family member at home. This subjective burden is an important predictor of negative health outcomes.

Conflict Tactics Scale An instrument developed by Murray Straus to measure the extent of domestic violence based on frequency and severity of incidents.

crisis episodes Significant events that are likely to lead to seeking help from professionals, changing caregiving conditions, and precipitating decision making.

cycle of abuse A tendency for family violence to repeat itself from one generation to the next, as abused girls and daughters of abused mothers grow up to become abused women, and abused boys or sons of abusive fathers grow up to become abusive husbands or fathers.

domestic violence Family violence; violence against any member of the household, including a child, spouse, parent, or sibling.

intimate partner violence (IPV) Physical abuse between the members of a couple. It may be reciprocal ("common couple violence") or directed by one partner against the other, and it may occur between cohabiters and legally married couples.

status inconsistency Lack of congruence between the various indicators of social class, such as education and occupation, or wealth and prestige.

stressor Something that causes stress; a challenge or threat.

Critical Thinking Questions

1. Why are some groups in society (such as single mothers) especially vulnerable to chronic stress? Is their vulnerability based on larger structural problems inherent to their populations or on a lack of coping resources?

2. Does the view of older adults as burdensome and unproductive members of society make them more susceptible to abuse? Or are other factors more important in increasing their risk of violence?

3. What are the most important reasons women do not leave violent situations, and how may the importance of these factors vary over a woman's life cycle?

4. How does abuse of older adults differ from abuse of children in its causes and consequences? Explain.

5. How has modern technology changed the way abusive partners target and torment their victims?

6. Does a sharp increase in the amount of family stress automatically increase the risk and level of violence within the family? If not, why?

Weblinks

Ontario Women's Justice Network
www.owjn.org
This site offers legal information related to violence against women, specifically on justice and legal issues regarding rural, immigrant, transgender, and impoverished women.

Canadian Mental Health Association
www.cmha.ca
This site provides a wide range of information on mental health issues in Canada, including resources to better understand and prevent stress and violence.

Native Women's Association of Canada
www.nwac.ca/home
This site provides important resources for Indigenous women in Canada, including a violence prevention kit that helps female Indigenous youth recognize and leave abusive situations at www.nwac.ca/policy-areas/violence-prevention-and-safety.

Canadian Research Institute for the Advancement of Women
www.criaw-icref.ca
This site provides excellent and comprehensive information on the issues facing rural, immigrant, and low-income women.

Canadian Network for the Prevention of Elder Abuse
www.cnpea.ca
This wonderful source of information on the abuse of older adults in English and French provides information on policy and practice for older adult issues in Canada, along with helpful links and resources to learn more about older adult abuse prevention.

Ontario Ministry of the Status of Women
www.women.gov.on.ca/english/index.shtml
This site provides specific information on women's legal, wellness, and child issues, along with resources for young women about sexual harassment and equality issues.

Chapter 9

Divorce and Ending Relationships

Trends, Myths, Children, and Ex-Spouses

Merzzie/Shutterstock

CHAPTER OUTLINE

- Divorce Rates
- Divorce and Society
  - Separation and Divorce in the Immigrant Population
- A Historical, Crossnational Overview of Divorce
  - Social Changes
  - Legal Changes
- Causes of Divorce
  - Micro-sociological Causes
- Meso-sociological Causes
- Macro-sociological Causes
- Effects of Divorce
  - Effects on Both Spouses
  - Effects on Women
  - Effects on Children
  - Relations with Parents
  - Effects on Older Adults
- Concluding Remarks

LEARNING OBJECTIVES

1 Understand different approaches to measuring divorce rates and what they mean for divorce risk.

2 Define and interpret micro-sociological, meso-sociological, and macro-sociological causes of divorce.

3 Comprehend the causes and effects of divorce on the couple.

4 Understand the effects of divorce and parental repartnering on children.

5 Evaluate the effects of divorce on society.

6 Analyze the relationship between immigration and divorce.

7 Dispel myths about divorce.

8 Explain the legal issues of divorce and cohabitation, both historical and current.

Divorce is often hard to understand. The factors leading to divorce are complex, as are the consequences for the individuals involved and for society. Another challenge is that close couple relations have changed so much recently, as we saw in Chapter 4, with the growing popularity of cohabitation. Cohabiting relationships that end are not counted as divorces. So, the greater the number of couples who cohabit, the lower the divorce rate will fall. Adding even more complexity, divorce rates are sometimes misleading, as we shall soon see. So, for divorce, as with much else about families, the numbers do not speak for themselves.

We often hear that one-half of all marriages end in divorce. It is certainly scary if people believe that their own marriage stands only a 50 percent chance of surviving. However, this figure is misleading: Different methods of measurement lead to different statistical outcomes and sociological conclusions.

DIVORCE RATES

To explain why divorce rates are misleading at times, we must explain what the various indicators of divorce mean. There are several ways to compute divorce rates, and meanings depend very much on the method of calculation. The *crude divorce rate*, for example, is calculated as the number of divorces in a given year (say, in 2013) divided by the mid-year population in 2013, multiplied by 100 000 (see Figure 9.1). This yields low rates because the denominator includes everyone in the population, many of whom are not at all at risk of divorce since they are children, single, or already divorced.

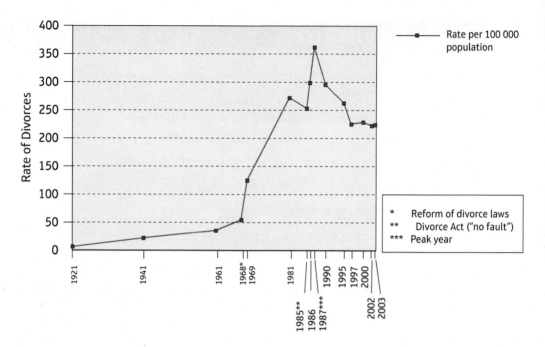

Figure 9.1 Divorce rate per 100 000 population in Canada, 1921–2003

Source: Data from Ambert, Anne-Marie. 2005. Divorce: Facts, causes and consequences. The Vanier Institute of the Family. Data retrieved December 9, 2005, from www.vifamily.ca/library/cft/divorce_05.html.

By contrast, another measure of divorce is based on the number of marriages in a given year. By this calculation, the number of *divorces* in 2013 is divided by the number of *marriages* in 2013. This overestimates divorce risk and lends itself to attention-catching statements (e.g., "One-half of all current marriages will end in divorce") that titillate but do not inform. Those married in 2013 are *not* those at risk of divorce in 2013! As well, if the number of marriages in any given year declines, as it has in the past decade in Canada, and the number of divorces stays the same (see Figure 9.2), it may appear as if the risk of divorce is rising when it is not. As you can see, this way of calculating divorce rate and risk is very misleading. It can be a "false fact" reported as true and then interpreted by couples as a serious risk. This is inappropriate and needlessly frightening.

Better measures of divorce risk, though too rarely provided for public discussion, consider the population at risk of a divorce and *only* that population. Thus, the population at risk of a divorce in 2013 are those (and only those) who are married at the beginning of 2013 *and earlier*. This estimate can be improved by standardizing for age and other social characteristics that are known to influence people's inclination to divorce. Since older people divorce less than younger people do, for example, we would do well to compute divorce rates on a "standard population" with the same

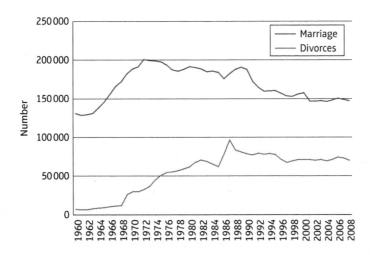

Figure 9.2 Number of marriages and divorces, Canada, 1960 to 2008

Source: Statistics Canada. 2012. Juristat Bulletin "Divorce cases in civil court, 2010/2011." Catalogue no. 85-002-X. Retrieved February 2013 from www.statcan.gc.ca/pub/85-002-x/2012001/article/11634-eng.htm. Reproduced and distributed on an "as is" basis with the permission of Statistics Canada.

supposed age structure at two points in time. Only in this way would we know whether divorce-proneness was increasing or whether changes in population makeup (such as population aging or immigration of young people) were causing the *appearance* of more divorce-proneness.

Yet another approach is to calculate a rolling divorce rate, which measures the number of people in the population ever divorced as a fraction of the population ever married. This method has advantages and disadvantages. One disadvantage is that this method is biased by cohort and period. Large cohorts (or generations) of people (such as the baby boom generation) have an especially large effect on this kind of estimate. So, this approach, too, can be misleading.

The most refined method of measurement gives the closest approximation for the divorce rate in a lifetime. It looks at couples who married 30 years ago and what proportion of that population has since divorced. Since couples rarely divorce after 30 years of marriage (Ambert, 2005b)—although this is changing now, with more later-life divorces (Brown and Lin, 2012)—the actual divorce rate is significantly lower than the widely quoted "half of all marriages." According to the best estimate, the number of Canadian marriages that end before the thirtieth anniversary is just over one-third (Clark and Crompton, 2006). However, this method is not widely used.

One final measure, which to our knowledge is never used in official data, calculates the number of adult years lived outside marriage. If our purpose in computing divorce rates were to gauge people's desire to be married and stay married, nothing would show the societal rejection of marriage more than a continuous decline in the time people spent being married. Similarly, increases in person-years spent cohabiting could also be viewed as a rejection of traditional marriage. However, the goal of computing divorce rates is not only to measure the societal rejection of marriage, but also to help sociologists develop and test theories about the factors that contribute to the survival and breakdown of marriages. In turn, this helps us understand something about the conditions that make for better and worse family functioning.

An interesting illustration of the advantage of organizing survey data in original ways to answer sociological questions comes from Canadian sociologists Clark and Crompton (2006). The authors analyzed data from the 2001 General Social Survey (GSS) to find out whether people face differential risks of divorce after their first, second, and third marriages. Figure 9.3 presents their breakdown of the data. Looking at divorce in this way, we first see that most ever-married Canadians (89 percent) only marry once (Clark and Crompton, 2006: 24). In addition, 69 percent of ever-married people remain with their first spouse, and people who do this, on average, remain married for 23.5 years. Only about 23 percent of people dissolve their first marriage after an average of 11 years together (Clark and Crompton, 2006: 23). This study has not been updated.

A lot more could be said about the challenges of divorce rates. Demographers spend a great deal of time perfecting these measures, and those who watch rates, like the readers of this text as well as policy-makers, should be careful to know what is

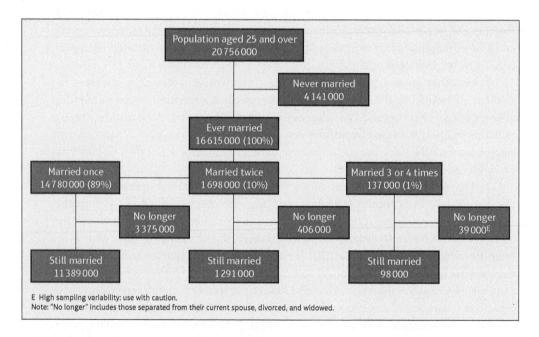

Figure 9.3 Risk of marriage dissolution after first, second, and third marriages

Source: Warren, Clark, & Susan Crompton. 2006. Till death do us part? The risk of first and second marriage dissolution. Ottawa: Statistics Canada. Catalogue no. 11-008. *Canadian Social Trends*. p. 24. Reproduced and distributed on an "as is" basis with the permission of Statistics Canada.

being measured and how. Generally, the best rate is one that correctly measures the risks of experiencing something such as divorce by those who are most at risk for divorce. It is wise never to trust a rate without knowing what question you are trying to answer; equally, never accept a rate as valid unless you know how it was created and what it shows.

DIVORCE AND SOCIETY

Many questions involving divorce need answering in sociology as well as in allied disciplines such as psychology and economics, as divorce affects many people. As we shall see, divorce solves some problems and creates others—problems between people and their children, parents, siblings, and friends.

Sociologists hope to gain insights from research on divorce about the nature of social bonding, the effects of economy and culture on personal relations, and the causes and effects of divorce. At the micro level, family sociologists try to understand why individual couples divorce. To do this, they examine family dynamics and interaction patterns, the expectations people have about married life, who they choose to marry and why, and people's subjective assessments of available alternative mates. An important consideration currently is whether wives have independent earnings and whether husbands have full-time jobs (Killewald, 2016). They also examine the effects on divorcing spouses, their children, and other family members. Then, they consider how people may individually work to reduce the harmful effects of divorce.

At the macro level, sociologists debate how to measure divorce, how to measure "a marriage or relationship breakdown," and how to measure the link between relationship breakdown and legal divorce. Often relationships break down long before divorce occurs, so separation may be a better indicator than divorce of marital problems. As we have noted, with dramatic increases in cohabitation, divorce rates are no longer reliable indicators of relationship breakdown. However, even in the past, they may not have been good indicators. And today's higher rates of cohabitation may lead to even higher rates of divorce in future—since cohabiters who then marry may be more likely to divorce (Le Bourdais, Neil, and Turcotte, 2000). However, higher cohabitation rates can also lead to lower divorce rates, since cohabiters are not at risk for legal divorce. And as cohabitation becomes more and more socially acceptable, the relation of cohabitation with divorce, as discussed by Le Bourdais, Neil, and Turcotte (2000), may become less apparent. For example, Kulu and Boyle (2010) found in a study relying on life history data from Austria that even though cohabiters who marry seem to have a higher risk of divorce, once controls are used for standard characteristics, risks for divorce diminish. Their conclusion: "Premarital cohabitation decreases the risk of marital separation . . ." (879).

Macro-sociologists have examined the social, cultural, economic, and political forces that shape marriage. Their goal has been to find out what accounts for the long-term increase in divorce rates over much of the twentieth century and the current stabilization and decline in divorce (Amato, 2010). To find out, we examine such large-scale processes as industrialization and urbanization, the increasing participation of women in the labour force, and changes in the societal norms regulating marriage and family life. We also study the macro-level effects of high divorce rates on family and social life, parenting, and the distribution of income.

Despite relatively high divorce rates, the family is still the most important and most fundamental institution in society, as we have argued in earlier chapters. Therefore, it is understandable that some may interpret high divorce rates as a sign of societal breakdown. This interpretation, favoured by political conservatives today, began with the work of nineteenth-century sociologist Émile Durkheim in works like *Suicide* and *The Division of Labor in Society*. Political conservatives are also more likely to see divorce rates as proof of the decreasing value of marriage in our society today. However, some have argued the opposite—namely, that we value "good" marriages more than ever (Huston and Melz, 2004). Today, we expect more of marriage than merely housekeeping and reproduction, for example. So, we are more likely today to hold off marrying or to leave relationships in which we find ourselves unhappy.

Conservative sociologists, sometimes called "marriage promoters," also note that, even today, high divorce rates are associated with high suicide rates, suggesting that the divorce rate reflects distress or disorganization in the general population (see Popenoe, 1996, as a major proponent for this way of thinking). Positive correlations between divorce rates, suicide rates, and alcohol consumption per capita suggest a broad-based social characteristic—a **social pathology**, as early sociologists would have called it— that produces stress-related behaviours (Evans, Scourfield, and Moore, 2016)

However, liberal sociologists deny that divorce rates necessarily show **social disorganization** (see Cherlin, 2004; Smart and Neale, 1999; Stacey, 1996, for example). Divorce may not hamper a healthy family and social life if clear social norms specify what is to happen to the husband, wife, and children after a divorce. In societies that handle divorce well, such as Sweden, children continue to live with their kin, often with their mother and her relatives. For this and other reasons, they may suffer less from the separation of their parents than North American children, for example. In Sweden, divorce produces fewer stress-related outcomes. And there are examples of smooth divorce arrangements in our own society. For example, the transition is easier when fathers remain involved with their children after divorce, or even become more involved (Smart and Neale, 1999).

People in our society have trouble thinking about divorce in a calm, dispassionate way, sometimes instead viewing it in dramatic terms, as evidence of a "pathology" or "societal breakdown." There may be two explanations for this way of thinking. First, divorce is both a personal (emotional) and a religious (or ideological) matter. Leaders from many different religions argue that marriage is sacred and should not be dissolved. Politics also enters the debate, with socially conservative politicians and journalists debating more liberal people about the meaning of divorce and how societies ought to respond.

Second, we often have trouble remaining calm and dispassionate about divorce because we never prepare for divorce as we do for other major adult life experiences like education, employment, and marriage. Most young people, for example, say that they expect *never* to divorce (Vanier Institute of the Family, 2002). Although the odds favour marriages lasting, many do not. Yet people organize their lives and societal roles around the belief that long-term marriage is the most reasonable expectation (Beaupré, 2008). Some beliefs about marriage and divorce have not changed much in centuries, although historical and crossnational data show us that divorce practices surely have!

Separation and Divorce in the Immigrant Population

In general, marriage (as opposed to other intimate unions) is more common, and divorce is less common, in non-Western countries. There are exceptions such as Russia, where both marriage and divorce rates are high (Keenan, Grundy, Kenward, and Lyon, 2012), but Russia is a country that has been in turmoil since the end of the Soviet Union, with sharply reduced life expectancies, especially for men, and challenges with health, particularly prevalent alcoholism. However, overall it is the case that divorce is less common in the home countries of immigrants who come to Canada. This is because marriage is highly valued in traditional cultures. In these societies, women are often denied the right to divorce their mate on religious grounds, or they are permitted to do so but stigmatized afterward (see Ayyub, 2000, for an outline of divorce in the South Asian Muslim population). Immigrating to countries like Canada where the opportunity to divorce is more readily accessible gives many women the chance to exercise this choice that was unavailable before.

However, research shows that divorce is still not as common among immigrants as it is among the native-born in Canada (Se'ver, 2011). This is largely because of persisting traditional views of the process, which are mostly negative (Jaaber and Dasgupta, 2003). For example, some women view separation and divorce as a deliberate act of disobedience to their husband and an embarrassment to their family. On the other hand, immigration can be disruptive to identities and traditions and can lead for some to higher risks of marital dissolution (Shirpak, Maticka-Tyndale, and Chinichian, 2011). Chang (2003), who studied differences in reported reasons for divorce among Korean immigrant and white non-immigrant women, found that most immigrants divorce for clear reasons. These include the ex-husband's use of violence, severe financial problems, or other highly negative circumstances. By contrast, white non-immigrant women base their reasoning on vaguer concerns such as lack of emotional fulfillment. These different explanations reflect different cultural justifications for divorce.

No wonder immigrant women are clear and cautious: Immigrant women who do decide to divorce are at a higher risk for violence by their spouse than are native-born women in Canada (Spiwak and Brownridge, 2005). The increased risk is related to various factors: male dominance in patriarchical cultures, the financial dependence of women, and disagreement over various migration decisions (Morash, Bui, Zhang, and

Holtfreter, 2007; Spiwak and Brownridge, 2005; Yick, 2000). It should be noted, however, that underreporting of interpersonal violence by immigrant women tends to be high. Many are afraid to report to authorities—even more afraid than native-born women (see Morton, 2011: 303–304; Tyyskä, 2011).

A HISTORICAL, CROSSNATIONAL OVERVIEW OF DIVORCE

In industrial societies, divorce rates hit a peak in the second half of the twentieth century. This peak occurred because of changes in the social, economic, and legal institutions that shape family life and individual expectations of marriage. Divorce is nothing new, however, nor is it limited to Western industrial societies (see Phillips, 1988). What follows is a thumbnail sketch of the relevant socio-historical processes.

Social Changes

In preindustrial times, as we discuss in Chapter 2, most families were rural, land-based, self-sufficient units. They produced most of what they needed to feed, clothe, and house their own members. The division of labour was simple. Tasks and responsibilities were allocated according to age and gender. *Social differentiation* beyond that was slight, except for royalty and the aristocracies in some parts of the world.

With the onset of the Industrial Revolution about 200 years ago (mid-nineteenth century in Canada), however, the modern Western family lost its main economic function. Most production moved out of the household and into factories and (later) offices. These changes affected the strength of family ties and the family's ability to control its members. People's lives became more individuated and governed by market forces.

In the past hundred years, other functions of the family, such as the education and training of the young, increasingly have become the responsibility of the state. In Canada, compulsory education was the state response to unruly youth of the early industrial period. This meant that the family was no longer the only source of personal security. Of course, that period of state expansion is now at an end. With increasing job and policy insecurity (in pensions, social assistance, and so on), families may once again be becoming a crucial source of security for individuals (McDaniel, 2002; McDaniel, Gazso, and Um, 2013).

To be sure, the family was always, and is still, important. Especially today, it is only by pooling their members' incomes that many families keep themselves out of poverty and off social assistance (McDaniel, Gazso, and Um, 2013). Immigrant family members, in particular, pool their resources to achieve upward mobility.

Nonetheless, since the second half of the twentieth century, the family has been much less necessary for educational and other social purposes. As a result, people may invest less of themselves in the family. And the looser their ties become, the easier it is to sever them when problems arise or attractive alternatives beckon.

So, divorce rates rise (South, Trent, and Shen, 2001). Figure 9.4 shows the trends in marital status of Canadians at the end of the twentieth century, while Figure 9.5 charts the trends nearly up to the present. Since 1971, the proportion of married

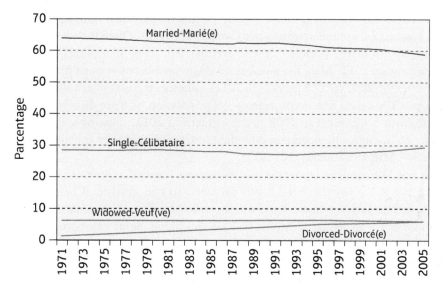

Figure 9.4 Population changes in marital status, Canada, 1971 to 2005

Source: Data from Statistics Canada. 2013. CANSIM Table 051-0042. Retrieved from http://www5. statcan.gc.ca/cansim/a26?lang=eng&retrLang=eng&id=0510042&paSer=&pattern=&stByVal=1&p1= 1&p2=-1& tabMode=dataTable&csid=.

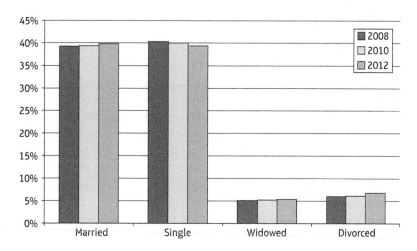

Figure 9.5 Population changes in marital status, Canada, 2008 to 2012

Source: Data from Statistics Canada. 2013. CANSIM table 051-0042. Retrieved February 2013 from www5.statcan.gc.ca/cansim/a26?lang=eng&retrLang=eng&id=0510042&paSer=&pattern=&stByVal= 1&p1=1&p2=-1&tabMode=dataTable&csid=.

people continued slowly to fall, while the proportion of divorced, cohabiting, and single people rose. By 2005, divorced people comprised 5.9 percent of the population age 15 years and older, compared to only 1.7 percent in 1975 (Statistics Canada, 2006a: 9). Also signalling the changed evaluation of family life, "the proportion of single people has been rising steadily since 1991 (27.1 percent), and by July 1, 2005, it had reached 29.3 percent" (Statistics Canada, 2006a: 8). There is a small change in the proportion of the population who are married, from 40.5 percent in 2008 to 39.7 percent by 2012. Also, the number of single people has seen an increase (from 29.3 percent in 2008 to 39.5 percent in 2012), although it has shown a slight decrease in the past few years. The percentage of the population who are divorced increased slightly from 5.9 percent in 2008 to 6.8 percent in 2012, showing a stabilizing of the rate of divorce when compared to the more rapid rises over other periods (see Figure 9.4; Statistics Canada, 2013d).

By this historical, and more current, reckoning, higher divorce rates are the result of a change in the ties that bind family members to one another. Where family ties once rested on life-and-death economic dependence and co-dependence, today they rest more often on fragile emotions of love and liking. Since emotional ties are by their nature more fickle than ties of economic dependence, we more easily sever them. However, not every couple that falls out of love gets a divorce, since divorce is a legal process and not a social or emotional one. Some couples, as we shall see, may not wish to end their marriages publicly at all. Others do.

Legal Changes

To understand divorce as a legal process, we must understand the laws governing divorce and how they have changed. Divorce laws in Canada and other Western countries have gradually loosened over the past two centuries. For example, during the colonial period in North America, divorce was illegal in the southern United States and Quebec. It was granted elsewhere only under narrowly defined circumstances such as adultery or after proof of seven years of desertion. Until the mid-twentieth century, Canadian law required an Act of Parliament for each divorce to be granted (Snell, 1983). Not surprisingly, divorces were granted most often to well-to-do and influential people. Before the 1968 Divorce Act (which accepted separation as a legitimate ground for divorce), most marriages "dissolved by taking other options, such as separation, desertion, or maintaining an 'empty shell' relationship by minimizing communication between partners" (McVey, 2008: 190).

There was a strong sense in the early 1900s in Canada that divorce was a moral and political issue, with bad implications for the country. Snell (1983: 113) quotes E.A. Lancaster, the Conservative member of Parliament for Lincoln, Ontario, 1900–1916: "Where will this country come to in twenty-five years if we are going to grant divorces because some woman has been disappointed in regard to her husband . . . The whole social fabric of the country would go to pieces."

Increasingly over the twentieth century, North American governments granted divorces on ever-widening grounds, such as marital cruelty, marital rape, sodomy, bestiality, homosexuality, and adultery. As divorce laws become more lenient, there was an accompanying rise in divorce rates. A turning point occurred in the late 1960s and early 1970s with the introduction of **no-fault divorce** laws in Canada and some jurisdictions in the United States. In Canada, the 1968 Divorce Act first enlarged the "fault grounds" under which a divorce could be granted, but also allowed divorce without accusations of wrongdoing in the case of "marital breakdown," which required three years of living apart, or five years if both spouses did not agree to divorce.

The 1985 Divorce Act considers marriage breakdown to be the only ground for divorce, although the older grounds such as adultery and cruelty are considered evidence of breakdown. It is no longer necessary for one spouse or the other to accept moral blame for the breakdown of the marriage. This change in approach reflects a gradual societal redefinition of divorce.

No longer does divorce have to be a stigmatizing process where one party is held responsible under the law. On the contrary, we now may be more likely to look critically at marriages that survive even though they are emotionally dead. These are marriages that we now think could end, freeing their participants to find emotional fulfillment in another union, or in living singly.

No-fault divorce laws implicitly define marriages in which couples are "incompatible" or have "irreconcilable differences" as grounds for divorce. Divorce, according to no-fault laws, then, could end marriages that are "irretrievably broken." The grounds for no-fault divorce are not inherently adversarial; they are based almost entirely on the loss of emotional connections. In earlier times, many marriages may have broken down emotionally or may never have been emotionally secure in the first place. It is only recently that the legal system has come to view this as reason enough to end a marriage.

In December 2002, the Government of Canada announced a new approach to divorce in Canada (Douglas, 2006). The purpose of proposed changes to the 1985 Divorce Act was, according to then Minister of Justice Martin Cauchon, to focus on children's needs primarily. Bill C-22, an Act to amend the Divorce Act, et al., would have replaced the terms *custody* and *access* in the Divorce Act with *parental responsibility* and *contact*. It also would have provided courts with a new list of factors to apply to decisions surrounding the post-separation parenting of children whose parents divorce (Douglas, 2006). Regrettably, the bill made no headway.

However, on May 1, 2006, amended Federal Child Support Guidelines came into force; these clarified the term *extraordinary expenses* to respond to judicial disagreement over the significance of the term. The guidelines also provided for education-related and extracurricular-activity extraordinary expenses to be added to child support amounts payable. They included new tables for setting child support levels, which reflected changes in tax structures in the provinces (Douglas, 2006).

- The divorced population in Canada in 2012 was 4.83 percent of the population, although this number did not include those living common-law. There was no significant change from 2008 (Statistics Canada, 2013d).

- More than one-third of marriages in Canada will end in divorce before the thirtieth wedding anniversary (Clark and Crompton, 2006). In 2011, the Vanier Institute, using data from Statistics Canada, published "Four in Ten Marriages End in Divorce" (see Figures 9.6a and 9.6b).

- Men between the ages of 20 and 64 are six times more likely to suffer from depression if they are divorced or separated than if they stay married. The figure is 3.5 times more likely for divorced or separated women (Rotermann, 2007).

- Divorced people also face higher risks of suicide (Ide, Wyder, Kolves, and De Leo, 2010) and higher risks of heart problems (Dupré, George, Liu, and Peterson, 2015).

- Forty-three percent of women who have undergone a marital breakup (divorce or separation) had a substantial decrease in household income in 2006, while 15 percent of separated or divorced men had a financial decline (Rotermann, 2007).

- In 1951, divorce accounted for only 3 percent of lone parents, but the proportion of divorced lone parents had increased tenfold, to 31 percent, by 2001 (Beaujot and Ravanera, 2008). In 2011, there were more than 1.5 million lone-parent families—16.3 percent of all census families—in Canada, an increase from 8 percent in 2006 (Statistics Canada, 2012a).

- Among seniors (age 65 and older), the proportion of divorced people tripled from 1.7 percent in 1981 to 5.1 percent in 2001 (Turcotte and Schellenberg, 2006: 139).

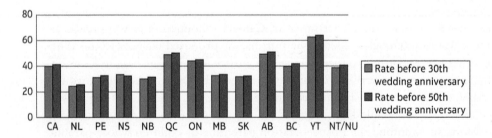

Figure 9.6a Percentage of couples who can expect to divorce before their thirtieth and fiftieth anniversaries

Source: Reprinted with permission from The Vanier Institute of the Family, 2011. Four in ten marriages end in divorce. *Fascinating Families*, Issue 41. www.vanierinstitute.ca/include/get.php?nodeid=132.

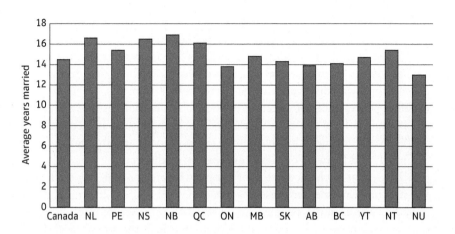

Figure 9.6b Average duration of marriage for divorced persons, Canada, 2011

Source: Reprinted with permission from The Vanier Institute of the Family, 2011. Four in ten marriages end in divorce. *Fascinating Families*, Issue 41. www.vanierinstitute.ca/include/get.php?nodeid=132.

CAUSES OF DIVORCE

In the discussion that follows, we speak of "causes," but we might as well use the word **determinants** or **predictors**. Many supposed causes of divorce intertwine with other causes. Their distinct, separate influence is hard to discover. The most we can say with certainty is that these are predictors—correlates that typically precede divorce and influence its likelihood in sometimes complicated ways.

Although underplayed in sociological discussion about the "cause" of divorce, a couple's emotional interaction and personal characteristics, such as being naturally more caring, compromising, or compassionate, can also play a role in marriages and subsequent divorces. This means that, although the importance of communication for the success of relationships is paramount (see Chapter 5), *knowing* how to communicate or problem solve may be still be inadequate if the marriage is not founded on mutual respect and admiration (Huston and Melz, 2004: 955). For instance, happy couples are more likely to have individual characteristics that make them more even-tempered and warm-hearted. They are also more likely to show goodwill toward their partners and therefore are more likely to work through any differences (Huston and Melz, 2004: 952).

Moreover, a couple's emotional climate and personal characteristics may clash from the beginning. Most people (wrongly) believe that unhappy marriages began as happy relationships and that conflicts that were unknown before developed during the marriage. On the contrary, Huston and Melz (2004: 952) found that most unhappy marriages fell short of happiness from the onset of the marriage. So, the reasons for divorce are complicated by the emotional climate of a marriage and the interplay of individual characteristics as well (Putnam, 2011).

We also distinguish among three levels of causal explanation: the micro, macro, and meso levels. By **micro-level** causes, we mean something close to the lived experience of people who divorce: attitudes, perceptions, sentiments, beliefs, and the like. We include the experiences of rejection, infidelity, and marital dissatisfaction in this category. By **macro-level** causes, we mean societal changes such as increased social tolerance of divorce, women's involvement in the workforce, and changes in divorce laws.

Finally, middle-range or **meso-level** causes of divorce are, typically, demographic predictors—that is, characteristics of people who are at a high risk of divorce. In this area, it is unclear whether these characteristics are causes, determinants, or merely predictors. For example, people who marry at an early age, or after only a short relationship, run an especially high risk of divorce, due to the stress, conflict, and dissatisfaction that arise when two immature people who do not know each other well try to work out a life together.

Precisely what we call the "cause" in the situation will vary from one analyst to another. Let us begin with the micro-sociological causes of divorce. They are the easiest causes to understand intuitively. However, they may not be the major factors leading to divorce—or, at least, to predicting it.

Micro-sociological Causes

From John Gottman's lifelong couples research we learn that some factors predictive of divorce occur when couples fall into escalating patterns of criticism and withdrawal, contempt and defensiveness. Much of this, he theorizes, is tied to how differences in psychological resiliency to stress are socialized and gendered (Gottman, 2014).

The second kind of micro-sociological reasons people cite to explain divorce typically describes the dynamics of the marriage relationship. As we said in Chapter 5, the quality of a relationship largely determines the stability of a marriage. Marriages likely to end in divorce have a typical profile. Usually, they are characterized by poor communication and poor conflict-resolution skills as well as a lack of commitment to the spouse or to the institution of marriage. The spouses may have few shared values and interests, and there is often a perceived inequity between spouses and limited respect, love, and affection on the part of one or both spouses. These are overall average traits and will not characterize each situation. We can imagine people in such relationships wanting and getting a divorce. However, because these are common problems of relationships, they are not good predictors. Even those on the inside of the relationship often cannot make that prediction.

Consider, instead, some life course (demographic) variables that make certain people more divorce-prone than others. These are better than micro-sociological variables at identifying conditions that produce tensions and unhappiness—which, in turn, increase the likelihood of divorce. Even if they do not seem to explain divorce as well, they are better at predicting it.

Meso-sociological Causes

Not everyone who marries gets divorced. In fact, the majority stay married, as discussed earlier. Moreover, the probability of divorce is spread unevenly throughout the population. Thus, to understand the causes of divorce we must look at who gets divorced.

Major life course and demographic variables correlated with a high divorce risk include young age at marriage, cohabitation before marriage, second or subsequent marriage, parental divorce, premarital pregnancy or childbearing, childlessness (or, conversely, having a large number of children), early stage of marriage, urban residence, residence in British Columbia or Alberta (or in Quebec), absence of religious belief or affiliation, and low socio-economic status.

Age at Marriage   Young age at marriage is probably the strongest predictor of divorce in the first five years of marriage (Amato, 2010; Ambert, 2002). Risks are especially high for people who marry in their teens. Various explanations for this have been ventured: Young people lack the emotional maturity needed for marriage, and they have ill-founded expectations of what married life holds in store. They are more likely to become disappointed and disillusioned with marriage, especially when they come upon plentiful alternatives to their current spouse (South, Trent, and Shen, 2001). As well, early marriage tends to reduce educational achievement. Those who marry young divorce more often because they have less education (and therefore a lower income) and fewer communication skills, which, in turn, can result in more misunderstandings and marital conflict.

Ironically, although those who marry young in our own society have high rates of divorce, young-marrying societies, in which the average age at marriage is low, have low rates of divorce. Typically, countries with low average ages of marriage have other features—for example, high rates of childbearing, strongly institutionalized religion, extended families, and restrictive divorce laws—that keep the divorce rates low for people of all ages. Latin American and Islamic societies share these features, as do some cultures in Africa and Asia (Emery, 2013).

Cohabitation   Cohabitation before marriage has, as we've said in earlier chapters, also been correlated with a higher risk of divorce. However, this fact needs careful interpretation. Societal and family pressures may push cohabiting people into marriage before they are ready, even if they are unsuited for marriage or for each other. Cohabitation, by hastening marriage, may increase the risk of separation and divorce (Ambert, 2002). On the other hand, couples in happy cohabiting relationships who succumb to societal pressures to marry, or slide into marriage (Stanley, Rhoades, and Markman, 2006), may find their relationship changed adversely by the social policies and laws that shape expectations about wives and husbands and supposedly encourage stability. Couples, in other words, may not be separating as much from each other as from the socially scripted roles and expectations that legal marriage entails. It would be interesting to find out how many couples who previously cohabited and subsequently married actually go back to living in a cohabiting relationship. Much has been learned about intimate unions from gay and lesbian couples, some of whom saw the reality that they could not legally marry in the past (in most jurisdictions) as strengthening their relationships (see Lehr, 1999; Rothblum, Balsam, and Solomon, 2011). In other words, couples are creating their own ways to be couples rather than working to fit into legally prescribed roles and obligations that some find constraining. Of course, that changed with the option for legalized gay and lesbian marriages in Canada beginning in 2005 and now in many other countries. Feminist sociology has found that legal marriage is often too constricting for women.

Still another possible explanation for this finding is **adverse selectivity**—that is, that the people who choose to cohabit are different from those who choose to marry without first cohabiting. In addition to selectivity, experiential aspects may be involved because cohabitating also has adverse influence on relationship quality, not only on relationship survival (Stanley, Rhoades, and Markman, 2006). These authors suggest that when couples cohabit, a kind of inertia builds and they end up sliding into marriage. This inertia comes more from shared property, pets, and children than from a high level of perceived compatibility and high level of commitment. One key to understanding the cohabitation effect on divorce is noticed in the fact that couples who were engaged before cohabiting tend to divorce less often than those who were not engaged before cohabiting. This seems to lend support to Stanley, Rhoades, and Markman's theory. Some conjecture holds that as more people—and more varied people—cohabit, cohabitation may no longer predict a higher risk of divorce. However, as of 2010, this did not seem to be the case. "Those who cohabited prior to engagement reported, on average, lower levels of positive attributes about their marriages, more negative interactions, and more proclivity toward divorce than did those who cohabited after making a clear and public commitment to the future (engagement or marriage)" (Stanley, Rhoades, Amato, Markman, and Johnson, 2010: 917). Therefore, cohabitation as a predictor variable for divorce risk continues to be examined in an effort to identify the key factors involved, such as the degree of intentionality toward marriage prior to cohabiting.

Second Marriages   Other things being equal, second marriages are more likely than first marriages to end in divorce. The risk in Canada is estimated to be about 10 percent higher than in first marriages (Ambert, 2002; 2005b). Data on marriages and divorces in Canada have not been collected recently. The probability that third marriages will end in divorce is higher still. (As well, subsequent marriages that end in divorce end more quickly than do first marriages.) Yet people still get married after a divorce. Approximately 70 percent of men and 58 percent of women in Canada (excluding Quebec) marry again following divorce. Remarriages are also more common among immigrants than among Canadian-born citizens (Ambert, 2005b; Wu, 1994).

This finding defies our common sense. One would expect remarriages—like cohabiting relationships—to have a lower divorce rate. People who had already gone through one divorce would, we imagine, be more careful when choosing their next mate. They would try harder to make their marriage work, to avoid the problems and costs associated with divorce. Some, in fact, do just this. When a second marriage endures, it often outlasts the first (Ambert, 2002; 2005b; Wu, 1994). Moreover, when remarriages work out, it is typically because the remarried people are older than average. Older people are less likely to divorce (although, as we have seen, this is changing). Young people who remarry are more likely to divorce than older people who remarry.

Another viable explanation is that people who have already been married choose cohabitation as a substitute to marriage the second time around. For these adults, cohabitation is a union in itself, one that will not end in marriage and that has a similar level of commitment as marriage (Ambert, 2005a; Beaupré, 2008). In this case, older cohabiters experience higher levels of happiness and stability than younger ones (King and Scott, 2005). Despite their success, these relationships are not counted as remarriages and, as such, do nothing to decrease the perceived overall risk of divorce in second marriages.

Adverse selectivity may *again* be the explanation for the higher divorce tendency in second and third marriages. People who experience a first divorce may be more willing to get a second. They may more readily see divorce as a solution to marital problems.

A competing theory argues that the stresses and strains of a remarriage are greater than those of first marriages. Second marriages may bring "baggage" from the first marriage or divorce, the (difficult) integration of stepchildren into reconstituted families, or the challenges of ongoing interactions with ex-spouses. Furthermore, fewer norms guide second marriages, although that is changing with their greater frequency. This makes remarriages more challenging. Both theories are compelling. We need more research to decide which explanation is better or whether both sets of factors come into play, with other factors still not well understood (Amato, 2010; Putnam, 2011).

Parental Divorce People whose parents divorced are more likely to divorce. They also have a greater tendency not to marry. However, the mechanism that transmits this inheritance is unclear. Perhaps people whose parents divorced are less likely to believe that marriages can last. That makes them more likely to opt for divorce when things get tough. They may have married before they were ready, out of fear that they would be alone (like their parents). They may have married before they understood what marriage was all about, because their parents' marriage did not last long enough for them to find out. On the other hand, they may be the victims of optimism. This does not mean, however, that if your parents are divorced, your risk of divorce is automatically high. It is not. Many children of divorced parents marry well and live happily.

Myth: Families where children live with their biological mothers are more stable across all situations.

- Fact: When a resident stepfather is present, the family is less stable than a family where the child is living with his or her biological father and a resident stepmother (Ambert, 2005b).

Myth: Higher divorce rates among children are a result of the conflict they saw in their families.

- Fact: This is not always true. Higher divorce risks also occur among adult children where their divorced parents had low levels of conflict. A sense of less commitment to each other may have been passed on to the children (Ambert, 2005b).

Myth: Step-parents have little connection with stepchildren.

- Fact: Many children enjoy the presence of a step-parent and benefit from the affection. Where stepfamilies endure, young adults are strongly attached to the reconstructed family (Ambert, 2005b).

Myth: After divorce, spouses are not concerned with what the ex-partner thinks.

- Fact: Perceptions of a former spouse can still have a powerful impact. Ex-wives' approval of the quality of fathering plays a role in how satisfied divorced fathers are (Cohen and Finzi-Dottan, 2005).

Myth: People with lower socio-economic status are least able to afford to leave their marriage and thus have lower risk of marital dissolution.

- Fact: People with less than high school education at the time of their first marriage face a 38 percent greater risk of divorce than those who completed high school. University graduates, on the other hand, are at 16 percent less risk for marital dissolution, suggesting that people with higher social status are happier and less likely to divorce (Clark and Crompton, 2006: 24).

Myth: Second marriages are more likely to end in divorce than first marriages.

- Fact: In reality, remarriages made after the age of 40 are more stable than first marriages, due to the partners' increased maturity. For example, the risk for marital dissolution of Canadians who remarried in their forties is half that of those who were younger than 30 (Clark and Crompton, 2006: 25).

One Canadian study (Corak and Heisz, 1999) compared children whose parents divorced with those who lost a parent to death. The researchers found, interestingly, that children who lose a parent to death have the same likelihood of marrying and of divorcing as anyone else.

The correlation of parental divorce with heightened divorce risk may be due, again, to adverse selectivity. People whose parents divorced were once a small minority. Today, they are not. Their parents' divorce stigmatizes them less and leaves them less ignorant about the variety of possible adaptations to marital conflict. They know that people survive divorce and that many people are better for doing so. If this explanation is so, we might expect that more people will have ideas for how to divorce less stressfully from watching their parents' divorce. However, demographically

According to Statistics Canada, "one characteristic of stepfamily parents is that they are more likely to be in a common-law union." According to data from the 2011 General Social Survey, 48 percent of parents ages 20 to 64 living in stepfamilies were living common-law. For parents in intact families, the proportion was 14 percent. Among parents in common-law relationships, those in stepfamilies were more likely than intact-family parents to want to marry.

When asked "Do you think you will ever marry (or marry again)?" 42 percent of stepfamily parents living common-law said yes. For intact-family parents, the proportion was 32 percent.

Source: Statistics Canada. 2011. *General Social Survey: Overview of Families in Canada—Being a parent in a stepfamily: A profile.* Catalogue no. 89-650-X–No. 002. http://www.statcan.gc.ca/pub/89-650-x/89-650-x2012002-eng.pdf

speaking, as the average age of the population increases, and as older people remarry less often and cohabit more often, we may see a decline in divorce.

Childbearing, before and after Marriage   Evidence documenting the relationship between premarital childbearing and the likelihood of divorce is overwhelming. For people who marry after having a child, the risk of divorce is high. Couples who marry after discovering that they are expecting a child may marry under extreme pressure to legitimate the birth of their child. This is not the best motivation to marry. The good news is that shotgun weddings (marrying quickly because of pregnancy) are less common than they used to be.

The relationship between the birth of children within marriage and the likelihood of divorce is strong but not straightforward. Couples who end up divorcing tend to have no children or have fewer on average than those who stay married (Ambert, 2002). The reasons may be unrelated to childbearing; it may be that most divorces occur within the early years of marriage. It is also likely that people who have no children may see themselves as freer to divorce than couples with children. Again, adverse selectivity is operating here.

However, children are quickly becoming less of a deterrent to divorce. The number of children affected by divorce and the fraction of divorces involving children have increased in recent years (Amato, 2010). Today, couples are less likely to stay together for the children.

Stage of Marriage   Duration of marriage is strongly negatively correlated with a propensity to divorce. That said, the lowest risk of divorce is in the first year of marriage (Statistics Canada, 2002a). The rate follows an inverted-U shape that is skewed toward the left. Before the first anniversary, divorce occurs in less than 1 in every 1000 marriages. After the first anniversary, the rate goes up to 4.3, and then jumps to 18.0 in the following year. The peak occurs at around the third and the fourth years, with 25.0 and 25.7 divorces, respectively. The curve goes down slowly each year after the fourth anniversary (Statistics Canada, 2004a). After 15 years of marriage, couples are less likely to divorce. The explanation is that the more time and energy people invest in their marriage, the higher are the costs of abandoning the marriage and starting a new life. Couples are more aware of being badly matched early in the marriage since the factors responsible for divorce (e.g., emotional satisfaction) carry more weight in the early years. As well, people think that, when a mistake has been made, it should be changed before it is too late. After about three years, relationships stabilize and many partners adjust.

On the other hand, with increases in longevity and more women having careers and means of living on their own, the rates of later-life divorce are increasing substantially. Brown and Lin (2012) estimate, based on U.S. national data, that the divorce rate among those age 50 and older doubled between 1990 and 2010. This suggests that people may be less willing to live out their later years in an unhappy marriage than they used to be. No similar studies have been done in Canada. Also, the longer a marriage goes on, the older the spouses tend to be, and the more likely they are to have grown up with cultural values in which marriage had much greater normative pull than it does today. We must wait another few decades before we find out the strength of this **cohort effect**—something that influences everyone of roughly the same age.

Place of Residence People living in urban centres are much more likely to divorce than people in rural areas. In some cases, this finding reflects a higher probability of divorce under the demands and stresses of urban life. However, in part these statistics also reflect adverse selectivity—specifically, the tendency for rural people to migrate to urban areas before, during, or after a divorce, or for younger people to migrate to cities for work or education and find themselves marrying there. A family farm or a rural small town can be a difficult place for divorced people, especially divorced women.

The effect of urban living is sometimes confounded by the divorce-increasing role of migration. When we control for many possible explanatory factors, rates of union instability are strongly related to recent and lifetime migration experience. Many immigrants come from cultures with strong family sanctions for lasting marriages. An alternative explanation is that when immigrants from countries in which marriage is seen primarily as a practical arrangement come to Canada and encounter the expectation that marriage should be based on passion and companionship, they may look at their own marriage from a different point of view and may become dissatisfied. A third possibility is that selectivity explains the finding. People who take the initiative of moving to a new country are risk-takers, willing to confront challenges and make changes in their lives. They may be more willing to consider divorce than the more cautious people who stay behind. Alternatively, they may experience greater stresses, which can cause even firmly based marriages trouble.

Religion Finally, the ethnic and religious composition of the population has something to do with the patterns of divorce. The risk of divorce is lower for foreign-born Canadians. Interestingly, the risk of divorce is no higher in Quebec, where cohabitation is much more common than it is in other provinces. That, of course, could be the reason, since cohabiters are not counted as divorced when the unions end. Wu (2000) noted that the risk of divorce is lower among Catholics and Protestants than among those with other or no religious affiliation. The more religious people are, the less likely they will be to opt for divorce, even if they are unhappy in their marriages. Couples in which the spouses belong to different religions are more likely to divorce than couples who belong to the same religion (Goode, 1993: 320; McDaniel, Boco, and Zella, 2013). But, in analyzing generational data in California, it is found that, once controlling for socio-economic status and other basic characteristics, the effects of religion (both affiliation and religiosity) on divorce disappear (McDaniel, Boco, and Zella, 2013).

Related to this is the overall **secularization** of societies such as Canada. With the massive move away from religion as a dominant social institution have come new norms. Among these, individual choice and liberalization of sexual beliefs and behaviours loom large. Marriage has become, for many, an individual choice rather than a covenant taken before God and extended family. Even couples who marry in churches tend to believe less in the religious covenant aspect now. Divorce, then, is seen more as a choice rather than as the breaking of a larger spiritual commitment or of an extended family network.

Socio-economic Status   Class, or **socio-economic status** (SES), is strongly correlated with probability of divorce. The divorce rate increases as one moves down the socio-economic ladder. Study after study confirms that, whatever the index of socio-economic status used—income, occupation, or education—we observe an inverse correlation between SES and divorce rates.

Economic stresses produce marital stresses. Moreover, the poor have less (economically) to lose from divorce and less to gain from staying married. However, differences in divorce rates by SES tend to be decreasing. This is in part a function of an increase in the divorce rate among middle- and upper-class people.

Goode (1993) suggests that this change is the result of a shift in the strongest variable in this pattern: the discrepancy between the husband's and the wife's incomes. Women with employment and incomes similar to that of their husbands can afford to divorce. This explanation assumes that women are more likely to want out than men. The more economically independent women become, the more likely they will be to leave their marriages when they want. This finding, however, recently has been found not to be the case. Killewald (2016) found that wives' incomes are not predictive of divorce; instead, what matters is whether the husband has full-time work. Along similar lines, some argue that marriage, though seemingly about love or emotional union, is still a way for women to gain economically, even in the second and third decades of the twenty-first century. Killewald's findings may confirm that the male breadwinner model is still in play. Women's desires for marriage to work reflect their economic needs for support and their wish to avoid poverty, according to this reasoning.

Of course, to confirm this hypothesis, we would have to look further at who initiates separation or files for divorce, and why. But that could be misleading, too.

An unexpected finding is the opposite link between class and divorce for women and for men. Evidence shows that the higher a man's income, the less likely he is to divorce. On the other hand, the higher a woman's income, the more likely she is to divorce (Wu and Schimmele, 2005b). The latter suggests that marriage represents economic dependence for women, though not for men. However, this theory does not explain why men are reluctant to divorce if they earn a high income.

On this topic, the findings are confusing. Some research finds that increases in wives' SES and labour force participation increase the probability of marriage disruption. For example, Wu (2000) found that, for women, having a job outside the home or being in school is associated with higher rates of divorce. When the wife's work status is higher than her husband's, the relationship can become unstable (Phillips and Griffiths, 2004; Tzeng and Mare, 1995). This, however, is a growing trend and may now be stabilizing unions (Glynn, 2012; Killewald, 2016). Most research finds that marital happiness and well-being increase as women's income increases. This happiness, in turn, decreases the likelihood of divorce (Rogers and DeBoer, 2001).

Couples with more education and a stronger attachment to the workforce generally have more stable marriages. In addition, these couples are most likely to be egalitarian. Given the importance of work in stabilizing marriage, it is no surprise that unemployed people have higher divorce risks than employed people. The receipt of family support income also increases the likelihood that a married woman will become divorced (Davies and Denton, 2001; Hoffman and Duncan, 1995). This does not mean that social transfers cause marital instability, but only that economic and other instabilities may be correlated.

Macro-sociological Causes

It should be clear by now that although the decision to divorce is one made by an individual couple, the decision is influenced strongly by large processes in the structure of society over which people have little, if any, control (Emery, 2013).

The institution of the family has changed a great deal over the past two centuries and even more so in recent decades. The ties of authority and economic dependence that bind family members together have weakened considerably. In addition, the legal structure forcing people to remain together has loosened, making divorce an attainable option for many people. Other important macro-level determinants of divorce include wars and migrations, economic cycles, gender roles, social integration, and cultural values. We will look at each of these factors in turn.

Economic Cycles   People are less likely to divorce during recessionary periods than during periods of economic prosperity (Hellerstein and Morrill, 2011). People feel freer to strike out on their own when economic opportunities exist. They are more wary of leaving a familiar home or relationship, even if it is unpleasant, in times of economic uncertainty. As well, they may need the advantage of pooling resources in couples or families to get by in tough economic times.

Moreover, divorce is costly. It requires establishing separate households, dividing the property, and establishing specific terms for the support of children. Legal costs can also be high. These expenses tax most people's financial resources even during prosperity and often become prohibitive in bad times. If this happens, the effect is short-lived. Or couples may opt to live separately in the same house for a period until they can afford separate homes. Although divorce rates drop during economic depressions, they rise rapidly when the depression ends.

On the other hand, according to White's (1990: 905) review of the sociological literature on divorce, "(t)he most sophisticated analysis of American time series data . . . finds that the effect of prosperity is to reduce divorce." Although prosperity may make divorce more feasible, the *benefits* of prosperity outweigh this effect on personal relationships (South, 1985). Thus, divorce rates may fall because financial security adds stability to personal relationships. At the least, the evidence on this is inconclusive.

Gender Expectations The evidence regarding the influence of gender expectations is difficult to interpret. Researchers have examined two hypotheses. First, when social structures allow women more economic independence from men and families, women have more freedom to divorce (Hetherington and Kelly, 2002; Popenoe, 1996; Stacey, 1996). Feminist theories enable us to see women's options in larger social and policy contexts, so that challenges such as discrimination against divorced lone mothers, particularly among women of colour or newer immigrants, lack of child care options, problems with credit ratings, and so on can come into play as women consider divorce (Se'ver, 2011: 251–252). Second, a growing similarity of women's and men's lives may produce less marital cohesion than complementary, reinforcing roles do. Both of these hypotheses imply that the more women become financially secure, the higher the divorce rate will be (Newman and Olivetti, 2015). Yet as women marry men of similar SES, it may be that the divorce gap between higher SES couples and others widens.

Evidence suggests that the most satisfying marriages (for both spouses) are those in which women's and men's roles in the household are more egalitarian, with men more sensitive and nurturing, and where husbands and wives share equally in making the decisions that affect their lives (Stacey, 1996). Antill and Cotton (1987) studied 108 couples and found that when both spouses are high on "feminine" characteristics such as nurturance, sensitivity, and gentleness, couples are happier than when one or both spouses are low on this cluster of characteristics. "**Femininity**" of both wives and husbands is positively associated with a smooth marital adjustment (Kalin and Lloyd, 1985). The explanation is that many of these qualities and characteristics are conducive to good interpersonal relationships. Relationships that both spouses view as equitable have the best marital adjustment. The greater the perceived inequity, the poorer the marital adjustment, and thus the higher the risk of divorce (Mahoney and

Knudson-Martin, 2009). Of course, equality in intimate relationships is hard to define by couples who may often disagree about whether they have equality in their relationships (Mahoney and Knudson-Martin, 2009).

The nature of the relationship between gender expectations and divorce-proneness is unclear. Historical and cross-cultural research is addressing the issues of (1) whether divorce rates and rates of female participation in paid work are intrinsically related, (2) whether the observed relationship is a passing effect of the tension between changing social expectations and lagging societal understandings of these changes, and (3) whether the divorce rate is as high as in countries that have had a longer history of female participation in the labour force (Emery, 2013; Se'ver, 2011).

Cultural Values and Social Integration Since the mid-twentieth century, the cultural value placed on marriage has been declining. Many scholars argue that formal marriage has lost much of its normative support and social appeal. Distinctions between marital and non-marital childbearing, and between marriage and cohabitation, have lost their normative force. Marriage and divorce are seen as formalities or sets of family options. That said, many couples will live together until they decide to have children, at which point they marry. Today, it is argued, we invest less, or at least differently, in family commitments, whether to parents, spouses, or children.

Another macro-level determinant of divorce is a society's degree of **social integration**. The higher the social integration, the lower the divorce rate. In a stable, highly integrated community, which could be a religious community or perhaps an ethnic community, consensus on social rules is strong and rule breakers are shunned. This happens especially when the rules broken bear on social institutions as central to the community life as "the family." The highly integrated community typically supports various "pro-family" ideals bearing on marriage, premarital or extramarital sexuality, or child obedience. In Canada, Muslim and some South Asian communities are particularly protective of their daughters. Girls are seen as holding a special place in the communities as "cultural vessels" (Tyyskä, 2011: 104). This can lead to girls in these communities leading double lives, with a foot in mainstream Canadian culture, where they seek acceptance, and a foot in their families' traditions. By getting a divorce, people, particularly women, risk incurring social stigma for flouting social norms and tearing the social fabric of their community. In these highly integrated communities, this is scary stuff and can be a definite deterrent to divorce.

EFFECTS OF DIVORCE

Divorce, like the breakup of any important relationship, can be messy and painful. Most couples decide to divorce only reluctantly over a long period. For many of them, considerable trauma is involved. Some may experience discrimination and may be, for a time, almost without friends. Some, notably women, suffer serious economic deprivation (Gazso and McDaniel, 2010).

In such a high-conflict time, outside intervention may become necessary to reduce the risk of harmful and potentially long-standing escalations. This is especially important when children are involved in a separation. The parents must make decisions about the children, child support, maintenance, and the division of marital assets, and they must negotiate liabilities. Family therapists or marriage counsellors can provide short-term or continuing support and insight to couples going through separation.

More recently, mediation has gained popularity among family therapists and divorcing couples (Emery, 2012). The main purpose of mediation is not to have the counsellor discuss with clients what they should do. Rather, the emphasis is on drawing "on the resources and knowledge of its participants to allow for creative solutions to the needs of the families who engage in this process" (Katz, 2007: 106). In other words, the role of the mediator is to promote an effective discussion between family members who, in the process, will discover the unique resources they have available and come up with solutions on their own.

The main differences between traditional therapy and mediation, according to Katz (2007), are the role played by the counsellor, the process engaged in, and the intended outcomes. Mediation always involves both parties with clearly defined goals, whereas therapy tries to understand the past and feelings are often worked through. Traditional therapy works with multigenerational genograms where the focus of mediation is only the relevant parties. In traditional therapy, the therapist intervenes to resolve mental health behaviour and relationship concerns; in mediation, the clients are assisted by a counsellor to use direct talk to negotiate and make decisions. Furthermore, since mediation emphasizes improving communication, it helps both parties move to common underlying interests from their previous fixed bargaining positions, with the overlying goal of creating a legally binding contract.

Effects on Both Spouses

One of the major effects of divorce is economic: For men and women, but especially women, incomes decrease. Economic distress is a large contributor to generalized psychological distress and to social policy challenges (Davies, McMullin, and Avison with Cassidy, 2001; Gazso and McDaniel, 2010). However, economic distress is only one aspect of divorce and its aftermath. The other side is the emotional stress of interpersonal conflict. But, of course, emotional distress can be made worse by financial worries. This begins well before the divorce and may reach its peak then. In the years immediately preceding divorce, people experience higher-than-usual levels of distress. However, conflict does not end with divorce. The effects of divorce on the divorcing adults, both material and emotional, can be surprisingly long-lasting for some (Gustafson, 2009; Mastekaasa, 1995; Soria and Linder, 2014). In a review of studies of divorce, Amato (2010) finds that pre-divorce marital discord conditions the effects of divorce on children.

Former spouses often disagree on the involvement of non-custodial parents in co-parenting. An overwhelming majority of residential parents feel that they have problems with the issue of visitation rights. A smaller but still large percentage of non-residential parents do, too. In addition, these problems do not go away quickly. For residential parents, visitation problems may be connected to feelings of hurt and anger about the divorce. They are also connected with concerns about the ex-spouse's parenting abilities, about child support, and sometimes about abuse of the child. Occasionally, especially in high-conflict divorces, one or both parents tend to idealize their role based on the belief that they are the only good role model for the child (Walters and Friedlander, 2016). This can increase stress, even when the other parent is found to be suitable by caseworkers. Children in high-conflict divorces tend to side with the parent most likely to gain custody in a "chameleon" strategy to protect themselves (Garber, 2014). In some countries, there is less conflict over custody, as custody arrangements are less variable (see Kalmijn, 2010). Public attitudes about parenting time and support after divorce can also influence how parents handle and adjust custody (Braver, Ellman, and Fabricius, 2015).

After divorce, most couples or parents find themselves unprepared for the new challenges they face and the inadequacy of counselling and support services. Even in the best post-divorce circumstances, many factors challenge a parent's efforts to maintain closeness with their children. A study by Yarosh, Chew, and Abowd (2009) found that parents and children faced communication challenges when children were away from the residential parent's home and visiting at the other parental house. Children found it difficult to carry on conversations about activities they did at the other parent's home and found phone conversations awkward. It was also difficult for them to think of meaningful topics for discussion. Ex-spouses were also hesitant to call their child while visiting for fear they would interrupt the flow of activities at the other house. Remarriage or a new partnership also added further complexity to interactions between ex-spouses as well as with children (Shaff, Wolfinger, Kowaleski-Jones, and Smith, 2008; Weiss, 1996).

Remarriage is associated with less frequent co-parental interaction, less reported parenting support from the former spouse, and more negative attitudes about the other parent for both women and men. For men, remarriage predicts lower levels of parenting satisfaction and involvement in children's activities (Christensen and Rettig, 1995). However, some research is finding that there are more benefits for children in remarried families than previous studies have indicated (Shaff et al., 2008).

Non-custodial fatherhood has increased due to increases in divorce and births outside of unions. The standard divorce—the mother with custody, the father with child support responsibilities and visiting rights—is the reality in most cases involving longer duration marriages, higher male income, and younger children. That said, joint or shared custody is becoming the norm in divorces where dependent children are involved (Bauserman, 2012; Cancian, Meyer, Brown, and Cook, 2014). Access to the children is seen as essential to some, but not all, non-custodial parents, and visiting

International Findings about Divorce

- As in Western societies, educational level in Japan is associated with divorce risk, which is lower among mothers with a university degree (Raymo, Iwasawa, and Bumpass, 2004). Divorced mothers in Japan have full custody of children. The parent without custody typically has no access to the child and is out of the child's life (Morely, n.d.).

- Russia has one of the world's highest divorce rates. Divorced Russian women with children have little likelihood of remarrying. One major reason for this is the shortage of men: Workers' mortality rates are high. There is a significantly higher proportion of women in their thirties than there are men (Nesterov, 2004).

- Although divorce is allowed, it is not widely practised in India. Where most marriages are arranged, women gain their social status from their husbands. When divorce occurs, the wife moves out. Her social connections also break down, as she is discouraged from befriending men and from socializing with married couples. The worry is that a divorced woman might be a marriage wrecker (Sonawat, 2001).

- Political and cultural resistance to divorce is strong in Italian society, where traditional family is deeply rooted. Italy has the lowest divorce rate in Europe, followed by Ireland, at 0.73 per 1000 population in 2003 (United Nations Demographic Yearbook, 2003). Yet separations occur, suggesting that unhappy married couples remain separated rather than taking legal steps to divorce (De Rose, 2001).

- In the Netherlands, adults who choose to remarry after a divorce are younger on average (42 to 47 years) than those who choose living apart together (59 to 64 years; De Jong Gierveld, 2004).

- Divorce in China is rare, at only 10 to 15 percent of the population. Society and neighbourhood groups become mediators when marriages fail, often preventing divorce. Divorced Chinese women are more likely to remarry than men and to remarry sooner (Dong, Wang, and Ollendick, 2002), unlike in the West.

is important to the quality of the subsequent father–child relationship (Peters and Ehrenberg, 2008). Access and child support are complementary, and joint custody tends to improve father–child relations, reduce parenting stress and conflict, and improve compliance (Bauserman, 2012). Most mothers are willing to allow visitation even if the father does not pay child support, thus acknowledging the importance of father–child relationships (Laakso, 2004).

By a large margin, in Canada fathers usually become the non-custodial parent through divorce, and this can lead to divorce-related emotional distress; dissatisfaction with custody, visitation, and child support arrangements; perception of divorce proceedings as unfair; and ongoing conflicts with former spouses (Dudley, 1996; Kruk, 2010). Moreover, this disempowerment, loss of legal custody, and relegation to the role of an economic provider can have a profound impact on a father's masculine identity (Kruk, 2010). Fathers often have limited contact with their children after divorce, and this contact decreases over time. With some divorced fathers, however, contact remains strong. Fathers are more likely to see preschool-aged children every week than they are to see school-aged children (Stephens, 1996). Poor adjustment to reduced contact with children appears to be one of the factors in divorcing fathers having a suicide rate seven to nine times higher than that of divorcing mothers (Ide, Wyder, Kolves, and De Leo, 2010).

Although the standard for custody decisions remains "best interests of the child" (Kelly, 2007; Scott and Emery, 2014), the legal systems in North America decide in 68 to 88 percent of cases that sole custody should go to the mother. Of course, mothers tend to be the primary caregivers. Fathers have primary custody in 8 to 14 percent of cases, and shared custody is the decision only 2 to 6 percent of the time (Braver, Ellmanm, Votruba, and Fabricius, 2010). By contrast, in Sweden, joint custody has reached levels of 30 to 40 percent. This greater gender equality in parenthood has led to increased female participation in the workforce (Juby, Le Bourdais, and Marcil-Gratton, 2005) and higher incomes for joint-custody mothers in Sweden.

Why do so many divorced fathers have reduced contact and visitation? Researchers offer many explanations. Divorcing parents in Canada have legal contests over access to the children twice as often as they do about child support (money) arrangements. It takes an average of a year and a half to resolve contested access cases (Statistics Canada, 2012h). For those involved, this extended uncertainty likely erodes father confidence in relations with the child. Non-residential fathers feel less competent and less satisfied in the role of father (Kruk, 2010). Typically, fathers of all kinds who identify strongly with the role of father are more frequently involved with their children. Non-residential fathers identify less strongly with the role (Juby, LeBourdais, and Marcil-Gratton, 2005; Minton and Pasley, 1996). Fathers may find it easier to modify the way they perceive themselves than to be assertive about custody or access when making parenting agreements, particularly when faced with a perceived choice of conflict over access and custody. However, research shows that joint custody need not translate to increased levels of parental conflict (Halla, 2013). Some research indicates that conflict negates the benefits children would otherwise gain from having access to their father. But in an analysis of 40 studies on joint custody, researchers found that "the children in shared parenting families had better outcomes on measures of emotional, behavioral, and psychological well-being, as well as better physical health and better relationships with their fathers and their mothers, benefits that remained even when there were high levels of conflict between their parents" (Nielsen, 2014: 613). Other studies find the opposite—that the mental health of children in joint custody situations is less good than when they live in a sole custody situation (Bergström et al., 2014). Still, for many fathers, interest in spending time with their children declines within the first year of divorce proceedings. Identity changes and uncertainty cause emotional disinvestment. Stress is a factor, as is the degree of involvement prior to divorce and whether abuse occurred in the family (Madden-Derdich and Leonard, 2000).

Prior to divorce, fathers are more emotionally invested in parenting and caregiving than their fathers might have been, thanks in part to education and egalitarianism inspired by second-wave feminism and education. Unfortunately, they seem to still carry the burden of past gender family roles into present-day family law decisions. Although the motherhood presumption (Russo, 1976) was invalidated in 1985, in 2010 children resided predominantly with their mother in 70 percent of divorced households (Statistics Canada, 2015). Unpaid caregiving remains predominantly a burden borne by women, compromising their availability for workforce participation. Thus, income after divorce recovers more slowly for women partially because women predominantly have sole custody in Canada. It appears that the ideal of sharing the burden of care equally between mothers and fathers encounters barriers in the family law divorce process, in social norms, and in a variety of related areas.

Effects on Women

This section emphasizes the adverse effects of divorce. However, we will begin by acknowledging that divorce may also have benefits. For example, divorced mothers whose marriages were difficult, and sometimes abusive, are typically relieved when their marriages are over. However, even among those who are happy to be out of a bad or intolerable relationship, a majority expresses concern about the situations they face after divorce. They tend to face diminished opportunities and perceived second-class treatment (Kurz, 1995; Warrener, Koivunen, and Postmus, 2013).

Because women and men have different experiences after a divorce, they behave differently. For example, separated men are six times as likely as married men to commit suicide, especially in the younger age groups (Barrett and Turner, 2005). However, separated women do not have much higher suicide rates than married women. After divorce, both male and female suicide rates rise (Ide, Wyder, Kolves, and DeLeo, 2010). Thus, as Durkheim said, marriage protects both sexes, but it does so differently. Women with more children have lower suicide rates than women with fewer children, for example. It is possible that their child-rearing responsibilities protect women against suicide. This protection erodes as their children become independent.

Divorce depresses both women and men, but not always and not in the same ways. But, of course, causality can work the other way too: Depression can pose challenges for a union and contribute to divorce (Davila, Stroud, and Starr, 2008). However, women undergoing divorce show greater increases in rates of depression. Men whose marriages are breaking up typically show higher rates of alcohol problems (Felix, Robinson, and Jarzynka, 2013; Wu and Hart, 2002), and risk of heart attack is higher for divorcees than for non-divorced persons and especially so for divorced women (Wu and Hart, 2002). Women report more distress but not more alcohol problems. These findings support the idea that men externalize their problems in response to circumstances that lead women to internalize. Women also show more symptoms of distress before the separation, whereas men display more symptoms after the final separation. Researchers must measure men's and women's well-being differently, and therapists need to help them in gender-appropriate ways. Feminist research has found that therapy is not always sensitive to gender needs and differences (Calixte, Johnson, and Motapanyane, 2010).

After divorce, women suffer a decline in their standard of living. A classic American study by Lenore Weitzman (1985) estimated a decline of 73 percent in women's standard of living, compared to a 42 percent decline for men in the first year after divorce. (For comparable Canadian data, see Finnie, 1993, which is discussed below. For more recent analyses, see Gadalla, 2009). This drop in standard of living occurs even among less advantaged subgroups, such as African American and Hispanic low-income adults. Most young minority men fare poorly after divorce in absolute economic terms. However, young minority women fare even worse, a disparity that stems, either directly or indirectly, from women's roles as primary caregivers for children (Smock, 1994). Reform of child custody standards has been recommended by various competing perspectives for more than 40 years, but inertia persists.

Finnie's (1993) Canadian research also demonstrates that both men's and women's income drops as a result of divorce, but women's income drops twice as much, on average. Men tend to recover lost income more quickly than women in the aftermath of divorce. As well, since men have higher income, they are less likely to be poor (Ambert, 2005b). The poverty triggered by marital dissolution is less likely to affect men than women (Vandecasteele, 2011). Thus, divorce is much more likely to plunge divorced women into poverty and keep them there for longer. This is especially true if they have children for whom they are solely or largely responsible.

Also, women usually get custody of the children, which means that fewer dollars have to support more people. And women with children may have stepped away from paid employment to work at home with the children while they are young, thus reducing their years of income and work experience. This also means reduced contributions to pension plans and risks of lower income in their older years, too (LaRochelle-Côté, Myles, and Picot, 2012). Low income is the cause of higher levels of life strains reported by separated women, according to a six-year longitudinal study (Nelson, 1994). On the other hand, some researchers find that "fathers are better off after divorce, for they can now spend most of their money on one person, themselves . . ." (Goode, 1993: 166). Some divorced fathers dutifully provide child support for their children after divorce, and researchers like Finnie (1993) have found that those fathers' incomes drop, though not as much as women's do.

Women's economic disadvantage after divorce is largely due to the traditional practice of investing male human capital in the wage labour market and female human capital in the family and home. This is a structural circumstance that feminist research has shown disadvantages women throughout their life courses, particularly if they withdraw from the paid labour force to raise children (Se'ver, 2011). The latter greatly disadvantages women after divorce, when women are likely to receive inadequate compensation for time spent out of the wage labour market. Even women with almost the same educational background as men are at a considerable disadvantage over time.

The impact of divorce is often lifelong; the healing and recovery processes take time. Healing is influenced by such variables as age of the woman and children, potential for employment, remarriage, coping skills, social networks, and income changes. Having a steady, satisfying job is associated with higher self-esteem and lower distress among divorced women. A good job provides meaning, social interaction and support, productivity, positive distraction, and, fundamentally important, income. Spiritual practice helps some women. Others change their behaviours to reduce stress. They may take up exercise or otherwise focus on nurturing a healthy body; they may take classes or take up hobbies to improve their mental well-being; they may revamp their personal appearance to give themselves a boost. (For more on this theme, see Wallerstein and Blakelee, 1990.) We will discuss more about life after divorce in Chapter 11, when we consider fresh family starts.

Effects on Children

In the past, many couples avoided divorce and stayed together "for the sake of the children." Their concern was, in some respects, justifiable. Divorce can have harmful effects on the children involved. However, research shows repeatedly that the effects of divorce on children as well as on parents depend very much on what is happening in the family before divorce and the quality of family relationships during and after the divorce (Amato, 2010; Amato and Booth, 1996; Amato, Loomis, and Booth, 1995; Smart and Neale, 1999; Stacey, 1996). If the family is violent or if family relationships are abusive and hostile, for example, then divorce might provide relief. The effects on children also depend on the society's or community's values. If, for example, a community believes that divorce is bad under almost all circumstances, the negative effects for all involved, including children, will be worse (Kalmijn, 2010).

Hetherington and Kelly (2002) suggest that the negative long-term effects of divorce on children may have become so exaggerated that it has become a self-fulfilling prophecy. For example, children of divorced parents can display poorer social and

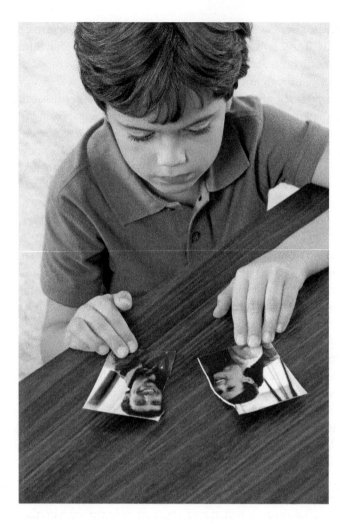

Children who have witnessed divorce, on average, show higher levels of depression, anxiety, and loneliness. Some children may even blame themselves for the divorce and may have particular difficulty in adjusting to new circumstances.

Pixland/Getty Images

psychological adjustment than children from non-divorced homes (Kunz, 1992: 352). More recent research, however, shows that a mother's education and income are crucial factors in the effects of divorce on children's achievements (Shaff et al., 2008).

However, if schools, counsellors, and parents are taught to look for these outcomes, that could account, in part, for why they find them more often. When the children grow up, they are much more likely than those from intact families to think that their own marriages may be in trouble. Were there other differences in these children prior to divorce? Are their subsequent expectations about their own marriages a result of childhood experience or of much-hyped research showing negative outcomes?

Research (Statistics Canada, 2005f) has found that the tension and turmoil leading up to a divorce are more harmful to children's mental health than the divorce itself.

If most of the damage is done to children who live in families where there is constant fighting, then staying together, especially for the sake of the children, may not be the wisest choice.

Parental divorce can increase the risk of adolescent depression in two ways. First, it may be a source of many secondary problems and stresses that cause depression. Second, it can alter youths' reactions to these stresses, sometimes increasing the depressive effects (Davila, Stroud, and Starr, 2008). Economic hardships, a common outcome of divorce for children, also increase the risk of depression, thus accounting for the greater vulnerability of youths in single-parent families to depression (Amato and Sobolewski, 2001; Aseltine, 1996). That these factors go together makes it challenging for researchers to sort out the independent effects of divorce per se.

On the other hand, separation and divorce can improve family functioning (Statistics Canada, 2005f), especially if custody rules are clear and agreed upon, civility is maintained, and peaceful order is beneficial to both parents. Mothers with joint custody report lower levels of parenting stress and better co-parental relations than sole-custody mothers (Bauserman, 2012). However, joint custody is known to be more probable as well as more workable for couples who get along better in the first place and put their children's interests above their own (Bauserman, 2012; Smart and Neale, 1999). This produces a happier set of parents, which will no doubt lead to better parenting.

Other things being equal, marriage or living in a stable, caring, long-term relationship is better for children than divorce. Children living in lone-mother families with no parental conflict and with continuing contact with the non-residential father still have lower levels of well-being, on average, than children who live in two-parent families without parental conflict. However, the well-being of children living in peaceful single-mother families is higher than that of children living in two-parent families with a lot of parental conflict. The degree of parental conflict after divorce is more important for the well-being of children than is contact with the absent father. That is, it is better for the children of divorce that the father does not come around if parental arguments break out when he does (Dronkers, 1996; Peters and Ehrenberg, 2008).

Beyond the effects on thinking and feeling, divorce is correlated with variations in children's behaviour. So, for example, in a family that is not abusive, divorce can be related to deterioration in children's school performance; increased proneness to crime, suicide, and out-of-wedlock births; lesser adult work performance; and the likelihood of the children themselves becoming divorced later in life (Galston, 1996; Shaff et al., 2008). The experience of divorce may weaken trust in people and institutions and impede the capacity to form stable, enduring relationships.

Parental divorce and remarriage have strong effects on children's attitudes toward premarital sex, cohabitation, marriage, and divorce, even after controlling for parental attitudes (Axinn and Thornton, 1993). Thus, children do not merely replicate their parents' values and attitudes toward non-marital sex, marriage, and divorce, but develop an approach that incorporates their life course experience. Kozuch and

Cooney (1995) as well as Amato (2010) note, however, that results from studies using parental marital status to predict young adults' attitudes have been inconsistent. In Kozuch and Cooney's survey of young adults from a variety of backgrounds, parental marital status predicted only two of the five attitudes toward marriage and family. By contrast, level of parental disagreement predicted four of the five.

Children of divorce often marry earlier, are more likely to cohabit, achieve less economically, and hold more pro-divorce attitudes. All of these factors account for some intergenerational transmission of divorce. However, holding these factors constant, behaviour problems play the largest part in this transmission of divorce. Children witnessing their parents' divorce are more likely than other children to learn behaviours that interfere with the maintenance of stable intimate relationships (Amato, 1996)—for example, to learn how conflict works but not how cooperation works. All of these findings, however, have become less and less common in children of divorce as divorce has become more common. In fact, children whose parents have divorced are now as diverse as children from intact families.

Divorce has been associated in the past with less formal schooling, possibly because young people with divorced parents may have less family financial support for pursuing postsecondary education. The support they receive is much more likely to come from their custodial than non-custodial parent. Thus, the lower educational and occupational attainment of children of divorce is more likely associated with reduced financial support than with a loss of confidence in higher education. Students who excel can easily find financial support for higher education, however, through scholarships or student loans.

Despite these seemingly negative outcomes for children of divorce, research indicates only a moderate risk of increased problem behaviours (20 to 25 percent of children of divorced families have problem behaviours compared to 10 percent of children of never-divorced families) (Kelly, 2003). Although 75 percent of college-aged children of divorced families have painful memories and feelings of loss as well as feel regret over missed time with fathers, researcher Joan Kelly (2003) points to evidence that negative memories do not necessarily translate into problems or limitations for the majority of college students who experienced the divorce of their parents. Neither exposure to parental divorce nor exposure to parental conflict affects the quality of attachment to adult intimates, nor the quality of parenting (Amato, 2010; Tayler, Parker, and Roy, 1995) "While some studies have reported adolescent boys to be at greater risk than girls, no gender differences specifically linked to divorce were found in other studies of adolescents and young adults" (Kelly, 2003: 245).

Challenges in adolescence are common, whatever kinds of families one comes from. Coming from a divorced family may add to the challenges of adolescence. However, coming from a divorced family does not, in the end, diminish an individual's ability to cope with new challenges. In fact, it might contribute to resilience.

Relations with Parents

Since divorce often results in the departure of the biological father from the family, father–child relationships are often most affected (Peters and Ehrenberg, 2008). In a study by Dunn, Cheng, O'Connor, and Bridges (2004), positive relationships between children and non-resident fathers were correlated with ongoing contact between child and father, the quality of the mother–child relationship, and the frequency of contact between the mother and her former partner. Increasingly, children and fathers do preserve a continuing relationship after the divorce. However, on average, adolescents in divorced families get less advice from their fathers and feel less satisfied with paternal support. Adolescents from intact families say that they have more positive

»» Causes and Effects of Divorce

- In general, marriage is less likely to result in divorce for people who marry later, did not live common-law before the wedding, have children, attend religious services, are university educated, and believe that marriage is important if they are to be happy (Clark and Crompton, 2006).

- According to data from the National Population Health Survey (NPHS), men and women who go through a divorce tend to have a higher risk of being depressed in the two years following the end of the relationship. The risk is especially great for divorced men, who are six times more likely to be depressed than those who remain married (Davila, Stroud, and Starr, 2008; Rotermann, 2007).

- Divorcing fathers are seven to nine times more likely to commit suicide than divorcing mothers, although both are at highest risk when the separation or divorce is recent (Kõlves, Ide, and De Leo, 2011; Yip, Yousuf, Chan, Yung, and Wu, 2015). Elevated risk exists even when depression is factored out, indicating a need to understand how societies and communities can better support divorcing parents (Stack and Scourfield, 2015). Male suicide was not as high in U.S. states that had less-gendered rates of shared custody (Halla, 2013).

- Problems in the realm of work and household labour as well as emotional and psychological relationship problems have become more important motives for a divorce, especially for women. This is consistent with the increase in emancipatory attitudes in the past decades (de Graaf and Kalmijn, 2006; Mahoney and Knudson-Martin, 2009).

- Older women who are divorced are more likely to live in low income than older women who are widowed. With the rising older population, more older women are at risk for entering poverty in the future (LaRochelle-Côté, Myles, and Picot, 2012; Turcotte and Schellenberg, 2006).

- Changes in father–child contact are more closely linked to the mother's subsequent remarriage than to the father's. Non-resident fathers sometimes reduce the frequency of visits when their children acquire a stepfather, but visits are not significantly reduced after the birth of a child in the father's new union (Juby, Billette, Laplante, and Le Bourdais, 2007).

- Divorce may be associated with increased levels of anxiety and depression in children. However, child antisocial behaviour decreases when marriages in highly dysfunctional families are dissolved (Strohschein, 2005).

emotional relationships with their fathers than do adolescents from divorced or remarried families. Adolescents who live with both parents may fight their fathers to achieve independence. However, this can be a good thing, related to the development of more self-esteem and a stronger ego identity (McCurdy and Scherman, 1996).

Amato and Booth (1996) used data from a 12-year longitudinal study of marital instability to examine the effects of divorce on parent–child relationships. The quality of the parents' marriage has both direct and indirect implications for later parent–child affection. Problems in the parent–child relationship before divorce, and low quality in the parents' marriage when children were (on average) 10 years old, led to low parental affection for the children when they were (on average) 18 years old. Divorce continued to undermine affection between fathers and children, although not between mothers and children. Thus, when there is a long history of turbulence and indifference, the break in a father–child relationship may predate divorce. Departure may reduce the child's access to his or her father. However, fathers who maintain contact remain important people in their children's lives and an important source of support in times of stress (Munsch, Woodward, and Darling, 1995; Peters and Ehrenberg, 2008; Smart and Neale, 1999).

As we have seen in previous chapters, there is a substantial amount of research on the lives of single mothers and the difficulties they face raising children. There is much less literature on father involvement in child rearing following a parental split. Edin, Tach, and Mincy (2009) used data from the Fragile Families and Child Wellbeing Study and from interviews with 150 unmarried fathers to understand contemporary non-marital father involvement. The authors found that "father involvement drops sharply after the parents' relationships end, especially when they enter subsequent relationships and have children with new partners" (Edin et al., 2009: 149).

As seen in Figure 9.7, father involvement is important not only for the welfare of the children involved but also because it affects the outcome of important deliberations about child custody and family reunification. For various reasons, unknown father cases rarely result in parent–child reunification. Mothers who are unable or unwilling to identify their child's likely father may have other characteristics that are related to the likelihood of an adoption outcome. The uncertainty about a father's identity may point to a broader family dysfunction, for example. As well, if an initial placement with a relative works out well, the caseworker may be reluctant to seek contact even with an identified father.

Compared with those who grew up in two-parent families, the adult children of divorced parents perceive their relationships with both mothers and fathers to be of lower quality. The quality is two or three times lower for fathers than for mothers. Usually, memories of parental conflict or other family problems can explain the effect of parental divorce on relationship quality. Adult children of divorce also have much less current contact with their parents than do adults from two-parent families (Webster and Herzog, 1995), although the effect on father–child relations is moderated by the degree to which divorce offered relief from the stress of interparental conflict, the

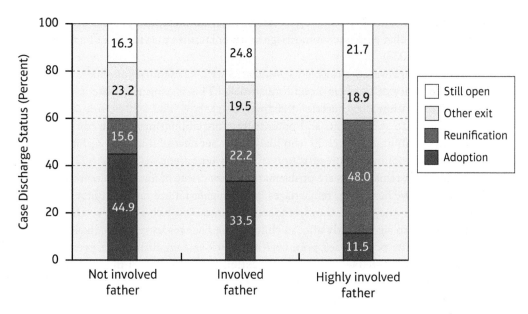

Figure 9.7 Discharge outcome by level of non-resident father involvement

Source: Prepared for U.S. Department of Health and Human Services et al. Washington, D.C. 2008.
More about the Dads: Exploring associations between nonresident father involvement and child welfare
case outcomes. http://aspe.hhs.gov/hsp/08/moreaboutdads/

father's resources, and the father's level of education (Kalmijn, 2015). Children evaluate their relationships with mothers more positively than those with fathers. They evaluate pre-separation relationships more positively than post-separation relationships, with some recovery after the passage of time. A positive relationship with one parent contributes negatively to the evaluation of the other parent after separation, suggesting that separation typically polarizes loyalties (Hoffman and Ledford, 1995; Walters and Friedlander, 2016). As divorce had become much more common in generations earlier, this means that fewer older people now may have close relations with their adult children, with implications for care as they age. This may also be true for parents of adult immigrants whose older parents may live in the homeland.

Stepfamilies Stepfamilies, often formed by the remarriage of biological parents after their divorce, are multiparent families that may give children as many as two full sets of parents (and siblings) and four sets of grandparents. The presence of loving parents and grandparents can be a real plus for a child, under the right circumstances. However, stepfamilies can pose problems too, for a variety of reasons. Stepfamilies are formed after divorce, and marital conflict precedes the divorce. So, there are problems to solve—bad feelings between the former spouses—even before the new families begin. These feelings can affect the relationship between children and the step-parent. Portrie and Hill (2005) found that a mother's conflicts with the former spouse have negative effects on children and their stepfathers. However, other research finds that a parent's remarriage and stepfamilies provide benefits to children (Shaff et al., 2008)

Chiefly, however, the problems associated with stepfamilies are due to the number and rapidity of changes a child must make. This is especially true if the remarriage occurs within a few years of the divorce.

Adapting to new parents and potentially more siblings may cause confusion and stress for the child. Even a child who likes his or her new siblings may feel in competition with stepsiblings for the affection of his or her parent.

Moreover, remarriages are problematic if they create an unstable environment for the child. As we have seen, remarriages have a higher failure rate than first marriages. However, when they work, they last for a long time. Research also shows that changes in parenting can significantly affect a child. These changes increase the likelihood that a child will suffer poor grades, poor health, low self-esteem, drug abuse, peer rejection, and lower self-reported well-being. At the extreme, a succession of divorces and remarriages presents an unstable environment, especially since expectations change with each new parent. We will talk more about remarriage and stepfamilies in Chapter 11.

In sum, for children, parents, and other relatives, divorce, like other major life events, has impacts. However, the extent or permanence of those impacts may be less negative than unending marital discord. Providing gender-equitable access to community supports and resources for those experiencing the stress of divorce can lead to more positive outcomes. Factors that reduce the adverse effects of divorce on children include a strong and clear sense that both parents still love them, an understanding that they are not to blame for the divorce, and regular visits with the non-custodial parent. Parental conflict, as we have said often, has a negative effect in both intact and divorced families (Weiner, Harlow, Adams, and Grebstein, 1995).

The impact of divorce on children varies enormously, depending on many factors, including the responsiveness of parents, schools, and communities. Overall, young adults are optimistic about marriage, and their parents' divorce does not have

⟫⟫ Stepfamilies

Stepfamilies can be classified as either *simple* or *complex*. In a simple stepfamily, all children are the biological or adopted children of one and only one married spouse or common-law partner. A complex stepfamily consists of any of the following:

■ Families in which there is at least one child of both parents and at least one child of only one parent

■ Families in which there is at least one child of each parent and no children of both parents

■ Families in which there is at least one child of both parents and at least one child of each parent.

In the 2011 Census, of the 3 684 675 couple families with children, 87.4 percent were intact families and 12.6 percent were stepfamilies (Statistics Canada, 2012a).

a large impact on their attitudes toward marriage and divorce (Landis-Kleine, Foley, Nall, Padgett, and Walters-Palmer, 1995).

Although divorce may sometimes cause problems, it sometimes also solves problems. Divorce spares many children serious problems. It may even bring benefits. People whose parents divorced during their adolescent years display a much higher level of moral development than those whose parents did not divorce (Kogos and Snarey, 1995). Underlying the development of moral judgment is an increased perspective-taking, necessary for children of divorce who witness differences in opinions between their parents. But, of course, witnessing differences of opinion is not limited to parents who divorce.

Effects on Older Adults

We have seen that today's older generation has more diverse family networks than previous generations. For example, older people today are more likely than previous cohorts to have experienced divorce. (For a look at the average age of Canadians who divorce, see Figure 9.8.) Therefore, it is important to understand how trends in family

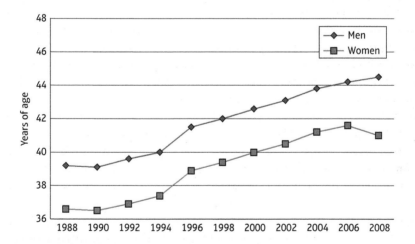

Figure 9.8 Average age at divorce, Canada, 1988 to 2008

Note: Average age at divorce is calculated using data from actual divorces occurring in a particular year.

Sources: Data from Skills Development Canada. 2012. Indicators of well-being in Canada. Retrieved from http://www4.hrsdc.gc.ca/.3ndic.1t.4r@-eng.jsp?iid=76&bw=1; For 1986 to 1996, Statistics Canada. 1999. Vital Statistics Compendium, 1996. Ottawa: Statistics Canada, Heath Statistics Division. Catalogue no. 84-214-XPE; For 1997 to 2003, Statistics Canada. Divorces. Shelf tables. Ottawa: Statistics Canada, 1999–2005; For 2004, Statistics Canada. 2008. 30 and 50 year total divorce rates per 1,000 marriages, Canada, provinces and territories (annual rate per 1,000 marriages) (CANSIM Table 101-6511). Ottawa: Statistics Canada; For 2006 to 2008, Statistics Canada, Health Statistics Division. 2011. Canadia

life and partnership dissolution may affect future support and care for older adults, given that their social networks are largely composed of family members (Askham, Ferring, and Lamura, 2007; LaRochelle-Côté, Myles, and Picot, 2012).

On the one hand, there is the belief that the experience of divorce weakens family ties, thereby reducing family support. There is evidence that divorce can have negative effects on support at older ages (Curran, McLanahan, and Knab, 2003; Kalmijn, 2007; Shapiro, 2003). It has been suggested that older people who have gone through divorce experience decreased contact and relationship quality with adult children as well as perceived support from children when compared with those in intact marriages (Curran et al., 2003; Kalmijn, 2007). Furthermore, a Canadian study has shown that divorce followed by remarriage among older couples is accompanied by decreased support from networks of friends (Schlesinger and Schlesinger, 2009).

On the other hand, it has been suggested that the deleterious effects of partnership dissolution for support in later life may be disappearing (Thornton and Young-DeMarco, 2001). For instance, Glaser, Stuchbury, Tomassini, and Askham (2008) found that partnership dissolution did not have a detrimental association with late-life support. In fact, separated older parents (age 70 and older) were significantly more likely to receive help from their adult children than married older parents. This research also found that the level of family support increased with increasing age and the health needs of the older person, regardless of family history (Glaser et al., 2008). Thus, a changing notion of the definition of "family," a greater acceptance of divorce, and an increasing tolerance of different family forms could be contributing to the stability of intergenerational support relationships.

CONCLUDING REMARKS

As we have seen, divorce is both a micro-level and a macro-level phenomenon, with both micro- and macro-level effects. Little synthesis between macro- and micro-level analyses has been achieved. We are still far from having a comprehensive theory that predicts who will divorce and why, but our sociological insights are increasing.

The past 30 years have not fulfilled legislators' objectives in adopting no-fault divorce, although it is more prevalent now. Family lives have improved with expanded choice and happiness. Some have remarked on how the combined effect of increased divorce rates and increasing levels of childbearing in cohabiting relationships have ensured that more than half of the children born in the 1980s will be raised in single-parent families or in families where parents are not married for all or part of their lives. The decline of marriage has also led to paternal disinvestments in children. Divorced men are less likely to support children financially than men who live in intact families. Increased maternal earning capacity or improved public investment has not compensated for the decline in paternal support (Whitehead, 1996).

The conservative approach, largely found south of the border, to the problems of divorce, teen pregnancy (a problem in the United States but not in Canada), suicide, violence, and substance abuse is to blame the emerging culture of tolerance and the welfare state, contending that they undermine the benefits of self-reliance and community standards. The conservative definition of "family values" tends to be far too narrow. However, the perspective rightly emphasizes the role of family in child rearing, whatever form it takes.

Progressives tend to recognize that increased unemployment, rising competition, and the need for dual-earner households have threatened the traditional family in some ways, or at least have posed challenges. However, they may overemphasize the extent to which government services can replace effective family bonds (Giele, 1996). Among socially conservative people, strategies to encourage the reinstitutionalization of the traditional family would include restricting the legal benefits of family life and of marriage. These would begin with tighter controls on entry into marriage, more difficulties in leaving a marriage through divorce, and legally defining marriage as a moral duty between partners, rather than as a personal contractual decision (Schneider, 1996). Some conservatives even suggest that marriage is the best solution to poverty for women.

Although it is not the job of sociologists to favour one side or the other, it is part of our responsibility to collect and examine evidence that would support one side or another. Here, sociology has an important role to play in the process by which a democratic society makes the policies and laws that govern family life.

The evidence shows us that divorce tends to be correlated with unhappiness and trouble. The question is, does divorce cause the unhappiness and trouble or do unhappiness and trouble cause divorce? Furthermore, does divorce prolong unhappiness and trouble or cut it short? While it is foolhardy to generalize about all divorces, there is no evidence to show that divorce is the cause of most family-related unhappiness. Although it is true that people benefit from stable family lives when those families are functioning well, it is also true that people suffer from family lives when those families function badly.

For better or worse, it is up to the participants to decide whether their family life works well or badly. Outsiders' impressions count for little. What counts is a person's individual experiences in families. If the people involved think that their family is working well, then to all intents and purposes, it is. If not, and efforts to correct the situation do not work, then divorce makes good sense—for the sake of the children as well as the spouses themselves, and sometimes for the sake of the extended family. After all, a child can experience good parenting without his or her father and mother living together. On the other hand, conditions of stress, violence, unhappiness, and depression make good parenting almost impossible. We must assume that most parents take these factors into account when they decide to stay together or divorce. This being so, the conservative viewpoint on divorce has little to offer us. The traditional family that conservatives crave may never have existed and may not have been the happiest of families in any case, particularly for women.

CHAPTER SUMMARY

In this chapter, we looked at the rise and now stability in divorce experienced since the middle of the twentieth century in most industrial societies. As social scientists, we look at the nature of social bonding, and our discussions on divorce cover not only some of the reasons behind increased divorce rates, but also the effects of divorce prevalence on individuals and society as a whole. Although these trends show a dramatic change in family structure and the functions the family plays in our lives, research has shown that our beliefs and attitudes about the role of the family have not kept pace. This makes the task of assessing the real impacts of divorce a bit more difficult, yet even more needed.

Historically, divorce has worried social scientists and policy-makers alike. This concern has grown with the increase of divorce rates worldwide. Divorce rates have now stabilized or declined in Canada and the United States as well as in other parts of the world. Social, legal, and cultural changes have all played a part in divorce trends.

Generally, causes of divorce should more accurately be called predictors, since it is easier to note relationships between variables than to pin down a clear cause-and-effect relationship. Factors influencing the likelihood of divorce are found at the micro, meso, and macro levels. Micro-level factors include poor communication, poor conflict-resolution skills, lack of commitment, lack of shared interests, and perceived inequity. Meso-level factors include age at marriage, marital duration, location, religiosity, class, and race. Macro-level factors include war, economic cycles, and cultural values.

The effects of divorce were then considered. Divorce can be a time of stress for spouses and children. Both men and women suffer a decline in standard of living, but men's incomes drop less and rebound faster. This effect is especially important for women, since they are most commonly the prime caregivers of children after a divorce. While there is dispute as to why it occurs (Adams, 2006), fathers become less connected to their children after divorce, although some do remain closely involved in parenting. Divorced fathers do less parenting than married fathers, although this is not always by choice. They provide less monetary resources than their married counterparts, and these funds do not seem to stretch as far. In some cases, debilitating impacts of marital and postmarital discord affect the self-esteem and job performance of both parents, and custodial parents face overwhelming time constraints when the non-custodial parent is not available to help. Evolving a family law culture that ceases to reward negative portrayals and reduces incentives for combative stances between former partners can do much to improve outcomes for all involved in divorce. Fault-finding for temporary gains in divorce settlements may reduce the resiliency and earning capacity of providers, resulting in higher, though less visible, long-term costs of perceived winning. A cooperative stance toward co-parenting and sharing resources naturally reduces the negative impacts of divorce (Lens, Katz, and Suarez, 2016).

Children tend to be distressed immediately after a divorce but gradually adjust. Finally, with a growing senior population in Canada, it is important to understand the trends and effects of separation and divorce in this population, especially how this affects intergenerational relationships in families. Women, in particular, who are divorced later in life are more apt to be poor in their later years, although both men and women who divorce are poorer than couples who remain married, and divorced persons have less retirement savings than married people.

The harmful effects of divorce are often talked about (McLanahan, Tach, and Schneider, 2013). Yet it is important to recognize that many of the harmful effects observed stem not from divorce per se but from poor family interactions prior to, during, and after the divorce. Hence, it may be important and helpful for families to seek professional help during this emotionally stressful time. Family therapy and mediation are just two examples of options available for people going through separation and divorce. A new focus on resiliency appears to be a useful recent trend in the helping professions (Black and Lobo, 2008; Walsh, 2002, 2015). We concluded the chapter with a look at some popular political viewpoints on divorce. There is a movement in the United States urging legal and policy changes to discourage divorce, in an attempt to alleviate some of the social burdens that divorce produces. We find many of the proposed solutions incomplete and ineffective because of the narrow interpretations of the problem, which label divorce rather than poor family interactions as the culprit.

Key Terms

adverse selectivity A tendency for people who choose to engage in a given behaviour to be, by nature of the kind of people they are, also at risk for a given outcome; selectivity may create the appearance of cause-and-effect relationships where they do not exist.

cohort effect The accumulated experience of going through life in the same set of years. For example, people born in the period 1924 to 1928 experienced World War II as teenagers and the postwar economic boom as young marrieds, and may have certain views or attitudes in common because of these experiences.

determinant A factor that contributes to an outcome (such as divorce) without necessarily being the direct or principal cause.

femininity A cluster of characteristics, such as nurturance, sensitivity, and gentleness, traditionally considered natural to women but that can be found in men or women.

macro-level The broad level of examining a social phenomenon, focusing on changes that affect society as a whole.

meso-level A middle range at which a social phenomenon may be examined, focusing on demographics—the characteristics of the people affected.

micro-level The smallest level at which a social phenomenon may be examined, the level of interactions between individuals and effects on individuals.

no-fault divorce Divorce granted because of marital breakdown rather than because of specific wrongdoing (e.g., adultery) on the part of one spouse or the other.

predictor A characteristic that is correlated with and precedes an outcome but may not be a direct cause.

secularization A move away from religion as an organizing principle of society.

social disorganization A breakdown of societal functioning.

social integration The state of societies that are closely knit and stable, in which people hold similar world views and there is a strong consensus on social rules.

social pathology A broad-based distress or disorganization within society.

socio-economic status Class; standing in society in terms of income, education, and prestige.

Critical Thinking Questions

1. In this chapter, you learned the importance of understanding the variation in divorce rates. (a) Formulate a sociological research question about divorce and propose how you would gather and analyze data on divorce rates. (b) Discuss how changes in the legal aspects of divorce may make it difficult to study the history of family breakdown and analyze divorce trends.

2. Discuss possible interventions that would lessen the negative impacts of divorce. For each approach, specify whether it addresses the micro-level, meso-level, or macro-level causes of divorce.

3. Children can be greatly affected by divorce. When parents repartner, children can find themselves living with more than one set of parents and in different homes with different rules. Discuss effective ways that stepfamilies can organize themselves to reduce conflict and stress.

4. The population of older adults in Canada is undoubtedly growing. Can you think how this may contribute to novel challenges faced by families, or the society at large, when either the parents or the grandparents divorce?

5. "Divorce rates are no longer a useful way of studying relationship dissolution, since so many people don't even bother getting married when they form a relationship." Do you agree with this statement? Why or why not?

Weblinks

Department of Justice: About Divorce and Separation
www.justice.gc.ca/eng/fl-df/divorce/sd.html
This site provides a list of links and information to help understand the legal issues and the process of divorce in Canada.

Ontario Association for Marriage & Family Therapy
http://rmft.oamft.com
This site is a resource for marriage and family therapists, as well as for the public interested in finding a therapist in Ontario or finding out about the profession in general.

Canadian Divorce Laws

www.canadiandivorcelaws.com

This site is a guide to the legal situation in Canada, written by a lawyer. It provides access to a library of articles on issues such as child support, child custody, spousal support, property division, and divorce procedure.

Ministry of the Attorney General—Family Law

www.attorneygeneral.jus.gov.on.ca/english/family

This site provides the public with comprehensive information about family law, the family court system, and legislation in Ontario.

Stepfamily Forum

www.stepfamily.net

This online forum and social networking site supports stepfamilies through sharing and discussion.

Organisation for Economic Co-operation and Development and (OECD) Family Database

www.oecd.org/els/family/database.htm

This OECD database includes crossnational information on family outcomes and policies as categorized under four broad headings: the structure of families, the labour market position of families, public policies for families and children, and child outcomes.

Families Change

www.familieschange.ca

This site, developed by the Province of British Columbia, provides easy-to-understand pamphlets and information about separation and divorce for kids, teens, and adults.

Chapter 10
Family Transitions and Diversity

Marc Debnam/DigitalVision/Getty Images

CHAPTER OUTLINE

- Introduction
- What Is a Family Transition?
- Social Change in Expected Transitions
- Family Transitions in the Past
- Family Transitions Past and Present: Immigrants and Transnational Families
- Transitions during Childhood
- Transitions to New Family Structures
- Transitions in Care Arrangements
- Delayed Home-Leaving

- Smaller Households and Single-Person Households
- Cohabitation, Marriage, and Relationship Dissolution
- Remarriage and Blended Families
- Money and Relationships
- Indigenous Families
- Lone-Parent Families
- Families and Disabilities
- New Contexts for Childbearing and Parenting
- Transitions in Midlife and for Seniors
- New Kinds of Close Relations
- Concluding Remarks

LEARNING OBJECTIVES

1 Understand the social change that has occurred in family transitions and how contemporary transitions compare to those experienced by previous generations.

2 Identify the transitions in family structure and care experienced by children and understand how the experiences of children today differ from previous generations.

3 Explain why household size is declining, and account for the growing popularity of living alone.

4 Describe some of the connections between cohabitation, marriage, relationship dissolution, and remarriage.

5 Describe the change that has occurred in the expected transitions for adults in midlife and for seniors.

6 Outline the challenges faced by lone parents, newcomers, Indigenous families, and families with a disabled family member.

7 Consider how childbearing and parenting have changed.

INTRODUCTION

Family transitions are inevitable as individuals transition from their families of origin to their own relationships, living arrangements, and families. In this chapter, we explore the varied family transitions experienced by individuals over the life course from childhood to adulthood. The prevalence of divorce and parental relationship dissolution means that many Canadian children will experience multiple family transitions during childhood. Transitions for adults have been transformed by the popularity of cohabitation, diversity in types of intimate relationships and families, and ideological change in how people think about personal fulfillment, sexuality, and intimate and family relationships. This diversity is celebrated and reflected in mainstream media and popular culture, such as in television shows like *Modern Family*.

In this chapter, we look at the kinds of transitions Canadians experience, particularly as they form intimate relationships and experience relationship breakup, possible subsequent relationships, and family reconfiguration. In their decisions about whether to partner, what kind of family they choose to build, or what kind of new relationships and families they experience due to unforeseen circumstances or circumstances not of their choosing, people create and recreate close relations. We are at a point in history where people are questioning how they might be defined by their intimate relationships and family ties and what these relationships will look like.

Modern Family is a popular American television program that began in 2009 and depicts the lives of three different kinds of families (nuclear, blended, and same-sex) in which parenthood is variously defined by biology, remarriage, and adoption. The show reflects broader societal changes and raises questions about how we might define and actively create families.
FOX/Photo 12/Alamy Stock Photo

Not only is there greater choice in relationships, but more people are also deciding to live alone and are defining their lives in ways that differ from previous generations. Given these trends, the question arises as to whether individuals place less importance on family relationships and are less likely to define themselves by their family or romantic relationships.

We also take a look at how social and technological changes offer opportunities for a redefinition of families, parenthood, and intimate relationships. All of these changes mean that there are greater choices for individuals, but they also mean that individuals may not be able to look to earlier generations, such as parents and grandparents, as examples in forging their private lives. The challenges faced by many Canadian families, particularly lone-parent, transnational and immigrant families, Indigenous families, and families experiencing the disability of a family member are also addressed in this chapter.

WHAT IS A FAMILY TRANSITION?

Family transitions are varied, can be planned or unplanned, and occur when an individual experiences a new living arrangement, intimate partnership, family structure, or substantive change in his or her family, such as a move into or out of paid employment or caregiving or the new realities faced when a family member has a disability. Transitions can shrink a household to a single-person household, a single parent with children, or empty nesters, and can also expand a household as new family members are added. Transitions extend beyond a change in partners or household membership to include transitions into or out of roles such as parent, single parent, step-parent, grandparent, empty nester, working parent, and non-working or retired parent, step-parent, or grandparent. Caregiving roles also change over an individual's lifetime and include the care of children and the elderly, disabled, injured, ill, or dying family member. Sometimes, caregiving roles follow more predictable life course sequencing, such as a parent caring for a child or aging parent, and sometimes they are unpredictable, such as a grandparent raising a grandchild, a parent caring for a seriously ill or disabled adult child, a young adult caring for a spouse who has suddenly become ill or disabled, or a child having to provide assistance to an ill or disabled parent. The term *sandwich generation* is used to describe individuals who are providing care simultaneously to young children and to aging parents. What makes the situation facing the sandwich generation particularly challenging as compared to earlier generations is that most of these individuals are also in full-time employment.

The underlying factors that might lead to transition are far ranging and are illustrated if we consider relationship dissolution. Breakups can be mutually agreed upon and amicable or unilateral and highly conflictual, such as when violence or emotional abuse necessitates exiting a relationship. Transitions sometimes happen as welcomed anticipated life events, such as a marriage, but sometimes happen when things do not go as expected or planned, such as an unplanned pregnancy or a partner leaving the relationship. Adaptations to transitions vary and are shaped by the amount of support an individual receives (Cooke, 2013; Fox, 2009), the resources the individual has to deal with the transition, and the individual's own level of resiliency to personal challenges. Challenges and stresses are not exclusive to difficult and unplanned family transitions such as the death of a family member or the end of a relationship. Challenges and stresses also follow welcomed, anticipated events such as marriage or the birth of a planned child. For example, research on the transition to parenthood suggests that many new mothers feel unprepared for the demands of mothering, and this is evidenced by the high prevalence of postpartum depression, baby blues, and other emotional difficulties faced by mothers (Rosenberg, 1987; Yount and Smith, 2012). Mothers who have greater social support are less likely to face these problems as compared to mothers who have little social support (Albuja, Lara, Navarrete, and Nieto, 2017; Chong, Gordon, and Don, 2017; Fox and Worts, 1999; Yount and Smith, 2012). Research on newly married couples reveals that many people experience stress with the labour, time, and expenses related to planning a wedding, and couples often underestimate how expensive a wedding will be, leading many into debt (Currie, 1993; Ingraham, 1999).

The root causes of transition are varied; they can be economic, or they can arise due to ideology, such as gender ideologies about appropriate roles for men and women. Economic pressures can precipitate a transition; for example, research done by Sassler and Miller (2011b) found that economic pressures, namely the high cost of housing, led many women to suggest cohabitation to their boyfriends. Research on divorced women finds that those with low income are likely to repartner because they require male economic support, whereas divorced women with higher incomes have lower rates of repartnering, as their financial resources afford them the opportunity to remain single (Goode, 1993). The opposite is true for divorced men; remarriage is more likely among higher-income men (Crosbie-Burnett, Skyles, and Becker-Haven 1988; Ihinger-Tallman and Pasley, 1987). Transitions are also tied to gender ideologies. For instance, the same research by Sassler and Miller (2011b) that showed that women initiated conversations about cohabitation with boyfriends because of economic pressures found that this same group of women believed that they needed to wait for their boyfriends to propose. These women did not initiate proposals or marriage; instead, they were "doing gender" (West and Zimmerman, 1987), in a sense, by waiting for boyfriends to ask them to get married. These women held the belief that men should make decisions about engagement and marriage. The fact that these women were waiting for marriage proposals reflected the power dynamics in their relationships; women lacked the power to move the relationship toward marriage. (Sassler and Miller, 2011b).

Contemporary Canadian families are diverse, and as such sociologists have turned their attention toward examining family processes rather than examining particular family structures. In considering family transitions and diversity, we observe individuals designing families anew, or rejecting family and intimate relationships, and negotiating with former family members or partners on such issues as how to co-parent children. An understanding of family dynamics gives us an appreciation of how individuals and families actively seek to meet the needs and challenges of intimate relationships and family life.

SOCIAL CHANGE IN EXPECTED TRANSITIONS

It is becoming normative for people to experience numerous relationships, living arrangements, and family reconfigurations. Younger generations experience a prolonged transition to adulthood as increased credentialism and the requirements of postsecondary education often result in the postponement of marriage and childbearing. Earlier generations faced a more continuous life course trajectory of completing their education, seeking employment, getting married, and having children. Younger generations are more likely to experience a discontinuous life course trajectory, whereby the sequencing of phases is less straightforward than it was for earlier generations. For instance, many people today return to postsecondary education to further their careers or to build new careers once they already have a family that they need to support. They might do so because of unemployment, underemployment, blocked job opportunities, low incomes, health issues, economic restructuring, corporate downsizing, or job dissatisfaction.

Young adults experience transitions that look different than those in their parents' and grandparents' generation. Unlike earlier generations, young adults today are more likely to live with their parents into adulthood or return to live with their parents several times. They are more likely to cohabit as compared to getting married as their first relationship and to experience numerous relationships. Serial monogamy refers to having one monogamous relationship at a time, but a person might have a number of different partners because of relationship breakup, divorce, death of a partner, or some other reason. Many individuals, some of whom are previously divorced, opt for dating rather than maintaining a monogamous relationship with one person. Sexual relations do not always occur within the context of an ongoing relationship. This is true not only of childless singles, but also of single parents who might opt for sexual relations outside of a relationship in order to maintain a separation between their family roles and their sex lives. The time pressures of single parenting may preclude romantic relationships, and some individuals opt to have sex outside of a relationship context. These sexual relationships take varying forms, including "one-night stands" or "hookups" for casual sex and "friends with benefits," where two people engage in a temporary or ongoing sexual relationship without the requirements of emotional support, commitment, or monogamy. Single, cohabiting, and married individuals and parents also move into and out of polyamorous relationships, which involve multiple partners (Boyd, 2017; Scheff, 2014).

Young adults are more likely to delay marriage, remain single, have fewer children, cohabit, and experience relationship dissolution or divorce as compared to earlier generations. They are also more likely to have children within the context of a cohabiting relationship, to have children with different partners, and to be a stepparent as compared to earlier generations. A growing number of Canadian children have been born to unmarried parents, particularly in Quebec. For instance, 1 in 3 births in this country are to unmarried women, most of whom are cohabiting (Marcil-Gratton and Le Bourdais, 1999, 2004). In Quebec, the rate is approximately 60 percent (Marcil-Gratton and Le Bourdais, 1999, 2004). Some sociologists have suggested that many lower socio-economic groups cohabit instead of marry because of a lack of resources. This is particularly true in the United States, where more whites than blacks marry and more well-educated Americans than less-educated Americans marry (Banks, 2011).

Family transitions continue throughout adulthood following divorce or widowhood as some individuals pursue later-life relationships. One change from earlier generations is the increase in divorce among older people. Phrases like "grey divorce" and "silver separations" have been used to describe older couples who divorce after decades-long marriages (LaRochelle-Côté, Myles, and Picot, 2012). Rates of remarriage for divorced or widowed individuals decline with age, yet many senior Canadians repartner. A significant recent change is that rates of remarriage or cohabitation following divorce are declining (Ambert, 2009). Divorced Canadians are taking longer to remarry or cohabit with a new partner, and an increasing number of divorced Canadians, particularly those with children, are not repartnering (Ambert, 2009).

FAMILY TRANSITIONS IN THE PAST

While some of the transitions we examine in this chapter are unique to the twentieth and twenty-first centuries, individuals have always experienced family transition over the life course. An example of this is remarriage. Prior to the twentieth century, when life expectancy was shorter, many married individuals remarried following the death of a spouse in order to maintain the economic viability of a household. The larger numbers of women who died during childbirth prior to the early twentieth century resulted in many blended or reconstituted families as men remarried. In preindustrial society, the labour of husbands and wives was required for agricultural or artisan households to survive, thus remarriage and reconstituted families were common, as were adoption and fostering. Reconstituted or **blended families** in the past came about due to parental death; today these families are primarily the result of divorce or relationship breakdown. Although the cause of family reconfiguration has changed, the economic vulnerability of single parents, particularly female lone parents, remains historically constant (Gordon and McLanahan, 1991).

FAMILY TRANSITIONS PAST AND PRESENT: IMMIGRANTS AND TRANSNATIONAL FAMILIES

Family transitions have always been a reality for newcomers to Canada confronted with the enormous economic and social challenges that accompany the settlement process. The immigration experience has the potential to strengthen or strain family relationships, challenge or undermine parent–child relationships, and redefine relations between spouses. It is important to point out that there is no singular, homogenous immigrant experience. More recent sociological research on the immigrant experience challenges earlier research by showing the diversity of the experience and highlighting how the immigration experience varies by many factors, such as the extent of support received either informally by friends and family or formally through institutions such as settlement agencies and socio-demographic variables such as race, ethnicity, religion, social class, gender, and age (Creese, Dyck, and McLaren, 2008).

In the first few decades after World War II, immigrants came largely from Europe, and these immigrants experienced much more upward social mobility as compared to more recent waves of immigrants. Since the 1990s, Canada has seen many more immigrants from China, Southeast Asia, the Middle East, Latin America, the Caribbean, and other parts of the world. This more recent groups of immigrants have faced a greater likelihood of downward social mobility, as foreign educational and workplace credentials are not always recognized by Canadian employers. One consequence is that rates of childhood poverty are much higher for the children of newcomers as compared to the children of Canadian-born parents (Polanyi, Mustachi, Kerr, and Meagher, 2016).

Parent–child relationships and spousal relationships are affected by the settlement process and can sometimes be transformed. Research done on parent–child relationships among earlier waves of newcomers to Canada revealed that children often served as cultural interpreters or translators for parents who needed help with English (Tyyska and Colavecchia, 2001). This can undermine parental authority, as parents become reliant on the language skills and assistance of their children. Research on immigrant youth has found that these youth report having to straddle two different cultures simultaneously in order to meet the expectations of their immediate and extended family and Canadian peers (Creese, Dyck, and McLaren, 2008). Tensions and conflict can arise if youth challenge the customs, religious practices, and social mores of their parent's country of origin in an attempt to conform to peer pressure and the influence of the wider Canadian society.

The settlement process can also challenge and transform gender relations and marital relations. Many highly educated immigrants who arrived since the 1990s have faced underemployment and unemployment. Newcomers who are accustomed to a more traditional nuclear family arrangement of a male breadwinner may face difficulty adapting to female employment in Canada. This is particularly true when wives have an easier time finding and keeping employment as compared to husbands. Even though earlier research on newcomers emphasized greater opportunities for gender equality and female financial independence, this is not always the reality for immigrant women (Man, 2004).

The term **transnational families** is applied to those families, both immediate and extended kin, who are separated geographically for varying lengths of time, including permanently. Often, the geographical separation is the outcome of immigration policy that prevents family members from moving to a new country together, such as Canada's Live-in Caregiver Program and the Seasonal Agricultural Workers Program. Transnational couples are separated when a migrant spouse comes to work in Canada, leaving behind a spouse. Migrant parents may leave behind non-migrant children, as is the case for many women who come to work as nannies and caregivers under the current Live-in Caregiver Program (Arat-Koc, 2006) and those who came under earlier immigration policies, such as those that resulted in large numbers of African-Caribbean women coming to work in Canada in order to provide financial support to their children in their country of origin (Crawford, 2011). Migrants may also leave behind older parents and siblings.

Although we may hear the term being used more frequently, transnational families are not new. They existed for earlier waves of immigrants, but the availability and lowered costs of new communications technologies, social media, and air travel have created opportunities for denser ties among transnational families. The high cost of air travel, long-distance phone calls, and lack of internet prior to the mid-1990s presented challenges to transnational families wanting to maintain connection. Inexpensive or free modes of communication make it easier for transnational families to keep in touch, and new technologies such as social media, video conferencing, and Skype allow family members to hear and see each other. Transnational caregiving entails much of the same kinds of care work done in families who are not separated geographically, such as maintaining strong ties with extended family and meeting the emotional and health needs of family members. Among the Indian immigrants to Canada interviewed by Somerville (2008), this transnational caregiving was gendered, as women assumed a disproportionate amount of the care work in transnational families.

The term *astronaut family* has been used by some writers to describe those families where typically the breadwinner has returned to work in the country of origin for a prolonged period of time (Kim, 2015; Man, 2015; Waters, 2002). For instance, a family has immigrated to Canada and the father returns to China for months at a time to work and support his wife and children, sometimes referred to as "satellite kids," in Canada. The term *parachute kids* has also been used by some writers to describe the situation where children in their late teen years have been transplanted into North American society and both parents have returned to the country of origin for employment or other reasons (Kim, 2014). Sometimes these young adults are left in the care of relatives, but the absence of daily parental supervision may give the appearance that these young adults have simply parachuted into the country on their own. The term also includes minors under the age of 18 who are studying in Canada, the United States, or elsewhere and may live in a school residence, with extended family, or with hired help. Transnational families challenge the notion that we might use co-residence as a way to define a family. Transnational families are yet another example that families are socially constructed and that membership is not limited to co-residence but determined and maintained by individuals themselves.

TRANSITIONS DURING CHILDHOOD

Transitions to New Family Structures

Children experience family transition in the event of parental divorce or parental relationship dissolution, and many Canadian children will live in more than one type of family structure before they reach adulthood and leave home. Thus, needing to adjust to changing families is becoming a more familiar experience for Canadian children, who may experience multiple transitions: from an original two-parent home, to a single-parent home, to a new blended family arrangement with new family members such as stepsiblings, step-parents, and other extended kin such as grandparents, aunts, and uncles. With increases in same-sex couples, the legalization of same-sex marriage in 2005, and increasing numbers of same-sex couples adopting children (Goldberg, 2012; Goldberg, Smith, and Perry-Jenkins, 2012; Raleigh, 2012), more children are now being raised by same-sex parents. Although there are no Canadian statistics on this, a growing number of children have transitioned from an opposite-sex parental home to a same-sex parental home. Many families headed by same-sex parents today had children within the context of a previous heterosexual relationship (Arnup, 2012; Dunne, 1998). The popularity of cohabitation and the instability of cohabiting relationships mean that some children have lived with or spent considerable time with numerous partners of one or both parents. Children who have developed an attachment to a parent's partner may experience loss or disruption in caregiving relationships when the parental relationship ends.

Children born to parents who have children from previous relationships do not always live with both parents. Some live with only one parent because of constraints preventing the couple from sharing a home. This can arise when partners decide that merging households would not be in the best interests of all of the children involved. Sometimes this living arrangement stems from geographical distance between partners who are in a long-distance relationship and may live in different cities, provinces, or countries. One partner may not be able to move because of custody arrangements with a former spouse. A child may live with only one of his or her parents, typically the mother, while the other parent visits, possibly during periods when children from a previous relationship spend time with the former spouse. There are also some Canadian children whose parents are legally separated or divorced yet live under the same roof because they cannot afford to maintain two residences. This arrangement may last for a short period of time, such as a one-year legal "in-house" separation while custody, access, and financial matters are resolved, or for a much longer period of time due to financial constraints. While all of these possibilities may sound quite complicated, they are a reality for Canadian children whose parents are no longer together. Transitions have become normative for a growing number of Canadian children.

Since rates of divorce began climbing in the 1960s, there has been ongoing concern and scholarly attention paid to the issue of the well-being of children following parental divorce or relationship breakup. The concerns are around children's emotional and physical well-being, their academic outcomes, and their later life outcomes such as level of educational attainment. This research suggests that there is variation in children's adjustment and resiliency following parental relationship dissolution (Amato and Sobolewski, 2001; Cherlin, 2001; Cherlin, Kiernan, and Chase-Lansdale, 1995; Fomby and Cherlin, 2007; Furstenburg and Cherlin, 1991). Children fare best when they are not exposed to a high level of parental conflict and when their daily routines are maintained (Chase-Lansdale, Cherlin, and Kiernan, 1995; Morrison and Cherlin, 1995). The adverse consequences of parental divorce are difficult to disentangle from the consequences of having fewer economic resources, as most women experience a decline in income following divorce. The tendency to focus on the potentially adverse consequences obscures more positive consequences that can also arise. Many people end relationships or get a divorce because they want to create a healthier home environment for their children free of parental conflict and other problematic issues such as abuse and addiction. Research on children who have gone through parental divorce finds that some develop coping skills, an ability to manage conflict and difficult situations, greater emotional resilience, and independence (Smart, 2006). Divorce can lead to an expansion of social networks and support for children, who might gain additional family members such as step-parents, stepsiblings, step-grandparents, cousins, aunts, uncles, and so on.

Less is known about the impact on children of multiple family transitions, such as going from a traditional nuclear family to a single-parent household or to a blended family with stepsiblings, step-parents, and new extended kin networks. Given that second marriages have higher rates of divorce than first marriages, that cohabiting relationships are less stable than marital relationships, and that an increasing number of divorces result in children living in two homes, there are children who have gone from living with both parents, to living with a single parent or moving between two households, to living with new step-parents, and back to living with a single parent only. That is a lot of transition and upheaval, and we do not know enough about how this affects children over the short or long term. Unfortunately, the fragility of adult intimate relationships is experienced in concrete terms by children who may experience a drop in economic resources; residential and schooling moves; the loss of adult and peer support; and the loss of familiar people, homes, schools, and neighbourhoods.

Transitions in Care Arrangements

Family composition or structure is one kind of transition; children also experience transitions in their care arrangements. This may arise following parental relationship dissolution but may also follow changes in the employment status of parents. A majority of Canadian children are taken care of in their first year of life by mothers on maternity leave. Most Canadian children experience transition at the age of 1 from care provided by their mother to another kind of care, as most women return to paid employment following the end of their maternity leave. In a study of parents in Ontario and Quebec, McKay and Doucet (2010) found that fathers deferred to mothers' preferences in making decisions about who would take parental leave and for how long. These decisions were shaped by women's breastfeeding, perceptions of workplace norms, and existing parental leave policy. Eligibility restrictions for women and Quebec's paternity leave facilitated men taking parental leave.

A majority of children are placed in unregulated, informal care arrangements because spots in regulated licensed daycare centres are scarce and expensive. Even though caregiving is performed disproportionately by women, more fathers are caring for their newborn children and more fathers are becoming "stay-at-home fathers." According to Statistics Canada, 20 percent of fathers received parental leave benefits in 2006 as compared to only 3 percent in 2000 (Marshall, 2008). Sometimes fathers become caregivers because of unemployment, but sometimes they actively decide to become the primary caregiver (Doucet, 2006). One of the more positive outcomes of divorce or relationship dissolution is that increasing joint physical custody may pull fathers who were previously less involved in caregiving into greater levels of caregiving and a closer relationship with their children. Another positive aspect of divorce is that there is the potential for greater accountability in parenting and oversight in those situations where problematic behaviours such as abuse and addiction are affecting children. In an intact marriage, these problems can remain invisible and not addressed, but in the context of divorce there is the potential for these problems to be addressed by lawyers, mediators, family court judges, child custody assessors, and child welfare officials.

DELAYED HOME-LEAVING

Delayed home-leaving has been increasing in Canada (Mitchell, 2006; Statistics Canada, 2007) and in many other industrialized countries as adult children require the support of parents to pursue postsecondary education and also because of unstable employment, dissolved relationships, and the rising costs of home ownership. Young adults are more likely to live at home for longer than their parents' generation did and are more likely to become "**boomerang kids**" who move back into the parental home, perhaps even several times, in adulthood. This has been described as the "revolving door" through which adult children leave and come back several times, perhaps with a spouse or children. It has also been described as the "cluttered nest." The "empty nest" period of parents is now shorter due to delayed home-leaving. Not only are younger adults taking longer to set up their own households, but the sequencing of major life transitions and milestones is less linear and predictable as compared to their parents' generation.

According to the 2011 Census, 42 percent of Canadians ages 20 to 29 lived with their parents (Statistics Canada, 2012c). There has been a significant increase in young adults living with parents in the last three decades. For example, in 2011, 59 percent of 20- to 24-year-olds and 25 percent of 25- to 29-year-olds lived with parents as compared to 41.5 percent of 20- to 24-years-olds and 11 percent of 25- to 29-year-olds in 1981 (Statistics Canada, 2012c). Economic pressures facing young adults, including low incomes, increasing student debt, the rising costs of postsecondary education, and expensive home ownership, mean that the transition to full independence in adulthood is prolonged. Postsecondary education is taking longer, and many young people face student debt when they finish college or university. In a 2011 *Globe and Mail* article, the Canadian Federation of Students stated that the average student debt load after graduation was $27 000 (Mason, 2011). Other media reports suggest that the debt load is closer to $37 000 (Del Campo, 2013).

Economic support is only one reason why young adults continue or return to live with parents. Much of the rise in delayed home-leaving is tied to the fact that even though cohabitation is popular among young Canadians, there has been a long-term decline in the number of young Canadians who are living with a partner. According to the 2011 Census, approximately 30 percent of Canadians in their twenties were living with a partner as compared to almost 52 percent in 1981 (Statistics Canada, 2012c). The increased instability of cohabiting relationships and the prevalence of divorce and single parenthood result in many young adults returning to the parental home for financial and emotional support and help with child care. The notion that most of these adults are financially exploiting their parents is inaccurate, as research shows that many individuals in this circumstance report mutually supportive relationships and reciprocity (Mitchell, 2006).

Children from blended families leave home earlier than children whose parents have not divorced. This may lead to long-term economic disadvantage, as these children may not receive the same level of economic or emotional support as children whose parents have not divorced. For example, rates of home ownership are higher for young adults who live with their parents in their early to mid-twenties; early departures from the parental home are associated with lower rates of home ownership (Turcotte, 2007). Early home-leaving among children in blended families may have long-term economic consequences, particularly if it coincides with early childbearing and uncompleted education (Mitchell, 1994, 2006). Children in blended families may be leaving the parental home due to family problems; females from blended families have a much higher probability of leaving the parental home before the age of 18 as compared to males (Mitchell, 1994, 2006). There are notable gender differences in delayed home-leaving, as males are more likely than females to live at home. This is partially because females cohabit or marry earlier than males and also partner and establish households with older males.

SMALLER HOUSEHOLDS AND SINGLE-PERSON HOUSEHOLDS

Household size has declined over the past five decades. In 1961, 32 percent of Canadian households contained five or more people, but by 2011 only 8 percent of households contained five or more people (Statistics Canada, 2012b). In 1961, only 9 percent of households contained only one person; in 2011, close to 28 percent of households were one-person households (Statistics Canada, 2012b). The shrinking of households is partially due to declining fertility, which has multiple causes, including female labour force participation dampening women's fertility; delayed fertility, which shortens women's reproductive years; greater access to contraception and abortion; and the high costs of raising children. Not all couples have children, as an increasing number of married couples are voluntarily childless. Smaller households reflect an aging population consisting of widowed seniors and a growth in divorced seniors. They also reflect increases in single-parent households and in Canadians who have previously been married or cohabited deciding not to repartner. The prevalence of one-person households promotes greater social acceptance of this living arrangement, and in turn this reduces the stigma that might have served as a significant obstacle to living alone in the past.

Among earlier generations, it was not uncommon for people to live on their own for a period of time before marriage. In contemporary society, living alone can be a temporary and transitional stage to a new relationship or a permanent arrangement, either by choice or because of the end of a relationship or the death of a partner. Among those who live alone are individuals who would prefer to live with a partner but are not in a relationship, those who may be in a relationship but prefer to live alone or where circumstances are preventing them from living with a partner (living alone together [LAT] couples), and those who want to live alone regardless of their current or future relationship status. In 2011, for the first time, there were more one-person households than couple households with children (Statistics Canada, 2012a), and this trend has continued. There has been a trend toward one-person households for more than five decades (Statistics Canada, 2012a). There are provincial differences, and Quebec has the highest number of one-person households (Census shows new face of the Canadian family, 2012). In 2011, 1 in 5 adults lived alone (Statistics Canada, 2012a). Canadians over the age of 65 are most likely to live alone. The proportion of men and women living alone increases with age, and given women's longer life expectancy, there are more senior women than senior men living alone. Widowhood is an expected life event for most Canadian women.

Just as economic resources facilitate the opportunity of living alone, so too do changes in societal values and ideas about people who remain unattached. At one time there was considerable stigma associated with remaining single, and that stigma coerced many into marriage (Adams, 1997). The discourse surrounding remaining single, particularly for women, has shifted in a short period of time, and there are many more role models of singlehood today than in the past. This reduces stigma and results in greater numbers of individuals feeling that it is acceptable to remain single. As more individuals experience relationship dissolution, they gain experience in being single, and this familiarity provides a point of comparison for people to make more informed decisions about the relative advantages and disadvantages of being in a relationship. People who have lived independently for a period of time may feel less inclined to share their living space if they have grown accustomed to their own space, routines, and habits. New reproductive technologies reduce pressure about when and if children are a possibility and provide the option of single parenthood. Social media and online dating provide more convenient opportunities for unattached individuals to have social connections, date, and have sexual encounters or relationships outside of a relationship context. As more Canadian males and females remain single, there is greater acceptance of this choice as compared to earlier generations.

COHABITATION, MARRIAGE, AND RELATIONSHIP DISSOLUTION

Decisions about cohabitation, marriage, and remarriage are shaped by numerous factors, including personal values, financial considerations, and family law. Decisions about whether to cohabit, marry, or merge households among couples where one or both partners have children from a previous relationship are further influenced by considerations such as whether various family members, such as stepsiblings, might get along and existing custody arrangements that require parents to stay within a certain geographical location. Relationship dissolution is affected by family law such as guidelines around the division of assets, child support, and spousal support. These realities may deter cohabitation or remarriage; for instance, individuals who receive spousal support may fear that a new cohabiting relationship or remarriage will affect the spousal support they receive or that a subsequent union dissolution will have negative financial consequences in terms of the division of assets, child support (including child support to stepchildren), and spousal support. Older Canadians wanting to ensure that their estate is inherited by adult children and grandchildren may avoid remarriage because marriage voids existing wills.

Cohabitation has become popular not only among young Canadians but also among older Canadians and Canadians who have previously divorced. The popularity of cohabitation reduces the number of people getting married and increases the age at marriage, as premarital cohabitation delays the timing of marriage (Manning, Brown, and Payne, 2014). There are many reasons why couples decide to cohabit, including love, shared housing costs, and interest in determining compatibility for marriage (Huang, Smock, Manning, and Bergstrom-Lynch, 2011). Gender differences have also been uncovered in terms of how men and women view cohabitation; research by Huang and colleagues (2011) found that men are more likely to emphasize that cohabitation provides greater opportunities for sex, whereas women are more interested in cohabitation as a step toward marriage. More women than men express concern that cohabitation delays marriage, whereas more men than women express concern about their loss of sexual freedom (Huang et al., 2011). Cohabitation is found among individuals of all income levels, but there is some evidence to suggest that as income increases, so too does the likelihood of marriage (Sassler and Miller, 2011a). The transition to cohabitation is faster among working-class couples because of financial pressures, whereas middle-class cohabitants are more likely than working-class cohabitants to get engaged (Sassler and Miller, 2011a).

The timing of cohabitating relationships is influenced by pregnancy and an individual's experiences in their family of origin, specifically whether they experienced parental divorce or parental conflict. Drawing on longitudinal data on 2174 individuals in Germany, Feldhaus and Heintz-Martin (2015) found that individuals whose parents separated or divorced left home at a younger age and were more likely to cohabit with a partner rather than marry. Pregnancy often precedes the decision to cohabit. Lichter and colleagues (2016) examined how pregnancy affected cohabitation, marriage, and the stability of relationships. The authors found that 1 in 5 pregnancies led quickly to either cohabitation or marriage, but that cohabiting relationships were more unstable than marital relationships. A small number of couples who cohabited following pregnancy married, but these marriages tended to dissolve. Lichter and colleagues (2016) suggest that couples who are committed to each other opt for marriage after pregnancy, and that this is what distinguishes them from the cohabiting relationships that are unstable. Overall, cohabiting following a pregnancy does not lead to relationship stability or marital stability (Lichter, Michelmore, Turner, and Sassler, 2016).

There is some evidence to suggest that divorce is more likely among people who cohabit prior to marriage, although this association may be eroding as cohabitation becomes more prevalent. Moreover, it seems that level of commitment appears to be more important than cohabitation itself in predicting union stability; Manning and Cohen (2012) found that marital instability was associated with level of commitment prior to cohabitation rather than with premarital cohabitation. Rhoades, Stanley and Markman (2006) found that men who were engaged to their spouses while they cohabited were more dedicated to their spouses than men who were not engaged when they began cohabiting with their spouses.

REMARRIAGE AND BLENDED FAMILIES

Rates of divorce in Canada are lower than in the United States, and most divorced people remarry or form a new cohabiting relationship. Rates of divorce are higher for second marriages, and this reflects many causes, including the greater financial challenges faced by blended families and the greater challenges in step-parenting and establishing harmony among children from different parents. Premarital cohabitation predicts divorce, and postdivorce cohabitation delays remarriage and increases the chance of a second divorce (Xu, Bartkowski, and Dalton, 2011). Marital stability is also linked to an older age at marriage (Gager, Yabiku, and Linver, 2016). More divorced men than women remarry, and the likelihood of remarrying following divorce is reduced if one has children, particularly for women. Children limit the time available to search for a marriage partner and may also deter potential partners, who may be reluctant to assume parenting and financial responsibilities for someone else's child (Goldscheider, Kaufman, and Sassler, 2009). That said, 1 in 10 children in Canada in 2011 lived in stepfamilies, measured for the first time on the 2011 short-form census (Statistics Canada, 2012a, 2012d). An increasing number of divorced individuals, particularly women, are deciding against repartnership following divorce. Remarriage is less common after widowhood (Connidis, 2001), and this reflects the fact that divorce tends to occur earlier in life than widowhood. Men are more likely to remarry following the death of a wife (Wu, Schimmele, and Ouellet, 2015), and high-income men are even more likely to remarry. Since women have a longer life expectancy than men, widowed men have a larger pool of potential spouses than women.

Intergenerational transmission of divorce is the idea that divorce is more prevalent among people who have experienced parental divorce. Using longitudinal data on 2174 individuals in Germany, Feldhaus and Heintz-Martin (2015) found that individuals who experienced a parental separation or divorce were more likely to divorce and that these effects were stronger for individuals who experienced a parental breakup before the age of 7. Diekmann and Schmidheiny (2013) found support for the intergenerational transmission of divorce in 13 Eastern and Western European countries and in North America. Amato and Patterson (2017) found that parental divorce is also associated with relationship dissolution among cohabiting couples. The intergenerational transmission of relationship stability is linked to the quality of parent–child relationships and parent relationships; Fasang and Raab (2014) found evidence that the intergenerational transmission of marriage and divorce patterns is associated with close emotional bonds between parents and children, and other researchers have identified exposure to parental conflict as an important variable. Children exposed to long-term parental conflict have a higher rate of relationship dissolution as adults, regardless of whether their parents divorced (Gager et al., 2016). Children exposed to high parental conflict for a short period of time preceding a parental divorce seem to recover from this adversity, as their rate of relationship dissolution as adults matches that of children raised in low-conflict intact families (Gager et al., 2016). The key factor seems to be the length of time that children are exposed to conflict; longer exposure leads to future relationship instability. Children raised in single-parent homes experienced lower conflict than children raised in intact high-conflict homes (Gager et al., 2016). Some researchers argue that the intergenerational transmission of divorce has weakened over time (Wolfinger, 2011), particularly as divorce has become more prevalent.

Blended families are remarried or cohabiting families in which one or both partners bring children into the new relationship. Blended families have also been described as reconstituted families or binuclear families (Church, 1996). Step-parents face challenges associated with parenting their partners' children and dealing with former spouses, whereas children face challenges associated with dealing with new stepsiblings, step-parents, and other extended family members. An increasing number of children are sharing equal time with both parents, which necessitates going back and forth between two households with different family members. This can be difficult and even chaotic, especially for children who prefer routine. Holidays can be problematic if there is conflict about how parents will share time with their children. The absence of children can be particularly difficult for parents who immersed themselves in caregiving before divorce. Research suggests that children do better when there is consensus in parenting approaches between step-parents and parents (Allan, Crow, and Hawker, 2011; Saintjacques, 1995).

The majority of couples succeed in meeting the challenges of a second marriage (Birditt and Antonucci, 2012). Meyerstein (2000) suggests that preparation is highly useful in a successful second marriage. Research on stepmothers finds that many women underestimate the challenges of a blended family, including increased domestic labour and caregiving and increased interpersonal negotiations with former spouses and extended family (Church, 1996). Step-parenting can be stressful, and stepmothering is often more challenging than stepfathering because of the added unpaid labour that women perform (Allan, Crow, and Hawker, 2011; Morrison, Thompson-Guppy, and Bell, 1986). Immigrants are more likely to remarry than are non-immigrants, most likely due to a preference for marriage in their culture as well as other factors such as financial dependency (Berger, 2000).

Discontinuity of relationships between children and their grandparents is of great concern to grandparents, who are increasingly using legal means to assert their right to access. Grandparents who have no or limited access to grandchildren have started online and offline education and support groups to exchange support with others going through the same experience. Studies show that grandparents (mostly paternal grandparents) are most at risk of losing contact with their grandchildren (Ahrons and Tanner, 2003; Kruk, 1995). Low rates of contact occur when the grandparent is related to the children's non-resident parent or when the children live with a step-parent (Lussier, Deater-Deckard, Dunn, and Davies, 2002). The primary mediators in ongoing grandparent–grandchild relationships are daughters-in-law. Disrupted contact is found to have adverse consequences for the grandparents. The consequences for grandchildren are less known. Yet a continuous relationship with grandparents can be of benefit, particularly when the grandparents themselves have a stable relationship. They can set positive examples and serve as a source of stability (Milan and Hamm, 2003).

MONEY AND RELATIONSHIPS

Historically, marriages were **endogamous**, meaning that people married within their own social class, race, ethnicity, and religion. Marriage as a social institution was viewed as an economic alliance between two families. Obligations of support were transparent, and individuals married to advance or reinforce their family's social class status. Thus, the idea that money is an important element in marriage is not new. In the past, marriage provided economic opportunism that was experienced by entire families; economic opportunism within relationships and marriages still exists but is more likely to be experienced by individuals who "marry up" rather than by entire families. Economic considerations factor into decisions about whether and when to partner and repartner and are also sometimes implicated in relationship dissolution.

Research on money in families suggests that many couples get joint bank accounts in their transition to marriage (Colavecchia, 2005). Separate bank accounts are more common among new relationships (Colavecchia, 2005), common-law relationships (Heimdal and Houseknecht, 2003; Singh and Lindsay, 1996; Treas and Widmer, 2000; Vogler, 2005), and relationships where one or both spouses have previously been divorced (Burgoyne and Morison, 1997; Fishman, 1983; Lown and Dolan, 1995; Pasley, Sandras, and Edmondson, 1994). Joint accounts may then lead to joint credit cards, jointly owning a vehicle, joint home ownership, and perhaps other joint debts such as lines of credit, home equity lines, and business loans. Financial risk exists when credit, such as credit cards, lines of credit, and car or business loans, is held by two people. An individual with bad credit may rely on his or her partner for access to credit if the partner has a better credit history. Financial risk emerges during relationships if finances and debts are merged and during relationship dissolution if one person is unable to pay back the debt or an individual's good credit is damaged. Many newly single individuals, particularly women, realize that they may have no credit history if they failed to establish and maintain their own credit history while they were married or cohabiting. Strong credit is required for mortgages and business and car loans; many women who have not maintained credit in their own name find that they are not able to qualify for mortgages and other loans once they are single. A drop in income and material standard of living often follows relationship dissolution; low income is a reality for many divorced women.

INDIGENOUS FAMILIES

In this section we examine contemporary issues facing Indigenous families in Canada, and these are contextualized within a broader historical view of the impact of colonialism on Indigenous groups. Indigenous groups face significant economic inequalities and lack of access to health care, employment opportunities, and social services, which affect the health and well-being of families and children.

Approximately 1.5 million Canadians have an Indigenous identity according to the 2011 National Household Survey; this represents approximately 4.3 percent of the Canadian population (Statistics Canada, 2013a). The Indigenous population is increasing at almost four times the rate of population increase for non-Indigenous people in Canada (Statistics Canada, 2013a), and the Indigenous population is young compared to the non-Indigenous population. Indigenous children age 14 and younger represent 28 percent of the total Indigenous population; non-Indigenous children in the same age group represent only 16.5 percent of the total non-Indigenous population (Statistics Canada, 2013a). Indigenous youth ages 15 to 24 years make up

>>> Colonialism and Indigenous Groups in Canada

Contemporary Indigenous poverty and child poverty must be understood within a broader historical context of the impact of colonialism and the social, political, and economic disadvantages created by the Indian Act (Fiske and Johnny, 2014). Two aspects of colonial rule, the reserve system and residential schooling, have had lasting adverse consequences for Indigenous groups. Among the many problematic aspects of the Indian Act were rules around the determination of Indian status. Gender discrimination was embedded in definitions of Indian status, as Indigenous women who married non-Indigenous men lost status, as did their children. Indian status had economic implications, such as tax implications and implications for access to reserve housing and other services.

The term **intergenerational trauma** (Czyzewski, 2011; Marsh, Cote-Meek, Young, Najavits, and Toulouse, 2016) describes how the legacy of colonialism and the residential school system continues to affect Indigenous families and communities. The physical, emotional, and sexual abuse that happened in residential schools hurt children, and the forcible abduction of Indigenous children from their parents damaged parent–child relationships. Indigenous parents today have been raised by parents and grandparents

who were victims of the residential school system, and the traumas experienced by individuals can ripple through families and adversely affect their children and grandchildren (Noormohamed et al., 2012).

The Truth and Reconciliation Commission of Canada conducted a comprehensive commission of residential schools between 2008 and 2015. The Commission set out to document the abuses in these schools and to offer recommendations for the Canadian government and all citizens aimed at addressing the harm caused by the residential school system. In its final report, the Commission described the treatment of Indigenous groups by the Canadian government as physical, biological, and cultural genocide:

> States that engage in cultural genocide set out to destroy the political and social institutions of the targeted group. Land is seized, and populations are forcibly transferred and their movement is restricted. Languages are banned. Spiritual leaders are persecuted, spiritual practices are forbidden, and objects of spiritual value are confiscated and destroyed. And, most significantly to the issue at hand, families are disrupted to prevent the transmission of cultural values and identity from one generation to the next. In its dealing with aboriginal people, Canada did all these things. (Truth and Reconciliation Commission of Canada, 2015)

18 percent of the total Indigenous population; non-Indigenous youth in the same age group represent approximately 13 percent of the total non-Indigenous population (Statistics Canada, 2013a).

Indigenous children are less likely to live with two parents and more likely to live with a single parent, in foster care, with a relative, or with a grandparent (with no parent present) as compared to non-Indigenous children. Only half of Indigenous children live with both of their parents, compared to 76 percent of non-Indigenous children (Statistics Canada, 2013a). More than one-third of Indigenous children live in a single-parent family, compared to 17 percent of non-Indigenous children. Almost half of all children age 14 and younger in foster care are Indigenous (Nearly half of children in foster care are Aboriginal, 2013). A much higher proportion of Indigenous children are living in skip-generation families with one or two grandparents and no parent (Nearly half of children in foster care are Aboriginal, 2013). Research on grandparent-led families indicates that these families are often led by grandmothers who live on low incomes. A higher proportion of Indigenous children are being raised by young parents and with a greater number of siblings (Statistics Canada, 2008a). According to a 2006 Statistics Canada report, "About 28% of Inuit children, 17% of First Nations children living off reserve, and 11% of Métis children were living in families with 4 or more children. This is compared to 8% of non-Aboriginal children in Canada. Among children under six years old, 26% of Inuit children, 27% of First Nations children living off reserve and 22% of Métis children had mothers between the ages of 15 to 24; this is compared to 8% of non-Aboriginal children" (Statistics Canada, 2008a). Many Indigenous children are being raised by young parents who experience strained economic circumstances and heavier caregiving responsibilities associated with multiple children. Multiple children impose greater financial and time challenges, and many of these young Indigenous parents are in fact single parents. In an analysis of 2006 Census data, Garner, Guimond, and Senecal (2013) found that Indigenous women are more likely than non-Indigenous women to be adolescent mothers and are less likely to graduate high school. They are more likely to live on low incomes in overcrowded housing that requires major repair.

Indigenous women have higher rates of fertility than non-Indigenous women; the fertility of Indigenous women is double that of non-Indigenous women. Rates of teen pregnancy are much higher among Indigenous women; among Indigenous women, the rate is 7 times greater, and among females under the age of 15, the rate of pregnancy is 18 times higher than that of other Canadians (UNICEF Canada, 2009). Early parenting is associated with less access to employment, education, and child care; only approximately half of Indigenous youth complete high school (UNICEF Canada, 2009). Although the impact of early childbearing among Indigenous women is often portrayed negatively, it varies tremendously depending on a woman's own personal circumstances. Using life course interview data, Cooke (2013) found that the impact of early childbearing for Indigenous women living in Canadian cities was variable and shaped by the amount of support they received and their strategies for managing parenthood.

Indigenous women have higher rates of lone parenthood and experience lengthier periods as single parents, including remaining single parents throughout their lives (Hull, 2001). The higher prevalence of single-parent families among Indigenous groups is also related to higher rates of cohabitation among Indigenous people (Aboriginal Affairs and Northern Development, 2012) and to the fact that cohabiting relationships are more unstable than marital relationships. Indigenous children face a greater likelihood of poverty as compared to non-Indigenous children, and this is linked to poorer health outcomes.

>>> Indigenous Families and Access to Health Care

Indigenous families tend to be larger and are more likely to live in overcrowded houses as compared to non-Indigenous families. Overcrowded housing leads to social problems such as tensions, conflict, and violence. Rates of domestic violence are higher in Indigenous communities. Overcrowded housing is also linked to the transmission of infectious illnesses and diseases such as respiratory infections, hepatitis A, and tuberculosis. Approximately 40 percent of Indigenous children under the age of 14 live in a crowded home; this is six times the rate experienced by non-Indigenous children (UNICEF Canada, 2009). Housing on reserves is more likely to be in need of repair and to have environmental hazards such as harmful mould and mildew, which leads to higher rates of asthma and respiratory infections; rates of illnesses like bronchitis and pneumonia are higher among the Indigenous population.

Indigenous people have less access to health care; those living in remote northern communities, in particular, do not have access to regular physician care. Among the Indigenous population, rates of infant mortality are three to seven times the national average, mostly due to respiratory infections and sudden infant death syndrome. Rates of maternal smoking are higher among Indigenous women, and there is a link between sudden infant death syndrome and maternal smoking during pregnancy and an

infant's exposure to secondhand smoke. Sudden infant death syndrome is three times higher among Indigenous communities as compared to non-Indigenous communities (University of Ottawa, 2015). Risk factors for sudden infant death syndrome include low socio-economic status, a mother who is a teen, and a mother who receives less prenatal care. Each of these factors exists in Indigenous communities. There are also higher rates of children born with alcohol spectrum disorder among the Indigenous population. Rates of teen pregnancy are higher in the Indigenous population and are particularly high for adolescents age 15 and younger. The cold climate of northern Indigenous communities is associated with a higher incidence of respiratory infections. There is evidence to suggest that Indigenous children have significantly higher rates of untreated ear infections and hearing loss (UNICEF Canada, 2009). Indigenous children have much lower rates of vaccination and experience more vaccine-preventable illnesses such as smallpox and measles (UNICEF Canada, 2009). The lack of access to doctors and medical care in many communities adversely affects children's health, as illnesses are not diagnosed and treated. Lack of medical care for chronic diseases is problematic given that rates of chronic illness such as diabetes are higher among the Indigenous population. There are much higher rates of sexually transmitted infections, human

(continued)

immunodeficiency virus (HIV), and acquired immune deficiency syndrome (AIDS) among Indigenous communities. Not only do Indigenous communities experience a lack of health care, but they also experience a lack of social services and child welfare services.

Access to clean water, adequate housing, and affordable nutritious foods are issues that have yet to be resolved for many Indigenous communities. Indigenous people are much more likely to experience food insecurity as compared to non-Indigenous people. Many Indigenous communities have been living under boil water advisories for years, and clean water is critical for health and safe food preparation. Nutritious food is not affordable in remote northern communities, and there is concern that younger generations are not learning about traditional food practices, hunting, fishing, and gathering from older generations (Earle, 2011). These issues affect the health and well-being of Indigenous families and lead to problems such as obesity and diabetes for both children and adults. These long-term economic and environmental problems are linked to social problems like suicide, mental health issues (Marsh et al., 2016), violence, substance abuse (Marsh et al., 2016), and family breakdown. The health issues and inequalities facing Indigenous groups are complex; Marsh and colleagues (2016) argue that strengthening cultural identity and Indigenous healing practices is beneficial in treating Indigenous people with substance abuse and mental health issues.

Higher rates of childhood poverty also reflect the prevalence of single-parent households. Indigenous children living on reserve are more likely to live with both parents as compared to those living off-reserve. Sixty percent of status Indian children living on reserve live in poverty, and 41 percent of status Indian children living off-reserve live in poverty. In comparison, 13 percent of non-Indigenous, non-racialized, non-immigrant Canadian children live in poverty (MacDonald and Wilson, 2016). Indigenous women who live off-reserve are much more likely to experience household moves as compared to Indigenous women living on reserve and non-Indigenous women (Aboriginal Affairs and Northern Development, 2012). Household moves are made due to relationship dissolution, low income, constrained employment opportunities, lack of affordable housing and child care, and access to social services and child care. Repeated moving has negative repercussions for adults and children, as it leads to stress, disrupted daily routines, and a loss of familiar social networks. It is particularly problematic for children, as household moves typically lead to a change in schools, which leads to a loss of friends, support networks, and familiar school personnel, homes, and neighbourhoods.

LONE-PARENT FAMILIES

Lone-parent families can be the result of divorce, relationship breakdown, widowhood, and planned or unplanned pregnancy that happens outside of the context of a relationship. It can be a choice made by an individual who decides to have a child on her own, either because she has not found a partner or because she opts to be a single parent for any number of reasons, including an assessment that parenting alone would be better than parenting with a problematic male partner (Wiegers and Chunn, 2017). The term *choice mom* is used by some women who actively seek parenthood on their own, and there are numerous online support groups and blogs written by and devoted to choice moms. Language such as "choice mom" is an attempt to challenge negative assumptions about single parents and to reframe lone parenthood in a more positive light. New reproductive technologies provide opportunities for men and women to become single parents, with or without biological connection to their child. There has been a growth in single-parent households in Canada. By 2006, the percentage of children age 15 and younger who lived with lone parents had reached 18.3 percent, and from 2006 to 2011 lone-parent families increased 8.0 percent (Statistics Canada, 2012a). In Canada, the percentage of children age 15 and younger who lived with lone parents was 12.4 percent in 1986, 16.0 percent in 1996, and 18.3 percent in 2006; in the 2011 Census, lone-parent families represented 16.3 percent of the population (Statistics Canada, 2012a). In other words, there has been a steady increase in the number of children growing up in single-parent households. Census data are cross-sectional data, or data taken at one point in time; therefore, they are limited in revealing children's lifetime experiences in single-parent versus two-parent families.

>>> Counting Single-Parent Families

Census data only give us the number of children at one point in time who are living in a single-parent household; if we tracked children from birth to 18 years of age, we would find an even higher number who have experienced a single-parent household at some point during their childhood. The amount of time that a child lives in a single-parent household varies tremendously. Some children have only ever experienced this type of family structure, while other children have only experienced this living arrangement for a temporary period, such as during a parental separation before the parents reconcile or the time until a single parent finds a new partner. Cohabitation with a new partner might be abrupt or more gradual as the new partner spends increasing amounts of time in the home.

Cross-sectional data such as census data do not capture change over time in children's experiences of living in a single-parent household, the increasing complexity of households and relationships, or who provides daily care to children. Census data cannot differentiate between single-parent households that are transitional and temporary and those that are more permanent. Longitudinal data are needed to track children's experiences of living in a single-parent household over time. For instance, a child may be living with a parent who is in a new relationship where there is partial or gradual cohabitation; as well, the nature of the relationship between a new partner and children can be minimal or more involved, where the new partner is involved in caregiving responsibilities such as taking children to school, activities, and meal preparation. Further methodological limitations of census data include the challenges of enumerating children of divorced parents where parents

(continued)

have shared access (joint physical custody) and children live equally in both homes. Since 1986, the census has recognized joint custody arrangements and has asked respondents to include children only if they live in that home "most of the time." For children who spend equal time with each parent, the census gives a specific day (e.g., May 10, 2016) and asks respondents to include the children if they were living in the home on that particular day. The census does not provide clarification for situations where a child has been in both parental homes on that particular day. The 2016 Census was worded in the following way:

> Children in joint custody should be included in the home of the parent where they live most of the time. Children who spend equal time with each parent should be included in the home of the parent with whom they are staying on May 10, 2016. (Census, 2016)

Macro data such as census data give us information about household membership yet provide little information about who performs child care. For example, many children living in two-parent homes might in fact receive all or most of their care from one parent. This may occur for any number of reasons, ranging from hours of work or work-related travel preventing one parent from spending time with children to lack of involvement in caregiving because of other reasons such as serious illness, substance abuse, or mental health issues.

The majority of single parents in Canada are women. Female lone-parent families in 2011 accounted for 12.8 percent of all census families, while male lone-parent families represented 3.5 percent (Sinha, 2014b). Single-parent households are more common in the United States: 27.3 percent of all families in 2009 were single-parent families (Vespa, Lewis, and Kreider, 2013). Although most single parents are women, single-father families are increasing in Canada and the United States. Between 2006 and 2011, lone-father households in Canada increased by 16.2 percent, compared with only a 6 percent jump in single-parent families headed by women (Sinha, 2014b). Although joint physical custody has been increasing, most children live with their mother following parental separation or divorce. According to the 2011 General Social Survey, 70 percent of separated or divorced parents stated that their children lived with the mother, 15 percent stated that their children lived with the father, and 9 percent stated that the children spent equal time with both parents (Sinha, 2014b). Eighteen percent of non-resident parents stated that they did not spend any time with their child in the previous year (Sinha, 2014b). Approximately 35 percent of parents stated that major decisions regarding schooling, health, and religion were made jointly (Sinha, 2014b).

Single-parent families are structured by gender in that the majority are led by women and more female-headed families live in poverty. In Canada, female-headed families are three times as likely to live in poverty compared to male-headed families. According to the 2011 Census, 21 percent of single mothers in Canada live in poverty as compared to 7 percent of single fathers (Canada without Poverty, 2017). Caragata and Liegghio (2013) studied single mothers on social assistance and explored the intersections between their mental health and poverty. The researchers highlight how the mental health of single mothers is rooted in the material conditions of these women's lives and the challenges they face in raising children on their own. Blacks (Sudarkasa, 2007) and Indigenous people have higher rates of single-parent households, and newcomers have lower rates of single-parent households. Some scholars have linked the rise in single-parent families headed by women in Canada and the United States, and in particular among blacks and African Americans, to welfare policy (Sudarkasa, 2007). It has been argued that the strict eligibility criteria for welfare meant that women could not collect government benefits if they lived with others, such as male partners, parents, and other extended kin. Over time, this reduced black and African American fluid and multigenerational households to two-generation single parent and children households. (Sudarkasa, 2007).

Fortunately, low income among single mothers has improved over the decades from 54 percent in 1976 to 21 percent in 2008 (Williams, 2010). Higher rates of labour force participation of single mothers have lifted more women out of poverty (Sauve, 2002). The situation of some single mothers has worsened considerably due to a lack of affordable housing and child care. Research by the Canadian Homelessness Research Network (Gaetz, Donaldson, Richter, and Gulliver, 2013) suggests that women with children, particularly lone mothers, may be the fastest-growing group among the homeless. Partnership provides protection against poverty due to shared living expenses, pooled income, and shared child care. Many women fall into poverty upon relationship dissolution and divorce, creating pressure for women to repartner in order to raise the standard of living for their children. Women who have labour force interruptions due to childbearing and child care face the cumulative economic disadvantage of a lack of work experience and blocked career progression. During marriage or cohabitation, many women forgo building their own careers and focus on the careers of their husbands or male partners. The longer-term consequences of doing so are often not appreciated until the relationship ends. Typically, men's economic circumstances improve after divorce, while women's worsen. It is important to point out that not all single mothers are economically disadvantaged. There has been an increase in births to older unmarried women in their late thirties and early forties, many of whom have higher levels of educational attainment, high incomes, and fewer children.

Despite matrimonial property laws that give women an equal division of assets in the matrimonial home, a single mother may not be able to pursue home ownership (and the associated benefits of building equity) if her income is not sufficient to qualify for a mortgage on her own. Some individuals may need to ask others, such as parents, to co-sign in order to be approved for a home mortgage. Relationship breakdown forces many women out of home ownership and into rental apartments or homes. Renting precludes women from building equity and may force women to relocate to less desirable neighbourhoods where there is access to rental accommodation. The intention of legislated child and spousal support is to equalize the material standard of living across parental households after divorce. This is beneficial to the lower-earning spouse, typically the mother, but the trend toward joint physical custody reduces the amount of child support a woman can receive. Many Canadian children experience a difference in the standard of living in maternal and paternal households. Although child support is mandated by law, it is not always paid in full or paid on time.

Part of the explanation for the high rates of child poverty in Canada is related to the low incomes of single-parent families, particularly those headed by women, and the lack of compliance with child support payments and Section 7 expenses. Given that women assume a disproportionate responsibility for caregiving and that their incomes tend to drop after divorce while men's incomes tend to increase after divorce, non-compliance with child support payments and Section 7 expenses further disadvantages the children of divorce. Children are economically disadvantaged following divorce, and any analysis of the impact of divorce on children cannot overlook this reality.

There is also growing recognition that the impact of divorce on children is not exclusively negative; positive impacts include being protected from violence and parental conflict and increased independence and coping abilities among children

»» Child Support Compliance

According to the 2011 General Social Survey, only 75 percent of Canadians receiving child support reported receiving the entire amount, 13 percent reported receiving half or more of the required amount, and 8 percent reported receiving less than half of what they should have received (Sinha, 2014b). Many custodial parents receive child support payments late or not at all. According to the 2011 General Social Survey, 24 percent of Canadians said that their child support was sometimes or always late, 41 percent reported that payments were missed or not received in their entirety, and 25 percent stated that most payments were missed (Sinha, 2014b). Some women make informal agreements to forgo child support or accept lower child support payments as a strategy to reduce conflict with a former spouse and gain leverage in having children spend more time in their home. While most divorcing couples have written divorce agreements, the extent to which these are followed over the long term is not known.

Individuals can also attempt to amend agreements if their financial circumstances change. For example, an individual who remarries and has more children can go back to family court and argue for lower child support payments because his or her economic circumstances have now changed with the additional children to support.

In addition to child support, individuals may also be required to pay additional expenses related to their children. These are referred to as Section 7 expenses and can be found in the Federal Child Support Guidelines. These expenses include those related to child care, medical and dental expenses, schooling and postsecondary education, and extracurricular activities. The extent to which individuals pay Section 7 expenses when they are required to is unknown, although we can surmise that since a large number of parents are not compliant with child support payments, rates of noncompliance for Section 7 expenses are likely even higher.

(Ferri, 1993; Smart and Neale, 1999). Children can become more emotionally resilient and develop conflict management skills (Smart and Neale, 1999). Many single-parent homes are exceptionally successful at meeting the emotional, social, and physical needs of children despite the absence of a second adult to assist with economic or caregiving support. Higher-income single parents benefit from having the economic resources to outsource tasks like housework and yard work and perhaps to work fewer hours, thus freeing up time for caregiving. They are in an advantaged position compared to low-income single parents who may have to work more hours in paid employment to make ends meet and may have no other choice but to use less than ideal child care arrangements because regulated child care is not affordable or available.

FAMILIES AND DISABILITIES

The experiences of families where one or more family members have a disability are varied, from families where the family member has experienced a disability or multiple disabilities from birth, to those where the disability or illness is experienced later in life, to those where the type of disability remains constant, to those where the disability changes and perhaps worsens over time. Disabilities vary in terms of how many disabilities an individual might have, the difficulties the individual with the disability faces, and the extent to which the disability limits daily activities. The onset of disability or serious illness in a family member or the sudden worsening of an

>>> Families and Disability

Approximately, 3.7 percent of Canadian children under the age of 15 have one or more disabilities (Statistics Canada, 2008b). Using the four categories of mild, moderate, severe and very severe disability, more than one-quarter of Canadian adults have very severe disabilities and almost 23 percent have severe disabilities (Statistics Canada, 2013b). More than 80 percent of disabled Canadian adults use some kind of assistive device, such as a wheelchair, hearing aid, or specialized computer (Statistics Canada, 2013b). Rates of disability are higher for women, and this is true of all age groups (Statistics Canada, 2013b). Rates of disability increase with age. There are many disabled Canadian parents who provide care to children, many Canadians who provide care to an older or disabled parent, and a significant number of Canadians described as the **sandwich generation**, who provide care to children and parents simultaneously. Considerable stigma and discrimination exist toward parents who are disabled and toward individuals who decide to become parents despite having a disability. Disabilities continue to be misunderstood in society, leading to the problem of people believing that disabled parents cannot provide good care to their children. Some disabled parents fear losing custody of their children due to their disability (Disabled parents fight to keep newborn at home, 2012; Tomasi, 2015) existing medical condition in either a child or a parent marks a challenging transition for family members, who face heightened caregiving responsibilities that must be managed alongside other responsibilities such as breadwinning and care of other children or family members. There are added financial costs associated with managing a disability or caring for someone who is gravely ill that create economic strains and logistical challenges for family members. Added financial costs might include improving the accessibility of homes and vehicles, missed work and pay, transportation to and from medical appointments and treatments, cost of medications, cost of medical devices such as portable oxygen machines and walkers, and hidden costs such as paying for parking at hospitals. In circumstances where a parent's disability, medical crisis, or terminal illness prevents or reduces the parent's ability to work or provide care, additional responsibilities shift to the other parent and to other family members such as older children or other relatives. A disability or medical crisis that results in a parent leaving paid employment either temporarily or permanently may shift family roles and have a significant economic impact on all family members, who now may have to make ends meet on one paycheque instead of two.

The growth of non-standard and precarious employment means that an increasing number of Canadians do not have any kind of workplace long-term disability coverage that can provide financial support in the event that they cannot work. A worsening disability or illness brings a set of emotional challenges as well; family or spousal relationships might be adversely affected by disability or illness. In those instances where families are facing the terminal illness of a family member, plans for the future need to be made as families face the transition to a new family structure. For instance, the death of one parent marks the transition to a new single-parent family.

NEW CONTEXTS FOR CHILDBEARING AND PARENTING

Among earlier generations of Canadians, childbearing was expected to occur within the context of marriage. Unmarried women who became pregnant faced enormous stigma if they tried to raise a child on their own, leading many to give their babies up for adoption, and dating couples who were confronted with an unplanned pregnancy sometimes decided to get married because of that pregnancy. Today, marriage and fertility no longer go hand in hand, as revealed by the increase in cohabiting couples who have children, married couples who are voluntarily childless, and women and men who decide to have children as single parents. There has been an increase in the number of people **co-parenting**. The term *co-parenting* has been associated with divorced couples raising children after divorce. However, co-parenting has expanded to include two or more people who wish to have and raise a child together. Two people who are not in a relationship may decide to co-parent, or a couple may decide to co-parent with a third individual. Co-parenting provides greater parenting options to single individuals and same-sex couples.

Verbal or written agreements that outline issues such as access, decision making, and financial contributions are made in advance of the birth of the child.

Marriage and heterosexuality are no longer prerequisites to parenthood due to women's increased financial independence and new reproductive technologies such as **in vitro fertilization (IVF)** and surrogacy. For example, single gay men are increasingly pursuing surrogacy to become single parents (Cribb, 2016). Although same-sex marriage was legalized in Canada in 2005, there have always been LGBTQ (lesbian, gay, bisexual, transgender, queer, and questioning) individuals; however, discrimination and homophobia prevented many people from pursuing non-traditional non-heterosexual relationships (Adams, 1997). What is new is that LGBTQ families receive greater societal recognition and support, policy entitlements such as pensions and medical benefits, and protections under the law (Goldberg, Moyer, Weber, and Shapiro, 2013). LGBTQ families continue to face discrimination by the larger society; those living in urban settings have greater access to support as compared to those living in rural areas (McCarthy, 2000).

New reproductive technologies like IVF are expensive; they are not affordable for low-income families. In 2010, Quebec became the first province to offer a program to cover all costs of IVF treatments but has since made reductions to coverage (Panitch, 2015). Ontario introduced some financial support for women who need IVF, and other provinces like Manitoba offer tax credits to help offset the costs of IVF (Ferguson, 2015). Zelkowitz and colleagues (2015) found that government funding for IVF in Quebec reduced disparities in access to IVF. Specifically, it improved access for newcomers, low-income women, and women with lower levels of education.

There has been an increase in the number of older mothers (Morgan, Merrell, and Rentschler, 2015) and in the number of older single mothers, reflecting the fact that there has been an increase in never-married women in Canada (Statistics Canada, 2012b). In contrast, rates of teen pregnancy have generally been on the decline due to access to contraception and abortion. Both planned and unplanned pregnancies are reflected in the number of single women in their twenties, thirties, and forties who become single parents. Lone parenthood in Canada differs from that in the United States, where there are larger numbers of single parents and lone parenthood happens at earlier ages. In the United States, earlier childbearing is associated with higher rates of poverty and poorer outcomes for children, such as in educational attainment (Dryburgh, 2001).

Earlier research looking at whether family structure (two parents versus single parent) predicts child outcomes such as educational attainment, substance abuse, or risk-taking behavior often suggested poorer outcomes for children of single parents. These types of studies cannot be taken as proof that single-parent households are disadvantageous for children because it is difficult methodologically to disentangle the impact of family structure from variables such as socio-economic status, children's exposure to parental conflict, and the number and kinds of transitions children may have experienced in their lives. Children raised by single parents may have had to endure parental conflict before the relationship breakdown, difficult financial circumstances, and multiple transitions such as residential moves and school changes. The transition to a single-parent home is multifaceted; although it may lead to more strained financial circumstances, it might also be beneficial in terms of protecting children from parental conflict or abuse. Single parents may be more effective in their parenting because they no longer have to compromise with another parent or live with a problematic spouse. The growing number of more economically advantaged women who become single parents shifts the discourse around lone parenthood because economic vulnerability is not a salient issue for these parents.

There are more options today for individuals to become lone parents, such as artificial insemination, IVF, informal access to sperm for conception, private adoptions, and foreign adoptions. Until recently, adoption processes favoured two-parent heterosexual families. Same-sex couples can now adopt children through the Children's Aid Society, and single parents are not explicitly excluded from foreign or domestic adoptions as they once were. Individuals who want to adopt must still go through screening processes, but it is now possible for individuals and same-sex couples to adopt. Many Canadians have pursued foreign adoption in countries like China, where a one-child policy has led to many baby girls being in need of adoption. Raleigh (2012) examined whether there was any association between the race of adopted children and the relationship status and sexual orientation of adoptive parents in the United States. She found that same-sex and single parents were the most likely to adopt non-white children and that although white parents are more likely to adopt Hispanic and Asian children, white single parents and same-sex adoptive parents are more likely to adopt black children. There are at least two possible reasons for these findings: First, non-traditional adoptive parents have more flexible conceptions of family and kinship, which makes them more open to transracial adoption. Second, single parents and same-sex parents may have fewer options in the adoption marketplace (Raleigh, 2012).

Fostering provides another avenue for some Canadians to pursue adoption of a child they have cared for as a foster parent. The number of children living in foster care homes was counted for the first time by the 2011 Census, and approximately 30 000 children and youth were in foster care (Foster children counted in Canadian census for 1st time, 2012). Indigenous children are vastly over-represented at all levels of intervention in the child welfare system and in some provinces constitute 80 percent of the children in foster care (Foster children counted in Canadian census for 1st time, 2012).

New reproductive technologies have fundamentally challenged the idea that parenthood is defined by biology. Individual men and women can use new reproductive technologies to have children without having a biological connection to those children. Surrogacy has become increasingly popular as individuals struggle with infertility, but surrogacy has also offered new possibilities for individuals to have children who they may or may not be connected to biologically. With traditional surrogacy, a surrogate uses her own egg and is artificially inseminated with sperm. The surrogate has a biological connection to the child and agrees to terminate her parental rights after the birth. The child is then adopted by the couple who arranged for the surrogate. With gestational surrogacy, the surrogate has no biological connection to the child because another woman's egg or a donor's egg is used. Either a donor egg or donor sperm or both donor egg and donor sperm can be used for gestational surrogacy. Individuals who hire a gestational surrogate and use donor egg and sperm have no biological connection to the child, yet have the societal recognition of being that child's parent. For most of human history, a younger age and heterosexual orientation were requirements for procreation. Age and sexual orientation no longer determine childbearing as new reproductive technologies open up greater possibilities for parenthood to be determined socially rather than biologically. New technologies are also allowing for the possibility of having three biological parents, as in the case of the first baby born who had DNA from one father and two mothers due to a hereditary life-threatening disease carried by the mother. In this case, the DNA of the mother was removed and replaced with the DNA of another woman in order to avoid having the baby inherit the disease (Clarke-Billings, 2016).

These new reproductive possibilities have transformed parenthood and led to an increase in legal challenges about parental rights (Kroløkke, Foss, and Pant, 2012). Despite the fact that same-sex marriage was legalized in 2005, automatic parental rights for same-sex parents does not exist in Canada. Non-biological same-sex parents must hire a lawyer to help them adopt their children. At the time of writing, the issue of automatic parental rights for same-sex partners has been brought before the courts and government, and it seems that these rights will be extended to same-sex parents soon (MacLachlan and Noseworthy, 2016). Feminists express concern about the implications of new reproductive technologies for women (McDaniel, 1988) because poor women can be exploited as reproducers. As fertility becomes commodified, economically marginalized women can be exploited (Kroløkke, Foss, and Pant, 2012), and solutions to ethical questions have not kept pace with these technologies. One example of this is the issue of children born to anonymous donors having the right to know the identity of the donors or to gain access to the medical history of the donors. For example, individuals who were produced using donor eggs or sperm argue that they have the right to know their biological lineage to ensure that they do not procreate with someone they are biologically related to. As donor eggs and sperm become more prevalent, there is an increased likelihood of individuals who were each produced using donor egg or sperm wanting to conceive and wanting to ensure that they are not biologically related to each other. Along these lines, there have been calls for either a voluntary or a mandatory donor registry in Canada. Regulatory frameworks to help navigate these ethical issues have yet to be established.

TRANSITIONS IN MIDLIFE AND FOR SENIORS

Among Canadians in midlife (i.e., in their forties or fifties), there is diversity in terms of relationship status and parenting. Some people are in their first marital or cohabiting relationship, while others are in second or subsequent marital or cohabiting relationships.

Humble (2013) explored the transition to marriage for midlife to later-life same-sex Canadian couples and how this transition was shaped by their lifetime experiences of homophobia. Among these couples, marriage was not an immediate reaction to the legalization of same-sex marriage in Canada; rather, same-sex individuals engaged in a process of determining their rationale for deciding to get married.

Parenting status can range from childlessness to being the parent or step-parent of a young child to being the parent of an adult child to perhaps even being a grandparent. With longer life expectancies and declining fertility, many of us will spend more years caring for aging parents than raising children, and many Canadians will have more parents than they do children. Most seniors live alone or with a spouse (Canada Year Book, 2011). Empty nests are a reality for most Canadians but they often occur later than they did in the past. Retirees are a rapidly growing group, and the number of seniors living in Canada is predicted to rise from 4.2 million to 9.8 million between 2005 and 2036 (Turcotte and Schellenberg, 2006). Senior Canadians tend to live in small households with only one or two people, and senior women are more likely to live alone because of widowhood. Many senior women live on low incomes, which reflects lower lifetime earnings and retirement savings. Following the death of a spouse or divorce, many women become financially vulnerable; women without husbands are more financially vulnerable than men without wives. Many midlife and senior Canadians have experienced divorce or relationship dissolution. More men than women remarry, and remarriage declines with age.

Senior Canadians tend to have regular contact with siblings and children; about half of all seniors live within 10 kilometres of at least one of their children (McDaniel, 2005). An increasing number of Canadians are raising grandchildren, often because the parents of these children are unable to raise them due to substance abuse, incarceration, or health issues. A majority of these grandparents are senior women, and many are parenting on their own on limited income. This unanticipated transition can be stressful, particularly when grandparents are also dealing with difficult circumstances such as substance abuse or incarceration that are affecting their adult child (Lumpkin, 2008; Thomas, 1995).

Widowhood is an expectable life event, and it is occurring later in life than it used to. Older men with health problems are more likely to have a wife at home who can provide care, whereas older women with health problems are less likely to have a husband at home and more likely to move in with relatives or into a care facility. Wu, Schimmele, and Ouellet (2015) found that widowers are more likely to remarry than widows, and remarriage is most likely to occur within 10 years of a spouse dying; after this period, remarriage is uncommon. Widows and widowers are more likely to remarry than to cohabit; however, cohabitation is more common in Quebec. Research on widows suggests that the grieving process is helped by support from family, peers, siblings, and other community members (Connidis, 2001). As a consequence of societal homophobia, individuals who lose a same-sex partner may not receive the same level of support as those who lose an opposite-sex partner (Connidis, 2001).

Diversity at midlife is further revealed when we consider that some in midlife are empty nesters whose adult children have set up their own households while others have adult children continuing to live in the parental home or who have come back to live in the parental home after living on their own for a period of time. Employment, marriage, and childbearing were the main reasons why earlier generations of adult children established their own households, but today young adults often leave the parental home for educational and employment opportunities or even just to live independently from their parents (Beaupré, Turcotte, and Milan, 2006). Adult children who leave home due to marriage and childbearing are less likely to return to the parental home as compared to those adult children who leave for other reasons (Beaupré, Turcotte, and Milan, 2006). Adult children may live with their parents for emotional and financial support as they pursue postsecondary education and build careers, and they may also return to live with parents following relationship dissolution, particularly if they have children and need help with caregiving (Mitchell, 2006). The popularity of cohabitation, which is more unstable than marriage, is another reason that many adult children return to live with parents.

The lengthening time spent in postsecondary education and the increasing costs associated with postsecondary education leave many students with large student loans. Many Canadians facing unemployment or blocked job opportunities return to school with hopes of a career change and better employment prospects. As more adult children live with their parents, the social stigma attached to this living arrangement is eroded. Although many individuals receive financial support from parents, primarily in the form of free or low-cost housing, it would be incorrect to characterize these living arrangements as exploitive because there is a lot of evidence that adult children provide support and companionship to parents and that there is reciprocity in these relationships (Mitchell, 2006). In terms of social policy, it seems that the family home is becoming a kind of safety net for youth who cannot establish themselves in independent residences (Mitchell, 2006; Mitchell and Gee, 1996; Statistics Canada, 2012c).

NEW KINDS OF CLOSE RELATIONS

In addition to the types of relationships already discussed, other forms of family are emerging. The definition of *family* is becoming more fluid and dependent on circumstances. Economic hardship may result in multifamily households, but there are also instances of more affluent newcomer Canadians selecting multifamily and three-generation households as a way to preserve culture, language, religion, and heritage. Relationship dissolution and the need to pool resources can create new but healthy families where children have the support of multiple adults. For example, a three-generation family may consist of a grandmother and two grown daughters, one of whom is a single mother with a daughter. This is just one of the families described in Fox and Fumia's (2001) study of unconventional families. In a study of women living in co-op housing in Toronto where rent was geared to income, Worts (2005) found that the shared outdoor space facilitated collective caregiving among mothers living in the co-op and challenged the privatized nature of caregiving. Consider the scenario of a widowed mother of a disabled teen renting her basement apartment to a single mother and exchanging child care to facilitate the employment schedules of both lone parents. While the women may not have defined each other as "family," their exchange of resources ensures the well-being of both women and their children. In the absence of wider social support, such as affordable and flexible child care that meets the needs of parents who work evenings and weekends or affordable care for disabled children or the elderly, many Canadians facing economic insecurity seek unconventional living and care arrangements. Families, living arrangements, and households are being transformed as individuals seek solutions to their caregiving, financial, emotional, and social needs.

CONCLUDING REMARKS

We explored varied transitions and diversity in families in this chapter. The transitions and new kinds of close relations discussed here are not the full list of possible ways in which family life changes and we change family for ourselves. Sometimes we can actively make informed decisions about families and relationships, but sometimes these choices and decisions are out of our hands and made by others, such as by our spouse or partner. Transitions can be happily or unhappily anticipated, but sometimes transitions are unexpected and sometimes they are out of our control, such as when a spouse dies or becomes disabled or when people have to flee relationships in order to keep themselves and their children safe. Choices can be freely made, but often choices are constrained by economic circumstances and the availability of social support. There are more options available today for families and intimate relationships as compared to earlier generations, yet many Canadians face significant economic, social, and health challenges, particularly single parents, Indigenous people, and Canadians with a disabled family member.

CHAPTER SUMMARY

This chapter discusses transitions to different family situations experienced in childhood and throughout the life course, including singlehood, lone-parent families, second or subsequent relationships or remarriage, stepfamilies, and living arrangements among middle-aged and older Canadians. Family transitions are not new, but some of the choices now available to us are new, such as new contexts for childbearing that are independent of age, gender, marital and relationship status, heterosexuality, and biology. Transitions can provide new benefits and opportunities but can also be fraught with hardship, such as the financial difficulties following single parenthood or relationship dissolution. Yet these transitions are mediated by factors such as socioeconomic status and availability of support. Families are actively created, are fluid, and extend beyond the walls of individual households, as is the case for transnational families, children of divorced parents, LAT (living apart together) couples, and older Canadians in romantic relationships who wish to maintain separate households and separate finances in order to preserve their estates for their children and grandchildren upon their death. In summary, transitions can be voluntary or involuntary, anticipated or unanticipated, and positive or negative experiences, or even a combination of these elements. From lone-person households to multifamily households to cluttered nests, the variation in families, intimate relationships, and living arrangements could not be greater. Individuals experience a multitude and fluidity of close relations throughout their lives, and these relations are shaped by wider social, economic, and legal forces.

Key Terms

blended family Typically, a family comprising two previously married spouses, with children, who marry each other and bring their children together in a new family.

boomerang kid A young adult who returns to the parental home after a period of living independently.

co-parenting Occurs when two or more people have and raise a child together, even if they have never previously been in a romantic relationship. Co-parenting provides greater parenting options to single individuals and same-sex couples. Verbal or written agreements that outline issues such as access, decision making, and financial contributions are made in advance of the birth of the child.

endogamous marriage A marriage between individuals who marry within their own social class, race, ethnicity, and religion.

in vitro fertilization Commonly known as *test-tube fertilization*; conception that occurs by bringing together ova and sperm using medical procedures.

intergenerational trauma The abuses experienced by Indigenous people in residential schools affected parent–child relationships, the legacy of which persists and has spanned generations.

sandwich generation Individuals who are simultaneously providing care to children and to parents.

transnational families Families made up of members who are separated geographically for extended periods of time.

Critical Thinking Questions

1. Poverty is more prevalent among lone-parent families, Indigenous families, senior women, and families with a disabled family member. Identify the factors that contribute to the economic insecurity faced by these groups.

2. We experience greater choices in the decisions we make about our intimate relationships as compared to earlier generations. Outline what this variety entails and why these choices exist.

3. What are the consequences of relationship dissolution for adults and for children?

4. How are the experiences of children and young people today different than those of earlier generations?

5. Describe the new contexts for parenthood that exist today. How is parenthood today different than in earlier times?

6. What are the ways in which concerns about money intersect with issues related to relationship formation and dissolution?

Weblinks

National Centre for Truth and Reconciliation
http://www.trc.ca/websites/trcinstitution/index.php?p=905
This site provides links to resources such as the Truth and Reconciliation Commission reports and findings, links to exhibitions and collections, and educational resources for students and teachers.

Department of Justice: Voice and Support: Programs for Children Experiencing Parental Separation and Divorce
www.justice.gc.ca/eng/rp-pr/fl-lf/divorce/2004_2/annexa.html
The Department of Justice has compiled a list of supports offered by province. These include community-based programs, court-based programs, and other organizations that provide a range of support services, including counselling.

Ontario Ministry of Children and Youth Services: Special Needs
www.children.gov.on.ca/htdocs/english/specialneeds/index.aspx
This site provides access to resources and support for parents of children with disabilities. The site includes support for mental health, fetal alcohol syndrome, autism, and many other issues. Support for Indigenous families is also provided.

LGBTQ Parenting Network
http://lgbtqpn.ca/our-work/
Community-based organizing and support for LGBTQ parents offering education, awareness, and access to various forms of support.

The Vanier Institute of the Family
http://vanierinstitute.ca/
A Canadian organization devoted to studying Canadian families and disseminating information to the public about pressing issues and emerging trends in families.

Council of Canadians with Disabilities
www.ccdonline.ca/en/
A national organization devoted to disability and inclusiveness providing information on support services.

Chapter 11

A Glimpse into the Future

Where Do Families Go from Here?

Gladskikh Tatiana/Shutterstock

CHAPTER OUTLINE

- Family Life in the Twenty-First Century
- Families in the Connected Society
  - Technology and Family Relations
  - Comparing Communication Technologies
- Communication Technology and the Forming of Relationships
- Technology for Family Caregiving
- New Reproductive Technologies
- The Growth of Individualization
- A New Culture of Intimate Life
- Likely Changes in the Future

- Dual-Income Families
- Refilled Nests
- Nominal and Virtual Families
- Increased Diversity
- Policy Challenges
- Concluding Remarks

LEARNING OBJECTIVES

1 Show an understanding of the role of technology in our personal relationships.

2 Describe the crucial role that technology plays in children's lives.

3 Analyze how technology is used in creating and maintaining romantic relationships.

4 Recognize the challenges that technology creates for our intimate relationships.

5 Assess future trends in family roles and transitions.

6 Assess the changing social and personal expectations for relationships.

In this chapter, we consider what the future holds for families. Methodically predicting the future has important practical value, since thinking about the future can help us avoid the mistakes of the past.

We cannot predict perfectly, as a record of many inaccurate past predictions proves, yet preparation is always better than being taken by surprise. Our close relations—especially our family relations—are intricate, varied, and always changing. We end this text by addressing the *likely* changes to family life in the future, and the forces—especially technological forces—behind those changes.

In the future, some family problems of the present will likely persist, and new problems will emerge. A future of families without problems is unthinkable, if only because we continue to create new problems as we go along. Like much else in the past hundred years, the problems of the next hundred years will probably involve changes in science and technology, travel and communication, and war and intergroup conflict. Since we will likely continue to live in a global society, humanity's problems will be progressively global in scope. Human health is continually improving, yet family concerns about health and health risks will continue to grow. Medical technology will improve, but new illnesses will also develop, and new disasters will force us to cope in different ways.

Most important, since we increasingly rely on information and technology, our problems will increasingly be concerned with information flow and with the use, abuse, and malfunction of technology. Our ability to solve family problems will need better social science and more social science–based policies.

FAMILY LIFE IN THE TWENTY-FIRST CENTURY

In this chapter, we focus on the important role of technology in changing family life. This is not to underestimate the importance of the economy in family life. The shortage of well-paying, secure jobs for young people will continue to play an important role in the formation and dissolution of families around the world, Canada included. It will also continue to affect people's childbearing decisions—whether and when to have children—and families' migration decisions.

The job shortage facing young and middle-aged Canadians is often attributed to globalization—the exodus of well-paying unionized manufacturing jobs out of Canada (and other industrialized countries) to lower-wage societies in the southern hemisphere. This assessment is justified: The Canadian economy has lost hundreds of thousands of well-paying, often unionized manufacturing jobs in the past 30 years. However, many of these losses have been because of automation, not globalization—that is, because of the replacement of human workers by machines, especially by intelligent, computer-controlled machines. This automation process will continue and even accelerate in the foreseeable future, continuing to undermine the availability of well-paying, secure jobs for young people and, accordingly, continuing to undermine the formation, health, and stability of families in Canada.

What should be said here, then, is that automation is part of a global, economic process of change that started nearly two centuries ago and shows no sign of abating. The pace of technological change in the past decade—let alone in the past century—has been daunting to even the most technologically aware people. Many social theorists wrongly think that technological changes inevitably produce social changes (Dumitrica and Wyatt, 2015). In their theories, technological changes and innovations have large and even drastic effects on societies, social institutions, and individuals, resulting in various ethnic, cultural, and social concerns. In their minds, people and societies always must react to, adjust to, or repair changes caused by new technology.

It's true that technology influences culture. However, mindless technology does not drive social change; human decisions are also involved. Social change is the co-production of economic and political imperatives, social values, and technical and social inventions. Technological opportunities at the wrong place or the wrong time will have little or no effect. However, under the right circumstances, technological innovations will often have dramatic and often unforeseen effects.

One of the most fundamental understandings to emerge from sociology is that technology is more than hard wires and virtual buttons. So, for example, sociologists have found that new technologies have not transformed family or personal communications fundamentally in the past 10 years, or 100 years. Instead, we humans have adapted these new technologies for current purposes. Our ideas about family life and our uses of new technology to put these ideas into effect have changed together, influencing one another. Present-day family life has changed so much that, for many, direct communication is no longer as easy as it once was. The technological boom in family communication (e.g., via email, text messaging, and video chat) reflects the demands of a changing society more than it reflects any inherent aspect of the technologies themselves (West and Heath, 2011).

Yet the technological explosion changes families too, in multifaceted ways. For example, reproductive technologies that allow clinically infertile people to become parents raise new and difficult questions. Equally challenging are the questions posed by medical technology that extends lives for longer than ever before.

Other concerns arise from the cultural effects of new technology. For example, routines such as family dinners—an important part of identity development—have become less common with the use of microwave ovens and prepared fast or frozen foods, which ease the time pressure that so many families experience today. As well, because of texting on mobile devices, family members may be physically together (e.g., at a family meal) but not really interacting. Rather than sharing time together, family members may also eat alone, standing in the kitchen, before racing off to their next activity.

Information and communication technologies (ICT) have helped some people to set their own work hours at home, released from the hubbub of commutes, office gossip, and the 9-to-5 routine. But these "teleworkers" must make choices about the maintenance of the work–family boundary and their transitions between work and family roles (Fonner and Stache, 2012). Factors that influence these choices include the degree to which the individual identifies with the institutional ideal of 9-to-5 work. They are not a simple result of technological change, and they cannot be solved by new technology alone, as we see in the box on the next page.

Many teleworkers feel a continuing tension between the positive flexibility that their work-from-home arrangement allows and the (sometimes) negative need for discipline to get their paid and domestic work done. On the one hand, telework can be both professionally and personally gratifying, giving the individual a better sense of control and a greater level of autonomy. On the other hand, it can be challenging to care for families and work in the same space at the same time (Gold and Mustafa, 2013). One study of married Canadian teleworkers with school-aged children found that participants appreciated the time they saved by not having to commute (Hilbrecht, Shaw, Johnson, and Andrey, 2008). However, they mainly reallocated this time to domestic chores, child care, or paid work, not to leisure or self-care. Thus, teleworking—often touted as a solution to women's "double shift"—may instead allow that double shift to occur in the same physical space. We may not learn the long-term family implications of these changes in work for many years.

Today, technologies offer families new ways to start and prolong close relations, but they also pose new challenges to our relationships. In this chapter, we focus on information technology as one example of new technology. Like earlier social inventions—think of the development of cities, factories, automobiles, telephones, and television—information technologies like smartphones, social media, tablets, and

Does Telecommuting Suit Everyone?

Carla Holub says that she has yet to experience a drawback to her telecommuting arrangement (Marowits, 2016). The Calgary-based WestJet sales agent says that she's been working from home for three years now. She saves money on lunches and coffee that she used to buy from shops near her office, no longer needs to pay for gas to get to and from work, and can forgo parking fees. The best part, though, is that Holub can redirect the two hours she used to spend commuting to taking her children to their hockey and dance lessons.

Research shows that not everyone is as enthusiastic about telecommuting as Holub, however. In their analysis of survey data from Edmonton, Habib, Sasic, and Zaman (2012) found that many workers were reluctant to try telecommuting. The mode of transportation their participants typically used to get to work influenced their willingness to work from home. Surprisingly, drivers—even those with long commute times—were not especially likely to telecommute. However, workers who relied on public transit or carpools were often more enthusiastic about telecommuting if their usual trip to the office demanded significant walking, waiting, or transferring. One of the main concerns with telecommuting that participants highlighted was that working from home would prevent them from maintaining a divide between their professional and private lives and complicate the division of household labour.

Many of the consequences of telecommuting that employers view positively may not be so great for telecommuting workers themselves. For example, some studies show that telecommuters are more productive, since they redirect up to 60 percent of the time they formerly spent travelling to doing their paid work (Immen, 2013). Telecommuting has also been said to allow workers to remain productive on their sick days, when they're at home caring for their children or parents, or while recovering from surgery (Immen, 2013). Employers undoubtedly benefit from telecommuters' longer hours, but workers who are expected to be constantly available may come to suffer from a lack of work–life balance.

Sources: The Globe and Mail, January 15. Retrieved from https://www.theglobeandmail.com/report-on-business/ careers/the-future-of-work/the-benefits-of-telecommuting/ article7362816; Marowits, R. 2016. More employees working from home in shift to "telecommuting". *Toronto Star*, May 23. Retrieved from https://www.thestar.com/business/2016/05/23/more-employees-working-from-home-in-shift-to-telecommuting.html.

email have already changed, and will continue to change, families and family lives (see Silva, 2010).

ICT affect families in several ways, as we will see (King-O'Riain, 2015). First, ICT affect our culture as a whole, and thus affect families indirectly. Second, ICT directly affect the ways in which family members communicate with one another and with non-family members. Third, ICT provide a way of delivering services—for example, teaching and providing therapy—thus giving people unequalled access to information and advice about families and family life, both good and bad. However, as we see in the box on the next page, ICT do not solve all of our problems.

Writer Eliana Dockterman recalls how the movie *Her* hit all too close to home. Sitting beside her visiting boyfriend, who lives 4000 kilometres away, Dockterman watched the film and realized that it spoke to the worst parts of long-distance dating (Dockterman, 2014). Misunderstandings when you cannot see your partner's body language, a lack of physical intimacy, and frustration from missed calls are all problems that persist despite apps like Skype and FaceTime.

Dockterman's relationship epitomizes the most popular understanding of long-distance courtships: couples who are physically separated for prolonged periods of time. However, researchers have proposed that work arrangements involving exceptionally long commutes can also cause a relationship to feel like a long-distance one. Sandow (2014) notes that some workers travel for hours every day, eliminating time they have to spend with their partners and hindering their ability to share domestic chores evenly. Others work far enough from home that they need to stay in temporary accommodations—such as a hotel or rented apartment—during the week and return home to be with their partners on weekends. This arrangement is especially common among older, married couples who have settled down and are unwilling to uproot their lives and move when one partner is offered a job opportunity far away (Landesman and Seward, 2013). Presumably, ICT are even less helpful for these long-distance commuters and their partners; the strain placed on their relationship is not because of one partner's physical absence for months at a time, but rather to the extensive travelling that consumes time they might otherwise spend with their significant other.

Sources: Based on Dockterman, E. 2014. How Skype is sabotaging your long distance relationship. *Time*, February 12. Retrieved from http://time.com/7195/how-skype-is-sabotaging-your-long-distance-relationship/; Landesman, J., & R.R. Seward. 2013. Long distance commuting and couple satisfaction in Israel and United States: An exploratory study. *Journal of Comparative Family Studies 44*(6): 765–781; Sandow, E. 2014. Til work do us part: The social fallacy of long-distance commuting. *Urban Studies* 51(3): 526–543.

FAMILIES IN THE CONNECTED SOCIETY

Today, any discussion of close relations must consider virtual communities, and especially communities of close relations that exist in cyberspace. These relations are characterized by regular electronic contact but rare face-to-face contact. Because of the country's vast geography, Canada's researchers know a lot about long-distance communication issues. As a nation of large distances and sparse population, Canada has always relied on transport and communication technology to make social organization possible. As such, Canada has been a "connected" nation for many years, with Canadians ranking among the world's highest users of telephone, internet, and cable services.

As well, Canada is an immigrant society, and this, too, contributes to the need for long-distance communication. Many immigrants preserve regular connections with relatives and friends in their homelands through telephone, email, and other means. With the development of technologies such as Skype and FaceTime, geographically distant family members can feel physically present (King-O'Riain, 2015).

Family members can catch up "face to face" or leave these apps running while they go about their daily routines, making it feel as if their loved ones are participating. Table 11.1 gives some indication of the importance of these technologies in Canadian social life.

A few simple statistics tell the tale. As of 2013 (the most recent year for which we have reliable statistics), 99.3 percent of Canadians have either a cellphone or landline telephone (Statistics Canada, 2015a). As well, 85.6 percent have a computer at home, and 83.9 percent can access the internet from home. These numbers are much higher than in previous years and continue to increase quickly, reflecting the willingness of Canadians to remain connected in virtual communities. We are willing to pay steep prices for such connectivity: In 2014, Canadian households paid an average of $203.04 per month for their communications services.

As a result, ever-speedier delivery of information, goods, and services has become a common fixation. Smartphones, tablets, and laptops connect ever more people, creating the impression that we are continuously available to each other, regardless of location or time.

Researchers disagree about the overall effect of this use of ICT on family life (Lai and Gwung, 2013). The negative effects are evident. For example, work-related emailing and phone calls may intrude on family life, disturbing family rituals and cohesion.

Table 11.1 Canadian Wireline and Mobile Wireless Subscribers per 100 Households

Year	Wireline	Mobile wireless	Wireline and/ or mobile wireless	Wireline only	Mobile wireless only	Only wireline or wireless
2002	97.0	51.6	98.7	47.1	1.7	48.8
2003	96.3	53.9	98.8	44.9	2.5	47.4
2004	96.2	58.9	98.9	40.0	2.7	42.7
2005	94.0	62.9	98.8	36.0	4.8	40.8
2006	93.6	66.8	98.6	31.8	5.0	36.8
2007	92.5	71.9	98.8	26.9	6.3	33.2
2008	91.1	74.3	99.1	24.8	8.0	32.8
2009	89.3	77.2	99.3	22.1	10.0	32.1
2010	89.1	78.2	99.3	21.1	10.2	31.3
2011	86.5	79.4	99.3	19.9	12.8	32.7
2012	83.5	81.4	99.2	17.8	15.7	33.5
2013	78.9	84.9	99.3	14.4	20.4	34.8

Source: Statistics Canada. 2015. *Communications Monitoring Report 2015: Canada's Communications System: An Overview for Citizens, Consumers, and Creators.* Retrieved from: http://www.crtc.gc.ca/eng/publications/reports/policymonitoring/2015/cmr2.htm. Reproduced and distributed on an "as is" basis with the permission of Statistics Canada.

Early research highlighted the tendency of computers and other ICT to isolate families, individuate family members—separate them from one another in individual activities—and even produce addictive behaviour. For instance, Nie and Hillygus (2002) found that frequent internet use is associated with less time spent with family and friends and on social activities in general, as well as increased depression and loneliness. These problems have continued and perhaps even intensified.

However, the positive effects of ICT are evident as well. Increased connectivity makes it easier to contact friends, neighbours, acquaintances, spouses, children, parents, and siblings. Thanks to their portability, cellphones may increase and enhance family communication. Siblings, spouses, and parents and children routinely reach out to each other via text message or group chat apps while waiting for appointments, commuting, or at school or work (Lanigan, 2009). When family members contact each other spontaneously and with greater regularity, they show their commitment to and concern for one another, thereby strengthening their ties. So, far from destroying social life, some researchers find that virtual relations improve it. To the extent that ICT have positive effects on Canadian lives, many want to make access a right, not a privilege.

Youth are by far the most likely age group to be online, but caregivers and older adults have also benefited from technological advancement (Haight, Quan-Haase, and Corbett, 2014). Social media apps and instant communication programs can help children build and sustain new friendships, explore their interests, and express themselves (Moscovitch, 2007). Older adults—especially those who have immigrated recently, leaving friends and family behind—can stay in touch with old contacts via email or build new relations in online chat rooms (Zhang, 2016). And stressed caregivers who are pressed for time can get answers to their questions in seconds over the internet and confirm that advice with professionals working for services such as Telehealth.

So, overall, ICT have had different effects on social life and will continue to have unpredictable effects, at least for a while (Lai and Gwung, 2013).

Information technology is also becoming more and more necessary from an academic standpoint. In 2005, more than one-quarter of adult Canadians—an estimated 6.4 million—used the internet for education, training, or schoolwork (McKeown and Underhill, 2005). By 2009, when the most recent statistics became available, usage had increased substantially. By then, many postsecondary and training courses were being offered online, and many people were seeking information via the internet (Statistics Canada, 2010a).

Yet, despite its growing popularity, ICT access varies in different regions for different people (see Table 11.2), creating a so-called "digital divide." Low-income parents with less than a high school–level education are less likely than other Canadians to have internet access at home (Haight et al., 2014). Only 58 percent of Canadian households with an income under $30 000 have internet access at home, compared to 98 percent of Canada's highest-earning households (ACORN Canada, 2016). And, even if they could afford it, many people who live in rural, northern Canadian

Is Internet Access a Privilege or a Right?

The internet is considered such a vital service that low-income earners in Canada redirect money from their food and rent budgets to pay for it (Monsebraaten, 2016).

ACORN Canada, an organization representing 70 000 low- and moderate-income families in nine cities across Canada, issued a report in 2016 calling for an affordable home internet program (Monsebraaten, 2016). The advocacy group proposed that Canadians living below Statistics Canada's low-income measure should be eligible for a home internet package priced at $10 per month. The federal Canadian Radio-television and Telecommunications Commission (CRTC) should mandate this service, ACORN suggested.

Research shows that a low-income earner's inability to afford internet access limits his or her opportunities for a better future. Those without internet access cannot search job postings, submit resumes, or fill out online job applications. They also cannot research or apply for schools, participate in online skills development programs, or use any online service designed to support low-income earners. One study found that unemployed people who lacked internet access were more likely to give up their job searches (Beard, Ford, Saba, and Seals, 2012). Those who were able use the internet at home or even in public libraries were 50 percent more likely to persist.

A lack of internet access also harms the next generation. Many teachers use blogs, wikis, and online portals to provide their students with homework assignments, post reminders about upcoming deadlines, and distribute study notes and other resources (Portier, Peterson, Capitao-Tavares, and Rambaran, 2013). Some exams are even administered online, and many instructors request that students submit their essays and research projects digitally. Youth who lack internet access are thus placed at an academic disadvantage compared to their higher-income counterparts who can use these resources conveniently at home.

Sources: Based on Beard, T.R., G.S. Ford, R.P. Saba, & R.A. Seals. 2012. Internet use and job search. *Telecommunications Policy* 36: 260–273; Monsebraaten, L. 2016. Anti-poverty advocates call for affordable internet. *Toronto Star*, February 2. Retrieved from https://www.thestar.com/news/gta/2016/02/02/anti-poverty-advocates-call-for-affordable-internet.html; Portier, C.A., S.S. Peterson, Z. Capitao-Tavares, & K. Rambaran. 2013. Parent perceptions and recommendations about homework involving wikis and blogs. *Middle School Journal* 44(5): 6–14.

communities do not have reliable internet connections; the needed infrastructure is not yet in place.

The digital divide has an especially powerful effect on Indigenous communities in Canada. Some remote or rural communities lack the necessary infrastructure. With small populations of consumers dispersed over large geographic areas, internet service providers have little incentive to maintain service. And in urban areas that have the necessary infrastructure, low-income Indigenous people may struggle to afford a computer and internet service (Mignone and Henley, 2009). Yet access to these technologies would provide Indigenous communities with access to educational and employment opportunities, allow them to share their language and cultural history, and allow them to access online health care services and support groups.

Table 11.2 Canadian Home Internet Access by Province, 2005–2009

Location of access = Home Internet access

Geography[3]	2005	2007	2009
Newfoundland and Labrador	45.9	56.6	65.3
Prince Edward Island	52.2	63.9	72.9
Nova Scotia	59.0	64.3	74.4
New Brunswick	49.4	58.4	70.5
Quebec	52.5	63.1	72.9
Ontario	66.5	70.9	77.9
Manitoba	57.5	64.1	71.7
Saskatchewan	58.3	68.8	75.8
Alberta	63.9	73.3	81.7
British Columbia	63.3	73.6	83.0

Source: Statistics Canada. 2010. *Canadian Internet use survey, Internet use, by location of access, Canada, provinces and selected census metropolitan areas (CMAs).* Retrieved from: http://www5.statcan. gc.ca/ cansim/a47. Reproduced and distributed on an "as is" basis with the permission of Statistics Canada.

Connectedness has a huge effect on people's lives. In a postindustrial, information-based economy, connectivity affects people's employability—their chances of getting a good job or any job at all. All of these factors have an effect on family life, since, as we have stressed in other chapters, the demands of work (including schoolwork) always influence the quality of close relations. Canadians' unequal access to the internet and social media, and their unequal computer literacy, also affects people's educational and occupational attainment and, indirectly, their family well-being.

We cannot predict how quickly this digital divide will shrink. In the long run, ICT may give traditionally disadvantaged and isolated families new opportunities to improve their social condition. This will indirectly improve family life, while also changing the face of work and community life. However, we are far from seeing this happen.

Technology and Family Relations

Changes in technology that simplify contact among family and friends often contribute to the quality and cohesion of relationships. Over the past 150 years, changes in communications and transport technologies have made contact among kin, whether they live near one another or great distances apart, less expensive, faster, and easier. As email and internet use spreads, geographic constraints on social relations continue to lessen (Silva, 2010).

Yet despite the constant changes in the technological context of social relations, most social research continues to find that people form and preserve close relations mainly through face-to-face interaction (Farrell, VandeVusse, and Ocobock, 2012). Among strongly tied (i.e., closely related) people, easy, cheap technologies such as email and phone calls have augmented but not replaced in-person contact. In their study of Torontonians' interactions in the pre- and post-internet years, Mok, Wellman, and Carrasco (2010) found that high-quality close relations continue to depend on physical proximity. People who call and email each other the most also see each other the most. By contrast, any form of contact with friends and relatives who live too far away to visit in person tends to drop off. Phone calls, emails, and other types of digital communication are used to sustain contact between face-to-face meetings and to plan those meetings; however, they do not replace in-person interaction.

Comparing Communication Technologies

One strategy for predicting how technology will affect close relations in the future is to examine how technology has affected close relations in the past. Here, we consider how the telephone and email have affected relations so far, and how these and other, newer innovations may continue to affect these relations in the future.

The Telephone   The telephone is hardly new or innovative, yet it remains a popular way for physically separated family members to maintain contact. Whether they allow children to call their errand-running parents or spouses to maintain long-distance relationships, phone calls are preferred over other modes of communication for their immediacy and simplicity. They provide direct, real-time contact within seconds, keep conversations private, and allow people to express their views in their own voice (as opposed to in writing).

Yet surprisingly, the effects of the telephone on social life have been modest. At most, the telephone has helped family members to stay in touch between face-to-face meetings. It has not replaced, or even come to be considered an equivalent to, in-person meetings (Lanigan, 2009).

Note that the telephone—like other forms of communication—has had both positive and negative effects on close relations. Couples in long-distance relationships often report that, despite the ease and affordability of phone calls, they still feel that they need to visit each other in person to preserve their relationship. Sometimes, the needed technology (such as reliable internet) may not be available and long-distance phone calls are costly. And if couples are in different time zones, real-time contact may have to be reserved for special occasions; often, one partner will be busy at work or school while the other is asleep (Tseng, 2016).

Frequent contact can also be frustrating and upsetting for siblings in transnational families. Increasingly in Canada, families are scattered over two or more nations, as parents move abroad to work, send some of their children to different countries to attend school, and send others back to the homeland, thinking that is in their best interests (Mummert, 2009). Some siblings may know each other only through photographs and phone calls. Having been raised by different parents or caregivers, in different countries, with different linguistic and cultural norms, phone calls between these siblings may be unnerving. If one sibling has flourished in a new home while another has missed out on educational and occupational opportunities, contact may also cause frustration, jealousy, or resentment.

Email Email is even cheaper than telephone communication. Like the telephone, email allows escape from continued contact, if that is desired. It gives a person time to think and reflect before initiating or responding to contact. Email does not interrupt in the same way as the telephone, nor is it dependent on both people being available at the same time. However, email carries dangers of its own. Faceless anonymity increases the risk of indiscretion, misunderstanding, and misquoting (Lanigan, 2009). The shield of visual and vocal anonymity may encourage blunt disclosure and self-misrepresentation. Couples in long-distance relationships often report that the lack of body language and other visual cues can make it hard to interpret their partners' meanings and feelings in emails. For family members in different time zones, communicating only through delayed emails can be frustrating and may reinforce the perception of distance (Tseng, 2016).

Technology has also made it harder for parents to censor and control the material their children interact with (Lanigan, 2009). For example, parents today are unlikely to be the first to discuss sex with their children. As in the past, youth are likely to begin discussing sex with their friends, not their parents; however, today, those friends are also likely to introduce each other to internet pornography, much of which is free and easily accessible (Weber, Quiring, and Daschmann, 2012). Rather than discussing sex in mature, respectful ways with their parents (or teachers), many children are first exposed to graphic, often violent and sexist pornography, which can shape their understandings of "appropriate," "normal" sexual activity.

Research confirms that parents are often unaware of their children's online activities (Sorbring and Lundin, 2012). In the past, parents could more easily supervise their children, since most of their children's interactions with friends and family happened at home, in friends' homes, on the playground, and so on. Today, however, youth text, Snapchat, or instant message their friends with great frequency, from any location they like. Parents are unable to monitor interactions they do not know are occurring.

One concern is that the internet has opened up a new realm for school bullies to attack their targets: Typically, boys report receiving physical threats while girls report receiving defamatory comments and online "slut shaming" (Sorbring and Lundin, 2012). Whereas traditional bullying is contained at school, cyberbullying can reach a target anywhere, at any time. And even parents who experienced bullying themselves may be less able to empathize with their children who are targeted by this cyberbullying.

Thus, families need to strike a delicate balance: Parents must support safe internet use that lets their children preserve friendships and access important information for school, but they must also set boundaries for their children. The challenge here is that many youths know more about the internet than their parents; some parents rely on their children to help them with tasks they used to perform independently, such as paying bills online or negotiating with internet or television providers. This reliance can confuse parent–child relationships, making it even harder for parents to enforce rules.

The effects of technological innovation on other types of family relationships can be considered using family development theory. The premise of this theory is that families continuously change with changes in social expectations, changes in environmental constraints, and the changing needs of family members (e.g., biological, psychological, and social needs). As families change and restructure, they engage in new developmental tasks, or activities that prepare them for coming stages.

Traditional "stages" include marriage without children, marriage with various-aged children (e.g., infant, preschool, school-aged, adolescent, young adult), marriage with children who live outside the household, grandparenting, and marriage in late life. As we have seen in earlier chapters, these traditional stages and relationships have been expanded today to include divorce and remarriage, cohabitation, the rise of childbearing as a "discretionary option," and the legalization of same-sex marriages.

The research questions offered by family development theory are: How does technology influence family change over time? Specifically, how does the use of ICT influence the norms and roles of family members? How do families use technology in the developmental tasks that contribute to life course transitions? In what ways is the use of technology different across various stages of development? Does technology affect or contribute to the experience of off-time or non-normative stage transitions? Finally, how does family development differ in families with continuous access to technology and in families without such access? An example of this developmental process is the need to grapple with new opportunities for cheating on one's spouse, and therefore new ways to deal with cheating.

Use of computers and smartphones at home will likely affect some stages of family life more than others. For example, these devices could harm new marriages more easily than longer-lived marriages. However, the new communication opportunities can also help new marriages between people who are technologically savvy. Couples today stay up to date on each other's lives by following each other on Facebook, Twitter, Instagram, Snapchat, and so on. This allows new couples to learn each other's lifestyles, preferences, and daily routines quickly. But it can also cause feelings of being left out—say, if one partner is on a trip or enjoying an event without the other— or of jealousy—say, if one partner is documented on social media spending much of his or her time with friends who could be potential dating partners (Tseng, 2016).

On the other hand, ICT can help busy working couples to coordinate chores and child care or to stay in touch while at the office. In these cases, ICT help to sustain and strengthen connections. Similarly, ICT can ease the sometimes-painful transition that parents experience when their children move away from home for the first time. While away at college or university, both children and their parents can feel at ease knowing that their loved ones are just a phone call or Skype session away

In a world filled with Tinder users, definitions of relationships and infidelity are becoming unclear. One popular question that online dating apps force us to ask is: Does online flirting count as cheating, even if you never meet in person?

The answer, according to one report by JDate and ChristianMingle, is yes. Fifty-one percent of male participants and 68 percent of female participants said that they thought texting or chatting with someone else online was being unfaithful (Cortese, 2014). However, that still leaves about half of men and 30 percent of women who think that cyber-relationships are acceptable, even if you have a "real" relationship. Some of these people say they do not think that online flirtations count as cheating because no physical contact is involved.

On the other hand, it may also be easier to detect (both physical and emotional) infidelity today than it was in the past, thanks to the same technologies. Couples are now able to monitor each other's behaviour from afar by checking their public Twitter, Facebook, Instagram, and Snapchat profiles (Rueda, Lindsay, and Williams, 2015). Some secretly read through each other's texts, emails, and direct messages in search of the online flirtations described above. One app called Karelog (or Boyfriend Log) eventually had to be redesigned: It allowed suspicious girlfriends to track the location of their boyfriends' phones and view their call history, raising concerns about privacy laws (Gregg, 2013). Thus, ICT may provide greater opportunities for infidelity of different sorts, but they can also hinder one's ability to cheat without getting caught.

Sources: Based on Cortese, A. 2014. Can virtual flirtation be considered cheating? *The Huffington Post*, August 5. Retrieved from http://www. huffingtonpost. com/alexa-cortese/can-virtual-flirtation-be-considered- cheating_b_5647386.html; Gregg, M. 2013. Spouse-busting: Intimacy, adultery, and surveillance technology. *Surveillance & Society* 11(3): 301; Rueda, H., M. Lindsay, & L. Williams. 2015. "She posted it on Facebook": Mexican American adolescents' experiences with technology and romantic relationship conflict. *Journal of Adolescent Research 30*(4): 419–445.

(Lanigan, 2009). Email, text messages, and Skype are also helping relatives in different parts of the world to stay in touch and helping adult children to check in on their aging parents.

Communication Technology and the Forming of Relationships

Technology not only helps to maintain relationships, but also increasingly helps to create them. In the past, people traditionally initiated dates and romantic relationships through face-to-face interaction, but people today increasingly use Facebook or online dating sites for the same purpose (Sautter, Tippett, and Morgan, 2010).

Most online daters seek, or say they seek, long-term partners and list the advantages of internet dating as convenience, privacy and confidentiality, and the opportunity to meet people they otherwise never would (Kang and Hoffman, 2011). Online romantic relationships are thus rapidly becoming commonplace for many single Canadians.

They are not as common, however, among recent immigrants or particular ethnic groups, including Muslims and southern Asians (Sautter, Tippett, and Morgan, 2010).

Online dating sites typically claim that they rely on complicated algorithms that match users with a perfect mate. Using these sites, online daters open themselves up to meeting countless more people than they would by searching for partners in conventional ways. However, online dating profiles also allow users to depict themselves in favourable (and sometimes untruthful) ways. For example, Toma, Hancock, and Ellison (2008) compared the information presented in online daters' profiles with objective measurements of their physical features. They found that, in profiles, men were more likely to exaggerate their height (upward), while women were more likely to exaggerate their weight (downward). Participants also admitted that their profile photos did not accurately reflect their appearance. Thus, like traditional face-to-face dating, selecting a partner online can have drawbacks as well as benefits.

Much less research has been conducted on the ways older adults use online dating sites, but we do know that many have turned to the internet to meet potential romantic partners (Wada, Mortenson, and Clarke, 2016). Traditional dating sites such as eHarmony have seen increased numbers of older adults using their services. As well, many new sites, such as Senior Friend Finder, Senior Match, and Senior People Meet, cater exclusively to clientele over age 50. So, online dating isn't helping only young adults to meet their future life partners; it's also helping older adults who are divorced, widowed, or never-married to find partners. Some of the strengths (and peculiarities) of these sites are discussed below.

The online relationships of older adults resemble those of their younger counterparts. Namely, both older and younger adults are typically looking to develop intimate, meaningful, and long-lasting relationships online. Both younger and older men often prioritize physical attractiveness in a potential date, whereas both younger and older women typically look for men with high status and high incomes (Alterovitz and Mendelsohn, 2009).

However, one study found that older online daters are more selective than younger ones with regards to the race, religion, income, age, and height of their potential mates (McIntosh et al., 2011). They are also willing to travel greater distances than young people to meet a promising potential partner. So, older adults may be interested in meeting the "right" person but not interested in meeting just anyone.

Because online dating has become widespread only within the last 10 or 20 years, we do not know yet whether these online daters will have stronger, longer-lasting relationships or more precarious ones than couples who form in other ways. We do know that, given the expanded possibility of meeting people, the types of relationships formed will be more diverse. Future research will need to address several questions: Are these relationships more or less prone to breakups and divorces than relationships formed in other ways? Will spouses feel insecure or suspicious that their partner may be meeting someone else online? Will parents who met online have different attitudes about their children's dating? Will they be more open to internet use by their children?

Exclusive Dating Apps: Classist or Realistic?

Many say they enjoy online dating because it offers a huge pool of diverse candidates, but today that diversity is in jeopardy. Tinder Select, Bumble VIBee, Luxy, and Raya are just a few offshoots of traditional dating apps that are invite only. These selective sites boast that they offer only the "highest-quality" singles, hand-picked from the dating masses (Beaulieu, 2017). For example, Luxy applicants must have their minimum $200 000 annual incomes verified to be granted access to the app and its supposedly more desirable users (Haynes, 2017).

As classist and exclusionary as they sound, invite-only apps are not that surprising. We like to think that love knows no boundaries and overcomes all odds. Until now, the online dating world has fed these fantasies by encouraging us to think that we may stumble upon our soul mates as we swipe through photos of thousands of strangers (Forani, 2017; Haynes, 2017). But, in reality, dating and mating happen through social institutions that push people into relationships with others like themselves (Dribe and Nystedt, 2013). The marriage of a one-percenter to a high

school–educated minimum-wage earner is a fantasy largely reserved for romantic fiction.

Online dating apps that let users sort profiles by income level or place high earners and otherwise attractive matches into separate dating pools more accurately reflect reality (Forani, 2017). By narrowing overwhelming numbers of candidates down, selective dating apps may give more people a better shot at finding a compatible partner.

Sources: Based on Beaulieu, M. 2017. Tinder Select makes swiping super exclusive. *CBC*, March 14. Retrieved from http://www.cbc.ca/life/wellness/tinder-select-makes-swiping-super-exclusive-1.4025220; Dribe, M., & P. Nystedt. 2013. Educational homogamy and gender-specific earnings: Sweden, 1990–2009. *Demography* 50: 1197–1216; Forani, J. 2017. Dating apps and the elite go exclusive. *Toronto Star*, April 18. Retrieved from https://www.thestar.com/life/relationships/2017/04/18/dating-apps-and-the-elite-go-exclusive.html; Haynes, G. 2017. From Raya to Tinder Select: The world of elite dating apps. *The Guardian*, March 8. Retrieved from https://www.theguardian.com/technology/shortcuts/2017/m.

We also know that a large number of people who use online dating sites do not meet anyone they contact and do not even intend to do so when they first set up their profiles. In 2013, 66 percent of people with online dating profiles reported having gone on a date with someone from an online dating site (Smith and Duggan, 2013). At least some of the remaining 34 percent may engage in "cyber-relationships": They instant message, chat over the phone, Skype, and may even have cybersex, but never meet in person. These relationships may unfold over great geographic distance, and partners may achieve intense emotional connections (Kang and Hoffman, 2011).

Other relationships may serve as fun distractions or an escape from the stress of the daily grind (Wang and Chang, 2010). Many people adopt bogus names and identities for their interactions online. Deception can be part of the fun of cyberspace, a type of social gaming.

Either way, many people say that they find online relationships easier than face-to-face ones, at least in some respects. For one, a sense of distance and seeming anonymity reduce the anxiety that some people experience about showing their feelings or fears (Tait and Jeske, 2015). Perhaps for this reason, some people report feeling that they can come to know each other intimately much more quickly online than in face-to-face relationships. Finally, some may turn to online relationships as a means of escaping stressful or unsatisfying in-person relationships (Cravens, Leckie, and Whiting, 2013).

So, cyber-relationships can help single people to form new bonds, but they can also threaten existing relationships. Cybersex constitutes a blatant form of infidelity, so what are we to make of cyber-relationships that unfold across hundreds or thousands of kilometres? Similarly, should we consider it emotional infidelity when a partner engages in online flirtations or "likes" or comments on someone else's social media content? By largely erasing the physical aspect of betrayal and stressing the emotional aspect, cyber-relationships and flirtations may redefine how our culture thinks about fidelity. Some of these issues are explored in the box below.

>>> Is Online Dating Doomed?

Evolutionary anthropologist Dr. Anna Machin says that the casual encounters typical of Tinder users go against human hardwiring (Llorente, 2017). But while long-term love might drive our society by supporting reproduction, that does not explain the huge popularity of dating apps designed exclusively to help people "hook up."

These apps have changed the dating game. Instead of limiting your selection to the people you might casually bump into in your neighbourhood, you can now swipe through hundreds of thousands of profiles of people with whom you may have otherwise never crossed paths (Jeffries, 2012). Some apps are explicitly designed to facilitate casual encounters. Couchsurfing.com, for example, matches residents in more than 100 000 cities around the world with travellers who will be visiting their neighbourhood on their next vacation (Zigos, 2013). Hosts offer their couch, but the unspoken agreement is that the guest's stay will be more than platonic.

Machin admits that convenience and variety are perks for people who have trouble finding partners, but she also highlights that these same factors can be drawbacks: We can start drowning in that massive pool of potential candidates. And rather than settling down with someone we click with, we're always tempted to keep swiping, to see if we can get someone even better (Llorente, 2017).

Machin predicts that the online dating scene will quickly revolutionize to bring back more face-to-face contact, instead of facilitating cyberconnections between people who may never meet (Llorente, 2017). But others disagree, noting that plenty of millennials seem intent on preserving their "freedom" and avoiding commitment, rather than desperately trying to settle down (Jeffries, 2012). Given the relative youth of online dating, only time will tell if we're in for a return to more traditional courtships or if digitally facilitated hook-ups are here to stay.

Sources: Based on Jeffries, S. 2012. Is online dating destroying love? *The Guardian*, Feburary 6. Retrieved from https://www.theguardian.com/lifeandstyle/2012/ feb/06/ is-online-dating-destroying-love; Llorente, J.L. 2017. Dr. Anna Machin. University of Oxford. Retrieved from http://www.ox.ac.uk/research/research-in-conversation/ love/dr-anna-machin; Zigos, J. 2013. Couchsurfing's sex secret: It's the greatest hook-up app ever devised. *Business Insider*, December 7. Retrieved from http:// www.businessinsider.com/ couchsurfing-the-best-hook- up-app-2013-12.

Research is already beginning to show that social media use can cause conflict and jealousy among partners that eventually leads to breakups and divorce (McDaniel, Drouin, and Cravens, 2017). Older research focused on pornography and on feelings of sexual betrayal when one partner discovered the other's use of explicit online photos and videos (Cravens et al., 2013). More recent research, however, has highlighted the interactive nature of social media: Today, partners are more likely to engage in two-way flirtations online by liking or commenting on someone else's photos or by chatting in real time, instead of the one-way interaction they would have with pornography. One study found that posting selfies on Instagram can lead to relationship conflict: Partners may get jealous when the photograph generates attention from viewers, and the individual posting the selfie may develop a cyber-relationship with those who "like" or comment on the photo, which could ultimately lead to in-person infidelity, relationship conflict, and a breakup (Ridgway and Clayton, 2016).

If infidelity is discovered on social media, breakup or divorce may be more likely. For example, research finds that conflict is likely to ensue if a person's "relationship status" is misleadingly set to "single" on Facebook. Photos, comments, chat windows, and other forms of communication on Facebook, Twitter, Instagram, and so on may also reveal that one partner is having an affair. Often, mutual friends and family members view these profiles, becoming aware of the affair before the non-cheating partner. If infidelity has been made public knowledge in this way, the non-cheating partner may feel even more betrayed, which could influence the decision to break up (Cravens et al., 2013).

Technology for Family Caregiving

Cyberspace is not only a place for meeting and mating with people or for keeping in touch with family and friends. It is also a storehouse of useful information for people facing challenges. Increasingly, people look to cyberspace for answers to questions about health, jobs, and family relations.

Researchers have paid special attention to the possible uses of the telephone and internet as means of delivering practical and social support to caregivers. For example, one study used an in-home device to provide care instructions and emotional support for caregivers of veterans with functional impairments (Griffiths et al., 2010). Results showed that caregivers felt relieved after learning more about their care recipients' conditions and how best to support them. Caregiver burden was also reduced because participants did not have to spend time travelling to appointments; instead, they efficiently received information in their homes.

Another study examined the effect of phone calls to caregivers of people who had sustained a traumatic brain injury (TBI) (Powell et al., 2016). Compared with a control group of unsupported caregivers, those who received the phone calls reported feeling like they had more support, that they were better able to obtain the information they needed, and that they could care for themselves more adequately. They even felt they had developed superior coping skills six months after the TBI survivor had been released from hospital.

The internet can also be a source of support for caregivers and recipients. Online chat groups eliminate time and distance barriers and limits on group size; they increase variety and diversity of support, anonymity, pre- and post-group support, and opportunities for expression. For example, CancerChatCanada offers real-time group chat sessions guided by professional therapists. In a study of 102 patients, caregivers, and survivors who used the service, Stephen and colleagues (2014) found that participants appreciated the convenience of using the service from home; felt less inhibited and better able to express themselves in an online, anonymous forum; and felt safe discussing their fears and concerns, knowing that other participants were going through similar experiences.

Another study examined the results of online support groups for hospice patients and family members (Buis, 2008). Results showed that interactions designed to provide emotional support—for example, messages of encouragement and comfort—were most common. However, some users also sought information in the online group, especially regarding medication and treatment.

Internet support groups can also have positive effects on caregiver well-being. For instance, research shows that internet interventions for caregivers of people with dementia often boost confidence and self-efficacy while reducing depression (Boots et al., 2014). Caregivers also benefit from social interactions with other caregivers. Not only do these contacts reduce feelings of social isolation, but they also reaffirm that others are enduring similar experiences. These internet interventions thus have the potential to provide low-cost, effective social support for caregivers. And today, family caregiver support is much needed: Care for older adults is becoming a central part of many people's lives as our population ages and formal caregiving services become less accessible and more costly. However, as with other uses of ICT, some risks are inevitable. Potential disadvantages of seeking support and assistance online include the chance of destructive interactions, a lack of clear and accountable leadership, and limited access to non-computer-using populations. Cyberbullying, exploitation, and violence are also worrisome (Kowalski, Limber, and Agatson, 2012).

Technology can also help support independent living: a preference of an increasing number of people of all ages who require care or support (Klinenberg, 2012). For example, automated medication reminders, video surveillance, mobile emergency response systems, and fall detection systems can all help create safe spaces for older adults to age in place (Rashidi and Mihailidis, 2013). Wearable technology can also monitor heart rate, blood pressure, and other vitals, so that older adults and their caregivers can track their own health from home (Wagner, Basran, and Bello-Haas, 2012). Many of these systems are still new, but they may be used with greater frequency in the future to provide older adults and their caregivers with a greater sense of security and safety.

More common today is the use of websites like WebMD, which provide health care information for specific conditions. Use of these sites can help older adults and

Research regarding the effects of communication technologies on family life is ongoing. With decreasing privacy, online safety is of most concern at this time.
Antonio Guillem/123rf.com

their caregivers to make informed decisions on the care they receive, who provides it, and the costs involved. The internet can also provide people with quick feedback on how their lives and medical condition are affected by their compliance with medication, exercise, and diet. This type of information can lighten the burden on family members who act as caregivers and, at the same time, help older adults retain the sense of autonomy so important to well-being.

NEW REPRODUCTIVE TECHNOLOGIES

New reproductive technologies make it possible to separate fertilization from child-bearing and parenting. In this way, these technologies have the potential to revolutionize family life. Often, however, technologies are used to advance traditional goals by traditional social means—through families, kinship networks, communities, churches, schools, and so on.

Many cultures link heritage and status to "biological" children—children who are genetically related to their parents (Mamo and Alston-Stepnitz, 2015). So, in most parts of the world, "blood ties" are central to kinship. This is largely why some ethnic groups curtail women's freedom to the extent they do: They see women as the vessels of culture transmission. As a result, infertility causes people great anxiety, self-doubt, and depression, especially in societies that consider having children equivalent to entering normal adulthood. There, fertility clinics increasingly offer hope.

Today, more low-fertility couples can now reproduce than in the past. This helps to perpetuate the ideal of the "normal" family with biological children and reinforces, to some degree, the social pressure on all couples to reproduce. For example, many women who have undergone successful fertility treatment want to stay home from work to care for their child after spending so much time and effort trying to reproduce. Rather than challenging traditional views of family, these new technologies appear to reinforce them. The wish to create a "normal" and socially accepted family unit remains strong in modern societies.

The same can be said of selective abortion of female fetuses, a practice that is common in ethnic groups whose culture prefers boys. Fetus sex is determined by ultrasound, a technology typically used to assess the health of the fetus. Increasingly, technologies such as amniocentesis tests are also being used to screen fetuses for signs of irregular development and genetic abnormalities. Parents who learn that their child is not developing normally also have the option to abort their pregnancy. Research finds that up to 85 percent of parents may opt to abort a pregnancy if they expect the child to be born with a severe defect (Balkan et al., 2010). For example, parents may be more inclined toward abortion if they are told their child will be born in great pain and will only live for weeks or days (Hester, Lew, and Swota, 2015).

Amniocentesis tests are known to carry risks, including miscarriage, which deters some women from having them. But as testing procedures become less invasive and more reliable, we may expect to see even more parents participate in fetal screening. For example, a new DNA-based test called MaterniT21 screens for Down syndrome using only a blood sample from the mother (Kaposy, 2013). When these prenatal tests diagnose fetuses with Down syndrome, parents abort the pregnancy between 60 and 90 percent of the time. Some research suggests that the rate of these selective abortions is declining as more individuals become more accepting of people with disabilities. Nevertheless, disability studies scholars suggest that selective termination can be considered a form of eugenics. It can also serve to painfully remind people with disabilities that they have yet to be fully accepted in our society.

Contributing to the problem is the fact that many doctors and even genetic counsellors report feeling inadequately trained to provide parents with the support they need to make this important decision. Researchers have pointed out that parents may feel pressure to abort a child who may be "abnormal" in any way because of persistent stigmatization of people with disabilities and the social pressure to have "normal" children (Jotkowitz and Zivotofsky, 2010).

Similar questions of ethics arise when the mother undergoing fetal screening is a surrogate. Biologically infertile couples, same-sex couples, and single adults are increasingly willing to pay for children they are unable to have themselves (Mamo and Alston-Stepnitz, 2015). Their desire to fill the traditional parenting role is currently being met by nontraditional, technologically advanced, globalized systems.

Sperm and eggs are routinely donated or sold, while surrogate mothers "rent" their wombs (and the rest of their bodies) before giving birth to a child they may never see again and have no legal rights to (Sarojini, Marwah, and Shenoi, 2011).

Increasingly, people view surrogacy as a transaction; the surrogate mother may receive payment or may have her medical bills, prenatal care, and other related expenses covered (Watson, 2016). Since it is now an international industry worth billions of dollars, some have even referred to the act of surrogacy as "outsourcing" the physical labour of child production (Pelzman, 2013: 387). However, conceptualizing surrogacy in these financial terms can be problematic; namely, if the terms of the contract are not met and a healthy child is not delivered, commissioning parents may request a "refund" or refuse to accept the child.

Such practices support our argument that technology tends to be a co-producer of social change. Often, technology is the handmaiden of human ambitions, however forward or backward those may be. If technology is to be understood in terms of social values and social organization, changes in family life must also be understood in those terms. However, social changes bring conflicting interests and conflicting values. What social changes, if any, would you recommend to deal with the problem described in the box on the next page?

THE GROWTH OF INDIVIDUALIZATION

With industrialism and post-industrialism came changes that ultimately allowed people to lead more separate, yet interdependent, lives. This has had a major effect on family life. Let us focus on one aspect of this change—what we call the *individualization* of people's lives (Worts, Sacker, McMunn, and McDonough, 2013). With individualization, we see more variety, fluidity, and idiosyncrasy in all major family processes: in migration, marriage, divorce, childbearing, family decision making, and the relation of work life and family life. We expect people to be self-sufficient actors in their economic, household, leisure, and intimate relations.

Individualization of social roles means the empowerment of women through higher levels of formal education and more participation in the paid labour force. The rise of a service economy creates more employment opportunities for women and thus speeds up this process. Any growth in jobs that free people from family dependency and control increases the variety, fluidity, and idiosyncrasy of people's private lives. Nevertheless, people still need and want the emotional attachments of family life.

When people can choose their own lives—for example, their mate, their living arrangement, or the number of children they will bear—they exercise this choice. This produces heightened satisfaction—at least, at the time of the decision—but also social changes. More choice also produces more confusion and ambivalence about how, and when, to limit choice. For example, do we support or oppose birth control awareness among teenagers? Do we allow abortion after sexual abuse or violent sexual assault, but not in other cases when women seek it?

In 2011, Crystal Kelley hesitantly signed a surrogacy contract that allowed the commissioning parents to request an abortion if three-dimensional ultrasound revealed a severe fetal abnormality (Keating, 2016). When an ultrasound identified a heart defect and cleft lip in the fetus 20 weeks into the pregnancy, the commissioning parents began demanding that Kelley seek an abortion (Forman, 2015). To make matters worse, Kelley learned that she would not have parental rights in Connecticut after the child was born, so the baby girl would become a ward of the state. To keep the child from going into foster care, Kelley packed up her own children and moved to Michigan, where she would have legal rights as the child's mother. But with no job, Kelley knew she could not raise the baby herself. Eventually, a friend of a friend agreed to adopt her, giving Kelley's story a happy ending. However, we can only imagine what happens to other unwanted children following their birth.

Kelley's experiences highlight the many risks associated with surrogacy, as well as the ethical dilemmas for which we have yet to develop solutions. First, although commissioning parents place a great deal of faith in them, contracts are rarely enforceable (Forman, 2015). Second, without a uniform approach to surrogacy across the globe, parental rights can shift if a surrogate moves to a different area, as Kelley did. Third, we remain unable to determine whether the ultimate right to a child should rest with the commissioning parents or the surrogate—and given the unique circumstances that surround most surrogacies, we likely never will (Shaw, 2016). Fourth and finally, cases like Kelley's raise interesting questions in the abortion debate: Surrogates retain autonomy and control over their own bodies, and should have the right to decide whether they undergo an abortion or not, but they are not the ones intending to raise the child—which, in Kelley's case, would have involved extensive caregiving responsibilities for a child with a disability (Walker and Zyl, 2015).

Sources: Based on Forman, D.L. 2015. Abortion clauses in surrogacy contracts: Insights from a case study. *Family Law Quarterly* 49(1): 29–53; Keating, C. 2016. Surrogate mom gives birth to baby girl with serious birth defects despite parents' order to abort: "She is everything i believed she would be." *People*, March 3. Retrieved from http://people.com/babies/ surrogate- crystal-kelley-baby-with-birth-defects-parents-order-to- abort/; Shaw, J. 2016. What do gestational mothers deserve? *Ethical Theory and Moral Practice* 19(4): 1031–1045; Walker, R., & L. Zyl. 2015. Surrogate motherhood and abortion for fetal abnormality. *Bioethics* 29(8): 529–535.

The result of struggles for and against change in family life is hard to predict. However, it seems likely that anything that (1) slows the growth of opportunities after an earlier growth, (2) increases the individualization of lives faster than the creation of new cultural meanings and norms, or (3) otherwise produces uncertainty and confusion (e.g., war or environmental disaster) will increase support for a backward-looking mythology of the family.

How do people cope with the ambivalence and confusion of intimacy and close relations these days? Typically, they develop new social forms and invent new lifestyles to deal with the doubts they face. Formal changes include laws and policies such as new legislation to define marriage and its rights and duties, to support gender equity and affirmative action for women, to improve child care, and to encourage fertility control. Informal changes include efforts people make in their own lives to negotiate new social roles and norms. For example, people work out new ways to discipline the children of their spouse's first marriage, interact with their mother's new boyfriend, or get to know a co-worker's same-sex spouse.

A new way of understanding the role of intergenerational caregiving, especially the care of older adults, has become increasingly vital. Many people who provide care and support to their aging parents today refuse to see themselves exclusively as caregivers (Guberman, Lavoie, Blein, and Olazabal, 2012). With careers, children, passion projects, and countless other endeavours occupying their time, the caregiver role becomes just one of many aspects of identity. In the past, serving as a caregiver may have been more widely expected and accepted. But today, our society values constant productivity and self-improvement. Caregivers are accordingly expected to juggle multiple roles to be considered "successful."

A NEW CULTURE OF INTIMATE LIFE

Out of all these changes, a new culture of intimate life emerges. Social and cultural changes, in turn, bring pressure for further changes by government and business. For example, the growth in part-time work, work sharing, and workplace child care all reflect, in part, new ideas about the necessary relationship between work and family life.

In turn, these changes further increase choice, confusion, and cultural change, so the cycle of family change continues. With few exceptions, this cycle works similarly in all societies. Bearing that in mind, what kinds of families are likely to result from this continuing individualization? At least four main kinds of nuclear family are likely to appear, which differ along two main dimensions: what we can call (1) role separability and (2) personal interchangeability.

Role separability in families refers to the separation of being a spouse from being a parent. Many North American households are made up of cohabiting couples with children, or reconstituted or blended families, where spouses may or may not parent one another's children. A second dimension, **personal interchangeability**, refers to the choice of a spouse based on his or her ability to fill certain roles, rather than for that individual's unique characteristics. People who marry for love choose a mate for his or her unique characteristics. People who marry for instrumental reasons are more interested in a mate who is a good provider or who can produce healthy offspring. Personal interchangeability is well suited to societies with high rates of mortality. By contrast, purely romantic marriages are unpredictable and unstable.

Now we can cross-classify nuclear families along these two dimensions. Doing so yields four possibilities: We call them (1) corporate, (2) collected, (3) concatenated, and (4) cyclical families.

Inseparable family roles and personal interchangeability characterize the **corporate family**. In this corporate family, people can come and go without changing the essential structure of the family. The husband serves as father to the younger generation in the household—children, apprentices, and household servants—and the wife serves as mother, whoever the natural parents of these children may be.

We use this antiquated definition of a younger generation because the corporate family existed in the nineteenth and early twentieth century. It is a patriarchal family in which a double standard prevails and in which men are dominant. Today, the corporate family—once the dominant model in Western societies—has lost its support in law and public opinion, at least in Canada. In the more religious United States, such a patriarchal model of the family still prevails in traditional circles, despite the mass culture's commitment to romantic choice.

Only in a society dominated by the corporate family can people think and speak of "the family" as a well-defined social institution. The state protects the institution of "the family." In culture and by law, "the family" has social importance, enjoys its own resources, and commands its members' loyalties. This family underlines its members' duty to the group. As Sacks (1991) says, such families exist because of choices people do *not* make: To be a child is to accept the authority of parents one did not choose. To be a parent is to accept responsibility for a future one may not live to see (Sacks, 1991: 56–57).

This family is best suited to a theocratic, undifferentiated social structure. There, the state, the law, and religion are closely tied together and lean the same way on family matters. In societies where the corporate family dominates, competing models of life—for example, notions that people have rights and liberties—and competing institutions (such as the secular school) hold little sway.

By contrast, separable roles and interchangeable performers characterize the **collected family**. It is similar to Duberman's (1975) "reconstituted" family, which follows the remarriage of partners who have children from previous unions. Like the corporate family, the collected family needs family members to conform to traditional notions of husband, wife, father, mother, and child. However, given the complexities of remarriage, family members concede the impossibility of compelling mates to be both good spouses *and* good parents to the resident children (Ebersohn and Bouwer, 2015).

In these families, the unit roles—not the family as a whole—are the locus of loyalty, meaning, and resources. Children are allowed to feel close to their mother, for example, without feeling obliged to love her intimate partner or call him "Daddy." Societies like our own—with growing numbers of reconstituted families—are beginning to recognize the special needs of collected families. For example, the state increasingly delivers benefits to partners *or* parents *or* children, not to the "family head" of earlier days. In this system, one cannot assume that the family has a "head" or even that the traditional idea of "family head" has any meaning today.

A third family type, the **concatenated family**, is exactly opposite to the corporate family, since separable roles and unique performers characterize it. From the outside, the concatenated family looks like a chance event, a slow collision of individuals in time and space. The concatenated family is nothing more than a household at a particular moment. Here, family members vest meanings, loyalties, and resources in particular people, not in roles. Families exist only through sharing these meanings and resources. As a result, family members must constantly affirm and renegotiate the bases for this sharing.

Here, the meaning of intimate partner or parent is no longer certain. Occasionally, definitions will mesh for long periods. In any event, we cannot assume, in these families, that members will have a permanent commitment to "the family" or even to their current partner and children. The concatenated family is an extreme version of radical individualism. It assumes that people ought to have continuous, unlimited free choice in their living arrangements. This freedom is subject only to the legal protection of minors from the results of a family breakdown and of all family members from household violence. Supporters of this family type see family life as a lifestyle or individual choice—so far as the adults are concerned, a supermarket for intimate relations.

In this system, mating is motivated by considerations of the spouse's unique characteristics, which may not continue to allure. Childbearing is motivated by a biological drive to reproduce or by self-expression—a form of psychic consumption of children for personal pleasure. Under these conditions, marital dissolutions will likely be frequent. Not surprisingly, this family system creates many potential kinship connections—for example, many sets of grandparents. However, more mothers than fathers will remain with their children in the case of a divorce. So, in practice, concatenated families (with children) are more matrifocal. Women and children remain in the household, while men come and go. In North America and Europe, concatenated families are still far from the average.

Like the corporate family, the **cyclical (or recycled) family** features traditional (inseparable) roles. But unlike the corporate family, the cyclical family lacks interchangeability. Each is a "return engagement" occurring *because of* the unique relationship of the members. This return engagement may be a second marriage of the same people, which is rare but does occur. More often, during this second parenthood people are called on to parent their now-adult children (referred to earlier as "boomerang children") a second time.

For example, the percentage of young Canadian adults living with their parents has risen greatly (see Figure 11.1). In 1981, 26.9 percent of 20- to 29-year-olds lived with their parents, either because they had never left or because they returned home after initially moving out. By 2011, that number had risen to 42.3 percent (Statistics Canada, 2015b). The result is a complex household that *looks* like a corporate family but has none of the predictability or normative power of that older arrangement. Many reasons account for the return of adult children: unemployment, inadequate income for accommodation, or the need for extra education or babysitting help. Unique family situations result from an interaction between the reasons for return and the expectations of the children and parents.

We can wonder whether the change from corporate families to collected, concatenated, and cyclical families is as certain as it seems. Some wishful thinkers want (and

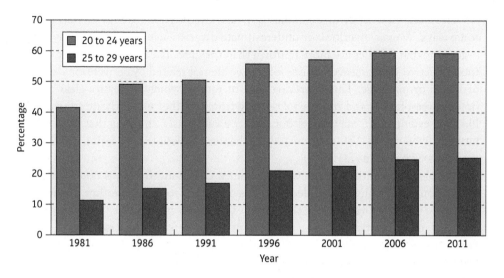

Figure 11.1 Percentage of young adults ages 20 to 24 and 25 to 29 living in the parental home, Canada, 1981–2011.

Source: Statistics Canada. 2015. *Living arrangements of young adults aged 20 to 29.* Retrieved from: http://www12.statcan.gc.ca/census-recensement/2011/as-sa/98-312-x/98-312-x2011003_3-eng.cfm. Reproduced and distributed on an "as is" basis with the permission of Statistics Canada.

some policy-makers encourage) mothers of preschool children to leave the workforce and devote their adult lives to family. If they did so, family incomes would drop greatly. As illustration, in 2008—the most recent year for which we have reliable data—women contributed 42 percent to the total household income in Canada (Statistics Canada, 2009). Even after considering the costs that they would not incur by mothers leaving the workforce, such as daycare and other work-related expenses, families would still suffer a net loss of income. The loss would be greatest for the 31 percent of Canadian dual-income families in which the wife earns more than the husband (Milligan, 2013). However, nothing suggests a return to old, restrictive family forms—at least not in Canada.

LIKELY CHANGES IN THE FUTURE

When Canadians discuss family today, they talk about two things. They stress that families, and what happens with families, matter to them. They also talk about the diversity of families today in comparison to the past. We hear about married couples with or without children, common-law or cohabiting couples with or without children, female- or male-headed single-parent families, adoptive families, foster families, empty nesters, gay or lesbian families, and so on. At times, the impression may be that a smorgasbord of choices about how to live in families exists.

However, viewing diverse families only as varied structures may be deceptive in some ways. We may overlook or underestimate diversity *within* various family forms, suggesting that families are more uniform than they are. The term *family* itself may be too restrictive, ignoring everyone to whom we are not related by conventional notions of blood or marriage. This restrictive idea of family, which suggests a clear distinction between family and friends, takes away from us other ways to care for those we like. For example, we may parcel out our love cautiously, thinking that family has a monopoly on caring. Yet, as discussed in Chapter 10, people may define many different kinds of people as family.

People are inventing new ways to be family. **Other-mothering** is one such family innovation, which allows extended relations or friends to fill the mother role for children who are not biologically their own. Other-mothering does break from the nuclear family tradition in some ways, yet it may reinforce that tradition in others. For example, Lange and Greif (2011) found that when mothers developed substance abuse problems, their own mothers felt obligated to step in and care for their children. This particular instance of other-mothering may reinforce traditional conceptions of family roles by suggesting that child care is "women's work" and that female relatives—but not biological fathers or grandfathers—have an obligation to mother any and every family member.

Similarly, Chib, Malik, Aricat, and Kadir (2013) note an increase in the number of women mothering from afar. As growing numbers of women leave their children behind to accept work in different countries, those children are left with various "replacement" mothers, including their biological fathers, grandparents, aunts, uncles, family friends, and so on. In addition, women often mother their distant children "transnationally," using phone calls, Skype, text messages, emails, social media, and various other ICT to remain in close contact. Many transnational mothers leave their children behind only to accept work as live-in nannies and thus insert themselves into new families as "surrogate mothers," often spending more time with the children they nanny than do the biological parents of those children.

Overall, Canadians are living in and thinking about increasingly diverse families. Statistics Canada (Milan, 2015) reveals nine changes to or features of family life that we can reasonably expect to see continue in the coming years:

1. Fewer couples are getting legally married.
2. More couples are breaking up.
3. Families are getting smaller.
4. Children are experiencing more transitions as their parents change their marital status.
5. Family violence continues to be under-reported.
6. Multiple-earner families have become the norm.
7. Women continue to do most of the juggling involved in balancing work and home.

8. Socio-economic inequality between families is worsening.

9. The future will have more aging families.

As social scientists and as citizens, we have several ways of responding to these trends. First, we can continue to watch the data and report whether these trends are continuing. Second, we can make and test theories about the reasons for these trends. Third, we can propose and evaluate social policies that will increase the benefits and decrease the harms associated with these trends. Fourth, we can lead public discussions about the ways we can promote the trends we favour and slow down the trends we dislike.

We have proposed throughout this text that, inevitably, more people will cohabit, divorce, and bear fewer children and, by implication, that children will experience more transitions as parents change their relationships (item 4 in the list above). Not only are these trends universal in industrial societies, but they are unlikely to reverse themselves and they result from the growth of human freedom—a quality most of us would want to promote. Also, families and populations will continue to age—a sure result of the decline in childbearing.

We can scarcely imagine social conditions that would lead Canadians to return to low rates of cohabitation or divorce or to high birth rates. So we must think about the problems these conditions create and the ways in which we can reduce the associated harm. Consider, for example, the changes associated with the rise to dominance of the multiple-earner family, a family form that is likely to become even more common in the future.

Dual-Income Families

Dual-income families are important harbingers of family change. As discussed earlier, the proportion of families with women who work outside the home has grown steadily. This pattern is not likely to change. The economy needs the wages and skills of women too much, and governments need the taxes that women contribute. Career and job commitments may lead to postponed weddings and to more commuting relationships in the future. Women may delay childbearing, but the emotional value placed on children will still mean that most couples will have children at some point.

In years to come, life with children and two incomes will continue to challenge both work and family for both men and women. With changes in the global marketplace, men's work may not be as privileged as it was in the past, when only men were viewed as family providers. Women increasingly are taking on the role of family provider, even where a man is present, as men's work becomes more precarious and insecure. More husbands may follow their spouses' career or job opportunities. This means changes in the roles and expectations of spouses and in the ways children come to see what mothers and fathers are and do.

Refilled Nests

For a time, the common pattern was that children grew up and left the family home when they could make their own way in the world. However, as discussed in Chapter 10, couples who thought that their children had grown up and "flown away" soon experienced a **refilled nest** with adult children who returned to (or never left) school, had trouble finding or keeping jobs, got divorced, or even had children of their own (Oksanen, Aaltonen, Majamaa, and Rantala, 2017).

The future therefore may be like the past. Some families live in refilled nests only out of necessity, and see themselves as pooling housing and resources to survive. Others, however, may see huge creative possibilities in refilled nests—grandparents providing child care while parents work, sharing housework among more family members, reducing environmental problems by having fewer accommodations, and developing new ways of intergenerational caring for older adults.

Nominal and Virtual Families

In the future, we are also likely to see an increase in the number of non-standard "virtual" families and increased confusion about how these families should be treated, relative to what we are calling "nominal" families. *Nominal families* are those empowered (by law) to care for their members—in particular, for children, older adults, and people with disabilities or severe illnesses. *Virtual families* do the actual work of caring for these family members. To be sure, in many households, virtual families *are* nominal families—that is, the working family unit coincides in structure with the legal definition of family. But as domestic arrangements continue to diversify, a broad and non-traditional range of caregivers is increasingly taking up family responsibilities. Virtual families may include grandparents, aunts, uncles, cousins, friends, and even neighbours.

To understand the difference, consider Kay, a 24-year-old university student. Kay lived in Toronto for the past seven years with her younger brother; her mother's mother, Bea; and Bea's second husband, Harold. Kay's younger sister, Jo, lives in a group home in Oshawa; she attends school only sporadically and periodically gets into trouble with the law. Bea has refused to let her come home, because Jo has stolen money from Bea in the past to buy drugs. Kay's estranged mother, a drug addict, lived in Sudbury until last spring, when she died of a drug overdose. Kay has met her father only once, although he lives in Toronto with a wife and young children. Kay is emotionally closest to her grandmother, her sister, and an aunt—her mother's sister—who lives in Ottawa. Kay has recently moved to Montreal, where she will live with a close friend from high school and attend a different university. Question: Who are the members of Kay's "family"? Answer: It's hard to say. Gazso and McDaniel (2014) have studied what they call "families by choice," finding that many people, perhaps especially those who earn low incomes, make families for themselves.

Canadian policy-makers often think in terms of nominal families. Virtual families, in contrast, reflect the true diversity of our nation's family landscape. Only after we have adequately defined "families" can we study their formation, functioning, and dissolution. With virtual families, this may mean studying intimate, long-lived support networks—networks of kin and friends who care for Canada's children, older adults, and people with disabilities or severe illnesses.

How does this notion of nominal versus virtual family connect with shifting patterns of family structure, formation, and dissolution, and what are the policy implications? Take, as an example, the issue of custody rights following divorce. In most jurisdictions, when a couple divorces, only they—as heads of a nominal family—have automatic rights to child custody and access. Yet in Canada's increasingly diverse family landscape, new partners, grandparents, uncles and aunts, friends, older siblings, fictive kin, and others—potential members of a virtual family—may play at least as big a role as one or both biological parents in caring for those children. Current legal and social policies assign to parents the default right to these children, but other people who have accepted responsibility for them may be refused rights to custody or access.

The policy challenges, then, are to recognize the limits of traditional legal and social definitions in capturing the modern diversity of family structures, to better document the practical and often inventive networks of caregiving that families create to promote their own well-being, and to ensure that social programs and services are delivered with these realities of Canadian family life in mind.

We need to learn a great many things about virtual and nominal families in Canada. For example:

■ What is the (empirical) overlap between nominal families and virtual families in Canada today? In other words, what proportion of families is both nominal and virtual? How does this overlap vary regionally, and by various groupings, such as age, ethnicity, and so on?

■ How well do people do in virtual families, compared with people in nominal families? Are we right to assume that people in well-functioning virtual families (whether or not these families are also nominal) are the happiest and healthiest Canadians?

■ What factors affect the well-being of people in virtual families? In particular, are virtual families hampered by not enough income or not enough rights to perform their family-like roles?

■ What factors affect the formation, maintenance, and dissolution of virtual families? What factors influence members of these families to continue supporting one another? And, for virtual families, what defines "formation" and what defines "dissolution"?

■ How are virtual families—their formation, dissolution, and well-being—affected by any of the following trends: increases in cohabitation; immigration; poverty and unemployment, especially among the young (e.g., boomerang generation); globalization and increased people living apart together (LAT); improved new communications technology for holding family members together at a distance; in-home work; young mothers working outside the home; increased longevity; prolonged survival of people with disabilities or severe illness; same-sex union formation; and individualization of women's lives? What effects do these trends have on family problems, such as domestic violence?

■ Finally, if we do not know the answer to any of these questions, how could we find out?

Increased Diversity

Previous chapters have noted that Canada faces a future of increased immigration and interaction between cultures from all over the world. The resulting increased diversity—especially in metropolitan areas where newcomers often concentrate—will lead to even further modifications to family forms.

Immigration is not the only source of increased variety. The trend toward diversity in close relations across the life cycle reveals a clear pattern of individualization of family life. People live longer today than ever before. In the lifetime allotted to each of us, we can—and likely will—live in many kinds of families, even if our family lives are stable and secure. Children grow up and leave home eventually—even if it takes them longer than it used to. Couples find themselves in different family situations by living year after year. The longer we live, the more family diversity we will face. The life cycle perspective offers a different view of diversity and one well worth considering, if for no other reason than to promote tolerance of other ways of being close in families.

Policy Challenges

Societies are not especially good at guessing the challenges they will face in a few years. But growing inequalities between families are already posing major policy challenges today and will likely continue to do so in the future (McDaniel, Gazso, and Um, 2013).

In 2014, the richest 1 percent of Canadian tax filers accounted for 10.3 percent of the country's total income, down from a peak of 12.1 percent in 2006 (Statistics Canada, 2016), while incomes remained stagnant for the poorest 20 percent. The result is increasing family income inequality in Canada, a trend obvious since 1980. From 1999 to 2012, the net worth of Canadian families increased by 73 percent; however, much of this growth went to already-wealthy families (see Table 11.3). Among Canadian families in the top income quintile, net worth increased by 80 percent during this time frame. Among those in the bottom income quintile, it increased only 38 percent. That said, income inequality has always been greater in Canada than it is in Europe, though considerably lower than it is in the United States. The most recent available statistics, for 2010, show a Gini index (which measures the inequality of family incomes) of 33.7 in Canada compared with 41 in the United States (World Bank, 2017). See Figure 11.2.

Regrettably, this income inequality translates into differences in information availability as well. As we see in Table 11.4, some groups of people have much more access to internet-based information than others. The result is what has often been called a "digital divide," in this case between older and younger people.

Another inequality we see in families is the gendered difference in employment rates between men and women, as illustrated in Figure 11.3. This, too, has important consequences for income inequality, between families and within families.

Largely because of these differences in employment and access to information, income inequality is not spread evenly around the population. Statistics Canada reports that a few Canadian groups are especially subject to long-term or persistent economic deprivation. They include "seniors, children, people living in lone parent families (lone parents), recent immigrants, off reserve Aboriginal people, people with activity limitations, and non-elderly unattached individuals" (Murphy, Zhang, and Dionne, 2012).

Traditionally, government support and tax policies have reduced family income inequalities. However, transfer payments did less in the 1990s and 2000s

Table 11.3 Family Income and Net Worth by Income Quintile, 1999 and 2012

	Average			Median		
	1999	2012	1999 to 2012	1999	2012	1999 to 2012
	dollars		percentage change	dollars		percentage change
Income	**63,300**	**74,800**	**18.2**	**49,700**	**57,000**	**14.7**
Bottom quintile	12,600	13,600	7.9	14,000	14,700	5.0
Second quintile	30,400	34,600	13.8	30,500	34,600	13.4
Middle quintile	49,900	57,200	14.6	49,700	57,000	14.7
Fourth quintile	76,000	88,100	15.9	75,700	86,900	14.8
Top quintile	147,500	180,600	22.4	123,900	149,500	20.7
Net worth	**319,800**	**554,100**	**73.3**	**137,200**	**243,800**	**77.7**
Bottom quintile	79,500	109,300	37.5	7,600	8,700	14,5
Second quintile	175,100	267,400	52.7	70,900	113,500	60.1
Middle quintile	261,800	453,300	73.1	135,100	236,900	75.4
Fourth quintile	360,700	641,000	77.7	203,700	388,200	90.6
Top quintile	721,900	1,300,100	80.1	424,900	879,100	106.9

Source: Uppal, S., & LaRochelle-Cote, S. 2015. Changes in wealth across the income distribution, 1999 to 2012. Statistics Canada. Retrieved from: http://www.statcan.gc.ca/pub/75-006-x/2015001/article/14194-eng.htm. Reproduced and distributed on an "as is" basis with the permission of Statistics Canada.

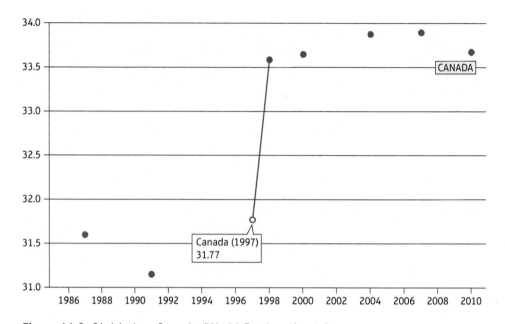

Figure 11.2 Gini index, Canada (World Bank estimate)

Source: World Bank. 2017. Gini Index (World Bank Estimate). Retrieved from: http://data.worldbank. org/indicator/SI.POV.GINI?end=2010&locations=CA&start=1985&view=chart.

to mitigate the market effects of income inequality than they did in the 1980s (Tarroux, 2012).

Will continuing declines in government support for low-income families further increase inequality? Research evidence suggests that this is a great problem for all of society. In pioneering research, Wilkinson (1994) showed that mortality rates and life expectancies in the industrialized world are more closely related to income inequality than to per capita income or per capita economic growth. Despite an overall increase in Canadian life expectancies, shorter life expectancies are found in poorer neighborhoods—and the poorer people are, the shorter are their life expectancies (Greenberg and Normandin, 2015).

Canada's future thus depends on addressing the widening gap between the rich and the poor. Today, children born into poor families are likely to grow up to be poor themselves. Growing up in poverty reduces children's life chances: Their lack of financial resources means that they have fewer educational and occupational opportunities (Caucutt, Lochner, and Park, 2016). In turn, they have greatly reduced chances of making a better future for themselves. But with the current shortage of government programs for low-income families with children, the cycle of poverty is likely to continue (Seguin et al., 2012).

A second major policy challenge is child care, as discussed earlier. If mothers of young children continue to work for pay in the numbers they currently do, and if

Table 11.4 Age Differences in Internet Use

Location of use	Age group	2010	2012
Internet use from any location	Total, Individuals aged 16 years and over	80.3	83.4
	Individuals aged 16 to 24 years	97.5	98.6
	Individuals aged 25 to 44 years	93.0	95.5
	Individuals aged 45 to 64 years	80.1	83.8
	Individuals aged 65 years and over	40.2	47.5
Internet use from home	Total, Individuals aged 16 years and over	77.2	80.8
	Individuals aged 16 to 24 years	94.0	95.5
	Individuals aged 25 to 44 years	89.3	92.6
	Individuals aged 45 to 64 years	76.7	80.8
	Individuals aged 65 years and over	38.9	46.2
Internet use from work	Total, Individuals aged 16 years and over	30.7	33.2
	Individuals aged 16 to 24 years	27.2	33.7
	Individuals aged 25 to 44 years	46.2	49.9
	Individuals aged 45 to 64 years	30.3	31.5
	Individuals aged 65 years and over	3.6	4.5
Internet use as a student from school	Total, Individuals aged 16 years and over	14.3	14.5
	Individuals aged 16 to 24 years	60.9	64.5
	Individuals aged 25 to 44 years	12.6	11.7
	Individuals aged 45 to 64 years	2.8	3.1
	Individuals aged 65 years and over	F	0.6[E]

Source: Statistics Canada. *Canadian Internet use survey, Internet use, by location of use, household income and age group for Canada and regions.* Retrieved from: http://www5.statcan.gc.ca/cansim/a26?lang=eng&id=3580154. Reproduced and distributed on an "as is" basis with the permission of Statistics Canada.

"mother work" remains mainly a woman's domain, some solutions to caring for children must be found. The lengthy public deliberation on the pros and cons of child care drags on, but children are not getting the care they need.

This issue is central to the future of families, since without some solution, couples may have little choice but to restrict their childbearing even further or to forgo parenthood altogether (McKenna, 2015). Our entire society would suffer as a result.

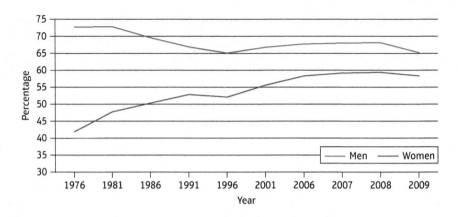

Figure 11.3 Employment rates of women and men, 1976 to 2009

Source: Statistics Canada. 2017. *Paid work.* Retrieved from: http://www.statcan.gc.ca/pub/89-503-x/ 2010001/article/11387-eng.htm. Reproduced and distributed on an "as is" basis with the permission of Statistics Canada.

Child care is also important to gender equality, since affordable child care makes it easier for women to contribute to society in ways that do their talents and education justice.

We openly admit the centrality of families to our individual lives and happiness, and to our collective future. Yet we seem reluctant to meet the needs of families by developing creative solutions to the problems they are facing today. Although the general public and policy-makers agree that the family is important, the government has, with public support, increasingly clawed back funding for social programs intended to support families (McKenna, 2015).

The authors of an analysis of data from the National Longitudinal Survey of Children and Youth (NLSCY) end with a "blueprint for a family-enabling society." The first recommendation is constructive collaboration among all levels of government, parents, teachers, and children themselves to set the conditions for improving results for children. The Early Childhood Development (ECD) Accord between the provinces and the federal government in 2000 identified four areas of cooperation: promoting healthy pregnancy, birth, and infancy; improving parenting and family supports; strengthening early childhood development, learning, and care; and strengthening community supports.

The second recommendation is investment in human capital, based on lifelong learning. To achieve this, we need seamless and universal support for families, from conception to kindergarten. Older children, strongly influenced by classroom and school environments, need continuing educational and social supports to stay in school.

The third recommendation is social inclusion. Successful communities bolster results for their least advantaged children. Finally, we need an increased capacity for program evaluation, oversight, and research. We need to examine policies to see if they are making the intended difference.

The United Nations Convention on the Rights of the Child was confirmed by Canada in 1991. Respect for children is implicit in the research collected and in the conclusions of the NLSCY study. However, respect for children must be put into practice to build a family-enabling society and to have positive results for vulnerable children. Children must be viewed as having inherent rights as human beings. They must also be seen as people with a need for autonomy. We have made important progress, but much work remains to be done to accomplish these goals.

CONCLUDING REMARKS

Two views of history are directly useful for our glimpse into the future of families. Consider first the image of the present as the peak of progress; according to this view, the future advances in the same direction as it has in the past. A contrasting view, equally prevalent, is that we used to have, or be, something wonderful, but with time, what was good slipped away and was replaced by a society with fewer clear values, more social problems, less stability, and less certainty.

We consider both views simplistic. So, we end this book with a call for modest optimism about the future of the family. In all likelihood, the future holds new and unforeseen problems that will challenge many families and their members—in addition to all of the problems we are already experiencing and can expect to continue. However, the future will also hold new opportunities for change and improvement.

So far, no one has found a technological fix for the kinds of organizational, interpersonal, and emotional problems that normally arise in ordinary family life. We do not foresee an easy solution to the problems of family life through genetic engineering, artificial intelligence, faster computers, smarter houses, better electrical appliances, or little white pills that can satisfy our human needs for love, meaning, belonging, attachment, and communication. However, families themselves will continue to deal with these needs and, often, to meet them. Through continuing study, we can hope to learn more about how healthy families work and how to help less healthy families do the same.

CHAPTER SUMMARY

In this chapter, we mulled over the future of close relations, while acknowledging that social prediction is far from a perfect science or art.

We began with an examination of the new communication technologies, virtual communities, and the role of families in the "connected society." We noted that new technologies increase the reach of family life, instead of limiting it, as critics had feared. We cannot predict all of the effects of cyberspace on family life, but we noted that two major communication technologies—telephone and email—did not transform family life as drastically as people had expected. On the contrary, they allowed people to pursue their most cherished goals more efficiently.

ICT pose problems with sexuality, specifically cybersex and the potential for online infidelity and cyberbullying. Mating and dating online create new ethical issues and may force families to rethink what they mean by commitment in the face of extended sexual opportunities. The same technology that extends the reach of mating and dating also extends the reach of caregiving. So, just as technology lures people away from their families, it also allows them to pay closer attention to their family members' needs, if they wish.

The new reproductive technologies also show the importance of human agency. These new technologies offer new opportunities and new ethical challenges, but they are being used to further traditional pronatalist agendas.

The most dramatic future changes to family life are extensions of a change that has been in process for centuries: the individualization of family life. More families are rethinking spousal and parental roles and shifting away from uniform corporate family structures to various collected, concatenated, and cyclical family structures.

We noted various trends in this chapter. For example, families continue to get smaller, children experience more transitions as parents change their marital status, family violence continues to be under-reported, multiple-earner families have become the norm, socio-economic inequality between families is worsening, and the future will have more aging families.

Dual-income families will continue to be important carriers of family change. In years to come, life with children and two incomes will continue to challenge both work and family for both men and women.

Family nests can refill readily when adult children bring their own children and possibly spouses back to the family home. The increase in boomerang families will place new demands on parents and children alike. In short, the longer we live, the more family diversity we will face.

Growing family inequalities pose a major policy challenge today. In the past 20 years, income inequalities have widened in Canada. The concern for the future is whether continuing declines in government support for low-income families will further increase family inequality in Canada. Family policy challenges are complex and diverse, and their solution may be central to the future of families and of us all.

Key Terms

collected family A structure that requires family members to conform to traditional notions of husband, wife, father, mother, and child. However, given the complexities of remarriage, family members concede the impossibility of compelling mates to be both good spouses *and* good parents to the resident children.

concatenated family A family exactly opposite to the corporate family, characterized by separable roles and unique performers. The concatenated family is nothing more than a household at a particular moment in time.

corporate family A family in which people can come and go without changing the essential structure of the family. The husband serves as father to the younger generation in the household—children, apprentices, and household servants—and the wife serves as mother, whoever the natural parents of these children may be.

cyclical (or recycled) family A family form featuring traditional (inseparable) roles but no role interchangeability. Instead, the performances of its members are unique. Each is a "return engagement" occurring *because of* the unique relationship of the members.

other-mothering Close parental-type care provided by extended relations or friends.

personal interchangeability Choosing a spouse based on his or her ability to fill certain roles rather than for the individual's unique characteristics.

refilled nests Family homes to which adult children have returned, possibly bringing their own children or spouses.

role separability The separation of being a spouse from being a parent.

Critical Thinking Questions

1. What is the effect on intimacy of always being connected to the world via one electronic medium or another? Is there a difference between using ICT to maintain relations with people who are at a distance and doing so to maintain relations with people with whom we share a close environment?

2. Consider two stereotypes: first, that older adults do not use computers—especially not the internet—and, second, that older adults do not have sex. How do these stereotypes influence research and hence knowledge about computer-mediated communication and the nature of online romantic relationships for older adults?

3. How do computer-mediated relationships (CMRs) compare to face-to-face relationships in terms of intimacy and gender roles? Are the dating scripts different for CMRs, in your opinion?

4. How can women today balance work–family conflict without returning to traditional family forms? Is formal, government-funded child care a reasonable option? If so, what improvements can be made to our presently overburdened system to make child care more accessible to more families?

5. Why does one have to keep in mind the distinction between nominal versus virtual family, and what are the policy implications? Discuss how closing the gap between virtual and nominal families will change family life in the future.

Weblinks

Online Dating University
www.onlinedating.org
This site provides reviews of different dating sites based on many criteria, including user base, user profile characteristics, reviews from other users, and fees.

Center for Genetics and Society

www.geneticsandsociety.org

The Center for Genetics and Society is a non-profit information and public affairs organization that endorses responsible uses and effective societal governance of the new human genetic and reproductive technologies. This site provides background information about emerging reproductive technologies and the issues and policies surrounding them.

The Center for Internet Addiction Recovery

www.netaddiction.com

This site provides information about internet addiction, including compulsive surfing, online affairs, and cybersex addiction. It also offers self-tests and treatment resources.

CaringInfo

www.caringinfo.org

This site is based on a national consumer and community engagement initiative to improve care at the end of life. It provides free resources and information to help people make decisions about end-of-life care and services before a crisis.

References

Abad, Neetu S., & Kennon M. Sheldon. 2008. Parental autonomy support and ethnic culture identification among second-generation immigrants. *Journal of Family Psychology* 22: 652–657.

Abada, T.S., & M. Gillespie. 2007. Family diversity and children's behavioral outcomes in Canada: From structure to process. *Sociological Focus* 40(4): 413–435.

Abma, J.C., & G. Martinez. 2006. Childlessness among older women in the United States: Trends and profiles. *Journal of Marriage and Family* 68(4): 1045–1056.

Aboriginal Affairs and Northern Development. 2012. *Aboriginal Women in Canada: A Statistical Profile from the 2006 Census.* Catalogue no. 978-1-100-20156-6. Retrieved from https://www.aadnc-aandc.gc.ca/DAM/DAM-INTER-HQ/STAGING/texte-text/ai_rs_pubs_ex_abwch_pdf_1333374752380_eng.pdf

Abortion Rights Coalition of Canada. 2017. Statistics: Abortion in Canada. Retrieved from http://www.arcc-cdac.ca/backrounders/statistics-abortion-in-canada.pdf

Abraham, M., & E. Tastsoglou. 2016. Addressing domestic violence in Canada and the United States: The uneasy co-habitation of women and the state. *Current Sociology Monograph* 64(4): 568–585. Abu-Laban, Sharon, & Susan A. McDaniel. 2004. Aging women and standards of beauty. In Nancy Mandell (Ed.), *Feminist Issues: Race, Class and Sexuality* (4th ed.). Toronto: Prentice-Hall.

ACORN Canada. 2016. Internet for all: Internet use and accessibility for low-income Canadians. Retrieved from https://www.acorncanada.org/sites/acorncanada.org/files/Internet%20for%20All%20report.pdf

Adams, M.-L. 1997. *The Trouble with Normal: Postwar Youth and the Making of Heterosexuality.* Toronto: University of Toronto Press.

Adams, Michele A. 2006. Framing contests in child custody disputes: Parental alienation syndrome, child abuse, gender, and fathers' rights. *Family Law Quarterly* 40(2): 315–338.

Adeagbo, Oluwafemi. 2015. Do according to your time, preferences and abilities: Exploring the division of household labour among interracial gay partners in post-apartheid South Africa. *South African Review of Sociology* 46(4): 39–58.

Ahmad, Farah, Angela Shik, Reena Vanza, Angela Cheung, Usha George, & Donna E. Stewart. 2004. Popular health promotion strategies among Chinese and East Indian immigrant women. *Women and Health* 40(1): 21–40.

Ahrons, C., & J.L. Tanner. 2003. Adult children and their fathers: Relationship changes 20 years after parental divorce. *Family Relations* 52(4): 340–351.

Ajrouch, Kristine J., Kathryn M. Yount, Alba M. Sibai, & Pia Roman. 2013. A gendered perspective on well-being in later life. In Susan A. McDaniel & Zachary Zimmer (Eds.), *Global Ageing in the Twenty-First Century: Challenges, Opportunities and Implications.* (pp. 49–78). Farnham, Surrey, UK: Ashgate.

Alam, S.S., Yeow, P., & Loo, H.S. (2011). An empirical study on online social networks sites usage: Online dating sites perspective. *International Journal of Business and Management, 6(10),* 155–161.

Albanese, P. 2009. *Child Poverty in Canada.* Don Mills, ON: Oxford University Press.

Alberta Justice. 2002. Alberta's Adult Interdependent Relationship Act and you. Retrieved August 5, 2005, from http://www.justice.gov.ab.ca/home/default.aspx?id=3550

Albuja, Analia F., M. Asunción Lara, Laura Navarrete, & Lourdes Nieto. 2017. Social support and postpartum depression revisited: The traditional female role as moderator among Mexican women. *Sex Roles* 77(3–4): 209–220.

Allan, G., G. Crow, & S. Hawker. 2011. *Stepfamilies.* Basingstoke, UK: Palgrave Macmillan.

Alterovits, S.S.R., & G.A. Mendelsohn. 2009. Partner preferences across the life span: Online dating by older adults. *Psychology and Aging* 24(2): 513–517.

Altintas, Evrim, & Oriel Sullivan. 2016. Fifty years of change updated: Cross-national gender convergence in housework. *Demographic Research* 35: 455–469.

Amato, P., & J.M. Sobolewski. 2001. The effects of divorce and marital discord on adult children's psychological well-being. *Journal of Marriage and the Family* 58: 356–365.

Amato, P.R., & B. Hohmann-Marriott. 2007. A comparison of high- and low-distress marriages that end in divorce. *Journal of Marriage and Family* 69(3): 621–638.

Amato, P.R., & D. Previti. 2003. People's reasons for divorcing: Gender, social class, the life course, and adjustment. *Journal of Family Issues* 24(5): 602–626.

Amato, Paul R. 1996 August. Explaining the intergenerational transmission of divorce. *Journal of Marriage and the Family* 58.

Amato, Paul R. 2010. Research on divorce: Continuing trends and new developments, *Journal of Marriage and Family* 72(3): 650–666.

Amato, Paul R., & Alan Booth. 1996 May. A prospective study of divorce and parent–child relationships. *Journal of Marriage and the Family* 58: 356–365.

Amato, Paul R., Laura Spencer Loomis, & Alan Booth. 1995. Parental divorce, marital conflict and offspring well-being during early adulthood. *Social Forces* 73(3): 895–915.

Amato, Paul R., & Sarah E. Patterson. 2017. The intergenerational transmission of union instability in early adulthood. *Journal of Marriage and Family* 79(3): 723–738.

Amato, Paul R., & J.M. Sobolewski. 2001. The effects of divorce and marital discord on adult children's psychological well-being. *American Sociological Review* 66: 900–921.

Ambert, Anne-Marie. 2002. *Divorce: Facts, Causes, and Consequences*. Ottawa: Vanier Institute of the Family.

Ambert, A.-M. 2009. *Divorce: Facts, Causes and Consequences* (3rd ed.). Ottawa: Vanier Institute of the Family.

Ambert, A.-M. 2012. *Changing Families: Relationships in Context* (2nd Canadian ed.). Toronto: Pearson Education Canada.

Ambert, Anne-Marie. 2005a. *Cohabitation and Marriage: How Are They Related?* Ottawa: Vanier Institute of the Family. Retrieved November 15, 2005, from http://www.vifamily.ca/library/cft/cohabitation.html

Ambert, Anne-Marie. 2005b. *Divorce: Facts, Causes and Consequences*. Ottawa: Vanier Institute of the Family. Retrieved December 9, 2005, from www.vifamily.ca/library/cft/divorce_05.html

Ammar, Nawal H. 2007. Wife battery in Islam: A comprehensive understanding of interpretations. *Violence against Women* 13: 516–526.

Amnesty International. 2014. *Violence against Indigenous Women and Girls in Canada: A Summary of Amnesty International's Concerns and Call to Action*. Ottawa: Author.

Anderssen, E. 2013, June 1. Dirty work: How household chores push families to the brink. *The Globe and Mail*. Retrieved from http://www.theglobeandmail.com/life/relationships/dirty-work-how-household-chores-push-families-to-the-brink/article12300024/?page=all

Andreassen, R. 2017. New kinships, new family formations and negotiations of intimacy via social media sites. *Journal of Gender Studies* 26(3): 361–371.

Angus Reid Group. 1999. *Family Matters: A Look at Issues Concerning Families and Raising Children in Canada Today*. Toronto: Angus Reid Group.

Anitha, S. 2011. Legislating gender inequalities: The nature and patterns of domestic violence experienced by South Asian women with insecure immigration status in the United Kingdom. *Violence Against Women* 17(10): 1260–1285.

Ansara, D.L., & M.J. Hindin. 2011. Psychosocial consequences of intimate partner violence for women and men in Canada. *Journal of Interpersonal Violence* 26(8): 1628–1645.

Antill, John K., & Sandra Cotton. 1987. Self disclosure between husbands and wives: Its relation to sex roles and marital happiness. *Australian Journal of Psychology* 39(1): 11–24.

Arat-Koc, S. 2001. *Caregivers Break the Silence: A Participatory Action Research on the Abuse and Violence, Including the Impact of Family Separation Experienced by Women in the Live-in Caregiver Program*. Toronto, ON: INTERCEDE.

Arat-Koc, S. 2006. Whose social reproduction? Transnational motherhood and challenges to feminist political economy, pp. 75–92. In Meg Luxton & Kate Bezanson (Eds.), *Social Reproduction: Feminist Political Economy Challenges Neo-Liberalism*. Montréal & Kingston: McGill-Queen's University Press.

Arendell, T. 1992. After divorce: Investigations into father absence. *Gender & Society* 6(4): 562–586.

Arnup, K. 2012. Out in the world: The social and legal context of gay and lesbian families, pp. 1–26. In T.R. Sullivan (Ed.), *Queer Families, Common Agendas: Gay People, Lesbians and Family Values*. New York: Routledge.

Aseltine, Robert H. Jr. 1996 June. Pathways linking parental divorce with adolescent depression. *Journal of Health and Social Behavior* 37.

Ashcraft, A., & K. Lang. 2006. *The Consequences of Teenage Childbearing* (No. w12485). Cambridge, MA: National Bureau of Economic Research.

Askham, J., Ferring, D., & Lamura, G. 2007. Personal relationships in later life, pp. 186–208. In J. Bond,

S. Peace, F. Dittmann-Kohli, & G.J. Westerhof (Eds.), *Ageing in Society*. London: Sage.

Attané, Isabelle. 2012. Being a woman in China today: A demography of gender. *China Perspectives* 5–15. Retrieved from http://chinaperspectives.revues.org/6013

Attree, Pamela. 2005. Parenting support in the context of poverty: A meta-synthesis of the qualitative evidence. *Health & Social Care in the Community* 13(4): 330–337.

Aubrey, J.S. 2004. Sex and punishment: An examination of sexual consequences and the sexual double standard in teen programming. *Sex Roles* 50(7–8): 505–514.

Aujla, W., & A.K. Gill. 2014. Conceptualizing honour killings in Canada: An extreme form of domestic violence? *International Journal of Criminal Justice Sciences* 9(1): 153–166.

Averett, K.H. 2016. The gender buffet: LGBTQ parents resisting heteronormativity. *Gender & Society* 30(2): 189–212.

Axinn, William G., & Arland Thornton. 1993. Mothers, children, and cohabitation: The intergenerational effects of attitudes and behavior. *American Sociological Review* 58(2): 233–246.

Ayers, P., & J. Lambertz. 1986. Labour and love: Women's experience of home and family, 1850–1940, pp. 195–210. In J. Lewis (Ed.), *Labour and Love*. Oxford, UK: Blackwell.

Ayoob, Keith-Thomas. 2011. Solving childhood obesity: Parents may be more powerful than policies. *Childhood Obesity* 7: 271–273.

Ayyub, Ruksana. 2000. Domestic violence in the South Asian Muslim immigrant population in the United States. *Journal of Social Distress & the Homeless* 9: 237–248.

Bacigalupe, G., & S. Lambe. 2011. Virtualizing intimacy: Information communication technologies and transnational families in therapy. *Family Process* 50(1): 12–26.

Badenes-Ribera, L., D. Frias-Navarro, A. Bonilla-Campos, G. Pons-Salvador, & H. Monterde-i-Bort. 2015. Intimate partner violence in self-identified lesbians: A meta-analysis of its prevalence. *Sexuality Research and Social Policy* 12(1): 47–59.

Baines, C.T., P.M. Evans, & S.M. Neysmith. 1998. Women's caring: Work expanding, state contracting, pp. 3–22. In C.T. Baines, P.M. Evans, & S.M. Neysmith (Eds.), *Feminist Perspectives on Social Welfare*. Toronto: Oxford University Press.

Baker, A. 2007. Expressing emotion in text: Email communication of online couples. In *Online matchmaking* (pp. 97–111). Hampshire, England: Palgrave Macmillan.

Baker, M. 2009. Restructuring reproduction: International and national pressures. *Journal of Sociology* 44(1): 65–81.

Baker, Maureen. 1995. *Canadian Family Policies: Cross-National Comparisons*. Toronto: University of Toronto Press.

Baker, Maureen. 2005b. Families, the state and family policies, pp. 259–276. In Maureen Baker (Ed.), *Families: Changing Trends in Canada* (5th ed.). Toronto: McGraw-Hill Ryerson.

Baker, N.L., J.D. Buick, S.R. Kim, S. Moniz, & K.L. Nava. 2013. Lessons from examining same-sex intimate partner violence. *Sex Roles* 69(3–4): 182–192.

Bakker, Arnold B., Evangelia Demerouti, & Ronald Burke. 2009. Workaholism and relationship quality: A spillover–crossover perspective. *Journal of Occupational Health Psychology* 14(1): 23–33.

Baldassar, L. 2007. Transnational families and the provision of moral and emotional support: The relationship between truth and distance. *Identities: Global Studies in Culture and Power* 14(4): 385–409.

Balkan, M., S. Kalkanli, H. Akbas, A. Yalinkaya, M. Alp, & T. Budak. 2010. Parental decisions regarding a prenatally detected fetal chromosomal abnormality and the impact of genetic counseling: An analysis of 38 cases with aneuploidy in southeast Turkey. *Journal of Genetic Counseling* 19(3): 241–246.

Ballingall, A. 2016. Survivors of 12 Huronia-style institutions will split $36 M class-action settlement. *Toronto Star*, March 27. Retrieved February 20, 2017, from https://www.thestar.com/news/gta/2016/04/27/twelve-more-huronia-style-institutes-get-36m-class-action-settlement.html

Banks, R.R. 2011. *Is Marriage for White People? How the African-American Marriage Decline Affects Everyone*. New York: Plume.

Barer, M.L., R.G. Evans, & C. Hertzman. 1995. Avalanche or glacier? Health care and demographic rhetoric. *Canadian Journal on Aging* 14(2): 193–224.

Barlow, J., N. Smailagic, C. Bennett, N. Huband, H. Jones, & E. Coren. 2011. Individual and group-based parenting programs for improving psychosocial outcomes for teenage parents and their children: Review. *Cochrane Database of Systematic Reviews* 3: 1–97.

Barnett, Mark A., Steven W. Quackenbush, & Christina S. Sinisi. 1996. Factors affecting children's, adolescents', and young adults' perceptions of parental discipline. *Journal of Genetic Psychology* 157(4): 411–424.

Barney, D. 2004. *The Network Society*. Cambridge, UK: Polity.

Barrett, Anne E., & R. Jay Turner. 2005. Family structure and mental health: The mediating effects of socioeconomic status, family process, and social stress. *Journal of Health and Social Behavior* 46(2): 156–169.

Basile, K.C., J.E. Hall, & M.L. Walters. 2013. Expanding resource theory and feminist-informed theory to explain intimate partner violence perpetration by court-ordered men. *Violence against Women* 19(7): 848–880.

Bassey Etowa, J. 2012. Becoming a mother: The meaning of childbirth for African–Canadian women. *Contemporary Nurse* 41(1): 28–40.

Bassuk, Ellen, Ree Dawson, & Nicholas Huntington. 2006. Intimate partner violence in extremely poor women: Longitudinal patterns and risk markers. *Journal of Family Violence* 21(6): 387–399.

Bastida, Elena. 2001. Kinship ties of Mexican migrant women on the United States/Mexico border. *Journal of Comparative Family Studies* 32: 549–569.

Battams, N. 2017. A snapshot of population aging and intergenerational relationships in Canada. *Statistical Snapshots*. Retrieved from http://vanierinstitute. ca/snapshot-population-aging-intergenerational-relationships-canada

Bauer, Gerrit. 2016. Gender roles, comparative advantages and the life course: The division of domestic labour in same-sex and different-sex couples. *European Journal of Population: Dordrecht* 32(1): 99–128.

Baumgartner, S.E., S.R. Sumter, J. Peter, & P.M. Valkenburg. 2012. Identifying teens at risk: Developmental pathways of online and offline sexual risk behavior. *Pediatrics* 130(6): e1489–e1496.

Bauserman, Robert. 2012. Meta-analysis of parental satisfaction, adjustment, and conflict in joint custody and sole custody following divorce. *Journal of Divorce and Remarriage* 53(6): 464–488.

Baxter, J. 2000. The joys and justice of housework. *Sociology* 34(4): 609–631.

Baxter, L., & West, L. 2003. Couple perception's of their similarities and differences: A dialectical perspective. *Journal of Personal and Social Relationships*, 20(4): 491–514.

BBC News. 2005. Japan's fertility hits record low, June 1. Retrieved from http://news.bbc.co.uk/1/hi/world/asia-pacific/4599071.stm

BBC News. 2016, September 30. Migrant child brides put Europe in a spin. Retrieved from http://www.bbc.com/news/world-europe-37518289

Beatty, B.B., & L. Berdahl. 2011. Health care and Aboriginal seniors in urban Canada: Helping a neglected class. *The International Indigenous Policy Journal* 2(1).

Beaujot, R. 2000. *Earning and Caring in Canadian Families*. Peterborough, ON: Broadview Press Ltd.

Beaujot, Roderic, & Zenaida Ravanera. 2008. Family change and implications for family solidarity and social cohesion. *Canadian Studies in Population* 35(1): 73–101.

Beaupré, P. 2015. *Intimate Partner Violence*. Ottawa: Statistics Canada. Retrieved from http://www.statcan.gc.ca/pub/85-002-x/2014001/article/14114/section02-eng.htm#a2

Beaupré, P., & E. Cloutier. 2007. *Navigating Family Transitions: Evidence from the General Social Survey, 2006*. Catalogue no. 89-625-XIE—No. 002. Ottawa, ON: Statistics Canada, Social and Aboriginal Statistics Division. Retrieved from http://www.statcan.gc.ca/pub/89-625-x/89-625-x2007002-eng.pdf

Beaupré, P., P. Turcotte, & A. Milan. 2006. When is junior moving out? Transitions from the parental home to independence. *Canadian Social Trends*. Ottawa: Statistics Canada. Catalogue no. 11-008: 9-15.

Beaupré, Pascale. 2008. I do . . . Take Two? Changes in Intentions to Remarry among Divorced Canadians during the Past 20 Years, Ottawa: Statistics Canada. Retrieved from http://www.statcan.gc.ca/pub/89-630-x/2008001/article/10659-eng.htm

Bejanyan, Kathrine, Tara C. Marshall, and Nelli Ferenczi. 2015. Associations of collectivism with relationship commitment, passion, and mate preferences: Opposing roles of parental influence and family allocentrism. *PLoS One* 10(2): e0117374.

Belknap, J., D.L. Larson, M.L. Abrams, C. Garcia, & K. Anderson-Block. 2012. Types of intimate partner homicides committed by women: Self-defense, proxy/retaliation, and sexual proprietariness. *Homicide Studies* 16(4): 359–379.

Bengston, Vern L., Timothy J. Biblarz, and Robert E. L. Roberts. 2002. *How Families Still Matter: A Longitudinal Study of Youth in Two Generations*. Cambridge, U.K. Cambridge University Press.

Bennett, J. 2016. The agony of the digital tease. *The New York Times*, July 8. Retrieved from https://www.nytimes.com/2016/07/10/fashion/dating-text-messages-breadcrumbing.html?_r=2

Bergdall, A.E., J.M. Kraft, K. Andres, M. Carter, K. Hatfield-Timajchy, & L. Hock-Long. 2012. Love and hooking up in the new millennium: Communication technology and relationships among urban African American and Puerto Rican young adults. *The Journal of Sex Research* 49(6): 570–582.

Berger, R. 2000. When remarriage and immigration coincide: The experience of Russian immigrant stepfamilies. *Journal of Ethnic & Cultural Diversity in Social Work* 9: 75–96.

Berger, R.M. 1990. Passing: The impact on the quality of same-sex couple relationships. *Social Work 35*: 328–332.

Bergstrand, C., & J.B. Williams. 2000. Today's alternative marriage styles: The case of swingers. *Electronic Journal of Human Sexuality 3*. Retrieved from http://www.ejhs.org/volume3/swing/body.htm

Bergström, Malin, Emma Fransson, Anders Hjern, Lennart Köhler, & Thomas Wallby. 2014. Mental health in Swedish children living in joint physical custody and their parents' life satisfaction: A cross-sectional study. *Scandinavian Journal of Psychology 55*(5): 433–439.

Bernard, Jessie. 1973. *The Future of Marriage*. New York: Bantam.

Betts Adams, K. 2006. The transition to caregiving: The experience of family members embarking on the dementia caregiving career. *Journal of Gerontological Social Work*, 47(3/4): 3–29.

Bezanson, K. 2014. Putting together a life: Families, coping, and economic change, 1997–2008, pp. 429–448. In B. Fox (Ed.), *Family Patterns, Gender Relations* (4th ed.). Don Mills, ON: Oxford University Press.

Bibby, Reginald. 2004. *A Survey of Canadians' Hopes and Dreams*. Ottawa: Vanier Institute of the Family.

Bibby, Reginald W. 2009. *The Emerging Millennials: How Canada's Newest Generation Is Responding to Change and Choice*. Lethbridge, AB: Project Canada Books.

Bibby, Reginald W. 2011. *Beyond the Gods and Back: Religion's Demise and Rise and Why It Matters*. Lethbridge, AB: Project Canada Books.

Biblarz, T.J., & S. Stacey. 2010. How does the gender of parents matter? *Journal of Marriage and Family 72*(1): 3–22.

Binstock, G., & A. Thornton. 2003. Separations, reconciliations, and living apart in cohabiting and marital unions. *Journal of Marriage and the Family 65*(2): 432–443.

BioPortfolio. 2006. Retrieved from http://www.bioportfolio.com/cgi-bin/acatalog/info_996.html

Birditt, K.S., & T.C. Antonucci. 2012. Till death do us part: Contexts and implications of marriage, divorce and remarriage across adulthood. *Research in Human Development 9*(2): 103–105.

Birenbaum-Carmeli, Daphna. 1998. Reproductive partners: Doctor woman relations in Israeli and Canadian IVF contexts, pp. 75–92. In Nancy Scheper-Hughes & Carolyn Sargent (Eds.), *Small Mall Wars: The Cultural Politics of Childhood*. Berkeley: University of California Press.

Birman, Dina, & Tina Taylor-Ritzler. 2007. Acculturation and psychological distress among adolescent immigrants from the former soviet union: Exploring the mediating effect of family relationships. *Cultural Diversity & Ethnic Minority Psychology 13*: 337–46.

Black, Keri, & Marie Lobo. 2008. A conceptual review of family resilience factors. *Journal of Family Nursing 14*(1): 33–55.

Blackmon, Amy Dixon. 2000. Empathy in marriage: Implications for marital satisfaction and depression. *Dissertation Abstracts International: Section B: The Sciences and Engineering 61*(5-B), 2746.

Blackstock, Cindy, Nico Trocme, & Marlyn Bennett. 2004. Child maltreatment investigations among Aboriginal and non-Aboriginal families in Canada. *Violence against Women 10*(8): 1–16.

Blair, B.L., & A.C. Fletcher. 2011. The only 13-year-old on planet Earth without a cell phone: Meanings of cell phones in early adolescents' everyday lives. *Journal of Adolescent Research 26*(2): 155–177.

Blaisure, K.R., & K.R. Allen. 1995. Feminists and the ideology and practice of marital equality. *Journal of Marriage and the Family 57*(February): 5–19.

Bloch, Lian, Claudia M. Haase, & Robert W. Levenson. 2014. Emotion regulation predicts marital satisfaction: More than a wives' tale. *Emotion 14*(1): 130–144.

Blumberg, R.S. 1991. Income under female versus male control: Hypotheses from a theory of gender stratification and data from the Third World, pp. 97–127. In R.S. Blumberg (Ed.), *Gender, Family and Economy: The Triple Overlap*. Newbury Park, CA: Sage.

Bogle, K. 2008. *Hooking Up: Sex, Dating and Relationships*. New York: NYU Press.

Bogle, K.A. 2008. *Hooking Up: Sex, Dating, and Relationships on Campus*. New York: NYU Press.

Bombay, A., K. Matheson, & H. Anisman. 2014. The intergenerational effects of Indian Residential Schools: Implications for the concept of historical trauma. *Transcultural Psychiatry 51*(3): 320–338.

Bonikowska, Aneta, John F. Helliwell, Feng Hou, & Grant Schellenberg. 2013. *An Assessment of Life Satisfaction Responses on Recent Statistics Canada Surveys*. Ottawa: Statistics Canada.

Bonke, J., & B. Jensen. 2012. Paid and unpaid work in Denmark—Towards gender equity. *Electronic International Journal of Time Use Research 9*(1): 108–119.

Boots., L.M.M., M.E. Vugt, J.M. Knippenberg, G.I.J.M. Kempen, & F.R.J. Verhey. 2014. A systematic review of Internet-based supportive interventions for caregivers of patients with dementia. *International Journal of Geriatric Psychiatry 29*(4): 331–344.

Borell, K., & S.G. Karlsson. (2002). *Reconceptualizing Intimacy and Ageing: Living Apart Together.* Paper presented at International Symposium, Reconceptualizing Gender and Ageing, Centre for Research on Ageing and Gender, University of Surrey, 25–27 June.

Bos, H., & T.G. Sandfort. 2010. Children's gender identity in lesbian and heterosexual two-parent families. *Sex Roles* 62(1–2): 114–126.

Bouchard, Geneviève. 2014. How do parents react when their children leave home? An integrative review. *Journal of Adult Development* 21(2): 69–79.

Bowlby, J. 1969. *Attachment and Loss: Vol. 1. Attachment.* New York: Basic Books.

Boyce, Cheryl A., & Andrew J. Fuligni. 2007. Issues for developmental research among racial/ethnic minority and immigrant families. *Research in Human Development. Special Issue: Social context, cultural processes and mental health across the life span among ethnically diverse populations* 4: 1–17.

Boyd, J.-P. 2017. *Polyamory in Canada: Research on an Emerging Family Structure.* Ottawa: Vanier Institute of the Family. Retrieved from http://vanierinstitute.ca/polyamory-in-canada-research-on-an-emerging-family-structure

Boyd, Monica, & Elizabeth Grieco. 2003. Women and migration: Incorporating gender into international migration theory. Retrieved September 12, 2008, from http://www.migrationinformation.org/issues_mar03.cfm

Boyd, Monica, & Anne Li. 2003. May–December: Canadians in age-discrepant relationships. *Canadian Social Trends* 70: 29–33.

Bradbury, Bettina. 1984. Pigs, cows and boarders: Non-wage forms of survival among Montreal families, 1861–1891. *Labour/Le Travail* 14: 9–46.

Bradbury, Bettina. 1996. Pigs, cows and boarders: Non-wage forms of survival among Montreal families. *Labour/Le Travail* 14: 9–46.

Bradbury, Bettina. 2001. Social, economic, and cultural origins of contemporary families, pp. 69–95. In Maureen Baker (Ed.), *Families: Changing Trends in Canada* (4th ed.). Toronto: McGraw-Hill Ryerson.

Brady, M., S. Dawe, & R. Richmond. 1998. Expanding knowledge among Aboriginal service providers on treatment options for excessive alcohol use. *Drug and Alcohol Review* 17(1): 69–76.

Braver, Sanford, Ira Ellmanm, Ashley Votruba, & William Fabricius. 2011. Lay judgments about child custody after divorce. *Psychology, Public Policy, and Law* 17(2): 212–240.

Braver, Sanford L., Ira Mark Ellman, & William V. Fabricius, 2015. Public sentiments about the parenting time adjustment in child support awards. *Family Law Quarterly*, forthcoming. Retrieved from https://ssrn.com/abstract=2628455

Broll, R. 2014. Criminals are inside of our homes: Intimate partner violence and fear of crime. *Canadian Journal of Criminology and Criminal Justice* 56(1): 1–21.

Brotman, S. 1998. The incidence of poverty among seniors in Canada: Exploring the impact of gender, ethnicity and race. *Canadian Journal on Aging* 17(2): 166–185.

Brown, Jennifer S.H. 1980. *Strangers in Blood: Fur Trade Company Families in Indian Country.* Vancouver: University of British Columbia Press.

Brown, Jennifer S.H., 1992. A Cree nurse in the cradle of Methodism: Little Mary and the Egerton R. Young family at Norway House and Berens River, pp. 93–110. In Bettina Bradbury (Ed.), *Canadian Family History: Selected Readings.* Toronto: Copp Clark Pitman.

Brown, Susan L., & I-Fen Lin. 2012. The gray divorce revolution: Rising divorce among middle-aged and older adults, 1990–2010, *The Journals of Gerontology* 67(6): 731–741. Retrieved from http://psychsocgerontology.oxfordjournals.org/content/67/6/731.full.pdf+html

Brownridge, Douglas A. 2010. Intimate partner violence against Aboriginal men in Canada. *The Australian and New Zealand Journal of Criminology* 43: 223–227.

Brozowski, K., & D.R. Hall. 2010. Aging and risk: Physical and sexual abuse of elders in Canada. *Journal of Interpersonal Violence* 25(7): 1183–1199.

Brumer, Anita. 2008. Gender relations in family—farm agriculture and rural—urban migration in Brazil. *Latin American Perspectives* 35: 11–28.

Brym, Robert J., & Rhonda L. Lenton. 2001. *Love Online: A Report on Digital Dating in Canada.* www.msn.ca. Retrieved June 14, 2009, from http://www.nelson.com/nelson/harcourt/sociology/newsociety3e/loveonline.pdf

Brzozowski, J.A., A. Taylor-Butts, & S. Johnson. 2006. Victimization and offending among the Aboriginal population in Canada. *Juristat: Canadian Centre for Justice Statistics* 26(3): 1.

Buddington, Steve A. 2002. Acculturation, psychological adjustment (stress, depression, self-Esteem) and the academic achievement of Jamaican immigrant college students. *International Social Work* 45: 447–464.

Bui, Hoan N., & Merry Morash. 2007. Social capital, human capital, and reaching out for help with domestic violence: A case study of women in a Vietnamese—American community. *Criminal Justice Studies: A Critical Journal of Crime, Law and Society* 20: 375–390.

Buis, L.R. 2008. Emotional and informational support messages in an online hospice support community. *Computers, Informatics, Nursing* 26(6): 358–367.

Bulanda, Jennifer. 2011. Gender, marital power, and marital quality in later life. *Journal of Women & Aging* 23(1): 3–22.

Bumpass, L.L., R.K. Raley, & J.A. Sweet. 1995. The changing character of stepfamilies: Implications of cohabitation and nonmarital childbearing. *Demography* 32(3): 425–436.

Burczycka, M. 2014. *Trends in Self-Reported Spousal Violence in Canada, 2014*. Ottawa: Statistics Canada. Retrieved from http://www.statcan.gc.ca/pub/85-002-x/2016001/article/14303/01-eng.htm

Burgoyne, C.B. 1990. Money in marriage: How patterns of allocation both reflect and conceal power. *The Sociological Review* 38(4): 634–665.

Burgoyne, C.B., & V. Morison. 1997. Money in remarriage: Keeping things simple and separate. *The Sociological Review* 45(3): 363–395.

Bushfield, S.Y., T.R. Fitzpatrick, & B.H. Vinick. 2008. Perceptions of "impingement" and marital satisfaction among wives of retired husbands. *Journal of Women & Aging* 20(3–4): 199–213.

Caldwell, John C., P.H. Reddy, & Pat Caldwell. 1984. The determinants of family structure in rural south India. *Journal of Marriage and the Family* 46(1): 215–229.

Calixte, S.L.L., J.L. Johnson, & J.M. Motapanyane. 2010. Liberal, Socialist and Radical Feminism, pp. 1–39. In Nancy Mandell (Ed.), *Feminist Issues* (5th ed.). Toronto: Pearson.

Calliste, Agnes. 2001. Black families in Canada: Exploring the interconnections of race, class and gender, pp. 401–419. In Bonnie J. Fox (Ed.) *Family Patterns, Gender Relations* (2nd ed.). Toronto: Oxford University Press.

Campbell, Kelly, & David W. Wright. 2010. Marriage today: Exploring the incongruence between Americans' beliefs and practices. *Journal of Comparative Family Studies* 41(3): 329–345.

Campbell, Lorne, & Sarah Moroz. 2014. Humour use between spouses and positive and negative interpersonal behaviours during conflict. *Europe's Journal of Psychology* 10(3). doi:10.5964/ejop.v10i3.763

Canada, Department of Justice. 2006. *Research Report: Polygyny and Canada's Obligations under International*

Human Rights Law. Retrieved from http://www.justice.gc.ca/eng/rp-pr/other-autre/poly/chap1.html

Canada without Poverty. 2017. *Poverty, Just the Facts.* Retrieved from http://www.cwp-csp.ca/poverty/just-the-facts/#demo

Canada Year Book. 2011. *Seniors, chapter 28.* Catalogue no. 11-402-X. Retrieved from http://www.statcan.gc.ca/pub/11-402-x/2011000/pdf/seniors-aines-eng.pdf

Canada's Aboriginal policies amounted to cultural genocide. 2015. *Yukon News*, June 3. Retrieved from http://yukon-news.com/letters-opinions/canadas-aboriginal-policies-amounted-to-cultural-genocide

Canadian Centre for Policy Alternatives. 2004. Medicare still on life support: Health care accord flawed by poor accountability and enforcement. Retrieved April 18, 2006, from http://www.policyalternatives.ca/index.cfm?act=news&do=Article&call=983&pA=BB736455

Cancian, Maria, Daniel R. Meyer, Patricia R. Brown, & Steven T. Cook. 2014. Who gets custody now? Dramatic changes in children's living arrangements after divorce. *Demography* 51(4): 1381–1396.

Cannon, C.E.B., & F.P. Buttell. 2016. The social construction of roles in intimate partner violence: Is the victim/perpetrator model the only viable one? *Journal of Family Violence* 31(8): 967–971.

Cantillon, S., & B. Nolan. 2001. Poverty within households: Measuring gender differences using nonmonetary indicators. *Feminist Economics* 7(1): 5–23.

Caradec, V. 1997. Forms of conjugal life among the young elderly. *Population: An English Selection* 9: 47–74.

Caragata, Lea, & Maria Liegghio. 2013. Mental health, welfare reliance, and lone motherhood. *Canadian Journal of Community Mental Health* 32(1): 95–107.

Caucutt, E.M., L. Lochner, & Y. Park. 2016. Correlation, consumption, confusion, or constraints: Why do poor children perform so poorly? *The Scandinavian Journal of Economics* 119(1): 102–147.

Caughy, Margaret O'Brien, Saundra Murray Nettles, & Patricia J. O'Campo. 2008. The effect of residential neighborhood on child behavior problems in first grade. *American Journal of Psychology* 42: 39–50.

CBC News. 2005. Gay teen wins fight over Catholic prom. Retrieved from http://www.cbc.ca/news/canada/gay-teen-wins-fight-over-catholic-prom-1.348831

CBC News. 2005, March 9. Marriage by the numbers. *CBC News Online.*

CBC News. 2014. CBC News poll on discrimination. Retrieved from http://s3.documentcloud.org/documents/1362391/cbc-discrimination-poll-november-2014.pdf

Census. 2016. *Census of Population Questions, Short Form*. Ottawa: Statistics Canada. Retrieved from http://www12.statcan.gc.ca/census-recensement/2016/ref/questionnaires/questions-eng.cfm

Census shows new face of the Canadian family. 2012. *CBC News*, September 19. Retrieved from http://www.cbc.ca/news/canada/census-shows-new-face-of-the-canadian-family-1.1137083

Chalmers, Lee, & Anne Milan. 2005. Marital satisfaction during the retirement years. *Canadian Social Trends*. Ottawa: Statistics Canada. Catalogue no. 11-008.

Chan, T.W., & A. Koo. 2011. Parenting style and youth outcomes in the UK. *European Sociological Review* 27(3): 385–399.

Chang, Janet. 2003. Self-reported reasons for divorce and correlates of psychological well-being among divorced Korean immigrant women. *Journal of Divorce & Remarriage 40*: 111–28.

Chappell, Neena. 2013. The cultural context of social cohesion and social capital: Exploring filial caregiving. In Susan A. McDaniel & Zachary Zimmer (Eds.), *Global Ageing in the Twenty-First Century: Challenges, Opportunities and Implications*. (pp. 235–252). Farnham, Surrey, UK: Ashgate.

Chappell, N.L., C. Dujela, & A. Smith. 2015. Caregiver well-being: Intersections of relationship and gender. *Research on Aging 37*(6): 623–645.

Charleyboy, Lisa. 2014. Looking for First Nations love: Indigenous dating life "complex." *CBC News*. Retrieved September 15, 2016, from http://www.cbc.ca/news/aboriginal/looking-for-first-nations-love-indigenous-dating-life-complex-1.2615016

Charter, David. 2016, September 29. Migrant child brides can stay with husbands. *The Times*. Retrieved from http://www.thetimes.co.uk

Chase-Lansdale, P.L., A.J. Cherlin, & K.E. Kiernan. 1995. The long-term effects of parental divorce on the mental health of young adults: A developmental perspective. *Child Development 66*(December): 1614–1634.

Cheah, Charissa S.L., & Valery Chirkov. 2008. Parents' personal and cultural beliefs regarding young children. *Journal of Cross-Cultural Psychology 39*(4): 402–423.

Cheal, D. 1993. Changing household financial strategies: Canadian couples today. *Human Ecology 21*(2): 197–213.

Cheal, David. 1991. *Family and the State of Theory*. Toronto: University of Toronto Press.

Cheal, David. 2002. *Sociology and Family Life*. London: Palgrave.

Chen, C.K., D. Uzdawinis, A. Scholmerich, & G. Juckel. 2014. Effects of attachment quality on caregiving of a parent with dementia. *The American Journal of Geriatric Psychiatry 22*(6): 623–631.

Chen, R.K., M.G. Brodwin, E. Cardoso, & F. Chan. 2002. Attitudes toward people with disabilities in the social context of dating and marriage: A comparison of American, Taiwanese, and Singaporean college students. *Journal of Rehabilitation 68*(4): 5.

Cherlin, A.J. 2001. New developments in the study of nonmarital childbearing, pp. 390–402. In Lawrence Wu & Barbara Wolfe (Eds.), *Out of Wedlock: Causes and Consequences of Nonmarital Fertility*. New York: Russell Sage Foundation.

Cherlin, A.J. 2004. The deinstitutionalization of American marriage. *Journal of Marriage and the Family 66*: 848–861.

Cherlin, A.J. 2009. *The Marriage-go-round: The State of Marriage and the Family in America Today*. New York: Alfred A. Knopf.

Cherlin, A.J., K.E. Kiernan, & P.L. Chase-Lansdale. 1995. Parental divorce in childhood and demographic outcomes in young adulthood. *Demography 32*(August): 299–318.

Cheung, A.K., & S.Y. Choi. 2016. Non-traditional wives with traditional husbands: Gender ideology and husband-to-wife physical violence in Chinese society. *Violence Against Women 22*(14): 1704–1724.

Cheung, Maria. 2008. Resilience of older immigrant couples: Long-term marital satisfaction as a protective factor. *Journal of Couple & Relationship Therapy 7*: 19–38.

Chib, A., S. Malik, R.G. Aricat, & S.Z. Kadir. 2013. Migrant mothering and mobile phones: Negotiations of transnational identity. *Mobile Media & Communication 2*(1): 73–93.

Chibber, Karuna S., Karl Krupp, Nancy Padian, & Purnima Madhivanan. 2012. Examining the determinants of sexual violence among young, married women in southern India. *Journal of Interpersonal Violence, 27*(12): 2465–2483.

Choi, Hye Jeong, Joris Van Ouytsel, & Jeff R. Temple. 2016. Association between sexting and sexual coercion among female adolescents. *Journal of Adolescence 53*: 164.

Chong, Alexandra, Alynn E. Gordon, & Brian P. Don. 2017. Emotional support from parents and in-laws:

The roles of gender and contact. *Sex Roles* 76(5–6): 369–379.

Chou, W.Y.S., Y.M. Hunt, E.B. Beckjord, R.P. Moser, & B.W. Hesse. 2009. Social media use in the United States: Implications for health communication. *Journal of Medical Internet Research*, 11(4): e48.

Chow, Chong Man, Duane Buhrmester, & Cin Cin Tan. 2014. Interpersonal coping styles and couple relationship quality: Similarity versus complementarity hypotheses. *European Journal of Social Psychology* 44(2): 175–186.

Christensen, Donna-Hendrickson, & Kathryn D. Rettig. 1995. The relationship of remarriage to postdivorce co-parenting. *Journal of Divorce and Remarriage* 24: 1–2.

Church, E. 1996. Kinship and stepfamilies. In M. Lynn (Ed.), *Voices: Essays on Canadian Families*. Scarborough, ON: Nelson.

Church, E. 2016, January 3. Eldercare is the new childcare professor says. *The Globe and Mail*. Retrieved from http://www.theglobeandmail.com/news/national/elder-care-is-the-new-child-care-professor-says/article27989811/

Citizens for Public Justice. 2012. *Poverty Trends Scorecard 2012*. Retrieved from http://www.cpj.ca/files/docs/poverty-trends-scorecard.pdf

Civettini, Nicole. 2016. Housework as non-normative gender display among lesbians and gay men. *Sex Roles* 74(5–6): 206–219.

Clark, Warren, & Susan Crompton. 2006. Till death do us part? The risk of first and second marriage dissolution. *Canadian Social Trends*. Ottawa: Statistics Canada. Catalogue no. 11-008: 23–32.

Clarke, Harriet, & Stephen McKay. 2014. Disability, partnership, and parenting. *Disability & Society* 29: 543–555.

Clarke-Billings, C. 2016. World's first baby born with three biological parents. *MSN News*, September 27. Retrieved from http://www.msn.com/en-ca/news/world/worlds-first-baby-born-with-three-biological-parents/ar-BBwHGH4?li=AA59G3&ocid=spartandhp

Cleland, H. 2017, March 31. The problem with the Trudeau's government 18-month maternity leave plan. *MSN Money*. Retrieved from http://www.msn.com/en-ca/money/topstories/the-problem-with-the-trudeau-government%E2%80%99s-18-month-maternity-leave-plan/ar-BBz6dE0?ocid=spartandhp

Clements, C.M., C. Oxtoby, & R.L. Ogle. 2008. Methodological issues in assessing psychological adjustment in child witnesses of intimate partner violence. *Trauma, Violence, & Abuse* 9(2): 114–127.

Cohen, Orna, & Ricky Finzi-Dottan. March 2005. Parent–child relationships during the divorce process: From attachment theory and intergenerational perspective. *Contemporary Family Therapy* 27(1): 81–99.

Colavecchia, S. 2005. Family finances: A sociological study of the earning, managing, and spending of money in marital relationships. (Unpublished doctoral dissertation). University of Toronto, Toronto, ON.

Colavecchia, S. 2008. Doing Moneywork: Le travail domestique des femmes dans la gestion des finances familiales, pp. 183–218. In H. Belleau & C. Henchoz (Eds.), *L'usage de l'argent dans le couple: Pratiques et perceptions des comptes amoureux*. Paris: L'Harmattan.

Colavecchia, S. 2009. Moneywork: Caregiving and the management of family finances, pp. 417–427. In B. Fox (Ed.), *Family Patterns: Gender Relations* (3rd ed.). Toronto, ON: Oxford University Press.

Colavecchia, Sandra. 2016. Families. In Robert Brym (Ed.), *New Society* (8th ed.). Toronto, ON: Nelson.

Collard, C., & S. Kashmeri. 2011. Embryo adoption: Emergent forms of siblingship among Snowflakes™ families. *American Ethnologist* 28(2): 307–322.

Collins, Randall. 1992. Love and property, pp. 119–139. In *Sociological Insight: An Introduction to Nonobvious Sociology*. New York: Oxford University Press.

Coltrane, Scott. 1998. *Gender and Families*. Thousand Oaks, California: Pine Forge Press.

Comeau, Tammy Duerden, & Anton L. Allahar. 2001. Forming Canada's ethnoracial identity: Psychiatry and the history of immigration practices. *Identity* 1: 143–160.

Confer, J. C., Perilloux, C., & Buss, D. 2010. More than just a pretty face: Men's priority shifts toward bodily attractiveness in short-term versus long-term mating contexts. *Evolution and Human Behavior* 31(5): 348–353.

Conger, R.D., T.J. Schofield, & T.K. Neppl. 2012. Intergenerational continuity and discontinuity in harsh parenting. *Parenting* 12(2–3): 222–231.

Connidis, Ingrid Arnet. 2001. *Family Ties and Aging*. Thousand Oaks, CA: Sage.

Connolly, J., A. Nocentini, E. Menesini, D. Pepler, W. Craig, & T. Williams. 2010. Adolescent dating aggression in Canada and Italy: A cross-national comparison. *International Journal of Behavioral Development* 34: 98–105.

Cooke, Martin. 2013. And then I got pregnant: Early childbearing and the First Nations life course. *International Indigenous Policy Journal* 4(1).

Coontz, S. 1992. *The Way We Never Were: American Families and the Nostalgia Trap*. New York: Basic Books.

Coontz, Stephanie. 2005. *Marriage, a History: From Obedience to Intimacy, or How Love Conquered Marriage*. New York: Viking.

Corak, Miles, & Andrew Heisz. 1999. *Death and Divorce: The Long-Term Consequences of Parental Loss on Adolescents*. Analytical Studies Branch Research Paper Series. Ottawa: Statistics Canada. Catalogue no. 11F0019MIE999135.

Costigan, C., & T.F. Su. 2008. Cultural predictors of the parenting cognitions of immigrant Chinese mothers and fathers in Canada. *International Journal of Behavioral Development 32*(5): 432–442.

Costigan, C.L., & D.P. Dokis. 2006. Relations between parent–child acculturation differences and adjustment within immigrant Chinese families. *Child Development 77*(5): 1252–1267.

Cousino, M.K., & R.A. Hazen. 2013. Parenting stress among caregivers of children with chronic illness: A systematic review. *Journal of Pediatric Psychology 38*(8): 809–828.

Coyte, Peter C., & Patricia McKeever. 2016. Home care in Canada: Passing the buck. *Canadian Journal of Nursing Research Archive 33*(2): 11–25.

Craig, Lyn, & Janeen Baxter. 2016. Domestic outsourcing, housework shares and subjective time pressure: Gender differences in the correlates of hiring help. *Social Indicators Research 125*(1): 271–288.

Cranswick, K., & D. Dosman. 2008. Eldercare: What we know today. *Canadian Social Trends 86* Catalogue no. 11-008-X. Retrieved from http://www.statcan.gc.ca/pub/11-008-x/2008002/article/10689-eng.htm

Cravens, J.D., K.R. Leckie, & J.B. Whiting. 2013. Facebook infidelity: When poking becomes problematic. *Contemporary Family Therapy 35*(1): 74–90.

Crawford, Charmaine. 2011. Transnational motherhood: The experiences of working-class African-Caribbean women in Canada (Doctoral dissertation). *Dissertation Abstracts International, A: The Humanities and Social Sciences 71*(9).

Crawford, D., & J.M. Ostrove. 2003. Representations of disability and the interpersonal relationships of women with disabilities. *Women & Therapy 26*(3–4): 179–194.

Crawford, L.A., & K.B. Novak. 2008. Parent–child relations and peer associations as mediators of the family structure–substance use relationship. *Journal of Family Issues 29*(2): 155–184.

Crawford, M., K. Brown, K. Walsh, & D. Pullar. 2010. From domestic violence to sustainable employment. *Forum of Public Policy 2*: 1–12.

Crawley, T. 2017. Accused Bountiful polygamist told police he didn't know wife was 15 years old. *The Globe and Mail*, April 24. Retrieved from https://www.theglobeandmail.com/news/british-columbia/accused-bountiful-polygamist-told-police-he-didnt-know-wife-was-15-years-old-trial/article34802914

Creese, G., I. Dyck, & A.T. McLaren. 2008. The flexible immigrant? Human capital discourse, the family household and labour market strategies. *Journal of International Migration and Integration/Revue de l'integration et de la migration internationale 9*(3): 269–288.

Cribb, R. 2016. Growing evidence shows men choosing single fatherhood via surrogacy. *The Toronto Star*, December 18. Retrieved from https://www.thestar.com/news/canada/2016/12/18/single-males-seeking-canadian-surrogates.html

Critically Thinking about Policy. 2008, October 25. *Increasing Hardships for Single Mothers*. Retrieved from http://criticallythinkingaboutpolicy.blogspot.ca/2008/10/increasing-hardships-for-single-mothers.html

Cronk, L., & B. Dunham. 2007. Amounts spent on engagement rings reflect aspects of male and female mate quality. *Human Nature 18*(4): 329–333.

Crosbie-Burnett, M., A. Skyles, & J. Becker-Haven. 1988. Exploring stepfamilies from a feminist perspective. In S. Dornbusch & M. Strober (Eds.), *Feminism, Children and the New Families*. New York: Guildford Press.

Cross, Gary, & Richard Szostak. 1995. Women and work before the factory, pp. 37–51. In Gary Cross & Richard Szostak (Eds.), *Technology and American Society: A History*. Englewood Cliffs, NJ: Prentice Hall.

Crossley, Thomas F., & Lori J. Curtis. 2006. Child poverty in Canada. *Review of Income and Wealth 52*(2): 237–260.

Curran, Melissa, Nancy Hazen, Deborah Jacobvitz, & Amy Feldman. 2005. Representations of early family relationships predict marital maintenance during the transition to parenthood. *Journal of Family Psychology 19*(2): 189–197.

Curran, S., McLanahan, S., & Knab, J. 2003. Does remarriage expand perceptions of kinship support among the elderly? *Social Science Research 32*(2): 171–190.

Currie, D. 1993. Here comes the bride: The making of a modern traditional wedding in Western culture. *Journal of Comparative Family Studies 24*(3): 403–419.

Curtis, Josh, & Julie McMullin. 2016. Older workers and the diminishing return of employment: Changes in age-based income inequality in Canada, 1996–2011. *Work, Aging and Retirement* 2(3): 359–371.

Czyzewski, Karina. 2011. Colonialism as a broader social determinant of health. *International Indigenous Policy Journal* 2(1).

Dahinten, V. Susan, Jennifer D. Shapka., & J. Douglas Willms. 2007. Adolescent children of adolescent mothers: The impact of family functioning on trajectories of development. *Journal Youth and Adolescence* 36: 195–212.

Dahinten, V. Susan, & J. Douglas Willms. 2002. The effects of adolescent child-bearing on children's outcomes, pp. 243–258. In J. Douglas Willms (Ed.), *Vulnerable Children: Findings from Canada's National Longitudinal Survey of Children and Youth.* Edmonton: University of Alberta Press, and Ottawa: Human Resources Development Canada, Applied Research Branch.

DAIP. Domestic Abuse Intervention Programs: Home of the Duluth Model. Retrieved October 20, 2017, from http://www.theduluthmodel.org

Dakin, John, & Richard Wampler. 2008. Money doesn't buy happiness, but it helps: Marital satisfaction, psychological distress, and demographic differences between low- and middle-income clinic couples. *American Journal of Family Therapy* 36(4): 300–311.

Dancet, E.A.F., I.W.H. Van Empel, P. Rober, W.L.D.M. Nelen, J.A.M. Kremer, & T.M d'Hooghe. 2011. Patient-centred infertility care: A qualitative study to listen to the patient's voice. *Human Reproduction* 26(4): 827–833.

Davies, Dominic. 2000. Sex and relationship facilitation project for people with disabilities. *Sexuality and Disability* 18(3): 187–194.

Davies, Lorraine, Julie Ann McMullin, & William R. Avison, with Gale L. Cassidy. 2001. *Social Policy, Gender Inequality and Poverty.* Ottawa: Status of Women Canada.

Davies, Sharon, & Margaret Denton. 2001. *The Economic Well-Being of Older Women Who Become Divorced or Separated in Mid and Later Life.* Social and Economic Dimensions of an Aging Population Research Papers, Number 66. Hamilton, ON: McMaster University.

Davila, Joanne, Catherine B. Stroud, & Lisa R. Starr. 2008. Depression in Couples and Families, pp. 467–491. In Ian H. Gotlib & Constance L. Hammen (Eds.), *Handbook of Depression* (2nd ed.). New York: Guildford Press.

DeBoer, Danelle D. 2002 December. The effect of infertility on individual well-being. *Dissertation Abstracts International, A: The Humanities and Social Sciences* 62(6), 2249–A.

Decuyper, M., M. De Bolle, & F. De Fruyt. 2012. Personality similarity, perceptual accuracy, and relationship satisfaction in dating and married couples. *Personal Relationships* 19: 128–145.

De Graaf, Paul M., & Matthijs Kalmijn. 2006. Divorce motives in a period of rising divorce. *Journal of Family Issues* 27(4): 483–505.

De Jong, G.J. 2015. Intra-couple caregiving of older adults living apart together: Commitment and independence. *Canadian Journal on Aging* 34(3): 356–365.

de Jong Gierveld, J., M. Broese van Groenou, A.W. Hoogendoorn, & J.H. Smit. 2009. Quality of marriages in later life and emotional and social loneliness. *Journals of Gerontology Series B: Psychological Sciences and Social Sciences* 64(4): 497–506.

De Jong Gierveld, Jenny. 2004. Remarriage, unmarried cohabitation, living apart together: Partner relationships following bereavement or divorce. *Journal of Marriage and the Family* 66(1): 236–243.

Del Campo, R. 2013. Average student graduates university with $37,000 in debt. *CTV Kitchener News*, May 7. Retrieved from http://kitchener.ctvnews.ca/average-student-graduates-university-37-000-in-debt-1.1271240

De Leeuw, S., M. Greenwood, & E. Cameron. 2010. Deviant constructions: How governments preserve colonial narratives of addictions and poor mental health to intervene into the lives of Indigenous children and families in Canada. *International Journal of Mental Health and Addiction* 8(2): 282–295.

del Mar Sánchez-Fuentesa, María, Pablo Santos-Iglesias, & Juan Carlos Sierra. 2014. A systematic review of sexual satisfaction. *International Journal of Clinical and Health Psychology* 14: 67–75.

DeMaris, Alfred. 2007. The role of inequity in marital disruption. *Journal of Social and Personal Relationships* 24(2): 177–195.

de Munck, V. C., & Korotayev, A. V. 2007. Wife–Husband Intimacy and Female Status in Cross-Cultural Perspective. *Cross-Cultural Research*, 41 (4), 307–308, 329.

Denton, W.H., B.R. Burleson, B.V. Hobbs, M. Von Stein, & C.P. Rodriguez. 2001. Cardiovascular reactivity and initiate/avoid patterns of marital communication: A test of Gottman's psychophysiologic model of marital interaction. *Journal of Behavioral Medicine* 24(5): 401–421.

DePaulo, Bella M., & Wendy L. Morris. 2006. The unrecognized stereotyping and discrimination against singles. *Current Directions in Psychological Science* 15(5): 251–254.

De Rose, Alessandra. 2001. Separation and divorce: Effect on family structures and life conditions. *Labour* 14(1): 145–160.

DeVault, M. 1991. *Feeding the Family: The Social Organization of Caring as Gendered Work*. Chicago: University of Chicago Press.

Devries, K.M., J.C. Child, L.J. Bacchus, J. Mak, G. Falder, K. Graham, C. Watts, & L. Heise. 2014. Intimate partner violence victimization and alcohol consumption in women: A systematic review and meta-analysis. *Addiction* 109(3): 379–391.

Dickason, Olive. 2002. *Canada's First Nations: A History of Founding Peoples from Earliest Times*. Don Mills, ON: Oxford University Press.

Diekmann, Andreas, & Kurt Schmidheiny. 2013. The intergenerational transmission of divorce: A fifteen-country study with the fertility and family survey. *Comparative Sociology* 12(2): 211–235.

Di Giulio, G. 2003. Sexuality and people living with physical or developmental disabilities: A review of key issues. *The Canadian Journal of Human Sexuality* 12(1): 53.

Ding, Shijun. 2004. The rural elderly support in China and Thailand. *Geriatrics and Gerontology International* 4: 56–59.

Disabled parents fight to keep newborn at home. 2012. *CBC News*, May 1. Retrieved from http://www.cbc.ca/news/canada/toronto/disabled-parents-fight-to-keep-newborn-at-home-1.1185318

Divale, William, & Albert Seda. 2001. Modernization as changes in cultural complexity: New cross-cultural measurements. *Cross-Cultural Research* 35: 127–153.

Dobransky, K., & E. Hargittai. 2006. The disability divide in internet access and use. *Information, Communication and Society* 9: 313–334.

Doherty, D., & D. Berglund. 2012. *Psychological Abuse: A Discussion Paper*. Ottawa: Public Health Agency of Canada. Retrieved from http://www.phac-aspc.gc.ca/sfv-avf/sources/fv/fv-psych-abus/index-eng.php

Dong, Qi, Yanping Wang, & Thomas H. Ollendick. 2002. Consequences of divorce on the adjustment of children in China. *Journal of Clinical Child and Adolescent Psychology* 31(1): 101–110.

Doosje, Bertjan, Krystyna Rojahn, & Agneta Fischer. 1999. Partner preference as a function of gender, age, political orientation and level of education. *Sex Roles* 40(1–2): 45–60.

Doucet, D. 2006. *Do Men Mother? Fathering, Care and Domestic Responsibilities*. Toronto: University of Toronto Press.

Douglas, Kristen. 2006. *Divorce Law in Canada*. Ottawa: Government of Canada, Law and Government Division. Retrieved from http://www.parl.gc.ca/information/library/PRBpubs/963-e.html

Dronkers, Jaap. 1996. *The Effects of Parental Conflicts and Divorce on the Average Well-Being of Pupils in Secondary Education*. American Sociological Ass'n is located in Washington, DC.

Dryburgh, H. 2001. *Changing Our Ways: Why and How Canadians Use the Internet*. Ottawa: Statistics Canada. Catalogue no. 56F0006XIE. Retrieved from http://www.statcan.gc.ca/pub/56f0006x/56f0006x2000001-eng.pdf

Dua, Enakshi. 1999. Beyond diversity: Exploring the ways in which the discourse of race has shaped the institution of the nuclear family, pp. 237–260. In Enaskshi Dua (Ed.), *Scratching the Surface: Canadian Anti-Racist Feminist Thought*. Toronto: Women's Press.

Dubé, J., & M. Polèse. 2015. The view from a lucky country: Explaining the localised unemployment impacts of the Great Recession in Canada. *Cambridge Journal of Regions, Economy and Society* 9: 235–253.

Duberman, Lucile. 1975. *The Reconstituted Family: A Study of Remarried Couples and Their Children*. Chicago: Nelson-Hall Publishers.

Dubinsky, Karen. 1999. *The Second Greatest Disappointment: Honeymooning and Tourism at Niagara Falls*. Toronto: Between the Lines.

Dudley, James R. 1996. Noncustodial fathers speak about their parental role. *Family and Conciliation Courts Review* 34(3).

Duffey, T.H., H.R. Wooten, & C.A. Lumadue. 2004. The effect of dream sharing on marital intimacy and satisfaction. *Journal of Couple & Relationship Therapy* 3: 53–68.

Duffy, Anne, & Nancy Mandell. 2001. The growth in poverty and social inequality: Losing faith in social justice, pp. 77–114. In Dan Glenday & Ann Duffy (Eds.), *Canadian Society: Meeting the Challenges of the Twenty-First Century*. Toronto: Oxford University Press.

Dumitrica, D., & S. Wyatt. 2015. Digital technologies and social transformations: What role for critical theory? *Canadian Journal of Communication* 40(4): 589–596.

Duncan, S., & M. Phillips. 2010. People who live apart together (LATs)—How different are they? *The Sociological Review* 58(1): 112–134.

Dunetz, J. 2017. Latest disturbing narcissist trend: Sologamy, or marrying yourself. *Constitution*, May 16. Retrieved from http://constitution.com/latest-disturbing-narcissist-trend-sologamy-marrying/

Dunn, Judy, Helen Cheng, Thomas G. O'Connor, & Laura Bridges. 2004. Children's perspectives on their relationships with their nonresident fathers: Influences, outcomes and implications. *Journal of Child Psychology and Psychiatry* 45(3): 553–566.

Dunne, G. 2000. Opting into motherhood: Lesbians blurring the boundaries and transforming the meaning of parenthood and kinship. *Gender and Society* 14(1): 11–35.

Dunne, G.A. 1997. *Lesbian Lifestyles: Women's Work and the Politics of Sexuality*. London, UK: Macmillan.

Dunne, G.A. 1998. Pioneers behind our own front doors: Towards new models in the organization of work in partnerships. *Work Employment and Society* 12(2): 273–295.

Dunne, G.A. 2000. Opting into motherhood: Lesbians blurring the boundaries and transforming the meaning of parenthood and kinship. *Gender and Society* 14(1): 11–35.

Dupre, Matthew E., Linda K. George, Guangya Liu, & Eric D. Peterson. 2015. Association between divorce and risks for acute myocardial infarction. *Circulation: Cardiovascular Quality and Outcomes* 8(3): 244–251.

Duxbury, Linda, & Christopher Higgins. 2012a. *Impact of Gender and Life-cycle Stage on the Findings: The 2012 National Study on Balancing Work and Caregiving in Canada*. Retrieved from http://newsroom.carleton.ca/wp-content/files/2012-National-Work-Key-Findings-Gender-and-Lifecycle.pdf

Duxbury, Linda, & Christopher Higgins. 2012b. *Revisiting Work Life Issues in Canada: The 2012 National Study on Balancing Work and Caregiving in Canada*. Retrieved from http://newsroom.carleton.ca/wp-content/files/2012-National-Work-Long-Summary.pdf

Dwairy, Marwan, & Kariman E. Menshar. 2006. Parenting style, individuation, and mental health of Egyptian adolescents. *Journal of Adolescence* 29: 103–117.

Dworsky, Amy, Keri-Nicole Dillman, Robin M. Dion, Brandon Coffee-Borden, & Miriam Rosenau. 2012. *Housing for Youth Aging out of Foster Care: A Review of the Literature and Program Typology*. Washington, DC: Office of Policy Development and Research, U.S. Department of Housing and Urban Development.

Dziak, E., B.L. Janzen, & N. Muhajarine. 2010. Inequalities in the psychological well-being of employed, single and partnered mothers: The role of psychosocial work quality and work–family conflict. *International Journal for Equity in Health* 9(1): 6–14.

Earle, L. 2011. *Traditional Aboriginal Diets and Health*. Prince George, BC: National Collaborating Centre for Aboriginal Health (NCCAH). Retrieved from http://www.nccah-ccnsa.ca/docs/social%20determinates/1828_NCCAH_mini_diets_health_final.pdf

Eastwick, Paul W., Alice H. Eagly, Peter Glick, et al. 2006. Is traditional gender ideology associated with sex-typed mate preferences? A test in nine nations. *Sex Roles* 54(9): 603–614.

Eastwick, Paul W., & Eli J. Finkel. 2008. Sex differences in mate preferences revisited: Do people know what they initially desire in a romantic partner? *Journal of Personality and Social Psychology* 94(2): 245–264.

Eaton, Asia Anna, & Suzanna Rose. 2011. Has dating become more egalitarian? A 35 year review using sex roles. *Sex Roles* 64(11): 843–862.

Eaton, Linda Carole. 2000 August. A study of the correlation between the coming-out process and the first long-term homosexual relationship between gay males. *Dissertation Abstracts International, A: The Humanities and Social Sciences* 61(2): 782-A–783-A.

Ebersohn, S., & A.C. Bouwer. 2015. A bio-ecological interpretation of the relationship challenges in the context of the reconstituted family. *South African Journal of Education* 35(2): 1–11.

Echenberg, Havi, James Gauthier, & André Léonard, 2011. Current and Emerging Issues: Some Public Policy Implications of an Aging Population, 41st Parliament, 16–17. Retrieved from http://parl.gc.ca/Content/LOP/ResearchPublications/CurrentEmergingIssues-e.pdf#page=18

Edin, Kathryn, & Rebecca Joyce Kissane. 2010. Poverty and the American family: A decade in review. *Journal of Marriage and the Family* 72(3): 460–479.

Edin, Kathryn, Laura Tach, & Ronald Mincy. 2009. Claiming fatherhood: Race and the dynamics of paternal involvement among unmarried men. *The ANNALS of the American Academy of Political and Social Science* 162(1): 149–177.

Edwards, K.M., K.M. Sylaska, & A.M. Neal. 2015. Intimate partner violence among sexual minority populations: A critical review of the literature and agenda for future research. *Psychology of Violence* 5(2): 112–121.

Eibach, R.P., & S.E. Mock. 2011. Idealizing parenthood to rationalize parental investments. *Psychological Science* 22(2): 203–208.

Eichler, M. 1983. *Families in Canada Today: Recent Changes and Their Policy Consequences*. Toronto, ON: Gage.

Eichler, M., P. Albanese, S. Ferguson, N. Hyndman, L.W. Liu, & A. Matthers. 2010. *More Than It Seems: Household Work and Lifelong Learning.* Toronto, ON: Women's Press.

Eichler, M.R. 2012. Marriage in Canada. *The Canadian Encyclopedia.* Retrieved from http://www.thecanadianencyclopedia.ca/en/article/marriage-and-divorce

Eichler, Margrit. 1997. *Family Shifts: Families, Policies and Gender Equality.* Toronto: Oxford University Press.

Eichler, Margrit. 2001. Biases in family literature, pp. 51–66. In Maureen Baker (Ed.), *Families: Changing Trends in Canada* (4th ed.). Toronto: McGraw-Hill Ryerson.

Elder, Glen H. Jr. 1992. Models of the life course. *Contemporary Sociology 21*: 632–635.

Elder, Glen H. Jr., Monica Kirkpatrick Johnson, & Robert Crosnoe. 2004. The emergence and development of life course theory, pp. 3–19. In Jeylan T. Mortimer & Michael J. Shanahan (Eds.), *Handbook of the Life Course.* New York: Kluwer.

El-Ghannam, Ashraf R. 2001. Modernisation in Arab societies: The theoretical and analytical view. *International Journal of Sociology and Social Policy 21*: 88–131.

Elias, B., J. Mignone, M. Hall, S.P. Hong, L. Hart, & J. Sareen. 2012. Trauma and suicide behaviour histories among a Canadian indigenous population: An empirical exploration of the potential role of Canada's residential school system. *Social Science and Medicine 74*(10): 1560–1569.

Emery, Robert E. 2012. *Renegotiating Family Relationships: Divorce, Child Custody and Mediation* (2nd ed.). New York: Guildford Press.

Emery, Robert E. 2013. *Cultural Sociology of Divorce: An Encyclopedia.* Thousand Oaks, CA: Sage.

Engels, F. 2010. *The Origins of the Family, Private Property and the State.* London, UK: Penguin Classics. (Original work published 1884.)

Engels, Frederick. [1884]1972. *The Origin of the Family, Private Property and the State.* New York: Pathfinder.

England, P. 2005. Gender inequality in labor markets: The role of motherhood and segregation. *Social Politics: International Studies in Gender, State and Society 12*(2): 264–288.

Epstein, M., J.P. Calzo, A.P. Smiler, & L.M. Ward. 2009. Anything from making out to having sex: Men's negotiations of hooking up and friends with benefits scripts. *Journal Sex Research 46*(5): 414–424.

Epstein, R. 1999. Lesbian families, pp. 107–130. In M. Lynn (Ed.), *Voices: Essays on Canadian Families.* Toronto: Nelson Canada.

Epstein, Robert, Mayuri Pandit, & Mansi Thakar. 2013. How love emerges in arranged marriages: Two cross-cultural studies. *Journal of Comparative Family Studies 44*(3): 341–360.

Ermisch, John. 2008. Origins of social immobility and inequality: Parenting and early child development. *National Institute Economic Review 205*: 62–71.

Esping-Andersen, G. 1999. *Social Foundations of Post Industrial Economics.* Oxford University Press, New York.

Espiritu, Yen Le. 2001. We don't sleep around like white girls do: Family, culture, and gender in Filipina American lives. *Signs 26*(2): 415–440.

Evans, J., & S. Rodger. 2008. Mealtimes and bedtimes: Windows to family routines and rituals. *Journal of Occupational Science 15*(2): 98–104.

Evans, Rhiannon, Jonathan Scourfield, & Graham Moore. 2016. Gender, relationship breakdown, and suicide risk: A review of research in Western countries. *Journal of Family Issues 37*(16): 2239–2264.

Faludi, S. 2013, October 22. Facebook feminism, like it or not. *The Baffler.* Retrieved from https://thebaffler.com/salvos/facebook-feminism-like-it-or-not

Farhat, Tilda, Denise Haynie, Faith Summersett-Ringgold, Ashley Brooks-Russell, & Ronald J. Iannotti. 2015. Weight perceptions, misperceptions, and dating violence victimization among U.S. adolescents. *Journal of Interpersonal Violence 30*: 1511–1532.

Farrell, Betty, Alicia VanderVusse, & Abigail Ocobock. 2012. Family change and the state of family sociology. *Current Sociology 60*(3): 263–301.

Fasang, Anette Eva, & Marcel Raab. 2014. Beyond transmission: Intergenerational patterns of family formation among middle-class American families. *Demography 51*(5): 1703–1728.

Feldhaus, Michael, & Valerie Heintz-Martin. 2015. Long-term effects of parental separation: Impacts of parental separation during childhood on the timing and the risk of cohabitation, marriage, and divorce in adulthood. *Advances in Life Course Research 26*: 22.

Felix, Daniel S., W. David Robinson, & Kimberly J. Jarzynka. 2013. The Influence of Divorce on Men's Health. *Journal of Men's Health.* 18 January 2013. http://www.sciencedirect.com/science/article/pii/S1875686712000954

Felson, R.B., & S.F. Messner. 2000. The control motive in intimate partner violence. *Social Psychology Quarterly 63*(1): 86–94.

Ferguson, C.J., C. San Miguel, & R.D. Hartley. 2009. A multivariate analysis of youth violence and aggression: The influence of family, peers, depression, and media violence. *The Journal of Pediatrics* 155(6): 904–908.

Ferguson, Rob. 2015, October 1. Ontario to cover in-vitro fertilization treatments. *Toronto Star.*

Fernandes, E. 2009. Swinging paradigm: An evaluation of the marital and sexual satisfaction of swingers. *Electronic Journal of Human Sexuality 12.* Retrieved from https://www.psychologytoday.com/files/attachments/134956/the-swinging-paradigm.pdf

Ferri, E. 1993. Socialization experiences of children in lone parent families: Evidence from the British National Child Development Study. In J. Hudson & B. Galaway (Eds.), *Single Parent Families: Perspectives on Research and Policy.* Toronto: Thompson.

Fetner, T. 2008. *How the Religious Right Shaped Lesbian and Gay Activism.* Minneapolis: University of Minnesota Press.

Finances Quebec. 2017, March 8. Daily daycare costs. Retrieved from http://www.budget.finances.gouv.qc.ca/Budget/outils/garde_en.asp

Fincham, Frank D., & Steven R.H. Beach. 2006. Relationship satisfaction, pp. 579–594. In Anita L. Vangelisti & Daniel Perlman (Eds.), *The Cambridge Handbook of Personal Relationships.* New York: Cambridge University Press.

Fingerman, Karen L., & Susan T. Charles. 2010. It takes two to tango: Why older people have the best relationships. *Current Directions in Psychological Science 19*(3): 172–176.

Fingerson, Laura. 2000. *Do Parents' Opinions Matter? Family Processes and Adolescent Sexual Behavior.* Paper presented to the American Sociological Association (ASA).

Finlay, Barbara, Ellen van Velsor, & Mary Ann Hilker. 1982. Household and family structure over the life cycle in the industrializing south: A comparative historical test. *International Journal of Sociology of the Family 12*(1): 47–61.

Finnie, Ross. 1993. Women, men, and the economic consequences of divorce: Evidence from Canadian longitudinal data. *Canadian Review of Sociology and Anthropology 30*(2): 205–241.

Fishman, Barbara. 1983. The economic behavior of stepfamilies. *Family Relations 32:* 359–366.

Fiske, J.A., & R. Johnny. 2014. The Lake Babine First Nation family: Yesterday and today, pp. 413–428. In Bonnie Box (Ed.), *Family Patterns, Gender Relations* (4th ed.). New York: Oxford University Press.

Fitzgerald, B. 1999. Children of lesbian and gay parents: A review of the literature. *Marriage and Family Review 29*(1): 57–76.

Fitzpatrick, T.R., & B. Vinick. 2003. The impact of husbands' retirement on wives' marital quality. *Journal of Family Social Work 7*(1): 83–100.

Flandrin, J-L. 1979. *Families in Former Times: Kinship, Household and Sexuality in Early Modern France.* Cambridge: Cambridge University Press.

Fleming, R. 1997. *The Common Purse: Income Sharing in New Zealand.* Auckland, New Zealand: Aukland University Press.

Fleras, Augie, & Jean Leonard Elliott. 2003. *Unequal Relations: An Introduction to Race and Ethnic Dynamics in Canada* (4th ed.). Toronto: Prentice Hall.

Fletcher, J.M., & B.L. Wolfe. 2012. The effects of teenage fatherhood on young adult outcomes. *Economic Inquiry 50*(1): 182–201.

Fleury, Dominique. 2008. Low-income children. *Perspectives on Labour and Income 9* (5): 14–23. Statistics Canada Catalogue no. 75-001-XIE. http://www.statcan.gc.ca/pub/75-001-x/2008105/pdf/10578-eng.pdf

Fomby, P., & A.J. Cherlin. 2007. Family instability and child well-being. *American Sociological Review 72:* 181–204.

Fonner, Kathryn L., & Lara C. Stache. 2012. All in a day's work, at home: Teleworkers' management of micro role transitions and the work–home boundary. *New Technology, Work and Employment 27*(3): 242–257. http://onlinelibrary.wiley.com/doi/10.1111/j.1468-005X.2012.00290.x/pdf

Forman-Hoffman, V.L., K.K. Richardson, J.W. Yankey, S.L. Hillis, R.B. Wallace, & F.D. Wolinsky. 2008. Retirement and weight changes among men and women in the health and retirement study. *The Journals of Gerontology: Series B, Psychological Sciences and Social Sciences 63*(3): 146–153.

Foster children counted in Canadian census for 1st time. 2012, September 12. *The Canadian Press,* September 12. Retrieved from http://www.cbc.ca/news/canada/foster-children-counted-in-canadian-census-for-1st-time-1.1137081

Fox, B. 2009. *When Couples Become Parents: The Creation of Gender in the Transition to Parenthood.* Toronto, ON: University of Toronto Press.

Fox, B., & M. Luxton. 2014. Analyzing the familiar: Definitions, approaches, and issues at the heart of studying families, pp. 2–30. In B. Fox (Ed.), *Family Patterns, Gender Relations* (4th ed.). Don Mills, ON: Oxford University Press.

Fox, B.J., & D. Fumia. 2001. Pathbreakers: Unconventional families of the nineties, pp. 458–469. In B.J. Fox (Ed.), *Family Patterns, Gender Relations.* New York: Oxford University Press.

Fox, B.J., & D. Worts. 1999. Revisiting the critique of medicalized childbirth: A contribution to the sociology of birth. *Gender and Society* 13(3): 326–346. doi:10.2307/190258

Fox, Bonnie J. 1993. The rise and fall of the breadwinner—homemaker family, pp. 147–157. In Bonnie J. Fox (Ed.), *Family Patterns, Gender Relations*. Toronto: Oxford University Press.

Fox, Bonnie J. 2001. The formative years: How parenthood creates gender. *La Revue Canadienne de Sociologie et d'Anthropologie/The Canadian Review of Sociology and Anthropology* 38(4): 373–390.

Fox, Bonnie J., & Meg Luxton. 2001. Conceptualizing family, pp. 22–33. In Bonnie J. Fox (Ed.), *Family Patterns, Gender Relations* (2nd ed.). Toronto: Oxford University Press.

Francis-Tan, Andrew, & Hugo M. Mialon. 2015. A diamond is forever and other fairy tales: The relationship between wedding expenses and marriage duration. *Economic Inquiry* 53(4): 1919–1930.

Frank, Kristyn, & Feng Hou. 2015. Source-country gender roles and the division of labor within immigrant families. *Journal of Marriage and Family* 77(2): 557–574.

Franko, D.L., D. Thompson, S.G. Affenito, B.A. Barton, & R.H. Striegel-Moore. 2008. What mediates the relationship between family meals and adolescent health issues. *Health Psychology* 27(2S): S109.

Fraser, C., E. Olsen, K. Lee, C. Southworth, & S. Tucker. 2010. The new age of stalking: Technological implications for stalking. *Juvenile and Family Court Journal* 61(4): 39–55.

Frias, Sonia M., & Ronald J. Angel. 2007. Stability and change in the experience of partner violence among low-income women. *Social Science Quarterly* 88(5): 1281–1306.

Frideres, J.S. 2007. Building bridges: Aboriginal, immigrant, and visible minority families in the twenty-first century, pp. 195–212. In David Cheal (Ed.), *Canadian Families Today: New Perspectives*. Toronto: Oxford University Press.

Friedman, May. 2015. Mother blame, fat shame, and moral panic: 'Obesity' and child welfare. *Fat Studies* 4: 14–27.

Friendly, M. 1994. *Childcare Policy in Canada: Putting the Pieces Together*. Toronto, ON: Addison-Wesley.

Fu, Xuanning. 2008. Interracial marriage and family socio-economic well-being: Equal status exchange or caste status exchange? *Social Science Journal* 45: 132–155.

Furnham, A., & A. McClelland. 2015. What women want in a man: The role of age, social class, ethnicity, and height. *Psychology* 6: 278–290.

Furstenberg, F.F. Jr., & Andrew J. Cherlin. 1991. *Divided Families: What Happens to Children when Parents Part*. Cambridge, MA: Harvard University Press.

Gabbay, N., & M.F. Lafontaine. 2017. Understanding the relationship between attachment, caregiving, and same sex intimate partner violence. *Journal of Family Violence* 32(3): 291–304.

Gadalla, T. M. 2009. Impact of marital dissolution on men's and women's incomes: A longitudinal study. *Journal of Divorce and Remarriage* 50(1): 55–65.

Gaetz, S., J. Donaldson, T. Richter, & T. Gulliver. 2013. *The State of Homelessness in Canada 2013*. Homeless Hub Paper #4. Retrieved from http://homelesshub.ca/sites/default/files/SOHC2103.pdf

Gager, Constance, Scott Yabiku, & Miriam Linver. 2016. Conflict or divorce? Does parental conflict and/or divorce increase the likelihood of adult children's cohabiting and marital dissolution? *Marriage and Family Review* 52(30): 243–261.

Gailey, Jeannine A. 2012. Fat shame to fat pride: Fat women's sexual and dating experiences. *Fat Studies* 1: 114–127.

Galston, William A. 1996. Braking divorce for the sake of children. *The American Enterprise* 7 (May/June). *Globe and Mail*, 2000, 49.

Galvin, Kathleen M., Dawn O. Braithwaite, & Carma L. Bylund. 2015. *Family Communication: Cohesion and Change*. New York: Routledge.

Garber, Benjamin D. 2014. The chameleon child: Children as actors in the high conflict divorce drama. *Journal of Child Custody* 11(1): 25–40.

Gareis, K.C., R.C. Barnett, K.A. Ertel, & L.F. Berkman. 2009. Work–family enrichment and conflict: Additive effects, buffering, or balance? *Journal of Marriage and Family* 71: 696–707. doi:10.1111/j.1741-3737.2009.00627.x

Garg, R., E. Levin, D. Urajnik, & C. Kauppi. 2005. Parenting style and academic achievement for East Indian and Canadian adolescents. *Journal of Comparative Family Studies* 36(4): 653–661.

Garner, Rochelle, Eric Guimond, & Sacha Senecal. 2013. The socio-economic characteristics of First Nation teen mothers. *International Indigenous Policy Journal* 4(1): 1–25.

Gatter, Caroline, Kathleen Hodkinson, & Monika Kolle. 2016. On the differences between Tinder™ versus online dating agencies: Questioning a myth. An exploratory study. *Cogent Psychology* 3(1).

Gaudie, J., F. Mitrou, D. Lawrence, F.J. Stanley, S.R. Silburn, & S.R. Zubrick. 2010. Antecedents of teenage pregnancy from a 14-year follow-up study using data linkage. *BMC Public Health* 10(1): 1.

Gaunt, Ruth. 2006. Couple similarity and marital satisfaction: Are similar spouses happier? *Journal of Personality* 74(5): 1401–1420.

Gazso, A., & S.A. McDaniel. 2010. The risks of being a lone mother on income support in Canada and the USA. *International Journal of Sociology and Social Policy* 30(7/8): 368–386. doi:10.1108/01443331011060724

Gazso, Amber, & Susan McDaniel. April 2009. *The Risky Business of Being a Lone Mother on Income Support in Canada and the U.S.* Paper presented at the Pacific Sociological Association meetings, San Diego.

Gazso, Amber, & Susan A. McDaniel. 2010a. The Great West 'Experiment:' Neo-Liberal Convergence and Transforming Citizenship in Canada. *Canadian Review of Social Policy*, 63/64: 15–35.

Gazso, Amber, & Susan A. McDaniel. 2014. Families by choice and the management of low income through social supports. *Journal of Family Issues*, forthcoming.

Gee, Ellen M. 1986. The life course of Canadian women: An historical and demographic analysis. *Social Indicators Research* 18: 263–283.

Geier, K. 2013, March 31. Review: Sheryl Sandberg's Lean In. *Washington Monthly*. Retrieved from http://washingtonmonthly.com/2013/03/31/review-sheryl-sandbergs-lean-in/

George, J., & S.M. Stith. 2014. An updated feminist view of intimate partner violence. *Family Process* 53(2): 179–193.

Gerson, K. 1985. *Hard Choices: How Women Decide about Work, Career, and Motherhood*. Los Angeles: University of California Press.

Getch, Y. 2012. Feelings of family caregivers, pp. 29–43. In R.C. Talley & J.E. Crews (Eds.), *Multiple Dimensions of Caregiving and Disability*. New York: Springer.

Ghimire, Dirgha J., William G. Axinn, Scott T. Yabiku, & Arland Thornton. 2006. Social change, premarital nonfamily experience, and spouse choice in an arranged marriage society. *American Journal of Sociology 111*: 1181–1218.

Gibson, M.F. 2016. This is real now because it's a piece of paper: Texts, disability and LGBTQ parents. *Disability & Society* 31(5): 641–658.

Giddens, Anthony. 1992. *The Transformation of Intimacy: Sexuality, Love, and Eroticism in Modern Societies*. Cambridge: Polity Press.

Giele, Janet Zollinger. 1996. Decline of family: Conservative, liberal and feminist views. In David Popenoe, Jean Bethke Elshtain, & David Blankenhorn (Eds.), *Promises to Keep: Decline and Renewal of Marriage in America*. Lanham, MD: Rowman & Littlefield Publishers, Inc.

Giesbrecht, M., F. Wolse, V.A. Crooks, & K. Stajduhar. 2015. Identifying socio-environmental factors that facilitate resilience among Canadian palliative family caregivers: A qualitative case study. *Palliative and Supportive Care* 13: 555–565.

Glantz, M.J., M.C. Chamberlain, Q. Liu, C.C. Hsieh, K.R. Edwards, A. Van Horn, & L. Recht. 2009. Gender disparity in the rate of partner abandonment in patients with serious medical illness. *Cancer* 115(22): 5237–5242.

Glaser, K., R. Stuchbury, C. Tomassini, & J. Askham. 2008. The long-term consequences of partnership dissolution for support in later life in the United Kingdom. *Ageing & Society* 28(3): 329–351.

Glenwright, Brittni, & Darren M. Fowler. 2013. Implications of egalitarianism and religiosity on relationship satisfaction. *Interpersona* 7(2): 215–226.

Glynn, Sarah Jane. 2012. *The New Breadwinners: 2010 Update, Rates of Women Supporting Their Families Economically Increased Since 2007*. Center for American Progress. http://www.americanprogress.org/wp-content/uploads/issues/2012/04/pdf/breadwinners.pdf

Godoy-Ruiz, P., B. Toner, R. Mason, C. Vidal, & K. McKenzie. 2015. Intimate partner violence and depression among Latin American women in Toronto. *Journal of Immigrant and Minority Health* 17(6): 1771–1780.

Gold, M., & M. Mustafa. 2013. Work always wins: Client colonisation, time management and the anxieties of connected freelancers. *New Technology, Work and Employment* 28(3): 197–211.

Goldberg, A.E., L.A. Kinkler, H.B. Richardson, & J.B. Downing. 2011. Lesbian, gay, and heterosexual couples in open adoption arrangements: A qualitative study. *Journal of Marriage and Family* 73(2): 502–518.

Goldberg, A.E., A.M. Moyer, E.R. Weber, & J. Shapiro. 2013. What changed when the gay adoption ban was lifted? Perspectives of lesbian and gay parents in Florida. *Sexuality Research and Social Policy* 10(2): 110–124.

Goldberg, Abbie E. 2012. *Gay Dads: The Transition to Adoptive Parenthood*. New York: New York University Press.

Goldberg, Abbie E., Julianna Z. Smith, & Maureen Perry-Jenkins. 2012. The division of labour in lesbian, gay, and heterosexual new adoptive parents. *Journal of Marriage and Family* 74(4): 812–828.

Goldscheider, F., G. Kaufman, & S. Sassler. 2009. Navigating the new marriage market: How attitudes toward partner characteristics shape union formation. *Journal of Family Issues* 30(6): 719–737.

Gonzalez, K.A., S.S. Rostosky, R.D. Odom, & E.D.B. Riggle. 2013. The positive aspects of being the parent of an LGBTQ child. *Family Process* 52(2): 325–337.

Goode, William. 1993. *World Changes in Divorce Patterns*. New Haven: Yale University Press.

Goode, William J. 1982. *The Family*. Englewood Cliffs, NJ: Prentice-Hall.

Gordon, Linda, & Sara McLanahan. 1991. Single parenthood in 1900. *Journal of Family History* 16(2): 97–116.

Gordon, P.A., M.K. Tschopp, & D. Feldman. 2004. Addressing issues of sexuality with adolescents with disabilities. *Child and Adolescent Social Work Journal* 21(5): 513–527.

Gotta, G., R. Green, E. Rothblum, S. Solomon, K. Balsam, & P. Schwartz. 2011. Heterosexual, lesbian, and gay male relationships: A comparison of couples in 1975 and 2000. *Family Process* 50: 353–376.

Gottman, John Mordechai. 2014. *What Predicts Divorce? The Relationship between Marital Processes and Marital Outcomes*. New York: Psychology Press.

Government of Canada. 2008. *Statement of Apology to Former Students of Indian Residential Schools*. Retrieved March 21, 2017, from http://www.aadnc-aandc.gc.ca/eng/1100100015644/1100100015649

Grable, John E., Sonya Britt, & Joyce Cantrell. 2007. An exploratory study of the role financial satisfaction has on the thought of subsequent divorce. *Family and Consumer Sciences Research Journal* 36: 130–150.

Graham, James M., & Zoe B. Barnow. 2013. Stress and social support in gay, lesbian, and heterosexual couples: Direct effects and buffering models. *Journal of Family Psychology* 27(4): 569–578.

Graham, K., S. Bernards, S. Wilsnack, & G. Gmel. 2011. Alcohol may not cause partner violence but it seems to make it worse: A cross national comparison of the relationship between alcohol and severity of partner violence. *Journal of Interpersonal Violence* 26(8): 1503–1523.

Green, Alan G., & David Green. 2004. The goals of Canada's immigration policy: A historical perspective. *Canadian Journal of Urban Research* 13: 102–139.

Greenberg, L., & C. Normandin. 2015. *Disparities in Life Expectancy at Birth*. Ottawa: Statistics Canada. Retrieved from http://www.statcan.gc.ca/pub/82-624-x/2011001/article/11427-eng.htm

Greene, K., & S.L. Faulkner. 2005. Gender, belief in the sexual double standard, and sexual talk in heterosexual dating relationships. *Sex Roles* 53(3–4): 239–251.

Gregg, M. 2013. Spousebusting: Intimacy, adultery, and surveillance technology. *Surveillance & Society* 11(3): 301–310.

Griffiths, P.C., N. Davis, J. Lin, D. Wachtel, S. Ward, J. Painter, . . . & T.M. Johnson. 2010. Using Telehealth technology to support family caregivers: Description of a pilot intervention and preliminary results. *Physical & Occupational Therapy in Geriatrics* 28(4): 307–320.

Grover, Shawn, & John F. Helliwell. 2014. *How's Life at Home? New Evidence on Marriage and the Set Point for Happiness*. Cambridge, MA: National Bureau of Economic Research.

Guberman, Nancy, Jean-Pierre Lavoie, Laure Blein, & Ignace Olazabal. 2012. Baby Boom Caregivers: Care in the Age of Individualization. *The Gerontologist* 52(2): 210–218. Retrieved from http://0-gerontologist.oxfordjournals.org.darius.uleth.ca/content/52/2/210.full.pdf+html

Guerriere, D., A. Husain, B. Zagorski, D. Marshall, H. Seow, K. Brazil, & P.C. Coyte. 2016. Predictors of caregiver burden across the home-based palliative care trajectory in Ontario, Canada. *Health and Social Care in the Community* 24(4): 428–438.

Gunby, J., F. Bissonnette, C. Librach, & L. Cowan. 2010. Assisted reproductive technologies (ART) in Canada: 2006 results from the Canadian ART Register. *Fertility and Sterility* 93(7): 2189–2201.

Gupta, S. 1999. The effects of marital status transitions on men's housework performance. *Journal of Marriage and Families* 61: 700–711.

Gustafson, Kaaryn. 2009. Breaking vows: Marriage promotion, the new patriarch, and the retreat from egalitarianism. *Stanford Journal of Civil*

Rights and Civil Liberties 2(5): 269–277. http://hei-nonline.org/HOL/LandingPage?collection=jour nals&handle=hein.journals/stjcrc15&div=13& id=&page

Hadas, Doron, Gila Markovitzky, & Miri Sarid. 2008. Spousal violence among immigrants from the former Soviet Union—general population and welfare recipients. *Journal of Family Violence* 23: 549–555.

Hahn, J.W., M.C. McCormick, J.G. Silverman, E.B. Robinson, & K.C. Koenen. 2014. Examining the impact of disability status on intimate partner violence victimization in a population sample. *Journal of Interpersonal Violence* 29(17): 3063–3085.

Haight, M., A. Quan-Haase, & B.A. Corbett. 2014. Revisiting the digital divide in Canada: The impact of demographic factors on access to the Internet, level of online activity, and social networking site usage. *Information, Communication & Society* 17(4): 503–519.

Hall, H.R., S.L. Neely-Barnes, J.C. Graff, T.E. Krcek, R.J. Robers, & J.S. Hankins. 2012. Parental stress in families of children with a genetic disorder/disability and the resiliency model of family stress, adjustment, and adaptation. *Issues in Comprehensive Pediatric Nursing* 35(1): 24–44.

Halla, Martin. 2013. The effect of joint custody on family outcomes. *Journal of the European Economic Association*, 11(2): 278–315.

Halpern-Meekin, S., W. Manning, P. Giordano, & M. Longmore. 2013. Relationship churning in emerging adulthood: On/off relationships and sex with an ex. *Journal of Adolescent Research* 28(2): 166–188.

Hamilton, L., S. Cheng, & B. Powell. 2007. Adoptive parents, adaptive parents: Evaluating the importance of biological ties for parental investment. *American Sociological Review* 72(1): 95–116.

Hamplová, D. 2003. Marriage and educational attainment: A dynamic approach to first union formation. *Czech Sociological Review* 39(6): 841–863.

Harrison, Deborah. 2002. *The First Casualty: Violence against Women in Canadian Military Communities*. Toronto: Lorimer.

Harrison, Deborah, Karen Robson, Patrizia Albanese, Chris Saunders, & Christine Newburn-Cook. 2011. The impact of shared location on the mental health of military and civilian adolescents in a community affected by frequent deployments. *Armed Forces & Society* 37(3): 550–560.

Hartley, S.L., L.M. Papp, & D. Bolt. 2016. Spillover of marital interactions and parenting stress in families of children with autism spectrum disorder. *Journal of Clinical Child & Adolescent Psychology*: 1–12.

Hartos, Jessica L., & Thomas G. Power. 2000 September. Relations among single mothers' awareness of their adolescents' stressors, maternal monitoring, mother–adolescent communication, and adolescent adjustment. *Journal of Adolescent Research* 15(5): 546–563.

Harvard Men's Health Watch. 2010, July. *Marriage and Men's Health*. Retrieved from http://www.health. harvard.edu/newsletter_article/marriage-and-mens-health

Hassouneh-Phillips, Dena, & Elizabeth McNeff. 2005. I thought I was less worthy: Low sexual and body esteem and increased vulnerability to intimate partner abuse in women with physical disabilities. *Sexuality and Disability* 23(4): 227–240.

Hawkins, Alan J., Victoria L. Blanchard, Scott A. Baldwin, & Elizabeth B. Fawcett. 2008. Does marriage and relationship education work? A meta-analytic study. *Journal of Consulting and Clinical Psychology* 76(5): 723–734.

Hayes, G. 2017. Cushioning, breadcrumbing or benching: The language of modern dating. *The Guardian*, May 8. Retrieved from https://www. theguardian.com/lifeandstyle/2017/may/08/ cushioning-breadcrumbing-benching-language-modern-dating

Hayford, S.R. 2013. Marriage (still) matters: The contribution of demographic change to trends in childlessness in the United States. *Demography* 50(5): 1641–1661.

Heath, M. 2016. Testing the limits of religious freedom: The case of polygamy's criminalization in Canada, pp. 157–179. In J. Bennion & L. Fishbayn Joffe (Eds.), *Polygamy: The New Marriage Rights Frontier*. Boulder, CO: University Press of Colorado.

Heiman, J.R., J.S. Long, S.N. Smith, W.A. Fisher, M.S. Sand, & R.C. Rosen. 2011. Sexual satisfaction and relationship happiness in midlife and older couples in five countries. *Archives of Sexual Behavior* 40(4): 741–753.

Heimdal, Kristen R., & Sharon K. Houseknecht. 2003. Cohabiting and married couples' income organization: Approaches in Sweden and the United States. *Journal of Marriage and Family* 65(3): 525–538.

Helbig, Sylvia, Thomas Lampert, Michael Klose, & Frank Jacobi. 2006. Is parenthood associated with mental health? Findings from an epidemiological community survey. *Social Psychiatry and Psychiatric Epidemiology* 41(11): 889–96.

Hellerstein, Judith K., & Melinda Sandler Morrill. 2011. Booms, Busts, and Divorce. *The Berkeley Electronic Journal of Economic Analysis and Policy* 11(1): 1935.

Henningsen, David Dryden, Mary Braz, & Elaine Davies. 2008. Why do we flirt? Flirting motivations and sex differences in working and social contexts. *Journal of Business Communication* 45 (4): 483–502.

Henripin, Jacques, & Yves Peron. 1971. Demographic transitions in the province of Quebec. In David Glass & Roger Ravelle (Eds.), *Population and Social Change*. London: Edward Arnold.

Henry, N.J.M., C.A. Berg, T.W. Smith, & P. Florsheim. 2007. Positive and negative characteristics of marital interaction and their association with marital satisfaction in middle aged and older couples. *Psychology and Aging* 22: 428–441.

Henry, Ryan G., & Richard B. Miller. 2004. Marital problems occurring in midlife: Implications for couples therapy. *American Journal of Family Therapy* 32: 405–417.

Henshel, A.-M. 1973. Swinging: A study of decision making in marriage. *American Journal of Sociology* 78(4): 885–891.

Hertz, L. 1986. *The Business Amazons*. London, UK: Andre Deutsch, Ltd.

Hester, D.M., C.D. Lew, & A. Swota. 2015. When rights just won't do: Ethical considerations when making decisions for severely disabled newborns. *Perspectives in Biology and Medicine* 58(3): 322.

Hetherington, E. Mavis, & John Kelly. 2002. *For Better or for Worse: Divorce Reconsidered*. New York: W. W. Norton.

Hilario, C., D. Vo, J. Johnson, & E. Saewyc. 2014. Acculturation, gender, and mental health of Southeast Asian immigrant youth in Canada. *Journal of Immigrant and Minority Health* 16(6): 1121–1129.

Hilbrecht, M., S.M. Shaw, L.C. Johnson, & J. Andrey. 2008. I'm home for the kids: Contradictory implications for work–life balance of teleworking mothers. *Gender, Work & Organization* 15(5): 454–476.

Hiotakis, Samantha. 2005. An investigation of familial variables associated with marital satisfaction. *Dissertation Abstracts International: Section B: The Sciences and Engineering* 66(5-B), 2877.

Ho, C., D.N. Bluestein, & J.M. Jenkins. 2008. Cultural differences in the relationship between parenting and children's behavior. *Developmental Psychology* 44(2): 507.

Ho, G.W.K. 2013. Acculturation and its implications on parenting for Chinese immigrants: A systematic review. *Journal of Transcultural Nursing* 25(2): 45–158.

Hochschild, A.R. 1989. *The Second Shift: Working Parents and the Revolution at Home*. New York, NY: Viking.

Hochschild, A.R. 1997. *The Time Bind: When Work Becomes Home and Home Becomes Work*. New York, NY: Henry Holt & Co.

Hoeve, M., J.S. Dubas, V.I. Eichelsheim, P.H. Van Der Laan, W. Smeenk, & J.R. Gerris. 2009. The relationship between parenting and delinquency: A meta-analysis. *Journal of Abnormal Child Psychology* 37(6): 749–775.

Hofferth, S., & F. Goldscheider. 2016. Family heterogeneity over the life course, pp. 161–178. In Michael J. Shanahan, Jeylan T. Mortimer, & Monica Kirkpatrick Johnson (Eds.), *Handbook of the Life Course, Volume II*. New York and London: Springer International.

Hoffman, Charles D., & Debra K. Ledford. 1995. Adult children of divorce: Relationships with their mothers and fathers prior to, following parental separation, and currently. *Journal of Divorce and Remarriage* 24(3–4).

Hoffman, Martin L. 1979. Development of moral thought, feeling, and behavior. *American Psychologist* 34(10): 958–966.

Hoffman, Saul, & Greg Duncan. 1995 Winter. The effect of incomes, wages and AFDC benefits in marital disruption. *Journal of Human Resources* 30.

Hoffner, C. 2008. Parasocial and online social relationships, pp. 309–333. In S.L. Calvert & B.J. Wilson (Eds.), *The Handbook of Children, Media, and Development*. Somerset, NJ: Wiley.

Holtmann, C. 2016. Christian and Muslim immigrant women in the Canadian Maritimes: Considering their strengths and vulnerabilities in responding to domestic violence. *Studies in Religion* 45(3): 397–414.

hooks, bell. 2013, October 28. Dig deep: Beyond lean in. *The Feminist Wire*. Retrieved from http://thefeministwire.com/2013/10/17973/

Hooks, Gwen. 1997. *The Keystone Legacy: Reflections of a Black Pioneer*. Edmonton, AB: Brightest Pebble Publishing.

Howell, Nancy, with Patricia Albanese & Kwaku Obosu-Mensah. 2001. Ethnic families, pp. 116–142. In Maureen Baker (Ed.), *Families: Changing Trends in Canada* (4th ed.). Toronto: McGraw-Hill Ryerson.

Howland, C.A., & D.H. Rintala. 2001. Dating behaviors of women with physical disabilities. *Sexuality and Disability* 19(1): 41–70.

Hsiung, P., & K. Nichol. 2010. Policies on and experiences of foreign domestic workers in Canada. *Sociology*

Compass 4(9): 766–778. doi:http://dx.doi.org/10.1111/j.1751-9020.2010.00320.x

Huang, Frederick Y., & Salman Akhtar. 2005. Immigrant sex: The transport of affection and sensuality across cultures. *American Journal of Psychoanalysis* 65: 179–188.

Huang, Penelope M., Pamela J. Smock, Wendy D. Manning, & Cara A. Bergstrom-Lynch. 2011. He says, she says: Gender and cohabitation. *Journal of Family Issues* 32 (7): 876–905.

Huck, Barbara. 2001 February/March. Love in another world. *The Beaver: Canada's History Magazine*: 12–19.

Hughes, K., & A. Funston. 2006. Use and value of ICTs for separated families. *Telecommunications Journal of Australia* 56(2): 76–85.

Hull, J. 2001. *Aboriginal Single Mothers in Canada, 1996: A Statistical Report*. Ottawa: Indian and Northern Affairs Canada. Catalogue no. R2-164/1996E. Retrieved from http://publications.gc.ca/collections/Collection/R2-164-1996E.pdf

Humble, Âine M. 2013. Moving from ambivalence to certainty: Older same-sex couples marry in Canada. *Canadian Journal on Aging* 32(2): 131–144.

Humensky, J.L. 2010. Are adolescents with high socio-economic status more likely to engage in alcohol and illicit drug use in early adulthood? *Substance Abuse Treatment, Prevention, and Policy* 5(1): 1.

Humphreys, Terry, & Ed Herold. 2007. Sexual consent in heterosexual relationships: Development of a new measure. *Sex Roles* 57: 305–315.

Husaini, Zohra, & Jagjeet Bhardwaj. 2010. *Anecdotal Report on the Incidence of Forced Marriage in Western Canada Submitted to Justice Canada by Indo-Canadian Women's Association*. Department of Justice, Canada. Retrieved from http://justice.gc.ca/eng/rp-pr/cj-jp/fv-vf/fmwc-mfoc/fmwc-mfoc.pdf

Huston, Ted L., & Heidi Melz. 2004. The case for (promoting) marriage: The devil is in the details. *Journal of Marriage and Family* 66(4): 943–958.

Hwang, Wei-Chin. 2006. Acculturative family distancing: Theory, research, and clinical practice. *Psychotherapy: Theory, Research, Practice, Training* 43(2006): 397–409.

Hyman, Ilene, Sepali Guruge, & Robin Mason. 2008. The impact of migration on marital relationships: A study of Ethiopian immigrants in Toronto. *Journal of Comparative Family Studies* 39: 149–163.

Iacovetta, Franca. 1992. *Such Hardworking People: Italian Immigrants in Post-War Toronto*. Montreal and Kingston: McGill-Queen's University Press.

Ide, Naoko, Marianne Wyder, Kairi Kolves, & Diego De Leo. 2010. Separation as an important risk factor for suicide: A systematic review. *Journal of Family Issues* 31(12).

Ihinger-Tallman, M., & K. Pasley. 1987. Divorce and remarriage in the American family: A historical review. In K. Pasley & M. Ihinger-Tallman (Eds.), *Remarriage and Stepparenting: Current Research and Theory*. New York: Guilford Press.

Immigration, Refugees and Citizenship Canada. 2016, October 31. *Notice—Supplementary Information 2017 Immigration Levels Plan*. Retrieved from http://www.cic.gc.ca/english/department/media/notices

Indigenous and Northern Affairs Canada. 2015. *Matrimonial Real Property on Reserves*. Retrieved from https://www.aadnc-aandc.gc.ca/eng/1100100032553/1100100032557

Ingraham, C. 1999. *White Weddings*. New York: Routledge.

Insights West. 2014. *Nearly All Chinese and South Asian British Columbians Have Faced Discrimination: Poll*. Retrieved from http://www.insightswest.com/news/nearly-all-chinese-and-south-asian-british-columbians-have-faced-discrimination

Ireton, J. 2017. Raising Elaan: Profoundly disabled boy's co-mommas make legal history. *CBC News*, February 21. Retrieved from http://www.cbc.ca/news/canada/ottawa/multimedia/raising-elaan-profoundly-disabled-boy-s-co-mommas-make-legal-history-1.3988464

Islam, F., N. Khanlou, & H. Tamim. 2014. South Asian populations in Canada: Migration and mental health. *Asia-Pacific Psychiatry* 8(1): 32–43.

Isler, A., F. Tas, D. Beytut, & Z. Conk. 2009. Sexuality in adolescents with intellectual disabilities. *Sexuality and Disability* 27(1): 27–34.

Iveniuk, James, Linda J. Waite, Edward Laumann, Martha K. McClintock & Andrew D. Tiedt. 2014. Marital conflict in older couples: Positivity, personality, and health. *Journal of Marriage and Family* 76(1): 130–144.

Jaaber, R., & S. Das Dasgupta. 2003. Assessing social risks of battered women. *Praxis International* 10: 14. Available at http://www.praxisinternational.org/library_frame.html under Library: Advocacy.

Jackson, Jeffrey, Richard B. Miller, Megan Oka, & Ryan G. Henry. 2014. Gender differences in marital satisfaction: A meta-analysis. *Journal of Marriage and Family* 76(1): 105–129.

Jackson, S.M., & F. Cram. 2003. Disrupting the sexual double standard: Young women's talk about heterosexuality. *British Journal of Social Psychology* 42(1): 113–127.

Jansen, Lisanne, Tigjem Weber, Gerbert Kraaykamp, & Ellen Verbakel. 2016. Perceived fairness of the division of household labor: A comparative study in 29 countries. *International Journal of Comparative Sociology* 57(1–2).

Jarman, J., R. Blackburn, & G. Racko. 2012. The dimensions of occupational gender segregation in industrial countries. *British Journal of Sociology* 46(6) 1003–1019.

Javaid, A. 2015. The role of alcohol in intimate partner violence: Causal behaviour or excusing behaviour? *British Journal of Community Justice* 13(1): 75–92.

Javed, N. 2008. GTA's secret world of polygamy. *The Toronto Star*, May 24. Retrieved from https://www.thestar.com/news/gta/2008/05/24/gtas_secret_world_of_polygamy.html

Jensen, T.M., K. Shafer, S. Guo, & J.H. Larson. 2017. Differences in relationship stability between individuals in first and second marriages. *Journal of Family Issues* 38(3): 406–432.

Jepson, Lisa K., & Christopher A. Jepson. 2002. An empirical analysis of the matching patterns of same-sex and opposite-sex couples. *Demography* 39(3): 435–453.

Johnson, M.D., & J.R. Anderson. 2013. The longitudinal association of marital confidence, time spent together, and marital satisfaction. *Family Process* 52(2): 244–256.

Johnson, M.P. 2011. Gender and types of intimate partner violence: A response to an anti-feminist literature review. *Aggression and Violent Behaviour* 16: 289–296.

Jones, C., L. Clark, J. Grusec, R. Hart, G. Plickert, & L. Tepperman. 2002. *Poverty, Social Capital, Parenting and Child Outcomes in Canada: Final Report.* Working Paper Series. Ottawa: Human Resources Development Canada.

Jones, C., L. Marsden, & L. Tepperman. 1990. *Lives of Their Own: The Individualization of Women's Lives.* Toronto, ON: Oxford University Press.

Jones, D.N., & Figueredo, A.J. 2007. Mating Effort as a Predictor of Smoking in a College Sample. *Current Research in Social Psychology,* 12(13): 186–195.

Jones, Elise F., Jacqueline Darroch Forrest, Noreen Goldman, Stanley Henshaw, Richard Lincoln, Jeannie Rosoff, Charles F. Westoff, & Deidre Wulf. 1993. *Teenage Pregnancy in Industrialized Countries.* New Haven: Yale Univerity Press.

Jones, K., P. Eathington, K. Baldwin, & H. Sipsma. 2014. The impact of health education transmitted via social media or text messaging on adolescent and young adult risky sexual behavior: A systematic review of the literature. *Sexually Transmitted Diseases* 41(7): 413–419.

Jones, Melanie. 2010. Systemic/Social Issues Aboriginal Child Welfare. *Relational Child & Youth Care Practice,* 23(4): 17–30. Retrieved from http://encore.uleth.ca:50080/ebsco-web/ehost/pdfviewer/pdfviewer?sid=b97fd556-b536-460a-beef-cc17aa7bac1e%40sessionmgr114&vid=2&hid=123

Jordan, Karen M., & Robert H. Deluty. 2000. Social support, coming out, and relationship satisfaction in lesbian couples. *Journal of Lesbian Studies* 4(1): 145–164.

Joseph, R.A., L.M. Goodfellow, & L.C. Simko. 2014. Double ABCX model of stress and adaptation in the context of families that care for children with a tracheostomy at home: Application of a theory. *Advances in Neonatal Care* 14(3): 172–180.

Jotkowitz, A., & A.Z. Zivotofsky. 2010. The ethics of abortions for fetuses with congenital abnormalities. *European Journal of Obstetrics & Gynecology and Reproductive Biology* 152: 148–151.

Juby, H.N., N. Marcil-Gratton, & C. Le Bourdais. 2004. *When Parents Separate: Further Findings from the National Longitudinal Survey of Children and Youth.* Catalogue no. 2004-FCY-6E. Ottawa: Department of Justice Canada.

Juby, Heather, Jean-Michel Billette, Benoit Laplante, & Celine Le Bourdais. 2007. Nonresident fathers and children. *Journal of Marriage and Family* 28(9): 1220–1245.

Juby, Heather, Celine Le Bourdais, & Nicole Marcil-Gratton. 2005. Sharing roles, sharing custody? Couples' characteristics and children's living arrangements at separation. *Journal of Marriage and the Family* 67: 157–172.

Justice, J. 2016, September 7. Sologamy: Disturbing marriage perversion trend rising rapidly. *Charisma News.* Retrieved from http://www.charismanews.com/culture/59745-sologamy-disturbing-marriage-perversion-trend-rising-rapidly

Kalil, A., & M. Rege. 2015. We are family: Fathers' time with children and the risk of parental relationship dissolution. *Social Forces* 94(2): 833–862.

Kalin, Rudolf, & Carol A. Lloyd. 1985. Sex-role identity, sex-role ideology and marital adjustment. *International Journal of Women's Studies* 8(1): 32–39.

Kalmijn, M. 2007. Gender differences in the effects of divorce, widowhood, and remarriage on intergenerational support: Does marriage protect fathers? *Social Forces* 86(3): 1079–1104.

Kalmijn, Matthijs. 1991. Shifting boundaries: Trends in religious and educational homogamy. *American Sociological Review* 56(6): 786–800.

Kalmijn, Matthijs. 2010. Country differences in the effects of divorce on well-being: The role of norms, support and selectivity. *European Sociological Review* 26(4): 475–490.

Kalmijn, Mathijs. 2015. How childhood circumstances moderate the long-term impact of divorce on father–child relationships. *Journal of Marriage and Family* 77(4): 921–938.

Kalmijin, Matthijs, & Christiaan Monden. 2011. The division of labor and depressive symptoms at the couple level: Effects of equity or specialization? *Journal of Social and Personal Relationships* 29(3): 358–374.

Kalmijn, Matthijs, & Frank Van Tubergen. 2010. A comparative perspective on intermarriage: Explaining differences among national-origin groups in the United States. *Demography* 47(2): 459–479.

Kang, Tanya, & Lindsay H. Hoffman. 2011. Why would you decide to use an online dating site? Factors that lead to online dating. *Communication Research Reports* 28(3): 205–213.

Kaposy, C. 2013. A disability critique of the new prenatal test for Down syndrome. *Kennedy Institute of Ethics Journal* 23(4): 299–324.

Karraker, A., J. DeLamater, & C.R. Schwartz. 2011. Sexual frequency decline from midlife to later life. *Journals of Gerontology Series B: Psychological Sciences and Social Sciences* 66(4): 502–512.

Kashyap, Lina. 2004. The impact of modernization on Indian families: The counselling challenge. *International Journal for the Advancement of Counselling* 26: 341–350.

Katz, Elana. 2007. A family therapy perspective on mediation. *Family Process* 46(1): 93–107.

Katz, Jennifer, & Laura Myhr. 2008. Perceived conflict patterns and relationship quality associated with verbal sexual coercion by male dating partners. *Journal of Interpersonal Violence* 23(6): 798–814.

Kaufman, G., & F. Goldscheider. 2007. Do men "need" a spouse more than women? Perceptions of the importance of marriage for men and women. *The Sociological Quarterly* 48: 29–46. doi:10.1111/j.1533-8525.2007.00069.x

Kaukinen, C., R.A. Powers, & S. Meyer. 2016. Estimating Canadian childhood exposure to intimate partner violence and other risky parental behaviors. *Journal of Child Custody* 13(2): 199–218.

Kawabata, Y., L.R. Alink, W.L. Tseng, M.H Van Ijzendoorn, & N.R. Crick. 2011. Maternal and paternal parenting styles associated with relational aggression in children and adolescents: A conceptual analysis and meta-analytic review. *Developmental Review* 31(4): 240–278.

Keenan, K., E. Grundy, M.G. Kenward, & D.A. Lyon. 2012. Alcohol and harm to others in Russia: Longitudinal analysis of couple drinking and subsequent divorce. *Journal of Epidemiology and Community Health* 66. Retrieved from http://jech.bmj.com/content/65/Suppl_1/A23.3.short

Kellogg, Nancy D., Thomas J. Hoffman, & Elizabeth R. Taylor. 1999 Summer. Early sexual experiences among pregnant and parenting adolescents. *Adolescence* 34(134): 293–303.

Kelly, Joan B. 2003. Changing perspectives on children's adjustment following divorce: A view from the United States. *Childhood* 10(2): 237–254.

Kelly, Joan B. 2007. Children's living arrangements following separation and divorce: Insights from empirical and clinical research. *Family Process* 46(1): 35–52.

Kelly, Mary Bess. 2010. The processing of divorce cases through civil court in seven provinces and territories. *Juristat*. Ottawa: Statistics Canada, Catalogue no. 85-002-X.

Kemp, C.L., & M. Denton. 2003. The allocation of responsibility for later life: Canadian reflections on the roles of individuals, government, employers and families. *Ageing & Society* 23: 737–760.

Kerr, Don, & Roderic Beaujot. 2003. Child poverty and family structure in Canada, 1981–1997. *Journal of Comparative Family Studies* 34(3): 321–335.

Kiecolt-Glaser, Janice K., & Tamara L. Newton. 2001. Marriage and health: His and hers. *Psychological Bulletin* 127(4): 472–500.

Killewald, Alexandra. 2016. Money, work, and marital stability assessing change in the gendered determinants of divorce. *American Sociological Review* 81(4): 696–719.

Kim, Ann. 2015. Structuring transnationalism: The mothering discourse and the educational project. In Guida Man & Rina Cohen (Eds.), *Engendering Transnational Voices: Studies in Family, Work, and Identity*. Waterloo, ON: Wilfrid Laurier University Press.

Kim, J., & K.A. Gray. 2008. Leave or stay? Battered women's decision after intimate partner violence. *Journal of Interpersonal Violence* 23(10): 1465–1482.

Kim, S.Y., Y. Wang, D. Orozco-Lapray, Y. Shen, & M. Murtuza. 2013. Does "tiger parenting" exist? Parenting profiles of Chinese Americans and adolescent developmental outcomes. *Asian American Journal of Psychology* 4(1): 7.

Kim, Tae-Sik. 2014. A qualitative inquiry into the life experiences of unaccompanied Korean adolescents in the United States. *The Qualitative Report* 19(20): 1–22.

Kim-Goh, Mikyong, & Jon Baello. 2008. Attitudes toward domestic violence in Korean and Vietnamese immigrant communities: Implications for human services. *Journal of Family Violence* 23: 647–654.

Kimuna, Sitawa R., Yanyi K. Djamba, Gabriele Ciciurkaite, & Suvana Cherkuri. 2012. Domestic Violence in India: Insights from the 2005–2006 National Family Health Survey. *Journal of Interpersonal Violence* 28(4): 773–807.

King, Rosalind Berkowitz, & Kathleen Mullan Harris. 2007. Romantic relationships among immigrant adolescents. *International Migration Review* 41: 344–370.

King, Thomas. 2012. *The Inconvenient Indian: A Curious Account of Native People in North America.* Toronto: Doubleday Canada.

King, V., & M.E. Scott. 2005. A comparison of cohabiting relationships among older and younger adults. *Journal of Marriage and Family* 67: 271–285.

King-O'Riain, R.C. 2015. Emotional streaming and transconnectivity: Skype and emotion practices in transnational families in Ireland. *Global Networks* 15(2): 256–273.

Kingsbury, M., J.B. Kirkbride, S.E. McMartin, M.E. Wickham, M. Weeks, & I. Colman. 2015. Trajectories of childhood neighbourhood cohesion and adolescent mental health: Evidence from a national Canadian cohort. *Psychological Medicine* 45(15): 3239–3248.

Kinsey, A.C., W.B. Pomeroy, & C.E. Martin. 1948. *Sexual Behavior in the Human Male.* Bloomington, IL: W.B. Saunders Company.

Kinsey, A.C., W.B. Pomeroy, C.E. Martin, & P.H. Gebhard. 1953. *Sexual Behavior in the Human Female.* Bloomington, IL: W.B. Saunders Company.

Klein, David M., & James M. White. 1996. *Family Theories: An Introduction.* Thousand Oaks, California: Sage.

Klesse, C. 2006. Polyamory and its "others": Contesting the terms of non-monogamy. *Sexualities* 9(5): 565–583.

Klinenberg, Eric. 2012. *Going Solo: The Extraordinary Rise and Surprising Appeal of Living Alone.* New York: Penguin.

Knee, Raymond C., Cynthia Lonsbary, Amy Canevello, & Heather Patrick. 2005. Self-determination and conflict in romantic relationships. *Journal of Personality and Social Psychology* 89: 997–1009.

Knudson-Martin, C. 2013. Why power matters: Creating a foundation of mutual support in couple relationships. *Family Process* 52: 5–18. doi:10.1111/famp.12011

Kobayashi, A. 1992. The Japanese–Canadian redress settlement and its implications for race relations. *Canadian Ethnic Studies* 24(1): 1–19.

Kogos, Jennifer L., & John Snarey. 1995. Parental divorce and the moral development of adolescents. *Journal of Divorce and Remarriage* 23(3–4).

Kohli, M., M. Rein, A. Guillemard, & H. Van Gunsteren. 1991. *Time for Retirement: Comparative Studies of Early Exit from the Labour Force.* Cambridge: Cambridge University Press.

Kõlves, Kari, Naoko Ide, & Diago De Leo. 2011. Marital breakdown, shame, and suicidality in men: A direct link? *Suicide and Life-Threatening Behavior* 41(2): 149–159.

Komter, A. 1989. Hidden power in marriage. *Gender and Society* 3(2): 187–216.

Korpi, W., T. Ferrarini, & S. Englund. 2013. Women's opportunities under different family policy constellations: Gender, class and inequality tradeoffs in Western countries re-examined. *Social Politics* 21(1): 1–40.

Kowalski, Robin M., Susan P. Limber, & Patricia W. Agatson. 2012. *Cyberbullying: Bullying in the Computer Age.* Chichester, Sussex: Wiley.

Koyama, N.F., A. McGain, & R.A. Hill. 2004. Self-reported mate preferences and feminist attitudes regarding marital relations. *Evolution and Human Behavior* 25(5): 327–335.

Kozuch, Patricia, & Teresa M. Cooney. 1995. Young adults' marital and family attitudes: The role of recent parental divorce, and family and parental conflict. *Journal of Divorce and Remarriage* 23(3–4).

Kreager, D.A., & J. Staff. 2009. The sexual double standard and adolescent peer acceptance. *Social Psychology Quarterly* 72(2): 143–164.

Kroløkke, C., K.A. Foss, & S. Pant. 2012. Fertility travel: The commodification of human reproduction. *Cultural Politics* 8(2): 273–282.

Kronby, Malcolm C. 2010. *Canadian Family Law* (10th ed.). Mississauga, ON: J. Wiley.

Kruger, Helga, & Rene Levy. 2001. Linking life courses, work and the family: Theorizing a not so visible nexus between women and men. *Canadian Journal of Sociology* 26(4): 145–166.

Kruk, E. 1995. Grandparent–grandchild contact loss: Findings from a study of grandparent rights members. *Canadian Journal on Aging* 14(4): 737–754.

Kruk, Edward. 2010. Parental and Social Institutional Responsibilities to Children's Needs in the Divorce Transition: Fathers' Perspectives. *The Journal of Men's Studies* 18(2): 159–178.

Kulik, L. 2001. The impact of men's and women's retirement on marital relations: A comparative analysis. *Journal of Women & Aging* 13(2): 21–37.

Kulu, Hill, & Paul J. Boyle. 2010. Premarital Cohabitation and Divorce: Support for the "trial marriage" Theory? *Demographic Research* 23(31): 879–904.

Kunz, J. 1992. The effects of divorce on children, pp. 325–376. In S.J. Bahr (Ed.), *Family Research: A Sixty-Year Review, 1930–1990, Vol. 2*. New York: Lexington Books.

Kupperbusch, C., R.W. Levenson, & R. Ebling. 2003. Predicting husbands' and wives' retirement satisfaction from the emotional qualities of marital interaction. *Journal of Social and Personal Relationships* 20(3): 335–354.

Kurz, Demie. 1995. *For Richer or for Poorer: Mothers Confront Divorce*. New York: Routledge.

Kuvalanka, K.A., & A.E. Goldberg. 2009. Second generation voices: Queer youth with lesbian/bisexual mothers. *Journal of Youth and Adolescence* 38(7): 904–919.

Laakso, Janice. 2004, Spring. Key determinants of mothers' decisions to allow visits with non-custodial fathers. *Fathering*.

Lacey, K.K., D.G. Saunders, & L. Zhang. 2011. A comparison of women of color and non-Hispanic White women on factors related to leaving a violent relationship. *Journal of Interpersonal Violence* 26(5): 1036–1055.

Lai, C.H., & H.L. Gwung. 2013. The effect of gender and Internet usage on physical and cyber interpersonal relationships. *Computers & Education* 69: 303–309.

Lai, D.W. 2011. Abuse and neglect experienced by aging Chinese in Canada. *Journal of Elder Abuse and Neglect* 23(4): 326–347.

Lai, D.W., & C. Thomson. 2011. The impact of perceived adequacy of social support on caregiving burden of family caregivers. *Families in Society: The Journal of Contemporary Social Services* 92(1): 99–106.

Lampard, Richard. 2007. Couples' places of meeting in late 20th century Britain: Class, continuity and change. *European Sociological Review* 23.3: 357–371.

Landis-Kleine, Cathy, Linda Foley, Loretta Nall, Patricia Padgett; & Leslie Walters-Palmer. 1995. Attitudes toward marriage and divorce held by young adults. *Journal of Divorce & Remarriage* 23(3&4): 63–74.

Landry, Yves. 1992. Les filles duroi au xviie siècle: Orphelines en France (Girls in the seventeenth century: Orphans in France). *Pioniéres au Canada*. Montreal: Lemeac.

Lange, B., & S. Greif. 2011. An emic view of caring for self: Grandmothers who care for children of mothers with substance use disorders. *Contemporary Nurse* 40(1): 15.

Langford, R., P. Albanese, & S. Prentice (Eds.). 2017. *Caring for Children: Social Movements and Public Policy*. Vancouver, BC: UBC Press.

Lanigan, J.D. 2009. A sociotechnological model for family research and intervention: How information and communication technologies affect family life. *Marriage & Family Review* 45: 587–609.

Laplante, B. 2006. The rise of cohabitation in Quebec: Power of religion and power over religion. *The Canadian Journal of Sociology/Cahiers canadiens de sociologie* 31(1): 1–24.

Laplante, B. 2014. Normative groups: The rise of the formation of the first union through cohabitation in Quebec: A comparative approach. *Population Research and Policy Review* 33(2): 257–285. doi:10.1007/s11113-013-92794

LaPrairie, C. 2002. Aboriginal over-representation in the criminal justice system: A tale of nine cities. *Canadian Journal of Criminology* 44: 181.

Lareau, A. 2006. Concerted cultivation and the accomplishment of natural growth, pp. 335–344. In G. Handel (Ed.), *Childhood Socialization* (2nd ed.). New Brunswick, NJ: AldineTransaction.

LaRochelle-Côté, Sebastien, John Myles, & Garnett Picot. 2012. *Income Replacement Rates among Canadian Seniors: The Effect of Widowhood and Divorce*. Ottawa: Statistics Canada, Catalogue no. 11F0019M, no. 343. Retrieved from http://www.statcan.gc.ca/pub/11f0019m/11f0019m2012343-eng.htm

LaRossa, Ralph. 2004. The culture of fatherhood in the fifties: A closer look. *Journal of Family History* 29(1): 47–70.

Laslett, Peter. 1965. *The World We Have Lost: England Before the Industrial Age*. London, UK: Methuen.

Laumann, E., A. Nicolosi, D.B. Glasser, A. Paik, C. Gingell, E. Moreira, & T. Wang. 2004. Sexual problems among women and men aged 40–80 y: Prevalence and correlates identified in the Global Study of Sexual Attitudes and Behaviors. *International Journal of Impotence Research* 17: 39–57. doi:10.1038/sj.ijir.3901250

Laumann, E.O., J. Mahay, & Y. Youm. 2007. Sex, intimacy and family life in the United States, pp. 165–190. In M. Kimmel (Ed.), *The Sexual Self*. Nashville: Vanderbilt University Press.

Lawrence, Erika, Alexia D. Rothman, Rebecca J. Cobb, Michael T. Rothman, & Thomas Bradbury. 2008. Marital satisfaction across the transition to parenthood. *Journal of Family Psychology* 22(1): 41–50.

Leach, B. 1999. Rural retreat: The social impact of restructuring in three Ontario communities, pp. 84–104. In D.B. Knight & A.E. Joseph (Eds.),

Restructuring Societies. Ottawa, ON: Carleton University Press.

Le Bourdais, C., & É. Lapierre-Adamcyk. 2004. Changes in conjugal life in Canada: Is cohabitation progressively replacing marriage? *Journal of Marriage and Family* 66(4): 929–942. doi:10.1111/j.0022-2445.2004.000 63.x

Le Bourdais, C., G. Neill, & P. Turcotte. 2000. The changing face of conjugal relationships. *Canadian Social Trends*. Catalogue no. 11-008. Ottawa: Statistics Canada. Retrieved from http://www.statcan.gc.ca/pub/11-008-x/1999004/article/4910-eng.pdf

Le Bourdais, Celine, & Nicole Marcil-Gratton. 1996. Family transformations across the Canadian/American border: When the laggard becomes the leader. *Journal of Comparative Family Studies* 27(3): 415–436.

Le Bourdais, Celine, G. Neil, & Pierre Turcotte. 2000. The changing face of conjugal relationships. *Canadian Social Trends* 56: 14–17.

Lee, B.H., & L.F. O'Sullivan. 2014. The ex-factor: Characteristics of online and offline post-relationship contact and tracking among Canadian emerging adults. *The Canadian Journal of Human Sexuality* 32(2): 96–105.

Lee, E.A.E., & W. Troop-Gordon. 2011. Peer processes and gender role development: Changes in gender atypicality related to negative peer treatment and children's friendships. *Sex Roles* 64(1–2): 90–102.

Lee, Murray, & Thomas Crofts. 2015. Gender, pressure, coercion and pleasure: Untangling motivations for sexting between young people. *The British Journal of Criminology* (May): 454.

Lee, Sharon M., & Edmonston, Barry. 2013. Canada's immigrant families: Growth, diversity and challenges. *Population Change and Lifecourse Strategic Knowledge Cluster Discussion Paper Series/Un Réseau stratégique de connaissances Changements de population et parcours de vie Document de travail* 1(1), Article 4. Available at http://ir.lib.uwo.ca/pclc/vol1/iss1/4

Lee, S.J., & Y.G. Chae. 2007. Children's Internet use in a family context: Influence on family relationships and parental mediation. *CyberPsychology & Behavior* 10(5): 640–644.

Lee, Sunmin, Deborah Rohm Young, Charlotte A. Pratt, Jared B. Jobe, Soo Eun Chae, Robert G. McMurray, . . . June Stevens. 2012. Effects of parents' employment status on changes in body mass index and percent body fat in adolescent girls. *Childhood Obesity* 8: 526–532.

LeFebvre, L., K. Blackburn, & B. Nicholas. 2015. Navigating romantic relationships on Facebook: Extending the relationship dissolution model to social networking environments. *Journal of Social and Personal Relationships* 32(1): 78–98.

Lehmiller, J. J., & Agnew, C. R. 2008. Commitment in age-gap heterosexual romantic relationships: A test of evolutionary and socio-cultural predictions. *Psychology of Women Quarterly*, 32: 74–82.

Lehr, Valerie. 1999. *Queer Family Values: Debunking the Myth of the Nuclear Family*. Philadelphia: Temple University Press.

Lennon, M.C., & S. Rosenfield. 1994. Relative fairness and the division of housework: The importance of options. *American Journal of Sociology* 100(2): 506–531.

Lens, Vicki, Collen Carry Katz, & Kimberly Spencer Suarez. 2016. Case workers in family court: A therapeutic jurisprudence analysis. *Children and Youth Services Review* 68: 107–114.

Lesemann, F., & R. Nicol. 1994. Family policy: International comparisons, pp. 117–125. In M. Baker (Ed.), *Canada's Changing Families: Challenges to Public Policy*. Ottawa, ON: Vanier Institute of the Family.

Lever, Janet, Christian Grov, Tracy Royce, & Brian Joseph Gillespie. 2008. Searching for love in all the "write" places: Exploring internet personals use by sexual orientation, gender, and age. *International Journal of Sexual Health* 20(4): 233–246.

Levine, D.I., & G. Painter. 2003. The schooling costs of teenage out-of-wedlock childbearing: Analysis with a within-school propensity-score-matching estimator. *The Review of Economics and Statistics* 85(4): 884–900.

Li, P.S. 1996. *The Making of Post-war Canada*. Toronto: Oxford University Press.

Lichter, Daniel T., & Julie H. Carmalt. 2009. Religion and marital quality among low-income couples. *Social Science Research* 38: 168–187.

Lichter, Daniel T., Katherine Michelmore, Richard N. Turner, & Sharon Sassler. 2016. Pathways to a stable union? Pregnancy and childbearing among cohabiting and married couples. *Population Research and Policy Review* 35(3): 377–399.

Liefbroer, A.C., & E. Dourleijn. 2006. Unmarried cohabitation and union stability: Testing the role of diffusion using data from 16 European countries. *Demography* 43(2): 203–221.

Lilly, M.B., C.A. Robinson, S. Holtzman, & J.L. Bottorff. 2012. Can we move beyond burden and burnout to support the health and wellness of family caregivers to persons with dementia? Evidence from British Columbia, Canada. *Health and Social Care in the Community* 20(1): 103–112.

Ling, R., T. Julsrud, & B. Yttri. 2005. Nascent communication genres within SMS and MMS, pp. 75–100. In R. Harper, L. Palen, & A. Taylor (Eds.), *The Inside Text*. New York: Springer.

Lipman, Ellen L., David R. Offord, Martin D. Dooley, & Martin H. Boyle. 2002. Children's outcomes in differing types of single-parent families, pp. 229–242. In J. Douglas Willms (Ed.), *Vulnerable Children: Findings from Canada's National Longitudinal Survey of Children and Youth*. Edmonton: University of Alberta Press, and Ottawa: Human Resources Development Canada, Applied Research Branch.

Liu, M., & F. Guo. 2010. Parenting practices and their relevance to child behaviors in Canada and China. *Scandinavian Journal of Psychology* 51(2): 109–114.

Lloyd, Eva. 2008. The interface between childcare, family support and child poverty strategies under New Labour: Tensions and contradictions. *Social Policy & Society* 7(4): 479–494.

Lockerbie, S. 2014. Infertility, adoption and metaphorical pregnancies. *Anthropologica* 56(2): 463–471.

Logan, John Allen, Peter Hoff, & Michael Newton. 2008. Two-sided estimation of mate preferences for similarities in age, education, and religion. *Journal of the American Statistical Association* 103.482: 559.

Lou, E., R.N. Lalonde, & J.Y.T. Wong. 2015. Acculturation, gender, and views on interracial relationships among Chinese Canadians. *Personal Relationships* 22: 621–634.

Lown, J.M., & E.M. Dolan. 1995. Remarried families' economic behavior: Fishman's model revisited. *Journal of Divorce and Remarriage* 22(1–2): 103–119.

Lugo-Gil, Julieta, & Catherine S. Tamis-LeMonda. 2008. Family resources and parenting quality: Links to children's cognitive development across the first 3 years. *Child Development* 79(4): 1065–1085.

Lumpkin, J.R. 2008. Grandparents in a parental or near-parental role: Sources of stress and coping mechanisms. *Journal of Family Issues* 29(3): 357–372.

Lunau, Thorsten, Clare Bambra, Terje A. Eikemo, Kjetil A. van der Wel, & Nico Dragano. 2014. A balancing act? Work–life balance, health and well-being in European welfare states. *European Journal of Public Health* 24(3): 422–427.

Luong, M. 2008. Life after teenage motherhood. *Perspectives on Labour and Income* 20(2): 41.

Lupri, E., & J. Frideres. 1981. The quality of marriage and the passage of time: Marital satisfaction over the family life cycle. *Canadian Journal of Sociology/Cahiers canadiens de sociologie* 5(3): 283–305.

Lussier, G., K. Deater-Deckard, J. Dunn, & L. Davies. 2002. Support across two generations: Children's closeness to grandparents following parental divorce and remarriage. *Journal of Family Psychology* 16(3): 363–376.

Luxton, M. 1980. *More than a Labour of Love: Three Generations of Women's Work in the Home*. Toronto: Women's Press.

Luxton, Meg (Ed.). 1997. *Feminism and Families: Critical Policies and Changing Practices*. Halifax: Fernwood.

Luxton, Meg. 2001. Conceptualizing families: Theoretical frameworks and family research, pp. 28–50. In Maureen Baker (Ed.), *Families: Changing Trends in Canada* (4th ed.). Toronto: McGraw-Hill Ryerson.

Lynn, Marion. 2003. Single-parent families, pp. 6–54. In Marion Lynn (Ed.), *Voices: Essays on Canadian Families* (2nd ed.). Toronto: Thomson Nelson.

Lyons, H., W. Manning, P. Giordano, & M. Longmore. 2013. Predictors of heterosexual casual sex among young adults. *Archives of Sexual Behavior* 42(2): 585–593.

Lyssens-Danneboom, V., & D. Mortelmans. 2014. Living apart together and money: New partnerships, traditional gender roles. *Journal of Marriage and Family* 76(5): 949–966.

Lytton, M. 2017. I got really nervous the day before: Sologamy, the practice of marrying yourself, seems to be on the rise. *National Post*, May 19. Retrieved from http://news.nationalpost.com/news/world/i-got-really-nervous-the-day-before-sologamy-the-practice-of-marrying-yourself-seems-to-be-on-the-rise

Macdonald, D., & M. Friendly. 2014. The parent trap: Child care fees in Canada's big cities. *Canadian Centre for Policy Alternatives*. Retrieved from https://www.policyalternatives.ca/sites/default/files/uploads/publications/National%20Office/2014/11/Parent_Trap.pdf

MacDonald, D., & D. Wilson. 2016. *Shameful Neglect: Indigenous Child Poverty in Canada*. Ottawa: Canadian Centre for Policy Alternatives. Retrieved from https://www.policyalternatives.ca/sites/default/files/uploads/publications/National%20Office/2016/05/Indigenous_Child%20Poverty.pdf

MacInnes, Maryhelen D. 2011. Altar-bound? The effect of disability on the hazard of entry into a first marriage. *International Journal of Sociology* 41: 87–103.

MacLachlan, A., & A. Noseworthy. 2016. By ignoring parental rights, Ontario puts our daughter's welfare at risk. *The Globe and Mail*, June 2. Retrieved from http://www.theglobeandmail.com/opinion/by-ignoring-parental-rights-ontario-puts-our-daughters-welfare-at-risk/article30244298

Maclean's. 2014. Canada is leading the pack in mixed unions. Retrieved September 15, 2016, from http://www.macleans.ca/society/there-is-no-better-index-of-racial-and-cultural-integration-than-mixed-unions-and-canada-is-leading-the-pack

Madathil, Jayamala, & James M. Benshoff. 2008. Importance of marital characteristics and marital satisfaction: A comparison of Asian Indians in arranged marriages and Americans in marriages of choice. *The Family Journal* 16: 222–230.

Madden-Derdich, Debra A., & Stacie A. Leonard. 2000. Parental role identity and fathers' involvement in coparental interaction after divorce: Fathers' perspectives. *Family Relations* 49(3): 311–318.

Mahoney, Anne Rankin, & Carmen Knudson-Martin. 2009. Gender Equality in Intimate Relationships, pp. 3–16. In Anne Rankin Mahoney & Carmen Knudson-Martin (Eds.), *Couples, Gender and Power*. New York: Springer.

Mainland, Mike, Susan Shaw, & Andrea Prier. 2015. Fearing fat: Exploring the discursive links between childhood obesity, parenting, and leisure. *Journal of Leisure Research* 47(2).

Maiter, S., & U. George. 2003. Understanding context and culture in the parenting approaches of immigrant South Asian mothers. *Affilia* 18(4): 411–428.

Mamo, L., & E. Alston-Stepnitz. 2015. Queer intimacies and structural inequalities: New directions in stratified reproduction. *Journal of Family Issues* 36(4): 519–540.

Man, G. 2004. Gender, work and migration: Deskilling Chinese immigrant women in Canada. *Women's Studies International Forum* 27(2): 135–148. doi:10.1016/j.wsif.2004.06.004

Man, Guida. 2001. From Hong Kong to Canada: Immigration and the changing family lives of middle-class women from Hong Kong, pp. 420–438. In Bonnie J. Fox (Ed.), *Family Patterns, Gender Divisions* (2nd ed.). Toronto: Oxford University Press.

Man, Guida. 2015. Maintaining families through transnational strategies: The experience of mainland Chinese immigrant women in Canada. In Guida Man & Rina Cohen (Eds.), *Engendering Transnational Voices: Studies in Family, Work, and Identity*. Waterloo, ON: Wilfrid Laurier University Press.

Mandell, Nancy. 2011. Portraying Canadian Families, pp. 3–32. In Nancy Mandell & Ann Duffy (Eds.), *Canadian Families: Diversity, Conflict and Change* (4th ed.). Toronto: Nelson.

Manning, W.D., P.C. Giordano, & M.A. Longmore. 2006. Hooking up: The relationship contexts of nonrelationship sex. *Journal of Adolescent Research* 21(5): 459–483.

Manning, W.D., M.A. Longmore, & P.C. Giordano. 2005. Adolescents' involvement in non-romantic sexual activity. *Social Science Research* 34(2): 384–407.

Manning, W.D., P.J. Smock, & D. Majumdar. 2004. The relative stability of cohabiting and marital unions for children. *Population Research and Policy Review* 23(2): 135–159. doi:10.1023/B:POPU.0000019916.29156.a7

Manning, Wendy D., Susan L. Brown, & Krista K. Payne. 2014. Two decades of stability and change in age at first union formation. *Journal of Marriage and Family* 76(2): 247–260.

Manning, Wendy D., & Jessica A. Cohen. 2012. Premarital cohabitation and marital dissolution: An examination of recent marriages. *Journal of Marriage and Family* 74(2): 377–387.

March, James G., & Herbert A. Simon. 1958. *Organizations*. New York: Wiley.

Marcil-Gratton, N., & C. Le Bourdais. 1999. *Custody, Access and Child Support: Findings from the National Longitudinal Survey of Children and Youth*. (Research Report CSR-1999-3E.) Ottawa: Department of Justice Canada.

Marcil-Gratton, N., & C. Le Bourdais. 2004. *When Parents Separate: Further Findings from the National Longitudinal Survey of Children and Youth*. (Research Report 2004-FCY-6E.) Ottawa: Department of Justice Canada.

Marks, M.J., & R.C. Fraley. 2005. The sexual double standard: Fact or fiction? *Sex Roles* 52(3): 175–186.

Marks, M.J., & R.C. Fraley. 2006. Confirmation bias and the sexual double standard. *Sex Roles* 54(1–2): 19–26.

Marsh, J. 2016. The rise of romance gaming: Is the perfect boyfriend inside your phone? *CNN*, December 12. Retrieved from http://www.cnn.com/2016/11/21/asia/romance-gaming-japan

Marsh, Teresa Naseba, Sheila Cote-Meek, Nancy L. Young, Lisa M. Najavits, & Pamela Toulouse. 2016. Indigenous healing and seeking safety: A blended implementation project for intergenerational trauma and substance use disorders. *International Indigenous Policy Journal* 7(2).

Marshall, K. 2006. Converging gender roles. *Perspectives on Labor and Income* 7(7). Catalogue no. 75-001-X1E. Ottawa, ON: Statistics Canada. Retrieved from http://www.statcan.gc.ca/pub/75-001-x/10706/9268-eng.htm

Marshall, K. 2008. Fathers' use of paid parental leave. *Perspectives on Labor and Income* 9(6): 1–24. Catalogue no. 75-001-X. Ottawa: Statistics Canada. Retrieved from http://www.statcan.gc.ca/pub/75-001-x/2008106/article/10639-eng.htm

Marshall, K. 2010. Employer top-ups. *Perspectives*. Catalogue no. 75-001-X. Ottawa, ON: Statistics Canada. Retrieved from http://www.statcan.gc.ca/pub/75-001-x/2010102/pdf/11120-eng.pdf

Marshall, K. 2011. Generational change in paid and unpaid work. *Canadian Social Trends* 92: 13–24.

Marshall, T. 2008. Cultural differences in intimacy: The influence of gender-role ideology and individualism–collectivism. *Journal of Social and Personal Relationships* 25(1): 143, 155.

Martinengo, Giuseppe, Jenet I. Jacob, & E. Jeffrey Hill. 2010. Gender and the work–family interface: Exploring differences across the family life course. *Journal of Family Issues* 31(10): 1363–1390.

Mason, G. 2011. The crushing weight of student debt. *The Globe and Mail*, July 7. Retrieved from http://www.theglobeandmail.com/news/british-columbia/the-crushing-weight-of-student-debt/article625694

Mason, Mary Ann, Arlene Skolnick, & Stephen D. Sugarman (Eds.). 2003. *All Our Families: New Policies for a New Century* (2nd ed.). New York: Oxford University Press.

Mastekaasa, Arne. 1995. Divorce and subjective distress: Panel evidence. *European Sociological Review* 11(2).

Matthey, Stephen, Bryanne Barnett, Judy Ungerer, & Brent Waters. 2000. Paternal and maternal depressed mood during the transition to parenthood. *Journal of Affective Disorders* 60(2), 75–85.

Mattingly, Marybeth J., & Robert N. Bozick. 2001. *Children Raised by Same-Sex Couples: Much Ado about Nothing.* Southern Sociological Society (SSS).

Maxwell, Krista. 2014. Historicizing historical trauma theory: Troubling the trans-generational transmission paradigm. *Transcultural Psychiatry* 51(3): 407–435.

McCabe, Marita P., & George Taleporos. 2003. Sexual esteem, sexual satisfaction, and sexual behavior among people with physical disability. *Archives of Sexual Behavior* 32(4): 359–369.

McCarthy, L. 2000. Poppies in a wheat field: Exploring the lives of rural lesbians. *Journal of Homosexuality* 39(1), 75–94.

McConnell, D., R. Breitkreuz, & A. Savage. 2011. From financial hardship to child difficulties: Main and moderating effects of perceived social support. *Child: Care, Health and Development* 37(5): 679–691.

McCurdy, Susan J., & Avraham Scherman. 1996. Effects of family structure on the adolescent separation–individuation process. *Adolescence* 31(122).

McDaniel, B.T., M. Drouin, & J.D. Cravens. 2017. Do you have anything to hide? Infidelity-related behaviors on social media sites and marital satisfaction. *Computers in Human Behaviour* 66: 88–95.

McDaniel, S., A. Gazso, & S. Um. 2013. Generationing relations in challenging times: Americans and Canadians in mid-life in the Great Recession. *Current Sociology* 61(3): 301–321.

McDaniel, S.A. 1988. A new stork rising? Women's roles and reproductive changes. *Transactions of the Royal Society of Canada* 3: 111–122.

McDaniel, S.A. 1992. Caring and sharing: Demographic aging, family and the state, pp. 121–144. In J. Hendricks & C. Rosenthal (Eds.), *The Remainder of Their Days: Impact of Public Policy on Older Families*. New York: Garland.

McDaniel, S.A. 1997. Serial employment and skinny government: Reforming caring and sharing among generations. *Canadian Journal on Aging* 16(3): 465–484.

McDaniel, S.A. 2005. The family lives of the middle-aged and elderly in Canada, pp. 181–199. In M. Baker (Ed.), *Families: Changing Trends in Canada* (5th ed.). Toronto: McGraw-Hill Ryerson.

McDaniel, Susan, Adebiyi Germain Boco, & Sara Zella. 2013. Changing patterns of religious affiliation, religiosity and marital dissolution: A 35-year follow-up study of members of three generation families. *Journal of Divorce & Remarriage* 54: 629–657.

McDaniel, Susan A. 1996a. The family lives of the middle-aged and elderly in Canada, pp. 195–211. In Maureen Baker (Ed.), *Families: Changing Trends in Canada* (3rd ed.). Toronto: McGraw-Hill Ryerson.

McDaniel, Susan A. 2002. Women's changing relations to the state and citizenship: Caring and intergenerational relations in globalizing western democracies. *Canadian Review of Sociology and Anthropology* 39(2): 1–26.

McDaniel, Susan A., & Paul Bernard. 2011. Life Course as a Policy Lens. *Canadian Public Policy* 37, Supplement, (April): S1–S13.

McDaniel, Susan A., Amber Gazso, & Karen Duncan. 2016. Relative prospects of children as they age: Canadians and Americans in mid-life in the Great Recession frame future generations. *Journal of Aging Studies* 37(April): 69–80. Retrieved from http://www.sciencedirect.com/science/article/pii/S0890406515301304

McDaniel, Susan A., Amber Gazso, Hugh McCague, & Ryan Barnhart. 2013. Les disparités en matière de santé au fil du vieillissement: une comparaison du parcours de vie des premiers baby-boomers et des pré-babyboomers au Canada (Health Disparities as We Age: A Life Course Comparison of Canadian Early Boomers with Pre-Boomers). *Sociologie et Sociétés* XLV(1): 43–65.

McDaniel, Susan A., Amber Gazso, & Seonggee Um. 2013. Generationing Relations in Challenging

Times: Americans and Canadians in Mid-Life in the Great Recession. *Current Sociology* 61(3): 301–321.

McDaniel, Susan A., & Robert Lewis. 1998. Did they or didn't they? Intergenerational supports in families past: A case study of Brigus, Newfoundland, 1920–1945, pp. 475–497. In Lori Chambers & Edgar-Andre Montigny (Eds.), *Family Matters: Papers in Post-Confederation Canadian Family History*. Toronto: Canadian Scholars Press.

McDaniel, Susan A., & Zachary Zimmer. 2013. Global ageing in the twenty-first century: Where to from here? pp. 309–318. In Susan A. McDaniel & Zachary Zimmer (Eds.), *Global Ageing in the Twenty-First Century: Challenges, Opportunities and Implications*. Farnham, Surrey, UK: Ashgate.

McDonald, H. 2011, February 15. Travelers attack Channel 4 over My Big Fat Gypsy Wedding. *The Guardian*, p. 12.

McDonald, Ted, Elizabeth Ruddick, Arthur Sweetman, & Christopher Worswick (Eds). 2010. *Canadian Immigration: Economic Evidence for a Dynamic Policy Environment*. Montreal and Kingston: Queen's Policy Studies Series, McGill-Queen's University Press.

McGill Institute for Health and Social Policy. 2012. Raising the global floor. Retrieved from http://raisingtheglobalfloor.org/index.php

McGlone, J. 1980. Sex differences in human brain asymmetry: A critical survey. *The Behavioral and Brain Sciences 3*: 215–223.

Mchitarjan, I., & R. Reisenzein. 2014. Towards a theory of cultural transmission in minorities. *Ethnicities* 14(2): 181–207.

Mchitarjan, I., & R. Reisenzein. 2015. The culture-transmission motive in immigrants: A world-wide internet survey. *PLoS ONE* 10(11): e0141625. doi:10.1371/journal.pone.0141625

McIntosh, W.D., L. Locker, K. Briley, R. Ryan, & A.J. Scott. 2011. What do older adults seek in their potential romantic partners? Evidence from online personal ads. *The International Journal of Aging and Human Development* 72(1): 6–82.

McIntyre, L., J.V. Williams, D.H. Lavorato, & S. Patten. 2013. Depression and suicide ideation in late adolescence and early adulthood are an outcome of child hunger. *Journal of Affective Disorders*, 150(1), 123–129.

McKay, Lindsey, & Andrea Doucet. 2010. Without taking away her leave: A Canadian case study of couples' decisions on fathers' use of paid parental leave. *Fathering* 8(3): 300–320.

McKenna, E. 2015. The freedom to choose: Neoliberalism, feminism, and childcare in Canada. *The Review of Education, Pedagogy, and Cultural Studies* 37: 41–52.

McKeown, Larry, & Cathy Underhill. 2005. Learning online: Factors associated with use of the Internet for education purposes. *Education Matters*. Ottawa: Statistics Canada. Catalogue no. 81-004-XIE. Retrieved from http://www.statcan.gc.ca/pub/81-004-x/2007004/10375-eng.htm

McLanahan, Sara. 2009. Fragile families and the reproduction of poverty. *The Annals of the American Academy 621*: 111–131.

McLanahan, Sara, Laura Tach, & Daniel Schneider. 2013. The causal effects of father absence. *Annual Review of Sociology 39*: 399–427.

McLaren, Angus, & Arlene Tigar McLaren. 1986. *The Bedroom and the State: The Changing Practices and Politics of Contraception and Abortion in Canada, 1880–1980*. Toronto: McClelland & Stewart.

McLaren, Angus, & Arlene Tigar McLaren. 1997. *The Bedroom and The State: The Changing Practices and Politics of Contraception And Abortion in Canada, 1880–1997*. (2nd ed.). Toronto: McClelland & Stewart.

McLean, Lorna. 2004. To become part of us: Ethnicity, race, literacy and the Canadian Immigration Act of 1919. *Canadian Ethnic Studies/Etudes Ethniques au Canada 35*: 1–28.

McMahon, M. 1995. *Engendering Motherhood: Identity and Self-Transformation in Women's Lives*. New York, NY: The Guilford Press.

McNaughton, Darlene. 2011. From the womb to the tomb: Obesity and maternal responsibility. *Critical Public Health 21*: 179–190.

McNulty, J.K., C.A. Wenner, & T.D. Fisher. 2016. Longitudinal associations among relationship satisfaction, sexual satisfaction, and frequency of sex in early marriage. *Archives of Sexual Behavior 45*: 85.

McRae, S. 1987. The allocation of money in cross-class families. *The Sociological Review 35*(1): 97–122.

McVey, Wayne W., Jr. 2008. Is separation still an important component of marital dissolution? *Canadian Studies in Population 35*(1): 187–205.

McWilliams, Summer, & Anne E. Barrett. 2014. Online dating in middle and later life: Gendered expectations and experiences. *Journal of Family Issues 35*(3): 411–436.

Meetoo, V., & H.S. Mirza. 2007. There is nothing "honourable" about honour killings: Gender, violence and the limits of multiculturalism. *Women's Studies International Forum 30*(3): 187–200.

Ménard, F.-P. 2011. What makes it fall apart? The determinants of the dissolution of marriages and common-law unions in Canada. *McGill Sociological Review* 2: 59–76.

Mensah, J., & C.J. Williams. 2013. Ghanaian and Somali immigrants in Toronto's rental market: A comparative cultural perspective of housing issues and coping strategies. *Canadian Ethnic Studies* 45(1): 115–141.

Mernitz, Sara E., & Claire Kamp Dush. 2016. Emotional health across the transition to first and second unions among emerging adults. *Journal of Family Psychology* 30(2): 233–244.

Meyer, S. 2012. Why women stay: A theoretical examination of rational choice and moral reasoning in the context of intimate partner violence. *Australian & New Zealand Journal of Criminology* 45(2): 179–193.

Meyerstein, I. 2000. Case studies: The remarriage box ritual: Helping stepfamilies differentiate between fear and reality. *Family Therapy Networker* 24(4).

Miall, Charlene E., & Karen March. 2005a. Open adoption as a family form: Community assessments and social support. *Journal of Family Issues* 26(3): 380–410.

Mignone, J., & H. Henley. 2009. Impact of information and communication technology on social capital in Aboriginal communities in Canada. *Journal of Information, Information Technology, and Organizations* 4: 127–145.

Milan, A. 2013. *Marital Status: Overview, 2011.* Catalogue no. 91-209-X. Retrieved from http://www.statcan.gc.ca/pub/91-209-x/2013001/article/11788-eng.pdf

Milan, A. 2015. *Marital Status: Overview, 2011.* Ottawa: Statistics Canada. Retrieved from http://www.statcan.gc.ca/pub/91-209-x/2013001/article/11788-eng.htm

Milan, A. 2016. Diversity of young adults living with their parents. *Insights on Canadian Society.* Catalogue no. 75-006-X. Ottawa: Ministry of Industry. Retrieved from http://www.statcan.gc.ca/pub/75-006-x/2016001/article/14639-eng.pdf

Milan, A., & B. Hamm. 2003. Across the generations: Grandparents and grandchildren. *Canadian Social Trends* (Winter): 2–7. Retrieved from http://www.statcan.gc.ca/pub/11-008-x/2003003/article/6619-eng.pdf

Milan, A., L.-A. Keown, & R.U. Covadonga. 2011. *Women in Canada: A Gender-Based Statistical Report: Families, Living Arrangements and Unpaid Work.* Catalogue no. 89-503-X. Retrieved from http://www.statcan.gc.ca/pub/89-503-x/2010001/article/11546-eng.pdf

Milan, Anne, Irene Wong, & Mireille Vézina. February 2014. Emerging trends in living arrangements and conjugal unions for current and future seniors.

Statistics Canada. Catalogue no. 75-006-X. *Insights on Canadian Society.*

Mileham, Beatriz Lia Avila. 2007. Online infidelity in Internet chat rooms: An ethnographic exploration. *Computers in Human Behavior* 23(1): 11–31.

Milhausen, R.R., & E.S. Herold. 2002. Reconceptualizing the sexual double standard. *Journal of Psychology & Human Sexuality* 13(2): 63–83.

Millar, Paul, & Anne H. Gauthier. 2002. What were they thinking? The development of child support guidelines in Canada. *Canadian Journal of Law and Society* 17(1): 139–162.

Millar, Wayne, & Surinder Wadhera. 1997. A perspective on Canadian teenage births, 1992–1994: Older men and younger women? *Canadian Journal of Public Health* 88: 333–336.

Miller, E., R. Chen, N.M. Glover-Graf, & P. Kranz. 2009. Willingness to engage in personal relationships with persons with disabilities: Examining category and severity of disability. *Rehabilitation Counseling Bulletin* 52(4): 211–224.

Miller, R.B., C.S. Hollist, J. Olsen, & D. Law. 2013. Marital quality and health over 20 years: A growth curve analysis. *Journal of Marriage and Family* 75: 667–680.

Milligan, K. 2013. What the data shows about female breadwinners in Canada. *Maclean's,* June 10. Retrieved from http://www.macleans.ca/economy/business/what-the-data-shows-about-female-breadwinners-in-canada

Milligan, Kevin. 2005. Subsidizing the stork: New evidence on tax incentives and fertility. *Review of Economics and Statistics* 87(3): 539–555.

Milligan, Kevin, & Mark Stabile. 2011. Do child tax benefits affect the well-being of children? Evidence from Canadian child benefit expansions. *American Economic Journal: Economic Policy* 3(3): 175–205.

Minnotte, K.L., M.C. Minnotte, & J. Bonstrom. 2015. Work–family conflicts and marital satisfaction among US workers: Does stress amplification matter? *Journal of Family and Economic Issues* 36(1): 21–33.

Minton, Carmelle, & Kay Pasley. 1996. Fathers' parenting role identity and father involvement: A comparison of nondivorced and divorced, nonresident fathers. *Journal of Family Issues* 17(1).

Miranda, A., R. Tarraga, M.I. Fernandez, C. Colomer, & G. Pastor. 2015. Parenting stress in families of children with autism spectrum disorder and ADHD. *Exceptional Children* 82(1).

Mirdal, Gretty M. 2006. Stress and distress in migration: Twenty years after. *The International Migration Review* 40: 375–389.

Mitchell, B. 1994. Family structure and leaving the nest: A social resource perspective. *Sociological Perspectives* 37(4): 651–671.

Mitchell, B. 2006. *The Boomerang Age: Transitions to Adulthoods in Families*. Piscataway, NJ: Transaction Publishers.

Mitchell, B., & E.M. Gee. 1996. Young adults returning home: Implications for social policy, pp. 61–71. In B. Galaway & J. Hudson (Eds.), *Youth in Transition: Perspectives on Research and Policy*. Toronto: Thompson Educational Publishing.

Mitchinson, Wendy. 2002. *Giving Birth in Canada: 1900–1950*. Toronto: University of Toronto Press.

Mitra, Monika, Vera E. Mouradin, & Maria McKenna. 2013. Dating violence and associated health risks among high school students with disabilities. *Maternal and Child Health Journal* 7: 1088–1094.

Mock, R. 2011. The top 5 myths and truths about online dating for the 50-plus singles. *PR Newswire*, August 22, p. 6.

Mohr, J., & R. Fassinger. 2006. Sexual orientation identity and romantic relationship quality in same-sex couples. *Personality and Social Psychology Bulletin* 32: 1085–1099.

Mok, D., B. Wellman, & J. Carrasco. 2010. Does distance matter in the age of the Internet? *Urban Studies* 47(13): 2747–2783.

Möller, K., C. Philip Hwang, & B. Wickberg. 2006. Romantic attachment, parenthood and marital satisfaction. *Journal of Reproductive and Infant Psychology* 24(3): 233–240.

Mooney-Somers, F., & S. Golombok. 2000. Children of lesbian mothers: From the 1970s to the new millennium. *Sexual and Relationship Therapy* 15(2): 121–126.

Moore, F.R., & C. Cassidy. 2007. Female status predicts female mate preferences across nonindustrial societies. *Cross-Cultural Research* 41(1): 66–74.

Moore, F.R., C. Cassidy, M.J.L. Smith, & D.I. Perrett. 2006. The effects of female control of resources on sex-differentiated mate preferences. *Eution and Human Behavior* 27(3): 193–205.

Moore Lappé, Frances. 1985. *What to Do after You Turn Off the TV: Fresh Ideas for Enjoying Family Time*. New York: Ballantine Books.

Morash, Merry, Hoan Bui, Yan Zhang, & Kristy Holtfreter. 2007. Risk factors for abusive relationships. *Violence against Women* 13: 653–675.

Moreau, C., S. Boucher, M. Hebert, & J. Lemelin. 2015. Capturing sexual violence experiences among battered women using the revised sexual experiences survey and the revised conflict tactics scales. *Archives of Sexual Behaviour* 44(1): 223–231.

Morely, Jeremy D. n.d. *Japanese Family Law—or the Lack Thereof!* Retrieved on December 9, 2005, from http://www.international-divorce.com/d-japan.htm

Morgan, P.A., J.A. Merrell, & D. Rentschler. 2015. Midlife mothers favor "being with" children over work and careers. *Work* 50(3): 477–489.

Morrison, D.R., & A.J. Cherlin. 1995. The divorce process and young children's well-being: A prospective analysis. *Journal of Marriage and the Family* 57(August): 800–812.

Morrison, K., A. Thompson-Guppy, & P. Bell. 1986. *Stepmothers: Exploring the Myth*. Ottawa: Canadian Council on Social Development.

Morrow, Marina, Olena Hankivsky, & Colleen Varcoe. 2004. Women and violence: The effects of dismantling the welfare state. *Critical Social Policy* 24(3): 358–384.

Morton, Mavis. 2011. Violence in canadian families across the life course , pp. 277–322. In Nancy Mandell & Ann Duffy (Eds.), *Canadian Families: Diversity, Conflict and Change* (4th ed.). Toronto: Nelson.

Morton, Suzanne. 1992. The June bride as the working-class bride: Getting married in a Halifax working-class neighbourhood in the 1920s, pp. 360–379. In Bettina Bradbury (Ed.), *Canadian Family History: Selected Readings*. Toronto: Copp Clark Pitman.

Moscovitch, A. 2007. *Good Servant, Bad Master? Electronic Media and the Family*. Ottawa: Vanier Institute of the Family. Retrieved June 13, 2009, from http://www.vifamily.ca/library/cft/media07.html

Mossakowski, Krysia N. 2008. Dissecting the influence of race, ethnicity, and socioeconomic status on mental health in young adulthood. *Research on Aging* 30(6): 649–671.

Mossman, M.J. 2003. Conversations about families in Canadian courts and legislatures: Are there lessons for the United States? *Hofstra Law Review* 32(1): 171–200.

Muehlenhard, Charlene L., Terry P. Humphreys, Kristen N. Jozkowski, & Zoë D. Peterson. 2016. The complexities of sexual consent among college students: A conceptual and empirical review. *The Journal of Sex Research* 53(4–5): 457–487.

Mummert, G. 2009. Siblings by telephone: Experiences of Mexican children in long-distance childrearing arrangements. *Journal of the Southwest* 51(4): 503–521.

Munsch, C.L. 2015. Her support, his support: Money, masculinity, and marital infidelity. *American Sociological Review* 80(3): 469–495.

Munsch, Joyce, John Woodward, & Nancy Darling. 1995. Children's perceptions of their relationship with coresiding and non-coresiding fathers. *Journal of Divorce and Remarriage* 23(1–2).

Murdock, George. 1949. *Social Structure*. New York: MacMillan.

Murphy, B., X. Zhang, & C. Dionne. 2012. *Low income in Canada: A multi-line and multi-index perspective*. Ottawa: Statistics Canada. Retrieved from http://www.statcan.gc.ca/pub/75f0002m/75f0002m2012001-eng.pdf

Myers, Jane E., Jayamala Madathil, & Lynne R. Tingle. 2005. Marriage satisfaction and wellness in India and the United States: A preliminary comparison of arranged marriages and marriages of choice. *Journal of Counseling & Development* 83(2): 183–190.

Myers, Scott M. 2006. Religious homogamy and marital quality: Historical and generational patterns, 1980–1997. *Journal of Marriage and Family* 68(2): 292–304.

Myrskylä, M., & R. Margolis. 2014. Happiness: Before and after the kids. *Demography* 51(5): 1843–1866.

Najman, Jake, Mohsina Khatun, Abdullah Mamun, Alexandra Clavarino, Gail M. Williams, James Scott, . . . , & Rosa Alati. 2014. Does depression experienced by mothers lead to a decline in marital quality? A 21-year longitudinal study. *Social Psychiatry and Psychiatric Epidemiology* 49(1): 121–132.

National Child Benefit. 2009. NCB: A unique partnership of the Government of Canada, provinces and territories and First Nations. Retrieved April 19, 2009, from http://www.nationalchildbenefit.ca/eng/06/ncb.shtml

Nearly half of children in foster care are Aboriginal: Statistics Canada. 2013. *ATPN National News*, May 8. Retrieved from http://aptnnews.ca/2013/05/08/nearly-half-of-children-in-foster-care-aboriginal-statistics-canada

Nelson, F. 1996. *Lesbian Motherhood: An Exploration of Canadian Lesbian Families*. Toronto: University of Toronto Press.

Nelson, F. 2000. Lesbian families: Achieving motherhood. *Journal of Gay and Lesbian Social Services* 10(1): 27–46.

Nelson, Geoffrey. 1994, January. Emotional well-being of separated and married women: Long-term follow-up study. *American Journal of Orthopsychiatry* 64: 150–160.

Nesterov, Andrey. 2004, June 25. Eighty percent of marriages in Russia end up in divorce. Pravda, 25 June. Retrieved December 9, 2005, from http://english.pravda.ru/main/18/90/359/13194_divorce.html

Nesteruk, Olena, & Alexandra Gramescu. 2012. Dating and mate selection among young adults from immigrant families. *Marriage and Family Review* 48(1): 40–58.

Newman, Andrew F., & Claudia Olivetti. 2015. *Career Women and the Durability of Marriage*. Working paper, Boston University.

Newman, Matthew L., Carla Groom, Lori Handelman, & James Pennebaker. 2008. Gender differences in language use: An analysis of 14,000 text samples. *Discourse Processes* 45(3): 211–236.

Nguyen, Linda. 2013. 2013. Financial stress takes heavy toll on couples: Money might tear you apart. *The Canadian Press*, February 13. Retrieved from http://www.canadianbusiness.com/lifestyle/financial-strain-can-result-in-heavy-toll-on-relationships-poll

Nie, Norman H., & D. Sunshine Hillygus. 2002. The impact of Internet use on sociability: Time-diary findings. *IT & Society*, 1(1): 1–20.

Nielsen, Linda. 2014. Shared physical custody: Summary of 40 studies on outcomes for children. *Journal of Divorce & Remarriage* 55(8): 613–635.

Nielsen, Mark R. 2002. Are all marriages the same? Marital satisfaction of middle-class couples. *Dissertation Abstracts International, A: The Humanities and Social Sciences* 63(11), 4108-A–4109-A.

Noel, Melanie, Carole Peterson, & Beulah Jesso. 2008. The relationship of parenting stress and child temperament to language development among economically disadvantaged preschoolers. *Journal of Child Language* 35(4): 823–843.

Noormohamed, R., L. Ireland, S. Goulet, T. Cochrane, C. Daniels, L. Beatt, . . . , & C. Morgan. 2012. *Intergenerational Trauma and Aboriginal Youth: A Scoping Review*. Calgary: City of Calgary, Family, and Community Support Services.

Nyman, C. 1999. Gender equality in the most equal country in the world: Money and marriage in Sweden. *The Sociological Review* 47(4): 766–793.

O'Connor, J. 2012. Trend of couples not having children just plain selfish. *National Post*, September 19. Retrieved from http://news.nationalpost.com/opinion/joe-oconnor-selfishness-behind-growing-trend-for-couples-to-not-have-children

Oksanen, A., M. Aaltonen, K. Majamaa, & K. Rantala. 2017. Debt problems, home-leaving, and boomeranging: A register-based perspective on economic consequences of moving away from parental home. *International Journal of Consumer Studies* 41(3): 340–352.

Omand, G. 2017. Long-awaited criminal trial against accused Bountiful polygamists to begin. *The Globe and Mail*, April 17. Retrieved from https://www.theglobeandmail.com/news/british-columbia/long-awaited-criminal-trial-against-accused-bountiful-polygamists-to-begin/article34727709

Ontario Ministry of Labour. 2015. *Equal pay for equal work.* Retrieved from https://www.labour.gov.on.ca/english/es/pubs/guide/equalpay.php

Orfali, K. 2011. The rhetoric of universality and the ethics of medical responsibility, pp. 57–75. In Catherine Myser (Ed.), *Bioethics around the Globe.* New York: Oxford University Press.

Organisation for Economic Co-operation and Development. 2011. *Key Characteristics of Parental Leave Systems.* Retrieved from https://www.oecd.org/els/soc/PF2_1_Parental_leave_systems.pdf

Orr, A.J. 2011. Gendered capital: Childhood socialization and the "boy crisis" in education. *Sex Roles* 65(3–4): 271–284.

Osborne, C., W.D. Manning, & P.J. Smock. 2007. Married and cohabiting parents' relationship stability: A focus on race and ethnicity. *Journal of Marriage and Family* 69(5): 1345–1366. doi:10.1111/j.1741-3737.2007. 00451.x

Osborne, C., & S. McLanahan. 2007. Partnership instability and child well-being. *Journal of Marriage and Family* 69(4): 1065–1083. doi:10.1111/j.17413737.2007.00431.x

Owen, J., & F.D. Fincham. 2010. Effects of gender and psychological factors on "friends with benefits" relationships among young adults. *Archives of Sexual Behavior* 40(2): 311–320.

Ozawa, M.N., & H.-S. Yoon. 2002. The economic benefit of remarriage: Gender and income class. *Journal of Divorce & Remarriage* 36(3–4).

Pahl, J. 1983. The allocation of money and the structuring of inequality within marriage. *The Sociological Review* 31(2): 237–262.

Pahl J. 1999. *Invisible Money: Family Finances in the Electronic Economy.* Cambridge, UK: Polity Press.

Palameta, B. 2003, August. Who pays for domestic help? *Perspectives on Labour and Income.* Catalogue no. 75-001-XIE. Retrieved from http://www.statcan.gc.ca/pub/75-001-x/75-001-x2003008-eng.pdf

Panitch, Melanie. 2008. *Disability, mothers, and organization: Accidental activists.* New York: Routledge.

Panitch, Vida. 2015. Assisted reproduction and distributive justice. *Bioethics* 29(2): 108–117.

Park, K. 2002. Stigma management among the voluntarily childless. *Sociological Perspectives* 45(1): 21–45.

Parker, George. 2014. Mothers at large: Responsibilizing the pregnant self for the obesity epidemic. *Fat Studies* 3: 101–118.

Parusel, Bernd. 2016. Unaccompanied minors in Europe: Between immigration control and the need for protection, pp. 139–160. In Gabriella Lazaridis (Ed.), *Security, Insecurity and Migration in Europe.* New York: Routledge

Pasley, K., E. Sandras, & M.E. Edmondson. 1994. The effects of financial management strategies on quality of family life in remarriage. *Journal of Family and Economic* 15(1): 53–70.

Paterson, S. 2011. Rethinking the dynamics of abusive relationships: The implications of violence and resistance for household bargaining. *Review of Radical Political Economics* 43(2): 137–153.

Paul, E.L., B. McManus, & A. Hayes. 2000. Hookups: Characteristics and correlates of college students' spontaneous and anonymous sexual experiences. *The Journal of Sex Research* 37(1): 76–88. doi:10.1080/00224490009552023

Peiser, Nadine C., & Patrick C.L. Heaven. 1996, December. Family influences on self-reported delinquency among high school students. *Journal of Adolescence* 19(6): 557–568.

Pelletier, D. 2016. The diffusion of cohabitation and children's risks of family dissolution in Canada. *Demographic Research* 35(45): 1317–1342.

Pelzman, J. 2013. Womb for rent: International service trade employing assisted reproduction technologies (ARTs). *Review of International Economics* 21(3): 387–400.

Peplau, Letitia Anne, & Adam W. Fingerhut. 2007. The close relationships of lesbian and gay men. *Annual Review of Psychology* 58: 405–424.

Perkins, J.J., R.W. Sanson-Fisher, S. Blunden, D. Lunnay, S. Redman, & M.J. Hensley. 1994. The prevalence of drug use in urban Aboriginal communities. *Addiction* 89(10): 1319–1331.

Perreault, S. 2011. Violent victimization of Aboriginal people in the Canadian provinces, 2009. *Juristat: Canadian Centre for Justice Statistics* 30(2): 1A.

Perreault, S., & S. Brennan. 2010. Criminal victimization in Canada, 2009. *Juristat: Canadian Centre for Justice Statistics* 30(2): 1G.

Perunovic, Mihailo, & John G. Holmes. 2008. Automatic accommodation: The role of personality. *Personal Relationships* 15: 57–70.

Peters, Brad, & Marion F. Ehrenberg. 2008. The influence of parental separation and divorce on father–child relationships. *Journal of Divorce and Remarriage* 49(1–2): 78–109.

Peters, J., T.K. Shackelford, & D.M. Buss. 2002. Understanding domestic violence against women: Using evolutionary psychology to extend the feminist functional analysis. *Violence and Victims* 17(2): 255.

Peterson, B.D., M. Pirritano, U. Christensen, & L. Schmidt. 2008. The impact of partner coping in couples experiencing infertility. *Human Reproduction* 23(5): 1128–1137.

Phillips, Bruce, & William Griffiths. 2004. Female earnings and divorce rates: Some Australian evidence. *Australian Economic Review* 37(2): 139–152.

Phillips, Roderick. 1988. *Putting Asunder: A History of Divorce in Western Society.* Cambridge, UK: Cambridge University Press.

Phipps, S.A. 2009. Lessons from Europe: Policy options to enhance the economic security of Canadian families, pp. 552–573. In B. Fox (Ed.), *Family Patterns: Gender Relations* (3rd ed.). Toronto, ON: Oxford University Press.

Phipps, S.A., & P.S. Burton. 1998. What's mine is yours? The influence of male and female income on patterns of household expenditure. *Economica* 65(260): 599–613.

Pilkington, Pamela, Lisa Milne, Kathryn Cairns, James Lewis, & Thomas Whelan. 2015. Modifiable partner factors associated with perinatal depression and anxiety: A systematic review and meta-analysis. *Journal of Affective Disorders* 178: 165–180.

Pitrou, A. 2005. The irreplaceable third age: Between family, work and mutual support, pp. 113–128. In L.O. Stone (Ed.), *New Frontiers of Research on Retirement.* Catalogue no. 75-511-XIE. Ottawa, ON: Statistics Canada. Retrieved from http://www.statcan.gc.ca/pub/75-511-x/75-511-x2006001-eng.pdf

Pitt, R.S., J. Sherman, & M.E. Macdonald. 2015. Low-income working immigrant families in Quebec: Exploring their challenges to well-being. *Canadian Journal of Public Health* 106(8): 539–545.

Polanyi, M., J. Mustachi, M. Kerr, & S. Meagher. 2016. *Divided City: Life in Canada's Child Poverty Capital.* 2016 Toronto Child and Family Poverty Report Card. Toronto: Childcare Resource and Research Unit.

Pong, Suet-ling, Lingxin Hao, & Erica Gardner. 2005. The roles of parenting styles and social capital in the school performance of immigrant Asian and Hispanic adolescents. *Social Science Quarterly* 86: 928–950.

Poortman, A.-R., & B. Hewitt. 2015. Gender differences in relationship preferences after union dissolution. *Advances in Life Course Research* 26: 11–21.

Popenoe, D. 1993. American family decline: 1960–1990: A review and appraisal. *Journal of Marriage and the Family* 55: 527–555.

Popenoe, David. 1996. Modern marriage: Revising the cultural script, pp. 247–270. In David Popenoe, Jean Bethke Elshtain, & David Blankenhorn (Eds.), *Promises to Keep: Decline and Renewal of Marriage in America.* Lanham, MD: Rowman & Littlefield Publishers, Inc.

Portrie, Torey, & Nicole R. Hill. 2005. Blended families: A critical review of the current research. *The Family Journal: Counseling and Therapy for Couples and Families* 12(4): 445–451.

Pot, N., & R. Keizer. 2016. Physical activity and sport participation: A systematic review of the impact of fatherhood. *Preventive Medicine Reports* 4: 121–127.

Powell, J.M., R. Fraser, J.A. Brockway, N. Temkin, & K.R. Bell. 2016. A Telehealth approach to caregiver self-management following traumatic brain injury: A randomized controlled trial. *Journal of Head Trauma Rehabilitation* 31(3): 180–190.

Pratt, G. 2009. Circulating sadness: Witnessing Filipina mothers' stories of family separation. *Gender, Place and Culture* 16(1): 3–22. doi:10.1080/09663690802574753

Prentice, Susan. 2007. Less access, worse quality: New evidence about poor children and regulated child care in Canada. *Journal of Children & Poverty* 13(1): 57–73.

Prestigiamo, A. 2017. Sologamy: The saddest trend you've ever heard of. *The Daily Wire*, May 15. Retrieved from http://www.dailywire.com/news/16451/sologamy-apparently-people-are-marrying-themselves-amanda-prestigiacomo#

Price, C.A., & E. Joo. 2005. Exploring the relationship between marital status and women's retirement satisfaction. *The International Journal of Aging and Human Development* 61(1): 37–55.

Prince, Michael J. 2009. *Absent Citizens: Disability Politics and Policy in Canada.* Toronto: University of Toronto Press.

Purvin, Diane. 2007. At the crossroads and in the crosshairs: Social welfare policy and low-income women's vulnerability to domestic violence. *Social Problems* 54(2): 188–210.

Putnam, Richard R. 2011. First comes marriage, then comes divorce: A perspective on the process. *Journal of Divorce and Remarriage* 52(7): 557–564.

Pyper, W. 2006. *Perspectives on Labor and Income: Balancing Career and Care.* Catalogue no. 75-001-XIE, Vol. 7, no. 11. Retrieved from http://www.statcan.gc.ca/pub/75-001-x/11106/9520-eng.htm

Quach, Andrew S., & Elaine A. Anderson. 2008. Implications of China's open-door policy for families: A family impact analysis. *Journal of Family Issues* 29: 1089–1103.

Qin, D.B. 2009. Being "good" or being "popular": Gender and ethnic identity negotiations of Chinese immigrant adolescents. *Journal of Adolescent Research* 24(1): 37–66.

Raffaelli, M., & L.L. Ontai. 2001. 16 years old and there are boys calling over to the house: An exploratory study of sexual socialization in Latino families. *Culture, Health, and Sexuality* 3: 295–310.

Raleigh, Elizabeth. 2012. Are same-sex and single adoptive parents more likely to adopt transracially? A national analysis of race, family structure, and the adoption marketplace. *Sociological Perspectives* 55(3): 449–471.

Raley, R.K., & L. Bumpass. 2003. The topography of the divorce plateau: Levels and trends in union stability in the United States after 1980. *Demographic Research* 8(8): 245–260.

Randall, A.K., & G. Bodenmann. 2009. The role of stress on close relationships and marital satisfaction. *Clinical Psychology Review* 29: 105–115.

Rashidi, P., & A. Mihailidis. 2013. A survey on ambient-assisted living tools for older adults. *Journal of Biomedical and Health Informatics* 17(3): 579–590.

Ravanera, Zenaida R., Fernando Rajulton, & Thomas K. Burch. 1998. Early life transitions of Canadian women: A cohort analysis of timing, sequences, and variations. *European Journal of Population* 14(2): 179–204.

Raymo, James M., Miho Iwasawa, & Larry Bumpass. 2004. Marital dissolution in Japan: Recent trends and patterns. *Demographic Research* 11: 396–419.

Reading, C.L., & F. Wien. 2009. *Health Inequalities and the Social Determinants of Aboriginal Peoples' Health*. Prince George, BC: National Collaborating Centre for Aboriginal Health.

Reaume, Geoffrey. 2012. Disability history in Canada: Present work in the field and future prospects. *Canadian Journal of Disability Studies* 1(1): 35–81.

Reay, B. 2014. Promiscuous intimacies: Rethinking the history of American casual sex. *Journal of Historical Sociology* 27(1): 1–24.

Regan, Pamela, Saloni Lakhanpal, & Carlos Anguiano. 2012. Relationship outcomes in Indian-American love-based and arranged marriages. *Psychological Reports* 110(3): 915–924.

Regmi, P. R., van Teijlingen, E. R., Simkhada, P., & Acharya, D. R. 2011. Dating and sex among emerging adults in Nepal. *Journal of Adolescent Research*, 26(6): 675.

Regnerus, Mark D. 2006. The parent–child relationship and opportunities for adolescents' first sex. *Journal of Family Issues* 27(2): 159–183.

Rehman, Uzma, Jackie Gollan, & Amanda Mortimer. 2008. The marital context of depression: Research, limitations, and new directions. *Clinical Psychology Review* 28(2): 179–198.

Reitz, J. 2007. Immigrant employment success in Canada, part 1: Individual and contextual causes. *Journal of International Migration and Integration/Revue de l'integration et de la migration internationale* 8(1): 11–36.

Remennick, Larissa. 2000, December. Childless in the land of imperative motherhood: Stigma and coping among infertile Israeli women. *Sex Roles* 43(11–12): 821–841.

Rhoades, G.K., S.M. Stanley, & H.J. Markman. 2006. Pre-engagement cohabitation and gender asymmetry in marital commitment. *Journal of Family Psychology* 20: 553–560.

Richards, J. 2010. *Reducing Lone-Parent Poverty: A Canadian Success Story*. C. D. Howe Institute Commentary (No. 305, June 2010). Retrieved from https://www.cdhowe.org/sites/default/files/attachments/research_papers/mixed//commentary_305.pdf

Richards, T.N., E. Tomsich, A.R. Gover, & W.G. Jennings. 2016. The cycle of violence revisited: Distinguishing intimate partner violence offenders only, victims only, and victim–offenders. *Violence and Victims* 31(4): 573–590.

Richmond, C.A.M. 2009. The social determinants of Inuit health: A focus on social support in the Canadian arctic. *International Journal of Circumpolar Health* 68(5): 471–487.

Ridgway, J.L., & R.B. Clayton. 2016. Instagram unfiltered: Exploring associations of body image satisfaction, instagram #selfie posting, and negative romantic relationship outcomes. *Cyberpsychology, Behavior, and Social Networking* 19(1): 2–7.

Riessman, C.K. 1990. *Divorce Talk: Women and Men Make Sense of Personal Relationships*. New Brunswick, NY: Rutgers University Press.

Rijken, A.J., & E.-M. Merz. 2014. Double standards: Differences in norms on voluntary childlessness for men and women. *European Sociological Review* 30(4): 470–482.

Risman, B., & D. Johnson-Sumerford. 1998. Doing it fairly: A study of post-gender marriages. *Journal of Marriage and the Family* 60: 23–40.

Robles, Theodore F., R.B. Slatcher, J.M. Trombello, & M.M. McGinn. 2014. Marital quality and health: A meta-analytic review. *Psychological Bulletin* 140(1): 140–187.

Rock, P. 2016. *The Making of Symbolic Interactionism*. New York: Springer.

Roelfs, David, Eran Shor, Rachel Kalish, & Tamar Yogev. 2011. The rising relative risk of mortality for singles: Meta-analysis and meta-regression. *American Journal of Epidemiology* 174(4): 379–389. doi:10.1093/aje/kwr111

Rogers, Stacy J., & Danelle D. DeBoer. 2001. Changes in wives' income: Effects on marital happiness, psychological well-being, and the risk of divorce. *Journal of Marriage and the Family* 63(2): 458–472.

Rosenberg, Harriet. 1987. Motherwork, stress and depression: The costs of privatized social reproduction, pp. 181–197. In H.J. Maroney & M. Luxton (Eds.), *Feminism and Political Economy*. Toronto: Methuen.

Rosenfeld, M.J. 2008. Racial, educational and religious endogamy in the United States: A comparative historical perspective. *Social Forces* 87(1): 1–31.

Rosenfeld, M.J., & R.J. Thomas. 2012. Searching for a mate: The rise of the Internet as a social intermediary. *American Sociological Review* 77(4): 523–547.

Rosenthal, Carolyn. 1985. Kinkeeping in the familial division of labor. *Journal of Marriage and the Family* 47: 965–974.

Ross, L., R. Epstein, C. Goldfinger, L. Steele, S. Anderson, & C. Strike. 2008. Lesbian and queer mothers navigating the adoption system: The impacts on mental health. *Health Sociology Review* 17(3): 254–266.

Roterman, Michelle, Sheila Dunn, & Amanda Black. 2015. *Oral Contraceptive Use among Women Aged 15 to 49: Results from the Canadian Health Measures Survey*. Ottawa: Statistics Canada. Retrieved from http://www.statcan.gc.ca/pub/82-003-x/2015010/article/14222-eng.htm

Rotermann, M. 2007. Marital breakdown and subsequent depression. *Health Reports* 18(2): 33–44.

Rotermann, M. 2012. Sexual behaviour and condom use of 15- to 24-year-olds in 2003 and 2009/2010. *Health Reports* 23(1). Ottawa: Statistics Canada. Retrieved from http://www.statcan.gc.ca/pub/82-003-x/2012001/article/11632-eng.pdf

Rothbaum, F., M. Pott, H. Azuma, K. Miyake, & J. Weisz. 2000. The development of close relationships in Japan and the United States: Paths of symbiotic harmony and generative tension. *Child Development* 71(5): 1121–1142.

Rothblum, Esther D., Kimberly F. Balsam, & Sondra E. Solomon. 2011. Narratives of same-sex couples who had civil unions in Vermont: The impact of legalizing relationships on couples and on social policy. *Sexuality Research and Social Policy* 8: 183–191.

Rowland, D.T. 2007. Historical trends in childlessness. *Journal of Family Issues* 28(10): 1311–1337.

Rowntree, S.B. 1910. *Poverty: A Study of Town Life*. London, UK: MacMillian.

Royal Canadian Mounted Police. 2017. The effects of family violence on children—Where does it hurt? Retrieved from http://www.rcmp-grc.gc.ca/cp-pc/chi-enf-abu-eng.htm

Russell, Mary, Barbara Harris, & Annemarie Gockel. 2008. Parenting in poverty: Perspectives of high-risk parents. *Journal of Children and Poverty* 14(1): 83–98.

Russo, Nancy Felipe. 1976. The motherhood mandate. *Journal of Social Issues* 32(3): 143–153.

Sacks, Jonathan. 1991. The *Persistence of Faith: Religion, Morality and Society in a Secular Age*. The 1990 Reith Lectures. London: Weidenfeld and Nicolson.

Saewyc, Elizabeth M., Darlene Taylor, Yuko Homma, & Gina Ogilvie. 2008. Trends in sexual health and risk behaviours among adolescent students in British Columbia. *Canadian Journal of Human Sexuality* 17: 1–13.

Saintjacques, M.C. 1995. Role-strain prediction in step-families. *Journal of Divorce and Remarriage* 24(1–2): 51–72.

Salisbury, D.L. 1997. Retirement planning and personal responsibility: The changing shape of the three-legged stool. *Generations* 21(2): 23–26.

Saltes, Natasha. 2013. Disability, identity and disclosure in the online dating environment. *Disability & Society* 28: 96–109.

Samuel, Lina. 2010. South Asian women in the diaspora: Reflections on arranged marriage and dowry among the Syrian Orthodox community in Canada. *South Asian Diaspora* 5(1): 91–105.

Sarojini, N., V. Marwah, & A. Shenoi. 2011. Globalisation of birth markets: A case study of assisted reproductive technologies in India. *Globalization and Health* 7: 27.

Sassler, S., & A.J. Miller. 2011. Waiting to be asked: Gender, power, and relationship progression among cohabiting couples. *Journal of Family Issues* 32(4): 482–506. doi:10.1177/0192513X10391045

Sassler, Sharon, & Amanda J. Miller. 2011a. Class differences in cohabitation processes. *Family Relations* 60(2): 163–177.

Sautter, Jessica M., Rebecca M. Tippett, & S. Philip Morgan. 2010. The social demography of Internet dating in the United States. *Social Science Quarterly* 91: 554–575.

Sauve, R. 2002. *Job, Family and Stress among Husbands, Wives and Lone Parents 15–64 from 1990–2000*. Ottawa: Vanier Institute of the Family. Retrieved from http://www.vifamily.ca

Scanzoni, John. 2000. *Designing Families: The Search for Self and Community in the Information Age.* Thousand Oaks, CA: Pine Forge Press.

Scaramella, Laura V., Tricia K. Neppl, Lenna L. Ontai, & Rand D. Conger. 2008. Consequences of socioeconomic disadvantage across three generations: parenting behavior and child externalizing problems. *Journal of Family Psychology* 22(5): 725–733.

Scheff, E. 2015. *The Polyamorists Next Door: Inside Multiple-Relationships and Families.* Lanham, MD: Rowman & Littlefield.

Schieman, S., M. Young, & P. Glavin. 2014. *A Brief Description of the Canadian Workforce: Findings from the 2012–2014 Canadian Work, Stress, and Health Study.* Toronto, ON: University of Toronto.

Schimmele, C.M., & Z. Wu. 2016. Repartnering after union dissolution in later life. *Journal of Marriage and Family* 78(4): 1013–1031.

Schlesinger, R.A., & B. Schlesinger. 2009. Canadian-Jewish seniors: Marriage/cohabitation after age 65. *Journal of Gerontological Social Work* 52(1): 32–47.

Schneider, Carl E. 1996. The law and the stability of marriage: The family as a social institution, pp. 187–213. In David Popenoe, Jean Bethke Elshtain, & David Blankenhorn (Eds.), *Promises to Keep: Decline and Renewal of Marriage in America.* Lanham, MD: Rowman & Littlefield Publishers, Inc.

Schoenfeld, Elizabeth, Timothy J. Loving, Mark T. Pope, Ted L. Huston, & Aleksandar Stulhofer. 2016. Does sex really matter? Examining the connections between spouses' nonsexual behaviors, sexual frequency, sexual satisfaction, and marital satisfaction. *Archives of Sexual Behavior* 46(2): 489–501.

Schrodt, Paul, Paul Witt, & Jenna Shimkowski. 2014. A meta-analytical review of the demand/withdraw pattern of interaction and its associations with individual, relational, and communicative outcomes. *Communication Monographs* 81(1): 28–58.

Schulz, Marc S., Carolyn Pape Cowan, & Philip A. Cowan. 2006. Promoting healthy beginnings: A randomized controlled trial of a preventive intervention to preserve marital quality during the transition to parenthood. *Journal of Consulting and Clinical Psychology* 74(1): 20–31.

Schulz, R., & P.R. Sherwood. 2008. Physical and mental health effects of family caregiving. *American Journal of Nursing* 108(Suppl. 9): 23–27.

Schvaneveldt, Paul L., Jennifer L. Kerpelman, & Jay D. Schvaneveldt. 2005. Generational and cultural changes in family life in the United Arab Emirates: A comparison of mothers and daughters. *Journal of Comparative Family Studies* 36(1): 77–91.

Schwartz, Christine, & Robert Mare. 2005. Trends in educational assortative marriage from 1940 to 2003. *Demography* 42.4: 621–646.

Scott, Elizabeth S., & Robert E. Emery. 2014. Gender politics and child custody: The puzzling persistence of the best-interest standard. *Law & Contemporary Problems* 77: 69.

Scrim, K. 2016. *Aboriginal Victimization in Canada: A Summary of the Literature.* Ottawa: Department of Justice. Retrieved from http://www.justice.gc.ca/eng/rp-pr/cj-jp/victim/rd3-rr3/p3.html

Sears, H., & S. Byers. 2010. Adolescent girls' and boys' experiences of psychologically, physically, and sexually aggressive behaviors in their dating relationships: Co-occurrence and emotional reaction. *Journal of Aggression, Maltreatment & Trauma* 19: 517–539.

Seguin, L., B. Nikiema, L. Gauvin, M. Lambert, M.T. Tu, & L. Kakinami. 2012. Tracking exposure to child poverty during the first 10 years of life in a Quebec birth cohort. *Canadian Journal of Public Health* 103(4): 270.

Serewicz, Mary, Claire Morr, & Elaine Gale. 2008. First-date scripts: Gender roles, context, and relationship. *Sex Roles* 58(3–4): 149–164.

Serina, A.T., M. Hall, D. Ciambrone, & V.C. Phua. 2013. Swinging around stigma: Gendered marketing of swingers' websites. *Sexuality & Culture* 17(2): 348–359.

Serran, Geris, & Philip Firestone. 2004. Intimate partner homicide: A review of the male proprietariness and the self-defense theories. *Aggression and Violent Behavior*, 9: 1–15.

Sev'er, A. 1992. *Women and Divorce in Canada.* Toronto: Canadian Scholars' Press.

Se'ver, Aysan. 2011. Marriage go-round: Divorce and remarriage in Canada, pp. 243–274. In Nancy Mandell & Ann Duffy (Eds.). *Canadian Families: Diversity, Conflict and Change* (4th ed.). Toronto: Nelson.

Shackelford, T.K., & J. Mouzos. 2005. Partner killing by men in cohabiting and marital relationships: A comparative, cross-national analysis of data from Australia and the United States. *Journal of Interpersonal Violence* 10: 1310–1324.

Shaff, Kimberly Anne, Nicholas H. Wolfinger, Lori Kowaleski-Jones, & Ken R. Smith. 2008. Family Structure Transitions and Child Achievement. *Sociological Spectrum: Mid-South Sociological Association* 28(6): 681–704.

Shalabi, D., S. Mitchell, & N. Andersson. 2015. Review of gender violence among Arab immigrants in Canada: Key issues for prevention efforts. *Journal of Family Violence* 30: 817–825.

Shankar, J., G. Das, & S. Atwal. 2013. Challenging cultural discourses and beliefs that perpetuate domestic violence in South Asian communities: A discourse analysis. *Journal of International Women's Studies* 14(1): 248.

Shapiro, A. 2003. Later-life divorce and parent–adult child contact and proximity. *Journal of Family Issues* 24(2): 264–285.

Sherkat, Darren E. 2004. Religious intermarriage in the United States: Trends, patterns, and predictors. *Social Science Research* 33(4): 606–625.

Shi, Liping. 2000, February. The communication structure of intercultural married couples and their marital satisfaction. *Soshioroji* 44(3): 57–73.

Shields, M. 2002. Shift work and health. *Health Reports* 13(4). Catalogue no. 82-003. Retrieved from http://www.statcan.gc.ca/pub/82-003-x/2001004/article/6315-eng.pdf

Shields, M. 2006. Unhappy on the job. *Health Reports.* Catalogue no. 82-003. Ottawa: Statistics Canada.

Shirpak, Khosro Refaie, Eleanor Maticka-Tyndale, & Maryam Chinichian. 2011. Post Migration Changes in Iranian Immigrants' Couple Relationships in Canada. *Journal of Comparative Family Studies* 42(6): 751–770.

Sierau, S., & P.Y. Herzberg. 2012. Conflict resolution as a dyadic mediator: Considering the partner perspective on conflict resolution. *European Journal of Personality* 26: 221–232. doi:10.1002/per.828

Silva, Elizabeth. 2010. *Technology, Culture and Family: Influences on Home Life.* Basingstoke: Palgrave.

Silverman, Elaine Leslau. 1984. *The Last Best West: Women on the Alberta Frontier, 1880–1930.* Montreal: Eden Press.

Simpson, Jeffry A., W. Steven Rholes, Lorne Campbell, Sisi Tran, & Carol L. Wilson. 2003. Adult attachment, the transition to parenthood, and depressive symptoms. *Journal of Personality and Social Psychology* 84(6): 1172–1187.

Sims-Gould, J., A. Martin-Matthews, & Monique, A.M. Gignac. 2008. Episodic crises in the provision of care to elderly relatives. *Journal of Applied Gerontology* 27(2): 123–140.

Singer, Merrill C., Pamela I. Erickson, Louise Badiane, Rosemary Diaz, Dugeidy Ortiz, Traci Abraham, & Anna Marie Nicolaysen. 2006. Syndemics, sex and the city: Understanding sexually transmitted diseases in social and cultural context. *Social Science & Medicine* 63: 2010–2021.

Singh, Supriya, & Jo Lindsay. 1996. Money in heterosexual relationships. *Australia and New Zealand Journal of Sociology* 32(4): 57–69.

Singh, Supriya. 1997. *Marriage Money: The Social Shaping of Money in Marriage and Banking.* Concord, MA: Paul & Company Publishers Consortium Inc.

Sinha, M. 2012a. *Family Violence in Canada: A Statistical Profile, 2010.* Ottawa: Canadian Centre for Justice Statistics.

Sinha, M. 2012b. *Portrait of Caregivers, 2012.* Ottawa: Statistics Canada. Retrieved from http://www.statcan.gc.ca/pub/89-652-x/89-652-x2013001-eng.htm#a2

Sinha, M. 2013. Portrait of caregivers, 2012. *Spotlight on Canadians: Results from the General Social Survey.* Catalogue no. 89-652-X—No. 001. Ottawa, ON: Social and Aboriginal Statistics Division. Retrieved from http://www.statcan.gc.ca/pub/89-652-x/89-652-x2013001-eng.pdf

Sinha, M. 2014a. Child care in Canada. *Spotlight on Canadians: Results from the General Social Survey.* Catalogue no. 89-652-X—No. 005. Ottawa, ON: Social and Aboriginal Statistics Division. Retrieved from http://www.statcan.gc.ca/pub/89-652-x/89-652-x2014005-eng.pdf

Sinha, M. 2014b. Parenting and child support after separation or divorce. *Spotlight on Canadians: Results from the General Social Survey.* Catalogue no. 89-652-X—No. 001. Ottawa, ON: Social and Aboriginal Statistics Division. Retrieved from http://www.statcan.gc.ca/pub/89-652-x/89-652-x2014001-eng.pdf

Sinha, M. 2015. *Family Violence against Children and Youth.* Ottawa: Statistics Canada. Retrieved from http://www.statcan.gc.ca/pub/85-002-x/2012001/article/11643/11643-3-eng.htm

Sitrin, Allison Gayle. 2001 September. The impact of the quality of marital adaptation on prenatal maternal representations and postnatal satisfaction with social support. *Dissertation Abstracts International: Section B: The Sciences & Engineering* 62(3-B), 1599.

Skew, A., A. Evans, & E. Gray. 2009. Factors affecting repartnering in Australia and the UK. *Journal of Comparative Family Studies* 40: 563–585.

Skinner, Kevin B., Stephen J. Bahr, D. Russell Crane, & R.A. Call Vaughn. 2002. Cohabitation, marriage, and remarriage: A comparison of relationship quality over time. *Journal of Family Issues* 23(1): 74–90.

Skinner, N.F., & K.B. Iaboni. 2009. Personality implications of adaption–innovation: IV. Cognitive style as a predictor of marital success. *Social Behaviour and Personality* 37(8): 1111–1113.

Slaughter, A.-M. 2013, March 7. Yes, You Can: Sheryl Sandberg's *Lean In*. *New York Times Sunday Book Review*. Retrieved from http://www.nytimes.com/2013/03/10/books/review/sheryl-sandbergs-lean-in.html

Slayter, E. 2009. Intimate partner violence against women with disabilities: Implications for disability service system case management practice. *Journal of Aggression, Maltreatment & Trauma* 18(2): 182–199.

Smart, C. 2006. Children's narratives of post-divorce family life: From individual experience to an ethical disposition. *The Sociological Review* 54(1): 155–170.

Smart, Carol, & Bren Neale. 1999. *Family Fragments?* Cambridge, UK: Polity Press.

Smith, Aaron, & Maeve Duggan. 2013. Online dating & relationships. *Pew Research Center, Internet & Technology*. Retrieved from http://www.pewinternet.org/2013/10/21/online-dating-relationships/

Smith, Jane E., V. Waldorf, & D. Trembath. 1990. Single White male looking for thin, very attractive . . . *Sex Roles* 23(11–12): 675–683.

Smith, T.W., C.A. Berg, P. Florsheim, B.N. Uchino, G. Pearce, M. Hawkins, & C. Olsen-Cerny. 2009. Conflict and collaboration in middle-aged and older couples: I. Age differences in agency and communion during marital interaction. *Psychology and Aging* 24: 259–273.

Smock, P. 2000. Cohabitation in the United States: An appraisal of research themes, findings, and implications. *Annual Review of Sociology* 26: 1–20.

Smock, Pamela J. 1994, September. Gender and the short-run economic consequences of marital disruption. *Social Forces* 73.

Snell, James G. 1983. The White life for two: The defence of marriage and sexual morality in Canada, 1890–1914. *Histoire Sociale/Social History* 16(31): 111–128.

Sociology Dictionary. 2017. Polygyny. *Open Education Sociology Dictionary*. Retrieved from http://sociologydictionary.org/polygyny

Somerville, K. 2008. Transnational belonging among second generation youth: Identity in a globalized world. *Journal of Social Science* 10: 23–33.

Sonawat, Reeta. 2001. Understanding families in India: A reflection of societal changes. *Psicologia: Teoria e Pesquisa* 17(2): 177–186.

Song, Jieun, Frank Floyd, Marsha Seltzer, & Jan Greenberg. 2010. Long-term effects of child death on parents' health-related quality of life: A dyadic analysis. *Family Relations* 59: 269–282.

Sorbring, E., & L. Lundin. 2012. Mothers' and fathers' insights into teenagers' use of the Internet. *New Media & Society* 14(7): 1181–1197.

Soria, Krista M., & Sarah Linder. 2014. Parental divorce and first-year college students' persistence and academic achievement. *Journal of Divorce & Remarriage* 55(2): 103–116.

South, S.J., & K.M. Lloyd. 1995. Spousal alternatives and marital dissolution. *American Sociological Review* 60(1): 21–35.

South, S.J., K. Trent, & Y. Shen. 2001. Changing partners: Toward a macrostructural opportunity theory of marital dissolution. *Journal of Marriage and the Family* 63: 743–754.

South, Scott. 1985. Economic conditions and the divorce rate: A time-series analysis of the children. *Journal of Marriage and the Family* 47(1): 31–42.

Southworth, C., S. Dawson, C. Fraser, & S. Tucker. 2005. *A High-Tech Twist on Abuse: Technology, Intimate Partner Stalking, and Advocacy*. Washington, DC: National Network to End Domestic Violence.

Spiwak, Rae, & Douglas A. Brownridge. 2005. Separated women's risk for violence: An analysis of the Canadian situation. *Journal of Divorce and Remarriage* 43: 105–117.

Sprecher, S. 2009. Relationship Initiation and Formation on the Internet. *Marriage & Family Review* 45(6–8): 761–782.

Sprecher, S., S. Treger, & J. Sakaluk. 2013. Premarital sexual standards and sociosexuality: Gender, ethnicity, and cohort differences. *Archives of Sexual Behavior* 42(8): 1395–1405.

Stacey, Judith. 1990. *Brave New Families*. New York: Basic Books.

Stacey, Judith. 1996. *In the Name of the Family: Rethinking Family Values in the Postmodern Age*. Boston: Beacon.

Stack, Steven, & Jonathan Scourfield. 2015. Recency of divorce, depression, and suicide risk. *Journal of Family Issues* 36(6): 695–715.

Stafford, Laura, Susan L. Kline, & Caroline T. Rankin. 2004. Married individuals, cohabiters, and cohabiters who marry: A longitudinal study of relational and individual well-being. *Journal of Social and Personal Relationships* 21(2): 231–248.

Stamp, P. 1985. Research note: Balance of financial power in marriage: An exploratory study of breadwinning wives. *The Sociological Review* 33(3): 546–557.

Stanik, C.E., & P.C. Ellsworth. 2010. Who cares about marrying a rich man? Intelligence and variation in women's mate preferences. *Human Nature* 21(2): 203–217.

Stanley, Scott M., Galena K. Rhoades, Paul R. Amato, Howard J. Markman, & Christine A. Johnson.

2010. The timing of cohabitation and engagement: Impact on first and second marriages. *Journal of Marriage and Family* 72(4): 906–918.

Stanley, Scott M., Galena K. Rhoades, & Howard J. Markman. 2006. Sliding versus deciding: Inertia and the premarital cohabitation effect. *Family Relations* 55(4): 499–509.

Statistics Canada. 1996a. *Life Events: How Families Change: Labour and Income Dynamics* 5(1). Ottawa: Statistics Canada.

Statistics Canada. 2002a. Changing conjugal life in Canada. *The Daily*, July 11. Retrieved December 9, 2005, from http://www.statcan.ca/Daily/English/020711/d020711a.htm

Statistics Canada. 2002e. *The Daily*, September 26. Retrieved April 25, 2006, from http://www.statcan.ca/Daily/English/020926/d020926c.htm

Statistics Canada. 2004a. Divorces. *The Daily*, May 4. Retrieved August 5, 2005, from http://www.statcan.ca/Daily/English/040504/d040504a.htm

Statistics Canada. 2004b. Births. *The Daily*, April 19. Retrieved October 16, 2005, from http://www.statcan.ca/Daily/English/040419/d040419b.htm

Statistics Canada. 2005b. Canada's Aboriginal population in 2017. *The Daily*, June 28. Retrieved October 16, 2005, from http://www.statcan.ca/Daily/English/050628/d050628d.htm

Statistics Canada. 2005c. *Family Violence in Canada: A Statistical Profile.* Ottawa: Statistics Canada. Catalogue no. 85-224-XIE.

Statistics Canada. 2005d. Study: Mature singles who don't expect to marry. *The Daily*, June 7. Retrieved November 18, 2005, from http://www.statcan.ca/Daily/English/050607/d050607a.htm

Statistics Canada. 2005f. Divorce and the mental health of children. *The Daily*, December 13. Retrieved December 14, 2005, from http://www.statcan.ca/Daily/English/050309/d050309b.htm

Statistics Canada. 2006. *Aboriginal Children's Survey.* Catalogue no. 89-634-X. Ottawa: Statistics Canada. Retrieved from http://www5.statcan.gc.ca/olc-cel/olc.action?objId=89-634-X&ObjType=2&lang=en&limit=0

Statistics Canada. 2006. General Social Survey: Paid and unpaid work. *The Daily*, July 19. Retrieved from http://www.statcan.gc.ca/daily-quotidien/060719/dq060719b-eng.htm

Statistics Canada. 2006a. *Annual Demographic Statistics, 2005.* Ottawa: Statistics Canada. Catalogue no. 91-213.

Statistics Canada. 2007. *The Daily*, September 12. Retrieved from http://www.statcan.gc.ca/daily-quotidien/070912/dq070912a-eng.htm

Statistics Canada. 2008a. *Aboriginal Children's Survey, 2006: Family, Community and Child Care.* Catalogue no. 89-634-X—No. 001. Ottawa, ON: Social and Aboriginal Statistics Division. Retrieved from http://www.statcan.gc.ca/pub/89-634-x/89-634-x2008001-eng.pdf

Statistics Canada. 2008b. *Participation and Activity Limitation Survey 2006: Families of Children with Disabilities in Canada.* Catalogue no. 89-628-X-No. 009. Ottawa, ON: Social and Aboriginal Statistics Division. Retrieved from http://www.statcan.gc.ca/pub/89-628-x/89-628-x2008009-eng.pdf

Statistics Canada. 2009. *Study: Hours and Earnings of Dual-Earner Couples.* Retrieved June 13, 2009, from http://www.statcan.gc.ca/daily-quotidien/090424/dq090424beng.htm

Statistics Canada. 2011. *Fifty Years of Families in Canada: 1961 to 2011. Families, Households and Marital Status, 2011 Census of Population. Census in Brief.* Catalogue no. 98-312-X2011003. Ottawa: Author.

Statistics Canada. 2010a. Internet use by individuals, by type of activity. Statistics Canada. http://www.statcan.gc.ca/tables-tableaux/sum-som/l01/cst01/comm29a-eng.htm

Statistics Canada, 2011a. Canada Vital Statistics, Marriage Database and Demography Division (population estimates), Ottawa: Statistics Canada. http://www4.hrsdc.gc.ca/.3ndic.1t.4r@-eng.jsp?iid=78

Statistics Canada. 2011a. *Conjugal Status (3), Opposite/Same-sex Status (5) and Presence of Children (5) for the Couple Census Families in Private Households of Canada, Provinces, Territories and Census Metropolitan Areas, 2011 Census.* Catalogue no. 98-312-XCB2011046. Retrieved from http://www12.statcan.gc.ca/census-recensement/2011/dp-pd/tbt-tt/Rp-eng.cfm?LANG=E&APATH=7&DETAIL=0&DIM=0&FL=C&FREE=0&GC=0&GID=0&GK=0&GRP=1&PID=102659&PRID=0&PTYPE=101955&S=0&SHOWALL=0&SUB=0&Temporal=2011&THEME=0&VID=0&VNAMEE=Conjugal%20status%20%283%29&VNA

Statistics Canada. 2011a. *Education in Canada: Attainment, Field of Study and Location of Study.* Catalogue no. 99-012-X2011001. Ottawa, ON: Statistics Canada. Retrieved from http://www12.statcan.gc.ca/nhs-enm/2011/as-sa/99-012-x/99-012-x2011001-eng.pdf

Statistics Canada, 2011b. *Families, Living Arrangements and Unpaid Work.* Catalogue No. 89-503-X. http://www.statcan.gc.ca/pub/89-503-x/2010001/article/11546-eng.pdf

Statistics Canada. 2011b. Study: Generational change in paid and unpaid work. *The Daily*, July 12. Retrieved from http://www.statcan.gc.ca/daily-quotidien/110712/dq110712c-eng.htm

Statistics Canada. 2011b. *Women in Canada: A Gender-Based Statistical Report*. Catalogue no. 89-503-X. Ottawa: Ministry of Industry. Retrieved from http://www.statcan.gc.ca/pub/89-503-x/89-503-x2010001-eng.pdf

Statistics Canada. 2011g. *Women in Canada: A Gender-Based Statistical Report*. Ottawa: Statistics Canada. http://www.statcan.gc.ca/pub/89-503-x/2010001/article/11388-eng.htm#a4

Statistics Canada. 2012. *Census in Brief: Living Arrangements of Seniors, no. 4* Catalogue no. 98-312-X2011003. Ottawa, ON: Ministry of Industry. Retrieved from http://www12.statcan.gc.ca/census-recensement/2011/as-sa/98-312-x/98-312-x2011003_4-eng.pdf

Statistics Canada. 2012a. Canadian households in 2011: Type and growth families, households and marital status, 2011 Census of Population. *The Census in Brief, no 2.* (Catalogue no. 98-312-X2011003). Retrieved from http://www12.statcan.gc.ca/census-recensement/2011/as-sa/98-312-x/98-312-x2011003_2-eng.pdf

Statistics Canada. 2012a. *CANSIM Table 102-4503: Live births, by age of mother, Canada, provinces and territories.* Retrieved from http://www5.statcan.gc.ca/cansim/a26?lang=engandid=1024503andp2=46

Statistics Canada. 2012a. *Living arrangements of young adults aged 20 to 29: Families, households and marital status, 2011 Census of Population. The Census in Brief 3.* Catalogue no. 98-312-X2011003. Ottawa: Author.

Statistics Canada. 2012a. *Portrait of Families and Living Arrangements in Canada (from the 2011 Census of Canada short form).* http://www12.statcan.gc.ca/census-recensement/2011/as-sa/98-312-x/98-312-x2011001-eng.cfm#a1

Statistics Canada. 2012b. *Fifty years of families in Canada: 1961 to 2011: Families, households and marital status, 2011 Census of Population. Census in Brief.* Catalogue no. 98-31-X2011003. Retrieved from http://www12.statcan.gc.ca/census-recensement/2011/as-sa/98-312-x/98-312-x2011003_1-eng.pdf

Statistics Canada. 2012b. *Portrait of Families and Living Arrangements in Canada (from the 2011 Census of Canada short form).* Catalogue no. 98-312-X2011001.

Retrieved from http://www12.statcan.gc.ca/census-recensement/2011/as-sa/98-312-x/98-312-x2011001-eng.pdf

Statistics Canada. 2012c. CANSIM 102-4507. *Live births, by age and marital status of mother*, Canada. Retrieved from http://www5.statcan.gc.ca/cansim/a47

Statistics Canada. 2012d. *Living arrangements of young adults aged 20 to 29: families, households and marital status, 2011 Census of Population. The Census in Brief, no 3.* Catalogue no. 98-312-X2011003.

Statistics Canada. 2012c. *Low Income in Canada—A Multi-line and Multi-index Perspective.* Catalogue no. 75F0002M—No. 001. Retrieved from http://www.statcan.gc.ca/pub/75f0002m/75f0002m2012001-eng.pdf

Statistics Canada. 2012d. *Portrait of Families and Living Arrangements in Canada (from the 2011 Census of Canada Short Form).* Catalogue no. 98-312-X2011001. Retrieved from http://www12.statcan.gc.ca/census-recensement/2011/as-sa/98-312-x/98-312-x2011001-eng.pdf

Statistics Canada. 2012g. *2012 Canadian Survey on Disability: Learning Disabilities among Canadians aged 15 years and Older, 2012.* Catalogue no. 89-654-X. Retrieved on February 22, 2017, from http://www.statcan.gc.ca/pub/89-654-x/89-654-x2014003-eng.htm

Statistics Canada. 2012h. Divorce cases in civil court, 2010/2011. Catalogue no. 85-002. Retrieved from http://www.statcan.gc.ca/pub/85-002-x/2012001/article/11634-eng.htm

Statistics Canada. 2013a. *Aboriginal Peoples in Canada: First Nations People, Métis and Inuit National Household Survey, 2011.* Catalogue no. 99-011-X2011001. Ottawa: Statistics Canada. Retrieved from http://www12.statcan.gc.ca/nhs-enm/2011/as-sa/99-011-x/99-011-x2011001-eng.pdf

Statistics Canada. 2013a. *Births by marital status and age, CANSIM table 102-4507.* Ottawa: Statistics Canada. Retrieved from http://www5.statcan.gc.ca/cansim/a26?lang=eng&id=1024507

Statistics Canada. 2013b. *Disability in Canada: Initial Findings from the Canadian Survey on Disability: Factsheet.* (Catalogue no. 89-654-X—No. 002). Retrieved from http://www.statcan.gc.ca/pub/89-654-x/89-654-x2013002-eng.pdf

Statistics Canada. 2013d. Living apart together. *The Daily*, March 5, 2013.

Statistics Canada. 2013g. *National Household Survey 2011. Immigration and Ethnocultural Diversity in*

Canada. Retrieved from http://www12.statcan.gc.ca/nhs-enm/2011/as-sa/99-010-x/99-010-x2011001-eng.cfm#a4

Statistics Canada. 2014. *Canadian income survey, 2012.* Retrieved from http://www.statcan.gc.ca/daily-quotidien/141210/dq141210a-eng.htm

Statistics Canada. 2015. *Families, Living Arrangements and Unpaid Work.* Catalogue no. 89-503-x. Retrieved from http://www.statcan.gc.ca/pub/89-503-x/2010001/article/11546-eng.htm#a12

Statistics Canada. 2015. *Lone-parent families.* Retrieved from http://www.statcan.gc.ca/pub/75-006-x/2015001/article/14202/parent-eng.htm

Statistics Canada. 2015. *Parenting and child support after separation or divorce.* Catalogue no. 89-652. Retrieved from http://www.statcan.gc.ca/pub/89-652-x/89-652-x2014001-eng.htm

Statistics Canada. 2015a. *Communications Monitoring Report 2015: Canada's Communications System: An Overview for Citizens, Consumers, and Creators.* Ottawa: Author. Retrieved from http://www.crtc.gc.ca/eng/publications/reports/policymonitoring/2015/cmr2.htm

Statistics Canada. 2015a, November 23. Employment insurance coverage survey, 2014. *The Daily.* Ottawa, ON: Statistics Canada. Retrieved from http://www.statcan.gc.ca/daily-quotidien/151123/dq151123b-eng.pdf

Statistics Canada. 2015a. Same-sex couples and sexual orientation . . . by the numbers. *The Daily.* Retrieved from http://www.statcan.gc.ca/eng/dai/smr08/2015/smr08_203_2015

Statistics Canada. 2015b. Employment Insurance Coverage Survey, 2014. *The Daily,* November 23. Ottawa: Statistics Canada. Retrieved from http://www.statcan.gc.ca/daily-quotidien/151123/dq151123b-eng.pdf

Statistics Canada. 2015b. *Living arrangements of young adults aged 20 to 29.* Retrieved from http://www12.statcan.gc.ca/census-recensement/2011/as-sa/98-312-x/98-312-x2011003_3-eng.cfm

Statistics Canada. 2015b. *Survival to Success: Transforming Immigrant Outcomes—Report from the Panel on Employment Challenges of New Canadians.* Catalogue no. Em16-7/2015E-PDF. Retrieved from https://www.canada.ca/en/employment-social-development/programs/foreign-credential-recognition/consultations.html?=undefined&wbdisable=true

Statistics Canada. 2016. *Family Violence in Canada: A Statistical Profile, 2014.* Ottawa: Author. Retrieved from http://www.statcan.gc.ca/pub/85-002-x/2016001/article/14303-eng.pdf

Statistics Canada. 2016. *High-income trends among Canadian taxfilers, 2014.* Retrieved from http://www.statcan.gc.ca/daily-quotidien/161121/dq161121d-eng.htm

Statistics Canada. 2016. *Satisfaction with work-life balance: Fact sheet.* Catalogue no. 89-652-X2016003. Ottawa, ON: Ministry of Industry. Retrieved from http://www.statcan.gc.ca/pub/89-652-x/89-652-x2016003-eng.pdf

Statistics Canada. 2016a. *Family Violence in Canada: A Statistical Profile.* Catalogue number no. 85-002-X. Retrieved from http://www.statcan.gc.ca/daily-quotidien/160121/dq160121b-eng.htm

Statistics Canada. 2016b. *Unpaid work.* Retrieved from http://www12.statcan.gc.ca/census-recensement/2011/consultation/92-140/A16-eng.cfm

Statistics Canada. 2017a, May 3. Age and sex, and type of dwelling data: Key results from the 2016 Census. *The Daily.* Retrieved from http://www.statcan.gc.ca/daily-quotidien/170503/dq170503a-eng.pdf

Statistics Canada. 2017b. *Employment by Industry and Sex.* CANSIM Table 282-0008. Retrieved from http://www.statcan.gc.ca/tables-tableaux/sum-som/l01/cst01/labor10a-eng.htm

Stein, Gabriela L., Alexandra M. Cupito, Julia L. Mendez, Juan Prandoni, Nadia Huq, & Diana Westerberg. 2014. Familism through a developmental lens. *Journal of Latina/o Psychology* 2(4).

Stenberg, U., C.M. Ruland, & C. Miaskowski. 2010. Review of the literature on the effects of caring for a patient with cancer. *Psycho-Oncology* 19(10): 1013–1025.

Stephen, J., K. Collie, D. McLeod, A. Rojubally, K. Fergus, M. Speca, . . . , & K. Burrus. 2014. Talking with text: Communication in therapist-led, live chat cancer support groups. *Social Science & Medicine* 104: 178–186.

Stephens, Linda S. 1996. Will Johnny see Daddy this week? An empirical test of three theoretical perspectives of post-divorce contact. *Journal of Family Issues* 12(4).

Stith, S.M., T. Liu, L.C. Davies, E.L. Boykin, M.C. Alder, J.M. Harris, . . . , & J.E.M.E.G. Dees. 2009. Risk factors in child maltreatment: A meta-analytic review of the literature. *Aggression and Violent Behavior* 14(1): 13–29.

Stone, J., A. Berrington, & J. Falkingham. 2014. Gender, turning points, and boomerangs: Returning home in young adulthood in Great Britain. *Demography* 51(1): 257–276.

Story, Nathan T., Cynthia A. Berg, Timothy W. Smith, Ryan Beveridge, Nancy J. M. Henry, & Gale Pearce. 2007. Age, marital satisfaction, and optimism as predictors of positive sentiment override in middle-aged and older married couples. *Psychology and Aging* 22: 719–727.

Straus, Murray A. 1996. *Identifying Offenders in Criminal Justice Research on Domestic Assault.* Beverley Hills, CA: Sage Publications.

Strohschein, Lisa. 2005. Parental divorce and child mental health trajectories. *Journal of Marriage and Family* 67(5): 1286–1300.

Strokoff, Johanna, Jesse Owen, & Frank D. Fincham. 2015. Diverse reactions to hooking up among U.S. university students. *Archives of Sexual Behavior* 44(4): 935–943.

Strong-Boag, Veronica. 2000. Long time coming: The century of the Canadian child? *Journal of Canadian Studies* 35(1): 124–261.

Su, C., & M. Hynie. 2011. Effects of life stress, social support, and cultural norms on parenting styles among mainland Chinese, European Canadian, and Chinese Canadian immigrant mothers. *Journal of Cross-Cultural Psychology* 42(6): 944–962.

Sudarkasa, N. 2007. African American female-headed households: Some neglected dimensions, pp. 172–183. In H.P. McAdoo (Ed.), *Black Families.* Thousand Oaks, CA: Sage Publications.

Sugiman, P., & H.K. Nishio. 1983. Socialization and cultural duality among aging Japanese Canadians. *Canadian Ethnic Studies* 15(3): 17–35.

Sullivan, T. Richard (Ed.). 2012. *Queer Families, Common Agendas: Gay People, Lesbians and Family Values.* New York: Routledge.

Sumter, Sindy, Patti Valkenburg, & Jochen Peter. 2013. Perceptions of love across the lifespan: Differences in passion, intimacy, and commitment. *International Journal of Behavioral Development* 37(5): 417–427.

Sumter, Sindy R., Laura Vandenbosch, & Loes Ligtenberg. 2017. Love me Tinder: Untangling emerging adults' motivations for using the dating application Tinder. *Telematics and Informatics* 34(1): 67–78.

Sunahara, A.G. 1981. *The Politics of Racism: The Uprooting of Japanese Canadians during the Second World War.* Toronto: James Lorimer & Company.

Sundie, J. M. 2003. Conspicuous consumption as a mating strategy. *ProQuest Information & Learning* 64(3): 123–139.

Sutherns, Rebecca, & Ivy Lynn Bourgeault. 2008. Accessing maternity care in rural Canada: There's more to the story than distance to the doctor. *Health Care for Women International* 29: 863–883.

Swahn, Monica, Thomas Simon, Ileana Arias, & Robert Bossarte. 2008. Measuring sex differences in violence, victimization and perpetration. *Journal of Interpersonal Violence* 23.8: 1120–1138.

Swan, S.C., & D.L. Snow. 2002. A typology of women's use of violence in intimate relationships. *Violence Against Women* 8(3): 286–319.

Sydie, Rosalind A. 1987. *Natural Women, Cultured Men: A Feminist Perspective on Sociological Theory.* Toronto: Methuen.

Tach, L., & K. Edin. 2013. The compositional and institutional sources of union dissolution for married and unmarried parents in the United States. *Demography* 50(5): 1789–1818. doi:10.1007/s13524-013-0203-7

Tait, S.E., & D. Jeske. 2015. Hello stranger! Trust and self-disclosure effects on online information sharing. *International Journal of Cyber Behaviour, Psychology and Learning* 5(1): 42–55.

Taleporos, George, & Marita P. McCabe. 2001. The impact of physical disability on body esteem. *Sexuality and Disability* 19(4): 293–308.

Taleporos, George, & Marita P. McCabe. 2003. Relationships, sexuality and adjustment among people with physical disability. *Sexual and Relationship Therapy* 18(1): 25–43.

Talmon, Yonina. 1964. Mate selection in collective settlements. *American Sociological Review* 29: 491–508.

Tan, Orkun, & Bruce R. Carr. 2012. The impact of bariatric surgery on obesity-related infertility and in vitro fertilization outcomes. *Seminars in Reproductive Medicine* 30: 517–527.

Tannen, Deborah. 1993. *Gender and Conversational Interaction.* New York: Oxford University Press.

Tarroux, B. 2012. Are equalization payments making Canadians better off? A two-dimensional dominance answer. *The Journal of Economic Inequality* 10(1): 19–44.

Tastsoglou, E., & A. Dobrowolsky (Eds). 2006. *Women, Migration, and Citizenship: Making Local, National, and Transnational Connections.* Farnham, Surrey, United Kingdom: Ashgate Publishers.

Tayler, Lyn, Gordon Parker, & Kay Roy. 1995. Parental divorce and its effects on the quality of intimate relationships in adulthood. *Journal of Divorce and Remarriage* 24(3–4).

Taylor, C.A., L. Hamvas, & R. Paris. 2011. Perceived instrumentality and normativeness of corporal punishment use among Black mothers. *Family Relations* 60(1): 60–72.

Taylor, C.A., J.A. Manganello, S.J. Lee, & J.C. Rice. 2010. Mothers' spanking of 3-year-old children and subsequent risk of children's aggressive behavior. *Pediatrics* 125(5): e1057–e1065.

Taylor-Butts, A. 2014. *Family Violence against Seniors*. Ottawa: Statistics Canada. Retrieved from http://www.statcan.gc.ca/pub/85-002-x/2014001/article/14114/section04-eng.htm

Teotonio, I. 2017. These kids are genetic siblings and each was born to a different mother. *The Toronto Star*, May 13. Retrieved from https://www.thestar.com/life/2017/05/13/these-kids-are-genetic-siblings-and-each-was-born-to-a-different-mother.html

Terrazas-Carrillo, E.C., & P.T. McWhirter. 2015. Employment status and intimate partner violence among Mexican women. *Journal of Interpersonal Violence* 30(7): 1128–1152.

Terriquez, V., & H. Kwon. 2015. Intergenerational family relations, civic organizations, and the political socialization of second-generation immigrant youth. *Journal of Ethnic and Migration Studies* 41(3): 425–447.

Thies, K., & Travers, J. 2006. *Handbook of human development for health care professionals*. Sudbury, MA: Jones & Bartlett.

Thomas, Madhavappallil, & Jong Baek Choi. 2006. Acculturative stress and social support among Korean and Indian immigrant adolescents in the United States. *Journal of Sociology and Social Welfare* 33: 123–143.

Thomas, T.N. 1995. Acculturative stress in the adjustment of immigrant families. *Journal of Social Distress and the Homeless* 4(2): 131–142.

Thomson, Elizabeth, Maria Winkler-Dworak, & Sheela Kennedy. 2013. The standard family life course: An assessment of variability in life course pathways. In Ann Evans & Janeen Baxter (Eds.), *Negotiating the Life Course: Stability and Change in Life Pathways*. Dordrecht: Springer.

Thomson, Elizabeth Jean, & Min Li. 1992. *Family Structure and Children's Kin*. Madison: University of Wisconsin Center for Demography and Ecology.

Thornton, A., & L. Young-DeMarco. 2001. Four decades of trends in attitudes toward family issues in the United States. *Journal of Marriage and the Family* 63(4): 1009–1037.

Tichenor, V.J. 1999. Status and income as gendered resources: The case of marital power. *Journal of Marriage and the Family* 61(3): 638–650.

Toma, C., J. Hancock, & N. Ellison. 2008. Separating fact from fiction: An examination of deceptive self-presentation in online dating profiles. *Personality and Social Psychology Bulletin* 34(8): 1023–1036.

Toma, Catalina L., & Jeffrey T. Hancock. 2012. What lies beneath: The linguistic traces of deception in online dating profiles. *Journal of Communication* 62(1): 78–97.

Tomasi, P. 2015. Parents with disabilities: These moms live in fear of losing their kids. *Huffington Post Canada*. Retrieved from http://www.huffingtonpost.ca/2015/05/10/parents-withdisabilities_n_7251484.html

Tornello, Samantha, Stacy M. Kruczkowski, & Charlotte J. Patterson. 2015. Division of labor and relationship quality among male same-sex couples who became fathers via surrogacy. *Journal of GLBT Family Studies* 11(4): 375–394.

Torppa, Cynthia Burggraf. 2002. *Gender Issues: Communication Differences in Interpersonal Relationships fact sheet*. Ohio State University Extension. Retrieved from http://ohioline.osu.edu/flm02/FS04.html. Reprinted with permission.

Treas, J. 1993. Money in the bank: Transaction costs and the economic organization of marriage. *American Sociological Review* 58(5): 723–734.

Treas, J., & E.D. Widmer. 2000. Whose money? Financial management in marriage: A multi-level analysis for 23 countries, pp. 1–14. In J. Weesie & W. Raub (Eds), *The Management of Durable Relations: Theoretical and Empirical Models for Households and Organizations*. Amsterdam: Thela Thesis.

Tremblay, D.-G. 2014. Quebec's policies for work–family balance: A model for Canada?, pp. 541–554. In B. Fox (Ed.), *Family Patterns: Gender Relations* (4th ed.). Toronto: Oxford University Press.

Trommsdorff, Gisela, Uichol Kim, & Bernhard Nauck. 2005. Factors influencing value of children and intergenerational relations in times of social change: Analyses from psychological and sociocultural perspectives: Introduction to the special issue. *Applied Psychology* 54(3): 313–316.

Trumbach, Randolph, 2013. *The Rise of the Egalitarian Family: Aristocratic Kinship and Domestic Relations in Eighteenth-Century England*. St. Louis: Elsevier.

Truth and Reconciliation Commission of Canada. 2015. *Honouring the Truth, Reconciling for the Future: Summary of the Final Report of the Truth and Reconciliation Commission of Canada*. Retrieved from http://nctr.ca/assets/reports/Final%20Reports/Executive_Summary_English_Web.pdf

Tseng, C.F. 2016. My love, how I wish you were by my side: Maintaining intercontinental long-distance relationships in Taiwan. *Contemporary Family Therapy* 38: 328–338.

Tsimicalis, A., B. Stevens, W.J. Ungar, M. Greenberg, P. McKeever, M. Agha, . . . , & R. Moineddin. 2012. Determining the costs of families' support networks following a child's cancer diagnosis. *Cancer Nursing 36*(2): 8–19.

Tumin, Dimitry. 2014. Marriage trends among Americans with childhood-onset disabilities, 1997–2003. *Disability Health Journal 9*: 713–718.

Turcotte, M. 2007. *Staying at Home Longer to Become Homeowners?* Ottawa: Statistics Canada. Retrieved http://www.statcan.gc.ca/pub/11-008-x/2007006/article/10378-eng.htm

Turcotte, M. 2013. *Insights into Canadian Families: Living Apart Together.* Catalogue no. 75-006-X. Ottawa: Ministry of Industry. Retrieved from http://www.statcan.gc.ca/pub/75-006-x/2013001/article/11771-eng.pdf

Turcotte, M. 2014. Canadians with unmet home care needs. *Insights on Canadian Society.* Catalogue no. 75-006-X. Ottawa, ON: Ministry of Industry. Retrieved from http://www.statcan.gc.ca/pub/75-006-x/2014001/article/14042-eng.pdf

Turcotte, Martin, & Grant Schellenberg. 2006. *A Portrait of Seniors in Canada.* Ottawa: Statistics Canada. Catalogue no. 89-519-XIE. Retrieved from http://www.statcan.gc.ca/pub/89-519-x/89-519-x2006001-eng.htm

Turner, Lynn H., & Richard West. 2014. The challenge of defining family. *The SAGE Handbook of Family Communication 10.*

Twenge, Jean M., W. Keith Campbell, & Craig A. Foster. 2003. Parenthood and marital satisfaction: A meta-analytic review. *Journal of Marriage and the Family 65*: 574–583.

Tyyska, V., & S. Colavecchia. 2001. *Study on Parenting Issues of Newcomer Families in Ontario: Report on Individual Interviews in Toronto.* Report for the Centre for Research and Education in Human Services (CREHS) and Joint Centre of Excellence for Research on Immigration and Settlement (CERIS). Retrieved from http://atwork.settlement.org/downloads/Parenting_Issues_Toronto_Interviews.pdf

Tyyskä, V., F.M. Dinshaw, C. Redmond, & F. Gomes. 2012. Where we have come and are now trapped: Views of victims and service providers on abuse of older adults in Tamil and Punjabi families. *Canadian Ethnic Studies 44*(3): 59–77.

Tyyskä, Vappu. 2011. Immigrant and racialized families, pp. 86–122. In Nancy Mandell & Ann Duffy (Eds.), *Canadian Families: Diversity, Conflict and Change* (4th ed.). Toronto: Nelson.

Tzeng, Jessie, & Robert Mare. 1995, December. Labor market and socioeconomic effects on marital stability. *Social Science Research 24.*

UNICEF. 2004. You and me together, ability forever. Retrieved from https://www.unicef.org/media/files/PreliminaryfindingsAfghanistandisabilityreport.pdf

UNICEF Canada. 2009. *Aboriginal Children's Health: Leaving No Child Behind: Canadian Supplement to the State of the World's Children.* Retrieved from http://www.unicef.ca/sites/default/files/imce_uploads/DISCOVER/OUR%20WORK/ADVOCACY/DOMESTIC/POLICY%20ADVOCACY/DOCS/Leaving%20no%20child%20behind%2009.pdf

United Nations. 2016, January 15. Protection of the family: Contribution of the family to the realization of the right to an adequate standard of living for its members, particularly through its role in poverty eradication and achieving sustainable development. UN-A-HRC-31-37, 24. Retrieved from https://documents-dds-ny.un.org/doc/UNDOC/GEN/G16/014/95/PDF/G1601495.pdf

United Nations Demographic Yearbook. 2003. *Table 25: Divorces and Crude Divorce Rate by Urban/Rural Residence.* Retrieved January 12, 2006, from http://unstats.un.org/unsd/demographic/products/dyb/dyb2.htm

United Nations, Department of Economic and Social Affairs, Population Division. 2015. *Trends in contraceptive use worldwide, 2015.* ST/ESA/SER.A/349. New York: Author.

University of Ottawa. 2015. *Sudden Infant Death Syndrome in Canada.* School of Epidemiology, Public Health and Preventive Medicine. Retrieved from http://www.med.uottawa.ca/sim/data/SIDS_e.htm

Uppal, S. 2015. Employment patterns of families with children. *Insights on Canadian Society.* Catalogue no. 75-006-X. Ottawa, ON: Statistics Canada. Retrieved from http://www.statcan.gc.ca/pub/75-006-x/2015001/article/14202-eng.pdf

Usher, P. 2016. Why women are choosing virtual boyfriends over real ones. *VOGUE,* March 5. Retrieved from http://www.vogue.com/article/virtual-romance-apps

Usita, P.M., S.S. Hall, & J.C. Davis. 2004. Role of ambiguity in family caregiving. *Journal of Applied Gerontology, 23*: 20–39.

Uskul, Ayse, Richard Lalonde, & Lynda Cheng. 2007. Dating among Chinese and European Canadians: The roles of culture, gender, and mainstream cultural identity. *Journal of Social and Personal Relationships 24*(6): 891.

Vall, B., J. Seikkula, A. Laitila, & J. Holma. 2016. Dominance and dialogue in couple therapy for psychological intimate partner violence. *Contemporary Family Therapy* 38: 223–232.

Vandecasteele, Leen. 2011. Life course risks or cumulative disadvantage? The structuring effect of social stratification determinants and life course events on poverty transitions in Europe. *European Sociological Review* 27(2): 246–263.

Van de Kaa, D. J. 1987. Europe's second demographic transition. *Population Bulletin* 42(1): 1–59.

Vandello, J.A., & D. Cohen. 2003. Male honor and female fidelity: Implicit cultural scripts that perpetuate domestic violence. *Journal of Personality and Social Psychology* 84(5): 997.

van Eeden-Moorefield, B., K. Pasley, E.M. Dolan, & M. Engel. 2007. From divorce to remarriage: Financial management and security among remarried women. *Journal of Divorce and Remarriage* 47(3–4): 21–42.

Vanier Institute of the Family. 1994. *Profiling Canada's Families*. Ottawa: Vanier Institute of the Family.

Vanier Institute of the Family. 2000. *Family Facts*. Retrieved May 12, 2005, from http://www.vifamily.ca/library/facts/facts.html

Vanier Institute of the Family. 2002. *Profiling Canada's Families II*. Ottawa: Vanier Institute of the Family.

Vanier Institute of the Family. 2004. *Profiling Canada's Families III*. Ottawa: Vanier Institute of the Family.

Vanier Institute of the Family. 2006. *Families Count: Profiling Canada's Families*. Ottawa: Vanier Institute of the Family.

Vanier Institute of the Family. 2010. *Families Count: Profiling Canada's Families IV*. Retrieved from http://vanierinstitute.ca/resources/families-count

Vanier Institute of the Family. 2010. *Fascinating Families 30*. Retrieved from http://vanierinstitute.ca/resources/fascinating-families/

Vanier Institute of the Family. 2010a. *Families Count—Profiling Canada's Families IV*. Ottawa: Vanier Institute of the Family.

Vanier Institute of the Family. 2010b. *Forming Unis—Again*. http://www.vanierinstitute.ca/modules/news/newsitem.php?ItemId=152#.UR1MY_LCTTo

Vanier Institute of the Family. 2013a. *Definition of Family*. http://www.vanierinstitute.ca/definition_of_family#.UdyJfFT4Dcc

Vanier Institute of the Family. 2016. *Infographic: Fifty years of family in Canada*. Retrieved from http://vanierinstitute.ca/infographics

Van Kirk, Sylvia. 1980. *Many Tender Ties: Women in Fur-Trade Society, 1670–1870*. Winnipeg: Watson & Dwyer.

Van Kirk, Sylvia. 1992. The custom of the country: An examination of fur trade marriage practices, pp. 67–92. In Bettina Bradbury (Ed.), *Canadian Family History: Selected Readings*. Toronto: Copp Clark Pitman.

Van Kirk, Sylvia. 2002. From marrying-in to marrying-out: Changing patterns of Aboriginal/non-Aboriginal marriage in colonial Canada. *Frontiers: A Journal of Women Studies* 23(3): 1–11.

Varela, Enrique R., Juan Jose Sanchez-Sosa, Angelica Riveros, Eric M. Vernberg, Montserrat Mitchell, & Joanna Mashunkashey. 2004. Parenting style of Mexican, Mexican American, and Caucasian-non-Hispanic families: Social context and cultural influences. *Journal of Family Psychology* 18: 651–57.

Vergun, Pamela Bea, Sanford M. Dornbusch, & Laurence Steinberg. 1996. *Come All of You Turn to and Help One Another: Authoritative Parenting, Community Orientation, and Deviance Among High School Students*. American Sociological Association paper.

Vespa, J., J.M. Lewis, & R.M. Kreider. 2013. *America's Families and Living Arrangements: 2012*. (P20-570). Washington, DC: U.S. Census Bureau. Retrieved from https://www.census.gov/prod/2013pubs/p20-570.pdf

Vezina, M. 2012. *2011 General Social Survey: Overview of Families in Canada—Being a Parent in a Stepfamily: A Profile*. Catalogue no. 89-650-X—No. 002. Ottawa: Social and Aboriginal Statistics Division. Retrieved from http://www.statcan.gc.ca/pub/89-650-x/89-650-x2012002-eng.htm#a13

Vezina, M., & M. Turcotte. 2010. *Helping a Parent Who Lives Far from Home: The Repercussions*. Ottawa: Statistics Canada.

Vilhauer, V. 2015. This is why ghosting hurts so much . . . and why it says nothing about your worthiness for love. *Psychology Today*, November 27. Retrieved from https://www.psychologytoday.com/blog/living-forward/201511/is-why-ghosting-hurts-so-much

Vincke, Eveline. 2016. The young male cigarette and alcohol syndrome: Smoking and drinking as a short-term mating strategy. *Evolutionary Psychology* 14(1).

Vittes, K.A., & S.B. Sorenson. 2008. Restraining orders among victims of intimate partner homicide. *Journal of the International Society for Child and Adolescent Injury Prevention* 14(3): 191–195.

Vogler, C. 2005. Cohabiting couples: Rethinking money in the household at the beginning of the twenty-first century. *The Sociological Review* 53(1): 1–29.

Vogler, C., M. Brockmann, & R.D. Wiggins. 2006. Intimate relationships and changing patterns of money management at the beginning of the twenty-first century. *British Journal of Sociology* 57(3): 455–482. doi:10.1111/j.1468-4446. 2006.00120

Vogler, C., C. Lyonette, & R.D. Wiggins. 2008. Money, power and spending decisions in intimate relationships. *The Sociological Review* 56(1): 117–143.

Vogler, C., & J. Pahl. 1994. Money, power and inequality within marriage. *The Sociological Review* 42(2): 263–288.

Wada, M., W.B. Mortenson, & L.H. Clarke. 2016. Older adults' online dating profiles and successful aging. *Canadian Journal on Aging* 35(4): 479–490.

Wadsby, Marie, & Gunilla Sydsjoe. 2001, December. *Frangraviditet till foeraeldraskap: En studie av parrelationen (From pregnancy to parenthood: A study of couples' relationships). Nordisk Psykologi* 53(4): 275–288.

Wagner, F., J. Basran, & V.D. Bello-Haas. 2012. A review of monitoring technology for use with older adults. *Journal of Geriatric Physical Therapy* 35(1): 28–34.

Wagner, K.D., A. Ritt-Olson, C.P. Chou, P. Pokhrel, L. Duan, L. Baezconde-Garbanati, & J.B. Unger. 2010. Associations between family structure, family functioning, and substance use among Hispanic/Latino adolescents. *Psychology of Addictive Behaviors* 24(1): 98.

Wagstaff, Danielle L., Danielle Sulikowski, & Darren Burke. 2015. Sex-differences in preference for looking at the face or body in short-term and long-term mating contexts. *Evolution, Mind and Behaviour* 13: 1–17.

Wainwright, Jennifer L., Stephen T. Russell, & Charlotte J. Patterson. 2004. Psychosocial adjustment, school outcomes, and romantic relationships of adolescents with same-sex parents. *Child Development* 75(6): 1886–1898.

Wall, G. 2010. Mothers' experiences with intensive parenting and brain development discourse. *Women's Studies International Forum* 33(3): 253–263.

Wallerstein, J., & S. Blakelee. 1990. *Second Chances: Men, Women, and Children a Decade after Divorce.* New York: Ticknor & Fields.

Walsh, Froma. 2002. A family resilience framework: Innovative practice applications. *Family Relations* 51(2): 130–137.

Walsh, Froma. 2015. *Strengthening Family Resilience.* New York: Guilford Press.

Walters, Marjorie Gans, & Steven Friedlander. 2016. When a child rejects a parent: Working with the intractable resist/refuse dynamic. *Family Court Review* 54(3): 424–445.

Walzer, S. 1998. *Thinking about the Baby: Gender and Transitions into Parenthood.* Philadelphia, PA: Temple University Press.

Wang, C.C., & Y.T. Chang. 2010. Cyber relationship motives: Scale development and validation. *Social Behaviour and Personality: An International Journal* 38(3): 289.

Wang, Fei-Ling. 2016. *Institutions and Institutional Change in China: Premodernity and Modernization.* New York: Springer.

Wang, M. 2007. Profiling retirees in the retirement transition and adjustment process: Examining the longitudinal change patterns of retirees' psychological well-being. *Journal of Applied Psychology* 92(2): 455.

Ward, C., & Terence J. 2004. Relation of shyness with aspects of online relationship involvement. *Journal of Social and Personal relationships,* 21(5): 611–623.

Waren, W., & H. Pals. 2013. Comparing characteristics of voluntarily childless men and women. *Journal of Population Research* 30(2): 151–170.

Warrener, Corinne, Julie M. Koivunen, & Judy L. Postmus. 2013. Economic self-sufficiency among divorced women: Impact of depression, abuse, and efficacy. *Journal of Divorce and Remarriage* 54(2): 163–175.

Wartime Day Nurseries Are Boon to Mothers Working in Industry. 1944, January 28. *Montreal Gazette.* Retrieved from https://news.google.com/newspapers?id=G78tAAAAIBAJ&sjid=opgFAAAAIBAJ&dq=wartime-day-nurseries+municipal&pg=6297,4028411&hl=en

Waters, Johanna L. 2002. Flexible families? Astronaut households and the experiences of lone mothers in Vancouver, British Columbia. *Social & Cultural Geography* 3(2): 117–133.

Watkins, N.K., & M. Waldron. 2017. Timing of remarriage among divorced and widowed parents. *Journal of Divorce & Remarriage* 58(4): 244–262.

Watson, C. 2016. Womb rentals and baby-selling: Does surrogacy undermine the human dignity and rights of the surrogate mother and child? *The New Bioethics: A Multidisciplinary Journal of Biotechnology and the Body* 22(3): 212–228.

Weber, M., O. Quiring, & G. Daschmann. 2012. Peers, parents and pornography: Exploring adolescents' exposure to sexually explicit material and its developmental correlates. *Sexuality and Culture,* 16: 408–427.

Webster, Pamela S., & Regula A. Herzog. 1995 January. Effects of parental divorce and memories of family problems on relationships between adult children and their parents. *Journal of Gerontology, Series B: Psychological Sciences and Social Sciences* 50B.

Wei, R., & V.H. Lo. 2006. Staying connected while on the move: Cell phone use and social connectedness. *New Media & Society* 8(1): 53–72.

Weiner, Jennifer, Lisa Harlow, Jerome Adams, & L. Grebstein. 1995. Psychological adjustment of college students from families of divorce. *Journal of Divorce and Remarriage* 23(3–4): 75–95.

Weinfeld, Morton. 2001. *Like Everyone Else . . . but Different: The Paradoxical Success of Canadian Jews.* Toronto: McClelland & Stewart.

Weiss, Jonathan A., Jennifer MacMullin, Randall Waechter, & Christine Wekerle. 2011. Child maltreatment, adolescent attachment style, and dating violence: Consideration in youths with borderline-to-mild intellectual disability. *International Journal of Mental Health Addiction* 9: 555–576.

Weiss, Robert S. 1996. Parenting from separate households, pp. 215–230. In David Popenoe, Jean Bethke Elshtain, & David Blankenhorn (Eds.), *Promises to Keep: Decline and Renewal of Marriage in America.* Lanham, MD: Rowman & Littlefield Publishers, Inc.

Weisshaar, K. 2014. Earnings equality and relationship stability for same-sex and heterosexual couples. *Social Forces* 93(1): 93–123.

Weisskirch, R.S. 2009. Parenting by cell phone: Parental monitoring of adolescents and family relations. *Journal of Youth and Adolescence* 38(8): 1123.

Weitzman, Lenore. 1985. *The Divorce Revolution: The Unexpected Social and Economic Effects for Women and Children in America.* New York: Free Press.

Welsh, S. 1999. Gender and sexual harassment. *Annual Review of Sociology* 25: 169–190.

West, C., & D. Zimmerman. 1987. Doing gender. *Gender & Society* 1: 125–151.

West, D., & D. Heath. 2011. Theoretical pathways to the future: Globalization, ICT and social work theory and practice. *Journal of Social Work* 11(2): 209–221.

White, L.K., & A. Booth. 1985. The quality and stability of remarriages: The role of stepchildren. *American Sociological Review* 50(5): 689–698.

White, Lynn. 1990. Determinants of divorce: A review of research in the eighties. *Journal of Marriage and the Family* 52(4): 904–912.

Whitehead, Barbara Dafoe. 1996. The decline of marriage as the social basis of childbearing, pp. 3–14. In David Popenoe, Jean Bethke Elshtain, & David Blankenhorn (Eds.), *Promises to Keep: Decline and Renewal of Marriage in America.* Lanham, MD: Rowman & Littlefield Publishers, Inc.

Whiting, J.B., M. Oka, & S.T. Fife. 2012. Appraisal distortions and intimate partner violence: Gender, power, and interaction. *Journal of Marital and Family Therapy* 38(s1): 133–149.

Whitty, M.T. 2005. The realness of cybercheating: Men's and women's representations of unfaithful Internet relations. *Social Science Computer Review* 23(1): 57–67.

Wickrama, K.A.S., C.W. O'Neal, & F.O. Lorenz. 2013. Marital functioning from middle to later years: A life course–stress process framework. *Journal of Family Theory & Review* 5: 15–34.

Wiegerink, D.J., M.E. Roebroeck, D.S., Van, H.J., Stam, & P. Cohen-Kettenis 2010. Importance of peers and dating in the development of romantic relationships and sexual activity of young adults with cerebral palsy. *Developmental Medicine & Child Neurology* 52(6), 576–582.

Wiegers, Wanda A., & Dorothy E. Chunn. 2017. Choice and sole motherhood in Canada, 1965–2010: An interview study. *Women's Studies International Forum* 61(March/April): 38–47.

Wienke, Chris, & Gretchen J. Hill. 2009. Does the "marriage benefit" extend to partners in gay and lesbian relationships? *Journal of Family Issues* 30(2): 259–289.

Wilkinson, Richard G. 1994. From material scarcity to social disadvantage. Daedalus: *Journal of the American Academy of Arts and Sciences* 123(4): 61–77.

Williams, A.M., J.A. Eby, V.A. Crooks, K. Stajduhar, M. Giesbrecht, & M. Vuksan. 2011. Canada's compassionate care benefit: Is it an adequate public health response to addressing the issue of caregiver burden in end-of-life care? *BMC Public Health* 11: 335.

Williams, C. 2008. Work–life balance of shift workers. *Perspectives on Labour and Income.* Catalogue no. 75-001-X. Ottawa, ON: Statistics Canada. Retrieved from http://www.statcan.gc.ca/pub/75-001-x/2008108/pdf/10677-eng.pdf

Williams, C. 2010. *Women in Canada: A Gender-Based Statistical Report Economic Well-being.* Catalogue no. 89-503-X. Ottawa: Statistics Canada, Social and Aboriginal Statistics Division. Retrieved from http://www.statcan.gc.ca/pub/89-503-x/2010001/article/11388-eng.pdf

Williams, L.A., L.S. Giddings, G. Bellamy, & M. Gott. 2016. Because it's the wife who has to look after the man: A descriptive qualitative study of older women and the intersection of gender and the provision of family caregiving at the end of life. *Palliative Medicine* 31(3): 223–230.

Williams, S., & L. Williams. 2005. Space invaders: The negotiation of teenage boundaries through the mobile phone. *The Sociological Review* 53(2): 314–331.

Williamson, Deanna L., & Fiona Salkie. 2005. Welfare reforms in Canada: Implications for the well-being of pre-school children in poverty. *Journal of Children & Poverty* 11(1): 55–76.

Willms, J. Douglas (Ed.). 2002. *Vulnerable Children: Findings from Canada's Longitudinal Survey of Children and Youth.* Edmonton: University of Alberta Press.

Willoughby, B.J., A.M. Farero, & D.M. Busby. 2014. Exploring the effects of sexual desire discrepancy among married couples. *Archives of Sexual Behavior 43*: 551.

Wills, C. 2001. Women, domesticity and the family: Recent feminist work in Irish cultural studies. *Cultural Studies 15*: 33–57.

Wilson, B. 2009. Estimating the cohabitating population. *Population Trends 136*: 21–27.

Wilson, G. 1987. *Money in the Family: Financial Organisation and Women's Responsibility.* Aldershot, UK: Avebury

Wilson, W.J. 1987. *The Truly Disadvantaged: The Inner City, the Underclass, and Public Policy.* Chicago, IL: University of Chicago Press.

Winch, Robert F. 1962. *The Modern Family.* New York: Holt.

Wolfinger, N.H. 2007. Does the rebound effect exist? Time to remarriage and subsequent union stability. *Journal of Divorce and Remarriage* 46(3–4): 9–20.

Wolfinger, Nicholas H. 2011. More evidence for trends in the intergenerational transmission of divorce: A completed cohort approach using data from the General Social Survey. *Demography* 48(2): 581–592.

Wong, J., & V. Tseng. 2008. Political socialisation in immigrant families: Challenging top-down parental socialisation models. *Journal of Ethnic and Migration Studies* 34(1): 151–168.

Woolley, F., & J. Marshall. 1994. Measuring inequality within the household. *Review of Income and Wealth* 40(4): 415–431.

World Bank. 2011. *World Development Indicators.* Washington, DC: Author.

World Bank. 2017. *Gini Index (World Bank estimate).* Retrieved from http://data.worldbank.org/indicator/SI.POV.GINI?locations=US&view=chart

World Health Organization. 2012. *Understanding and Addressing Violence against Women: Intimate Partner Violence.* Retrieved from http://apps.who.int/iris/bitstream/10665/77432/1/WHO_RHR_12.36_eng.pdf

Worley, Timothy, & Jennifer Samp. 2016. Complaint avoidance and complaint-related appraisals in close relationships: A dyadic power theory perspective. *Communication Research* 43(3): 391–413.

Worts, D. 2005. It just doesn't feel like you're obviously in: Housing policy, family privacy, and the reproduction of social inequality. *Canadian Review of Sociology and Anthropology* 42(4): 445–465.

Worts, D., A. Sacker, A. McMunn, & P. McDonough. 2013. Individualization, opportunity and jeopardy in American women's work and family lives: A multi-state sequence analysis. *Advances in Life Course Research* 18(4): 296–318.

Wozniak, D. 2014. Predatory marriage: A modern–day trap. *SisKinds: The Law Firm.* Retrieved from http://www.siskinds.com/predatory-marriage-a-modern-day-marriage-trap/

Wright, P.J. 2011. Mass media effects on youth sexual behavior assessing the claim for causality. *Annals of the International Communication Association* 35(1): 343–385.

Wu, Z., & C. Schimmele. 2009. Divorce and repartnering, pp. 1–25. In M. Baker, (Ed.), *Families: Changing Trends in Canada* (6th ed.). Toronto: McGraw-Hill Ryerson.

Wu, Zheng. 1994. Remarriage in Canada: A social exchange perspective. *Journal of Divorce and Remarriage 21* (3–4), 191–224.

Wu, Zheng. 2000. *Cohabitation: An Alternative Form of Family Living.* Don Mills, ON: Oxford University Press.

Wu, Zheng, & R. Hart. 2002. The effects of marital and nonmarital union transition on health. *Journal of Marriage and the Family* 64: 420–432.

Wu, Zheng, & Christoph Schimmele. 2005b. Divorce and repartnering, pp. 202–228. In Maureen Baker (Ed.), *Families: Changing Trends in Canada* (5th ed.). Toronto: McGraw-Hill Ryerson.

Wu, Zheng, Christoph M. Schimmele, & Nadia Ouellet. 2015. Repartnering after widowhood. *The Journals of Gerontology: Series B: Psychological Sciences and Social Sciences* 70(3): 469–507.

Xiaohe, Xu, & Martin King Whyte. 1990. Love matches and arranged marriages. *Journal of Marriage and the Family* 52(3): 709–722.

Xie, Yu, Yang Jiang, & Emily Greenman. 2008. Did send-down experience benefit youth? A reevaluation of the social consequences of forced urban–rural migration during China's cultural revolution. *Social Science Research* 37(2): 686–700.

Xu, Anqi, Xiaolin Xie, Wenli Liu, Yan Xia, & Dalin Liu. 2007. Asia: Chinese family strengths and resiliency. *Marriage & Family Review* 41(1–2): 143–164.

Xu, X., C. Hudspeth, & J. Bartkowski. 2006. The role of cohabitation in remarriage. *Journal of Marriage and Family* 68(2): 261–274,

Xu, Xiaohe, John P. Bartkowski, & Kimberly A. Dalton. 2011. The role of cohabitation in remarriage: A replication. *International Review of Sociology/Revue internationale de sociologie* 21(3): 549–564.

Yaffee, Jennifer Beth. 2003. The role of perceived attitude similarity in relationship satisfaction among heterosexual and lesbian couples. *Dissertation Abstracts International: Section B: The Sciences and Engineering* 63(12-B): 6148.

Yarosh, Svetlana, Yee Chieh Denise Chew, & Gregory D. Abowd. 2009. Supporting parent–child communication in divorced families. *International Journal of Human–Computer Studies* 67: 192–203.

Yick, Alice G. 2000. Domestic violence beliefs and attitudes in the Chinese American community. *Journal of Social Service Research* 27(1): 29–51.

Yip, Paul S.F., Saman Yousuf, Chee Hon Chan, Tiffany Yung, & Kevin C.-C. Wu. 2015. The roles of culture and gender in the relationship between divorce and suicide risk: A meta-analysis. *Social Science & Medicine* 128: 87–94.

Yoo, Hana, Suzanne Bartle-Haring, Randal Day, & Rashmi Gangamma. 2014. Couple communication, emotional and sexual intimacy, and relationship satisfaction. *Journal of Sex & Marital Therapy* 40(4): 275–293.

Yoshioka, M.R., L. Gilbert, N. El-Bassel, & M. Baig-Amin. 2003. Social support and disclosure of abuse: Comparing South Asian, African American, and Hispanic battered women. *Journal of Family Violence* 18(3): 171–180.

Young, M. 2010. Gender differences in precarious work. *Relations Industrielles/Industrial Relations* 65(1): 74–97.

Young, M., S. Schieman, & M. Milkie. 2014. Spouses' work-to-family conflict, family stressors, and mental health among dual-earner mothers and fathers. *Society and Mental Health* 4(1): 1–20.

Young, Michael. 1952. Distribution of income within the family. *British Journal of Sociology* 3: 305–321.

Yount, Kathryn M., & S. Megan Smith. 2012. Gender and postpartum depression in Arab Middle Eastern women. *Women's Studies International Forum* 35(4): 187.

Yum, Y., & Hara, K. 2005. Computer-mediated relationship development: A cross-cultural comparison. *Journal of Computer-Mediated Communication* 11(1): 133–152.

Yurchisin, J., K. Watchravesringkan, & D. Brown McCabe. 2005. An exploration of identity re-creating in the context of Internet dating. *Social Behaviour and Personality* 33: 735–750.

Zelkowitz, P., K.J. Looper, S.S. Mustafa, M. Purden, & M. Baron. 2013. Parenting disability, parenting stress and child behaviour in early inflammatory arthritis. *Chronic Disease and Injuries in Canada* 33: 81–87.

Zentner, M., & K. Mitura. 2012. Stepping out of the caveman's shadow: Nations' gender gap predicts degree of sex differentiation in mate preferences. *Psychological Science* 23(10): 1176–1185.

Zelkowitz, Phyllis, Leonara King, Rob Whitley, Togas Tulandi, & Carolyn Ells. 2015. A comparison of immigrant and Canadian-born patients seeking fertility treatment. *Journal of Immigrant and Minority Health* 17(4): 1033–1040.

Zhang, J. 2016. Aging in cyberspace: Internet use and quality of life of older Chinese migrants. *The Journal of Chinese Sociology* 3(26).

Zhang, S.Y., & S.L. Kline. 2009. Can I make my own decision? A cross-cultural study of perceived social network influence in mate selection. *Journal of Cross-Cultural Psychology* 40: 3–23.

Zhang, X. 2009. *Perspectives on Labor and Income: Earnings of Women with and without Children.* Catalogue no. 75-001-X. Ottawa, ON: Statistics Canada. Retrieved from http://www.statcan.gc.ca/pub/75-001-x/2009103/pdf/10823-eng.pdf

Zhenchao, Qian, & Daniel T. Lichter. 2007. Social boundaries and marital assimilation: Interpreting trends in racial and ethnic intermarriage. *American Sociological Review* 72: 68–94.

Zimmer, Zachary, & Susan McDaniel. 2013. Global ageing in the twenty-first century: An introduction, pp. 1–12. In Susan McDaniel & Zachary Zimmer (Eds.), *Global Ageing in the Twenty-First Century: Challenges, Opportunities and Implications.* New York: Routledge.

Zukewich, N. 2003. Work, parenthood and the experience of time scarcity. *Days of Our Lives: Time Use and Transitions over the Life Course.* Catalogue no. 89-584-MIE—No. 1. Ottawa, ON: Housing, Family and Social Statistics Division. Retrieved from http://publications.gc.ca/collections/Collection/Statcan/89-584-M/89-584-MIE2003001.pdf

Index

2001 Census of Canada, 401
2001 General Social Survey (GSS), 117, 296
2004 General Social Survey (GSS), 102
2006 Census of Canada, 185
2011 General Social Survey (GSS), 311
2011 National Household Survey (NHS), 39

A

Abad, Neetu S., 212
Abada, Teresa, 205
ABCX family crisis model, 256–257, 289
Aboriginal peoples of Australia, 18
abortifacients, 57, 66
abortion, 56–58
   legalizing of, 57
Abowd, Gregory D., 318
abusive relationships, 269–274
acculturation gap, 21, 28, 213, 258
acculturative stress, 258, 289
achieved status, 95
Adams, Mary Louise, 119
adolescent parenting, 171
   fathers, 185
   mothers, 185
   risks, 185
   unwanted, 185
   variations in, 184
adoption, 130, 186–187
Adult Independent Relationships Act (Alberta, 2003), 7
Adventures of Ozzie and Harriet, The, 18
adverse selectivity, 308, 309, 310, 312, 335
agricultural development, 14–15
Ahmad, F., 37
Amato, Paul R., 317, 328
American Revolution, 37
Andreassen, R., 141
Angel, Robert J., 280
Angelou, Maya, 197

anomie, 148, 179
Antill, John K., 315
arranged marriages, 75–76, 164
   Confucian ideology and, 76
   cultural reasons for, 75–76
   in pre-industrial countries, 75
   reasons for, 75
   South Asians and, 76
artificial intelligence, 411
Askham, J., 332
assisted fertility, 187–188
assisted human reproductive (AHR) technologies, 188
astronaut family, 346
attachment theory, 196–198
attractiveness, 79
authoritarian parenting style, 199, 216
authoritative parenting style, 199, 216

B

baby boom, 51, 183
Baello, Jon, 283
Baldassar, Lorraine, 215
Baldwin, James, 197
battered women, 279
Battle of the Plains of Abraham (*a.k.a.* Conquest) (1760), 34
Beckjord, E. B., 266
benching, 140
Bernard, Jessie, 96
bilateral kinship systems, 10, 28
biological determinism, 17
birth controls, 51, 55, 57
   improvements in, 183
birth rate, 50, 183, 216
   as political issue, 51
   changes in, 53
   decline in, 183
   Indigenous peoples, 53
Blackmore, Winston, 131
Blair, Bethany L., 214
blended families, 344
   remarriage and, 124–125, 354–356
Blood First Nations peoples, 32

bloodlines, 15
body images, 25
Bombeck, Erma, 4
boomerang kids, 349
Booth, Alan, 328
Bourgeault, Ivy Lynn, 184
Bowlby, John, 197
Brandt, Anthony, 4
Brault, Robert, 4
breadcrumbing, 140
Bridges, L., 327
Brown, Susan L., 312
Brym, Robert, 77
Bureau of Census (U.S.), 6
Bush, Barbara, 4

C

Canada Committee for the International Year of the Family, 6
Canada,
   birth rates as political issue in, 53
   child support in, 60
   contraceptive use in, 184
   dating and mating characteristics in, 97
   decline in birth rates in, 183
   decrease of family sizes in, 58
   divorce laws in, 302–303
   divorce statistics in, 293–294, 294f, 295f, 304
   families as producers in preindustrialized, 34
   families, profile of (*see* families, profile of)
   family income inequality in, 406
   family size as political issue in, 51
   immigration policies in, 38
   immigration to, 20
   importance of family to, 3
   interracial dating in, 90
   marriage rates in, 49, 295f
   multiple families in, 5–6

patrilineal system of kinship in, 10

population growth in, 47*f*

teenage rates of parenthood in, 184

trends in family structures in, 7

virtual and nominal families in, 405

Canadian Fertility and Andrology Society (CFAS), 188

Canadian Forces, 42

Canadian Pacific Railway, 38

capitalism, 16

   international, 21

caregiver burden, 260–267

caregiving family

   cyberspace and, 392–393

caregiving, 222, 341

   consequences of, 262–264

   coping with stress from, 265

   crisis episodes in, 263

   gender disparities in, 235–236

   and stress, 265

   transnational, 346

   types of, 223

casual sex, 131

Ceausescu, Nicolae, 57

celibate couples, 5

Census families, 5, 7

Census of Canada, 24, 27

   see also individually dated entries

Chae, Y. G., 215

Chang, Janet, 299

chastity, 76

Cheah, Charissa, 211

Cheal, David, 19

Cheng, H., 327

Chew, Yee Chieb, 318

child abuse, 278

child bearing, 56

   as predictor of divorce, 310

   decline in, 183

child care, 24, 247–250

   conflicts over, 172

   fathers and, 160, 248–249

   government support for, 408

   Live-in Caregiver Program, 249–250

child poverty, 59–60, 61, 360

   Indigenous peoples and, 61

   reasons for, 61

child support, 4, 364

   in Canada, 59–60

   in the United States, 60

Child Tax Benefit program, 60

childbearing, and parenting, 128–130, 366–369

childbirth,

   marriage satisfaction and, 158–161

children's viewpoint (of family), 11

children,

   ages of with older mothers, 6

   in industrialized Canada, 35

   parents, with disabilities, 239–240

   raising, 43

   sexual abuse of, 9

childless couples, 128–129

Chinese Exclusionary Act, 38

Chinese head tax (1885–1923), 38

Chirkov, Valery, 211

choice mom, 360

Chou, W. S., 266

Clark, Warren, 296

Clements, C. M., 287

cohabitation, 4, 6, 48, 114–116

   adverse selectivity and, 308

   as family transitions, 352–353

   as predictor of divorce, 308

   divorce rates and, 293, 295–296

   satisfaction in compared to marriage, 154

   see also common-law couple

cohort effect, 312, 335

cohorts, 43, 66

collected family, 398, 399, 412

collectivist cultures,

   parenting in, 212

colonialism, 32, 37, 357

common-law couple, 5, 7

   children of, 8

   see also cohabitation

common-law couple families, 112, 115–116

communication (in marriage), 174–175

   demand/withdrawal pattern of, 175

   idioms and, 175, 179

   non-verbal, 175–176

   quality of, 174

   quantity of, 174

communities, 14

   studies of, 14

companionship, 163

Compassionate Care Program, 243

compersion, 133

complementary needs theory (of mate selection), 73

concatenated family, 398, 399–400, 412

Confederation, 36

confirmation bias, 84, 85

conflict, 233

   stress and, 227–228

conflict management, 168–170

Conflict Tactics Scale, 269, 289

Confucian ideology, 76

connectivity, 380

consumerism, 27

contraception, 53, 184

   technology of, 57, 58

control and supervision, 198–199, 216

convergence theory, 25

Cooney, Teresa M., 326

co-parenting, 129–130, 141, 366–367

coping resources, 280

corporal punishment, 201

corporate family, 398–399, 413

Cotton, Sandra, 315

courtship, 18

   changes in, 48

Crawford, Lizabeth A., 205

crisis episodes, 263, 289

Crompton, Susan, 296

crude divorce rate, 293

cushioning, 140

Custom of Paris, 34

cybersex addiction, 390

cycle of abuse, 287, 289

cyclical (recycled) family, 398, 400, 413

D

Dakin, John, 173, 174

Darwin, George, 73

dating, 18

   in aging society, 88

   attractiveness and, 79

   culture of, 76

   and disabilities, 80–84

   flirting as part of, 80

   immigrants and, 88–90

   importance of meeting place for, 80

dating (*continued*)
  internet, 77–79
  interracial, 90
  market values in, 79
  multiculturalism and, 88–89
  myths, 78
  for overweight and other
    stigmatized people, 93–94
  personal decoration and, 79
  same-sex, 92
  seniors and, 88
  sexual behaviour and, 87
  sexual violence and, 102
  sexually transmitted diseases
    (STDs) and, 87
  technological approach to, 77
  violence and, 102–105
dating violence
  for overweight people, 103–104
  for people with disabilities,
    104–105
Davis, P., 263
De Jong, Gordon, 117
de Sévigné, Marquise, 4
definitions of family, 3–7, 27–28
  George Murdock's, 4–5
  importance of, 7
  inclusive approach to, 5
  process-based, 6–7
  Statistics Canada's, 5, 6, 7
delayed home-leaving, 349–351
demographers, 53, 66
  divorce rates and, 296
demographic transitions,
    54–56, 66
  birth controls and, 55
  effects of, 56
  first, 54
  second, 54–56
Denton, M., 63
dependency,
  as element of family, 8
depression, 152
  divorce and adolescent, 325
  divorce and, 322
  infertility and, 161
  marital quality and,
    173–174
  postnatal, 161
determinants (of divorce),
    305, 335
differences approach, 12
different family member
    approach, 11–12

discipline, 198–200
  induction and, 201
  internal moral control
    technique of, 201
  physical punishment threat,
    201
  power assertion technique
    of, 201
discontinuity, and social change,
    110–111
discrimination, 20
diversity, 406
  at midlife, 371
  in sexual relationships (see
    sexual relationships,
    diversity in)
  and social change, 110
diversity over time, 12
*Division of Labour in Society,
  The*, 298
division of labour, 35, 172
  by gender, 36
  in industrialized Canada, 35
  in pre-industrial Canada, 35
divorce
  adverse consequences of, 348
  high-conflict marriages, 123
  inequality and, 123
  low-conflict marriages, 123
  and relationship dissolution,
    121–124
Divorce Act (1968), 65, 121, 302
Divorce Act (1985), 303
Divorce Act (1986), 121
divorce rates, 121, 293–295
  after previous marriages,
    296–297, 296f
  cohabitation and, 293, 295–296
  crude, 293
  in China, 319
  and life expectancy, 112
  lifetime, 295
  measurements of, 293–295
  population at risk of, 294
  rolling, 295
  societal breakdown and, 298
  standard population, 294–295
Divorce Revolution, The, 60
divorce risk, 294
divorce, 3, 5–6, 49, 293
  causes and effects of, 327
  children and, 11
  communication with children
    effects of, 318

custody of children, 318
determinants, 305
economic effects of, 317–318
effects of, 316–319
effects on children of, 323–326
effects on elderly of, 331–332
fall in incomes after, 322
father–child relationship after,
    327–32
immigrants and, 299–300
international findings on, 319
laws, 302–303
legal changes and, 302–303
life-course approach to, 306
macro-level causes of, 306,
    314–316
marriage and, 149–150
mediation and, 317
meso-level causes of, 306,
    307–314
micro-level causes of, 306,
    306–307
myths and facts about, 310
no-fault, 303, 336
non-custodial fathers and,
    318, 319
parental as predictor of,
    309–311
predictors, 305
rates, 27
regulation of, 64–65
relationship with parents',
    327–331
religion and, 312–313
remarriage as predictor of, 309
social changes and, 300–302
traditional therapy and, 317
women and effects of,
    321–323
world view of, 65
domestic labour, 222–223
domestic violence, 9, 170–171,
    255, 289
  cycle of, 285–287, 286f
  effects of, 284–287
  witnessing, 287
Doucet, Andrea, 249
Down syndrome, 395
dual-earner families, 221
dual-income families, 403
Duberman, Lucile, 399
Dubinsky, Karen, 48
Dunn, J., 327
Dunne, G.A., 234

Durham Catholic District School Board, 92
Durkheim, Émile, 16, 46, 147, 148, 298, 321
Duxbury, Linda, 241
Dwairy, Marwan, 199

E

Early Child Development (ECD) Accord, 410
early retirement, 62
earnings, gender disparities in, 235–236
economic inequality, gender and, 135–136
economy of gratitude, 230
education,
    as achieved status, 95
    as criterion for marriage, 95
effective families, 8
Eichler, Margrit, 5, 65
elder care, 24, 62–63
Elder, Glen H., 11
elderly,
    effects of divorce on, 331–332
    internet (online) dating and, 389
    support for, 62–63
Eliot, George, 4
email, 386–388
embryo adoption, 128
emotional abuse, 269
Employment Standards Act (2000), 236
empty nest syndrome, 162
endogamous marriage, 356
endogamy, 96, 106
    for Indigenous people, 98–99
Engels, Friedrich, 14, 23
English Common Law, 33, 34
    inheritance under, 34
    marriage under, 33–34
Erikson, Erik, 197
Espiritu, Yen, 89
ethnic diversity, 7
    dating and, 88–91
Evans, Michael, 320
evolution of species theory, 73–74, 275
evolutionary perspective (of mate selection), 73–74
exchange theory (of mate selection), 73
exogamy, 91, 106

expressive exchanges, 73, 106
extended family, 6, 15, 28
    farmwork in preindustrialized Canada, 34
extended-kin headship, 15

F

Facebook, 167
fairness, perceptions of, 232–233
families
    and disabilities, 365–366
    dual-earner, 221
    persons with disabilities in, 64
    profile of (see families, profile of)
families, profile of, 112–130
    childbearing and parenting, 128–130
    cohabiting couples, 114–116
    common-law couple, 112, 115–116
    LAT relationships, 116–117
    LGBTQ families, 125–128
    living alone, 117–118
    lone-parent (single-parent), 112–113
    married-couple, 112, 113–114
    merge households decisions, 121
    remarriage and blended families, 124–125
    single-person households, 118–119
    stepfamilies, 113
family allowances, 60, 66
    in Quebec, 60
family as social creation, 16
family as social institution, 20
family cohesion, 198, 216
family diversity, 7
family dynamics, 19
family interactions, 19
family law, 7, 121
    after Conquest, 34
family over time approach, 13–14
family-oriented policy, 245
family planning, 184
family policy
    limitations of, 244–245
    private, 245
    typologies of, 245–246
family reunification, 4

family size,
    as political issue, 51
    changes in, 51–53
    increases in, 58
family stress, 256
    ABCX family crisis model of, 256
    effects on roles and relationships, 256
    stressor events, 256–257
family structures, 51–52
family transitions, 339–341
    blended families, 354–356
    in care arrangements, 349
    causes of, 342
    cohabitation, 352–353
    definition of, 341–343
    historic, 344
    immigrants and, 345–347
    marriage and, 352–353
    in midlife, 369–371
    money and, 356
    to new family structures, 347–348
    relationship dissolution and, 352–353
    remarriage as, 354–356
    for seniors, 369–371
    social change in, 343–344
    young adults and, 343–344
family violence, 255, 268–287
    abusive relationships, 269–274
    definitions of, 268
    emotional abuse, 269
    measuring, 268–274
    physical violence, 268
    sexual violence, 268
    see also sexual violence
family
    as recent social idea, 14
    as social institution, 18
    Census family, 5, 7
    collected, 398, 399, 412
    concatenated, 398, 399–400, 412
    convergence theory of, 25
    corporate, 398–399, 413
    cyclical (recycled), 398, 400, 413
    definitions of, 3–4
    dependency element of, 8
    differences, approach to, 12
    different family member, approach to, 11–12

family (*continued*)
  dual-income, 403
  economics factors on, 14–15
  Engels's theory of, 14–15
  extended, 6
  family over time theoretical
    approach, 13–14
  feminist theories of, 13–14,
    22*t*, 24
  future changes in, 401–403
  gay and lesbian, 7, 12
  household *versus*, 5–6
  households, 6
  immigration and, 20, 36–37
  impact of wars on, 41–42
  importance of, 3
  industrialization and, 25
  information communication
    technologies (ICTs) and,
    378–380
  intimacy element of, 8
  Le Play's theory of, 15
  life-course approach to, 11, 22*t*,
    26, 42–44
  Marxist theory of, 22*t*, 23–24
  modernization and effects of
    on, 44
  multiple, 5–6
  nominal, 404–406
  nuclear, 6, 18
  patriarchy and, 9
  pooling of resources within, 300
  post-structural approaches
    to, 21
  postmodern approaches to, 21,
    22*t*, 24–25
  power element of, 9
  protection element of, 9
  queer theories, 14
  religious approaches to, 16
  roles, 19
  sequencing of events in, 44
  sexual propriety norms of, 8–9
  sexuality element of, 8–9
  social and economic needs of, 9
  social support for, 59
  societal changes and, 7
  standard North American
    family (SNAF), 18
  structural functionalism
    approach to, 18–19,
    21–23, 22*t*
  symbolic interactionism
    approach to, 22*t*, 23

  technological changes and
    development of, 384–385
  theoretical approaches to,
    13–14
  traditional family, 3
  variety of forms of, 3
  violence as element of, 9–10
  virtual, 404
  women's role in, 16
Father Knows Best, 18, 41
Federal Support Child
  Guidelines, 303
female migration, 39
female singlehood, 119
femininity, 315, 335
feminist theories, 14, 20, 22*t*, 24
  on divorce predictors, 315
  research and, 20
  women immigrants and, 39
Ferguson, Christopher J., 287
fertility,
  assisted, 187–188
  declining rates of, 51–52, 58
  marriage and, 128–129
  rates of Indigenous peoples, 53
  rates, 55
  reasons for decline in rates
    of, 56
  teenage rates of, 184
feudalism, 72
filial piety, 45
financial cost model (of marriage
  dissatisfaction), 160
Finnie, Ross, 322, 323
First Nations peoples, 53
  parenting and, 210–211
  poverty and, 60
Fletcher, Anne C., 214
flirting, 80
fluidity, and social change, 110
forgiveness, 169
Foshee, Vangie A., 103
Foster, Craig, A., 191
Fox, Bonnie, 19, 160
Frias, Sonia, M., 280
Frideres, James S., 157
Funston, Andrew, 215

G

Gaunt, R., 156
gay and lesbian dating, 92
gay and lesbian families, 12
Gazso, Amber, 404
Gee, Ellen M., 54

gemeinschaft (rural community),
  34, 66
gender disparities, in earnings/
  caregiving, 235–236
gender equality, 35, 74–75
  divorce and, 315
  modernization and, 45
  parenthood and marriage, 160
gender inequalities, in unpaid
  labour, 230, 233
gender roles, 33
  in marriage, 171–173
gender socialization, 193–194, 216
gender
  dating violence and, 102–103
  and economic inequality,
    135–136
  roles in marriage, 171–173
genetic engineering, 411
genetic survival, 73
ghosting, 140
Giddens, Anthony, 19
Gignac, Monique A. M., 263
Gillespie, Michael, 205
Gini index, 406
Glaser, K., 332
glass ceiling, 240
glass escalator, 240
Global Initiative to End All
  Corporal Punishment, 201
globalization, 21, 27
Goethe, Johann Wolfgang
  von, 197
Goode, William, 25, 313
Gottman, J. M., 306
Great Depression (1930s), 53
  poverty during, 59–60
group marriage, 131
Guaranteed Income
  Supplement, 63
guilt, 228
Guruge, S., 157

H

Hall, Marc, 92
Harper, Stephen, 14, 245
Harris, K. M., 88, 89
Harrison, Deborah, 42
Hartley, Richard D., 287
Hassouneh-Phillips, Dena,
  81, 286
Helbig, Sylvia, 161
Hesse, B. W., 266
Hetherington, E. Mavis, 315, 323

heterosexual relationships, homosexual relationships vs., 156
Higgins, Christopher, 241
Hill, Reuben, 256
history of the family (as social idea), 14–16
HIV/AIDS, 4, 87
Hochschild, A. R., 230, 241
homogamy, 94, 106
    age, 96
    educational, 95
    ethnic, 96–97
    marital satisfaction and, 157
    propinquity (closeness) theory for, 94
    reasons for, 94
    religious, 98
homosexual relationships vs. heterosexual relationships, 156
honour killings, 281
hooking up, 101
Hooks, Gwen, 37
horizontal occupational sex segregation, 237
households, 5, 6
    decline in size of, 58
    economic and social needs of, 9
    family, 6
    modernization effects on, 44
    one-person, 58
    size, 351
    smaller/single-person, 351–352
    with children, 42–43, 43f
housework, 24
    conflicts over, 172
    mechanization of, 36, 67
Hudson's Bay Company, 32
Hughes, Katie, 215
Hunt, Y. M., 266
Huron peoples, 32
Huxley, Aldous, 197
Hwang, W.-C., 21
Hyman, I., 157
Hynie, Michaela, 213

I

idioms, 175, 179
immigration (immigrants), 4, 7, 12
    African Americans to Alberta, 37
    African Americans to Nova Scotia, 37

causes of family violence, 282–284
    changes in sources of, 39
    culture and, 20
    dating and 88–91
    divorce and, 299–300
    effects of family violence, 282–284
    European, 37, 39
    families preserving ethnic values, 283
    and family transitions, 345–347
    history of family, 36–38
    isolating effects of, 37
    marital satisfaction and, 157
    parent–teenager conflict, 89–91
    separation and, 299–300
    South Asian, 37
    visible minorities and, 38
    women and, 39
immigration policies, 38–41
    Chinese discriminatory, 38
    gender neutral, 39
    to provide labour, 38
in vitro fertilization, 128, 188, 367, 373
Indian Act, 12, 357
Indigenous families, 209–211, 356–360
    access to health care, 359–360
    causes of spousal violence in, 281
    colonialism and, 357
    diversity of, 32
    early contacts and, 32–33
    forced assimilation of, 12
    gender roles in, 33
    kinship and, 33
    parenting and, 210–211
    residential schools and, 12, 210
    settlers and, 33–34
    women's fertility rate, 358
Indigenous peoples
    birth rates, 53
    colonists' relationships with, 32
    endogamy for, 98–99
    first contacts with, 32
    fur traders and, 32
    mixed-race children, 32–33
    poverty amongst, 60
    property and, 33
individualization, 396–398

induction, 201, 216
Industrial Revolution, 35, 300
industrialization, 16, 26, 27
    changing of women's roles after, 44
    family and, 25
    in Canada, 35
    redefining family effect of, 44
industrialized Canada,
    agricultural family changes in, 35
    childhood in, 35
    division of labour in, 35
    household technology in, 35–36
infertility, 161–162
    stigma of, 18
information communication technologies (ICTs), 214, 378–379, 380, 382, 384
inheritance, 15
    English Common Law and, 33, 34
instrumental exchanges, 73, 106
interactional problem, 278
intergenerational trauma, 357
intermarriage, 96
    ethnic, 96–97
    social dilemma of, 97
internal moral control, 201, 216
internet (online) dating, 77–79, 391
    activities, 77
    changes in, 391
    dangers of, 78
    elderly and, 389
    gays and lesbians and, 79
    gender differences in, 78
    large database for, 77
    long-term relationships and, 389
    for people with disabilities, 83–84
    reasons for popularity of, 77
    similarity characteristic for, 77
internet,
    ages of users, 409
    educational usage, 382
    health care on, 392–394
interpersonal violence, 102–105
interracial dating, 90

intimacy, 5
  as element of family, 8
  emotional, 110
  friendship and, 167
  importance of, 166
  internet chat rooms and, 167
  marital quality and, 166–167
  patriarchy and, 166
  problems, 167
  sexual, 166–167
  social media and, 139–141
intimate-partner violence (IPV),
    271–273, 289
  Indigenous families and, 274
in vitro fertilization (IVF),
    128, 367
Inuit peoples, 54
IPV. see intimate partner
    violence (IPV)

J

Jacobi, Frank, 161
Japanese Canadians, 41–42
joint custody (co-parenting), 6
Judeo-Christian religious
    beliefs, 15
juvenile delinquency, 202

K

Kamp Dush, C. M., 155
Katz, Elana, 317
Kaufman, A. R., 51
Kelly, John, 323
Kemp, C. L., 62
Keystone Legacy, The, 37
kibbutz, 16
Kim-Goh, Mikyong, 283
kin-keepers, 11, 28, 225
King, R. B., 88
King, William Lyon Mackenzie, 60
kinship group, 10–11, 26
  Indigenous families as, 33
  bilateral, 10
  matrilineal, 10
  patrilineal, 10
Kozuch, Patricia, 325, 326

L

labour (work),
  domestic division of, 24,
    222–223
  immigration for supply of, 38
  paid, 221

separation from family, 16–17
  unpaid (*see* unpaid labour)
  women during World War II,
    41–42
labour market
  barriers in, 240
  primary, 236
  secondary, 236
Lampard, Richard, 80
Lampert, Thomas, 161
Lancaster, E. A., 302
Laslett, Peter, 70
Laumann, Edward O., 165, 166
Le Play, Frederic, 15
Leach, B., 235
*Lean In: Women, Work, and the Will
    to Lead* (Sandberg), 238
Leave It to Beaver, 18, 41
Lee, S. J., 215
legal rights, 4
Lenton, Rhonda, 77
les filles du roi (daughters of the
    King), 34
LGBTQ (lesbian, gay, bisexual,
    transgender, queer, and
    questioning) families, 110,
    125–128, 367. *see also* same-
    sex families
  societal homophobia
    and, 127
life expectancy, 43
life histories, 13
life-course approach, 11, 22t, 26
  cohorts and, 42
  principles of, 26
  to divorce, 306
  variations in family, 42–44
Lin, I-Fen, 312
literacy, 45
Live-in Caregiver Program,
    249–250, 346
living alone, 117–118
living apart together (LAT)
    relationships, 111, 116–117
Lockerbie, S., 130
lone-parent (single-parent)
    families, 8, 112–113, 185,
    360–365
  adolescent drug taking and, 205
  benefits of, 205–206
  children and, 328–329
  myths, 205
lone-parent households, 3
longitudinal data, 12

Longmore, Monica A., 124, 131
low-income families, 61
  government support for,
    407–408
  single mothers, 206
Lupri, Eugen, 157
Luxton, Meg, 19

M

macro-level causes of divorce,
    306, 314–316, 316
  cultural values and social
    integration, 316
  economic cycles, 315
  gender expectations, 315–316
Mahay, Jenna, 165
male viewpoint (of family), 11
Malinowski, Bronislow, 18
March, Isobel, 46
marital conflict, 169
marital infidelity, 167
marital quality, 147
  arranged marriages and, 164
  childbirth and, 158–161
  communication and, 174–176
  coping with conflict, 168–170
  depression and, 173–174
  financial stress and, 173–174
  forgiveness and, 169
  gender roles in marriage and,
    171–173
  homogamy and, 156–157
  immigrant couples and, 157
  in beginning cycle of marriage,
    157–163
  in later cycle of marriage, 163
  in midlife cycle of marriage,
    162
  infertility and, 161–162
  intimacy and, 166–167
  love and, 164–165
  power inequality and, 172
  retirement and, 163
  sexual satisfaction and,
    165–166, 167
  unemployment and, 174
  work stress and, 173–177
marital satisfaction, 98
  religious beliefs and, 98
  social similarity of partners
    and, 98
market economy, 27
marriage gradient, 96, 106
marriage promoters, 298

marriage rates, 27
marriage, 356
  age differences in, 96
  arranged, 75–76
  as marking a life transition, 48
  as moral organization of
    society, 16
  beginning cycle of, 158
  change in rates of, 49
  changes in attitude toward,
    48–49
  children and, 158–161
  cohabitation and, 45
  coping with conflict in,
    168–170
  declining rates of, 49
  difficulties, 152
  division of labour and, 72
  dynamics, 306
  education as criterion for, 95
  effects of war on, 41
  egalitarianism in, 44
  English Common Law and,
    33, 34
  expectations, 53
  and fertility, 128–129
  gender roles in, 171–173
  group, 131
  health and, 149–150
  heterosexual, 110
  importance of sexual
    intercourse in, 158
  in feudal times, 72
  later, 49
  midlife cycle of, 162–163
  predatory, 137
  reasons for a successful, 153
  second and divorce, 308–309
  societal rejection of, 295–296
  stage of, 311–312
  unhappiness in, 305
  well-being and, 149–150
  women's satisfaction in, 152
marriage bar, 123
married-couple families, 112,
  113–114
Martin-Matthews, Anne, 263
Marx, Karl, 14, 23
Marxist theory of family, 22t,
  23–24
Mason, R., 157
mate selection, 72
  cigarettes as part of strategy
    in, 101

complementary needs theory
  of, 73
conspicuous consumption as
  strategy for, 101
evolutionary perspective of,
  73–74
exchange theory of, 73
facial attractiveness in, 101
gender equality and, 74–75
goals of, 101
ideals of, 99–102
optimal mate and, 100–102
romantic love and, 164–165
social role theory of, 74
theories, 72–74
unrealistic beliefs in, 100
maternal wall, 240
mating, 77–79
mating myths, 78
matrilineal kinship group, 28
McDaniel, Susan A., 11, 404
McKinnon, Robert, 92
McNeff, Elizabeth, 286
mechanization of housework,
  36, 67
Menninger, Karl, 197
Menshar, K. E., 199
mental health, unpaid labour and,
  228–229
meso-level causes of divorce, 306,
  307–314, 335
  age at marriage, 307
  childbearing before and after
    marriage, 311
  cohabitation, 307–308
  marriage stage, 311–312
  parental divorce, 309–311
  place of residence, 312
  religion, 312–313
  second marriage, 308–309
  socio-economic status (SES),
    313–314
Métis peoples, 54
micro-level causes of divorce,
  306–307, 335
Middle Ages, 72
Millar, W. J., 185
millennial generation, 120
Mirdal, Gretty M., 282
Mitura, Klaudia, 75
mixed-race unions, 97
Modern Family (tv show), 340
modernism (modernization), 25
  effects of in India of, 45

effects on culture of, 45
effects on family, 44
gender equality and, 46
parent–child relationships
  and, 46
political will and ideology
  changes from, 45
societal changes from, 45
traditional values and, 45
money management, 134–139
  economic exploitation,
    136–137
  economic inequality, gender
    and, 135–136
  relationship dissolution,
    138–139
  relationship status and, 134–
    135
monogamy, 15, 133
Monsignor John Pereyma
  Catholic High School,
  Oshawa, 92
Moore-Lappé, Frances, 6
Morash, Merry, 283
Mormon community, and
  polygamy, 131–132
Morton, Suzanne, 72
Moser, R. P., 266
Mossman, Mary Jane, 138
multiculturalism, 88–89
multigenerational
  genograms, 317
multiple families, 5–6
Murdock, George, 4, 5
MySpace, 167

N
Nash, Ogden, 4
National Child Benefit
  program, 60
National Longitudinal Study of
  Children and Youth
  (NLSCY), 12, 206, 410
National Population Health
  Survey (NPHS), 327
neoliberalism, 138, 242–243
New France, 32
Nishio, Harry K., 42
no-fault divorce, 303, 336
  laws, 302–303
nominal families, 404–406
non-monogamy, 130,
  133–134
Novak, Katherine B., 205

nuclear family, 6, 28
  golden age of, 18
  structural functionalism and, 21

O

O'Connor, T. G., 327
occupational sex segregation, 237
Ogle, R. L., 287
Old Age Security, 63, 133
Old Testament, 15
older adults, emerging trends
  for, 112
online dating. *See* internet (online)
  dating
online support groups, 266
opposites attract, 73
optimal mate, 100–102, 106
Organisation for Economic
  Co-operation and Social
  Development (OECD), 184
Orr, Amy J., 193
other-mothering, 402, 413
outsourcing, 231
overweight/obese people
  dating for, 93–94
  dating violence for, 103–104
  and parenting, 194–196
Oxtoby, C., 287

P

paid labour, 221
  unpaid labour and,
    intersections between,
    234–240
parachute kids, 346
parent–child relationship
  effects of divorce on, 327–329
  long distance, 215
parent–child violence, 287
parental divorce, 309–311
parental involvement, 208, 216
parental leave, benefits, 246–247
parenthood, 183
  reasons for, 183–184
  teenage
  transition to and gender
    inequality, 160
parenting, 12
  adolescent, 184–185
  attachment theory, 196–198
  authoritarian style of, 199
  authoritative style of, 199
  caring for sick children,
    203–204

childbearing and, 128–130,
  366–369
control and supervision,
  198–200
cultural variations in, 211–214
disability and, 204
discipline, 200–203
emotional stability, 198
expressing love for children,
  196–198
gay and lesbian couples and,
  208–209
in internet age, 214–215
in poverty, 206–208
Indigenous families and,
  209–211
lone-parent, 206
long-term poverty and, 208
obesity and, 194–196
permissive style of, 199
process, 194
proverbs, 213
stepfamily, 311
unengaged style of, 199
parents of children with
  disabilities, 239–240
Parsons, Talcott, 18
patriarchy, 9, 15, 17, 28
patrilineal kinship group, 10, 28
pay equity, 236
permissive parenting style,
  199, 216
personal interchangeability,
  398, 413
pet care, 224
petting, 131
physical health, unpaid labour
  and, 228–229
physical violence, 268
Plato, 197
*Polish Peasant in Europe and
  America (1918–1920),
  The*, 212
polyaffectivity, 132
polyamory, 132–133
polyandry, 131, 143
polygamy, 131–132
polygyny, 131
population growth, 47*f*
pornography, 392
post-industrial society, 62
post-structural theories, 21
post-traumatic stress disorder
  (PTSD), 284

postmodern theories, 21, 22*t*,
  24–25
postnatal depression, 161
power assertion, 201, 216
power,
  as element of family, 8–9
pre-industrial Canada, 34
  division of labour in, 35
predatory marriage, 137
predictors (of divorce), 305, 336
  age at marriage, 307
  childbearing before and after
    marriage, 311
  cohabitation, 307–308
  cultural values and social
    integration, 316
  economic cycles, 314–315
  gender and, 315–316
  marriage stage, 311–312
  religion, 312–313
  second marriage, 308–309
  socio-economic status (SES),
    313–314
  urban compared to rural
    residence as, 312
primary labour market, 236
private family policy, 245
primary socialization, 192, 216
private property, 14, 23
*Prom Queen: The Marc Hall
  Story*, 92
pronatalist societies, 187
propinquity (closeness) theory,
  94, 106
protection,
  element of family, 9

Q

Quebec
  birth rate as political issue in, 53
  cohabitation rates in, 116
  family allowances in, 60
  gender imbalance in, 34
Québécois, 34
Québécoise, 34
queer theories, 14
quid pro quo sexual harassment,
  240

R

relationship dissolution
  divorce and, 121–124
  and family transitions, 352–353
  money and, 138–139

relationship statuses
  and money management,
    134–135
religion
  divorce and, 312–313
  family and, 15
remarriage, 112
  and blended families, 124–125
reproductive technologies, 128
research (family), 11
  feminism and, 19
restriction of freedom model
  (of marriage dissatisfaction),
    160
retirement, 163
  power relations in, 163
  relationship satisfaction
    during, 163
revenge of the cradle, 51, 67
rituals, 70
role conflict model (of marriage
  dissatisfaction), 160
role separability, 398, 413
roles in family, 23
romance apps, 141
romantic love, 72, 106
  emergence of, 72
  marriage satisfaction and,
    164–165
  people with disabilities
    and, 78
  social roles and, 72
Rowntree, S.B., 136
Royal Canadian Mounted Police
  (RCMP), 41

S

Sacks, Jonathan, 399
same-sex families, 7, 233–234. *see
  also* LGBTQ families
same-sex marriages, 3, 7, 347
  coming-out as part of quality
    of, 156
San Miguel, Claudia, 287
Sandberg, Sheryl, 238
sandwich generation, 223, 251,
  341, 365
satellite kids, 346
Scheff, Elisabeth, 132
Schlesinger, B., 163
Schlesinger, R. A., 163
secondary labour market, 236
secondary poverty, 136
second shift, 230

*The Second Shift: Working Parents
  and the Revolution at Home*
  (Hochschild), 230
secularization, 65, 67, 313, 336
  divorce and, 313
self-esteem, 286
separation, 299–300
September 11, 2001 attacks, 14
serial monogamy, 130
sex, 46
  premarital, 325
sexual abuse, 8–9
sexual activity, 87
sexual attitudes, 46–48, 86
  in Victorian times, 46
sexual behaviour
  cultural backgrounds and, 89
sexual dissatisfaction model (of
  marriage dissatisfaction), 160
sexual double standard, 84–87,
  106, 158
sexual harassment, quid pro
  quo, 240
sexual satisfaction, 165–166, 167
sexual scripts, 86, 106
sexual violence, 103, 268
sexuality, 25, 48
  as element of family, 8
  and social stigma, 81–82
  taboos, 9
sexually transmitted debt,
  137, 138
sexual relationships, diversity in,
  118, 130–134
  non-monogamy, 130, 133–134
  polyamory, 132–133
  polygamy, 131–132
  serial monogamy, 130
sexual scripts, 86
sexual violence, 268
Sheldon, Kennon M., 212
Silverman, E. L., 56
Sims-Gould, Joanie, 263
single mothers, 186
  myths about, 205
single-parent families. *See* lone-
  parent (single-parent) families
single-person households, 118–119
Skype, 250, 346, 380, 387, 388,
  390, 402
Snell, James G., 302
social attitudes, 16
social change, 110–112
  discontinuity, 110–111

diversity, 110
  in family transitions, 343–344
  fluidity, 110
  older adults, emerging trends
    for, 112
  young adults, emerging trends
    for, 111
social creation of family, 16
social differentiation, 300
social disorganization, 298, 336
social forces, 27
social inequalities, 20
  gendered, 20
social institution of family, 18
social integration, 316, 336
social isolation, 280, 283
social marginality, 212
social meanings, 23
social media
  and intimate relationships,
    139–141
social pathology, 298, 336
social policy
  child care, 247–250
  family policy (see family policy)
  neoliberalism, 242–243
  parental leave benefits,
    246–247
social reproduction, 222
social role theory (of mate
  selection), 74
social roles
  romantic love and, 72
social status
  dating violence and, 103–104
social stigma, sexuality and,
  81–82
social support, 59
  for families, 60
  for lone mothers, 59
social support network, 265–267
social unrest, 16
socialization, 192–193, 216
  agents of, 193
  bi-directional process of, 193
  gender by peers, 193
  gendered, 193–194
  primary, 192, 216
socially attached people, 147
socially unattached people,
  119–120, 148
socio-economic status (SES), 336
  as predictor of divorce, 313–314
  dating violence and, 103

sologamy, 120
spanking, 201
Spencer, Herbert, 17
spousal relationships, effect of
    disabilities, 177–179
spousal violence
    alcohol and drug abuse causes
        of, 280
    cultural attitudes cause of,
        280–281
    interactional cause of, 278
    lack of coping resources cause
        of, 280
    social isolation cause of, 280
    status inconsistency cause of,
        279–280
    traditional family values as
        cause of, 281–282
Sprecher, Susan, 77
stalled revolution, 231
standard employment, 236
standard North American family
    (SNAF), 18
Statistics Canada, 5, 6, 7, 43f,
        304, 311
    National Longitudinal Study of
        Children and Youth
        (NLSCY), 12
    poverty rates, 60
    Survey of Labour and Income
        Dynamics (SLID), 12
status inconsistency, 279, 290
stepfamilies, 113, 329–331
    classification of, 330
stepfamily parents, 311
Stewart, Martha, 36
stigmatization, 81–82
Straus, Murray, 289
street youth, 203
stress
    caregiving and, 265
    and conflict, 227–228
stressor events, 256–260, 290
    chronic stressors, 257, 259–260
    major life transitions, 257,
        258–259
    major upheavals, 257
    occasional stress, 257
structural functionalism, 18–19,
        21–23, 22t, 25
    nuclear family and, 21
    problems with, 21–23
structures of family, 25

Su, Chang, 213
suburbanism, 18
Sugiman, Pamela, 42
suicide, 147
    causes of, 147
Suicide, 147, 298
Survey of Labour and Income
    Dynamics (SLID), 12
survivors, 284–287
Sutherns, Rebecca, 184
symbolic interactionism, 19,
        22t, 23
    sharing of symbols and
        meaning in, 23
Szasz, Thomas, 197

T

Talmon, Yonina, 71
technological changes, 21, 139–141
    email, 386–388
    family development and,
        384–385
    household, 36
    impact on family of, 380–384
    labour-saving devices, 36
    new reproductive technologies
        (NRTs) and, 378, 394–396
    relationship challenges from,
        378, 384
    social change and, 377
    telephones, 385–386
telephone,
    social history of, 385–386
telework, 378
Temporary Foreign Workers
    Program, 38
Terence, Tracey, 77
theoretical approaches, 13–14
    big bang in, 19
    convergence theory, 25
    Engels's, 14–15
    feminist, 20, 22t, 24
    Le Play's, 15
    life-course, 11, 22t, 26
    Malinowski's, 18
    Marxist, 22t, 23
    patriarchal, 15
    post-structural, 21
    postmodern, 21, 22t, 24–25
    structural-functional, 18,
        21–23, 22t
    symbolic interactionism, 19,
        22t, 23

third shift, 241
Tomassini, C., 332
traditional family, 3, 26
transnational families, 346
transnational mothering,
        249–250
Troop-Gordon, Wendy, 193
Trudeau, Justin, 244, 245
Truth and Reconciliation
    Commission of Canada, 357
Tseng, V., 193
Twenge, Jean M., 191

U

unemployment insurance (UI), 60
unemployment, 21
unengaged parenting style,
        199, 216
United Empire Loyalists, 37
United Nations (UN), 6
United Nations Convention on
    the Rights of the Child, 411
unpaid labour, 220–221
    division of, 231–232
    gender inequalities in,
        230, 233
    measuring, 225
    and mental health, 228–229
    multifaceted, 224–225
    multiple meanings of,
        226–227
    paid labour and, intersections
        between, 234–240
    perceptions of fairness,
        232–233
    and physical health,
        228–229
    sick days, 225–226
    skills involved in, 229
    stress and conflict, 227–228
Upper Canada, 32
urbanization, 26, 26

V

Van de Kaa, Dirk, 55, 57
Vanier Institute of the
    Family, 6
vertical occupational sex
    segregation, 237
violence,
    against women, 9–10
    as element of, 9–10
    domestic, 9

family (*see* family violence)
gender and, 102–103
interpersonal, 102–105
intimate partner, 271
previous experience as cause
of, 278
see also family violence; sexual
violence
sexual, 102–103
virginity, 46
virtual families, 404–406
visible minorities, 38

W

Wadhera, S., 185
wage penalty, 237
Wampler, Richard, 173, 174
war,
effects on future generations
of, 42
impact on families, 41–42
Ward, Christopher C., 77
Weisskirch, R. S., 214
Weitzman, Lenore, 60, 322

welfare states, 27
Canada as, 61
welfare-to-work initiatives, 61
well-being,
comparison of in types
of relationships,
154–156
Wellman, Barry, 385
White, Lynn, 315
Whitehead, Barbara Dafoe, 13
Whyte, Martin King, 164
widowhood, 370
Wilkinson, Richard G., 408
Winch, Robert, 73
woman's viewpoint (of
family), 11
women's role in family, 16
during World War II, 18
women,
in corporate leadership, 238
as immigrants, 39
during World War II,
41–42
role changes after
industrialization, 44

Wong, J., 193
work. *See* labour (work)
work–life balance, 241–242, 246
World War II, 18
effects on families from Axis
power countries, 41
impact on families of, 41
women labourers during, 18–19
Wu, Zheng, 314

X

Xiaohe, Xu, 164

Y

Yarosh, Svetlana, 318
Youm, Yoosik, 165
young adults
emerging trends for, 111
and transitions, 343–344

Z

Zentner, Marcel, 75
Znaniecki, Florian, 212
zombieing, 140